Can they do that?

Can do

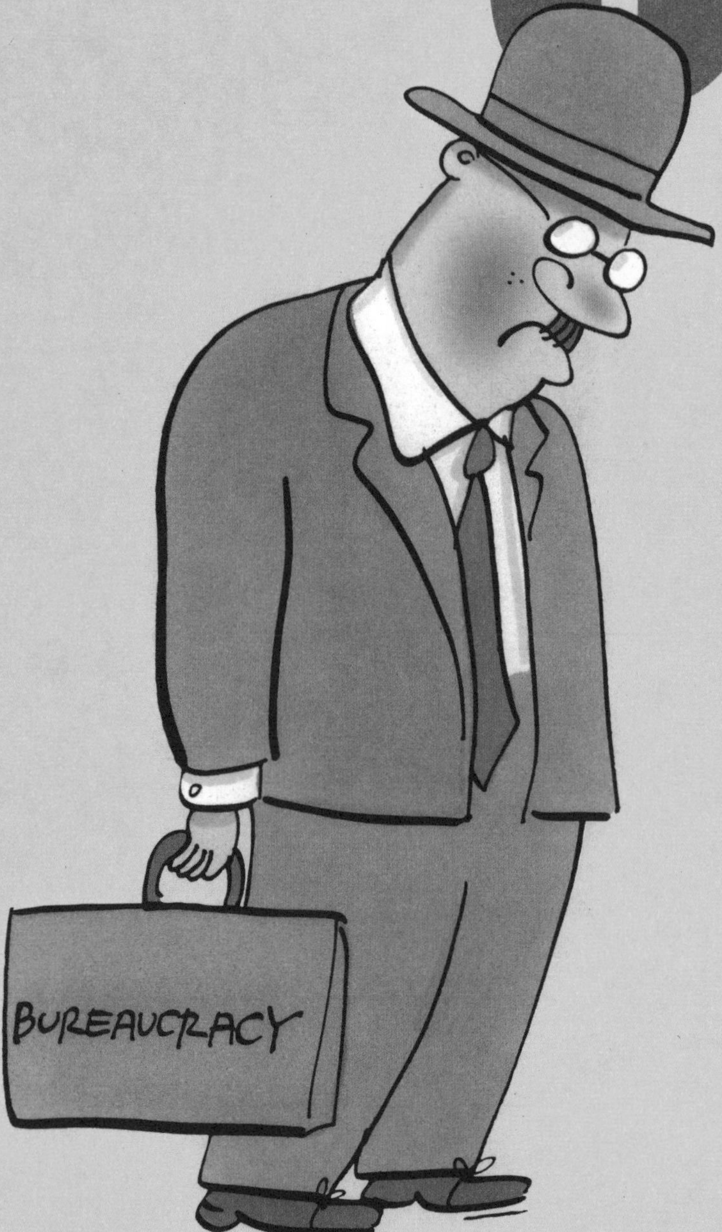

they
that?

Published by THE READER'S DIGEST ASSOCIATION LIMITED
London • New York • Sydney • Montreal

HOW TO USE THIS BOOK

Can They Do That? is divided into 15 chapters, each covering your rights in a different area of day-to-day life. Within each chapter, a variety of situations is dealt with in question and answer form to give you easy access to the vital information you need to know. In addition, single or double-page features tackle important, more involved areas, such as pensions or how to complain about the National Health Service. Flow charts, tables and checklists help you to identify your rights and the actions you should take.

Question

Answer

In some cases, the answer is followed by an **action plan**, giving you step-by-step guidance about how to assert your rights.

'Golden Rule' boxes give you key hints that will help you to avoid trouble in the first place or make sure that your complaint is taken seriously.

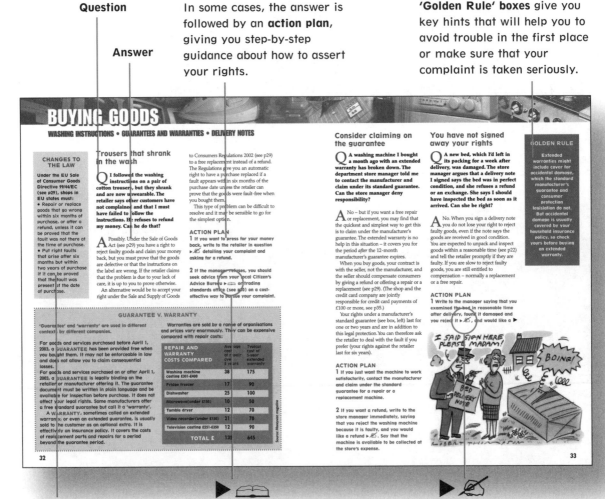

'Changes to the Law' boxes warn you of new legislation that has recently come into effect or is due to do so in the next few years, altering your rights.

Sometimes, a **word of warning** reminds you of key issues you should bear in mind before taking action.

This symbol refers you to the **Directory of Addresses** (pp458-466), where you will find contact details, including postal addresses, phone numbers, email addresses and web sites, of organisations mentioned in the text.

This symbol refers you to the **sample letters** section (pp418-457), where you will find a letter you can adapt for your particular situation. The sample letters are included in the CD that accompanies the book. Using the CD, you simply adapt the relevant letter, and then print it off.

CONTENTS

HOW TO COMPLAIN AND WIN

Can your GP refuse you the treatment you are sure you need? Can your bank make charges without letting you know first? What about the builder who repeatedly fails to follow your instructions ... or the teachers at your child's school who refuse to take action against bullying? Can they do that?

Whatever the answer, the key to asserting your rights is knowing how to make an effective complaint – in person, in writing or, ultimately, in court. There are four 'golden rules' of complaining: know your rights; keep your cool; be clear about your goals; and persist in getting what you want. Follow these when you have been cheated, ripped off or wronged, and whether you simply return faulty goods to a shop, appeal to a consumer watchdog or sue an organisation, you can fight back, and you can win.

FOUR GOLDEN RULES OF COMPLAINING

I MUST WARN YOU I'M A BLACK BELT IN PERSISTENCE

RULE ONE
Know your rights

Reading this book will give you a clear idea of your basic rights in all areas of everyday life – from your right to claim compensation for a late-running train to your rights as a tenant in rented property, from your entitlement to time off work for a family emergency to your child's entitlement to free school transport. Armed with this knowledge, you will be able to claim your rights with confidence.

COMPLAINTS

Be reasonable Rights are not always cut and dried, and you will find that the word 'reasonable' crops up repeatedly in the various laws quoted in the book. Reasonable is a term much used in law to describe something that is appropriate given the circumstances, that is not excessive or extreme. It can often help when you are faced with an unsatisfactory situation to ask yourself whether what has happened is reasonable under the circumstances. If not, you are probably within your rights to ask for matters to be corrected.

RULE TWO
Keep your cool

Your own attitude should be reasonable, too. When something goes wrong it is understandable if you feel anxious, upset or annoyed, but you are most likely to be effective if you stay calm and polite. Do not get angry or confrontational, and never resort to being rude or personally abusive. If you make the effort to explain the problem clearly and reasonably, many people are only too willing to try to put things right.

RULE THREE
Be clear about your goals

To make a successful complaint it is important to be clear from the outset what you want to achieve. Each problem can be resolved in a variety of ways – for example, if you have been sold a defective washing machine, you must decide whether you want a replacement, a refund or a credit note, or whether you are happy to accept a repair.

If the problem is with a service which has not been performed satisfactorily, are you prepared to give the tradesperson the opportunity to sort it out, or do you want to call in someone else to fix it and claim compensation?

If you know what you want from the beginning, you are more likely to be satisfied with the outcome.

RULE FOUR
Persist in getting what you want

If you do not get what you want straight away, you need to be persistent.
- Ask to talk to the boss or a supervisor if you are not making progress.
- Log all conversations, whether in person or by phone, including the date, time, and name and position of the person to whom you spoke.
- Do not let yourself be intimidated by statements designed to put you off, such as 'we don't offer refunds', or 'it's not company policy'. These are usually irrelevant to your legal rights (and possibly illegal).
- Provided that what you want is reasonable, do not allow yourself to be sidetracked by comments about the difficulty of meeting your demands, such as 'we'll lose money if we do that', or 'I'd have to ask the driver to do an extra run'. That is their problem, not yours.
- If initial approaches do not succeed, you may need to take things further – for example, by writing to the company head office, initiating a formal complaint or even threatening legal action.
- Keep a copy of all correspondence and any other paperwork relating to the complaint, such as quotations, invoices and receipts.

OMBUDSMEN AND REGULATORY AUTHORITIES

There are many bodies you can appeal to if you have tried other avenues of complaint and still not got a satisfactory result. They include the various ombudsmen and government-appointed watchdogs. An ombudsman – the term comes from an old Norse word meaning 'administration man' – investigates complaints about public services and also services which are not under government control, such as law and financial advice. For contact details, see the Directory of Addresses (pp458-466).

Advertising Standards Authority (ASA) Oversees content and quality of advertisements in the press, television and radio, and on street hoardings and billboards. See p24.

Financial Ombudsman Service Oversees most financial and insurance companies, including banks and building societies. See p141.

Financial Services Authority (FSA) Regulates companies providing financial services, including banks, building societies, insurance companies, financial advisers and stockbrokers. See p157.

Health Service Ombudsman Investigates complaints about the National Health Service (NHS). See p121.

Independent Police Complaints Authority Investigates complaints about police. See p256.

Information Commissioner Regulates controls on information under the Data Protection Act. See p383.

Legal Services Ombudsman Oversees the handling of complaints about lawyers. See p170.

Local Government Ombudsman Investigates complaints about local councils where there is evidence of maladministration and unfairness. See p193.

Mortgage Code Compliance Board (MCCB) Regulates mortgage providers and advisers. Due to be taken over by the Financial Services Authority on October 31, 2004. See p230.

National Care Standards Commission Regulates institutions providing care services such as care homes, children's homes, private hospitals and nurses' agencies. See p132.

National House-Building Council (NHBC) Sets standards for house building and provides consumer protection for new home buyers. See p219.

REGULATING THE UTILITIES

Each of the utilities has both a watchdog, set up by the government to safeguard the interests of the consumer, and a national regulatory authority. Approach the watchdog first with your complaint. The watchdog will refer any unresolved issues to the regulatory authority.

	Consumer watchdog	Regulatory body
Gas and electricity	EnergyWatch, see p66	Office of Gas and Electricity Markets (Ofgem), see p66
Water and sewerage	local WaterVoice Committees, see p72	Office of Water Services (Ofwat), see p72
Phones	Advisory Committee on Telecommunications (ACTs), see p74	Office of Communications (Ofcom), see p390

Occupational Pensions Regulatory Authority
Investigates and takes action if there is evidence of maladministration in an occupational pension scheme. See p165.

Office for Standards in Education (Ofsted)
Inspects and reports on state-funded and independent schools, including nursery schools, sixth-form colleges and colleges of further education. See p369.

Office for the Supervision of Solicitors
Deals with complaints about solicitors. See p170.

Office of Communications (Ofcom)
Regulates electronic communications industry, including phones and radio and television broadcasting. Investigates complaints about standards in radio and television. See p388.

Ombudsman for Estate Agents A private agency rather than a government-appointed ombudsman. It deals with complaints about estate agents. See p235.

Pensions Advisory Service Investigates complaints from members of the public about occupational or private pension funds. See p165.

Pensions Ombudsman Adjudicates in disputes about the way pension schemes are run. See p165.

Patient Advocacy and Liaison Service (PALS) Operated by individual National Health Service trusts to deal with patients' complaints about health service treatment. See p109.

Postwatch Investigates complaints from customers about postal services. See p77.

Press Complaints Commission (PCC) Investigates complaints about standards in newspapers and magazines. See p390.

Royal Institution of Chartered Surveyors (RICS) Regulates surveyors and investigates complaints about them. See p222.

BEFORE YOU COMPLAIN

If possible, always try to sort out a problem face to face or over the phone. Take the faulty iron back to the shop you bought it from; phone the bank about the wrong sum that was debited from your account – ask to speak to the manager.

Sometimes, problems are too complicated to resolve quickly in person. For example, if your new dishwasher floods the kitchen you may need time to assess the damage, find out who is responsible, check your legal rights and then gather the necessary evidence. In these cases, or if your initial requests for action have not been satisfactorily met, you may need to set out your grievance in writing.

Before putting pen to paper, there are three steps you need to take:
1 Find out to whom you should address your complaint – preferably a named individual.
2 Get the right advice.
3 Decide what you want.

STEP ONE
Find who to complain to
Usually, the best place to start is with the individual immediately responsible for your problem. Write to the carpenter stating that you really would like the shelves to be level; explain in a letter to the store manager just what is wrong with the lawnmower you purchased last week; inform your landlord in writing that your guttering is still leaking despite a promise to fix it.

If you are dealing with a large organisation, you may need to talk or write to someone higher up or more specialised – perhaps at its head office or in its complaints department.

Many big organisations – for example, the National Health Service (NHS) – have an official complaints procedure. The person you first deal with should be able to tell you what to do and who to contact. The details may be printed on a bill or in the organisation's literature. If not, phone and ask who deals with such complaints – get a name and job title, and address your letter to that person.

There may be times when you will want to go through an intermediary – for instance, your insurance company, which, after a car accident, will negotiate with the other driver's insurer. In such a case, the intermediary should tell you how to proceed.

Moving up the ladder If at first you do not get what you want, take your complaint further up the hierarchy. How many steps up you have to go will depend on the size of the organisation. If your grievance is with a sole trader, your next step may be limited to contacting the local trading standards office (see p30) or Citizens Advice Bureau ▶ ⌷ for advice on pursuing your complaint.

If you are having difficulty with a phone or utility company, work your way through the organisation's complaints procedure. If your grievance is not dealt with satisfactorily, contact the relevant watchdog or regulator and perhaps have your complaint referred to an ombudsman (see box, pp8-9).

Sometimes, you will have several avenues to choose from. For example, if you have suffered from poor medical care, you could contact your local Patient Advocacy and Liaison Service (PALS; see box, p109), use the NHS's complaints procedure (see pp114-115), submit a complaint about the doctor to the General Medical Council ▶ ⌷, contact your MP, start a legal case for compensation, or pursue a combination of these possibilities.

STEP TWO
Get the right advice

If your problem is complicated or you want to be sure of your legal position, or you have complained without success, you probably need specialist advice. This will help you to decide if your case is worth pursuing and, if so, how to proceed. You do not have to incur huge expense to get advice. For organisations that can help you, see the box opposite.

Check your insurance
Many people, often without realising it, have legal protection included in their insurance policies. First, check whether your house insurance (for claims about goods and services) or your motor insurance (for claims against other road users) covers you for relevant legal expenses. Travel insurance may also

cover you for legal expenses – if, for example, you have to make an injury claim (see p299) against someone as a result of an accident abroad.

If your insurance company does offer this kind of cover, there is usually a legal helpline you can call for initial advice. If you have a good claim, the insurance company may fund taking the case to court.

Free or cheap advice from a solicitor Many solicitors offer a free or low-cost initial consultation, and for certain claims you may then be able to use a 'no-win, no-fee' arrangement (see p299) to fund taking the case to court. If you have limited means, ask the solicitor or your local Citizens Advice Bureau ▶ ⌷ if public funding (see p15) is available to cover getting advice and help in court.

Specialist or professional associations Consider whether your problem could be assessed by any specialist organisation with an interest in helping you. Trade unions often give free legal advice to members about employment-related disputes and may fund taking a case to a court or tribunal if it appears that you are being treated unfairly or unreasonably.

Or you may belong to a professional association with experience of similar issues – for example, if you are self-employed and are having difficulty in getting a client to pay your bill. A commercial body may also be able to help – for example, motoring organisations often give free or low-cost legal advice to members.

Public bodies and charities Your local Citizens Advice Bureau (see box, opposite) offers free advice. You could also contact the relevant department of your local authority, such as the housing department or trading standards office. The network of Law Centres (see box, opposite) across England and Wales offers free and independent legal advice to people ▶ p13

Finding the best advice

A number of organisations can help you to complain and win. Some offer general advice and give you practical assistance in pursuing your claim; many operate networks of advice centres around England and Wales. They range from government departments to voluntary bodies, from commercial organisations to pressure groups that specialise in particular areas.

ORGANISATIONS THAT CAN HELP

For the addresses, phone numbers, emails and web sites of the following organisations, see the Directory of Addresses (pp458-466).

Citizens Advice Bureaux A network of offices staffed by trained volunteers who can advise on most legal or financial problems, including consumer rights, debt, personal injury, employment law, benefits and housing, effects of crime and personal rights.

Community Legal Service Coordinates a network of organisations offering legal advice and help. Also has a web site with a directory to help you to find solicitors and legal advice centres in your area, and an advice search facility, leading you to reliable legal information on other web sites.

Consumers' Association A body that campaigns for consumer rights. It offers general advice on consumer protection, and publishes the consumer magazine *Which?* and a range of books. Has a subscription-only online service.

Consumer Support Networks These link the services of trading standards offices, Citizens Advice Bureaux, independent advice agencies, and charities such as Age Concern to ensure that wherever you live and whichever organisation you approach for help you will have access to good-quality advice.

Department of Trade and Industry Government department which aims to promote good trading practices and protect consumers from improper business methods. Offers general advice but does not handle individual complaints.

Law Centres A network of more than 50 centres, staffed by lawyers offering free and independent legal advice. Mostly based in major cities and funded by local authorities. Overseen by Law Centres Federation.

Office of Fair Trading Government department which offers consumer information and investigates illegal trading activities, dubious advertising practices and complaints about unfair contract terms.

Trade associations Set up to protect the interests of their members and promote public confidence in them. Most have a code of practice for members, although these have no legal force and their sanctions are generally limited to a fine or expulsion from the association. Many associations offer conciliation and arbitration services for disputes between members and consumers. Using these can be simpler, faster and cheaper than taking legal action.

Trading standards offices All local councils have a trading standards office. Its functions include:
● dealing with suspected breaches of trading legislation, such as misleading pricing, food labelling and credit advertising, inaccurately described properties and holidays, and other breaches of the Trade Descriptions Act
● investigating illegal activities, such as a trader posing as a private individual (for example, at a car boot sale), attempting to deny your legal rights (such as displaying a 'no refunds' sign) or selling pirated goods (such as illegal copies of films, CDs or sportswear)
● taking action against traders who are breaching safety standards in the way they sell or hire out goods or services – for example, by selling contaminated food or unsafe prams, toys or electrical goods; by hiring out unsafe power tools; or supplying services while claiming to be members of a trade association (see above) when, in fact, they are not.

What makes a good letter of complaint?

When making a complaint, much depends on the impression you create with your letter. People are more likely to take you seriously if the letter is well-presented and its tone is moderate and lucid, as in the example below. For a wider selection of letters for different kinds of complaint, see pp418-457; see also the CD accompanying this book, which has copies of all the letters adaptable for your own purposes. If you are writing a letter yourself:

Do:
- address your letter to a named individual
- be polite – firm but reasonable
- state the problem clearly at the outset
- provide copies of any documentation, such as a quotation or receipt (keep the originals), or state what other evidence you can provide
- explain what you have already done to try to get redress
- state clearly what you want
- impose deadlines for actions, such as providing a replacement.

Do not:
- be apologetic, such as by writing 'I'm sorry to trouble you'
- use hesitant language, such as 'I think I should perhaps be entitled to a refund'. Instead, you should say 'I am therefore entitled to a refund'
- be vague – give precise details
- offer alternatives, such as 'I would like a refund or a credit note' – go for a refund first, even if you may be prepared to compromise later
- send your letter until you have checked the grammar and spelling or asked someone else to look it over for you (inaccuracies make your letter less forceful).

Mr Stanley Brown
Customer Complaints Manager
Bargain Electronics Ltd
Bigtown
ST44 4ST

4 Acacia Drive
Little Blandings
Shropshire
ST44 4RH

Email: John.Smith7676@freenet.co.uk   Tel: 01234-1231234

Dear Mr Brown

Re: Archway digital camcorder, model no: 44X44X4, purchase price £499.99

October 22, 2004

I bought this camcorder from your Littletown shop on October 19, 2004, paying the £499.99 purchase price by credit card. A copy of the original sales receipt is attached.

When I got it home and opened the camcorder packaging, I discovered that the lens mounting was badly cracked and that the zoom function did not work. I immediately telephoned your shop and was advised to contact you.

Under consumer legislation, goods are required to be of satisfactory quality and fit for their purpose. In this instance, the camcorder is defective. I have not misused it in any way. I am therefore claiming a full refund.

The camcorder is available for collection. Please contact me to discuss the arrangements.

If the matter is not resolved to my satisfaction in two weeks time, by November 5, 2004, I will be seeking advice on claiming a refund and all related expenses.

I look forward to hearing from you.

Yours sincerely

John Smith

John Smith

who live or work in the catchment area of each of the centres.

Many bodies, notably the Citizens Advice Bureaux, the housing charity Shelter ▶☒ and the various government departments, maintain extensive web sites covering your rights and offering advice. They are also members of networks such as the one run by the Community Legal Service (see box, p11), which aim to help consumers to get quick access to the most appropriate advice.

Some of these bodies also operate phone helplines offering free advice, such as ChildLine ▶☒ for children in trouble or NHS Direct (see box, p109), which provides advice about health and the NHS.

Advice about discrimination If you believe you have been subjected to discrimination or harassment – for example, if you believe you have been passed over for promotion because of your sex or race, or are being sexually harassed by your boss – contact one of the following bodies for advice:
- the Equal Opportunities Commission ▶☒ – to counter discrimination on grounds of sex
- the Commission for Racial Equality ▶☒ – race
- the Disability Rights Commission ▶☒ – disability. They may also be prepared to fund taking a case to court on your behalf.

STEP THREE
Decide what you want
Having received the best advice about what your rights are, you can decide what you want and what is feasible. Do not act in the heat of the moment or vent your feelings without thinking about the purpose of your complaint.

Sometimes, such as in dealings with the NHS or a government agency, your decision about what you want may be influenced by emotional factors. An explanation, apology or official investigation may be as important to you as the possibility of financial compensation. If you have a particular grievance, you may want to make a formal complaint, to see an individual disciplined or even to ensure that someone is prosecuted for a criminal offence.

In your private life, you may want to stop someone doing something which is a nuisance or hazardous to you. In many kinds of situation, you may want to have your expenses reimbursed if someone has caused you financial loss.

Knowing what you want, you will find it easier to make your complaint.

COMPLAINING IN WRITING

You know who to complain to, you have got the relevant expert advice and you know what you want. You have tried to resolve the problem in person, either face to face or over the phone. You are now in a position where you want to put your complaint in writing.

You can write a letter yourself (see box, opposite), or use a standard complaints procedure if the organisation has one. To help you to word your complaint, when you see the symbol ▶✍ in the text turn to pp418-457 for a sample letter, or use the CD that accompanies this book. It contains the same letters, which you can adapt on your computer and then print off.

Keep your letter to one page – other relevant details, such as a diary of events, can be included as separate documents. Send it by recorded or special delivery, which must be signed for on receipt, so that no one can deny having received it. Keep a copy and make a note of the response and what has been agreed.

One letter may be all that is needed to reach a satisfactory outcome. In other cases you may have to write several letters to negotiate a settlement.

Do not accept an unsatisfactory offer If you reach a stalemate in your negotiations, contact the governing body, watchdog or association that oversees the organisation, profession or trade concerned. It may have a conciliation, mediation or arbitration procedure to help you. Examples of such bodies include the Federation of Master Builders ▶☒ and the Society of Master Shoe Repairers ▶☒. Other organisations, such as the Royal Institution of Chartered Surveyors (RICS) ▶☒, use the scheme run by the Chartered Institute of Arbitrators ▶☒, which is legally binding and an alternative to going to court.

If your complaint involves a public service or a matter of general public concern, such as health service facilities or the activities of a local council, contact your local councillor or MP for help.

PREPARING TO GO TO COURT

If you have written letters, gone through the formal complaints procedures and got nowhere, you may be nearing the point at which you will have to consider court action.

Before going to court

Starting a legal action should always be a last resort. Before you take this step, ensure that you have exhausted all other options. The court will expect you to have done everything you can to reach an agreement in other ways. Make sure you have looked into all possible mediation or arbitration procedures.

You should also consider whether what you may gain from a court action will be worth the costs in time, stress and money (see box, right). For example, there may be little point pursuing an action for compensation against an unemployed individual or an insolvent company.

Nonetheless, if you cannot resolve your complaint in any other way, you may have no option but to sue. You do not necessarily need a lawyer for this, particularly if you decide to use the small claims procedure in your local county court (see box, p19). But if you are contemplating legal action, it is generally wise to consult an expert, at least to confirm that you have a good case.

DRASTIC I KNOW, BUT THINK OF THE MONEY WE'LL SAVE NOT GOING TO COURT

DUELLING PISTOLS

What can a court do?

It is important to bear in mind what a court can and cannot do for you. It can only intervene in disputes between individuals if the claim has a basis in law.

A court can help if, for example, you are:
- sold defective goods
- a victim of shoddy workmanship or poor health treatment
- injured at work
- subjected to harassment from your landlord
- subjected to threats of violence from a former spouse.

A court cannot help if you have no valid legal complaint – for example:
- if you agree to pay for something and then find you could have got it cheaper elsewhere
- if you exchange contracts to sell your house and then wish to back out of it
- if your electricity is cut off in a flood.

IS IT WORTH SUING?

Sometimes the cases for and against suing (taking someone to court in order to get redress for your grievances) can be finely balanced. The following checklist may help you to make the best decision.

For suing
- The threat of court proceedings is often enough to prompt the other side to settle.
- Suing will resolve the problem, provided you have a good case.
- Suing ensures that justice is done.

Against suing
- Cases are often protracted and time-consuming.
- Taking legal action can be stressful.
- Suing can sometimes be costly – even if you are not paying legal fees, the cost of your time and effort can be considerable.
- Suing is potentially very expensive if you lose – you could be ordered to pay the other side's costs.
- Even if you win a case for compensation, you may not get the money – for example, if the other party absconds.

PUBLIC FUNDING FOR LEGAL ACTION

Public funding (formerly called 'legal aid') may be available for legal cases involving child protection, medical negligence or domestic violence. It is also sometimes granted in disputes over housing, employment rights, social security entitlements and debt. It is taken from the Community Legal Service (CLS) Fund, administered by the Legal Services Commission ▶⌂.

Can you claim?
You can claim CLS funding if you cannot afford to pay for a solicitor. To decide whether you can have funding, the Legal Services Commission will consider:
- your gross income
- state benefits you receive
- your capital (savings) and your disposable income – how much money you have left after you pay all your bills.

What can you use the funding for?
If you fulfil the conditions and the Legal Services Commission believes your claim is likely to be successful, it may make funding available for:
- limited legal advice from a solicitor, including writing letters on your behalf – usually up to a maximum of two hours or £500
- a solicitor or barrister to argue for you in court.

To apply for public funding you should discuss the matter with your solicitor, who will be able to assess your likelihood of success and apply for it on your behalf.

For more information, contact the Legal Services Commission ▶⌂ for a copy of its leaflet, *A Practical Guide to Community Legal Service funding by the Legal Services Commission*, or you can download it from the Commission's web site.

Common types of legal claim

If you have a valid legal case for suing, it is most likely to fall into one of the following categories:
- breach of contract
- negligence
- breach of statutory (legal) duty.

In all three cases, you will have to prove that the person or organisation you are suing has failed to fulfil a contract or duty.

You will also have to go to court if you need to apply for a court order (see p16). This is an order issued by the court that obliges someone to do, or refrain from doing, something – for example, an 'occupation order' obliges one spouse (in, say, a domestic violence case) to leave the family home.

For an explanation of which court hears which cases, see the box on p17.

Breach of contract A contract is formed when you agree with a person or organisation that they will provide a service or supply goods, usually in exchange for money. So if you order a new dining table, hire a plumber or book a restaurant table, you are entering into a contract – whether or not there is anything in writing.

The law assumes certain terms – known as 'implied terms' – for particular types of contract, which are binding: for example, anything you buy from a shop must be of satisfactory quality, fit for the purpose for which it is normally intended and as described (see box, p29). You can also stipulate your own contract terms, usually in writing (for example, 'the building work to be completed by June 12').

If someone breaks the terms of a contract, you are entitled to compensation for any resulting losses, provided they were reasonably foreseeable. For instance, if a plumber installs your shower and it floods your bathroom, you are entitled to have the work put right and the damage to the ceiling underneath repaired. The expenses involved are a reasonably foreseeable consequence of the plumber's failure to do the job properly. But you cannot claim against the plumber because you could not wash your hair and so lost a modelling contract. This was not reasonably foreseeable.

Negligence In the eyes of the law, 'negligence' is failing to do something that a reasonable and careful person would do, or doing something that a reasonable and careful person would not do. If you are harmed, physically or in other ways, through someone else's negligence (for example, in a road accident or because a solicitor fails to advise you properly), you may be entitled to damages (money paid to you in compensation). To claim

damages, you have to prove all three of the following:
• that the person or organisation responsible owed you a 'duty of care' (see box, p21) – for example, an accountant's or a surveyor's duty to a client, or a driver's duty to other road users
• that the person or organisation breached this duty by failing to stick to reasonable standards which could have reduced your risk of harm – for instance, if a driver crashed into you while speeding, or hospital treatment went wrong because a junior doctor failed to get a second opinion from a senior colleague
• that the harm done to you was predictable and a direct result of an action or omission by the other person or organisation – for example, if you lost a court case because your solicitor failed to pursue it vigorously enough.

The last point can be complicated to prove if there are several possible causes of the problem or you had previous similar problems – for example, if you have neck pain after a car crash but you already had arthritis in your neck.

Breach of statutory duty This is similar to a negligence claim, except that the duty to take care of your safety has been laid down by Act of Parliament, making it a 'statutory duty'. For example, your employer can be held responsible if you are injured at work due to failure to maintain safe working practices, as laid down in the various health and safety regulations, such as the 1992 Manual Handling Operations Regulations (see question, p310).

Court orders A court order is any decision of a court which is binding on the person or organisation to whom it is addressed. Individuals can apply for a court order for a variety of reasons, such as to compel payment of a debt, to regain possession of a property let to a tenant, to determine child support or parental contact or to prevent a violent spouse from returning to the family home.

How to apply for a court order First of all, you need to fill in a form, which you get from your local county court or, for family matters, the family section of a magistrates' court.
• You take the completed form back to the court, where you will be asked to confirm that the information you have entered is correct, and to sign it, witnessed by court staff.
• The other person involved – the respondent – will be notified and a date will be set for a hearing before a judge, who will decide whether or not to grant the order. In an emergency (such as domestic violence), a court order may be sought without notice to the other party – this is known as an *'ex parte'* (from one side only) application.
• The order takes effect when it is physically handed to – 'served on' – the respondent, who is also given notice of a formal court hearing. This is when that person may contest the order, or give an undertaking to refrain from the behaviour that is being complained of – this is not, however, taken as an admission of guilt.

Once a court order is issued How long a court order remains valid depends on the kind of order. For example, an order obliging one ex-spouse to pay maintenance to the other after a divorce is enforceable only as long as the spouse receiving the payments stays unmarried. If that spouse remarries, he or she loses the right to maintenance.

Penalties for failing to comply with a court order can include arrest and imprisonment for contempt of court. ▶ p18

WHICH COURT WILL DECIDE YOUR CLAIM?

Most civil cases – disputes between individuals – are heard in local county courts. A few complicated or high-value claims – for more than £15,000 – go straight to the High Court, which also hears appeals if an earlier court decision is disputed. Family proceedings are dealt with confidentially in special sections of magistrates' courts.

Cases involving specific areas of the law, such as child support, disputes between employers and workers, and disputes about schools, may be heard in specialised tribunals. These are often run by lawyers who, although judges in rank and status, are known as chairmen. Tribunals are more informal and usually cheaper to use than the courts.

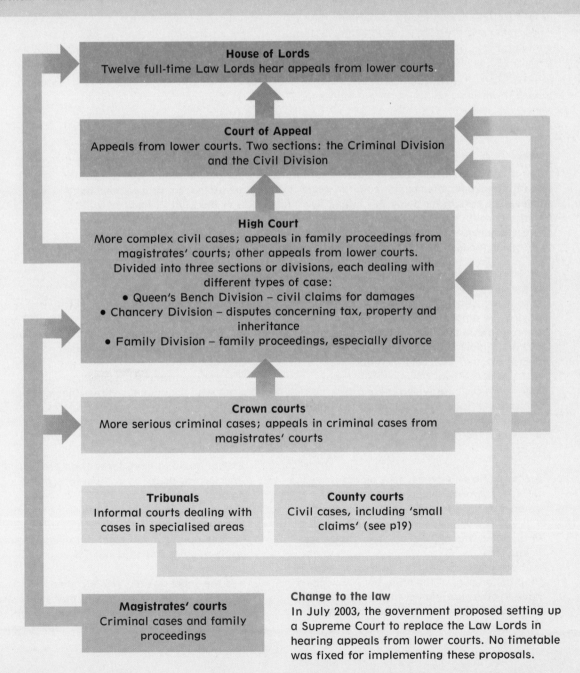

House of Lords
Twelve full-time Law Lords hear appeals from lower courts.

Court of Appeal
Appeals from lower courts. Two sections: the Criminal Division and the Civil Division

High Court
More complex civil cases; appeals in family proceedings from magistrates' courts; other appeals from lower courts.
Divided into three sections or divisions, each dealing with different types of case:
• Queen's Bench Division – civil claims for damages
• Chancery Division – disputes concerning tax, property and inheritance
• Family Division – family proceedings, especially divorce

Crown courts
More serious criminal cases; appeals in criminal cases from magistrates' courts

Tribunals
Informal courts dealing with cases in specialised areas

County courts
Civil cases, including 'small claims' (see p19)

Magistrates' courts
Criminal cases and family proceedings

Change to the law
In July 2003, the government proposed setting up a Supreme Court to replace the Law Lords in hearing appeals from lower courts. No timetable was fixed for implementing these proposals.

TAKING LEGAL ACTION

If you are sure you have a case and you have decided you want to take the matter to court, the next step is to decide whether you want to handle your action yourself, or use a solicitor.

Making a claim in a county court

Cases in county courts (see p17) are allocated to one of three 'tracks', depending on the value of the claim – how much you are demanding in compensation:

• multi track: cases worth more than £15,000
• fast track: cases worth between £5000 and £15,000. The trial should not last more than five hours to limit costs and keep the procedure simple.

• small claims track: cases worth up to £5000, or £1000 for personal injury cases (see pp302-303).

If your case is straightforward and your claim for £5000 or less, you may decide to use the small claims track (see box, opposite). It is especially suitable if someone owes you money and will not pay, or if you are having problems with goods or services. You do not need any previous experience of the law to use the small claims track and you should not need to hire a solicitor.

For anything other than a small claims case, you will almost certainly need a solicitor. If you have already taken professional advice, you may have found a solicitor you trust and who understands your case. If not, you need to find one. ▶ p20

SETTLING OUT OF COURT

Often it can be cheaper for both sides to settle a legal case before it gets to trial. Either side may make an offer to settle 'out of court' at any time after legal proceedings have started. The system for doing this is laid down in Part 36 of the Civil Procedure Rules. An offer to settle may be followed by some haggling. During this time, your solicitor labels any correspondence 'without prejudice'. This means that you are not legally bound by any suggestions made. You still have the right to change your mind and take the case to court.

If the other side makes an offer

1 Your opponents may offer to settle by paying the amount of money they consider appropriate to the clerk of the court (called a 'Part 36 payment'). You have 21 days to decide whether to accept the offer.
• If you accept, your opponents will pay your legal costs, provided these are 'reasonable' (see box, p21), up to the date of their 'Part 36 payment' into court.
• If you reject the offer, the case will go to court.

2 What happens next depends on how much the court awards you compared with the amount of the offer.
• If you are awarded more than the amount of the offer, you will get all your reasonable legal costs.
• If you are awarded the same as or less than the amount of the offer, your opponents have to pay your legal costs only up to the date of their payment into court. After that date, you will be responsible for all your costs and for the other side's costs.

If you make an offer

1 You may make an offer to settle at a price you consider appropriate and make a 'Part 36 payment' into the court. Your opponents then have 21 days to decide whether to accept.
• If your opponents accept, they will pay what you ask, including 'reasonable' legal costs.
• If they reject your offer, the case will go to court.

2 What happens next depends on how much the court awards you compared with the amount of your offer.
• If the court awards you the same as or more than your offer, your opponents may have to pay your full legal bill plus interest on those costs from the date of your offer to settle.
• If the court awards you less than your offer, the other side must still pay your legal costs, but the amount of costs allowed will be decided by the court.

Using the small claims procedure

The small claims procedure is the most straightforward of the three 'tracks' to which county court cases are allocated. You will have to pay up to £120 in court fees, depending on the amount of your claim, but if your action succeeds, the other party is usually asked to pay your costs in addition to the sum you are claiming. Generally, the upper limit for small claims is £5000 – or £1000 in personal injury cases – but more expensive claims may be treated as small claims if the court and defendant agree.

You should be able to run your case yourself, without a solicitor, using the procedure outlined below. For further information, contact the Court Service ▶▭, which publishes a series of pamphlets explaining how the small claims track works, or you can download them from the Court Service's web site. You can also get advice from your local Citizens Advice Bureau ▶▭ or Law Centre ▶▭.

HOW THE SMALL CLAIMS PROCEDURE WORKS

The purposes of the small claims track are to keep costs down by avoiding unnecessary court time and to be straightforward and informal. Cases are decided by a district judge (a judge who deals with county court cases only) in chambers, the rooms where the judge works. There is no full court session. The judge allows both sides to speak and seeks to maintain a balance between them. This means, for example, that if you represent yourself the judge will not allow a solicitor appointed by the other side to use legal jargon. Both sides must help the court to decide fairly.

How you make a claim

1 Fill in a claim form (available from your local county court or by downloading from the Court Service web site ▶▭). Provide details of who you are suing and the nature of the problem, and give a description of what happened. You must also state what, if anything, you have done to try to resolve the problem, and the sum you are claiming, with an explanation of how you arrived at the figure.

2 Take two copies of the claim form to your local county court or send it by recorded or special delivery. Alternatively you can file your claim online: go to the Court Service web site. Keep an extra copy of the form for yourself.

3 The court will send a 'summons' to the person or body you are claiming against (the defendant). This consists of your claim form plus other forms, including the 'defence form' for the defendant to fill in.

4 The defendant has 14 days to reply to the summons by filling in the defence form. If there is no reply, the court may enter judgment in default (that is, without the defendant's input) and award you compensation.

5 If the defendant decides to defend the claim, the court will set a date for a hearing, usually before a district judge. You must send the court any important documents relating to your case no later than 14 days before you see the judge. If both parties agree, the judge can deal with the claim without a hearing, on the basis of statements and documents.

Costs and fees

When you submit your claim form, you pay a small court fee – between £30 and £120 – based on a sliding scale according to the amount you are claiming. If your case is decided in your favour, you should be able to recover the court fees and certain other costs of bringing the action, such as the costs of commissioning experts' reports (up to £200), travelling and overnight expenses, and up to £50 per day for loss of earnings because you had to attend the hearing.

Finding and instructing a solicitor

The best way of choosing a solicitor is through personal recommendation. Ask your relatives, friends, neighbours and colleagues to see if anyone has had any experience of local solicitors. Try to find someone who is approachable, efficient, able to explain the legal process step-by-step and prepared to keep you informed as the case progresses.

Bear in mind that solicitors often specialise in particular areas of law, especially within large firms. One partner may deal with conveyancing, while others spend most of their time involved in divorce cases, or commercial or criminal work. Sometimes, the whole firm specialises in one type of legal work, such as personal accident. As a result, the solicitor who did your friends' conveyancing when they bought their house is not necessarily the best person to represent you if you have a claim against a utility company.

If nobody recommends a solicitor personally, you may find that someone else with whom you are dealing can supply you with a contact. For example, your insurance company may recommend someone on its own panel who has experience of dealing with your type of case.

You can also get a list of solicitors from your local county court office, or contact the Law Society ▶ ⌨, which supplies details of local solicitors and their areas of specialisation.

What to check Once you have a name, double-check that the solicitor handles your sort of case on a regular basis.

Contact the Law Society ▶ ⌨ for copies of its 'client's charter' and the pamphlet, *Your guide to using a solicitor*. These will give you useful advice on what you can expect from a solicitor and the kinds of questions you should ask when you have your first meeting with one.

Some solicitors offer a free initial interview, or you can arrange a short, fixed-fee interview to start off with. This gives you a chance to assess the solicitor, and during this first meeting you should also discuss fees and make sure that you understand, and can cope with, the likely cost. If you are not happy at this stage, go elsewhere.

Once you have found someone you trust, be sure to take notes during meetings and phone calls, so you know exactly what has happened, what to expect next and anything you need to do, such as gather evidence. Ask if you do not understand something.

Handing over the evidence Give your solicitor, or the court concerned, all documentary evidence of your claim. You should include a clear, brief diary of the events that led to your claim and an index of all the documents you are presenting.

If you leave anything out, the court could rule it 'inadmissible' – meaning that it will not be considered when your claim is decided. For example, if you fail to hand over a copy of the report you commissioned showing that the drains in your new house are faulty, this vital piece of evidence may not be taken into account in your claim against the surveyor who missed the problem. This will reduce your chances of getting compensation.

WHICH KIND OF LAWYER?

Broadly, there are two types of lawyer: barristers and solicitors.

Solicitors take instructions directly from you, the client. Your solicitor is your first point of contact and will do most of the work on your case. Solicitors may work in a general legal practice, or specialise in particular fields – for example, conveyancing or accident law.

Barristers are entitled to present a case in court. They usually specialise in a particular area of law, such as intellectual property or medical negligence. Your solicitor will instruct a barrister to assess and present your case in the higher courts – crown courts, the High Court, the Court of Appeal and the House of Lords (see p17). Some solicitors are now allowed to speak in court themselves in certain cases.

The final stage

The next step is for you or your solicitor to give the other side a final warning in writing. State that if you do not receive the payment or other response you are seeking within, say, 14 days, you will start legal action.

Even after legal proceedings have begun, there is a possibility that you will not have to go to court. Once the other party realises that you are serious enough to take legal action, they may choose to give you what you want or try to reach a compromise. Many cases are settled out of court (see box, p18), sometimes as late as the day before the hearing.

But even if your case does come to a hearing, you can approach it with confidence. If you have followed the steps recommended here, you will have your evidence in order and know that you have a good case – and a good chance of winning.

YOU AND YOUR RIGHTS: SOME COMMONLY USED TERMS

A number of legal terms appear frequently in this book. Often they are words or phrases which are widely used in ordinary speech but have a more specific meaning in law.

Burden of proof Responsibility for proving a case.

By-law Regulation laid down by a local authority, with the full force of law in that area.

Claimant The person who starts a law suit. Also known as a plaintiff.

Defendant The person against whom legal proceedings are brought.

Damages Money a court orders to be paid to someone in compensation for a wrong or injury.

Default Failure to comply with a court order within the specified time.

Duty of care A person's or organisation's duty to take reasonable care to avoid injury to anyone likely to be affected by that person's or organisation's actions or failure to act.

Injunction A court order obliging someone to do, or not to do, something.

Liability A legal responsibility for something or to do something.

Mortgage A legal agreement with a company lending money, usually to buy a home. It gives the lender conditional ownership of the home or other asset, until the borrower has repaid the loan.

Nuisance Damage or interference with public property (public nuisance) or individuals' private property or well-being on their land (private nuisance). Includes excessive noise or fumes.

Onerous Involving heavy, possibly excessive, obligations.

Plea A defendant's formal response to charges brought in court. It can be 'guilty' or 'not guilty'.

Reasonable A term to describe something that is appropriate given the circumstances (see p7).

Respondent A defendant in a divorce suit.

Statutory Laid down by an Act of Parliament, as in a 'statutory duty'.

Warrant A court document authorising the police or other law enforcement officials to carry out an action, such as a search or seizure.

BUYING GOODS

Shopkeepers can charge any price they like

Q **I saw a coat in a shop window marked £160 and went in to try one on. When I paid, the staff said that the price in the window was a mistake and that they had to charge £20 more. Can they do that?**

A Yes. A shopkeeper does not have to sell you something at a particular price, even if the item is wrongly labelled. But if the information about prices is deliberately misleading – say, for example, all the prices in the window are lower than those charged in the shop – the owner may be acting illegally.

Customers should be given accurate prices on labels, displays or shelves in shops, catalogues, advertisements and by phone. If shopkeepers compare their prices with those in another shop, the figures they quote should also be correct.

You cannot make the shop staff sell you the coat at the lower price, but you can report the matter to your local trading standards office ► ↦ (see p30), whose officers will investigate.

A poor deal is no reason for a refund

Q **I bought a new electric kettle from a major chain store and two weeks later I saw the identical brand and model much cheaper in a discount supermarket. I asked the chain store staff to refund my money or give me a store credit, but they refused. Can they do that?**

WHEN THE TIME FOR RETURNS IS UP

The law allows you a 'reasonable time' in which to examine goods you buy, reject them if they are faulty and ask for a refund.

'Reasonable time' is something the courts decide, according to circumstances. It depends on factors such as:
● your opportunity to examine the goods
● how obvious the defect is and whether the buyer could detect it early on
● at what stage the defect should have become apparent.
    For example, you may be expected to detect a problem in a perishable item, such as food, in a matter of hours or days, whereas a fault in a new car or a computer may take a few weeks to spot.

What you should do
The quicker you act, the fewer obstacles you will encounter in resolving any problems. Advise the shop of any foreseeable delays in checking the goods.
● Check goods soon after purchase to make sure they can do all you will want them to do.
● Put together self-assembly items to check all the parts are there.
● Switch on electrical items to see that they work.
● Send in any registration card and keep the receipt, credit card slip or other proof of purchase.

A Yes. As a UK consumer you are well protected against unsuitable, poor-quality or faulty goods, but you cannot demand a refund because you could have got a better deal elsewhere.

You should get the product you asked for

Q Before buying a backpack from a camping shop I asked if it was waterproof. The assistant said it was. But when I went on a camping holiday it rained and the backpack leaked, so all my gear got wet. The assistant says there's no obvious fault with the backpack and refuses to replace it or give me a refund. Can she do that?

A No. You should take it back to the shop again, and insist on a refund. As long as you reject the backpack within a reasonable time (see box, left) you are entitled to your money back because according to the law:
• Goods must do what they are intended to do (see p29). As long as you make it clear when you buy goods that you want them for a certain purpose, the product that is sold to you must be right for that purpose. It is reasonable to expect a backpack to be resistant to rain (but not to expect it to be waterproof if it is immersed in a river, for instance).
• Shopkeepers must give you accurate information about the goods they sell. The assistant told you that the backpack was waterproof, and this turned out to be false – a misrepresentation. If you buy on a shop assistant's assurance, you are entitled to return the item or sue the seller for compensation.

ACTION PLAN
1 Return the backpack to the store with your receipt or other proof that you bought it there, and speak to the manager. Say that because the

I'M TAKING MY BACKPACK BACK TO THE CAMPING SHOP... I MAY BE SOME TIME

ANTARCTIC EXPEDITION

backpack is not waterproof, it is not fit for its intended purpose, so the shop is in breach of contract. If you are not given a refund, ask for a receipt for the backpack and leave it in the shop.

2 Complain in writing ▶ ✍ , saying that you bought the backpack on an assurance that it was waterproof. This was a misrepresentation, and you are entitled to cancel the contract. Give the manager 14 days to take action.

3 If you get no response from the manager, contact your local Citizens Advice Bureau ▶ ◰ or trading standards office (see p30) for advice about pursuing your complaint.

4 If any of your possessions were damaged because they got wet inside the backpack, inform the shop and provide evidence of the damage and any financial loss you incurred.

BUYING GOODS

Persuaded by a misleading claim

Q **I signed up for a weight-loss programme after being given a guarantee that I would lose weight. Six months later, the only thing lighter is my bank account. Can I get my money back?**

A Possibly, but only if the guarantee was unqualified and formed part of your contract with the company. Sometimes a statement is no more than trader's puff, a description hyping up a product but not meant to be taken literally. If it is trader's puff, it cannot be relied on as a basis for a legal claim.

If you want to recover your money you may have to take legal action, in which case you would have to prove that you stuck to the programme and that your weight is now the same or greater than when you began.

Since April 1, 2003, and the Sale and Supply of Goods to Consumer Regulations 2002 (see p29), guarantees are legally binding. But this kind of claim often appears in the advertising for a service, then vanishes, or is hedged about with small print, when you sign on – hence the phrases often found on advertisements, such as 'only effective as part of a calorie-controlled diet'.

On the other hand, advertisements in any media are illegal if they are intended to deceive, and you should complain about the advertisement you answered to the appropriate advertising watchdog (see box, below). They cannot award compensation but a successful complaint may strengthen any case you might have against the weight-loss programme.

You would still have to prove your case in court. Since a claim will be complicated you should seek legal advice, bearing in mind that the cost might outweigh any possible compensation.

COMPLAINING ABOUT ADVERTISED GOODS

The Advertising Standards Authority (ASA) says that advertisements have to be 'lawful, decent, honest and true'. Advertisers must not use the word 'guarantee' in a way that causes consumers to be confused about their legal rights. They must spell out the major limitations of a guarantee in an advertisement (for example, 'only if used according to the manufacturer's instructions'). And they must make the full terms available to you on request.

If an advertisement infringes any of these regulations, you can complain to one of the bodies that deal with complaints about advertising, listed right (see also p45). They can order an advertisement to be amended or withdrawn, and they can obtain some degree of redress (if, for example, you order a pressure washer from a catalogue and the hose is shorter than the one shown in the catalogue). But they cannot get back any money you paid or lost on the basis of claims made in an advertisement.

Advertising Standards Authority (ASA) ▶ 🖃
Print and other non-broadcast media, including promotions, direct mail and mail order.
European Advertising Standards Alliance (EASA) ▶ 🖃
All media, including direct mail, in EU countries. Some non-EU countries and non-European countries are associate members.
Independent Committee for the Supervision of Standards of Telephone Information Services (ICSTIS) ▶ 🖃
Promotions and services involving the use of a phone connection (including Internet and interactive TV) to make a premium rate call.
Independent Television Commission (ITC) ▶ 🖃
Commercial television.
Radio Authority ▶ 🖃
Commercial radio.
Trading Standards ▶ 🖃 (see p30)
Shop window displays and point-of-sale material.

A contract to buy may not be binding

Q I paid £120 deposit when I ordered a new sofa. Three days later I lost my job and telephoned to cancel the order. The store's head of department refused to refund my deposit. Can she do that?

A Yes. When you agree, verbally or in writing, to buy something at a stated price, you make a contract with the seller. If you change your mind for any reason, the shopkeeper does not have to take the goods back or refund any deposit you have paid.

Do not commit yourself to a major purchase unless you can continue to pay for it if your financial situation changes. Your contract with the seller is binding unless the documents contain a statement saying that you can change your mind within a certain time.

The time limit for goods to be delivered

Q I ordered an extendable dining table, and said that I wanted it for a party six weeks later. Now, a week before the party the store manager has called to say that he can't guarantee delivery on time. I want to cancel the order, but he refuses to accept. Can he do that?

DELIVERY TIME

If the delivery date influences your decision to buy something, ask for it to be written on the order form or receipt. The law says that goods ordered from a shop must be delivered within a 'reasonable period', and this is open to interpretation unless you state when you order that 'time is of the essence to the contract'.

You cannot cancel a contract because delivery is slow. But at any point you can ask in writing for a delivery date, stating that time is now of the essence to the contract and giving the seller time to comply. If the goods do not arrive by the stated date, you can then cancel the contract.

The law is more specific about mail-order goods, which must arrive within 30 days (see p45).

A Yes. The manager need not accept your cancellation right away. But he will probably have to accept your right to cancel and receive a refund if the table is not delivered in time.

You have the right to cancel if you made it clear when you ordered the table that you wanted it on condition that it was delivered by a certain date. If that date is written on the order form or ▶

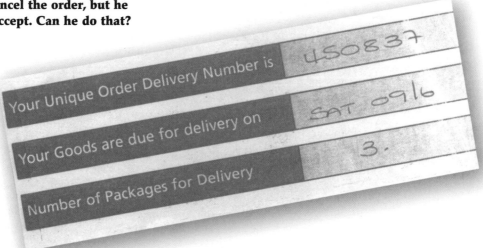

Your Unique Order Delivery Number is — 450837

Your Goods are due for delivery on — SAT 0916

Number of Packages for Delivery — 3.

BUYING GOODS

HIRE PURCHASE • RETURNING GIFTS • UNSOLICITED GOODS • UNSUITABLE GOODS

receipt, you can cancel the contract and pay nothing. A verbal understanding may be enough if the manager remembers that you made it clear when you ordered the table.

ACTION PLAN

1 Write to the manager immediately to say that you made it clear when you ordered the table that it was needed for the date of your party ▶✍. State that 'time is of the essence to the contract' and if the table does not arrive on time you will cancel the contract and request a full refund. Also say that if you incur extra expense as a result of non-delivery (if, for example, you hire a table) you expect to be reimbursed.

2 You may have to take legal action to recover the money.

3 If you paid by credit card, send a copy of your letter to the shop to the credit card company. It is equally liable with the shop for failure to deliver the goods (see p35).

The buyer may not be the legal owner

Q I've decided to sell a motorbike I bought on hire purchase. I'm told it's not mine to sell until I've paid all the instalments. Can this be right?

A Yes. When you buy something on hire purchase, the retailer sells it to the finance company with whom you make the agreement. Technically, you hire the goods for the period of the agreement, and at the end of that period you have an option to purchase it.

The motorbike becomes yours only when you have made the final payment.

Until then the finance company owns it, and you need the company's permission to sell it – you cannot sell it and continue to pay the hire purchase instalments.

If you eventually sell and need to prove ownership, the hire purchase documents do not count as proof – you have to show a receipt.

On the other hand, you can sell goods you bought with a credit card because when you pay with a card, you own the goods and you owe the debt.

The giver should return a gift

Q A friend bought me a ring as a birthday present, but it didn't fit. When I took it back to the jewellers, they refused to give me a refund even though I had the receipt. The manager said that the giver had to bring the goods back in person. Can he insist on this?

A Yes. A contract is made between the seller and the buyer, so the person who bought you the gift should return it to the shop. Moreover, if the ring was bought with a credit card, the refund must be made using the same card.

Check that your friend did not identify you as the recipient of the gift by writing your name on the receipt or invoice. The law makes it possible to give the recipient the right to return a gift if the purchaser made clear to the shop staff that another person was intended to benefit from the purchase. If your friend asked for your name to be written on the sales document, you would have the right to return it to the shop.

If you are not identified as the recipient, the manager does not have to offer you a refund, but many will offer a refund or credit as a goodwill gesture.

> **GOLDEN RULE**
>
> When you buy a gift, ask the sales staff to note the recipient's name on the sales receipt, invoice or guarantee, and endorse it. Most staff will agree, but the law allows them to refuse.

Receiving invoices for goods you did not order

Q I received a set of garden tools in the post, but I didn't order them. Next came a bill for £75, which I ignored. Now I've had a letter from the company that sent the tools threatening legal action. Can the company do this?

A No. You are under no obligation to do anything if you receive items you did not order or ask for (called 'unsolicited goods').

ACTION PLAN

1 Write to the company, with proof of postage, and keep a copy of your letter. Explain that you did not order the goods and ask them to arrange collection of the goods within 30 days (state the date). If the company has not arranged for collection or return postage by this date, the goods become yours to keep or dispose of as you see fit.

2 If you continue to receive demands, contact your local Citizens Advice Bureau ▶  or trading standards office (see p30) and ask them to investigate the matter.

Software that works – but on other computers

Q I bought some software, but it will not work on my computer. I told the sales assistant what type of computer I had, but she didn't tell me that the software wouldn't work on it. Now she refuses to take the software back. Can she do that?

A No. Under the Sale of Goods Act 1979 (as amended; see p29), any item you buy must be suitable for its purpose, including any purpose that you specify when you buy it. You made it clear that you wanted software that would work on your computer; it does not, so you are entitled to a full refund.

ACTION PLAN

1 Go back to the shop, taking some form of proof of purchase (a receipt, credit card slip or cheque book stub, for example), and ask to speak to the manager.

2 Explain that the software will not run on your hardware and that you told the sales assistant what type of computer you have, so you reject the software in accordance with your legal rights and want a full refund.

3 If you are refused a refund, contact your local trading standards office ▶ (see p30) or your local Citizens Advice Bureau ▶ about pursuing your claim.

BUYING GOODS

PROOF OF PURCHASE • EX-DISPLAY GOODS • FAULTY GOODS

OK SIR, THAT'S QUITE ENOUGH PROOF THANK YOU

CLOCKS AND WATCHES

CREDIT CARD BILL

DNA TEST

FINGER PRINTS

EYE WITNESS

Proof of purchase for goods bought

Q A watch I bought six months ago has started to lose time. When I took it back to the shop, the manager refused to repair it because I didn't have the receipt. Can he do that?

A No. A shopkeeper is not legally obliged to give you a receipt, so he cannot demand that you produce one. But he is entitled to ask for proof that you bought the watch from him before accepting responsibility for any faults.

Unless you paid in cash, you should have some documentary proof of your purchase that the shopkeeper can accept. Look through your old bank statements and cheque book stubs for a payment record. If you bought the watch with a credit card, look through your vouchers and statements. If you cannot find a voucher for the watch, contact the credit card company to see if they can provide you with a copy.

No refunds for goods with known faults

Q I bought a digital camera that was marked down because it was an ex-display model. Although it works, the casing is badly scratched in a couple of places, but the shop owner now refuses to take it back. Can she do that?

A Yes. You have no right to return the camera if the defect was – or should have been – obvious at the time when you bought it.

It is reasonable to expect an ex-display model to have some wear and tear to the casing, so the law regards this as a known fault at the time of purchase. If the camera works properly, it qualifies as of satisfactory quality and fit for the purpose for which it was bought.

Weatherproof boots should keep the rain out

Q Some boots I bought a month ago have started to leak. When I took them back to the shop I was told they shouldn't be worn in wet weather. Can the staff claim this?

A Yes, if it was made clear when you bought them that the boots were for party wear, say, or they are made of material that is not weatherproof. But if they are made of a hardwearing material, or described as 'all-weather boots', the staff are wrong. ▶ p30

YOUR RIGHTS AS A CONSUMER

As a consumer in the UK, you are protected from faults and mis-selling by the Sale of Goods Act 1979. Legislation introduced since 1979 has made changes to this Act, so it is referred to as the Sale of Goods Act 1979 (as amended). This legislation states that any goods should be:

Of satisfactory quality:
- in good condition
- safe to use
- generally free from faults or defects
- of reasonable appearance and finish
- durable for a reasonable time.

Fit for their purpose:
- suitable for the purpose for which such goods are generally sold
- suitable for any specific or particular purpose you specify when you buy them.

As described:
- corresponding with any description given, in words or pictures, for example on the label or packaging, in an advertisement or verbally by the seller.

A close match:
- must match any sample you were shown at the time you bought the goods.

- **Reasonable time** If any of these conditions are not met, you have the right to reject the goods and ask for a full refund. You must do this within 'a reasonable time' (see p22).
- **Wear and tear** and **misuse** The retailer who sold you the item is not liable for damage caused by normal wear and tear, or misuse of the item.
- **Loss of value** If you bought an item some time ago, have used it regularly, and then an inherent fault develops, the retailer may be liable to offer you compensation for 'loss of value' (usually equal to the amount it would cost to repair it).
- **Time limit** The trader is liable for up to six years. If you claim after six months from the date of purchase, you must prove that the item was faulty or incorrectly described when you purchased it, or has a fault that should not have developed in the time.

Consumer protection in EU member states

The European Directive 99/44/EC on the Sale of Consumer Goods gives consumers a minimum level of protection for goods bought across the EU. Member states can either let the Directive run alongside their own consumer legislation or incorporate it into domestic law.
- **If a product develops a fault within six months** you are automatically entitled to a replacement or a free repair, or a partial or full refund, unless the retailer can show that the merchandise was not faulty at the time of purchase, or could not be expected to last six months.
- **After six months and for up to two years** you are entitled to a replacement or a free repair if you can prove that the product was faulty when you bought it or that it could be expected to have lasted longer.

Alternatively, consumers can claim for faulty goods under the laws of the country concerned.

How the combined UK/EU regulations work

The Directive above was incorporated into UK law as the Sale and Supply of Goods to Consumers Regulations 2002 and applies to goods purchased on or after April 1, 2003. It does not replace the Sale of Goods Act 1979 (as amended), but it gives consumers a choice of options for goods bought in the UK.

If something you bought **recently** is faulty or was wrongly described, you can:
- EITHER immediately reject the goods and ask for a refund.
- OR ask for a free repair or a replacement. The shopkeeper can refuse only if he can prove that an item was not faulty when you bought it, or should not have developed the fault in the time. If a repair or replacement are not feasible, you can claim a full or partial refund.

For an item you bought **more than six months but less than six years ago** see **Time limit** above.

For detailed information about consumer rights, contact the DTI Consumer Gateway ▶ ⌂ or the Office of Fair Trading (OFT) ▶ ⌂.

The goods they sell must be accurately described, of reasonable quality, and fit for the purpose for which they are sold. It should be safe to assume that outdoor boots sold in Britain will keep your feet dry if worn in wet weather.

The law says that the retailer must prove that a defect was not there when the goods were sold (see p29). If the shop staff cannot prove this, you are entitled to a replacement or a free repair.

GOLDEN RULE

Act quickly to inspect goods you buy, and report any faults to the supplier straight away. The 'reasonable time' the law allows you to spot any faults (see p22) is very short when those faults are deemed obvious. For example, you should notice a plate of the wrong design in a dinner service, or a colour mismatch in a set of tiles as soon as you unpack them.

ACTION PLAN

1 Write to the manager ▶ ✎ , saying that the boots are defective and not fit for their purpose, that the shop is in breach of contract, and that you are entitled to your money back, a free repair or a replacement pair of boots that do not leak. Ask the manager to resolve your complaint within 14 days.

2 If you do not get a reasonable offer of redress within this time, contact your local Citizens Advice Bureau ▶ 📖 or trading standards office (see box, right) ▶ 📖 for advice about pursuing your complaint.

WORD OF WARNING

A shopkeeper need not accept as faulty goods that have been used for a purpose for which they were not intended.

Returning a mistaken purchase

Q I bought a roller blind for my kitchen, but when I got it home I saw that it didn't go with the colour scheme. I took it back to the shop without opening the package and asked for a refund, but the assistant pointed to a 'No Refunds' sign and offered me a credit note instead. Can he do that?

A Yes. As long as the blind was as described on its packaging (see p29), the manager does not have to refund the money. Shopkeepers do not have to compensate a customer for a mistaken purchase, but most will offer a credit note or the option to exchange the item for one of a different size or colour.

The shop's 'No Refunds' sign is not relevant. Customers have the right to a refund in certain circumstances (see p29), and a retailer cannot take this right away by putting up a sign. Signs restricting your rights, such as 'No Refunds', might not be legal and should be reported to your local trading standards office (see box, below).

If you make a similar purchase again, ask if you can return it unopened to claim a refund if it does not match your colour scheme at home. If the manager agrees in advance to allow a refund, his decision forms part of your contract with the shop. But be sure to talk to the manager or a senior staff member. It may be hard to prove that you got a binding assurance from a junior. If possible, get the agreement in writing. If the manager

TRADING STANDARDS OFFICES Every local authority in England and Wales has a trading standards office whose job is to enforce the law relating to commercial trading. Contact your local office for information about your rights as a consumer, and advice on any problem to do with buying and selling. The officers also help traders with information about their rights and obligations. To find your local office, phone your local council switchboard or search the Trading Standards web site www.tradingstandards.gov.uk

later retracts the offer, you can enforce your right to a refund if you have the offer in writing. For advice, contact your local Citizens Advice Bureau ▶ 📖 or trading standards office (see below).

3 If the manager will not refund your money, contact your local Citizens Advice Bureau ▶ 📖 or trading standards office (see box, opposite) for advice on pursuing your complaint.

Goods must match the sample shown

Q **Based on the sample I saw in the shop, I ordered tiles for my bathroom. When they arrived, their colour didn't match the sample. I want to reject them, but the manager says I should expect some variation. Can she refuse to give me a refund?**

A No. The law says that if you buy something from a sample, the goods must match the sample (see p29). If they do not, you are entitled to reject them and ask for your money back. But before taking any action, you should check that the manufacturer or the retailer did not display a disclaimer.

Some goods, such as hand-made fabrics, utensils and tiles, vary naturally in shape, texture or colour. If the retailer or the manufacturer displayed a notice on or near the tiles warning of such variations, you will be deemed to have accepted this when you ordered or bought them and you would not be able to claim a refund.

ACTION PLAN
1 Write to the shop manager, saying that you reject the tiles because they do not match the sample you were shown in the shop before you bought them. Ask for a full refund of the money you paid within 14 days, and quote any invoice or account number.

2 Take the letter with the tiles back to the shop, or say in the letter that the tiles are available for collection and post it to the manager.

Arranging for goods to be returned

Q **When our new double wardrobe was delivered, I found that the door wouldn't shut properly. I called the shop at once and the manager offered to deliver a replacement wardrobe when I returned the first one. Can she ask me to do that?**

A No. If goods are faulty, and provided that you notify the seller within a reasonable time (see p22), you are entitled to reject them and ask for a full refund, or to accept a replacement. Since the wardrobe is a bulky item that had to be delivered to you, it would be reasonable to ask the shop to collect it. (If the faulty item was small and light, it would be reasonable for you to return it yourself.) You must allow the seller reasonable time to arrange for collection and you must take care of it until it is collected.

Write to the manager, saying that you reject the wardrobe and that you want either a full refund or a replacement. Say that the wardrobe is available for collection, and ask the manager to let you know when it is to be picked up.

WORD OF WARNING
The Sale of Goods Act 1979 (as amended; see p29) says that if you reject goods and want a refund, you must show that they are faulty, except for goods purchased on or after April 1, 2003, in which case it is for the seller to prove that the goods are not faulty. If there is a dispute and you cannot prove your point, you will have to pay the cost of returning the goods.

BUYING GOODS

WASHING INSTRUCTIONS • GUARANTEES AND WARRANTIES • DELIVERY NOTES

CHANGES TO THE LAW

Under the EU Sale of Consumer Goods Directive 99/44/EC (see p29), shops in EU states must:
• Repair or replace goods that go wrong within six months of purchase, or offer a refund, unless it can be proved that the fault was not there at the time of purchase.
• Put right faults that arise after six months but within two years of purchase if it can be proved that the fault was present at the date of purchase.

Trousers that shrank in the wash

Q **I followed the washing instructions on a pair of cotton trousers, but they shrank and are now unwearable. The retailer says other customers have not complained and that I must have failed to follow the instructions. He refuses to refund my money. Can he do that?**

A Possibly. Under the Sale of Goods Act (see p29) you have a right to reject faulty goods and claim your money back, but you must prove that the goods are defective or that the instructions on the label are wrong. If the retailer claims that the problem is due to your lack of care, it is up to you to prove otherwise.

An alternative would be to accept your right under the Sale and Supply of Goods to Consumers Regulations 2002 (see p29) to a free replacement instead of a refund. The Regulations give you an automatic right to have a purchase replaced if a fault appears within six months of the purchase date unless the retailer can prove that the goods were fault-free when you bought them.

This type of problem can be difficult to resolve and it may be sensible to go for the simplest option.

ACTION PLAN

1 If you want to press for your money back, write to the retailer in question ▶ ✍ detailing your complaint and asking for a refund.

2 If the manager refuses, you should seek advice from your local Citizen's Advice Bureau ▶ 📖 or trading standards office (see p30) on a cost-effective way to pursue your complaint.

GUARANTEE V. WARRANTY

'Guarantee' and 'warranty' are used in different contexts by different companies.

For goods and services purchased before April 1, 2003, a GUARANTEE has been provided free when you bought them. It may not be enforceable in law and does not allow you to claim consequential losses.

For goods and services purchased on or after April 1, 2003, a GUARANTEE is legally binding on the retailer or manufacturer offering it. The guarantee document must be written in plain language and be available for inspection before purchase. It does not affect your legal rights. Some manufacturers offer a free standard guarantee but call it a 'warranty'.

A WARRANTY, sometimes called an extended warranty, or even an extended guarantee, is usually sold to the customer as an optional extra. It is effectively an insurance policy. It covers the costs of replacement parts and repairs for a period beyond the guarantee period.

Warranties are sold by a range of organisations and prices vary enormously. They can be expensive compared with repair costs:

REPAIR AND WARRANTY COSTS COMPARED	Average cost of repair over 5 years	Typical cost of 5-year extended warranty
Washing machine costing £301-£400	38	175
Fridge freezer	17	90
Dishwasher	25	100
Microwave (under £150)	10	50
Tumble dryer	12	70
Video recorder (under £150)	21	70
Television costing £251-£350	12	90
TOTAL £	135	645

Source: Moneywise magazine

Consider claiming on the guarantee

Q A washing machine I bought a month ago with an extended warranty has broken down. The department store manager told me to contact the manufacturer and claim under its standard guarantee. Can the store manager deny responsibility?

A No – but if you want a free repair or replacement, you may find that the quickest and simplest way to get this is to claim under the manufacturer's guarantee. The extended warranty is no help in this situation – it covers you for the period *after* the 12-month manufacturer's guarantee expires.

When you buy goods, your contract is with the seller, not the manufacturer, and the seller should compensate consumers by giving a refund or offering a repair or a replacement (see p29). (The shop and the credit card company are jointly responsible for credit card payments of £100 or more, see p35.)

Your rights under a manufacturer's standard guarantee (see box, left) last for one or two years and are in addition to this legal protection. You can therefore ask the retailer to deal with the fault if you prefer (your rights against the retailer last for six years).

ACTION PLAN

1 If you just want the machine to work satisfactorily, contact the manufacturer and claim under the standard guarantee for a repair or a replacement machine.

2 If you want a refund, write to the store manager immediately, saying that you reject the washing machine because it is faulty, and you would like a refund ▶ ✍ . Say that the machine is available to be collected at the store's expense.

You have not signed away your rights

Q A new bed, which I'd left in its packing for a week after delivery, was damaged. The store manager argues that a delivery note I signed says the bed was in perfect condition, and she refuses a refund or an exchange. She says I should have inspected the bed as soon as it arrived. Can she be right?

A No. When you sign a delivery note you do not lose your right to reject faulty goods, even if the note says the goods are received in good condition. You are expected to unpack and inspect goods within a reasonable time (see p22) and tell the retailer promptly if they are faulty. If you are slow to reject faulty goods, you are still entitled to compensation – normally a replacement or a free repair.

ACTION PLAN

1 Write to the manager saying that you examined the bed in reasonable time after delivery, found it damaged and you reject it ▶ ✍ , and would like a ▶

GOLDEN RULE

Extended warranties might include cover for accidental damage, which the standard manufacturer's guarantee and consumer protection legislation do not. But accidental damage is usually covered by your household insurance policy, so check yours before buying an extended warranty.

full refund. Say that the bed is available for collection and suggest some convenient dates and times. Alternatively, you could ask for a replacement bed.

2 If the manager refuses, write to the company's head office if it is part of a group, enclosing a copy of your original letter and asking for a refund or replacement ▶✍. Or seek advice from your local Citizens Advice Bureau ▶🖼 or trading standards office (see p30) about pursuing your claim.

WORD OF WARNING

Always inspect goods as soon as you get them home or on delivery, and report problems to the retailer immediately. Any delay could jeopardise your right to a refund or replacement.

WHAT COUNTS AS 'ACCEPTANCE'?

Under the Sale of Goods Act 1979 (as amended; see p29), you have the right within a 'reasonable time' after purchase (see p22) to reject goods that are faulty, unsuitable for their purpose or not as described, provided that you have not formally accepted them. Acceptance counts as:

An action that convinces the seller that you accept the goods
Example: confirming delivery in good condition.
BUT signing an 'acceptance note' on delivery, before you have inspected and checked the goods properly, does not count.

Altering the goods in any way
Examples: causing damage by using the goods carelessly or not following instructions; attaching an item to something such as a wall; decorating the goods, perhaps by painting them or modifying them in some way; removing a part of the goods, perhaps by cutting the labels out of clothing.

Keeping the goods for longer than a reasonable time
What is reasonable time depends on the type of goods (see p22), but any evidence that you have used them suggests you have accepted the goods.

Requesting a refund for a necessary repair

Q I bought a suitcase for a trip abroad, but on the journey the handle broke. The suitcase was under guarantee, but I had to use it so I had a repair done locally. On my return, I took the suitcase back to the store where I bought it. The manager said that by having it mended I had infringed the guarantee, and he refused to refund the repair. Can he do that?

A No. The store must refund the money you paid for the local repair and, if necessary, offer you a permanent repair free of charge.

Under the Sale of Goods Act 1979 (as amended; see p29), you could claim compensation for the repair and any loss of value. Although it might be difficult to claim a refund for goods you have altered, it is up to you to minimise any loss of value, and a temporary repair could be seen in that light.

ACTION PLAN

1 Take the receipts for the suitcase and the repair to the store and speak to the department manager. If the repair was a temporary one, ask for the cost to be refunded and for a permanent free repair to be carried out. If the repair was permanent, ask for the cost to be refunded.

2 If the manager refuses, write to the store's complaints department or head office, explaining the problem and enclosing copies of the receipts.

3 If this does not work, consult your local Citizens Advice Bureau ▶🖼 or local trading standards office (see p30) about pursuing your complaint.

Your rights after a guarantee expires

Q The amplifier on my hi-fi failed two weeks after the standard manufacturer's guarantee expired, but the repairs department at the store where I bought it says I'll have to pay to have it mended. Can they say that?

A No. A guarantee or warranty from the manufacturer is in addition to your legal rights. These protect you against the sale of faulty goods and are binding for six years after the purchase date. If you can show that the failure is caused by a fault in the equipment or its components that was there when you bought them, the trader must provide a free replacement or repair.

ACTION PLAN

1 Speak to the store manager and ask for the problem to be rectified.

2 If the manager refuses, inform him in writing that you will get an estimate for repair from an independent third party, which might suggest the cause of the problem. You will have to pay, but it may sway the manager and you can negotiate to recover the cost.

3 If the manager remains unwilling to offer a remedy, seek advice from your local Citizens Advice Bureau ▶🕮 or trading standards office (see p30) about pursuing your complaint.

PAYING BY CREDIT CARD

If you make any purchase of over £100 (and up to £30,000) on a credit card, you have a contract with the trader and with the credit card company, and the Consumer Credit Act 1974 makes them jointly liable for any problems that arise with the goods or service.

BUT this rule does not apply to debit cards (the money is taken out of your bank account) or charge cards (such as store cards, which must be paid off each month), and not to cheques or credit card cheques (cheques issued by the credit card company and debited to your credit card account when you write them). For these, and for transactions of less than £100, only the seller is liable.

AND some retailers make an extra charge for paying by credit card. A retailer who charges extra must display a notice prominently in the shop giving details of the price differences.

The legal benefits are:

• You can complain to the seller or the credit card company, or both, if goods or services are faulty or unsuitable, or if they are not delivered. This can be very useful if the trader is unhelpful.

• You have a right to take action against the card company for the full value of the transaction if the trader goes out of business or cannot be traced.

• For faulty goods purchased abroad and paid for by credit card, always copy any letters of complaint to the credit card company and ask for its help in resolving the complaint. Do not forget other sources of help and advice for foreign complaints, such as the European Consumer Centre ▶🕮 or the Better Business Bureaux ▶🕮 in the USA, Canada and Japan.

Reclaiming a deposit paid to a bankrupt shop

Q I ordered a kitchen range from a local supplier and paid £180 as a deposit. Yesterday I learned that the suppliers are now bankrupt. Can they keep my deposit?

A Yes. The Official Receiver (the person appointed by the court to take control of a bankrupt company's assets) can keep your deposit. You may be able to reclaim it if you paid by credit card as card payments of more than £100 give the buyer rights against the retailer and the card company (see box, above). ▶

BUYING GOODS

CREDIT AGREEMENTS • SALE PRICES

If you paid with a debit or charge card, cash or a cheque, you have less chance of reclaiming your deposit because you will have to pursue the supplier. You first need to find out whether the supplier ceased trading, went into liquidation or was run by a single owner (a 'sole trader') who declared bankruptcy as the legal position is different in each case.

To pursue a claim you need specialist advice. Bear in mind that insolvency proceedings may take a long time and that you may not recover any of your money, this course of action may not be worthwhile for £180.

If you proceed against the bankrupt store you should be invited to a creditors' meeting to be told how much money is left for people to whom the store owed money. If funds remain after those with a prior claim (such as employees, banks and government departments) are paid, you may get some or all of your money back.

ACTION PLAN

1 If you paid by credit card, write to the credit card company and ask if it can refund your deposit.

CREDIT AGREEMENTS

A credit agreement is any financial arrangement that enables you to spread payments over time. Cash loans, credit and charge cards, interest-free loans, hire-purchase agreements and conditional sale agreements are all credit agreements.

Most agreements for £50-£25,000 and involving more than four repayments are regulated by law. You must be given a written copy of the agreement, which should include details of any cancellation or early repayment rights. Common arrangements are:
• a credit sale – you own the goods from the start, but pay for them in instalments plus interest
• a department store credit agreement – a loan to buy specified items is arranged for you by the store through a finance company.

---

2 If you paid by debit card, charge card or cheque, write to the store manager outlining your claim. Send the letter to the store's business address, or the registered address if this is different (it should appear on the documents the store sent you).

3 Contact your local Citizens Advice Bureau ▶ ⬚ or trading standards office (see p30), who will be able to advise you on pursuing your claim. They may also be able to obtain information about the status of the business. This is useful if the head office is not local to you.

Using a department-store credit agreement

Q I ordered new carpets from a department store and signed a credit agreement to pay for them. We now want to cancel the agreement because we're moving house, but the manager says we can't do this. Can he say that?

A Probably, if you signed the agreement in the store (if you signed it in your own home, see p39). A credit agreement is similar to a credit card payment in that you have effectively bought the goods and now owe a debt. The only difference from a cash payment is that you borrowed the money.

The law allows you very little time to withdraw from a credit agreement if you sign it on business premises – only until the creditor (the company that advances the loan) has also signed the agreement. Once the creditor has signed, the agreement is legally binding on both sides. You can take action against the finance company if it breaks the agreement; and the company can

sue you if you break it. You cannot change your mind unless the agreement gives you a right to cancel, but you have rights if the goods prove defective (see p29).

ACTION PLAN

1 If it is only a day or two since you signed the agreement, call the finance company immediately and state your intention to withdraw. You can withdraw only if the company has not yet signed the agreement. If you can withdraw, confirm your intention to do so in writing.

2 If it is too late to withdraw, read the written documentation of your credit agreement carefully. If you find details of cancellation rights, write immediately to the finance company stating your intention to cancel the agreement, and send the letter by recorded delivery.

3 If you have no cancellation rights, contact the finance company and ask if the management will let you end the agreement before the carpets are delivered. They may charge a cancellation fee or administrative costs as well as repayment of any part of the loan already advanced.

A sale price must be a genuine reduction

Q I bought my daughter a hi-fi reduced from £499 to £250 in the sale. She told me she'd seen the identical system in the display window at £200 just before the sale. Can the shop staff do that?

A Probably not. Consumers are entitled to accurate pricing information on goods bought from shops, and the law says that goods offered as reduced, on special offer or on sale must have been displayed at the old price for

at least 28 consecutive days in the previous six months. Goods marked 'seconds' or 'special purchase' are the only exception.

If you are certain the goods had not been more expensive for 28 days before the sale, ask to see the manager and complain. You might be offered a discount. Alternatively, you can report the matter to your local trading standards office (see p30).

ACTION PLAN

1 Think back and reassure yourself that no one among the shop staff made clear to you that the goods had been on sale at the lower price during the previous 28 days. If the shop did not tell you the goods had been less expensive, contact them and ask them to explain.

2 If you are not happy with the explanation, report the matter to your local trading standards office (see p30).

BUYING GOODS

RETURNING SALE GOODS • DOORSTEP SELLING • SECOND-HAND GOODS

Most sale goods can be returned

Q **The clasp on a leather bag that I bought in a sale broke the third time I used it. The shop staff deny responsibility and have a 'no refunds or exchanges' policy for sale goods. Can they do that?**

A No. Your rights are the same for sale goods as for new goods unless they are on sale because of a fault that is obvious or pointed out when you buy them. You are entitled to a refund, replacement or repair, as long as there was no obvious problem with the clasp when you bought the bag, you have not mistreated it, and you claim within the time limits (see pp22 and 47).

ACTION PLAN
1 Return the bag to the shop with proof of purchase (see p28) and ask the manager for a refund, a free repair or a replacement. Ask for any agreement to be confirmed in writing.

2 If the manager refuses all three options, complain in writing ▶ ✍ to the manager or the head office.

3 If this does not work, contact your local Citizens Advice Bureau ▶ 📖 or trading standards office (see p30) about pursuing your complaint.

You are protected against doorstep selling

Q **Two days ago a doorstep salesman persuaded me to sign for £3500-worth of double glazing. Today I changed my mind and phoned to cancel, but the salesman said I couldn't. Can he say that?**

A No, you have a right to cancel. The salesman should have told you this when you signed the agreement. Since he did not, the contract is invalid and the company can be prosecuted and fined.

The law protects people who sign a contract to buy goods or services in their home following an 'unsolicited visit' from a salesperson. A visit is unsolicited if a salesperson calls on you unannounced, without an invitation, or you give a time to visit only after a phone call or a letter that you did not request.

If a salesperson calls on you without warning and you agree to a return visit at a later time, the visit is still considered an unsolicited one. But the law does not protect you if you invite a salesperson to visit – by phoning the company to ask for a quotation, for example.

If you sign a contract for double glazing after an unsolicited visit, and you are not paying for it with a credit or finance agreement given to you by the salesman, you have the right to a 'cooling-off period' of seven days in which to change your mind

If you signed a finance agreement that the salesman gave you, and you discussed it with him while he was in your own home (and not over the phone), you have the following rights:
• the finance company must send you a notice of the agreement by post, and you have a cooling-off period of five days from the day you received it in which to change your mind
• if you change your mind during the cooling-off period, you have a right to cancel the contract and owe nothing. You do not have to give reasons. If you paid a deposit, it should be returned in full.

If you cancel the agreement during the cooling-off period and the salesman left goods or parts with you, keep them for the company to collect. You do not have to arrange to return them.

ACTION PLAN

1 Write immediately to the sales company cancelling the contract, and keep a copy. Pay for recorded delivery as proof that the letter was received.

2 If you signed a finance agreement offered to you by the salesman, notify the finance company in writing that you have cancelled the agreement. Do this even if you have not received a notice from them confirming it.

3 Contact your local trading standards office (see p30) for advice. Tell them of a possible illegal trading practice.

WORD OF WARNING

Your right to a cooling-off period applies only to unsolicited visits, so unscrupulous salespeople may try to persuade you to sign a form or write a letter stating that you invited them in. Refuse to sign.

Second-hand goods should work properly

Q I bought a used freezer from a local second-hand shop. When I set it up at home I found that although it keeps food frozen, a persistent leak means there is always a puddle on the floor. I complained, but the manager says it's nothing to do with her. Can she deny responsibility?

A No. Second-hand goods are covered by the Sale of Goods Act 1979 (as amended; see p29), so you have the right to expect any used items you buy from a trader (but not from a private individual, see p41) to be fit for their intended purpose, of satisfactory quality, and to match any description or sample.

Although your freezer is doing the job for which it is intended, its quality is impaired because it is leaking. However, you have to match your expectations to

WHO TO LET INTO YOUR HOME

The National Doorstep Cold Calling Protocol is promoted by the police, the Trading Standards Institute and charities such as Help the Aged to provide reliable guidelines on which callers you should or should not allow to enter your home. The Protocol requires doorstep callers to make an appointment in advance whenever possible. It is not legally binding, but reputable companies expect their representatives to obey it, so do not admit doorstep callers into your house unless they:

- Declare their name and the organisation they represent.

- Give you an identification card with the name and logo of the organisation they represent and a photograph with which you can compare the caller's face – and explain that they will not enter the house until you do so. A reputable caller should also carry a large-print card with an enlarged photograph to show to customers with impaired vision.

- Explain the purpose of the visit.

- Give you the phone number of the organisation they represent and explain that you can use it to check their identification and the information they have given you. It should be a landline number (not a mobile or a cellphone) and be answered by a person, not a machine. It should be listed in the phone directory and on company advertising material. It should ideally be a freephone number.

- Ask you if you prefer to arrange to have someone else, such as a neighbour, present during the visit.

- Tell you that they will not enter your house without your permission.

- Ask you if you would prefer them to leave and return at another prearranged date and time.

See the Telephone Preference Service on p292 and the Mailing Preference Service on p293.

the price paid and the fact that the goods are used. You cannot expect the same degree of performance, reliability, finish or durability from second-hand goods as you would from new ones. ▶

BUYING GOODS

You should explain the problem to the shop manager and ask if anything can be done. Be ready to accept any reasonable offer. If necessary, ask your local Citizens Advice Bureau ▶ ⌷ or trading standards office (see p30) for advice.

WORD OF WARNING

When buying second-hand goods, ask specifically if anything is wrong with them. The seller is not allowed to give false or misleading information. If you are told that there are no major faults, and this turns but not to be true, you may be able to get your money back.

Buying goods from a private individual

Q **The second-hand television I bought from my neighbour turned out to be useless, and would cost more to repair than I paid him for it. Have I any comeback?**

A Probably not, unless he assured you that the television was in good working order. When you buy something from a private individual, you are not protected by the stipulations of the law (see p29) that goods sold must be of

---

BUYING FROM NON-PROFESSIONAL TRADERS

When buying from car-boot sales, the small ads in newspapers or someone in the pub, you are not protected by the Sale of Goods Act 1979 (as amended; p29), so inspect goods carefully before you commit yourself to buy.

• Never buy from an advertiser whom you can contact only through a mobile phone number, or who wants to meet in a public place or at your home or workplace.

• Ask for a receipt that includes the seller's name and address.

• Beware of goods that could be hazardous, such as electrical devices, car seats and furnishings that could give off toxic fumes in a fire, children's toys that could injure or choke, and children's clothing that might not be flameproof.

• Beware of stolen goods. Popular items include power

tools, garden ornaments and mountain bikes. If you suspect that something you bought may have been stolen, contact the police.

• Beware of pirated goods. Often, these are cheap, poor-quality video and audio tapes and CDs. Take the pitch number, if there is one, and note down the car registration number, and inform your local trading standards office (see p30).

• Regular sellers of new items at markets and car-boot sales are probably professional traders masquerading as private sellers (see box, right). Contact your local trading standards office (see p30).

satisfactory quality and fit for the purpose intended. For private sales generally, the principle caveat emptor ('let the buyer beware') holds.

You do have some protection. The goods must be as described. If a jacket you are told is made of leather turns out to be imitation leather, you can ask for your money back. Private sellers must not misrepresent the goods they sell. They should not lie about the age of an item, or tell you that it works if it does not.

It can be very difficult to get compensation from a private seller. Seek advice from your local Citizens Advice Bureau ▶ 📖 or trading standards office (see p30) about your complaint, although it might prove difficult to pursue it.

Auction goods must be described correctly

Q **At an auction I bid for a sofa bed in working order, and it proved defective. I called the auction house but they say I cannot return it. Can they do that?**

A Probably not. Any statement made by an auctioneer about the quality and function of goods at auction must be accurate. This is especially important if you did not have the chance to examine the goods before the auction or if you relied on notes in the auctioneer's sale catalogue, or on other expertise in assessing what you wanted to buy.

For goods bought on or after April 1, 2003, you can rely on the new consumer regulations and rights detailed on p29. But solutions such as repair, replacement, partial refund and full refund do not apply to second-hand goods if the auction house gives you the opportunity to attend the auction in person and inspect the goods for sale, and displays clear signs stating that consumer rights do not apply to second-hand goods. If the auction house does not make it

possible for the public to inspect auction items, then you can rely on your rights under the Sale of Goods Act 1979 (as amended; see p29). These rights also apply to telephone and Internet auctions.

ACTION PLAN

1 Contact the auctioneer and explain that you bought the sofa bed because it was described as 'in working order'. Say that the description was inaccurate because it does not work properly. The auctioneer or seller may let you return it for a refund, or offer a free repair or compensation for loss of value.

2 If you are not satisfied with the response, find out first whether the auctioneer excluded liability for faulty goods in the catalogue or on a notice at the saleroom. If so, you may still have an action against the seller, but you may need expert advice on how to proceed. Contact your local Citizens Advice Bureau ▶ 📖 or trading standards office (see p30).

PROTECTING YOUR INTERESTS AT AUCTION

- **Some auctioneers offer to let you pay an 'indemnity fee', which entitles you to reject goods within one month of purchase. This is a wise precaution, especially if the auctioneer excludes liability.**
- **If you pay with a credit card, you have extra protection if things go wrong (see p35).**

BUYING FROM PRIVATE INDIVIDUALS

When you buy goods privately, you have less protection than when you buy from a shop:

- **Rogue traders often masquerade as private sellers in order to avoid their obligations under the Sale of Goods Act 1979 (as amended; see p29), leaving you without protection against malfunctioning, shoddy or dangerous goods.**
- **Goods may be substandard, counterfeit or imported illegally.**
- **Rules to protect consumers may not apply or may be ignored. You are at risk of misleading pricing, poor food hygiene, unfair trading and price-marking practices, breaches of the Trades Descriptions Act and of safety standards applying to goods such as children's toys, pushchairs and prams, and heating appliances.**
- **If something goes wrong, it can be difficult to track down the seller, and even more difficult to claim compensation.**
- **Some goods are stolen. Even if you did not know this when you bought them, you cannot keep the goods in order to claim a refund from the seller – you must hand them in to the police, then find the seller and claim a refund.**

BUYING GOODS

DANGEROUS GOODS • MAIL ORDER

When something you buy causes you harm

Q I was drinking a cup of instant coffee when I saw that it contained tiny shards of glass. Luckily I managed not to swallow any glass. Am I entitled to compensation?

A Yes. In addition to your rights under the Sale of Goods Act 1979 (as amended; see p29) – which entitles you to a refund or replacement of the coffee from the trader – you have rights under the Consumer Protection Act to compensation for injury caused by a defective product. These rights are usually against the manufacturer of the goods.

If it is unclear who the manufacturer of the coffee was, and the staff at the shop where you bought it cannot tell you, you can sue the shop. If you are not harmed by the product, you are not entitled to compensation, although a letter to the shop or the manufacturer may result in a goodwill gesture.

This incident involves a safety issue that may affect other consumers, so you should report it without delay.

ACTION PLAN

1 Keep the cup with the coffee dregs and the jar of coffee. Contact your local trading standards office (see p30), which will be able to take action under the Consumer Protection Act and the Food Safety Act. The jar of coffee is needed as evidence and trading standards will give you a receipt for it.

2 If you are concerned about having sustained an injury, contact your GP for advice. You will need medical evidence should you wish to pursue a claim for personal injury.

3 Inform the shop manager of the action you have taken so far.

4 Decide what you want – a refund, a replacement with another brand of coffee or an apology. The trading standards office or your local Citizens Advice Bureau ▶ 🖾 can advise you on pursuing your claim.

If you are injured, you need specialist advice

Q My daughter was using her hair dryer, which is nine months old, and it caught fire. Her hair was singed, she burned her hand, and when she dropped the hair dryer the bedroom carpet was scorched. Can we make any claim?

A Yes. Your daughter may be entitled to compensation for personal injury under the Consumer Protection Act. You will have to show that she followed the manufacturer's instructions, that the appliance has not been altered in any way, that it has not been misused and that the item is less than three years old. You may also have a claim for damage to the carpet.

ACTION PLAN

1 Gather all the information you can about the hair dryer, including receipts, guarantee and original packaging – and contact your local trading standards office (see p30).

2 Contact your GP for treatment, advice and a consultation as soon as possible. You will need medical evidence should you wish to pursue a claim for personal injury. Take photographs of your injuries and of any damage to your property.

3 If the carpet needs to be replaced, obtain two or three quotations. If the replacement cost is more than £275, you may have a claim against the manufacturer of the hair dryer, although you may not be entitled to the entire replacement cost, particularly if it was an old carpet. The trading standards office can advise you about this.

4 Contact a solicitor specialising in personal accident claims for advice on making a claim. Many offer a free initial consultation.

WORD OF WARNING

You may fail in a claim for personal injury or property damage if the problem stemmed from anything that you did; for example, if you have rewired electrical equipment carelessly, or submerged the object in water.

ACTION PLAN

1 Write to the mail-order company, say that you have the right to cancel and ask for a refund. If you paid by credit card, contact the credit card company (see p35) and ask for advice.

2 If you do not receive a refund, write to the Advertising Standards Authority (ASA) ▶ ⌫ (see p24) and tell them that you have not received either the goods or a refund. The ASA will look into the affair and try to resolve it.

3 Inform your local trading standards office (see p30), who keep records about company trading practices.

4 Check whether the mail-order company belongs to the Mail Order Traders Association (MOTA) ▶ ⌫. If so, you can ask the MOTA conciliation service to help to resolve the dispute.

A long wait for mail-order goods

Q I have been waiting six weeks for a computer I ordered and paid for from a mail-order company. I now want to cancel the contract and receive a refund but the person I spoke to when I phoned said the company wouldn't allow it. Can the company just make me wait?

A No. If you buy goods by mail order, by phone or through the Internet, they should be delivered within 30 days (see pp44-45). If they do not arrive, you have the right to cancel the order and ask for a refund. You can, however, waive this right and agree to a later delivery when you place the order.

These rights, under the European Consumer Protection (Distance Selling) Regulations 2000 (see p45), apply only to goods bought in the EU.

BUYING GOODS

Protection for home shoppers

When you buy goods by mail order, telephone, fax, over the Internet or through a television shopping channel (but not online auctions), you have the same rights under the Sale of Goods Act 1979 (as amended; see p29) as when buying from a shop. If you buy the goods from a company within the EU, you have rights under the Consumer Protection (Distance Selling) Regulations 2000.

You can minimise the security and privacy risks of shopping on the Internet by looking for companies that carry the admark, TrustUK and Which? symbols, indicating that they follow a recognised code of good trading practice online.

If you want to cancel your order, or the goods do not arrive, or they are faulty, it is essential to act quickly (see p51).

The Office of Fair Trading (OFT) ▶ provides step-by-step advice on shopping on the Internet. You can get a copy of their free information leaflet from their publications order line 0870 60 60 321, or by downloading it from the web site **www.oft.gov.uk**

TRUSTWORTHY TRADING ONLINE

admark

The 'admark' icon on a web site, email, banner, popup or other online advertisement indicates that the company displaying it subscribes to the rule of the Committee of Advertising Practice ▶ ⌒ that advertising online should be 'legal, decent, honest and truthful'.

trust UK

The TrustUK hallmark on a company web site indicates that the company follows an approved code of practice for fair trading, secure payment, privacy and protection of children during online shopping.

SECURE INTERNET SHOPPING

Follow these rules to minimise the possibility of theft and other problems when you shop online:

• Deal only with traders who give a business name, geographical address and landline phone number. Try to deal with well-established companies with well-known names, or those recommended to you by people you know.
• Look for a statement on the web site indicating that the site is secure. This often takes the form of a secure site logo and a padlock symbol. If you cannot find one, do not deal with the company.
• Print out the 'terms and conditions' on the company's web site and check what protection you have against problems that may occur. Keep a copy of the printout.
• If you buy from outside the EU, you may have difficulty getting something done about undelivered, damaged or faulty goods; you may have less consumer protection; guarantees may

be difficult to enforce; legal action against a foreign supplier may be expensive and difficult to pursue; and electrical goods may be incompatible.
• Check the delivery charges. If you buy outside the EU, you may be liable for VAT, customs duty and other extra charges.
• Never give out credit card details unless you are on a secure site – check the screen for a padlock symbol at the bottom of each page.

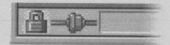

• Print out and keep your order and its confirmation in case of future disputes.
• When you pay by credit card, check your statement immediately it arrives and notify the credit card company at once of any discrepancy.

HOME SHOPPING IN THE EU

If you buy from an EU country you have rights under the European Consumer Protection (Distance Selling) Regulations 2000. These apply to goods but not services.

Your rights include:

• For most goods, you should have a cooling-off period of seven working days from the date you receive the goods, during which you may cancel your order (in writing, by letter, fax or e-mail) and owe nothing.

• You should be given information on your right to cancel. If not, the 'cooling off period' is extended to three months, or seven days from when you do receive the information.

• If you cancel your order, the company must refund any money paid within 30 days.

• If you bought the goods under a credit agreement suggested or organised by the seller, this is automatically cancelled if you cancel your order.

• The goods must be delivered within 30 days unless you agree otherwise.

MAKING COMPLAINTS

Check before ordering from mail-order, Internet or other distance-selling companies that the retailer is a member of one of the trade associations listed below. If you have a problem, you can contact the trade association for help. Several offer arbitration services whose decisions are binding on their members.

See p24 for bodies that handle complaints about advertisements, including those originating in EU countries outside the UK.

For complaints about transactions in a foreign country outside the EU contact a Citizens Advice Bureau or that country's Chamber of Commerce in the UK (details from the embassy or consulate).

To complain about	Contact
Mail-order traders	The Mail Order Trade Association (MOTA) ▶ ⌂
Direct marketing (advertisements citing the company's contact details, leaflets, inserts in magazines, catalogues and mailshots)	The Direct Marketing Association (DMA) ▶ ⌂
Internet traders	TrustUK ▶ ⌂ or any trade organisation to which a TrustUK web trader belongs
The content of a company's web site. Illegal activity by an Internet or other trader	Your local trading standards office (see p30), or the Office of Fair Trading ▶ ⌂
An Internet business in any country	www.Econsumer.gov, a US Federal Trade Commission web site providing contact information for consumer-protection bodies in participating countries
A trader you found through your Internet service provider (ISP)	Your Internet service provider (ISP)

To minimise the opportunity for fraud and theft:
• never send cash through the post
• do not send details of your bank or credit card account by fax or email
• only give bank account and credit card details to companies that you know to be members of MOTA, DMA or TrustUK or other trade associations.

How late can you make a complaint?

Q **My old hedge trimmer packed up last winter, so I bought a new one when I happened to be in a garden centre. I didn't need to use it for several months, and when I did I discovered it didn't work properly. The manager says it's too late to complain. Is that right?**

A No. The Sale of Goods Act 1979 (as amended; see p29) says you should check your purchases and report faults to the seller 'within a reasonable time' (see p22), so you may have left it too late to reject the hedge trimmer and ask for a refund. But you are entitled to compensation for up to six years if the goods were faulty when you bought them. In this case you can claim for loss of value – a repair or an amount equivalent to the cost of a repair.

In addition, under EU law (see p29), if a product develops a fault within six months you are entitled to a replacement or a free repair, unless the retailer can show that the merchandise was not faulty when you bought it or could not be expected to last that long. After six months it is up to you to show that the product was faulty when you bought it or should have functioned for longer.

ACTION PLAN

1 Take the hedge trimmer back to the garden centre and speak to the manager.

• If you bought it less than six months ago, explain that you are entitled to a replacement or a free repair. If the trimmer cannot be repaired, you can still claim some or all of your money back.

• If the trimmer is more than six months old, explain the circumstances and point out that you are entitled to have faulty goods repaired for up to six years after the date of purchase.

2 If the shop refuses a refund or repair, consult your local Citizens Advice Bureau ▶ ⌂ or trading standards office (see p30) about pursuing your claim.

WORD OF WARNING

Your rights are based on the assumption that the goods have been handled with care and kept under conditions that are reasonable for the type of product. If, for example, you kept the hedge trimmer in a damp, leaky shed all winter, you could not expect it to work in spring.

Claim for damage caused by faulty item

Q **My new dishwasher worked for six weeks, then flooded the kitchen, ruining a new floor. The suppliers agreed to repair or replace the dishwasher, but refuse to pay the cost of replacing the floor. Can they do that?**

A No. You are entitled to have faulty goods fixed and to compensation for any damage directly resulting from the fault – in this case to your floor.

You may have the option of taking action against the supplier, who is liable for the faulty dishwasher, and the manufacturer, who is liable for the flood damage, if the cost of repairing the damage exceeds £275. If you ▶ p48

TIME LIMITS FOR CLAIMING REFUNDS, REPAIRS AND REPLACEMENTS

Your rights	What you must do	You may lose your rights if:	How long you have to claim	Who to claim against	Legal basis
To reject goods that are faulty or described inaccurately and receive a full refund.	• Examine the goods as soon as possible. • Return the goods or make them available for collection.	• you accept the goods (see p34); • you knew of a fault or it was obvious, when you bought the goods; • you take too long to report the fault.	A 'reasonable time' after purchase (possibly a week or less).	The retailer.	Sale of Goods Act 1979 (as amended; see p29).
To get financial compensation for 'loss of value' of faulty goods (you may also choose to accept a replacement or free repair).	Demonstrate that the fault was there when you bought the goods, or that they could reasonably be expected to have lasted longer (see next item).	• you handle the goods carelessly; • you do not follow the manufacturer's instructions; • you damage or alter the goods.	Up to six years after purchase.	The retailer.	Sale of Goods Act 1979 (as amended; see p29).
To receive a refund, a partial refund, free repair or replacement of the faulty goods.	Inform the retailer (your rights are automatic if the goods are faulty).	• the retailer can prove that the goods were not faulty when you bought them or could not reasonably be expected to last that long.	Up to six months after purchase.	The retailer.	Sale and Supply of Goods to Consumers Regulations 2002 (see p29).
To receive financial compensation for personal injury, or for damage to property worth over £275 caused by the faulty goods.	Demonstrate that the fault was there when you bought the goods.	• you contribute to the damage by any action you take while using or handling the goods.	Up to three years after purchase.	The importer or manufacturer (or the retailer if you cannot identify the former).	Consumer Protection Act.
To cancel a contract signed in your home as a result of an unsolicited visit, and get a full refund, including return of any deposit paid.	Take care of any goods left at your home and make them available for collection.	• you sign a 'linked' credit agreement (offered by the sales company) but discussed over the phone, not face to face in your home.	Seven days after signing the contract, or five days after receiving the notice of agreement of a linked finance agreement.	The retailer, plus the finance company if there is a linked credit agreement.	Consumer Credit Act 1974; Consumer Protection Regulations 1987.
To cancel a contract entered into at home to buy goods in the EU and receive a full refund.	Look after goods left at your home and return them or have them ready for collection.		Seven-day cooling-off period starting from receipt of goods.		The Consumer Protection (Distance Selling) Regulations 2000 (see p45).

47

BUYING GOODS

WEAR AND TEAR • CORRECT LABELLING • SELF-ASSEMBLY INSTRUCTIONS

WHEN THE SELLER IS NOT LIABLE

A seller is not liable for normal wear and tear or for damage caused by the buyer. A seller's liability for something that develops faults after you bought it depends on the time since purchase, how long it is expected to last, and how it has been treated. If, for example, you spill coffee into your DVD player, leave it in high temperatures or treat it roughly, the seller may not be liable for subsequent faults.

bought the machine by credit card or with a loan, the credit card or finance company also has some legal responsibility (see p35). You may have more success pursuing your claim through them than through the trader or manufacturer.

A claim for compensation for damage can be complicated and you may need specialist advice.

ACTION PLAN

1 Take photographs of the damage. Gather as much documentation as you can about the floor – quotations and invoices for work – and any written statement about the cause of the damage. For example, the plumber whom you called out to deal with the flood may be willing to give a statement about what happened.

2 Talk to the manager of the company that sold you the dishwasher to say that you are aware of your rights, and to ask for compensation for replacing the floor.

3 If the manager refuses to accept that the dishwasher was responsible for the damage to the floor, set out your claim in a letter ▶ ✍ to the manager, and in another to the manufacturer. You should notify both of the problem, even if you later claim against only one.

4 If both the manufacturer and the shop dispute your claim for the cost of repairing your floor, contact your local Citizens Advice Bureau ▶ ⌂ or trading standards office (see p30) for advice on pursuing the claim.

WORD OF WARNING

A claim for damage to property resulting from faulty goods can take a long time to resolve. If the cost of replacing the floor is covered by your household insurance, you will probably find that this is your quickest and simplest option.

Is damage due to wear and tear or a fault?

Q I recently bought an expensive jumper. I have only worn it once and one of the seams has unravelled and come apart. The shopkeeper refuses to allow me a refund, replacement or repair, saying the problem is due to wear and tear. Can she do that?

A Probably not. You should be able to claim either a replacement jumper or a full refund.

Both the Sale of Goods Act and the Sale and Supply of Goods to Consumers Regulations 2002 (see p29) give you similar rights in this instance. You will find it is easier to make a claim under the latter because the Regulations put the burden of proof on the retailer to demonstrate that goods are not defective at the time of purchase.

ACTION PLAN

1 Write to the shopkeeper explaining that the jumper cannot have been of satisfactory quality because it fell apart so quickly and that you have the right to a full refund on these grounds.

2 If the shopkeeper refuses to give you a refund, consult your local Citizens Advice Bureau ▶ ⌨ or trading standards office (see p30) about pursuing your claim.

Goods must be labelled with the correct size

Q I bought a shirt labelled size 15½, my usual size. When I tried it on at home it turned out to be closer to a size 17. I took the shirt back and asked for a refund, but the shopkeeper refused, saying that it was up to me to select the correct size. Can he do that?

A No. If the size marked on the shirt is clearly inaccurate you are protected under the Sale of Goods Act 1979 (as amended; see p29) and you are entitled to a full refund. You should take the shirt back to the shop immediately, show proof of purchase and ask for a full refund, saying that you have the legal right to do so.

If you mistakenly buy clothing of the wrong size but which is correctly labelled, you are not entitled to return it unless it has a fault, and the shop can refuse a refund or exchange.

Self-assembly shelves that will not stand up

Q I followed the instructions when I put together a flat-packed self-assembly bookcase, but it's rickety and unstable. The shop manager says I must have assembled it badly and that the shop is not liable. Can she do that?

A Possibly. The shop manager may be able to show you evidence of identical self-assembly bookcases that are perfectly functional. She could then make a convincing argument that there was nothing wrong with the flat-packed bookcase or the instructions and that the fault lies in the way you assembled it.

You will have a stronger argument if you can show that the instructions are incorrect or seriously misleading. The instructions form part of the contract. If they are incorrect or misleading, they are not fit for their purpose and you are entitled to a full refund (see p29).

If the shopkeeper argues that you do not have the right to a refund because you have assembled – and therefore accepted – the bookcase, you can explain that assembly is part of the procedure for checking that the goods comply with the terms of the contract. It does not constitute acceptance of the goods.

Shopkeepers sometimes tell customers to pursue complicated complaints with the manufacturer – in this case, the firm that made the bookcase. As your sale contract is with the shop, not the manufacturer, it is up to the shop to deal with the problem. ▶

TOO BIG? NONSENSE! YOU'LL SOON GROW INTO IT SIR

BUT I'M SEVENTY THREE!

SHIRTS SHIRTS SHIRTS

BUYING GOODS

ACTION PLAN

1 If you think you can show that the bookcase was not fit for its purpose speak again to the shop manager, stating your case and claiming your refund under the Sale of Goods Act 1979 (as amended; see p29). If the instructions are difficult to follow, point out that it is in the shop's interest to resolve the problem.

2 If the manager continues to refuse your claim, put the case in writing and send it to the shop manager or, if the shop is part of a group, to the head office. The company may have a disputes resolution procedure or be able to send out an employee to check why your bookcase is unsteady.

3 As a last resort seek advice from your local Citizens Advice Bureau ▶ ⌐ or trading standards office (see p30) on pursuing your claim.

WHEN TO ACCEPT A CREDIT NOTE

If you buy goods that turn out to be faulty, unsuitable for their purpose, or were inaccurately described, the law allows you to claim a full or a partial refund, a free replacement or a repair.

• A retailer cannot deny you these legal rights, so cannot impose a 'no refunds' policy and offer you a credit note instead.

• If you make a mistake, perhaps about the size or colour of an item of clothing, a shopkeeper does not have to offer you a refund or change it, but may offer a credit note allowing you to buy something else of the same value from the same shop.

• Once you have accepted a credit note you cannot change your mind and insist on a refund.

• Check any conditions that apply to the credit note. Time limits are common.

Returning something bought abroad

Q On a trip to Paris I bought a pair of shoes. Two months later a heel fell off. I sent the shoes back to the shop with a copy of the receipt and a letter asking for a refund, but the staff have offered me a replacement pair of shoes instead. Can they refuse to give me a refund?

A No. Under the EU Sale of Consumer Goods Directive 99/44/EC (see p32), you have the right to a repair or replacement, or a partial or full refund, for goods that were faulty when you bought them. When a fault develops within six months of purchase, and it is reasonable to expect the item to last that long, it is presumed that the fault was present at the time of purchase unless the retailer can prove otherwise.

ACTION PLAN

1 Write to the shop manager saying that because the shoes were faulty when you bought them, you have the right to a replacement or refund under European Directive 99/44/EC on the Sale of Consumer Goods. Add that under the directive the shopkeeper must prove that the shoes were not faulty when you bought them.

2 If the manager does not offer a refund or some other acceptable form of redress, contact the European Consumer Centre ▶ ⌐ for advice.

3 If you paid by credit card and the shoes cost more than the equivalent of £100, you can approach the credit card company for assistance (see p35). Copy your complaint correspondence to the credit card company.

IF THINGS GO WRONG

If you buy something and things go wrong – the item does not work, does not match what you ordered, leaks, breaks down, falls apart, causes damage or shrinks – you need to act quickly. Collect the evidence, decide what you want, then assess your options and take appropriate action.

GATHER THE FACTS

Act promptly You may lose rights if you delay.

Stop using the faulty item Do not attempt to repair it yourself. If possible, replace the item in its original packaging and return it to the shop, or tell the trader that it is available for collection.

Keep all related paperwork such as advertising material, order forms, receipts, credit card slips, invoices, delivery notes, instructions and guarantee forms.

Keep a log of what happened For example:

- the date you bought or ordered the item

- what the salesperson said

- any special requirements you specified when you bought the item

- when you first became aware of a problem (give dates, if possible)

- what problems have occurred with the item

- anything you have done about the problem.

DECIDE WHAT YOU WANT

This might be:

- the delivery of goods that have not arrived

- replacement of a wrong item by the one that you ordered

- to set a firm delivery date

- to cancel an order

- to return goods for a full refund

- to have an item repaired

- to return an item and have it replaced with a new one

- a credit note

- some money back to compensate for a fault

- to claim under a guarantee or a warranty

- to complain about the trader

- compensation for damage or injury caused by faulty goods.

TAKE ACTION

- Establish what your legal rights are.

- Take the item back to the shop, or write, phone or email the company as appropriate.

- Try to negotiate a settlement.

- Write a formal letter to the company. Keep copies of all your letters and get a free certificate of postage as proof of posting.

- Be persistent. If you do not immediately get what you want, talk to the manager, write again, or write to the company's head office.

- If you paid with a credit card, notify the card company.

- Make a note of anything that has been agreed and keep copies of all correspondence.

- Report the trader to the Office of Fair Trading (OFT) ▶🖾, the Advertising Standards Authority (ASA) ▶🖾 or other appropriate organisation.

- Take advice in difficult cases. Contact your local Citizens Advice Bureau ▶🖾 or trading standards office (see p30).

BUYING SERVICES

An estimate is not a fixed price

Q I called a plumber to fix a leaking pipe. On the phone he quoted about £60, depending on how long the job took. It took him just over an hour, but he handed me a bill for £210. Can he do that?

A Yes. As your plumber said 'about £60' and qualified this by saying the price would depend on how long the job took, his statement was an estimate rather than a firm quotation.

Although the difference between an estimate and a quotation is not specified in law, it is generally taken that a quotation represents a firm price, whereas an estimate is a rough guide and not legally binding.

The final cost will depend on the time and skill involved and any parts used. Within limits the plumber is entitled to charge for these elements as he sees fit.

If you did not agree a firm price, you are still entitled to have the work done for a reasonable charge – even in an emergency, such as a serious leak.

What is reasonable is not legally defined (see box, right), but a charge may be regarded as unreasonable if it is significantly higher than the amount typically charged by comparable tradespeople in the same area.

ACTION PLAN
1 Tell the plumber that the charge does not seem reasonable. He may offer an explanation (for example, if an expensive fitting was required), or he may be willing to reduce the bill for you.

2 If you are not satisfied with the plumber's response, you should find out what is a fair price for the job from a trade association or by asking for quotations from other plumbers in your area.

3 If the bill is excessive in comparison with what other plumbers would charge, it may be unreasonable. You can offer to pay the plumber what you think is reasonable, and withhold the amount in excess of what other plumbers would charge, but you may have to defend this action if the plumber takes you to court. Seek advice from your local Citizens Advice Bureau ▶ ☐ or trading standards office (see p30).

4 If your plumber is a member of a trade organisation such as the Association of Plumbing and Heating Contractors ▶ ☐, or the Institute of Plumbing ▶ ☐, you may be able to use their conciliation and arbitration service to resolve the dispute. Their web sites provide information on how the complaints procedures operate.

WORD OF WARNING
If you want to be certain of the price for a job you can ask for an exact and firm quotation in writing first, but once you agree a definite price you cannot challenge it later as unreasonable.

Complain even if you have paid the builder

Q I agreed a builder's quotation to have a new door and lintel fitted, and paid in full when he said he had completed the work. I later found that the door wouldn't open and close properly, and then discovered that he hadn't installed a lintel as specified. When I

complained, the builder said that my payment for the work implied that it was satisfactory. Can he get away with this?

A No. If a job of work is not performed properly or according to agreed specifications, you are entitled to compensation – generally the amount it will cost to rectify the situation, even if this is more than the original contract price. But first give the builder the chance to remedy the defective work.

ACTION PLAN

1 Write to the builder explaining that you are not satisfied with the job, and why ▶ ✍. Say that you would like to give him a reasonable opportunity to put things right. Suggest a time limit for remedying the work, and give a date by which you want a reply.

IT OPENS DOESN'T IT?

THE SUPPLY OF GOODS AND SERVICES ACT 1982

A customer's rights when buying services from tradespeople and professionals are set out in this Act (amended by the Sale and Supply of Goods Act 1994). The Act states that work should be carried out:
• using reasonable skill and care – that is, to the standard that could be expected from a competent practitioner
• in a reasonable time – this depends on the circumstances, so agree dates in advance
• at a reasonable cost – if you have not agreed a price in advance, you have to pay only what other tradespeople or suppliers of the service would have charged for the same job
• any materials used must be of satisfactory quality, fit for their intended purpose and as described (see box, p29).

2 If the builder will not agree, you may have to take legal action to get compensation. You will need at least two formal quotations for the cost of remedying the defective work. You may also require a specialist report to show that the work was not up to standard and that a lintel is required, which you will have to pay for. It will help your case if you have written evidence that the lintel was part of the agreed job. Seek advice from your local Citizens Advice Bureau ▶ 📖 or trading standards office (see p30) about how to proceed.

3 If the builder is a member of the Federation of Master Builders ▶ 📖 (only about 10 per cent of builders are), you can use its complaints procedure or opt for independent arbitration through the federation.

BUYING SERVICES

SUBCONTRACTED WORK • INSPECTIONS • DISAPPEARING WORKMEN

Builder is responsible for subcontracted work

Q I had a kitchen extension built, but the tiling was shoddy. When I complained to the builder, he disclaimed any responsibility, saying that he'd subcontracted the work. Can he do that?

A No. Generally, if you hire a firm to do a complete job of work involving several different tradespeople, the main contractor is responsible for all the work, and that includes the actions of subcontractors.

ACTION PLAN

1 Point out to the builder that he is ultimately responsible for the work done on your kitchen extension and that the tiling is unsatisfactory. Tell him that you would like to give him the opportunity to put the matter right, and suggest a reasonable time limit for doing this.

2 If you do not get a satisfactory response from the builder, get quotations from two or three professional tiling firms for remedying the work.

3 Write to the builder pointing out that as the work on your kitchen has not been performed with reasonable care and skill, he is in breach of contract and you are entitled either to withhold from his bill the cost of re-tiling (generally, a sum equivalent to the cheapest quotation you have obtained), or to have the remedial work done and send him the bill ▶ ✍. Offer him a final opportunity to remedy the poor tiling.

4 Before you risk getting involved in a legal dispute with the builder, seek advice from your local Citizens Advice Bureau ▶ 📖 or trading standards office (see p30).

Inspect the work before you sign

Q I recently had some roofing work done on my house, and the roofer has asked me to sign a statement that I have inspected the work and am satisfied with it. Should I sign?

A No, not unless you have actually inspected the work and are happy with what has been done.

Some tradespeople ask you to sign this kind of statement immediately on completion of a job or shortly afterwards, in which case it is always wise to write 'unexamined' beside your signature. If you do this, you are more likely to be able to get the tradesperson to put things right if problems develop after completion of the work.

Similarly, you can write something that makes it clear you are not an expert – for example, 'as far as I can tell' – so that you are protected later if remedial work needs to be done.

Electrician performs a disappearing act

Q I booked an electrician to do some rewiring, and paid him a £50 deposit. When he started work he asked for £250 cash. I haven't seen him since and his phone is disconnected. Is there any way I can get my money back?

A Yes. The law says you are entitled to a refund if the electrician does not complete the job. In practice, you will have a chance of getting your money back only if you can trace the electrician, he is still in business, and you have a receipt for the cash you paid him.

ACTION PLAN

1 If you have an address for the electrician, write a letter asking when he plans to start work and giving him a reasonable deadline to complete it. Say that if the work is not done by this date you will cancel the contract and require your money back ▶✍. This gives you protection if you need to take him to court at a later date.

2 If you do not have an address, you need to track down the electrician. If he was running a limited company it should be registered at Companies House ▶🕮, where you will also find whether the company has gone into liquidation. If the electrician was working as an individual, check with the Insolvency Service ▶🕮 whether he has declared insolvency.

3 Talk to your local trading standards office, which may be aware of previous problems with this person.

4 If your letter and enquiries lead nowhere, or the electrician has gone out of business, take advice from your local Citizens Advice Bureau ▶🕮 or trading standards office (see p30).

LOOK FOR THE LOGO

Protect yourself from cowboys by employing a member of a recognised trade organisation or of the Quality Mark Scheme.

Building trade associations

The Council for Registered Gas Installers (CORGI) ▶🕮 is the national watchdog for gas safety and gas installation work. All work involving gas installations must be carried out by a CORGI registered firm.

The Federation of Master Builders (FMB) ▶🕮 promotes high-quality workmanship and professional business practices in the building trade.

The Institute of Plumbing (IOP) ▶🕮 is a professional body that promotes training and high-quality work in the plumbing trade.

Members of each association have agreed to follow a code of professional standards. The CORGI code is legally binding on CORGI installers. Each association:
- keeps a register of competent and qualified tradespeople who can be contacted through its web site
- provides practical and safety advice for customers
- has a complaints procedure.

The Quality Mark Scheme

The Department of Trade and Industry is developing the national **Quality Mark Scheme** ▶🕮 to protect consumers and promote legitimate firms. It has been piloted in Birmingham and Somerset and is gradually being extended nationwide.

The scheme covers 18 building trades involved in domestic maintenance, repair and home improvement work, and provides contact details of registered tradespeople who have demonstrated:
- workmanship skills
- good management practices and financial probity
- adherence to a code of practice for customer relations
- appropriate insurance cover.

All Quality Mark work will be backed by a scheme warranty, included as part of the quotation for a job, giving protection against poor workmanship, major defects and insolvency for up to six years. All Quality Mark traders will have a complaints system.

For more information on the scheme, or to use the register to find tradespeople in your area:
phone the Quality Mark hotline: 0845 300 8040
or visit the Quality Mark web site www.qualitymark.org.uk

BUYING SERVICES

How to get a good job done

There are a number of precautions you can take to safeguard your interests when you are having any sort of building, repair or decorating work done in your home. By selecting reputable, qualified builders and other tradespeople, by agreeing a contract for the work, either verbally or in writing, and by monitoring the work as it progresses, you can minimise the likelihood of problems and ensure that you have some legal comeback if anything does go wrong.

CHOOSING THE RIGHT PERSON

DO
- Select a tradesperson who has been personally recommended.
- Choose someone who is a member of a trade association (see box, p55). The association can often recommend a reliable tradesperson in your area. Members usually abide by the association's code of practice, and if necessary you can use its complaints procedure.
- Always get at least three quotes.
- Ensure that the quotes include precise specifications about fittings and materials.
- Make sure that the quote you accept is an exact and firm quotation so that it is legally binding and you cannot be asked to pay more.
- Specify a time for starting and completing the work (see box, p59).
- Have a written contract for major work, such as a loft conversion (see opposite).
- Pay by credit card if possible (see box, p35).
- Always get a receipt with the tradesperson's name and address on it.
- Ask about guarantees or (preferably) insurance-backed warranties for the work.
- Make sure the trader carries insurance in case of damage to your home or contents, or to a neighbour's property.
- Check that either the tradesperson's insurance or your own household insurance includes cover for death or personal injury due to the work.

DON'T
- Employ anyone who does not have a recognised business name and address, and a landline phone number.
- Engage anyone who cold-calls to tout for business.
- Allow yourself to be pressurised into having work done which you do not want.
- Agree to extra work on top of the original job, unless you are sure it is necessary.

Beware the trader who:
- suggests the need for extra items or procedures that other quotes have not mentioned
- finds allegedly serious problems with your property not related to the job in question
- talks up the difficulty of doing a straightforward job
- asks for cash upfront
- makes verbal promises that do not accord with the 'small print' of a contract.

AGREEING A CONTRACT

A contract may be made verbally, in writing, or by a combination of the two. All are equally valid in law, but a written contract makes it easier to prove what has been agreed.

In any contract for services you have rights under the Supply of Goods and Services Act 1982 (see box, p53), irrespective of what has actually been agreed between you and the supplier or tradesperson.

A written contract
It is always wise to have a written contract specifying what has been agreed so both parties are aware of their rights and obligations. This does not have to be a formal document, but ideally both of you should sign and date the contract and each keep a copy.

A contract for work should specify:
• complete details of the work that is to be carried out
• precise specifications for any fittings to be used, including materials and makes where appropriate
• details of any preparatory work
• details of how the job is to be finished off – for example, removing all rubbish and leaving the site clean and tidy
• a time for the work to start and an agreed completion date
• the total price and payment details – for example, payment on satisfactory completion or within 30 days; if staged payments are involved, details of exactly what must be completed before each payment is made
• details of any guarantees or warranties
• a statement of any insurance in force.

SCAMS TO WATCH FOR

Do not give in to heavy sales talk. And beware of people trying to entice you to employ them on the basis of:
• 'special deals' because they happen to be working in your area, have some leftover concrete in the mixer, and so on
• deals that will expire if you do not sign now or within a very short time ('only at this price until Friday')
• claims to have 'just noticed when passing/cleaning the windows/delivering something...' a problem with your property and an offer to fix it, or to know someone who can
• any offer requiring you to sign a contract for repeated payments
• any heavy pressure applied to persuade you to agree
• a request that you sign an apparently innocuous form ('just to say I've been') that you may not realise is a contract.

COUNTING THE COST

When you have hired someone to do a job for you, watch out for:
• workers who charge by the day then arrive late, take long breaks or leave early
• workers who disappear for implausible lengths of time to get supplies
• unsupervised goings on in your home if you have given tradespeople access while you are out
• problems 'discovered' while working on your home that can be fixed at the same time – for a price (it is not unknown for unscrupulous workers to exaggerate or even to create new problems)
• heavy mark-ups on fittings (charging you more than the retail price plus a reasonable cost for collecting the items)
• poor-quality fittings charged as more expensive ones
• unauthorised extra work added to the bill.

Cancelling work that is late starting

Q Nine months ago I agreed with a carpenter that he would line my new study with floor-to-ceiling bookshelves. He still can't give me a date when he will start, but when I said I wanted to cancel the job he threatened to sue me for breach of contract. Can he do that?

A Yes, but he may not succeed – and you have a possible counterclaim. If no time is stipulated in the contract for carrying out the work, the law states that it must be done within a reasonable time (see box, right, and p53), but this is not defined. In a dispute the court will decide.

HELLO, I'M JOSEPH... THE CARPENTER

BLIMEY YOU'VE TAKEN YOUR TIME!

To sue you, the carpenter would have to prove that a nine-month delay in starting the work was not unreasonable. What is more, you could argue in court that he was in breach of contract because of the unreasonable delay.

Rather than let matters get out of hand, your best course of action is to impose a deadline – you are always free to do this, even if no time was stipulated in the original contract.

ACTION PLAN

1 Write a letter to the carpenter stating that you wish the work to be completed ▸ ✎. Set a date that gives the carpenter reasonable notice to start work and allows a reasonable time to complete it. State that if the work is not completed by this date, you will cancel the contract.

2 If the carpenter is a member of a trade association (see box, p55), you may be able to use the association's complaints procedure if he does not respond satisfactorily.

3 Once the deadline for completion passes, if the work has not been completed write a letter cancelling the contract, stating the reason as failure to carry out the work by the specified date ▸ ✎. Keep a copy.

4 You are then free to obtain estimates from other tradespeople and engage someone else to do the work.

You need not accept substitute fittings

Q I had a new bathroom installed and left the workmen to it. When I got back from work one evening I found that the cupboard doors they'd fitted were made from chipboard covered with fake wood veneer, instead of the solid-wood louvered doors I had chosen. The manager says the doors supplied are of satisfactory quality and he's refusing to replace them. Can he do that?

A No, not if the type of doors you required was specified in your original agreement. When fittings are supplied as part of a service, they must conform to any description given when you entered into the contract as well as being of satisfactory quality and fit for the purpose intended (see boxes, p29 and p53). So you are entitled to have your chosen doors installed instead of those put in by the workmen.

ACTION PLAN

1 Write to the manager of the firm and explain what has happened ▶ ✍. Say that the doors are not the ones you chose and point out your rights under the Supply of Goods and Services Act 1982 (see box, p53) to have the fittings as described when you entered into the contract. Ask the workmen to replace the doors with the ones specified.

2 You are entitled to withhold part of the payment for the bathroom until the correct doors have been fitted.

3 If the doors you selected are not available, you have the right to choose an equivalent type or to ask for compensation.

4 If the firm does not take appropriate action, seek advice from your local Citizens Advice Bureau ▶ 🗪 or trading standards office (see p30). You might be able to claim compensation through the small claims service in your local County Court (see pp18-20).

Compensation for damage by workmen

Q I had a new washing machine installed and the first time it was used it flooded my kitchen and ruined the ceiling of the flat beneath mine. The company which installed it has fixed the leak and offered me a small sum in compensation, but the manager claims that the company isn't liable for the damage to my downstairs neighbour's flat. Can he do that?

A No. Your washing machine should have been installed using reasonable care and skill, and any fittings should have been of satisfactory quality and fit for carrying water to and from the machine via the pipework.

The company that installed the washing machine is liable for any damage resulting from its failure in this duty, including rectifying any damage to your neighbour's flat.

ACTION PLAN

1 Ask your neighbour to get two or three firm quotes (not estimates) for repairing her ceiling and any other damage that was done to the room below yours.

2 Write to the manager of the company pointing out that it is in breach of contract and liable for all the damage done as a result ▶ ✍. Enclose the quotes and ask him to add the cost of repairing your neighbour's property to the compensation owing to you. Say that you will pursue the company for the cost.

3 If you do not get a satisfactory response, seek advice from your local Citizens Advice Bureau ▶ 🗪 or trading standards office (see p30) about pursuing your claim for compensation and the cost of repairs.

MAKING TIME OF THE ESSENCE

Generally when you enter into a contract, the law does not regard a delay in carrying out the work as sufficient reason to cancel. You can avoid this by including in the original contract a date by which the work must be completed. This is called 'making time of the essence to the contract'. If you do this and suffer any financial loss as a result of delay, you may be able to claim compensation.

BUYING SERVICES

GUARANTEES • ADVERTISED SERVICES • HIRING TOOLS

When a guarantee proves useless

Q When my house was damp-proofed five years ago I was given a ten-year guarantee. Now several damp patches have appeared. The damp-proofing firm that did the work has been taken over by another company, which says it's not liable and will only deal with the problem if I pay its standard charges. Is this right?

A Yes. Your legal right to obtain compensation for defective workmanship for up to six years from the date of the contract can only be enforced against the original company. Any guarantees the firm gave (which are additional to your legal rights, and do not replace them) also operate only as long as the company continues trading. If a firm is taken over, the new company has no responsibility towards customers of the old company.

If you paid for the damp-proofing with a credit card or on a credit agreement, you may have rights against the card or finance company (see Golden Rule, opposite, and box, p35). If so, contact the company concerned, which remains liable for the cost of putting right any defective work.

If you have an insurance-backed warranty, contact the insurance company to start a claim. If you do not have a warranty and did not pay for the original work on credit, you have no redress in this situation and will have to pay the cost of any remedial work.

The price charged is not the one advertised

Q I answered an advertisement offering to clean carpets for an attractive price. I didn't ask for a quotation because I thought the price was as advertised. When the crew arrived, the supervisor refused to do the job for that price, insisting on an additional fee for removing stains. Can she do that?

A Yes. If you do not have a definite agreement, you cannot force the company to do the work. If the advertisement was misleading, you can complain about that, but you cannot compel the company to abide by the price stated. You may find that the small print in the advertisement covers the company against this kind of situation.

If you had received a firm contract or quotation (not an estimate) for the cost of cleaning the carpets, and assuming any time limit stipulated had not been exceeded, the company would be legally obliged to carry out the work at the agreed price. If it refused in these circumstances, you could sue it for breach of contract to obtain compensation, although any compensation would be minimal.

ACTION PLAN

1 If you received any paperwork confirming the appointment to clean your carpets, check whether the price is stated as firm, or whether there are any qualifications (such as 'as low as £...' or 'subject to...').

2 If you think you were given a firm price without qualifications, write to the company and say that you had a contract for cleaning your carpets at this price and would like the work carried out.

3 If you feel the advertisement or the price were misleading, complain to your local trading standards office, which will be able to advise you. In the event of the advertisement being misleading, the matter would be referred to the Advertising Standards Authority (ASA). At least you may be able to ensure that others are not similarly misled.

Hired equipment should not be defective

Q The circular saw I hired from a local power-tool supplier had a defective blade, which ruined the expensive piece of hardwood I was working on. The supplier refused to take any responsibility or offer a refund. Can she get away with this?

A No. All goods supplied as part of a service, or hired out, should be of satisfactory quality, fit for the purpose intended and as described.

The trader cannot limit liability for any of these points, so you are entitled to compensation. Depending on the circumstances, this could include a refund of the hire charge and compensation for the damage to your piece of wood.

Traders that hire out tools are legally obliged to maintain their equipment in a safe condition – each item should be properly serviced between each hire and supplied with a label confirming that this has been done. They must also give instructions on safe use.

It is worth reporting your complaint to your local trading standards office. It can prevent unsafe tools being hired out. Suppliers who breach safety standards and are found to hire out unsafe equipment can face fines and even custodial sentences.

ACTION PLAN

1 Write to the hire-firm manager stating that the firm was in breach of its contract to supply you with a satisfactory safe tool and that you would like compensation, including a refund of the hire charge and the cost of replacing your piece of damaged wood ▶ ✍. Give the manager 14 days to take action.

2 If you do not receive a satisfactory response and wish to pursue the case, seek advice from your local Citizens Advice Bureau ▶ ▭ or trading standards office (see p30).

WORD OF WARNING

Although hirers are responsible for ensuring that the tools they supply are safe to use, customers are responsible for following instructions and using the tools correctly. Many DIY accidents are due to improper use or failure to take appropriate safety precautions.

HIRING TOOLS

You have the same rights under the law when you hire tools or equipment as you would have if you had bought them. Equipment must be of satisfactory quality, fit for its purpose and match its description (see the Sale of Goods Act 1979 as amended, p29).

A high price to pay for repairs

Q I took a valuable watch to a jeweller for repair. I'm now disputing the cost of mending it, but the jeweller won't return the watch until I pay the bill. Can he do that?

A Yes. And the company could take you to court if you do not have sufficient justification for refusing to pay the repair bill.

Under the Supply of Goods and Services Act (see p53), you are entitled to have the work done at a reasonable cost if the price was not agreed in advance, and the trader is entitled to a reasonable fee for the service performed. The law does not define what is reasonable, so in disputed cases the matter may have to be settled in court.

If you take something to be repaired and fail to pay the bill, the trader has a legal right to retain the item until the debt is paid. So the jeweller can hold onto the watch until you pay the repair charge. If you want your watch back, you may have to pay up first and then argue about the cost afterwards.

Assuming the watch has been satisfactorily repaired, you will only be able to claim at most a proportion of the charge, and you will have to prove that the charge was excessive. You may need to pay to obtain an independent report on the watch and the work done.

ACTION PLAN

1 Go back to the shop and speak to the manager. Try to negotiate a compromise price for the repair.

2 If you cannot agree a price and you want to pursue a complaint, pay the bill in order to get your watch back, writing on the cheque or card voucher that you are paying under protest. Seek advice from your local Citizens Advice Bureau ▶ 🕮 or trading standards office (see p30) about pursuing your claim.

Shoe repairs not up to scratch

Q I took my shoes to the repairer to have new soles and heels, but the soles lasted less than three weeks. The repairer says he'll have to charge for re-soling. Shouldn't he replace the soles free of charge?

A Yes. Under the Supply of Goods and Services Act 1982 (see p53) you are entitled to expect a service to be carried out with reasonable care and

skill, and that any goods supplied as part of the service will be of satisfactory quality, fit for their intended purpose and matching any description given.

Your rights apply only if you have not subjected the shoes to an extraordinary challenge (such as long-distance walking or exposure to extreme heat).

ACTION PLAN

1 Take the shoes back to the repairer and explain that under the Supply of Goods and Services Act 1982 you are entitled to have your shoes repaired with reasonable skill and care, using suitable, good-quality soles. Say it is reasonable to expect new soles to last for longer than three weeks, and that you would like the shoes to be re-soled free of charge.

2 If this does not produce the desired response, seek advice from your local trading standards office (see p30).

3 If the repairer belongs to the Society of Master Shoe Repairers ▶ ⌨, you can ask it to investigate. Members must follow its code of practice, and the society has a free arbitration scheme to deal with customer complaints.

Clothing damaged at dry cleaners

Q I recently collected a silk blouse from the dry cleaners, to find it had been ruined. The cleaner pointed to a notice saying, 'We cannot accept responsibility for loss or damage, however caused'. Can she do that?

A No. Under the Supply of Goods and Services Act 1982 (see p53), all services should be carried out with reasonable care and skill. Traders cannot evade their duty to carry out a service

with reasonable care and skill by displaying a notice disclaiming responsibility for damage.

As your blouse has been ruined by the dry-cleaning process, you are entitled to financial compensation, but only at the current second-hand value. You are not entitled to claim the replacement cost of a new blouse.

Under the Unfair Contract Terms Act 1977, the company cannot limit its liability without good reason. The dry cleaners may suggest that the problem is the manufacturer's fault, for example, by giving incorrect care instructions on the label. If this is the case, it is up to you to prove where the fault lies – which may entail getting an independent report. Contact the Textile Services Association ▶ ⌨ for advice.

ACTION PLAN

1 Take the blouse back to the dry cleaners and ask to speak to the manager. Point out your rights under the Supply of Goods and Services Act 1982, and state that your ruined blouse is evidence that cleaning was not performed with reasonable care and skill. See what the manager is prepared to offer.

2 If you are not satisfied, write to the manager setting out the facts and demanding compensation for your ruined blouse ▶ ✍.

3 Check whether the cleaner is a member of the Textile Services Association (TSA) ▶ ⌨. If so, and you are still not satisfied with the cleaner's response, you may be able to use the association's conciliation service to resolve your complaint.

WORD OF WARNING

You do not have the same rights to compensation if a dry cleaner warns you that the item might be difficult to clean and you accept the risk.

> **GOLDEN RULE**
>
> Before going ahead with any kind of repair to an expensive item, always get a specific quotation in writing for the work.

Photographs lost at the processors

Q **I took my daughter's christening pictures to a photographic processor to be developed. When I went to collect them I was told the films had been lost. I asked about compensation, but the manager said he could only reimburse me for the cost of the film. Can he do that?**

A Probably not, but it may depend on the precise terms of your contract.

Photographic processors must exercise reasonable care and skill, including not losing films. So you are entitled to a refund of any processing costs you paid and to a replacement film. As you cannot remedy the loss of your photographs, it would also be reasonable for the processors to offer you compensation for your disappointment.

Check your receipt or collection ticket to see whether the company attempted to limit its liability to the cost of the film. Under the Unfair Contract Terms Act 1977, a trader cannot publish terms of business that limit his own liability in a way that allows him to provide an inadequate service. If the processors try to limit their liability to the cost of a replacement film, you could challenge this as an unfair contract term.

In one case, a claimant was awarded substantial costs in compensation for the loss of holiday photographs, suggesting that the court may recognise the emotional value of precious photographs and award compensation accordingly.

If the processors had made clear to you when you left the film with them that if you paid a higher charge they would accept full responsibility for any loss or damage, and you chose the standard service, any limitation of

liability would be regarded as reasonable because you had a choice between a service that provided full compensation and one that did not.

ACTION PLAN

1 Return to the shop and ask to speak to the manager, or write a letter ▶ ✍. Explain that under the Supply of Goods and Services Act 1982 (see p53) your films should have been handled with reasonable care and skill, and losing them proves that this was not the case. Say that the photographs had great personal value and you would like compensation for your disappointment at their loss.

2 If the company's offer is not satisfactory and you wish to pursue a claim, seek advice from your local Citizens Advice Bureau ▶ 📖 or trading standards office (see p30).

Compensation for poor hairdressing

Q **I went to the hairdresser for a very expensive perm. A few days later my hair started to fall out in patches. When I rang to complain the hairdresser would only offer a re-style and refused to refund my money. Can she do that?**

A Probably not. Everyone providing a service has to exercise reasonable care and skill, which the hairdresser evidently did not do in this case. She is also responsible for the products she used on your hair, whether or not she was aware of any problems.

When someone provides a defective service you are entitled to have the matter rectified, but as you have actually lost hair, this may not be possible.

GOLDEN RULE

Always examine any document and read all the small print carefully before signing. Make sure that any changes or additions agreed verbally are written into a contract.

Depending on the degree of damage to your hair, you may be entitled to a refund for the perm and perhaps compensation for the distress caused.

ACTION PLAN

1 Take photographs of the unsatisfactory perm. You will need this as evidence if your complaint is not resolved quickly and amicably.

2 Go back to the hairdresser and show her the state of your hair. Say that you do not think reasonable care and skill were exercised when she did your perm, and that if she cannot rectify the damage you would like a refund. Also ask if the salon belongs to a professional association, which might have a complaints procedure.

3 If the hairdresser cannot put the matter right and refuses to refund your money, ask another hairdresser for a second opinion – in particular, whether there is anything that can be done to repair the damage to your hair. If so, you are entitled to ask the original hairdresser to compensate you for whatever this would cost.

4 If there is nothing that will help your hair until it re-grows, you could take action against the hairdresser to get your money back and perhaps to claim compensation for your distress. Seek advice from your local Citizens Advice Bureau ▶ 🕮 or trading standards office (see p30).

5 If the perm cost more than £100 and you paid by credit card, you can claim compensation from the card company (see p35).

Abiding by a membership contract

Q I recently joined a local gym. Although my membership contract limits me to 'non-peak' hours, which are the same hours that I work, the gym's salesperson told me when I signed it that I would be allowed to use the facilities at any time. Now the gym is refusing me entry when I want. Can it do that?

A Yes. If you signed a contract limiting your membership to non-peak hours, you have little ground to stand on. Once you sign a contract you are bound by its terms, even if they are not what you expected.

If you relied on the terms offered by the salesperson, you could argue either that the gym allow you to use its facilities any time or that the contract be cancelled without penalty to you. To pursue your complaint, seek advice from your local Citizens Advice Bureau ▶ 🕮 or trading standards office (p30).

GOING ANYWHERE NICE THIS YEAR?

COURT!

The cost of constant power cuts

Q **I keep experiencing power cuts, leaving me without electricity for long periods. The final straw came last week when I had to throw out all the food stored in my freezer. Can I claim compensation from the electricity company?**

A Yes, probably. You may have a right to automatic compensation under the Guaranteed Standards Scheme (see p73). Usually this will cover you for loss of supply beyond a specified minimum time. The amount of compensation will depend on whether the loss of power was planned and notified, and on how long it took for the supply to be reconnected. You may also be able to claim compensation for the spoiled food in your freezer.

The utility companies' guaranteed standards do not replace your legal rights, so if your power cuts are due to a lack of reasonable care and skill on the part of the supplier you may also be able to recover your costs.

ACTION PLAN

1 Contact your electricity company and ask for a copy of its Guaranteed Standards to see whether you can claim automatic compensation for loss of supply.

2 Make a detailed log of the dates when the power cuts occurred, and draw up a list of all the food items you had to throw out each time. Calculate the approximate cost of replacing them all.

3 Write to the company and point out that you are having frequent power cuts, and that the consequence of the last one was that all your freezer food was ruined ▶ ✍. Enclose your list of items and ask for compensation for the spoiled food as well as any entitlement you have under the guaranteed standards scheme.

4 If you are not happy with the company's response, contact Energywatch ▶ ⌂ (see box, left), which can take up the matter with the electricity company on your behalf. If Energywatch cannot reach agreement with the company, it may refer your claim to Ofgem (the Office of Gas and Electricity Markets), the energy regulator ▶ ⌂, for a decision.

5 Alternatively, check your household contents insurance policy as you may be able to claim for the spoiled food under this.

WORD OF WARNING

Electricity companies cannot guarantee to supply you with power under all circumstances. Loss of supply beyond the company's control (for example, if there are heavy storms or lightning strikes) may not entitle you to compensation.

ENERGYWATCH is the independent consumer watchdog for the gas and electricity industries. It produces price comparison factsheets for electricity and gas suppliers and information on how to switch suppliers.

It also gives advice on pursuing complaints about energy suppliers. If a customer has a complaint that he or she cannot resolve satisfactorily with the company concerned, Energywatch will take up the matter with the company on their behalf. If appropriate, Energywatch may refer the complaint to Ofgem, the energy regulator.
- Consumer hotline: 08459 06 07 08
- Online service at: www.energywatch.org.uk

No bill – the supplier is at fault

Q **Since moving into my flat 18 months ago I've never had an electricity bill, despite regular requests. Now I've received a bill for £1500. The electricity company wants immediate payment and is threatening to take me to court. Can it do that?**

A No. And you have grounds for complaint about the company's threatened action. The company should at least offer you some means of paying off the debt by instalments.

Guidelines on good practice for energy suppliers issued jointly by Ofgem, the energy regulator, and Energywatch (see box, opposite) suggest that where the supplier is at fault – including where no bill has been sent for more than six months or where the company has failed to take into account your ability to pay – it should offer you redress.

If it is the supplier's fault that a debt has built up, the guidelines include reducing the debt or writing off debts over a certain age, or accepting payment spread over a period at least as long as the time it has taken the bill to build up.

Although the electricity company should have a strong incentive to resolve this matter to your satisfaction, redress is at the discretion of the supplier.

ACTION PLAN

1 **Write to the electricity supplier and in your letter:**
• **give the dates when you contacted them requesting a bill**
• **explain that the debt accumulated due to the supplier's billing failure, which occurred despite your repeated requests for a bill ▶ ✍**
• **point out that the threat to take you to court in this situation is contrary to good practice, and ask that it be withdrawn immediately**

• **ask that, as a minimum, you are offered a period of 18 months to pay the backlog by instalments**
• **ask that the supplier considers some form of appropriate redress.**

2 **If you do not receive a positive response, copy your letter to the electricity company to Energywatch (see box, opposite). Energywatch should be able to negotiate between you and the electricity supplier, and refer your complaint to Ofgem, the energy regulator, if appropriate.**

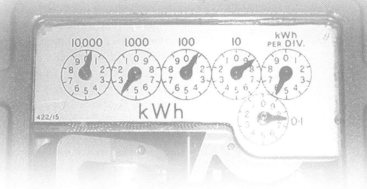

Challenging the meter reading

Q **I have been away for the past four months, yet my electricity bill is even higher than usual. When I challenged it, the electricity company said that it's based on a meter reading, and that I must pay up. Can it do that?**

A Yes, probably. Check both your bill and the meter reading carefully. If your reading is lower, contact the electricity company and give it the current figure. You will be sent an amended bill.

Although your bill is based on a correct meter reading, your previous bill may have been an estimated reading that was too low – in which case your latest bill will be correspondingly higher. ▶

> **GOLDEN RULE**
>
> To avoid being caught out by estimated meter readings – whether too high or too low – always check your bill and your meter and ask your supplier to amend your bill accordingly.

67

BUYING SERVICES

ELECTRICITY DISCONNECTION • FAULTY GAS BOILER • ENGINEER FAILS TO CALL

Check your bill to see whether the reading given for the start of the charging period – which should be the same as the final reading on your previous bill – is an estimate.

If the bills and the meter reading are apparently correct, but you still believe the amount recorded is too high, your meter may be faulty. Report this to the electricity company. You can ask the company for an independent check of the meter, but you may have to pay for this.

If you are unhappy with the way the company deals with your concerns, contact Energywatch (see box, p66), and your local trading standards office (see p30). Trading standards may be able to advise if it is a case of a defective meter.

You may be cut off for non-payment of a bill

Q I cannot afford to pay my electricity bill. The supplier has told me I will be disconnected. Can they do that?

A Yes, in theory, but it will not happen immediately. If you persistently fail to pay bills on time, the company may disconnect your supply or insist that you have a pre-payment meter installed to avoid further arrears.

Contact your electricity company as soon as possible to discuss alternative payment arrangements – there is usually a contact phone number on the back of your bill.

Rather than paying the whole bill at once, you may be able to pay by instalments through flexible or regular payment schemes, including budget schemes, which spread costs throughout the year. Most companies are also happy to offer advice on debt prevention to help you in future – for example, they may suggest ways in which you can increase energy efficiency and reduce heat loss in your home.

Contact Energywatch ▶ ⌁ (see box, p66) if you are not happy with the way your supplier deals with your problem.

The new boiler that fails to do the job

Q A gas company engineer installed a new central-heating boiler in our house. It has never heated up the water and radiators effectively, but the company refuses to come back to look at it. Can we do anything?

A Yes. Insist that the company rectifies the problem, and take action against it if it still refuses. Under the Supply of Goods and Services Act 1982, you are entitled to have a service carried out with reasonable skill and care, and to have materials used which are of satisfactory quality and fit for the purpose intended. If not, you can claim compensation.

ACTION PLAN

1 Write to the company, describing the problem and stating that the company is in breach of contract ▶ ✍ . Offer the company the chance to remedy the problem by a specific date, otherwise you will use another

engineer to resolve the problem and pursue the company for the cost of rectifying the problem.

2 If this does not produce the required response, get two or three quotes for whatever remedial work is needed from other companies. Seek advice from your local Citizens Advice Bureau ▶ 📖 or trading standards office (see p30) about pursuing a claim for compensation.

The gas engineer fails to appear

Q When my boiler broke down I made an appointment for the gas supplier's engineer to call. I took time off work and waited all day for him. He didn't turn up – or even phone to cancel. Can I claim compensation?

A Yes. All utility companies (gas, electricity, water and phone) abide by the Guaranteed Standards Scheme, which offers automatic compensation for missed appointments (see p73). If you had to take time off work for the appointment and lost money as a result you are not limited to the fixed compensation offered, and can claim for your lost wages as long as you made the company aware of this when you made the appointment.

ACTION PLAN
1 Write to the company and claim its fixed compensation for a missed appointment ▶ ✍. The amount may be stated on the back of a recent bill, or you can phone the company to find out what it is.

2 If you made the company aware that, in the event of a missed appointment, you might claim for lost wages, set out the details of your

claim in your letter. You may be asked to provide evidence of the amount you have lost.

3 If the company refuses to reimburse you, seek advice from your local Citizens Advice Bureau ▶ 📖.

SAFEGUARDING YOUR APPLIANCES

Many companies offer maintenance and breakdown plans which, for an annual fee, protect you against common breakdowns within the home. Although such policies can provide peace of mind – you know you will not be faced with a huge repair bill unexpectedly, and you have someone to call even if the heating fails on a bank holiday afternoon – they provide varying degrees of cover. Are all parts covered? Does a service mean a full service? Make sure you know what is – and what is not – included before you sign up.

Check the terms
• Read the policy carefully and check what it does and does not cover. For example, which parts of the heating system are included, and are you covered for replacement of a major item, such as the boiler, if it breaks down completely.
• Some companies may refuse to take on your appliance or system unless some remedial work is done first – for instance, a 'powerflush' on a central-heating system. If you are unsure whether any recommended work is necessary, seek a second opinion.
• Make sure that an annual service included in the plan is a full service. Some contracts provide what is described as an annual diagnostic service and safety check, which is a simple electrical probe analysis of the flue gases. A full service involves a more thorough investigation.
• Check the small print to find out what the procedure is if the engineers sent out cannot fix the problem. Will another engineer be called out? Will you be charged for his visit?

Ensure you get what you paid for
Once you have cover, be sure the annual maintenance visit takes place at precise yearly intervals. A persistent delay with increasing gaps year on year means that you are not getting what you paid for and may be entitled to a rebate.

Don't be fooled into upgrading
Watch out for claims that the manufacturer no longer makes spare parts for your model of boiler, accompanied by suggestions that you need to upgrade. Some consumers have been told this only to discover that the parts in question were standard components still available off the shelf.

Switching supplier without realising it

Q **An energy company salesman called at my home saying he was doing a survey on fuel costs. He took details of my bills and asked me to sign a form stating that he had called. Later I realised that my gas and electricity had been switched to a new supplier. Can they do that?**

A No. Electricity and gas suppliers must abide by guidelines on how they market their products. In particular, a utility supplier must not abuse customers' trust.

The supplier must check with you within 14 days of any new contract being signed in these circumstances to ensure that you are aware of having signed and are happy with the sales approach used. In addition, if you sign any contract at home as a result of an unsolicited visit by a salesperson, you may have a right to cancel the contract without penalty (see box, p38). In any event, you may also be entitled to compensation.

If the paperwork you signed appears to be a contract, it will not be binding if you were tricked into signing it.

ACTION PLAN

1 Ask the new company why it thinks you agreed to transfer your supply. If it says you signed a contract, ask for a copy to be sent to you. Explain to the company that you were not aware of having agreed to switch to a new supplier. In this situation, the company will usually cancel the transfer at this stage.

2 If the company refuses to cancel the transfer, complain to Energywatch ▶ ▭ (see box, p66), which will investigate your complaint and negotiate with the supplier on your behalf. If Energywatch cannot resolve the problem, it will refer your complaint to Ofgem, the energy regulator.

3 If the company attempts to hold you to a contract you feel tricked into signing, seek advice from Energywatch, your local Citizens Advice Bureau ▶ ▭ or trading standards office (see p30). If there is the possibility that your signature was forged, your complaint will be referred to the police.

HOLD ON, HE'S NOT OUR USUAL GAS MAN, MAUREEN

BEWARE OF UNSCRUPULOUS ENERGY SELLERS

In 2001/2 Energywatch (see p66) received 85,000 complaints from consumers about energy suppliers. Of people approached by doorstep sellers, three in five were unable to understand all the information given and one in five were given no information at all. Half of those approached felt subject to lying, intimidation, or bullying, and 1 in 25 were transferred to a new supplier without their consent. Some consumers' signatures had been forged in order to present a contract for transfer of supply.

Ignore energy supply salespeople who:
● say they are conducting a survey on energy use or offer you special deals or discounts on behalf of a reputable organisation such as Energywatch, Transco, Ofgem or a branch of government (these bodies do not employ doorstep representatives)
● claim to be from your existing supplier – perhaps showing you a false identity card – and offer a special deal, discount or new pre-payment meter key or card (your existing supplier would normally contact you by post).

Don't be fooled into:
● signing for a meter reading (you never need to sign anything when a meter is read)

● giving your signature in order to be sent more information
● signing up for a special deal ('you need to sign now to get this cheap rate')
● signing out of sympathy for the salesperson ('My boss needs proof that I called', or 'I won't get any commission without a signature')
● parting with cash – reputable companies never require cash in advance.

To reduce the risk of problems:
● shop around – if you are contemplating a change of supplier, research the different companies and deals available
● do not deal with cold-callers (by phone or on the doorstep) or people who approach you in public, for instance in supermarkets
● do not leave a salesperson unsupervised in your home
● never be pressurised into signing a contract on the spot
● do not sign anything unless you have decided you want to switch companies and have read the contract thoroughly
● if anyone refuses to leave until you sign something, call the police.

Gas company refuses to supply a new customer

Q I'm going to university and will be moving into a flat with a friend. The company currently supplying gas to the flat is insisting that in order to take over the supply, we either give them a large deposit, which we cannot afford, or have a pre-payment meter installed, which we don't want. Can they do that?

A Yes. If you are a new customer without a previous payment record, or if you have a poor payment record, an energy supplier can insist that you give adequate financial security, and may refuse to connect you until you do. The deposit must be a reasonable sum, and no more than the estimated annual winter usage over two quarterly bills. After one year, the supplier should review the position and refund your deposit if you have paid your bills in full.

Some companies may let you pay via a regular payment plan. Or they may allow you to nominate a guarantor, such as a parent, who will be responsible for paying your bills if you default. Again, if you pay your bills in full the supplier will usually release the guarantor from the arrangement after one year.

If you think that the supplier is asking for too high a deposit, write to the company and say so. If you are not satisfied with the response, contact Energywatch (see p66).

If you have problems getting a gas supply, seek advice from your local Citizens Advice Bureau ▶ 🖆.

Interruption to the water supply

Q **Without any warning, my water supply has been cut off for two days. No one can tell me when it will be back on again. Can the water company do this?**

A No, not normally. As a domestic consumer you are entitled to a constant water supply. If for any reason the water company has to interrupt supply for more than four hours, it must:
• give you 48 hours' notice in writing
• tell you when supply will be restored.

For an unplanned interruption (such as a burst water main), the water company has a set time (12 or 48 hours, depending on the type of leak) to restore supply. It must also, as soon as possible, inform you where you can get an alternative water supply and when its supply will be restored, and provide a phone number that you can call for further information.

If any of these guaranteed standards are not met, you are entitled to fixed compensation of £20 (barring exceptional circumstances, such as drought), but you must claim it in writing within three months.

Some water companies have compensation schemes with benefits in excess of the guaranteed standards (see box, opposite), so always check with the individual company.

WATERVOICE represents customers' interests in respect of price and service in the water and sewage industry. Through its nine regional WaterVoice committees in England and one in Wales, it takes up customers' complaints with the relevant companies.

To find the WaterVoice Committee for your water company, look in your local phone directory or visit the web site www.ofwat.gov.uk and click on the WaterVoice logo.

ACTION PLAN

1 Phone your water company and ask to speak to a supervisor. Point out that you are entitled to a constant supply of water and to reasonable notice if this is to be interrupted at any time. Ask why you have been without water, where you can obtain an alternative supply and when the service will be resumed.

2 If you do not get a satisfactory response, ask for details of the water company's complaints procedure and make a formal complaint. You must claim compensation in writing within three months of the interruption. In the event of a severe drought, compensation may be reduced.

3 If the complaints procedure does not produce a satisfactory outcome, you can contact the WaterVoice Committee for your local water company (see box, above) ▶ ▭. If the water company does not accept WaterVoice's recommendations, WaterVoice will refer your complaint to Ofwat, the regulator for the water and sewage industries, for arbitration.

Who pays for a water leak?

Q I live alone and my water supply is metered. My last bill was double the normal amount. I queried it and the water company identified the cause as a leak on my property. It tells me that I'm responsible. Is that right?

A Yes. The water company is responsible only for the water main in the street. You are responsible for all the plumbing and pipework within your house and for the supply pipe running from the house to the meter or to the stop tap in the street. As your water supply is metered, you are liable for the cost of any water lost through leaks in the supply pipe.

Water companies operate a code of practice on leaks for people with water meters, and this may give you some protection. You should contact the water company and ask for a copy of its code to see what it offers.

If you are unhappy with any offer made by the company, you can complain to your regional WaterVoice Committee (see box, opposite) ▶ ⌫ .

Who pays for a sewer to be unblocked?

Q My neighbour and I share a sewer pipe that keeps getting blocked. The water company says this may be because the pipework is old. It says we're responsible for the cost of replacing the pipe. Is that right?

A Yes. Water and sewerage companies are responsible for maintaining the public sewers. Householders are responsible for all the drains and sewers connecting their property to the public sewer, whether the pipework falls inside or outside the boundary of their property.

If houses share a sewer pipe, then all the householders (or landlords) involved share financial liability for repair or replacement costs. There are exceptions for older properties: if your house was built before 1937, ask your water company if it will determine who is responsible in your case.

GUARANTEED STANDARDS SCHEME

All utility companies must abide by the Guaranteed Standards Scheme, a customers' charter that guarantees certain standards of service. If these are not met, you can get automatic compensation. The standards cover many areas of potential conflict between the company and the consumer, including:

- sticking to the time of fixed appointments
- dealing with account queries
- responding to complaints
- installing meters
- interruptions to supply, including notification of planned interruptions and times for restoration of supply
- problems with supply
- compensation payments.

As well as the guaranteed standards, many companies offer their own, higher standards of service and compensation.

Your rights in law
Your entitlements under the Guaranteed Standards Scheme do not take away your ordinary rights in consumer law – so you can still take legal action if you have been given bad service.

How to get a copy
Your utility company will give you a copy of its guaranteed standards – the main terms may be listed on the back of your bill.

How to claim compensation
If you think you are entitled to a fixed compensation payment, notify the utility company involved. Usually, this type of compensation will be credited to your next bill.

Compensation may not be payable for problems due to exceptional circumstances, such as severe weather in the case of electricity supplies, drought in the case of water supplies or industrial action.

A long wait for a phone connection

Q **The phone company keeps promising to install my phone line 'within the next few days', but three months have gone by and I'm still without a service. Can I force it to carry out the work?**

A No, but you should be able to move things along, and you may be entitled to compensation if the terms of a contract have been breached. The time limit for providing you with a service depend on which phone company you are dealing with and what has been agreed between you.

Usually when you sign up with BT, for instance, a particular date for service provision will be agreed. If this date is breached you may be entitled to automatic compensation.

If you have signed on with another operator, your contract should say how long the company will take to connect to the service.

ACTION PLAN

1 Write to the company reminding it of the date you signed your agreement and, if you have one, the original date on which the company agreed to provide a service ▶ ✐. Ask what is the reason for the delay and when you can expect to have the phone line connected. Notify the company of any particular circumstances that might add urgency to your connection, such as a member of the household with mobility difficulties or a condition which might, on occasion, require urgent medical attention.

2 If the company will not give you a firm date for connection, or fails to meet a promised date, ask it for a copy of its complaints procedure and what compensation is available. You may be able to claim fixed compensation or a refund if the standard of service for connecting your line has not been met.

3 If you are unhappy with the response, complain to your local Advisory Committee on Telecommunications (ACTs) ▶ ⌂ or to Ofcom ▶ ⌂, the telecommunications regulator, about the poor service you have received and ask them to investigate. You might be better off cancelling the contract – most companies let you to this if connection standards are not met – and signing on with another provider.

Several days with a fault on the line

Q **There was a fault on my phone line, which I reported to the phone company. I was without a phone for four days waiting for the fault to be repaired, which caused me substantial loss of earnings. Can I claim compensation?**

A Yes, depending on your contract with the company and the extent to which you can prove your losses. Also, you can only claim for losses that you made the company aware of when you reported the fault. The company may exclude liability for matters outside its control, such as severe weather, and some companies will attempt to exclude liability for losses due to supply failure.

BT, for instance, accepts liability only for matters covered under its Customer

Service Guarantee. If a line fault is not fixed within a certain time, you can claim a refund of your line rental fee and either call diversion or compensation. But you have to claim this compensation; it will not be credited automatically to your next bill.

ACTION PLAN

1 Ask your phone company for its procedure when faults occur and what compensation is available.

2 Make a record of your losses. Can you prove the figure is correct? If you have the choice, decide whether you would be better off accepting fixed compensation or claiming for your actual losses.

3 If you are unhappy with the compensation offered, complain to your local Advisory Committee on Telecommunications (ACT) ▶ 🕮 or Ofcom ▶ 🕮. If you wish pursue the case, seek advice from your local Citizens Advice Bureau ▶ 🕮 or trading standards office (see p30).

WORD OF WARNING

If a phone company is slow to repair a fault, you may only be able to claim for losses that you made the company aware of when you reported the fault.

Mobile phone cancellation charge

Q **My mobile phone company no longer offers a competitive deal, but insists I pay a £60 fee if I cancel my contract. Can it do that?**

A Yes. If you pay a monthly charge to a mobile phone provider, this may tie you into a contract for 12 months or more. If you have signed such a contract, the company can penalise you for breaking it. You may also find that by

upgrading your phone, you have been tied into a new 12-month contract.

In addition, your phone may be 'locked', so that you cannot use it with another provider until your existing company 'unlocks' it, and for this you may have to give notice or pay a fee.

Ask the company what the £60 fee covers, and what is its locking policy. Check whether there is a notice or penalty period. It may be cheaper to give notice to terminate your contract, or to unlock your phone, than to pay the fee.

If your phone provider is no longer giving you the service described in your original contract, you might be entitled to compensation or to terminate the contract.

If you feel that the contract terms in your agreement may be unfair, or that your provider has breached its side of the bargain, seek advice from your local trading standards office (see p30). If the terms of the contract appear to breach the Unfair Terms in Consumer Contract Regulations (see box, above), trading standards will refer the contract to the Office of Fair Trading.

If you are unhappy with your service provider's behaviour, complain to Ofcom ▶ 🕮, the telecommunications regulator.

BUYING SERVICES

DELAYED POST • ITEMS DAMAGED IN POST • COURIER SERVICE

The high cost of a letter delivered late

Q The job application I sent by first-class post took 11 days to arrive, and missed the closing-date for applications. Can I claim compensation from Royal Mail?

A No. Target delivery times for standard first and second-class mail are aims, not guarantees. Compensation is available only for lost or damaged items, and then is limited to the market value of the item (in this case, the cost of the paper and envelope) or £27, whichever is the lower.

Royal Mail is not legally liable for the value of any message or information sent by standard mail, or for any 'consequential loss' arising from non or late delivery. There is no compensation for anxiety or inconvenience.

Royal Mail offers other types of services such as 'Recorded Signed For' and 'Special Delivery' (see box, right), which provide guaranteed delivery and various levels of compensation.

No compensation for breakable items

Q For her birthday I sent my granddaughter a china rabbit, costing £15, by Parcelforce standard service. The parcel arrived two weeks later, badly damaged, and the rabbit was broken. Parcelforce is refusing to pay compensation. Can it do that?

A Yes. The standard Parcelforce service pays compensation for lost or damaged items up to a maximum of £20. This covers only the value of the item – there is no compensation for delay.

SENDING VALUABLE ITEMS THROUGH THE POST

If you want something to reach the right person on time, and to know that you can claim compensation if it goes astray, Royal Mail offers two services that are generally more secure than standard post. Both are available at your local post office.

• **Recorded Signed For** proves that an item has been delivered to the address stated. It is suitable for documents, but not for valuable items (such as money or jewellery). Compensation if items are lost or damaged is limited to £28. Royal Mail aims, but does not guarantee, that first-class recorded items arrive the next day and second-class by the third working day. You can request, for a fee, a copy of the recipient's signature by phoning 0845 9272 100.

• **Special Delivery** is suitable for sending valuable items by post. Delivery is guaranteed by noon on the next working day. All items sent by special delivery are covered for £250 compensation if they are lost or damaged. You can pay extra to increase the level of compensation to £1000 or £2500. If the item is delivered late, the cost of postage is refunded.

To check that the item has arrived, use Track and Trace: phone 0845 927 2100 or visit www.postoffice.co.uk

The standard service provided by Parcelforce should not be used for sending breakable or valuable items such as glass or china, and such items are excluded from the compensation scheme. It is up to you to judge which parcel service is suitable, and to check that the insurance cover is adequate for the item you are sending.

Also, the responsibility for packaging lies with the customer, although Parcelforce produces guidance leaflets and will give advice. If you send an item that arrives damaged, Parcelforce may request that you send it the packaging for examination before paying compensation, and will not pay if it considers the packaging was inadequate.

If you have already taken this matter up with your local office, contact Postwatch, the postal services watchdog ▶ ⌂, which can investigate complaints about the Post Office, Royal Mail and Parcelforce.

Slow service by a courier company

Q **I used a courier company to send a gift of expensive chocolates, which I wanted to be delivered the same day. The parcel arrived four days late and the chocolates had melted. The courier company said it had no record of the collection and isn't responsible for the loss. Can it do that?**

A No. The company is responsible for handling your parcel with reasonable care and skill. This has clearly not happened as the contents have been damaged. It is your responsibility to inform the company if the goods require special handling, for example if they are perishable or breakable.

Also, it is not unreasonable to imply that 'time is of the essence' (see p59) to a contract with a courier company, since that is one of the main purposes for using that kind of delivery. The firm probably stipulates when delivery should occur (typically 'same day' or 'overnight'). If so, the courier is doubly in breach. It is possible that the company has an

exclusion clause covering late delivery or damage to perishable goods. If so, it would be up to a court to decide whether the clause is fair or not.

ACTION PLAN

1 Write to the courier firm enclosing evidence that you asked or paid for the delivery – a copy of the addressee form, a collection slip, chequebook stub or credit card receipt, for example. Point out that the company is in breach of contract and that you are entitled to compensation for the spoiled goods ▶ ✍. If the company has breached an agreement on delivery times, you can also ask for compensation for the delay.

2 If the company still refuses to acknowledge responsibility, seek advice from your local Citizens Advice Bureau ▶ ⌂ or trading standards office (see p30) on pursuing your claim for compensation.

The star of the show cancels a performance

Q **We booked stalls seats for an opera performance starring a famous tenor. On the night, he was indisposed and an understudy performed the role. We asked for our money back, but the management refused. Can they do that?**

A Yes. Opera houses and theatre companies work on the principle that the ticket is for the show rather than to see a named singer or actor. They protect themselves with small print on literature and tickets that gives them the right to change the performance to accommodate off-stage problems – for example, 'Tickets are sold subject to the theatre's right to make any alterations to the programme or cast as a result of circumstances beyond its reasonable control'. Opera and theatre companies usually have stand-ins ready to take the part of indisposed stars.

Managements may be prepared to try to resell tickets on the night for those people who do not want to watch the understudy, so enquire at the box office.

If the entire production is cancelled, perhaps for technical reasons, ticket holders are entitled to claim a refund.

Wheelchair access is not guaranteed

Q **I use a wheelchair, but neither of my local cinemas has wheelchair access so I can't go to see films. I thought that was illegal. Can I complain about it?**

A Yes, you can complain to the cinema managers and ask them if they have any plans to improve access under the Disability Discrimination Act 1995 (see box, below). Access for wheelchair users is one of the changes the cinema managers should consider but are not legally bound to provide (see box, below).

But they have to make such changes only if they are 'reasonable'. They do not have to do so if the cost of the work is disproportionately high – if, for instance,

---

DISABILITY DISCRIMINATION ACT 1995

The aim of the Act is to 'give disabled people important rights of access that others take for granted', and makes it illegal to treat disabled people less favourably because of their disability. Anyone providing goods, services or facilities to the public, whether charged for or free – including shops, cinemas, restaurants and hotels – must make reasonable steps to make sure that disabled people can use their services.

Services providers must:
• make reasonable adjustments to the way they deliver their services so disabled people can use them
• consider altering any physical feature of their building that makes access impossible or unduly difficult for disabled people.

In its Code of Practice to Rights of Access, Goods, Facilities, Services and Premises, the Disability Rights Commission ▶ ⌂ gives guidelines on how the Act should operate so that disabled people are not excluded from aspects of daily life. You can download it from www.drc.gb.org/sitemap

the building is listed and the alterations are not possible, or if the necessary changes would be too disruptive.

You could ask the managers if they could open an alternative entrance to allow wheelchair users to enter.

If a football match is abandoned

Q I took my 14-year-old son and three of his friends to a football match. Twenty minutes into the game the floodlights broke down and the match was abandoned. Am I entitled to a refund?

A Probably not, but when a match kicks off and is later abandoned, spectators are usually offered half-price tickets to see the replay. It depends on the club's ticketing regulations, and these may differ according to whether the match was in the Premiership, the FA Cup or another competition.

An announcement is usually made asking customers to keep their tickets and use them to claim reduced-price tickets for the replay. Alternatively, vouchers may be given out so that ticket-holders can claim reduced-price replay tickets.

When spectators are admitted to a stadium but the match is abandoned before kick-off, the spectators are usually offered free tickets for the rearranged match, but ticket-holders who ask for a refund may be given one.

ACTION PLAN

1 If you have not been offered half-price tickets to the replay, contact the club's box office to ask for them.

2 If you were offered reduced-price tickets but you do not want them, ask at the club's box office for a full refund. The club will probably want to maintain goodwill with its supporters, so ticket staff may agree to a refund.

Overpriced seats from a theatre-ticket booth

Q I bought two tickets costing £50 each from a theatre-ticket booth. At the theatre we were seated in the upper circle, and when I looked at my ticket stub, the price printed on it was £12.50. I went back to the booth the next day, but the man said the theatre had seated us in the wrong place and it wasn't his problem. Can he get away with that?

A Possibly not, but you will have to prove that the salesman did not tell you the real ticket price. If you paid cash, that may be impossible.

It is not illegal to sell tickets at inflated prices, and unauthorised ticket sellers act illegally only if they conceal the true face value of any ticket they sell. In this case the price printed on the tickets was not concealed. The tout relied on your not noticing it. ▶

To stay inside the borderline of legality, touts often ask customers to sign a receipt for their tickets. These show the price paid alongside the real seat price and amount to a signed statement that the buyer accepts the difference. If you signed a receipt for your tickets, you have no comeback against the seller.

ACTION PLAN

1 If you paid by cheque, you could consider stopping the cheque and issuing a new cheque for an amended amount representing the cost of the tickets and an amended service fee. Send this together with a covering letter explaining the reason for your actions. If you paid by credit card, advise them of your predicament and that you are taking the matter further.

2 No matter which payment method you used, contact your local trading standards office (see p30) and inform it of what has happened. Also contact the Society of Ticket Agents and Retailers (STAR) ▶ 📖 , whose members follow a code of practice and which offers an arbitration service in cases of dispute. If you bought the ticket in London, also contact the Society of London Theatre ▶ 📖 . Both organisations work with Trading Standards to monitor sharp practices.

Cancelling a restaurant booking can be costly

Q We booked a table for six at a restaurant, but had to cancel at the last minute because of illness. The manager is demanding compensation for loss of business. Can she do that?

A Yes. When you book a table, you make a contract with the restaurant. You undertake to turn up on the prearranged day at the prearranged time, and pay for the meal; the restaurant undertakes to serve the meal as described on the menu. The management can demand damages for breach of contract if the restaurant loses money because you do not turn up.

If you paid a deposit, you will forfeit this, and the management can charge you for loss of profits on your booking – the cost of the food and drink your party can reasonably be expected to have consumed.

But the restaurant management must try to reduce its losses by arranging for other customers to use your table. If they do fill the table, the management will not have suffered a loss and cannot claim damages against you.

In an attempt to crack down on no shows, some restaurant managers take credit card details when a booking is made by a customer and deduct a deposit, which the customers forfeit if they fail to appear.

Compensation for a double booking

Q We booked a table for eight at a restaurant to celebrate a wedding anniversary, but arrived to find that there was no table for us because the restaurant was full. Can we claim redress?

A Yes. By failing to provide a table or serve a meal that you booked, the restaurant management is in breach of its contract with you.

The amount you can claim depends on the importance of eating in that particular restaurant, and the trouble involved in making alternative arrangements. Your claim could include a sum to reflect your disappointment, distress, inconvenience and loss of enjoyment, plus the money you spent on finding another restaurant. This might include taxis for the guests to another venue, and the extra cost of ending up in a more expensive restaurant for the evening.

Your claim will carry more weight if you made it clear when you booked that it was for a special occasion.

ACTION PLAN

1 Write to the restaurant manager ▶ ✍ to complain that no table was available when you arrived for your booking. If you paid a deposit, ask for its return and for compensation. Say that when you booked, you stated that the booking was for a special occasion.

2 If the manager disputes your claim, collect evidence that you booked, such as a copy of an email, fax or letter to the manager or a record of a call on a phone bill, and write again, saying that you are prepared to take the matter further.

3 If the response is unsatisfactory, inform the restaurant that, if the matter is not resolved by a stated deadline, you are prepared to take out a claim using the small claims track in the county court (see p19). Your local Citizens Advice Bureau ▶ 📖 or trading standards office (p30) may help you to fill in the court forms.

WORD OF WARNING

When you make a restaurant booking for an important occasion, especially at a busy time of year such as Christmas, confirm the booking by email, fax or a letter, and ask for written confirmation from the restaurant.

Your coat goes missing while you dine out

Q We went out to a restaurant for dinner and my wife left her coat with the cloakroom attendant. At the end of the evening the coat was missing. The proprietors deny responsibility. Can they do that?

A Possibly, but only if they can show that the fault is not theirs – if, for example, you had hung your own coat on a hook without assistance from any staff. The management has a legal duty to take care of its customers' possessions, so even if the restaurant displayed a notice stating that 'The management accepts no responsibility for loss or damage to items left in the cloakroom', it cannot dodge its duty to take care of them.

You have a good case to argue that the restaurant failed in its duty if:
- the staff insisted that you hand your coat to the cloakroom attendant
- a ticketing system operates in the cloakroom, and it seems that the coat was handed to someone who had no ticket, or the wrong ticket
- there was a cloakroom charge (this would imply that you could expect a higher-than-otherwise level of care)
- the cloakroom attendant had left the coats unguarded. ▶

Give your contact details to the manager and wait for a few days to see if another customer contacts the restaurant to report that she has the wrong coat.

If the coat does not reappear and your home contents insurance includes cover for personal belongings outside your home, you can claim for the full cost of a replacement coat.

If all else fails, contact your local Citizens Advice Bureau ▶ ⌨ or trading standards office (see p30) for advice on pursuing a claim for your loss. It could mean using the small claims track in the county court (see p19).

Wrong information about ingredients

Q I am allergic to nuts. I recently suffered an allergic reaction after eating in a restaurant even though I asked beforehand about the ingredients in the dishes I wanted to choose, and the waiter assured me that my meal didn't contain nuts. Am I entitled to compensation?

A Yes. If you were misled about the food you ordered and you suffered as a result, you can seek compensation using the small claims track in the county court (see p19).

Winning a case is difficult without evidence. If you have an immediate allergic reaction to restaurant food, you may be able to obtain a sample of the food to take to your GP the next day for analysis, or to the environmental health office for the area where the restaurant is located, contactable through the local council switchboard. If you were with another person, that person may agree to act as a witness to your conversation with the waiter and to your allergic reaction.

It is also possible that the restaurant management may admit liability. Professional caterers recently admitted liability for serving a canapé that they knew contained peanuts to a person they had been told was allergic to nuts.

You need expert advice and for this you should contact your local trading standards office (see p30). The officers will advise you and could pursue the case on your behalf.

LEGAL PROTECTION WHEN EATING OUT

When you eat in a restaurant, you are protected by the following laws and regulations. You can download copies of laws pubished after 1982 from the HMSO web site ▶ ⌨, or buy printed copies from The Stationery Office (TSO) ▶ ⌨.

• **Price Marking (Food and Drink on Premises) Order 1979** states that the menu, and any minimum cover and service charges, must be displayed where people can read them before entering a restaurant.

• **Sale of Goods Act 1979** says that any goods, including food served, must be as described (so a vegetarian risotto should not be made with meat stock) and of satisfactory quality (see p29).

• **Trades Description Act 1968** makes it a criminal offence to give a false description of any goods or services, or false indications of their origin (so cheese described as 'buffalo mozzarella' must have been made from buffalo milk). Download from www.dti.gov.uk/ccp/topics1/guide/tda1968

• **Food Safety Act 1990** makes it an offence to sell food not of 'the nature, substance or quality demanded by the purchaser' and to describe food in a way that is likely to mislead.

• **Food Hygiene Regulations 1970** (amended 1990) regulate the cleanliness of kitchens and the hygiene of staff; state that food handlers must have recognised food hygiene training; and stipulate that cases of food poisoning in staff or customers must be reported to the environmental health authorities.

The cost of biting on an olive stone

Q I have spent £300 on dental repairs to my tooth after I damaged it biting into a stone in an olive described as 'pitted' on a restaurant menu. The restaurant owner refuses to reimburse the cost. Can I claim compensation?

A Yes. If you were served a dish of olives, all with stones, you might be able to claim the cost of the dental treatment and compensation for pain, distress and your loss of enjoyment of the meal.

When the restaurant management seated you at a table, they undertook to serve dishes as described on the menu. By serving olives with stones instead of pitted olives as described on the menu, they are in breach of contract. It is easier to make a claim for a breach of contract than it is for negligence.

If, at the time, you refused to pay for the dish containing the stony olive, or you paid 'under protest' – writing this phrase on the cheque, credit card slip or all copies of the bill – to indicate that the manager had not heard the last of that meal, you added weight to your argument.

But you must be sure that you were not served a dish of pitted olives among which was one stray olive with a stone. The staff may have taken the olives in good faith from a tin labelled 'pitted olives'. If the restaurant management can show that they took all reasonable steps to ensure that their labelling is correct, such as buying from reputable suppliers and testing the olives regularly, they might claim 'due diligence', and a court may not find in your favour.

You should report the incident to your local trading standards office (see p30), giving the endorsed payment record as evidence. Trading Standards ▶ (see p30) enforces the law relating to the quality of food served in restaurants.

WHY CAN'T YOU COMPLAIN POLITELY ABOUT THE OLIVE STONES LIKE OTHER PEOPLE, DEREK?

PHUT!

When a vegetarian dish contains meat products

Q At a restaurant I ordered an avocado mousse, which was labelled 'vegetarian'. A friend said later that it must have been made with gelatine – an animal product. I phoned the restaurant, but the manager refused to discuss the dish's ingredients. Can she do that?

A Yes, you cannot make restaurant staff discuss the ingredients of a meal.

'Vegetarian' has no legal definition, but the Vegetarian Society definition (a diet of grains, pulses, nuts, seeds, vegetables and fruits with or without dairy products and eggs) is accepted in many restaurants where vegetarian dishes are marked on the menu as 'suitable for vegetarians' or 'vegetarian dish of the day'. ▶

If you believe that a dish you are served, which is labelled vegetarian on the menu, may contain animal products such as fat or gelatine, you should ask the manager before you eat any of it. If you try a dish and taste meat or fish products, complain to the manager at once and ask to be served a vegetarian dish, or refuse to pay.

You could report the restaurant to your local trading standards office (see p30). It has the power to investigate the restaurant and, if justified, may bring an action against it under one of the laws governing the description and quality of food served in restaurants (see box, p82).

You do not have to pay for poor service

Q We enjoyed a good meal at a restaurant, but the service was surly and very slow so we deducted the service charge from the bill when we paid. The manager claimed that the service charge was part of the cost of the meal and couldn't be deducted. Can he be right?

A No. You do not have to pay for service that is unsatisfactory, even if the charge is described as compulsory on the menu and included in the bill.

It is illegal to order a meal in a restaurant with the intention of not paying for it, but a manager cannot claim that under the law you must pay the full bill for a meal in all circumstances. But you must be clear about why you are withholding payment of the charge.

You must also give the restaurant staff a chance to put things right, which means that if you are dissatisfied with the food or the service, complain to the waiting staff during the meal. If they do not respond, complain to the manager before you finish the meal.

If nothing is done to remedy the situation, you can deduct the amount shown as the service charge on the bill. As long as you make it clear to the manager that you have a genuine reason for not paying, you leave your name and address and show proof of identity, you cannot be accused of acting dishonestly.

If the menu states that a percentage charge is included in the meal price, you can reduce the bill by that percentage if the service has not been of a 'reasonable standard'. If the percentage was not specified, anything up to 15 per cent would be accepted as reasonable in law.

If pressure from the restaurant staff inhibits you from deducting the service charge, make it clear that you are paying 'under protest'. Write this on the back of both your and the restaurant's copy of the bill and/or on the reverse of the cheque or credit card slip. This strengthens your case if you decide to make a claim against the restaurant.

ACTION PLAN

1 If you paid the bill in full, write to the restaurant manager ▶ ✍, make clear that you are aware of your rights and ask for compensation.

2 If the manager refuses, tell him that, if the matter is not resolved by a stated deadline, you are prepared to make a claim using the small claims track in the county court (see p19). Your local Citizens Advice Bureau ▶ 📖 or trading standards office (see p30) may help you to fill in the court forms.

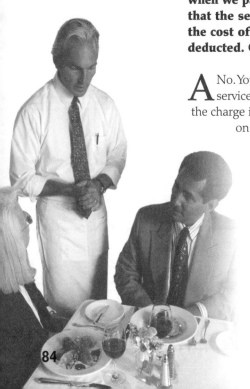

Minimum charge leaves a sour taste

Q **A friend and I met for an early evening drink. She had a mineral water and I had a glass of wine. The bill came to £20, which the manager says is their minimum charge. Can she charge so much?**

A Yes. A minimum charge (and a cover charge, which is in effect a fee for providing a table, table linen, glasses and other aspects of restaurant service) is legal as long as it is made clear to people who enter the restaurant.

By law (see box, p82), the charges have to be shown as prominently and clearly as the food prices. They need not be on the menu, but they must be displayed with the menu near the restaurant entrance. If a minimum charge or a cover charge are on view, you must pay them.

You can challenge a minimum charge if you think it is disproportionately high. You must make your views clear to the manager, pay the charge 'under protest' (see question, left), and then report the restaurant to the local trading standards office (see p30), which is responsible for policing the legislation governing restaurants (see box, p82).

If no minimum charge notice is displayed, yet you are presented with a bill laden down with a high minimum charge, you can refuse to pay it. You should also report the restaurant to the local trading standards office.

Food poisoning after eating at a restaurant

Q **I went out with a group of friends to a restaurant. The following day we all went down with food poisoning. We suspect that it was something we ate at the restaurant, but the manager denies responsibility. Can he do that?**

A Probably not. But the decision as to whether the restaurant is responsible for your illness depends on the evidence being made available to the local environmental health service at the earliest possible stage. Ideally, a sample should be taken of the meal you ate.

It is important that you and your friends visit your GPs immediately so that stool samples can be taken from you all. You should also contact your local environmental health service. The officers have powers to take samples of food from the restaurant kitchens, and to investigate whether the same bug is present in both sets of samples. They have powers to close restaurants, if necessary, while investigating the cause and eradicating the contamination.

It is essential to act quickly. Delays mean that there is an interruption in the chain of evidence, making it difficult to investigate and to prove contamination. If a day or two go by before you are able to report the incident, seek advice from your local environmental health service.

ACTION PLAN
1 Contact your local environmental health service immediately, through the switchboard of your local or district council. They will work with the service local to where the restaurant is located. Environmental health will take whatever steps are necessary to investigte the matter and will advise you on other action to take, such as seeing your GP. The environmental health service will inform you of analysis results.

2 If contamination is found, you may be able to claim compensation for personal injury against the restaurant owner, or if it is part of a chain, against the group. Your claim could include: the cost of the meal, loss of earnings and expenses directly incurred as a result of your illness and an amount for the illness. ▶

3 Contact the Office for the Supervision of Solicitors ▶ 📖 or look up www.justask.org.uk, tel: 0845 608 1122, to find a local solicitor who specialises in personal injury claims on a 'no-win no-fee' basis (see p299), as no financial assistance is available for personal injury claims. A free first interview with a solicitor might be enough to give you a plan of action for your claim. Or your local Law Centre ▶ 📖 might be able to offer advice.

4 If the environmental health service decide to take formal action against the restaurant in the criminal court, you could apply for a criminal compensation order instead of pursuing a civil action in the county court. Get advice from a solicitor or Law Centre in this eventuality.

GOLDEN RULE

Whenever possible, book weekend breaks through a tour operator. If overbooking occurs, the tour operator is responsible for dealing with the problem and paying compensation under the Package Travel, Package Holidays and Package Tour Regulations 1992 (see p98). If the alternative hotel you are offered is inferior in quality, you are entitled to refuse it, travel home and ask for compensation.

A hotel room is double-booked

Q My wife and I booked a room for a weekend in a three-star hotel in Dorset. When we arrived, the manager told us that no room was available. She offered to book us into another hotel, but could only find a room in a budget hotel. We refused the room and returned home. Can we claim compensation?

A Yes, but you must do so quickly or you will be deemed to have accepted the manager's offer.

You have no rights enshrined in law in this situation. But overbooking means that your plans must be changed, so the contract the hotel staff made with you when they accepted your booking has been broken.

This contract is made up of several pledges – for example, the booking

conditions printed in the hotel brochure, statements made in a written confirmation of your booking, and information given to you verbally by hotel receptionists. When a contract is breached in this way, you can claim compensation from the hotel.

For this reason, the management of almost every UK hotel (and many international chain hotels) has a policy of compensating people who make a booking but are refused a room on arrival because the hotel is full.

Although policies of different hotels differ in detail, this compensation should broadly cover transport to another hotel of comparable quality, the cost of the first night's stay, and one phone call (no matter how long-distance) to let family or work colleagues know about the change of hotel.

Since the alternative accommodation you were offered was inferior in standard to that of the hotel you booked – a budget hotel instead of a three-star hotel – you and your wife were right to refuse it. You have a case for claiming the cost of travel to the hotel and back home, refreshments during the journey and perhaps a sum for a disappointing weekend.

If the alternative accommodation had been of a similar standard to that in the hotel you booked, you could not normally claim extra compensation. The only exception would be if you had made it clear when you booked that you had a special reason to stay in that hotel – if, for example, you and your wife booked an anniversary visit to the hotel where you had spent your honeymoon, or a person with mobility problems booked the only hotel in a resort close to local amenities.

ACTION PLAN

1 Write immediately ▶ ✍ to the hotel manager, reiterating all that happened and stating that you rejected her offer

of alternative accommodation because it was not of comparable quality. Say that you are entitled to reasonable compensation, list the expenses you incurred, enclosing copies of receipts, and suggest a sum to compensate you for a disappointing weekend. If the hotel is part of a group or a chain, copy the letter to the head office. Keep copies of all correspondence.

2 If the manager does not respond within two weeks, or if the answer is unsatisfactory, try to negotiate, saying you are prepared to go to court.

3 If the response is not satisfactory, you could claim for compensation using the small claims track in the county court (see p19). Your local Citizens Advice Bureau ▶ 📖 or trading standards office (see p30) may help you to fill in the court forms.

Losing out when you cancel a hotel booking

Q I booked a weekend at a hotel in the UK, but I was ill and had to cancel. The manager won't refund my deposit. Can he do that?

A Yes. When your room reservation is accepted, you make a contract: the hotel management agrees to provide a room on the specified date, and you agree to turn up and pay for it.

The hotel management can therefore not only keep your deposit but also claim for loss of profits. In theory, it can sue you for breach of contract if you do not turn up. This is unlikely in practice, but such a claim could add up to about two-thirds of the full cost of the booking, once an allowance is made for food not eaten and laundry not used.

If, after receiving your cancellation, the hotel staff let your room to another guest, you are no longer liable to pay

compensation. But the booking terms may say that your deposit is not refundable.

If you have an annual travel insurance policy, it may cover you for UK holiday breaks, and you can claim to recover your lost deposit.

Notices disclaiming liability may be invalid

Q While staying in a hotel, my jewellery case and its contents worth more than £1000 were stolen from my room. The staff say a notice is displayed prominently in all the bedrooms disclaiming liability for guests' losses above £50. Can they get away with that?

A No, the hotel management cannot deny all responsibility for the theft of your jewellery just because a disclaimer was displayed in your room. Although the Hotel Proprietors Act 1956 allows the liability of hotels to be limited to £50 an item, or £100 in total if a disclaimer is displayed, this protection is invalidated if negligence by the staff caused the loss.

To pursue a claim against the hotel for the loss of your jewellery, you would have to prove that the management or staff behaved negligently and that their actions or omissions led to the theft. If, for instance, there was no one in reception to monitor people entering the hotel, you may have a case.

But if the notice recommended that guests use the safe in their room or at reception, and you ignored this advice, your claim would be weakened. And if you had left the door open when you were not in the bedroom, so encouraging opportunist theft, your action would count as negligent and you would probably stand little chance of winning a claim.

You might be able to claim on your home contents insurance for 'contents temporarily removed' as you were temporarily resident at the hotel.

ENTERTAINMENT & TRAVEL

CHANGE TO A PACKAGE HOLIDAY • TRAVEL INSURANCE • SURCHARGES

The tour operator changes your holiday

Q **My tour operator has changed the resort for a holiday that I booked six months ago. Can I cancel the holiday?**

A Yes. Under the Package Travel Regulations (see box, p98), tour operators must tell you about proposed changes to your holiday and give you the chance to cancel and claim a refund. You can also claim compensation if the changes cause you to lose money – for example, if you have to book a pricier holiday to stay in the same resort.

If you accept the change of resort, write to your tour operator to say that you do so under protest and reserve the right to claim compensation should the alternative not be satisfactory.

If you go on holiday and are taken to a different resort without having been informed about the change by the tour operator, you can request to be flown home if the alternative is wholly unacceptable; for example, if there is no wheelchair access for a wheelchair user. If you continue the holiday, you must lodge a complaint with the local tour representative immediately. If you fail to do so, it may affect your ability to make a claim on your return, should the alternative not be satisfactory.

WORD OF WARNING

Tour operators are allowed to make small adjustments to the holidays they sell, and usually state in the brochure in small print that they reserve the right to make minor alterations. In the case of a more substantial change, do not be put off by small print that sounds as if it is deterring you from cancelling.

You can choose your travel insurance

Q **My travel agent insists that I buy the agency's travel insurance as part of the holiday package. Can she do that?**

A No. According to the Package Travel Regulations (see p98), travel agents can insist that you take their insurance cover only if it is offered as an inclusive part of a package holiday. If insurance is not included in the package, you can buy it anywhere, or travel uninsured though this is not recommended. Some travel agents simply require that you have travel insurance to cover you for the period of the holiday.

Travel agents and tour operators also cannot charge you extra for a foreign package holiday if you do not buy travel insurance from them.

Cut-off point for surcharges

Q I recently booked a holiday and paid a deposit. Now the tour operator is demanding a £150 surcharge. Can it do that?

A Probably, but to be sure, you must find out whether the tour operator belongs to a trade association (see p92), then check the rules of that association.

Surcharges can be imposed to cover increases in the cost of transport, fuel, taxes, fees chargeable for services such as landing taxes or disembarkation fees at ports or airports, and the exchange rates used to calculate the holiday price.

Most package holidays sold in the UK are sold by members of the Association of British Travel Agents (ABTA). The ABTA Code of Conduct states that member tour operators must bear up to 2 per cent of any increased costs of the holiday before imposing a surcharge.

They may ask for surcharges up to 30 days before the scheduled departure date. If a surcharge is more than 10 per cent of the cost of the holiday, you can cancel the holiday and seek a refund. For rises up to 10 per cent, you must pay or abandon the holiday and your deposit.

Members must explain ABTA's rules on surcharges in the brochure – there is usually a paragraph in the small print. It should say what exchange rate was used to calculate the printed prices.

Other travel trade associations have similar rules, but tour operators that do not belong to a trade association are not bound by rules and their customers must pay or lose their deposit.

TRAVEL INSURANCE – ARE YOU COVERED?

Travel insurance policies vary in the cover they provide. Read the small print before you sign up to make sure that none of the exclusions apply to your situation or the type of trip you are planning.

Travel insurance normally covers you for:
- illness or injury while you are away
- loss or theft of your belongings
- loss or theft of money/travellers' cheques
- cancellation (as long as you take out the insurance as soon as you book the trip) and cutting short the trip
- delayed or missed departures
- liability for accidents to others
- air ambulance return to the UK in an emergency
- hijack.

Most standard policies exclude loss or damage caused by:
- your failure to obtain the required passport or visa
- exchanging currency
- dangerous pursuits, such as rock climbing or potholing (you may need specialist cover for an adventure holiday)
- deliberate risk-taking (except to save human life), including excessive drinking and drug-taking
- problems associated directly or indirectly with HIV/AIDS
- the outbreak of war or other hostilities, and civil disturbances.

Health insurance in Europe
If you do not have travel insurance when you travel to EEA countries (the majority of EU member states plus Iceland, Liechtenstein and Norway), be sure to get form E111. If you are taken ill, an E111 will entitle you to whatever reduced-cost or free medical treatment are available in the country you are in.

Form E111 is not a substitute for travel health insurance because:
- in many countries there are charges for treatments that are free on the NHS in the UK
- you must pay for the treatment, then claim for the permitted amount.

Form E111 is available from your GP's surgery or the post office, or you can download it from www.doh.gov.uk/traveladvice/forme111.htm Fill it in and have it signed by your GP. Then make five or six photocopies (to reclaim your money, you may have to hand over a copy each time you are treated).
The E111 booklet that comes with the form details the paperwork you need to request from doctors, hospitals and pharmacists in each country in order to make a claim.

Counting the cost of undeclared taxes

Q I saw a holiday advertised for £875. When I went to book it, the tour operator said I would have to pay extra to cover taxes. Can she do that?

A Yes, although it is not good practice on the tour operator's part and you have grounds to complain about the advertisement.

The Advertising Standards Authority (ASA, see p24) ▶ 📖 says that advertisements for holidays should be priced to include all taxes, such as Air Passenger Duty and airport taxes. But if there is a change in the tax or a new one is introduced unexpectedly, it would be reasonable to allow the operator to add this to the advertised price.

To complain about a misleading advertisement, write to the ASA. It cannot impose fines or award compensation, but it can request that advertisements be withdrawn and also that publications reject them. It can also draw the public's attention to a misleading advertisement by issuing a press release.

You can also inform your local trading standards office (see p30) as Trading Standards ▶ 📖 enforce pricing legislation, including instances of misleading prices in advertisements.

Booking by credit card protects deposits

Q We booked a holiday to India and paid a 50 per cent deposit by credit card. The tour operator was not an ABTA member and has now ceased trading. Can we get our money back?

A Yes. As long as the holiday cost between £100 and £30,000 you are covered by the Consumer Credit Act 1974, which makes the credit provider as liable as the supplier for delivering what you have paid (see p35). This legislation applies to credit cards but not debit cards.

If the tour company goes bust before your holiday, you can make the same claim against the credit provider as you would have brought against the supplier for breaking the contract.

Write immediately to the credit card company, stating your claim: a return of the 50 per cent deposit that you paid.

Unsuitable cabin for a disabled passenger

Q When I phoned to book a cruise, the company promised me a cabin suitable for a disabled passenger. But when I boarded, I found that mine was high up, and access to restaurants and other amenities was via companionways that I couldn't use. Shouldn't the cruise line provide accommodation suitable for disabled passengers?

A No. The cruise line is under no legal obligation to accommodate disabled passengers. The Disability Discrimination Act (see p78) stipulates that cruise line and ferry terminals in the UK must have facilities for disabled people, but its jurisdiction ends at the top of the boarding ramp.

Cruise lines and ferry companies are increasingly adapting their ships to cater for the needs of disabled passengers, with specially designed cabins and toilets, panic buttons, facilities for guide dogs and hearing-aid systems. But amenities vary, so if you plan a future trip, research each cruise line. The Passenger Shipping

Association ▶ 🕮 has a list of liners suitable for people with disabilities.

If you find a cruise line that offers disabled facilities, ask for your special needs to be written on the booking form (see Golden Rule, p95). They then form part of your contract with the cruise company, and if you are not provided with them, you have a case for legal action.

Timeshares have a ten-day 'get-out' clause

Q **While on holiday I went to a timeshare presentation. Under some pressure, I signed for a share in an apartment in the Algarve, Portugal. Now I have changed my mind, but I'm told I can't back out. Can the company prevent me from cancelling the deal?**

A Not if you signed in the past ten days. The European Directive on Timeshare (94/47/EC) states that you have a minimum of ten days from signing the contract during which you can withdraw. This is the minimum cooling-off period that must be applied throughout the EU, although some individual member states have given their consumers a longer period in their law. Portugal has the ten-day minimum. When you sign a timeshare agreement abroad, it is governed by the laws of that country, so your contract should specify the length of Portugal's cooling-off period (the EU Directive specifies that all contracts must be in the language of the buyer's home country).

If you signed for a timeshare in the UK (whether the property is in the UK or abroad) you have a 14-day cooling-off period (Timeshare Act 1992). During this time you can change your mind, cancel a finance or credit agreement you signed, and reclaim your deposit, and the seller cannot seek or accept money from you.

TIMESHARES, HOLIDAY PACKS AND CLUBS

A timeshare is a share in a property, usually a holiday home abroad, that allows use by several owners at agreed different times. Buyers are protected by the European Directive on timeshare 94/47/EC.

Before signing a timeshare contract:
• Ensure that everything is put in writing.
• Check that the contract is for a timeshare (which has protection, such as a cooling-off period to allow you to cancel if you have second thoughts) and not for a holiday pack or club (see below), which do not have the same protection.
• Check the maintenance charges carefully, since they can escalate considerably; and make sure that the resort has a democratically run owners' club and not a resort management company that could raise annual fees year after year.
• Find a lawyer who specialises in timeshare and knows the laws of the country where you intend to buy. Ask the lawyer to examine the contract before you sign.
• Deal only with timeshare companies that belong to the Organisation for Timeshare in Europe (OTE) ▶ 🕮. It provides a free advisory and conciliation service, and members have to abide by its code of practice.
• Do not sign until you get home and have taken legal advice.

Schemes related to timeshares have emerged that are not covered by the legislation:
Holiday packs are timeshares that run for less than three years, but may come with an option to extend the contract for as much as 50 years.
Holiday clubs are associations whose members either pay a fee or buy points that allow them to take holidays at various locations.

If you buy a timeshare or membership of a holiday club and find you have not got what you paid for, you may get your money back if you paid by credit card. But you are not protected against simply changing your mind.

WORD OF WARNING

Some companies are said to hunt out newly arrived holidaymakers, and persuade them during the early days of their holiday to sign for a timeshare, so that when they get back home after their fortnight's holiday, their right to back out of the agreement will have expired.

Financial protection for holiday booking

Several organisations exist that protect travellers against financial loss should the company they have booked through goes out of business before or during their trip. These include ABTA and AITO, which cover travel and holidays that do not include a flight, and ATOL, which covers holidays that include air travel. The Confederation of Passenger Transport Bonded Holidays Group ▶ ⌒ covers coach-trip holidays.

Least protection is available to travellers who book a scheduled flight (including low-cost flights), and to those who buy a holiday not as a prearranged package but as separate components of travel, accommodation, car hire and so on. If you put together a holiday package by booking the different elements from one web site, you will have limited protection, if any, unless you pay by credit card.

ABTA
Association of British
Travel Agents ▶ ⌒
The trade association for travel agents and tour operators. About 90 per cent of package holidays sold in the UK are handled by ABTA members, who follow a code of conduct covering brochure information, compensation and so on.

If an ABTA travel agent or tour operator:
● **fails before your holiday starts**, ABTA will refund your payments or arrange an alternative for you
● **fails while you are away**, ABTA will arrange for you to continue your holiday and return to the UK.

● If you have a dispute with a member, ABTA will help to settle it and offers an independent arbitration scheme.

AITO
Association of
Independent Tour
Operators ▶ ⌒
The association for independent and specialist holiday companies. It represents about 160 tour operators. AITO members protect money paid by customers for any holiday sold under the AITO logo.

If an AITO member:
● **fails before the start of your holiday**, AITO will refund your payments or make alternative arrangements for you
● **fails while you are away**, AITO will arrange for you to continue your holiday and return to the UK.

● If you have a dispute with a member, you can use AITO's independent dispute settlement service.

ATOL
Air Travel Organisers
Licensing ▶ ⌒
A protection scheme managed by the Civil Aviation Authority (CAA) for holiday packages sold by tour operators that include a flight. British firms must have an Air Travel Organisers Licence (an ATOL)

granted by the CAA before they can sell air-inclusive holidays.

If a tour operator or charter airline holding an ATOL:
● **fails before the start of your trip**, the CAA will refund money you paid for your holiday
● **fails while you are away**, the CAA will pay for you to continue your holiday and to travel back to the UK.

Is your flight ATOL-protected?
It is against UK law to sell package tours and holidays including a flight without ATOL cover.
● If you buy a ticket for a **scheduled** flight (including from a low-cost airline) direct from the airline, your flight is not ATOL-protected.
● If you buy a ticket for a **scheduled** flight from a travel agent who has ATOL protection, and you are given your ticket immediately, or within 24 hours if you book by phone or on the Internet, you are ATOL-protected. If the travel agent does not give you a ticket immediately, or within 24 hours, the travel agent must provide written details of its ATOL or tell you that you are not protected.
● If you book an ATOL-protected **charter** or **air-inclusive package holiday**, you are given an ATOL receipt printed with the travel organiser's ATOL number. You should be given this immediately if you book in person, or within 24 hours if you book by phone or on the Internet.

HOW TO AVOID FINANCIAL LOSSES

Both the type of trip you book and the way you book it affect who you claim compensation from if one of the companies concerned goes out of business. The table below shows the logos you should look for on company brochures, advertisements, web sites, invoices, receipts and correspondence for different types of holiday and travel bookings.

TYPE OF TRAVEL	HOW BOOKED	PROTECTION
Package holiday including a flight	booked through a tour operator's advertisement in a national newspaper:	ABTA · AITO PROTECTED · CREDIT CARD
Rhine river cruise	booked through a travel agent, drive there and back:	ABTA · AA RAC
Low-cost airline flight and a hotel	booked separately and directly through airline and hotel on the Internet:	ABTA · CREDIT CARD
Specialist holiday such as overland trek	booked through a small specialist tour operator:	AITO THE ASSOCIATION OF INDEPENDENT TOUR OPERATORS · CREDIT CARD
Scheduled flight and hotel	flight booked through airline, hotel booked directly:	CREDIT CARD
Scheduled flight only	booked through high-street travel agent:	ABTA · AITO PROTECTED
Package consisting of ferry and hotel	booked through travel agent's web site:	ABTA · AITO THE ASSOCIATION OF INDEPENDENT TOUR OPERATORS
Low-cost flight, ticket to sporting event, hotel	all booked separately on the Internet:	ABTA · CREDIT CARD
Package offer – flight to Milan, tickets for opera, one night in a hotel	booked through TV holiday channel:	ABTA · AITO PROTECTED · CREDIT CARD
Fly-drive holiday in Europe	booked through an Internet travel web site, with a major tour operator:	ABTA · AITO PROTECTED · AA RAC
Fly-drive holiday in USA	Booked through a tour operator	ABTA · AITO PROTECTED · CREDIT CARD

Sports facilities still under construction

Q We booked a hotel with multiple sports facilities for our family holiday through a tour operator. On arrival we found that the tennis courts and golf course were still being built. We had to pay to use facilities nine miles away, but the hotel manager refused to refund the cost of this. Can we claim compensation?

A Yes. You can claim for the cost of the holiday plus a sum for your disappointment from the tour operator. (You can make a similar claim if a hotel is still under construction or one described as quiet is noisy.)

When a tour operator accepts your booking and deposit, a contract is made.

The descriptions in the tour operator's brochure are part of the contract, so you are entitled to expect accommodation and facilities as specified in the brochure, at the price charged.

Tour operators must take 'all reasonable steps' to avoid incorrect descriptions. Your operator should have checked the readiness of the sports facilities at the hotel and told you well ahead of your departure that the brochure description was wrong.

While still on holiday, you must lodge your complaint with the tour operator's local representative. Keep a copy of the complaint log and give the local rep the opportunity to minimise any losses and costs you are likely to incur in getting the holiday you paid for. Gather evidence – such as photographs of tennis courts and golf course still under construction, and notices informing guests that these facilities are not yet available. Talk to other guests, and ask for the names and addresses of any who would back up your version of events.

Keep receipts relating to the extra expenditure you incurred, especially for taxi fares to other sports facilities and the charges for using them.

ACTION PLAN

1 When you return home, write to the tour operator ▶ ✍ enclosing copies of your evidence and asking for compensation.

2 Inform your local trading standards office (see p30) of your unsatisfactory holiday as Trading Standards enforce the Trades Description Act 1968 and the Package Travel Regulations 1992, which may be relevant to your complaint.

3 If you get an unsatisfactory response from the tour operator, seek advice from your local Citizens Advice Bureau ▶ 🕮 or trading standards office on pursing your complaint using the small claims procedure in the county court (see p19).

4 If the tour operator is a member of the Association of British Travel Agents (ABTA; see p92), you can use the low-cost ABTA arbitration procedure to claim compensation instead of the county court.

A brochure description masks a holiday hell

Q We booked an idyllic holiday advertised in a brochure, but the hotel turned out to be under the airport flightpath. We resent having paid for such a disrupted holiday. Shouldn't the tour operator give us our money back?

A Yes, the operator is responsible for the hotel and you can claim compensation for your ruined holiday.
Several laws protect consumers from 'holidays from hell'. For example, if a tour operator publishes a brochure, the information it contains must not be misleading. The Trades Description Act 1968 states that a holiday must be 'as described'. If the description states that it is a quiet hotel, that is misleading.

Log your complaint with the local tour representative and give him or her the opportunity to move you into another hotel. If you move without reference to the rep, you may have difficulty getting compensation on your return.

ACTION PLAN

1 Write to the tour operator urgently and say that the holiday was misdescribed because the hotel was described as quiet. Tell them that you are seeking advice to pursue a claim against them.

2 Inform your local trading standards office (see p30) about your complaint. You will need to show trading standards the holiday brochure and the tour operator's documentation and any other evidence you have gathered to support your claim.

3 If you get an unsatisfactory response from the tour operator, seek advice from your local Citizens Advice Bureau ▶ 🕮 or trading standards office (see p30) about pursuing your complaint using the small claims track in the county court (see p19).

4 If the tour operator is a member of ABTA, you can use the low-cost ABTA arbitration procedure to claim compensation instead of using the county court.

TRAVEL AGENTS AND TOUR OPERATORS – WHO IS LIABLE FOR WHAT

Travel agents usually book clients onto a package holiday with a tour operator. They can provide extras such as transport to an airport, currency exchange or car parking. They can also book transport and hotels independently. If an agent books you on the wrong train, fails to reserve a hotel room, or delays a booking so much that you lose a place on a popular holiday, you can claim compensation. When you book a holiday through a travel agent, the agent is acting on behalf of the tour operator, who bears legal responsibility for the holiday.

Tour operators are responsible for all the elements of the holiday – travel, accommodation, car hire and so on – and for providing the services requested on your behalf by the travel agent. Read the booking confirmation carefully to be sure the travel agent has included everything you expect.

No compensation for missed connection

Q My connecting flight from Manchester to London was delayed and I missed my flight to Vancouver, which was with a different airline. Am I entitled to compensation?

A No, because you bought two unrelated tickets for your domestic and transatlantic flights. This means that you had a contract with each airline and there is no obligation on either carrier to ensure that you make your connection. Flight times do not form part of the contract for carriage – the terms under which you buy your ticket. The International Air Transport Association (IATA) ▶ ⌧ recommends that when flight delays cause passengers to miss connecting flights, airlines should arrange onward flights with other carriers, reroute the passengers to their destination or offer a refund – but it cannot enforce its recommendations.

If you had bought a through ticket, so that one airline was committed to carry you from Manchester to Vancouver, and a delay occurred, that airline would be responsible for finding an alternative flight to your destination. You can usually also expect the airline to pay for meals and any necessary overnight stay in a hotel, although it is not obliged to do so.

If you have travel insurance (see p89), it may cover you for missed connections.

No recompense for a diverted flight

Q My flight was diverted because of fog and the plane landed in Bristol instead of Gatwick. I had to wait for several hours for a coach to take me to Gatwick and was not offered recompense of any kind. Can the airline refuse compensation?

A Yes. Airlines do not routinely offer cash compensation for delays and cancellations due to bad weather, even if they cause passengers financial loss. Regulations about compensation recognise that airlines do not control the weather, and that passenger safety must be their priority.

If you can show that the way the airline handled the delay and diversion caused you to lose money – for example, if you could have got to Gatwick by train in time for a business appointment, but the airline representative refused to pay for it – you may have a case for claiming some compensation.

If you have travel insurance, you may be able to claim on that.

If your flight is cancelled or there is a change of schedule before takeoff, a scheduled airline must offer to refund your money or propose an alternative arrangement. With most scheduled airlines you can ask to switch to another carrier, but the low-cost airlines do not have this arrangement.

THE SMALL PRINT ON AN AIR TICKET

The few lines of small print normally found on the back of an air ticket set out the conditions you accept when you pay for it, and the undertaking that the airline makes to fulfil its obligations. They are called the Contract of Carriage.

An airline's terms and conditions embrace the Warsaw Convention and other international agreements governing matters such as fares, currency, ticketing, cancellation, refunds and check-in.

The conditions also state that you cannot claim any compensation if airline delays deprive you of the enjoyment of your holiday for several days, or for loss of earnings caused by delays on your homebound journey.

Airlines' liability for flight delays

Q My scheduled flight to Hong Kong was delayed for more than 12 hours because of problems with the aircraft. The airline staff refused to offer a hotel, meals or a refund. Can they do that?

A Yes, but this is a grey area. One view is that under Article 19 of the 1929 Warsaw Convention (incorporated into English law by the Carriage by Air and Road Act 1979) airlines should compensate you if they do not get you to your destination within a 'reasonable time', and if the reasons are under their control. On a long-haul flight, this is generally taken to mean getting you to your destination within about six hours of your scheduled arrival time.

But Article 20 of the Convention says that as long as the airline has taken all necessary steps to avoid problems, or if it was impossible to take such steps, the airline is not liable to compensate you for costs or distress caused by a delay.

Even proposed new EU regulations on compensation for delays (see box, p98) take the view that airlines cannot be held responsible for delays caused by aircraft breaking down. If an airline can show that it has done everything possible to avoid the delay, it should not have to pay compensation.

Many airlines offer overnight accommodation and vouchers for meals during a long delay, so it is worth asking for these. And if you took out travel insurance when you booked, you may be able to claim for a long delay under the terms of your policy.

AIR TRANSPORT USERS COUNCIL

AUC

The AUC is an independent organisation, funded mainly by the Civil Aviation Authority (CAA) to represent air passengers' interests and rights. The AUC:
• publishes information about using air transport
• commissions research
• proposes new policies to the authorities that regulate air transport
• investigates complaints against airlines and other suppliers of air transport services, including airports (but not tour operators).

If you have a complaint:
• first try to resolve it with the airline, airport or provider of the service
• if the response is not satisfactory, contact the AUC ▶⎙ by letter or phone. Explain what happened and send tickets, copies of correspondence, the names and addresses of other passengers who will support you, and other evidence to back up your claim.

The AUC will advise you, and may take up your complaint and act as an arbitration service. If it finds in your favour it can put pressure on the airline or airport to give refunds or compensation.

ENTERTAINMENT & TRAVEL

OVERBOOKING • LOST LUGGAGE • AIRCRAFT SEATING

GOLDEN RULE

Take a note of the weight of your luggage when you check in, because you will need to quote this information if your baggage is lost en route and you then make a claim for compensation.

Compensation for an overbooked flight

Q My partner and I booked scheduled flights to Rome. We arrived to check in, but an hour before take-off we were told the flight was full due to overbooking. Can we claim compensation?

A Yes, you can claim a full refund or a seat on the next flight of your choice, plus compensation and one free phone call from the airline's check-in desk. As you were on a scheduled flight, your claim is against the airline.

Under EU regulations the airline must offer you cash compensation at the airport. You are currently entitled to about £120 for flights up to 3500 km (2175 miles) and £240 for longer flights. You can claim half these sums if the airline gets you to your destination within two hours of the scheduled arrival time for shorter flights and four hours for longer flights. You are also entitled to meals and overnight accommodation.

Airlines overbook flights because some passengers with flexible tickets may book a flight but decide at the last minute to take another, and airlines need to fill their aircraft. The airlines usually ask for volunteers to take a later flight, but if necessary passengers will not be allowed to take their seat ('bumped').

For more information, contact the Air Transport Users Council (see p97).

A flight arrives without passengers' luggage

Q My flight reached its destination, but my luggage didn't arrive until two days later, involving me in considerable extra expense. The airline has refused to reimburse me. Can they do that?

CHANGES TO COMPENSATION FOR FLIGHT DELAYS AND CANCELLATIONS

The Package Travel, Package Holidays and Package Tour Regulations 1992 are a set of regulations that control the sale and content of package holidays. They define what is a package (see question, p100), and require travel organisers to protect clients against financial failure, and give accurate descriptions and detailed information about the arrangements.

New legislation for delays, cancellations and overbooking
In July 2003, the European Parliament voted to extend these regulations by introducing new rules to limit overbooking and compensate passengers for delays and cancellations. They are likely to become EU law late in 2004. The rules apply equally to scheduled (including low-cost) and non-scheduled flights (such as charter flights for package holidays), and apply to passengers departing from EU airports; or from an airport outside the EU to an airport in an EU member state.

The rules state that if a flight is overbooked or cancelled, airlines must:
• pay up to £174 compensation of 900 miles or less; £277 for flights between 900 and 2200 miles; and £415 for flights of more than 2200 miles
• offer passengers a choice between an alternative flight at the earliest opportunity and a refund of the money they paid for their ticket.

Passengers facing long delays must be offered whatever refreshments, meals and hotels are needed during the delay, care for passengers with special needs, and a choice between an alternative flight and reimbursement of tickets.

For more detailed information contact the Air Transport Users Council (see p97), the Department of Trade and Industry (dti) ▶ ⌨ or download the latest details from www.hmso.gov.uk

A No. The 1929 Warsaw Convention (incorporated into English law by the Carriage by Air and Road Act 1979) allows you to claim about £15 per kilogram of checked-in baggage if your luggage is lost. The compensation is based on weight, not value, so it will be the same if your case was full of designer clothes and jewellery as if it was packed with old trainers and bicycle chains.

If your baggage is irretrievably lost and weighed below the standard allowance of 20 kilograms, you are entitled to about £300 in compensation.

ACTION PLAN

1 If your suitcase fails to appear on the baggage carousel, report it to the airline representative at the airport and ask for an Irregularity Report (PIR). Keep your baggage stub, which was attached to your ticket at check-in.

2 Ask the airline representative for funds to buy essential items such as toiletries and clothes to wear until your luggage appears. Some carriers pay in advance, usually about £75. If the baggage fails to appear, this sum is deducted from the final payment. Otherwise, keep all the receipts and then make a claim. On a homeward journey you would be offered nothing because the airlines assume that you have everything you need at home.

3 Check whether your travel insurance will reimburse any expenditure not covered by the airline's compensation. You cannot claim twice for the same things, so payments from the airline will be deducted from the final payout from the insurance company.

A family cannot ask to sit together

Q **We booked a flight and asked that our family of two adults and three children should sit together. At the check-in we were told that our seats were not adjacent. Could we have insisted that other passengers be moved so we could all be together?**

A No, unless your request to sit together was accepted in writing. A few holiday companies and airlines accept seat pre-bookings for parties for a small fee, but otherwise it is unusual for a group to be given a guarantee that they will be seated together on a flight. The best way for a family to get seats together is to arrive at the airport early and aim to be the first to check in.

Tall passengers who travel in economy class check-in early if they want to request seats facing the cabin bulkheads or by the emergency exits, which have extra leg room. This first-in-line tactic works even on the budget airlines, since passengers who are given the first batch of numbers are usually admitted into the aircraft first.

DIY holiday bookings on the Internet

Q **I booked a flight to Austria with a low-cost airline on the Internet, and then a hotel and car hire via links on the web site. When I collected the car, I presented the hire company's voucher, which I'd printed out when I booked. But the clerk said it was invalid and I had to pay again to hire a car. When I got home I spoke to an airline manager about the invalid car-hire voucher, but she said this was nothing to do with the airline. Can she be right?**

A Yes. Because you booked a flight, a hotel and car hire separately, you made three independent contracts, and the airline was responsible for the flight only. You must act quickly to try to recover your money from the car-hire company. If you took out travel insurance you may be able to claim under the policy.

'DIY packages' booked independently on the Internet may be cheaper than tour operators' packages, but if they are not 'package holidays' as defined by the law you have no comeback if things go wrong. A 'package' is strictly defined by the Package Travel Regulations 1992 (see p98). To qualify, a trip must be:
• sold or offered at an all-inclusive price
• include an overnight stay or last more than 24 hours
• include two or more of the following elements: transport; accommodation; and at least one other tourist service (for example, car hire, tickets for sports events, entertainment)
• prearranged (the elements must be offered together, even if you have choices, for example, between hotels).

If you had booked the flight, hotel and car hire through a travel agent or tour operator who has an ATOL and bonded insurance (see pp92–93), the travel organiser has to make alternative arrangements or pay you compensation if any problems occur.

ACTION PLAN

1 Check the voucher to see where the car-hire company is registered and whether the fee was debited from your account. If the company is registered in the EU, contact your local Citizens Advice Bureau ▶ 📖 and show the booking confirmation and evidence that the money was paid from your account.

2 As you were travelling within the EU, the Citizens Advice Bureau will contact the European Extra-Judicial Network, which operates a clearing-house for cases involving products and services bought in EU states. The CAB will try to resolve the dispute for you. If this fails, it will advise you about taking legal action abroad.

3 If it is a UK company, send copies of the confirmation and payment debit, and ask for a refund. If you cannot trace the company, or you get no reply, contact your local trading standards office (see p30) for advice.

4 If you paid by credit card, contact the card company, which has joint responsibility for the hire and may refund the money (see p35).

Unexpected charges for hire-car repairs

Q **After I returned from holiday recently, the car-hire company took £200 off my credit card for alleged damage to the car. To my knowledge, the car was undamaged. Can the company do that?**

DRIVING ABROAD

For detailed information about driving abroad, ask your insurer or, if you intend to hire a car, the car-hire company. The AA and RAC give full information on requirements in all European countries on their web sites: www.theaa.com (under Travel Services) for the AA; and www.rac.com (under European Motoring Adviser) for the RAC.

Contact the UK embassy, consulate or High Commission for countries outside Europe. Driving regulations may also be published on a country's official web site.

Driving licence

The full British licence is accepted in all EU countries, but elsewhere an International Driving Permit may be needed. The AA ▶☐ and RAC ▶☐ issue these and can tell you if you need one. Take your registration document V5 or VE 130 ('vehicle of hire' certificate) if you hired the car in the UK with you on the trip.

Rules of the road

Check for different national laws and regulations governing driving, especially:
- minimum driving age
- priority rules at junctions and roundabouts
- speed limits
- seat belt requirements
- rules for driving with children (in some countries, children under a certain age must not travel in the front seat).

Special equipment

Check what requirements and restrictions are compulsory in the countries you intend to visit. These may include:
- GB stickers
- headlight converters
- a red warning triangle
- snow chains
- an approved child seat
- a first-aid kit
- a spare set of light bulbs.

ADDITIONAL INSURANCE COVER FOR HIRED CARS

You may need extra insurance for the USA, Canada and some other countries, and an international Green Card – check what you need with your insurer.

If you hire a car, third-party insurance is included in the tariff. You can usually also buy extra cover from an insurer or from your car-hire firm:

Collision Damage Waiver (CDW) If the car is damaged, CDW limits your liability for physical damage to the car (but not for theft, attempted theft or vandalism – read the exclusions list carefully).

CDW is sold per vehicle by most car rental and insurance companies.

Super CDW This eliminates most of your financial liability if the car or its accessories are damaged (but theft, attempted theft and vandalism are common exclusions). Super CDW is not available in all countries.

Loss Damage Waiver The equivalent of CDW in Canada and the USA. It covers theft and vandalism of a rented car, as well as damage caused by accident.

Liability Insurance Supplement (LIS) This is available in Canada and the USA. It gives the hirer up to $1 million third-party liability coverage and legal defence and damages coverage.

A Yes. You will find a clause in the small print of the contract you signed giving the car-hire company the right to take cash from your credit card to cover dents and scratches, speeding fines and congestion charges, and to pay for filling up the tank with petrol.

You are responsible for the car until it has been checked in by an employee of the car-hire company. If you leave a car in a garage and drop off the keys outside office hours, then leave the country, you are still legally responsible for any damage found when the staff open up in the morning and check the car's condition.

For this reason, always check the car when you hire it and make a note of any damage or defects, and again when you have finished with it, and try to return the car during office hours so that you ▶

can make a final check with a company representative and agree extra charges for any damage found.

Some car-hire companies photograph each car with a digital camera before hire to show its condition, and again after it is returned. If a hire car collects any scrapes or dents while you are using it, you can photograph them yourself and use the photographs as evidence if you need to dispute the amount the company charges you for repairs.

Insurance policies are available that cap the amount you have to pay for repairs to a hire car (see p101).

ACTION PLAN

1 Contact the car-hire company and ask for details of the damage. If you are then certain that you are not responsible for whatever has happened to the car, argue that it occurred after you returned the car and that you should not have to pay.

2 Contact the credit-card company if the repairs cost £100 or more. It may be prepared to refund the money to you and pursue the matter with the car-hire company (see p35).

Travelling without a rail ticket

Q **When I arrived at the station, the ticket office was closed. On the train, the inspectors refused to sell me my usual Saver ticket and insisted that I pay the full-price fare. Can they do that?**

A No. The inspector should sell you exactly the same ticket as you would have bought had the ticket office been open. You should contact the train company and make a complaint.

Some stations that are staffed only at peak times are in regions where penalty fare schemes operate. These stations have machines that accept loose change and dispense a 'permit to travel' ticket. You should get a permit, and at the first opportunity change it for a ticket and pay the difference. If you travel without a permit or valid ticket for the journey, you will have to pay a penalty fare if you are stopped by a ticket inspector.

Compensation for late-running trains

Q **My morning train is consistently late or cancelled so that it's difficult to get to work and meetings on time. Can the rail franchise get away with this?**

A No, it must compensate you. You can also complain to the Strategic Rail Authority (see p105), who has powers to penalise the company if it does not improve the service.

The National Rail Conditions of Carriage (see box, opposite) specify that when 'delays, cancellations or poor service arise for reasons within a Train Company's control, you are entitled to compensation in accordance with the arrangements set out in the latest edition of that Train Company's "Passenger's Charter"'.

You can claim compensation if you arrive more than an hour late at your destination station. The minimum payable compensation is equal to 20 per cent of the amount you paid for your journey, and you are usually given travel vouchers, to be used in part-payment for tickets.

Many rail companies pay more than the minimum compensation – for example, 25 per cent to 60 per cent for delays of an hour, and up to 120 per cent for delays of 90 minutes to 2 hours. There are separate rates for season-ticket holders, who are compensated automatically when they renew their tickets. Ask for a copy of your train company's charter and a claim form from one of the company's ticket offices and check the rates.

You must make a claim within 28 days of the delay occurring, but the train company will probably consider a complaint about a series of delays and cancellations over a longer period if you can mark the delayed and cancelled services on a copy of a timetable. Take this to a ticket office, with the completed claim form and the tickets that were valid for the journeys.

In addition to paying compensation for delayed and cancelled trains, train companies must arrange to get passengers to their destination by other forms of transport, or arrange for overnight accommodation for any who are stranded.

YOUR RIGHTS ON THE RAILWAYS

Rail passengers' legal rights are set out in the National Rail Conditions of Carriage. These cover all scheduled non-international passenger services on the British railway network. When you buy a ticket to travel, you enter into an agreement underpinned by this document, which sets out your rights and any restrictions, and the minimum level of service you can expect. The Conditions of Carriage guarantee minimum rights – except on some discounted-fare journeys. Each train operator has, in addition, a set of by-laws, and some may offer you more extensive rights. These by-laws are part of your legal contract as a passenger, and you can be prosecuted if you breach them.

The National Rail Conditions of Carriage cover:
- the use and validity of tickets
- refund rights
- seating and reservations
- luggage and lost property
- parking of cars and bicycles at stations.

You can ask for a copy of the Conditions of Carriage at any station or download it at www.nationalrail.co.uk/info/conditions/conditions.htm

There need not be a seat for each passenger

Q I regularly have to stand in the corridor for my 70-minute train journey home from work. The ticket collector said that the company has no obligation to provide a seat. Can this be right?

A Yes. Train operators guarantee seats only to passengers who have a seat reservation. If the second-class carriages are full and there is space in first class, passengers with a second-class ticket can ask the ticket inspector if they can travel in first class without paying extra.

If you have a first-class ticket and there are no first-class seats, you can claim a refund of the difference in fare. If you reserved a seat and someone occupies it, you can claim compensation if you had to stand during all or part of the journey.

GOLDEN RULE

Under Section 38 of the Conditions of Carriage (see box, p103), you will have to pay the full first-class fare if you travel (sitting or standing) in a first-class carriage, unless you have permission from a ticket inspector or you paid the difference between standard and first-class fares before boarding the train.

Penalty fare for a crowded rail journey

Q I bought a second-class rail ticket. The second-class compartments were overcrowded, with people standing, so I found a seat in a first-class compartment. The ticket collector insisted that I pay a penalty fare. Can he do that?

A No. The inspector should ask you to pay the difference between the second and first-class fares. He should only have charged you a penalty fare if you were travelling without a valid ticket for your journey.

The National Rail Conditions of Carriage (see box, p103) state that when you have a second-class ticket and no standard seats are available, you should ask the ticket inspector's permission to sit in first class. If you ask first, the ticket inspector should allow you to do so for no extra charge as long as all the second-class seats are occupied and no first-class ticket-holder needs the empty first-class seat. If you just take a first-class seat without speaking to the inspector first, he or she will ask you to pay the difference between the fares.

If a seat becomes available in a second-class carriage, or a first-class ticket-holder requires your seat, the inspector can ask you to move.

ACTION PLAN

1 Write to or email the train company outlining your rights under the National Rail Conditions of Carriage ▶✎. State the date and time of travel and the service you used. Send your ticket and penalty-fare ticket. Keep copies of the letter and tickets.

2 The train company should refund the difference between the penalty fare and the supplement.

3 If you are not satisfied, contact your local Committee of the Rail Passengers' Council (see oppposite). If the Committee feels you have a good case, it may take up the complaint with the train company.

Compensation for train cancellations

Q I bought a ticket from a machine. After waiting an hour for a train, I decided not to travel after all. The ticket office was closed, so I couldn't complain. Can I claim a refund?

A Yes, if you bought the ticket less than 28 days ago. Take it to a ticket office at any of the train company's stations, explain what happened, and you should get a full refund. Had the ticket office been open, you could have claimed an immediate full refund. If you have to return to claim a refund, the company may deduct a small charge. A refund may be denied if the ticket expired more than 28 days ago or is damaged.

COMPENSATION FOR LOST BAGGAGE

Train passengers are expected to stay with their luggage and be responsible for it. Under Section 50 of the Conditions of Carriage (see p103), a train company will accept liability only if the loss or damage to the luggage is caused by neglect or is the fault of the company or its staff. The liability is limited to £1000, or the value of the item if less.

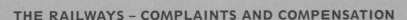

THE RAILWAYS – COMPLAINTS AND COMPENSATION

If you want to make a complaint about a rail service, contact the relevant train company. If the company is unhelpful, you can appeal to a higher authority. At the top of the hierarchy is the Office of the Rail Regulator ▶⌂, but you would complain to it only if you thought that a company supplying services to the railways was guilty of unfair competition. The Strategic Rail Authority can put pressure on Network Rail and the rail companies if many passengers complain about a problem.

Train operators
Role Operate the passenger train services and manage regional and local stations.
Complain to them about timetables, delays and cancellations, fares, service, stations.
How to complain In person to the station manager; on claim forms, available from ticket offices; on web sites (details from Rail Passengers' Council).

Rail Passengers' Council (RPC) and Committees
Role These government bodies monitor the train companies and look after passengers' interests. The Council coordinates the work of the eight regional Rail Passengers' Committees.
Complain to them about safety, trains, delays, cancellations, local stations, ticketing, punctuality, overcrowding, cleanliness, information boards.
How to complain First complain to the train operator. If the outcome is unsatisfactory, appeal to your regional Rail Passengers' Committee: call 020 7713 2700, write ▶⌂ or log on to the web site: www.railpassengers.org.uk The Committee will pursue the matter with the train operator.

Network Rail
Role A non-profit-making company with responsibility for maintaining, improving and upgrading the railway infrastructure.
Complain about track, signalling, bridges, level crossings, tunnels, vandalism, major stations such as London Waterloo or Manchester Piccadilly, safety.
How to complain Call the 24-hour helpline 0845 711 4141; in person to station managers; write ▶⌂.

Strategic Rail Authority (SRA)
Role To promote and improve the rail services – specifically to improve use and performance, and reduce overcrowding; regulates Network Rail.
Complain about Network Rail; the rail franchises, overcrowded trains, the train companies' provisions for disabled passengers. The SRA also deals with appeals against penalty fares.
How to complain Write ▶⌂ or email via the web site www.sra.gov.uk-contactpage

COMPENSATION FOR LATE-RUNNING AND CANCELLED TRAINS

Train operators must display performance details at all their major stations, giving the dates when punctuality and reliability fell below standard and triggered a compensation payment. When the service is so bad that a day is declared void, the operator can give a free day's travel to holders of monthly and annual season tickets.

Train operators do not have to award compensation if delays are caused by events outside their control, such as vandalism or a landslide. The minimum refunds are outlined below, but many operators set out higher compensation rates in their passengers' charter.

Single, return and weekly season ticket refunds
• At least 20 per cent for a journey delayed by at least 60 minutes.
• If your train leaves late but not late enough to qualify you for compensation, but you miss a connection and arrive at your final destination late enough to qualify for compensation, you can claim from the operator of the first train.
• If you do not travel because of a cancellation or delay, you can ask for an immediate full refund at the ticket office. But if you were told about delays or engineering work and decided to travel, you cannot claim compensation.

Monthly and annual season ticket refunds
• Compensation is based on the overall performance of the trains along the route.
• If performance targets are missed, you are offered a minimum discount of 5 per cent for poor punctuality, and 5 per cent for a high level of cancellation, when you renew your ticket.
• Season ticket holders are compensated when they renew their tickets, as long as they renew within four weeks of the old ticket expiring.

A reserved seat is already occupied

Q **I reserved a seat on a train, but the seat had been double booked and was occupied. I had to stand for more than half the journey. Can I demand compensation?**

A Yes. You have the right to a refund of the fee you paid to reserve the seat and also to compensation because you had to stand when you had a seat reservation. You must claim within 28 days of completing the journey.

The National Rail Conditions of Carriage (see p103) state that the compensation cannot be more than the full single fare for the journey you made.

ACTION PLAN

1 Take your ticket and seat reservation to one of the train company's ticket offices and ask for compensation. You will need to show the train's timetabled departure time.

2 If you have difficulty claiming your refund, contact your local committee of the Rail Passengers' Council (see p105), who will investigate on your behalf.

An injury occurs on a bus journey

Q **On a recent bus journey, I twisted my ankle when the bus jerked, and I tripped and stumbled. I had to get a taxi to the doctor's and for three days I couldn't work. Now the bus company says it isn't responsible for what happened. Can it refuse to pay compensation?**

A No. The company has a duty of care (see p117) to its passengers, and you can claim compensation for the pain and suffering caused by the injury, and for the taxi, the earnings you lost because you could not work, and other expenses such as paying for a childminder. If the effects of the accident reduce your long-term earning potential, you can also claim for that. You must show receipts for your expenses and proof that you were unable to work.

If the bus driver was forced to brake or swerve because of someone else's poor driving, the company can claim against that driver.

Claims under £50,000 are pursued through the county court (see p19), which uses previous cases involving similar injuries as a guide to damage levels. A settlement is often negotiated before the case gets to court.

ACTION PLAN

1 Check if the bus or coach company operate the service in partnership with local councils. If they do, contact the councils, the bus or coach operator and complain ▶✍. List the expenses you have incurred as a result of the injury and say how much compensation you want to claim.

2 If you do not get a satisfactory response, contact a solicitor who specialises in personal injury cases and can advise you on legal action.

WORD OF WARNING

The bus or coach operator may decide to pay some money into the court under a system called the Civil Procedure Rules Part 36. You have 21 days to decide whether to accept this sum. If you reject it and the court awards you a lower sum, you may be liable for the operator's legal costs from the date of the offer.

Compensation for coach-trip delays

Q I recently travelled by coach from Truro to Nottingham. The journey involved changing buses, but connecting services were delayed and I arrived five hours late, missing my granddaughter's birthday party – the reason for my trip. I have complained to the bus company, but they say they're not liable. Can they be right?

A Yes. Typically, the company will not accept liability for any loss or cost to passengers as a result of delays caused by factors beyond its control. This includes everything from traffic jams, accidents and severe weather to strikes, riots and vandalism. Rather than accept liability for damages, some coach companies make a small goodwill payment.

If the delay was caused by something that was clearly under the company's control, such as a mechanical breakdown of the coach, the company would be liable up to the limit specified in the Conditions of Carriage, the terms you accept when you buy a ticket. The Conditions of Carriage are displayed at ticket offices or are available on request.

If you missed a connection and faced a long wait for the next coach, and took a taxi or hired a car instead, you would have a case for claiming those expenses as long as you gave the company the opportunity to assist you in making alternative arrangements.

Taxi driver's estimate of a fare

Q When booking a taxi recently, I asked what the fare would be. At the end of the journey, the driver demanded a much higher fare than the one I'd been quoted. Do I have to pay?

A Yes. The fare you must pay at your destination is shown on the taxi meter, and it is an offence not to pay it. The meter monitors cab fares, working on a rate per mile, but when the speed goes below 10 miles per hour, it switches to registering time.

The meter only operates inside the cab's officially designated 'home territory'. If your journey takes you beyond it, the driver will tell you and may suggest a fixed fare or ask you to agree to pay the fare on the meter.

The cab driver can only estimate what the fare is likely to be for any journey.

A taxi driver who takes a long route

Q I recently took a taxi across London and the driver used an unnecessarily long route and made me late for an appointment. Did I have to pay the fare shown on the meter?

A Yes, you have to pay the metered fare at the end of any journey inside the taxi's home patch (see question, left).

Licensed drivers have a duty to use the best route. This may be the quickest route rather than the most direct one between two points that may be clogged with traffic. If you feel that a driver is taking a longer route than necessary, you should query it. The driver may explain, for example, that a road or a bridge is closed. If you do not believe the explanation, you can call the police, but the meter will run while you wait for them to respond.

To complain about a taxi or a private hire vehicle, contact your local council's licensing department, or, in London, the Public Carriage Office ▶ 🚕, part of Transport for London. These authorities investigate complaints and can suspend or revoke a driver's licence. If they find a complaint justified, the driver usually returns the overpayment or the fare.

YOUR HEALTHCARE

Shop around for the right doctor

Q I applied to register with a GP and was turned down, but no reason was given. Can I insist that the GP should take me on?

A No. You are entitled to be registered with an NHS doctor, but you cannot insist that a particular GP accept you as a patient. An NHS doctor can refuse to take you on without saying why. Equally, you can change your GP by asking another doctor to accept you – and you do not have to tell your current GP.

You should now try other doctors in the area – take time to find the right one. If you need medical attention before you find one, any local GP will provide immediately necessary treatment for up to 14 days.

Ask friends, neighbours and people in local pharmacies and health shops to recommend a good GP. Then you should visit the surgery – you can tell a great deal about a medical practice from a short visit. Is the waiting-room cheerful and clean? Are the receptionists welcoming? Are there magazines and children's toys? What posters and leaflets are on display?

ACTION PLAN
1 Ask for a list of NHS doctors from:
• **NHS Direct (see box, opposite)**
• **the local library**
• **your local Health Authority (listed in the phone directory).**

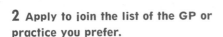

2 Apply to join the list of the GP or practice you prefer.

3 If three or more practices do not accept you, the local Health Authority will allocate a GP to you. Contact the authority, ask for a form and fill it in, giving the names of surgeries you tried. The authority can help if you need, for example, an interpreter.

How to get a second opinion

Q I find my GP unsympathetic and I'm not confident of his diagnosis of my medical problem. He says I don't have a right to a second opinion. Is this correct?

A Yes. GPs should consider seriously a patient's request for a second opinion from another GP or a hospital specialist, but they do not have to agree if they think it is unnecessary.

If your GP does not agree with your request for a second opinion, you can:
- see another GP in the practice
- call NHS Direct (see box, below) or visit an NHS walk-in centre (see box, p112)
- see a doctor privately (private GPs are listed in the local phone directory)
- ask your GP to refer you to a specialist privately
- change your GP.

> **NHS DIRECT** is a 24-hour helpline offering medical advice. It is staffed by nurses, who can tell you what to do if you or your family members are ill. They also give information on health conditions, local health services (including late-night pharmacies), and support organisations.
> - Phone helpline: 0845 4647
> - Online service at: www.nhsdirect.nhs.uk

If the GP's diagnosis proves to have been wrong and he would not agree to a second opinion, make a formal complaint (see pp114-115). You may be able to sue if the resulting delay in diagnosis caused you harm.

WORD OF WARNING
Trying to obtain another opinion behind your GP's back may damage your relationship. Try to discuss the matter with him again before making a move.

Can your GP remove you from the practice?

Q My GP struck me off her list because I refused to have a test. Can she do that?

A Yes. GPs can refuse to continue to treat any patient without giving a reason. Most often patients are excluded for aggressive behaviour, but your GP can remove you from her list if you refuse a test or other recommendation, even though you have the right to refuse. She must agree to see you for the next 14 days, while you find another doctor.

Patients are responsible for their own health

Q I'm a bit overweight and a heavy smoker. My doctor says she will refuse further treatment for my asthma unless I agree to take more responsibility for my own health. Can she do that?

A No. A doctor must treat you according to your medical needs, and cannot refuse to do so because your health problems seem to be self-inflicted.

Yet doctors must also operate within NHS budgets, and should take account of habits such as smoking when deciding whether patients would benefit from ▶

a treatment. For example, if you continue to smoke while receiving nicotine replacement therapy on the NHS, your treatment will be stopped. Ask your doctor what she meant. If she will not treat you for associated problems such as breathlessness, you have grounds to complain. But she may feel that certain treatments would be ineffective because of smoking or your weight, in which case you could ask for help to quit smoking or advice on dieting. If you find your doctor unsympathetic, consider changing GP.

If a doctor takes advantage

Q **I went to my usual practice for a routine pill check and saw a locum doctor. He insisted on examining my breasts and seemed to take far too long about it. A few days later I saw him in the street and he invited me to stop for a drink in a bar. Isn't that unethical?**

A Yes, and you should report the matter. Patients assume that doctors will not take advantage of their vulnerability when they allow them access to their bodies.

The doctor may have needed to make a thorough examination – which may have seemed prolonged – if he detected a cyst or a swelling, and this will be taken into consideration in any investigation. But doctors are not allowed to have sexual relationships with their patients, so he should not have invited you for a drink. And a doctor must not use the excuse of examining you to indulge in personal sexual gratification – to do so is serious professional misconduct.

ACTION PLAN

1 Report what happened to the practice manager or, if you prefer, to your GP when he or she returns.

2 If you are unhappy with the response, contact your local Patient Advisory Liaison Service (PALS; see box, p109) or, if a PALS has not yet been set up in your area, the Community Health Council/Patient Forum (details from your GP's practice manager, your area Health Authority or NHS Trust – listed in the phone directory). The advisers will investigate and can help you to make a formal complaint.

3 If the response is inadequate you can report the locum to the General Medical Council (GMC; see box, left).

WORD OF WARNING

A complaint to the GMC can have a devastating effect on a doctor's career, so consider taking such a step only if all other appropriate action has failed and the matter you are thinking of reporting to the GMC is very serious.

WHAT THE GMC CAN DO

The General Medical Council (GMC) ▶ ⌥ licenses doctors to practise medicine in the UK. It keeps a register of doctors who can practise, sets standards of conduct and clinical care and practice, and ensures that those on the register maintain them. It also issues guidelines for medical practice.

The GMC will investigate complaints from the public if they have implications for the doctor's fitness to practise. After a formal investigation it may act if:
- a doctor has been convicted of a criminal offence
- serious professional misconduct is alleged
- professional performance was seriously deficient
- a doctor with health problems continues to practise while unfit.

The GMC can: give advice or a warning, order the doctor to take further training, restrict or suspend registration, or bar the doctor from practising medicine.

Getting treatment while away from home

Q I became ill when staying with friends, and so I saw their GP, but he just said I should see my GP at home. Should he have treated me?

A Not necessarily. You are entitled to temporary treatment from a local GP if you are ill while away from home. But the doctor may decide that your medical problem does not need immediate treatment and advise you to wait to see your own doctor when you return home.

Keeping your medical records private

Q My mother's friend is a nurse at the group practice where I'm being treated for an eating disorder. She found my case notes, read them and told my mother. Is this allowed?

A No. Health professionals' regulatory bodies (see box, above right) warn that personal details – even the fact that someone is a patient – should be seen only by those directly concerned with the patient's care. National Health Service (NHS) staff, including secretaries, are bound to keep patients' records private.
   Exceptions to this rule occur when:
• patients consent to their details being passed on
• special factors come into play – for example, if a person drives when taking medication that affects concentration, or if a patient has a 'communicable' disease that must by law be reported to the authorities
• details are needed for NHS administrative purposes, in which case they are usually given without identifying the patient.

If your details are passed on in this way, you should be told. And the people to whom they are sent must be reminded that they, too, have a duty of confidentiality. You can object to details that might identify you being given to other people, and your objection should be recorded in your medical notes.

ACTION PLAN
1 Report what has happened to the practice manager, who may take the matter further.

2 If you are unhappy with the response, complain formally (see box, pp114-115).

3 You could try to sue the nurse for breach of confidentiality, but you will have to show that the unauthorised disclosure caused you serious damage.

LEGAL REGULATION OF HEALTH PROFESSIONALS

People practising in most healthcare professions are regulated by a professional body. These bodies have complaints procedures for patients and codes of practice, along with the power to take disciplinary action against members who do not follow their code of practice. Osteopaths and chiropractors are the only complementary therapists regulated by law (see box, p135).

Dentists
General Dental Council ▶ ⌂

Doctors
General Medical Council (GMC) ▶ ⌂

Nurses, midwives and health visitors
Nursing and Midwifery Council ▶ ⌂

Opticians
General Optical Council ▶ ⌂

Other medical professionals: art therapists, chiropodists/podiatrists, clinical scientists, dieticians, medical laboratory technicians, occupational therapists, orthodontists, prosthetists, physiotherapists, speech and language therapists, radiographers and paramedics
Health Professions Council ▶ ⌂

Your right to see your medical records

Q My doctor let me see my medical records, but they are incomplete and there are a couple of errors. When I returned them, the practice manager said I couldn't alter them in any way. Can they stop me correcting them?

A No, you are allowed to make corrections. You have the right to see all your health records, including those from dentists and opticians and from NHS and private practices, whether they are held on paper or as electronic files. There may be a small charge for this and for a copy of all or part of them. You can ask for a written explanation of anything you do not understand in the records, and you can point out any mistakes, including facts that are missing. Your comments will be added to your records and you will be sent a copy of the corrections. Details cannot be deleted from your records even if they are wrong, unless you apply for a court order.

Your doctor can withhold certain facts – for example, a note that you may have an illness, which is not yet confirmed, or comments relating to your family, such as a suspicion that there may be violence in the home.

HOW THE NHS IS ORGANISED

Health Authorities
In England, 28 Strategic Health Authorities assess regional needs, oversee and monitor GPs, hospitals and other healthcare services, and work with local authorities on health education and providing other health services. In Wales, 22 Local Health Boards oversee healthcare services and spending in their areas.

There are also some Special Health Authorities, which run particular services for the population as a whole, not just a particular region – for example, the National Blood Authority.

Primary care
GPs, community nurses, health visitors, dentists, opticians, pharmacists, chiropodists and others are the first people you contact if you need treatment – so they are said to provide 'primary care'.

Primary Care Trusts (PCTs)
In England, more than 300 Primary Care Trusts (PCTs) are responsible for organising the primary care in their areas. The PCTs make sure that there are enough GPs locally and that other pimary health services are being provided, including dentists, pharmacists and opticians. In large cities, they have walk-in centres, where patients can go without an appointment for treatment and advice.

PCTs have a responsibility to improve the health of the local community, to tackle health inequalities and to liaise with local authorities to ensure that health and social care policies are complementing one another.

You can obtain details of your local PCT from your library or your local Strategic Health Authority, or from the NHS web site ▶ ⌸.

Secondary care
This is specialist treatment, usually offered in hospitals. Except in an emergency, your GP usually arranges for you to receive secondary care.

Many hospitals or groups of hospitals are now organised as NHS trusts – for example, Guy's and St Thomas' Hospitals in London are part of the Guy's and St Thomas' NHS Trust. Trusts apply for funding to organise and provide secondary care services needed locally. They are responsible to the area Strategic Health Authority.

ACTION PLAN

1 Ask to see your records again by visiting, phoning or writing to the surgery or hospital ▶ ✎. You may have to make an appointment to see them, and fill in a form or show proof of identity. You do not have to say why you want to see them, unless you are thinking of taking action in the courts against your GP and want to see your records to look for evidence to support your action.

2 If you are refused access to all or part of your records, ask why. If you do not accept the answer, write, saying why, to your GP's practice or Primary Care Trust (see box, opposite) ▶ ✎ or, as a last resort, the Health Service Ombudsman (see p121). If you are taking legal action, ask a solicitor about applying for a court order.

3 If you get to see your records and something is wrong or missing, write a letter saying what it is. Ask for a correction to be noted in the records. If it is not made, ask to make a formal complaint (see pp114-115). Alternatively, ask for help at your local Patient Advisory Liaison Service (PALS – see p109) or, if you do not have access to a PALS, the Community Health Council/Patient Forum (details from your GP, NHS Trust, or area Strategic Health Authority – listed in the phone directory).

Children's medical records

Q My request to view my child's medical records has been refused. Can I insist on seeing them?

A No. Parents and guardians can apply for access to a child's medical records, and in most cases it will be granted. But if a doctor thinks it is in the

---

SEEING SOMEONE ELSE'S RECORDS

If you apply to see someone else's medical records, you may be given access if you are that person's parent or guardian or if you have the person's written permission. The doctor may withhold details that the patient asked not to be disclosed. You can also ask a relative or other person to apply to see your records on your behalf.

Similar rules apply to the records of those who have died. The representative of a deceased person – for example, an executor (see box, p401) – has the right to see the records, as does anyone with a claim against the estate (see box, p395). Access may be denied if the patient so requested – by a letter of wishes (see box, p396), say – when still alive.

---

child's best interests not to show them to the family, access can be refused.

A young person aged 16 or 17, or a child under 16 whom the doctor judges to be mature enough to consent to treatment (see box, p119), can insist on confidentiality. In such circumstances, the doctor may not disclose information to parents without the child's permission.

How to complain about the NHS

If you have concerns about care you receive from any part of the National Health Service, you can use the official NHS complaints procedures outlined here. It is your right to have your complaint fully investigated and it will not affect your medical care. You need to know how to make a formal complaint, what results to expect at each stage, and how to take your complaint to higher levels if you are dissatisfied with the initial outcome.

MAKING AN INFORMAL COMPLAINT

If you have a complaint about your treatment or against the attitude of NHS staff, it is usually best to speak first with someone directly concerned. This might be a receptionist, your dentist, optician or GP, a nurse or the practice manager, who may be able to resolve a problem readily and speedily.

MAKING A FORMAL COMPLAINT

For help with making a complaint, contact:
• NHS Direct (see box, p109)
• your local PALS (see box, p109) or, if a PALS has not yet been set up in your area, the Community Health Council/Patient Forum (details from your GP's practice manager or your area Strategic Health Authority or NHS Trust – listed in the phone directory)
• The Patients Association (details through NHS Direct), which publishes a booklet, *Making a Complaint*
• your local Citizens Advice Bureau.

To make a formal complaint:
• Ask for a copy of the NHS complaints procedure, available from all NHS practices and organisations, including hospitals, GPs' and dentists' surgeries, opticians and pharmacies.
• Make your complaint within six months of the incident or of your awareness of a problem, provided this is within 12 months of the original event. If you want to extend these time limits, ask the complaints manager at the surgery, pharmacy or other organisation to arrange it.
• Hand your complaint to the complaints manager, who must ensure that your complaint is investigated and that the staff involved in the problem deal with it as quickly as possible.
• You can use the NHS complaints procedure if you were treated on the NHS but in a private hospital (see question, p133).

You should receive:
• An acknowledgement within three working days.
• A written response from a GP, dentist, pharmacist or optician within ten working days.
• A written response from an NHS Trust or a Primary Care Trust (PCT; see box, p112) within 20 working days.
• A full explanation and, if appropriate, an apology.

WORD OF WARNING
An apology is not an admission of negligence. You will not get any financial compensation as a result of your complaint. For this you would need to take legal action.

TAKING LEGAL ACTION

The complaints procedure was established to avoid lawsuits, so even if you are thinking of sueing, most solicitors will advise you to pursue the NHS complaints procedure first. The NHS can refuse to look into a complaint if you are suspected of intending to take legal action.

STAGES OF A FORMAL COMPLAINT

1 Local resolution

This may involve:

• Conciliation. You or the service you are complaining to may suggest this – or you can contact the Patient Advocacy and Liaison Service (PALS – see p109) and ask a representative to arrange it. If you both agree, the complaints manager at the service you are complaining to or the PALS representative will appoint an independent conciliation service. Both sides then try to reach an agreement through a mediator.

• A local resolution meeting. This is an informal meeting with those involved, arranged by the complaints manager or your local PALS representative, to try to find a solution. You will be sent a written response to your complaint.

2 Independent review

If you are not happy with the outcome of a local resolution meeting you have the right to ask the complaints manager of the service you are complaining to, or your local PALS representative to arrange an independent review. You should do this within 28 days of receiving the written response to your initial complaint.

The review will be set in motion by a convenor – a non-executive director of the NHS

Trust, Primary Care Trust (PCT) or Health Authority responsible for the service involved – who may ask you to put your case in writing.

The convenor may:
• decide there is no more to be done
• suggest further investigation or attempts at local resolution
• suggest conciliation if this has not been tried
• convene a panel to investigate further.

You should receive the convenor's decision within four weeks. The review panel must report:
• within 30 working days of the panel being convened for a GP complaint
• within 50 working days for other complaints.

An independent review panel consists of a lay chairperson, the convenor and an independent third person. The panel may ask for expert medical advice, and will:
• re-examine the issues and prepare a report about its conclusions
• send you a copy of the report.

3 Health Service Ombudsman

If you are unhappy after going through the NHS complaints procedure, you can refer the matter to the Health Service Ombudsman, who investigates complaints about the NHS (see box, p121).

An employer and your medical records

Q I have chronic asthma and my employer has asked to see my medical records, or that I go to see a company doctor. Can she insist?

A No, but bear in mind that an employer may need medical information for reasons that could benefit you: for example, to assess your eligibility for company benefits such as pension schemes. Your employer will not normally want to see all your medical records or to read them personally. Instead, and with your consent, she may request a medical report from your GP or hospital specialist, or both. She may also ask you to see the company doctor, who may then contact your GP.

Doctors will disclose information only if you agree, unless they judge that you pose a danger to others – for example, if your job involves driving and you are on medication that affects alertness.

You are normally allowed to see the medical report before your employer sees it, and the doctor should ask you whether you want to do so. You can ask for inaccurate details to be amended, but having given consent to a report being drawn up for your employer, you cannot conceal or withhold specific details from it.

ACTION PLAN
1 Ask your employer why she needs your medical details, so that you can assess the likely consequences of allowing or refusing permission.

2 If you are worried that your condition might interfere with your job or part of it, ask the company doctor to recommend reasonable adjustments to allow you to continue in your job, or suggest alternative work you could do.

WORD OF WARNING
If you conceal details relevant to your job from your employer, you could jeopardise your job and future employment prospects if you are found out later on. You could also be legally liable for any resulting damage.

You have a right to confidential treatment

Q A friend and I have the same GP. Once when my friend was in the surgery, he overheard our GP talking to another doctor in the practice about my condition. Shouldn't they be more careful?

A Yes. All patients have a right to keep their medical details private. The General Medical Council (GMC; see box, p110) advises doctors not to discuss their patients where they can be overheard.

ACTION PLAN
1 Report what has happened to your GP, or, if you find it easier, to the practice manager.

2 If you are unhappy with the response you can make a formal complaint to the NHS (see pp114-115).

Your right to a home birth

Q I wanted to have my baby at home, but my GP says there are not enough midwives for this in my area. I would rather be at home when I have my baby, even without a midwife, but he says this is illegal. Can he be right?

A No. You are allowed to have your baby at home. The law states that nobody other than a doctor or a midwife can help a mother with the birth of her baby. But the government has made it clear that this law will not now be used to outlaw husbands, partners or relatives giving support and assistance to a woman who is in labour.

The law is less clear on whether you are entitled to a midwife's attendance, so keep telling your GP, midwife and obstetrician that you plan to give birth at home and that you expect a midwife to be provided. Alternatively, you can bypass the problem by booking a private midwife through the Independent Midwives Association ▶ ⌨.

A midwife will give full antenatal and postnatal care at home and assist at the birth. Midwives are independent practitioners and you do not need the support of your GP to book one.

ACTION PLAN

1 Write to the Supervisor of Midwives at your local hospital and the head of your local maternity unit (you can get contact details from the Director of Midwifery at the hospital or from your local Health Authority). Say that you plan to have your baby at home and would like a hospital or independent midwife to attend ▶ ✎.

2 If the replies are unhelpful, contact your local Patient Advisory Liaison Service (PALS – see p109) or, if a PALS has not yet been set up in your area, the Community Health Council/ Patient Forum (details from your GP's practice manager or your area Health Authority or NHS Trust – listed in the phone directory).

3 Contact the NCT (National Childbirth Trust) ▶ ⌨ or the Association for Improvements in Maternity Services ▶ ⌨ for advice and information.

Do I have to agree to a Caesarean?

Q **When I was in labour with my first baby I was persuaded to have a Caesarean, although I wasn't certain there were good medical reasons. I'm about to have my second baby and I want to give birth without a Caesarean this time. But doctors are recommending another Caesarean. Can they insist that I have one?**

A No. A surgeon cannot operate on you without your consent, so no doctor could insist that you have one. But there are risks in having a normal birth after a Caesarean, so talk to your doctors again and work out with them a realistic plan. They will be more likely to heed your wishes if they are discussed in advance.

Make a birth plan with the health professional who will attend your birth. This may be your GP, a community or private midwife, an obstetrician or the maternity staff at the hospital.

A birth plan is a short statement of your wishes for treatment at the various stages of pregnancy, in which ▶

> **NCT (NATIONAL CHILDBIRTH TRUST)** ▶ ⌨ is a charity that gives up-to-date information about pregnancy, childbirth and early parenthood. Parents can go to meetings, discussion groups and classes at its nationwide network of branches. The NCT publishes books and leaflets and sells maternity products. You can access information through its web site and ask questions through phone helplines. The antenatal advisers can help with information on how to go about making a birth plan.

you agree on what actions should be taken in situations that might arise during your labour. For example, if you want to state in your birth plan that you refuse to have a Caesarean, but your advisers disagree, you might all agree on a 'trial of labour': you go into labour naturally but you agree to a Caesarean if it becomes necessary. Ask for the birth plan to be attached to your medical notes, and make sure that it is attached.

A birth plan does not have to be written – a verbal statement is legally sufficient. But putting your wishes in writing reduces the chances of misunderstanding or dispute if for any reason you cannot state or enforce your views during your labour. It also gives you a chance to think ahead about the complications that may arise during labour, and how you wish to be treated.

For more information about making a birth plan and your rights during pregnancy, contact the NCT (National Childbirth Trust; see box, p117), and the Maternity Alliance ▶ 🖾, a charity that focuses on improving rights and services for pregnant women and new mothers.

WHAT HEALTHCARERS MUST DO

Everyone who works in healthcare has a legal obligation to give each patient the best possible care. Any failure in this 'duty of care' (see p21) may be regarded as negligence if it has caused a patient harm. A doctor's duty of care involves not only diagnosing a patient's condition and treating it but also, for example, explaining the condition and proposed treatment and making sure the patient understands the consequences. Failure to do these things or to rectify a problem that should have been treated count as negligence. And doctors are negligent if they do something that causes or contributes to a medical problem, or makes one worse.

This means that a doctor:
- **is not expected to be an expert in everything, but should treat patients using the care and skill it is reasonable to expect of other doctors in similar circumstances**
- **is not negligent if other doctors find his or her actions acceptable, even if there were several options and other doctors might have acted differently**
- **can be judged only according to the standards and knowledge available when the treatment took place.**

Examples of a breach of duty may include:
- **failure to diagnose a patient's condition when it is reasonable to expect a competent doctor to have done so**
- **failure to ask a patient to consent to treatment – the law defines this as an assault**
- **omitting to tell a patient about the risks and side effects of a proposed treatment**
- **neglecting to offer appropriate treatment when other responsible doctors would have done so**
- **unreasonable delays in diagnosis or treatment**
- **mistakes in diagnosis or treatment that a reasonably competent doctor would not have made.**

You cannot force an obstetrician to operate

Q **I want to have a Caesarean birth but my obstetrician refuses to agree to this beforehand. She says I have to wait and see what happens. Can she refuse?**

A Yes. You cannot compel any health professional to give you a treatment that seems unnecessary. Wanting a Caesarean is not a good enough reason to justify major surgery for which there is a risk of serious complications – surgeons have a 'duty of care' (see box, left).

You could agree a birth plan (see question, above) with the maternity staff who will look after you during labour, stating your wishes for its management and making clear your preference for a Caesarean. Alternatively, you could ask your doctor to refer you to a private obstetrician, who may be more willing to consider a Caesarean delivery.

When sterilisation does not work

Q I was sterilised after the birth of my second child, but was pregnant again in three months. Can I claim compensation?

A Possibly, if you can show that the surgery was carried out negligently, perhaps because a faulty technique was used. You could claim for the distress and inconvenience of an unwanted pregnancy and the physical effects of giving birth, and for the cost of a second sterilisation.

A claim for the costs of raising a child who would not have been born were it not for faulty treatment is complicated, but you could be awarded compensation for some of the losses and expense incurred. It would be a 'wrongful birth' claim – different from a 'wrongful life' claim sometimes brought by a disabled child who would not have been born if the disability had been detected during pregnancy. Consult a solicitor (see p20).

A teenager's right to contraception

Q I've discovered that our doctor has been prescribing the contraceptive pill for my teenage daughter without my consent. Can she do that?

A Yes. Your rights are limited. If your daughter is under 16 and you do not want contraceptives to be supplied to her, you can tell her doctor not to prescribe them and the doctor must obey you. But if she asks for contraception advice and a doctor judges her mature enough to understand the issues involved, the doctor can prescribe the Pill for her without your consent and without telling you. If your daughter is 16 she can agree to her own medical treatment, including contraceptive treatment (see box, above).

DO CHILDREN HAVE A SAY IN THEIR MEDICAL TREATMENT?

Children – legally, anyone under 16 – can agree to medical treatment on their own behalf if they are considered to possess what is called 'Gillick competence' – that is, if they are capable of understanding fully what is proposed. If so, parental rights in the matter cease.

Who decides? The treating doctor has the final decision. The courts will not usually intervene.

Can children refuse medical treatment? A child cannot usually refuse treatment, and parents can usually consent on their child's behalf. If treatment is refused, a doctor may take the case to the courts. They usually take the view that treatment is in the child's best interests and override refusals by a child of any age or by parents.

Legally, 16 and 17-year-olds are not children. They are defined as 'young people' and can make their own decisions about their medical treatment.

You cannot overrule her decisions. But before agreeing to prescribe, doctors would urge a girl to discuss this with her parents. Perhaps you can find a way of discussing the issue with your daughter.

Yes, you can refuse a vaccination

Q I don't want my baby daughter to have the MMR vaccination. Can I refuse it?

A Yes. As her parent, you can take decisions about your daughter's medical treatment until she is mature enough to decide for herself (see box, above), so you can refuse the measles, mumps, rubella (MMR) vaccination and give no reasons. Parents' refusal can be overruled only by a court order, and one is unlikely to be granted for a vaccination because in the UK vaccination is not compulsory.

A GP should at least assess the patient

Q In the evening my son had a high temperature and seemed disorientated. I phoned my GP, who suggested I give him paracetamol and plenty of liquid, but she didn't think it warranted a visit. The next morning I took him to casualty, where meningitis was diagnosed. Can a GP just decide not to visit?

A Yes. A GP does not have to visit you at home (most now prefer to see patients outside surgery times in a local out-of-hours centre). Unfortunately, the early symptoms of meningitis, which is rare, are very similar to those of a host of common children's complaints. It is every GP's nightmare to miss a meningitis case, but it sometimes happens.

But your GP may need to justify any failure to offer at least to assess your child, and she should have told you what to do if your son's condition did not improve. You may therefore have grounds for a formal complaint (see pp114-115). And if your son suffered harm as a result of the delay in diagnosis, there may be cause to sue the GP.

The surgeon cannot tell you everything

Q My surgeon neglected to tell me about adhesions – a complication of an operation I had recently to take out my appendix. I feel worse now than before my operation. Can I sue her?

A Probably not. All surgery involves some risk, and your surgeon should have warned you before you went into hospital for your operation about any serious complications associated with it, particularly if you asked specific questions about possible aftereffects.

Yet a surgeon does not have to tell you about all possible risks and complications. Although it is now common for patients to be given full information about their treatment, your surgeon was not negligent because she did not warn you about the uncomfortable complication you suffered. In all areas of medical practice the answer to such a question depends on what is regarded as reasonable practice and what any responsible surgeon should have told you (see box, p118).

Never assume that a surgeon will give you all the information about your operation. Always ask questions.

A patient's right to speed up treatment

Q My consultant says I need a hernia operation, but the earliest date the local hospital can offer me is in five months. I want to speed things up. Can I do that?

A Probably not. The NHS operates a form of rationing by queueing and is only obliged to provide treatment according to clinical need: patients judged to have the greatest need or possible benefit must be treated first. Decisions are usually based on a doctor's judgment as to the severity and urgency of each case. Patients have no rights to speed up treatment unless their condition changes.

Yet there are some avenues you might try. Check with your GP that the severity of your symptoms has been accurately assessed and recorded, and ask if you can be transferred to any other hospital with a shorter waiting list. You can also ask your GP for a private referral. Phone private hospitals and ask for their rates for a 'self-pay' hernia operation (rather than claim on private medical insurance for the cost of the operation, you pay for it). Ask to be quoted an all-inclusive price for surgery, anaesthetic, the stay in hospital, including food, and aftercare.

Taking part in clinical drugs trials

Q **My doctor has prescribed a new drug for me which she says is not widely available yet. I'm worried that I'm participating in a drugs trial without knowing it. Is that possible?**

A Yes, but unlikely. After extensive testing elsewhere, new drugs are tested on real patients before being marketed. A doctor must explain the test to the patient, give full information about the drug being tested and other available treatments, and ask the patient to sign a consent form. The patient can refuse. To fail to do any of these things amounts to misconduct and negligence, so you should ask the doctor if the drug is being tested as part of a clinical trial.

ACTION PLAN
1 Contact your local Patient Advisory Liaison Service (PALS – see box, p109) or Community Health Council/Patient Forum (details from your GP, area ▶

HOW THE HEALTH SERVICE OMBUDSMAN CAN HELP

The Health Service Commissioner, usually called the Ombudsman, investigates complaints about the NHS and is independent of the NHS.

THE HEALTH SERVICE OMBUDSMAN investigates complaints where there is evidence that hardship or injustice has been caused by:
- failure to provide a service
- failure in the service
- maladministration.

THE OMBUDSMAN DOES NOT:
- have to take up every complaint
- investigate a case that has not been through the NHS complaints procedure (see pp114-115)
- usually investigate a case that you could be expected to pursue in court, unless it is considered unreasonable to expect you to go to court – for example, because the costs would be very high.

If the ombudsman decides not to look into your complaint, you will be told why.

WHY INVOLVE THE OMBUDSMAN?
- Your complaint was not resolved for two months.
- You tried to get an independent review (see p115), but your request was turned down.
- The answer to your complaint was unsatisfactory.

WHEN TO COMPLAIN
Complain within a year of the incident or the date when you became aware of the matter you want to complain about.

HOW TO COMPLAIN
Write to the ombudsman explaining in detail why you are unhappy about how your complaint was handled ▶✍. You can complain on behalf of someone else, but you must explain why the person cannot do so and that you have his or her agreement.

WHAT WILL HAPPEN?
A statement setting out the matters to be looked into is sent to both sides. The hospital, GP, dentist or other service you are complaining about is asked for comments and relevant papers. These may include your medical records, but they are seen only by the ombudsman, who may want to interview you and others, and ask for independent medical advice from experts.

After an investigation, the ombudsman writes a detailed report and sends a copy to both parties. The ombudsman may recommend that you receive an apology, that a decision be altered, that costs be returned to you, or that the service introduces changes in the way it operates.

Health Authority or NHS Trust – listed in the phone directory) who may be able to find out about the drug.

2 If you are being used to test a trial drug without consent, you can report the doctor to the General Medical Council (GMC; see p110).

You cannot escape 'postcode prescribing'

Q A friend who lives 20 miles away has been receiving treatment for infertility paid for by the NHS, but my Health Authority refuses to do the same for me. They say they can refuse to fund treatments that are available in other areas. Can they do that?

A Yes. Each Health Authority can decide how to allocate its funds. This includes deciding what types of treatment to fund, to what level, and what proportion of the budget for an illness should be spent on, say, hospital care or investigations, or drugs used in its treatment.

When it comes to a particular kind of treatment or a drug, a Health Authority might decide that there are more urgent spending priorities for its patients. It may conclude that existing evidence does not show sufficient benefit to justify taking money from other services to pay for it.

The budget that is eventually allocated for a treatment will fund treatment for limited numbers of patients. Doctors must then decide who would benefit most from treatment.

You have the right to appeal against funding refusals. Talk to the Patient Advocacy and Liaison Service (PALS – see box, p109) or consider a formal complaint (see pp114-115). If an appeal fails, private treatment may be the only alternative.

Committing a relative to a psychiatric hospital

Q My sister has been behaving very strangely recently. We have a history of manic disorder in our family, and I'm worried that she might do something dangerous. She refuses to accept that anything is wrong and won't see her doctor. I want to get her admitted for psychiatric treatment. Can I do that?

A Yes. Contact your sister's GP and explain your worries about her behaviour. The GP may then be able to arrange for a 'mental health assessment' to be carried out. Alternatively, you could contact the social services department of the local council. They have a duty to respond when the nearest relative of someone in the area they cover requests a mental health assessment.

The assessment could lead to your sister being admitted to a psychiatric hospital against her will under the Mental Health Act 1983. This would happen if she is judged to be suffering from a mental disorder requiring further assessment or treatment, and admission is thought to be necessary in the interests of her own health or safety, or to protect others.

If your sister were admitted to hospital against her will, it would probably be under Section 2 of the Mental Health Act (see box, below). If her behaviour poses an immediate threat, an emergency application under Section 4 can be made for admission for up to 72 hours.

If someone who appears to be mentally disordered is behaving dangerously, the police have powers to remove that person to a 'place of safety' (usually, a psychiatric hospital) and, if necessary, get a court order to break into a house to do so.

ACTION PLAN

1 Contact your sister's GP and explain the situation. The GP may be able to arrange a mental health assessment.

2 If you are not happy with the GP's response, contact the local council's social services department.

3 Social services may say they cannot act because you are not the nearest relative. This is because the Mental Health Act has a list of categories of relative used to establish who someone's nearest relative is. Ask your local Citizens Advice Bureau ▶ 🕮 for help in identifying who counts as your sister's nearest relative – for example, it may be one of her children if she has any. Ask that person to make a formal request to social services for an assessment.

4 If your sister does anything that poses a threat to her own safety or that of other people, contact the police.

CAN YOU BE KEPT IN A PSYCHIATRIC HOSPITAL?

In the UK, an adult (anyone aged 18 or over) may be detained in a psychiatric hospital only if:
• the person has one of the mental disorders listed in the Mental Health Act 1983, *and*
• this disorder requires assessment or treatment in hospital, *and*
• the person is believed to be a danger to him or herself or to other people.

An application to detain someone against that person's will must be made by:
• a doctor, nurse or social worker who specialises in the mentally ill; *or*
• the person's nearest relative as defined by the Mental Health Act (see Action Plan, above).

In addition, two doctors must confirm in writing that the detention is valid (one doctor in an emergency).

How long someone can be detained depends on which section of the Mental Health Act is used. Under Section 2, the person is admitted ('sectioned') for an assessment, with treatment if necessary, and can be detained for up to 28 days.

Other sections commonly used are:
• Section 3: the person is sectioned for immediate treatment and can be detained for up to six months
• Section 4: an emergency admission for up to 72 hours initially
• Section 5: a 'voluntary patient' has asked to be sectioned and can be detained for up to 72 hours.

PATIENTS' RIGHTS

Patients held under the Mental Health Act can:
• ask another doctor to review the detention and decide whether it is appropriate
• appeal to an independent mental health review

tribunal to assess whether they should be kept in hospital. The hospital should provide application forms for a review, and staff or social workers should help an applicant to complete one.

YOUR HEALTHCARE

A GP'S REFERRAL • LEAVING HOSPITAL • CONSENT TO SURGERY • ORGAN DONORS

Can a GP refuse a referral to a specialist?

Q **My father suffered from a brain tumour in his later years, and as I get older I get increasingly worried that the same might happen to me. But my GP won't refer me to an NHS or a private specialist because she says brain tumours don't run in families. Can I insist?**

A No. GPs are not compelled to refer you for specialist assessment on the NHS or privately if they do not think it worthwhile. You are unlikely to secure an appointment with a specialist without your GP's help, since even specialists in the private sector will ask for a referral letter from your GP before seeing you.

They need to know that they have all the background information.

You should talk to your doctor again and explain how worried you are. A doctor must always consider that to refuse to investigate a problem that later proves detrimental could lead to a complaint or even court action.

Can you discharge yourself from hospital?

Q **I'm very anxious to leave hospital, but my doctor insists that I stay. Does she have the right to do that?**

A No. Adults (people aged 18 or over) have the right to decide what happens to their body. That includes the right to refuse medical treatment no matter what the possible consequences of a refusal might be. The doctor cannot keep you in hospital against your wishes even if she judges that you might suffer harm or die without treatment.

Adults can only be detained against their wishes under the mental health laws for treatment of a mental condition (see box, p123).

ACTION PLAN

1 If you are determined to leave, you should tell the doctor and other medical staff that you intend to discharge yourself from hospital, against medical advice if necessary, and explain that you are prepared to accept the consequences.

2 You may be asked to sign a form stating that you intend to discharge yourself against medical advice. You do not have to do this, but a refusal to do so will be noted by the staff on your hospital records.

Removing an organ without your consent

Q I'm going into hospital for investigative surgery for a lump on my womb. I'm worried that the surgeon may decide to remove the whole womb without my consent and I want to be sure he doesn't. Can I do that?

A Several court cases have emphasised that no surgeon should remove any part of your body without your consent, except in an emergency. In spite of that, it does happen. But if you register your wishes in advance, your surgeon is unlikely to ignore them. To do so would leave him open to charges of misconduct, negligence and assault.

Nevertheless, you should consider your options if you had a condition serious enough to justify removal of the whole womb. You could wait to see the results of the investigation before agreeing to further surgery, but a second operation will always carry a risk.

ACTION PLAN

1 Discuss the matter with the surgeon, or contact your GP, who may agree to act as advocate on your behalf.

2 Write a letter to the surgeon stating your wishes, and ask for it to be attached to your notes ▶✍.

3 Review your wishes with the surgeon and other ward staff when you are admitted to hospital.

What an organ donor card will ensure

Q I carry an organ donor card, but I'm told this won't ensure that my organs will be used for research or use by another person when I die. Can this be true?

A Yes. An organ donor card only indicates your wish to donate your organs for transplant into living people. You cannot use it to donate them for medical research. Although you have the right to decide to be an organ donor, doctors usually ask a donor's relatives for consent, and they would be unlikely to accept your organs if your family objected. Make your wishes clear to your family now, and tell your friends.

Always carry your organ donor card and add your name to the NHS Organ Donor Register ▶⌷, the national list of transplant donors. It will have your details on record in case your card cannot be found when needed. You could record your wishes in a 'living will' (see p126), and notify your GP.

It is also important to tell your relatives if you do not want parts of your body donated to others or used for research after your death. Unless you have stated this, your relatives can allow your organs to be donated.

To leave your body for medical research you must register your wishes before death with an institution, such as a medical school anatomy department. There is usually an authorisation form to fill in. You should tell your relatives and be sure they agree or the school may reject your body.

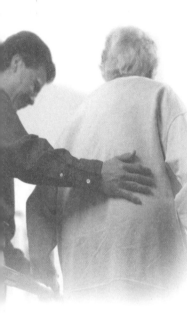

Turning off a life-support system

Q My brother was attacked and has been in a coma ever since. He's not expected to recover. We know he wouldn't want to exist like this, but the hospital doctors refuse to turn off his life support, although our parents have asked. Can we do anything to stop them keeping him in this situation?

A Probably not. If your brother had made a living will (see box, below) doctors would not continue to treat him. It does not matter whether this wish was explained formally in writing or verbally, but if a person's intentions are not written down, it is harder to prove them.

No one else, not even the next of kin, has a right to make treatment decisions for an adult. So if your brother is incapable of consenting to treatment, including life support, his doctors must treat him according to their view of his best interests. Doctors usually consult relatives about continuing life support, but you have no power to force them to do (or not to do) anything.

ACTION PLAN

1 Ask your brother's friends and other relatives whether he discussed his wishes in such a situation, and search for any written statement he may have made. Ask his GP and his solicitor, and check his will. Offer any evidence you find to the hospital consultant in charge.

2 Talk to the hospital doctors and find out whether they think there is any chance, however slim, that your brother might recover. They may be waiting before making a decision.

3 If the responses are unsatisfactory, contact your local Patient Advisory Liaison Service (PALS; see box, p109) or, if a PALS has not yet been set up in your area, your Community Health

---

A LIVING WILL

This is not a will, but an 'advance statement' or 'directive' – instructions about stopping life-prolonging treatment in the future if a person loses the ability to express his or her wishes. No law has been passed to make an advance statement legally valid, but the British Medical Association (BMA) says that where 'incompetent or unconscious patients have made a formal and specific statement applicable to the circumstances, doctors should regard it as potentially legally binding'. The legal view is that an advance statement is a refusal to have treatment, made in advance, and that in common law your wishes should be taken into account provided certain conditions are met:

• You must be 18 or over when you decide and must not have been influenced by anyone else.

• You should be 'of sound mind' and understand the consequences of refusing treatment.

MAKING THE WILL

1 Discuss your wishes with your GP, who should help you to draft your statement. The BMA recommends the 'model' statements developed by the HIV/AIDS charity, the Terrence Higgins Trust ▶ ☞ – even for people who do not suffer from HIV/AIDS.

2 Sign the statement and get it witnessed by two people who will not be involved in caring for you and will not benefit from your death.

3 Give copies to your next of kin, to a person who can take decisions about medical care for you, and to your doctor, to keep with your medical records. Keep the original with your will, or where it is likely to be found if you are ill.

Council/Patient Forum (details from your GP's practice manager or your area Health Authority or NHS Trust – listed in the phone directory).

Can I be denied the chance of resuscitation?

Q **I'm 82 and due to have a minor operation. I have chronic health problems and I worry that if something goes wrong surgeons may not resuscitate me. Can I be denied resuscitation?**

A No, a patient who wants to be resuscitated should never be denied it. But it can be difficult for doctors to decide, especially without long-term knowledge of the person's beliefs, whether a patient would wish to be resuscitated.

Recent NHS reforms have ensured that resuscitation will be discussed when patients are admitted to hospital. Your wishes are likely to be followed if you write a 'living will' (see box, opposite) and tell those who care for you.

ACTION PLAN

1 Talk to your GP before you go into hospital. A GP who understands your feelings can be an excellent advocate.

2 In hospital, ask that your wishes be formally recorded in your notes. You should also discuss them with the surgeon who will operate on you.

Is my consent needed for an HIV test?

Q **My obstetrician has just told me that my antenatal clinic results show that I'm negative for the HIV virus. I didn't know I'd been tested. Surely they should ask before testing?**

A Yes, they should. Medical staff must seek patients' consent for tests as well as treatment. Technically, testing without consent can count as assault.

If you ask a doctor to investigate an illness, you may be presumed to have given your consent to the necessary tests. Attending an antenatal clinic and giving a blood sample would normally imply that you agreed to the routine tests involved.

But this does not apply to HIV tests. Medical staff must ask for your consent, mainly because being HIV positive has such serious implications. The same is true of tests for other conditions, such as hepatitis B.

You have suffered no harm from having the test, however, so you have no grounds for taking legal action, but you could make a formal complaint (see pp114-115).

A negligence claim against a surgeon

Q **My father had a minor operation to remove a cyst on his neck. The surgeon cut through a nerve by accident and now my father can't speak properly. Can he do anything to ensure that the surgeon pays for his error?**

A Yes, several things. First, your father should decide what outcome he wants. It could be an apology, to ensure that the same thing does not happen to someone else, disciplinary action against the surgeon or compensation.

The more drastic the surgeon's action, the more prolonged and stressful the legal procedure against him is likely to be. So before considering legal action your father should ask the surgeon, by speaking to him or in writing, for an explanation. Then he needs to decide how much time he can devote to taking his case through the courts. ▶

ACTION PLAN

1 If the surgeon's explanation seems unsatisfactory, your father can make a complaint (see pp114-115) or report the surgeon to the General Medical Council (GMC; see box, p110), which will decide whether the surgeon's fitness to practise is in doubt.

2 If your father decides to take legal action you should contact Action for Victims of Medical Accidents (AVMA) ▶ ⌨ and ask for a list of solicitors who specialise in medical negligence.

Claiming compensation for birth defects

Q **Several things went wrong when I had my baby in hospital and she was diagnosed with cerebral palsy shortly after birth. She's now two and isn't developing properly and I'm told she could need lifelong care. I believe the hospital was at fault and I want to claim compensation on her behalf. Can I do that?**

A Yes, if you can prove that her injuries were the result of medical negligence. Such cases occur most often after induced birth, and delivery assisted with, for example, forceps, so you should collect all the evidence you can about what happened during and after the birth.

You can sue on your child's behalf as what is called her 'litigation friend', and have access to her medical records (see box, p113). You have the right to sue up to her 21st birthday, and if the claim is likely to succeed she will probably be granted public funding for legal action (see p15). Children usually qualify for public funding because their income only, not that of their parents, is taken into account.

ACTION PLAN

1 Contact Action for Victims of Medical Accidents (AVMA) ▶ ⌨ for a list of solicitors who specialise in medical negligence. A solicitor can start a court action and apply for legal aid on your behalf. Solicitors do not charge for initial advice.

2 If you sue while your daughter is still a child and compensation is awarded, it will normally be held in trust until her 18th birthday, but you can use some of the money for care needs. To do this, you must set up a trust fund – consult a solicitor (see p20). If your daughter is unable to manage her affairs as an adult, you must apply for a Court of Protection Order – again, consult a solicitor. The court will appoint a receiver (usually you or another close relative) to manage her affairs for her.

You have to prove the cause of your problem

Q **After a car accident a hospital doctor diagnosed a knee injury, but I have since found that my spine was injured in the crash. A consultant said my back injury is permanent, but would have been as bad even if the doctor had spotted it. She says I can't sue the hospital for negligence. Is that right?**

A Probably, if her assessment of your injury is right. To sue for negligence you will have to prove that the hospital doctor did something contrary to good medical practice or failed to take some necessary action, and that your injury was made worse as a direct result. This last requirement (called 'proof of causation') is usually the hardest to establish in medical negligence claims. If the consultant is correct, you will not be able to prove that the cause of your back problem was the initial failure to spot your back injury.

You can ask for a second opinion about your back, but unless another specialist suggests that the hospital doctor could have done anything to make a difference, you do not have a case. You can complain to the hospital (see pp114-115) if you feel that the hospital doctor should have spotted your back injury.

Compensation for ill-fitting dentures

Q I went to my NHS dentist for a set of dentures. The first set didn't fit and had to be replaced, at additional cost. Months later I'm still suffering pain and discomfort. Can I claim compensation?

A Possibly, but the likely outcome depends on the facts. Did you complain about the first set of dentures? Why didn't they fit? Have you talked to your dentist about the problems you have now? Perhaps you are one of the many people who take time to get used to dentures. You must make an appointment to see the dentist and ask why you are having such discomfort with your dentures.

If you are dissatisfied with the dentist's explanation, the interview with the dentist will have been worthwhile. You will need to be well-informed about the problem if you decide to make a formal complaint (see pp125-126) or take action for compensation.

ACTION PLAN

1 If the dentist's explanation seems unsatisfactory, try to negotiate. For example, you could ask for the dentures to be replaced free of charge. If the dentist refuses, ask for a written record of the treatment that has been carried out.

NHS DENTAL TREATMENT

Most people who are registered as NHS patients must pay 80 per cent of the costs of dental treatment (up to £360 in 2003). The following categories of people can claim free treatment.

You can get free treatment if you:
- are aged under 18
- are aged 18 and a full-time student
- are pregnant or have a baby born in the past 12 months.

You can apply for a refund after treatment starts if you:
- have a currently valid NHS Low Income Scheme HC2 Certificate. You are entitled to this if you do not have more than £8000 capital (£12,000 if you or your partner are 60 or over, or £16,000 if you live in a residential care or nursing home). To apply, fill in an HC1 form (available from your local Social Security Office or NHS hospital)
- are on Income Support
- are on Income-based Jobseeker's Allowance
- receive Working Tax Credit or Child Tax Credit
- receive Disabled Persons Tax Credit (you must have a Tax Credit NHS exemption certificate).

You may be eligible for a refund of some of the costs if you:
- have a currently valid NHS Low Income Scheme HC3 Certificate (which, unlike the HC2, offers limited, rather than full, help with costs).

2 Get a second opinion from another NHS dentist. You will have to pay the standard NHS fee for a check-up.

3 If you then feel you have grounds, ask at your dentist's surgery how you can use the complaints procedure. NHS and private dentists, and some dental insurance schemes, have a complaints procedure. If this fails, use the NHS complaints procedure (see pp114-115). ▶

129

4 If you think the dentist is guilty of professional misconduct, complain to the General Dental Council (GDC) ▶ 📖. The GDC regulates dentists (see box, p111) and can suspend or strike a dentist from its register. It does not award financial compensation.

5 If after taking your complaint through the official procedure you are not awarded financial compensation, contact the Law Society ▶ 📖 for a list of solicitors who specialise in medical malpractice and consult one about taking legal action against the dentist.

Can NHS dentists charge private rates?

Q **My dentist was treating me as an NHS patient, but last time I went, I was told he no longer takes NHS patients and would charge me the full private rate. Can the dentist just stop giving me NHS treatment?**

A That depends. Dentists are independent practitioners who are free to choose whether or not to accept NHS patients. They may choose to have both NHS and private patients.

Being accepted as an NHS patient entitles you to receive NHS treatment regularly, but if you do not see the dentist during the first 15 months after you register, your registration lapses and the dentist does not have to continue treating you under the NHS scheme.

ACTION PLAN
1 Ask the dentist whether your registration has lapsed and, if so, whether he is prepared to take you back as an NHS patient. If he refuses,

NHS Direct (see box, p109) will help you to find another dentist in your area who takes NHS patients.

2 If you feel you are being denied NHS treatment unfairly, you can make a formal complaint (see pp114-115).

Is my dentist doing unnecessary work?

Q **I suspect that my private dentist has been carrying out unnecessary work on my teeth. Can he get away with that?**

A No, but this can be difficult to prove. First, make an appointment to discuss your concerns with your dentist. Then if you still feel dissatisfied, ask for a second opinion from another dentist. Assessing a patient's dental fitness and the quality of work done is fairly straightforward. If this assessment helps you to prove that the dentist has done unnecessary work, you may have reason to complain and claim for compensation.

ACTION PLAN
1 Before seeking a second opinion, ask for a copy of your dental records (see question, pp112-113) to give to the dentist whom you have asked to examine the work already done.

2 If the second opinion confirms your suspicions, you can report the dentist to the General Dental Council (GDC) ▶ 📖, which will investigate and can suspend or strike him from its register. Or you can ask the Law Society ▶ 📖 for a list of solicitors specialising in medical malpractice, and take action for compensation to recover the costs of the unnecessary work and any remedial work, plus damages.

Should a dentist offer out-of-hours service?

Q **My young son had terrible toothache on a Saturday night and I called my dentist but there was only an answerphone message. Shouldn't she have an emergency service for nights and weekends?**

A Yes. All dentists, private and NHS, should provide an emergency service outside surgery hours. A rota system operates in most areas, so when you phoned the practice you should have heard a message telling you which dentist is on duty and giving you contact details. You should tell your dentist that you called and did not get this message.

If you are away from home or not registered with a dentist, contact NHS Direct (see box, p109). The nurse you speak to will find a walk-in centre or an emergency dentist nearby.

Are you being overcharged?

Q **I'm having dental implant treatment from my private dentist. I knew it would be expensive, but on the bill are items I didn't expect and the total is more than the estimate. Can the dentist charge what he likes?**

A Possibly – you can find out only by talking to your dentist. NHS dental charges are all preset, but private dentists can decide their own rates, which are likely to be more than twice as much.

If the dentist gave you an itemised estimate before the treatment, you should go through the account, noting the discrepancies from the estimate. Ask him to explain them. He may have had to do extra work in order to deal with complications.

Even if he did not give you a detailed estimate, speak to the dentist. Tell him that the bill is more than you expected, and ask him to explain his charges. Try to negotiate a reduction, and ask for warning in future if his charges are likely to rise.

Should my dentist wear rubber gloves?

Q **I noticed that my dentist was not wearing rubber gloves. Can he treat me without them?**

A Yes. Although most dentists wear gloves, to protect patients and staff against transmittable diseases, they do not have a legal duty to do so.

Why a health insurance claim may be rejected

Q **My health insurer has rejected my claim for heart surgery, which I'm told I need, but the insurers haven't given me a reason? Can they do that?**

A No, the insurers cannot refuse to give you a reason. You should contact your insurers and ask why they will not pay. There are many reasons for refusing, so when you apply for medical insurance, check the exclusions with the insurer and make sure you give all relevant details accurately and declare all your health conditions before you sign the policy. If you are not sure whether to mention a minor disorder, ask the insurer. If important information is wrong or missing and you make a claim, the company can refuse to pay or even cancel the contract.

Medical insurers will not usually cover you for any condition present before you took out the policy. Many chronic health conditions (long-term illnesses such as arthritis that may last for years) ▶

are not covered, nor are GP services or treatments regarded as a matter of choice, such as infertility treatment or cosmetic surgery. Many policies also exclude childbirth and the consequences of HIV infection.

Check the exclusions again before you book any treatment. If you arrange to have medical treatment and the insurer refuses your claim for it, you will have to pay for the treatment.

ACTION PLAN

1 If insurers will not pay a claim, but you think it is valid, ask if they have a complaints procedure. If they do, use it to make a formal complaint.

2 If the company's procedure fails you, take your claim to the Financial Ombudsman Service ▶ 🕮 (see box, p141).

NHS rights in a private hospital

Q I've been told that my local hospital will arrange for me to have my operation done in a private hospital, even though I'm an NHS patient. But a friend informed me that I have no rights if something goes wrong. Can that be true?

COMPLAINING ABOUT PRIVATE HEALTH TREATMENT

As a private patient you should complain to the doctor who treated you or the hospital or clinic you attended. Most major private hospital groups and medical insurance companies have a complaints procedure – the Independent Healthcare Association ▶ 🕮, a charity that presses for improved standards in private healthcare, has one for all its member institutions. Private clinics and hospitals, and doctors and other professionals in private practice, have third-party insurance, so if legal action arises (see below) any damages are paid by an insurance company.

LEGAL ACTION

If any aspect of your private care fails to meet minimum standards, no matter whether the care is paid for by you or a health insurance policy, you should consider legal action. Ask the Law Society ▶ 🕮 for a list of solicitors specialising in medical malpractice, who can advise you.

You can sue for:
• **Negligent treatment.**
• **Breach of contract:** as a private patient you have a contract with the doctor (as an NHS patient, you do not). So if the doctor fails to perform the services for which you paid, or if you received substandard treatment, you may be entitled to damages.

CARE STANDARDS

The National Care Standards Commission ▶ 🕮 in England and the Care Standards Inspectorate for Wales ▶ 🕮 are independent patient watchdogs that regulate private and voluntary health services.

If a private health provider handles a complaint unsatisfactorily, you can refer the matter to the area office of the Commission or Inspectorate. Ask for details of its complaints procedure. It will investigate your case, and if there is evidence of a breach in regulations or standards, it can order changes and improvements. Ultimately, it can close down clinics and hospitals. It cannot award financial compensation.

A No. You have the same rights as any other NHS patient. People being treated in private hospitals are entitled to transfer back to NHS care if they wish, or if a need arises for facilities that are only available locally in an NHS hospital.

When you are treated under the NHS in a private hospital, you can use the NHS complaints procedure (see pp114-115) and sue the NHS if anything major goes wrong.

Complaining to a private clinic

Q **I paid for a day-case cataract removal in a private clinic and told the nurse who took my details that I'm allergic to latex in surgical gloves. During the operation I had a severe reaction and had to stay in hospital for three days. The surgeon says it's not his fault because my allergy wasn't in my notes, and I think the nursing staff forgot to pass on the information. Can they get away with that?**

A No. The hospital system must ensure that important details given by a patient on arrival are communicated to the doctors and others responsible for the patient's care. But the surgeon should also have checked that you did not have any allergies.

You must decide what you want: an apology; reimbursement of fees you have paid, to make certain that a safe system is put in place; or compensation. Then check through the Independent Healthcare Association ▶ ⊂⊃ (see box, opposite) whether the clinic has a complaints procedure, and ask if you can use it to make a formal complaint.

Complementary treatment on the NHS

Q **I've been paying for private homeopathic treatment for arthritis for several months, but a friend tells me that I can get it on the NHS. Is that true?**

A Yes. Homeopathic medicine is available through the NHS and you can ask for it. But doctors do not have to provide any treatment, including homeopathy, unless they believe it is clinically necessary. Your friend might have been aware that homeopathy is the only form of complementary medicine that the NHS provides by law because it was included when the NHS was set up. There are a few NHS-staffed homeopathic hospitals in the UK and any GP can refer you to one.

You should see your doctor and explain how you think homeopathy is helping your arthritis. Many GPs are qualified in complementary therapies, so you could check beforehand with the practice to see if your GP has a special interest in homeopathy. Alternatively, contact the British Homeopathic Association ▶ ⊂⊃ or the British Medical Association (BMA) ▶ ⊂⊃ to see if you can find a GP in your area who is also a qualified homeopathic practitioner.

Chiropractors are regulated by law

Q For months I paid a chiropractor for regular treatment for my back pain, but noticed no improvement. In frustration, I went to my doctor and discovered that the problem was a cracked vertebra. I would like to make a claim against the chiropractor. Can I do that?

A Possibly, but it depends on what form of redress you want and whether the chiropractor was negligent. Chiropractors are registered and regulated by the General Chiropractic Council (GCC) ▶ ⌂, a legally recognised body that can take action if professional misconduct is alleged (see box, opposite). Before acting on a complaint, the GCC encourages patients to try to resolve the problem directly with the chiropractor.

ACTION PLAN

1 Make an appointment with your chiropractor to discuss your doctor's findings.

2 If you are not satisfied with the response, ask your chiropractor if you can complain formally – most have a complaints procedure. You should get an explanation and perhaps an apology.

3 If you are still unhappy, report the chiropractor to the GCC, providing a statement and medical evidence. If malpractice is proved, the GCC may reprimand or suspend the chiropractor, impose conditions on the practice, or strike the chiropractor from its register. The GCC cannot help with costs or award compensation.

4 If you think the chiropractor was negligent, consult a solicitor who specialises in medical malpractice about sueing for damages.

Taking action against a therapist

Q Although my treatment by a reflexologist made me ill, I've been told that I'll have much more trouble taking action against her than if I'd had conventional treatment. Can that be true?

A Partly. More than a quarter of us have used complementary medicine, but only chiropractors and osteopaths are governed by a regulatory body (see box, opposite). Yet all complementary therapists owe you a duty of care (see p116) and if they fail in this and a patient is harmed, they can be sued for negligence.

In law, doctors are judged according to the accepted standards of other doctors, but complementary therapists are not judged according to the accepted standards of other complementary practitioners. If they do something that most doctors would consider hazardous, they can be judged negligent – even if what they did is standard practice in their therapy. They are then liable for any harm to the patient that might result.

ACTION PLAN

1 Write to the complementary practitioner, giving details of your complaint ▶ ✍.

2 Check whether the therapist is a member of any professional body. If so, you could contact the body and ask for advice.

3 Talk to your solicitor and ask what your chances of success are if you sue the therapist.

Appeals against benefit tribunal decisions

Q I applied for a disability benefit, but my application was turned down. Can I appeal?

A Yes, you can appeal through the Appeals Service ▶ 📖, which will arrange an independent tribunal hearing to look into the legal validity of your benefit claim.

A tribunal (see box, p17) consists of a panel of three people:
• someone with legal training, who chairs
• a doctor
• someone with 'experience of disability'. This could be a disabled person, someone who has worked with disabled people or someone with a detailed understanding of the issues surrounding disability.

To appeal, you can fill in a form (from the office that refused your benefit) or write a letter ▶ ✎. If your appeal is accepted, an enquiry form (TAS 1) will be sent to you to fill in, with papers (called 'the submission' or 'the schedule of evidence') that outline your case and explain the decision to reject your claim.

The tribunal will ask you whether you want it to make a decision from written evidence or whether you would prefer to be there in person. A venue will be arranged as close as possible to where you live.

You can bring a friend for support or someone to speak for you, and you will be asked about special needs – for an interpreter, for example – or help with access. For help in filling in complex forms, and preparing for and ▶

attending the hearing, contact your local Citizens Advice Bureau ▶ 📖. For more information about how to appeal, contact the Department for Work and Pensions Disability Unit ▶ 📖.

ACTION PLAN

1 Send your appeal so that the Appeals Service ▶ 📖 receives it within four weeks of the date on the letter rejecting your application for disability benefit. Explain your claim and why you think its rejection is wrong. Give the date of the rejection letter, the reference shown on it, and your National Insurance number.

2 Complete and return the TAS 1 form within 14 days of receiving it. Your appeal will be stopped if you send it back late and if you do not reply to any enquiry or instruction.

3 Read the submission documents or show them to your representative if you have one. They will help you

---

DISABILITY BENEFIT

The main aim of disability benefit is to help with the costs of mobility and care. It is tax-free. You do not have to be means-tested to claim; rates vary according to the severity of the disability. You can claim:

DISABILITY LIVING ALLOWANCE (DLA)
This is the main benefit available to people with a disability. You can apply for DLA if:
• you are over 16 and under 65; and
• you have suffered from an illness or a disability for at least three months and it is expected to continue for another six months.

ATTENDANCE ALLOWANCE (AA)
This is equivalent to the DLA for people over 65 (see p351).

HOW TO CLAIM
Disability benefit claim packs are available from local benefits offices or by contacting the benefit enquiry line for people with disabilities. This is a confidential telephone advice and information service for disabled people and their carers and representatives, and it gives advice on how to fill in benefit forms. Call:
• 0800 882 200; or
• Textphone 0800 243 355 for people with speech or hearing difficulties.

For more information about disability benefits, contact the Department for Work and Pensions ▶ 📖.

---

prepare for the hearing. If you go to the tribunal hearing, take all the paperwork with you, or give it to your representative if you appoint one.

4 If you go to the tribunal hearing you will be met by a clerk who will explain the procedure before you go in and will ask if you have any additional papers you want the tribunal to consider. You can claim travel and other expenses and the clerk will help you with these.

STANDARDS YOU CAN EXPECT FROM THE NHS

The NHS Plan launched by the Department of Health (DoH) in 2000 set standards of service for all NHS organisations and professionals, from GPs, emergency services and hospitals to dentists and opticians. The DoH regularly updates and reviews the NHS Plan. For a summary, read *Your Guide to the NHS*, available from the DoH ▶▭. Or you can download it from www.nhs.uk/nhsguide/start.htm

Your legal rights

You have a right to expect the government to provide a Health Authority, hospitals and GPs for your area (see p112), emergency ambulance and hospital services, and the fast-track, no-appointment services, including NHS Direct (see box, p109), and, in major cities, NHS walk-in centres.

What can you do if standards are not met?

The standards set out in the NHS Plan (see box, below) are government policies, not citizens' rights. They do not carry legal weight. For example, if you are referred to hospital for tests and you are not offered care in a single-sex ward as directed in the NHS Plan, you cannot sue the government or the hospital for compensation.

But the government is increasing the pressure on NHS services to achieve the standards set by the plan, and it has introduced some systems for patients to get redress. For example, there is a scheme for patients whose operation is cancelled (see below).

Using the complaints procedure

If a service fails to meet the NHS Plan standards, but the DoH has not started a redress scheme, you can make a formal complaint (see pp114-115) against the service provider. If your complaint is successful, you should receive at least an apology and an explanation, and, where feasible, a service may be improved, restored or provided.

GPs, EMERGENCY SERVICES AND HOSPITALS

Standards for GPs
• **GPs** must provide access to appropriate general medical care 24 hours a day.
• **GPs** must give you an appointment and see you within 48 hours of asking.

Standards for emergency services
• **If you dial 999, an ambulance or paramedic unit** should arrive within 8 minutes of a call if the case is life-threatening; within 14 minutes in urban areas and 19 minutes in rural areas if the case is serious; but in less serious cases you may be put through to NHS Direct.
• **In a hospital accident and emergency department or minor injuries unit** you must be assessed by a nurse or doctor within 15 minutes of arrival and told how soon you will be treated. You should be found a bed within two hours of a decision to admit you.

Standards for hospitals
On referral to hospital you should:
• wait 26 weeks maximum for an outpatient appointment
• be seen within 30 minutes of an agreed time at an outpatient clinic
• wait 18 months maximum for in-patient treatment
• be seen by a specialist within two weeks of an urgent referral for suspected cancer
• be assessed by a specialist chest pain clinic within two weeks of referral if you are a first-time sufferer from suspected angina.

If your operation is cancelled, a hospital should:
• offer you another date no more than 28 days on, if your operation is cancelled for non-medical reasons on the day of surgery
• pay for alternative surgery at your convenience.

FINANCIAL & LEGAL SERVICES

Is the bank right to charge?

Q My bank statement shows that a charge has been added to my account without my authorisation. Can the bank do that?

A Yes, if the contract you have with the bank allows it to make the charge. When you became a customer, you entered into a contract (see p16) with the bank for its services.

The terms of this contract are set out in the bank's terms and conditions, and other literature. These should list the bank's charges and the circumstances in which they may be made. For example, most current account holders are allowed free banking while the account is in credit, with charges normally imposed on an overdraft.

The Banking Code (see box, opposite) states that your bank must notify you personally – for example, by letter – of any increase in charges at least 30 days before they are imposed. It should also give you 14 days' notice of charges it intends to make for its standard services.

ACTION PLAN

1 Ask for the latest rules for your account to see if they allow for charges to be made without first notifying you or asking for authorisation.

2 If you think they do not, talk to someone at the bank, who may be able to deal with the problem quickly.

3 If the response is unsatisfactory, ask to use the bank's official complaints procedure and for guidance on how to use it. Make a formal complaint, demanding that the charge be recredited to your account with any associated charges, such as loss of interest.

4 The bank should send you a final response. If you are unhappy with it or if you do not receive it within eight weeks, take your case to the Financial Ombudsman Service (see box, p141).

CAREFUL, IT'S A BANK MANAGER, I HEAR THEY CHARGE WITHOUT WARNING

Delay in paying money into a bank account

Q My salary is usually paid directly into my bank account on the first day of the month. But this month my rent cheque bounced because the salary wasn't credited until the fifth day. Am I entitled to claim compensation from the bank?

A Possibly, but you first need to find out what happened. You are probably paid by 'direct credit' – in other words, an electronic transfer direct from your employer's bank account to yours.

This type of payment is processed by the Bankers' Automated Clearing Service (BACS), usually on a cycle of three working days:
• Day one. The payer authorises payment. It is processed overnight by BACS.
• Day two. The bank receiving the payment processes it.
• Day three. Simultaneous settlement takes place, with payment deducted from the payer's account and credited to the recipient's account.

When the money reaches your account on day three it counts as 'cleared funds' and is normally available for you to use straight away, although some banks and building societies can set a period longer than three days. Check the terms and conditions for your account.

There are several possible reasons why your salary was credited to your account later than expected:
• Maybe your employer was late making the payment, in which case you should complain to whoever at work deals with payroll matters.
• Your employer may alter the date it pays you if the first of the month falls on a weekend or bank holiday.
• Clearing takes place over three working days, so weekends and bank holidays lengthen the delay between payment and being able to withdraw your money.

THE BANKING CODE

The Banking Code is a code of practice that UK banks and building societies should follow when dealing with the public. It covers current accounts, personal loans, savings and credit cards. It was set up by the British Bankers Association ▶ 🕮 and is monitored by the Banking Code Standards Board (BCSB) ▶ 🕮. You can get a copy of the code from the BCSB or download it from the BCSB's web site.

What the code promises
Under the code, banks and building societies promise to:
• act fairly and reasonably in all their dealings with the public
• help the public to understand how different financial products and services work
• deal quickly and sympathetically with clients when things go wrong.

If you think a bank or building society has breached the code, contact the BCSB. It will refer your case to the bank or building society to take action. If this does not resolve the problem, the BCSB can issue a warning to the bank or building society. You can also ask the Financial Ombudsman Service (see box, p141) to look into it.

If, having made these checks, you think the fault lies with the bank or clearing system, you should complain.

ACTION PLAN

1 Check the terms and conditions for your bank account to see how long it takes for credit items to clear.

2 If it took longer for your salary to clear than stated in the rules for your account, complain formally through the bank's complaints procedure.

3 Ask for compensation for any costs you incurred as a result, such as loss of interest or charges for a bounced cheque. You could also claim a proportionate sum – say £50 – for minor distress and inconvenience.

4 If the bank's final response states that it does not accept your argument, take your case to the Financial Ombudsman Service (see box, p141).

Bank delay causes a financial loss

Q I asked my bank for copies of my statements, which I needed to get a mortgage on a house I was about to buy. The clerk said it would take a few days, but that was weeks ago and the property purchase has fallen through. Can I sue the bank?

A Possibly. The Supply of Goods and Services Act 1982 (see box, p53) imposes on banks a duty to carry out their services with reasonable care and skill. If you told the bank that you needed the statements by a certain date and it did not provide them on time, you may have a case. You will have to prove that the bank did not fulfil its duty.

Do not be deterred from making a claim by the bank's terms and conditions, which probably contain clauses that exclude liability for losses resulting from the failure or unavailability of its services. In a similar case, the Financial Ombudsman (see box, opposite) ordered a bank to pay compensation to a customer. This precedent means that you may win compensation through the ombudsman.

ACTION PLAN

1 Explain to your bank manager what has happened as a result of the delay in sending the statements you requested and ask for compensation.

2 If the manager does not agree to compensate you, ask to make a complaint using the bank's formal complaints procedure.

3 If, having taken your complaint through the bank's formal procedure, you are still not satisfied with the outcome, you can complain to the Financial Ombudsman Service (see box, opposite).

Dealing with a direct debit error

Q I've set up a direct debit to pay the minimum monthly payment on my credit card. Last month the bank paid my credit card company £1500 above the agreed amount. As a result, I went overdrawn and have been charged interest. Can I get the money back and the interest refunded?

A Yes. If you neither authorised a larger payment nor were notified in advance that a larger sum would be paid, you have the right to a full and

---

DIRECT DEBIT GUARANTEE

A direct debit is an instruction to a bank to let an organisation take money from your account. Variable direct debit allows an organisation to change the amount collected.

Direct debits are made through the Direct Debit Scheme, managed by the Bankers' Automated Clearing Service (BACS; see question, p139), and are protected by a guarantee. This states that:
• If the amount to be paid or the payment date changes, the organisation you are paying will notify you in advance – normally ten working days before your account is debited.
• If an error is made by the organisation you are paying or by your bank or building society, your branch must give you a full and immediate refund of the amount paid.
• You can cancel a direct debit at any time by writing to the organisation which is debiting the payments. You should also send a copy of your letter to your bank or building society.

Banks and building societies are constantly monitoring the efficiency and security of the scheme. For example, before allowing an organisation to take money from your account by direct debit, your bank checks its financial standing.

immediate refund. Your bank is responsible for this error, even if it was made by your credit card issuer and not the bank itself. Also, your bank should refund the interest that was charged on the overdraft created by the error.

ACTION PLAN

1 Contact your bank ▶ ✍ and the organisation receiving your funds. Explain what happened and ask them to arrange for an immediate refund of the money paid above the monthly payment you authorised, including any interest on the overdraft.

2 If the unauthorised payment is not refunded to your account, plus any interest charged on the overdraft, ask to make a formal complaint using the bank's official complaints procedure.

3 If you are not satisfied with the response, take your case to the Financial Ombudsman Service (see box, right).

A need to close a joint bank account

Q My girlfriend and I had a joint bank account. We split up months ago, but she still writes cheques against the account. These are backed by her cheque guarantee card, so the bank staff won't stop them, and they say I'm responsible for her spending. Can they do that?

A Yes. When you have a joint account, each of you is responsible for the whole account, including any transactions made by the other. You may also find that if you want to close the account, the bank will keep it open until your ex-girlfriend has returned her ▶

THE FINANCIAL OMBUDSMAN SERVICE

This free, independent service helps to settle disputes between consumers and financial companies, such as banks and building societies. According to the rules of the independent financial watchdog, the Financial Services Authority (FSA; see box, p157), all companies offering current and savings accounts in the UK must sign up to the scheme. Banks offering accounts to UK customers but based in other European Economic Area (EEA) countries (the EU member states plus Iceland, Liechtenstein and Norway) are exempt.

The Financial Ombudsman Service considers complaints about:
• products and services from banks, building societies, insurance companies and investment companies' advisers
• mortgages from banks and building societies, and, from October 31, 2004, mortgages arranged by mortgage advisers. Until that date, mortgage advisers can choose, if they wish, to be covered by the ombudsman service, but from November 2004 they will be regulated by the FSA and must use it
• general insurance arranged by advisers who give information on, for example, car, home and holiday insurance. Until January 15, 2005, general insurance advisers can choose to use the ombudsman service, but it is not obligatory. After January 15, 2005, they will be regulated by the FSA and must use it (see box, p166).

The service does not accept complaints about loans and credit cards from companies that are not banks or building societies.

The ombudsman can consider a complaint only after:
• the company complaints procedure has been tried; *and*
• the company has not resolved the matter to your satisfaction, and has given you a final response; *and*
• you have given the company eight weeks to respond to your formal complaint and you have received no decision.

The ombudsman can order a company to pay compensation up to £100,000. The order is binding on the company, but the customer can still take the case to court if not satisfied.

To make a complaint you must fill in a complaint form. This is available from the Financial Ombudsman Service ▶ 🖾, or you can download it from the Service's web site.

card and cheque book. Your rights in this situation depend on whether you were aware of these 'onerous' terms (see box, p21) when you and your ex-girlfriend opened the account.

If you were aware of the terms and still opened the account, you accepted them and are liable for your ex-girlfriend's cheques. If the terms were not brought to your attention when you opened the account, you can challenge them as unreasonably heavy obligations.

To do so, you will have to use your bank's formal complaints procedure. Ask an adviser at the bank for details, and, in the meantime, ask for your losses to be limited by:
• not issuing new cheque books to your ex-girlfriend
• not renewing her guarantee card.

Dealing with a phantom cash withdrawal

Q **My bank statement shows a withdrawal from a cash machine of £100 which I never made. The bank says I'm liable. Is that true?**

A No. Under the Banking Code (see box, p139), unless the bank can show that you have acted fraudulently or without reasonable care, the most you would ever be liable for is £50 and often nothing at all.

You may be liable for a fraudulent withdrawal if you have not acted with reasonable care to protect your card from misuse. This would include:
• writing your personal identification number (PIN) on your card or on something else you keep with your card
• giving your PIN to another person
• opting for a PIN which is easy to guess, such as 1234 or your date of birth.

The onus is always on the bank to show that you did not act with reasonable care, not on you to prove your innocence.

ACTION PLAN

1 Write to your bank, referring to the Banking Code, and requesting that it refund you the £100.

2 If it refuses, ask to make a formal complaint using the bank's official procedure.

3 If you are not satisfied with the response, take your case to the Financial Ombudsman Service (see box, p141).

BIT OF AN OBVIOUS PIN NUMBER MR BOND?

007 STOLEN CREDIT CARD

Taking action over a forged cheque

Q My latest bank statement shows a cheque cashed against my account that I didn't write. I called my branch immediately to report a forgery. The manager I spoke to claims that it's too late to do anything about it. Can he do that?

A No. The bank should take action provided you bring the matter to its attention within six years of the forged cheque being drawn on your account.

If you alert the bank as soon as you can, you will not normally be liable for the amount written on the cheque and the money should be re-credited to your account. If the cheque has been forged, that is a criminal offence and the bank should notify the police.

You can be held liable for the sum on the cheque if you have infringed the banks' terms and conditions. This would include giving someone a blank cheque or leaving large gaps between words and figures on a cheque you have written, which might allow a fraudster to alter the details.

ACTION PLAN

1 Write to your bank manager, explaining what makes you think the forgery has taken place. Enclose a copy of your bank statement. Ask for the value of the cheque to be credited to your account.

2 If the manager refuses to credit your account, ask to make a complaint using the bank's official procedure.

3 If you are not satisfied with the outcome, take your complaint to the Financial Ombudsman Service (see box, p141).

Cheques written from a stolen cheque book

Q My cheque book was stolen. I didn't realise it had gone until several days later. I reported the loss to my bank, but the bank says I may be liable for any cheques written with a forged signature. Can it do that?

A No. Provided you notify your bank as soon as you become aware of the theft, you should not normally be liable for any cheques fraudulently written against your account. You should also report the theft to the police.

The terms and conditions of your account will usually require you to take reasonable care to guard against misuse of your cheque book. So, if you kept your cheque book and cheque guarantee card in the same bag or pocket and they were stolen together, you might be held liable for the amount of any fraudulent cheques written before the bank was notified.

When a cash machine swallows a card

Q A cash machine has kept my card, leaving me unable to pay for anything. The bank said it was following its normal procedures to protect customers from fraud and that it's not responsible for any inconvenience caused. Can it do that?

A Yes. Most banks and building societies state in their terms and conditions that they will return your card to you as soon as possible, but will not accept responsibility for any loss or inconvenience you suffer from being without the card.

▶

There are three reasons why your card might be swallowed by the cash machine:

- You (or someone else) repeatedly tried to key the PIN number, but got it wrong. This is a technique often used in card fraud and the machine is programmed to retain the card.
- The card is past its expiry date, in which case you should already have received a replacement card. If you have not, there is a risk that the new card was intercepted by fraudsters in the post.
- Criminals have been using a device often referred to as a 'Lebanese loop'. This is a plastic device which sits in the card slot of a cash machine. Your card appears to be retained but, once you have walked away from the machine, the criminals release the loop with your card inside and steal cash from your account or take your card shopping. Often, the thieves will stand by the machine and, seeing you are having difficulties, urge you to try again, giving them a chance to watch you as you key in your PIN and memorise it.

If your card is retained in a machine, notify your card issuer at once. It is a good idea to keep a separate note of the contact number, which can be found on the back of your card (see box, opposite).

- If your card is swallowed by a machine outside any bank that is open, go in and report it. The staff may be able to retrieve the card immediately or will forward it to your postal address.
- If you are not outside a bank, or it is not open, and you have a mobile phone, call while you are still at the machine and put a stop on the card. This defeats the Lebanese loop trick.
- If your card is retained by a machine while you are on holiday, and you have travel insurance (see box, p89), contact the insurer. Your cover may include a provision to get cash to you in an emergency. You will have to apply for a new card on your return home.

Money withdrawn with a stolen cash card

Q **My cash card was stolen and, before I could report it, the thief withdrew £750 from my account and made me £500 overdrawn. I thought the most I would be liable for was £50, but the bank says I must bear the whole loss because I had written my PIN on the card. Can it do that?**

A No. The maximum sum the bank manager can ask you to pay is £300: the amount you had in your account – £250 – plus the first £50 of the overdraft.

According to the Banking Code (see box, p139):
- if your card is lost, or stolen and misused, the most you will have to pay is £50; *but*
- if the bank can show that you did not

act with reasonable care to protect yourself from fraud (see question, p142), it can ignore the £50 limit.

Writing your PIN on the card does not show reasonable care, so the bank can ignore the £50 limit and could expect you to bear the full £750 loss – if you had £750 in your account at the time of the theft. But you did not: the bank cannot make you bear a cost greater than the amount you had in your account, and that was £250.

You should report the theft to the police, and speak or write to your bank manager ▶ ✍. Tell the manager that you wish to discuss how you might resolve the problem, based on the information contained in the Banking Code. Ask the bank to freeze interest on your account while the matter is being investigated.

Introductory credit card rate can be a trap

Q **Three months ago I changed to a new credit card because it offers a 0 per cent interest rate for the first six months. But on my latest statement I've been charged 15.9 per cent, even though I'm still within the initial six-month period. Can they do that?**

A Yes. Many credit cards offer an attractive introductory rate to encourage you to switch to them. But often this low – or even zero – rate of interest applies only to the balance transferred from your old card (or cards). It may not apply to new purchases made with the new card.

Moreover, what you pay off each month may go first to reduce the transferred balance. Only when this has been paid off completely do you start to reduce the amount borrowed for the new purchases.

If the low introductory rate applies solely to the transferred balance, it will only last as long as you are paying off that balance. So if you pay it off in three months instead of in six, the low interest rate period will last for only three months, not six.

If the fact that the percentage rate applied only to balances transferred from old cards was not clear in the advertisement, you may have a case for compensation. The bank would be in breach of the Banking Code, which stipulates that all advertising and promotional material should be 'clear, fair, reasonable and not misleading'.

You should make a complaint to the Bank Code Standards Board (BCSB; see box, p139), which, if it agrees with the complaint, can instruct the bank to clarify material. You could also contact your local trading standards office (see p30), who will investigate allegations of misleading advertising.

ACTION PLAN

1 Look through a selection of promotional material advertising the introductory rate. If you think the facts are unclear, write a letter of complaint to the Banking Code Standards Board (BCSB) ▶ 📖. Send a copy to your local trading standards office (see p30).

2 If the BCSB agrees that the facts are unclearly presented, complain to the card issuer. Point out that it is in breach of the Banking Code (see box, p139). Ask for the 0 per cent interest rate to be extended to new purchases for the introductory period, and for the higher interest rate you have been charged to be recredited to your account.

3 If the card issuer refuses your request, take your case to the Financial Ombudsman Service (see box, p141).

GOLDEN RULE

Cash cards and credit cards have a 24-hour phone number on the back which you should call if the card is stolen or lost. If you carry a card, make a note of the number and always keep it with you – but separately from the card. If a card is lost or stolen, report it straight away by phone, and follow up your call with a letter or email to the card issuer. You are legally liable for bills run up in your name, to a maximum of £50 in total, until the card company receives your notification.

Interest charged when the balance is paid

Q **I paid my credit card bill in full last month, but I was still charged interest. Can they do that?**

A Yes. In some circumstances you will run up an interest charge even when you pay off the whole balance.

This could happen if:

• You have used your card to obtain cash, including foreign currency. With many cards, interest is charged on cash withdrawals from the date of withdrawal right up to the date you pay off the full balance, not just the statement date.

• You did not pay off your bill in full the previous month. Different cards calculate interest in different ways and this applies to those cards where interest is charged right up to the date the balance is repaid, not just the statement date.

• You have one of the few cards that does not offer an interest-free period. This means you pay interest from the date of purchase up to the statement date or the date you pay the bill, regardless of whether you pay off the full balance.

A victim of credit-card 'skimming'

Q **I used my credit card in a French restaurant and now I find that £200 in phone calls to Paris have been charged to my account. Can my card company make me pay for the calls?**

A No. Under the Consumer Credit Act 1974, you are not liable for any loss due to misuse of your card details while your card remains in your possession. You have probably been a victim of a fraud known as 'skimming'. When you make a genuine transaction, your card is also swiped through the fraudster's machine, which copies the details carried on the card's magnetic stripe. These details are used to make a fake card. The fraudster then goes shopping and the transactions turn up on your credit card statement. Skimming typically happens in restaurants, bars, hotels and petrol stations, where your card may be briefly out of your sight.

Always check your credit card statement carefully and if it lists any transactions you did not make, call your card company immediately – there will be an emergency phone number printed on your statement. The card company will cancel your present card and issue you with a new one. You should also report the incident to the police.

Increased credit limit is not welcome

Q **I've had a letter from my credit card company saying it has increased my credit limit to £3000 – it was previously £1000. I don't want a higher limit. Can the company give me extra credit without asking?**

A Yes. As the law stands, it can do so, provided it is satisfied you can manage the extra credit. But you do not have to accept the higher limit. Under the Banking Code (see box, p139), the credit card company should assess whether it feels you will be able to repay before lending you money.

Periodically, the card company will review your credit limit and may take

---

GOLDEN RULE

Section 75 of the Consumer Credit Act 1974 gives you valuable protection when you use a credit card to buy things – including in some cases the right to a refund. So whenever possible pay for goods and services with a credit card rather than other types of plastic card – section 75 protection does not apply to purchases made using debit, cash or charge cards. (See also question, opposite.)

into account your past record of payments and details from your credit reference file. If you do not want the higher limit, contact your card company and ask it to reinstate the lower limit.

Claiming a refund under 'section 75'

Q **I signed up for a timeshare when I was on holiday in the Canaries and paid a £500 deposit with my credit card. Now I've been sent the details, the deal appears to be a rip-off, but the timeshare company won't give me my money back. I remembered reading that I could claim a refund from my credit card company instead, but it says it doesn't cover purchases made abroad. Can it do that?**

A Not according to the Office of Fair Trading. But this is a grey area of the law. Under section 75 of the Consumer Credit Act 1974, if you buy something costing more than £100 and up to £30,000 using your credit card and something goes wrong, you can claim

PIN AND CHIPS

By 2005, card companies expect to have replaced the magnetic stripe on all UK credit, debit and cash cards with microchips. Once the changeover is complete, you will key your personal identification number (PIN) into a credit card machine when you pay, instead of signing a paper slip.

The chip – essentially a tiny computer – will store your name and your card number and expiry date, plus extra identification, all in coded form. This coding, along with the extra security information carried by the chip, make the data very difficult to copy, so credit card companies hope that the change will help to prevent skimming.

against either the supplier or the card company (see box, p35). This gives you useful extra protection.

Most card companies claim that section 75 protection applies only to purchases you make in the UK. They do not consider that they have to meet claims if you bought abroad.

The Office of Fair Trading (OFT – the government department responsible for all matters relating to the Consumer Credit Act; see p11) ▶ see p11 thinks differently and has persuaded some card companies to treat overseas purchases in the same way as they treat UK transactions. A few card companies ▶

HOW TO GUARD AGAINST CREDIT CARD FRAUD

- Look after your credit cards as if they were cash.
- Learn your PIN by heart and do not write it down.
- Destroy the print-out notifying you of your PIN.
- Never tell anyone your PIN.
- Do not let your cards go out of your sight when using them to make payments.
- Check your statements carefully.
- Tell your card company immediately if you suspect your card has been used fraudulently.

have agreed that overseas claims are valid, while others have said they are prepared to honour such claims voluntarily, but retain the right to refuse.

Your best course of action is to contact your local trading standards office (see p30). It can advise you about your cancellation rights with timeshares and any action you might be able to take under section 75 of the Consumer Credit Act.

Is a parent liable for son's debts?

Q My 18-year-old son filled out a credit card application. Now he has run up a £2000 debt and the credit card company is asking me to pay the bill. Can it do that?

THE ANSWER'S STILL NO SON

LIVING IN A CARDBOARD BOX PLEASE HELP

A No, unless you agreed to act as a guarantor for your son's debts, which would be unusual in the case of a credit card.

In England and Wales, it is illegal for companies to offer credit facilities to people under the age of 18 (if this happens, report the matter to your local trading standards office – see p30). Once people reach 18 they may be bombarded with card offers. Companies take the commercial decision to sign up new clients and they must also accept the risk that some will run into problems handling the credit. They cannot look to parents to settle their adult children's debts.

A husband's card bill is not his wife's problem

Q My husband ran up thousands of pounds in debt on his credit card in hotel bills and meals out. Now the card issuer is pursuing me to pay the bill. Can it do that?

A No. You cannot be held responsible for debts your husband has run up on his own credit card. Credit cards are normally issued in the name of a single account holder and that person is solely responsible for the debts on the card.

The account holder can ask for other people to be made additional cardholders. In that case, the account holder is also responsible for any debts run up by the additional cardholders. But the additional cardholders cannot be held responsible for the debts of the account holder.

HOW BANKS OPERATE USING THE INTERNET

Many banks offer their customers accounts they can operate themselves through the bank's web site on the Internet. Customers can go to the web site to transfer money from one account to another, pay bills, check their account balance, see and print out statements, arrange overdrafts and carry out other transactions.

Internet banking is commonly called 'e-banking'. To prevent fraud from 'hackers' (thieves who break into Internet bank accounts to steal money),

customers are given passwords and other security codes to use when they access their accounts.

People using e-banking facilities can still pay money into an account using the post or by visiting a branch in the traditional way, and withdraw cash from one of the bank's branches or a cash machine.

The laws that govern banking – notably the Supply of Goods and Services Act 1982 (see box, p53) – apply equally to e-banking.

WHO REGULATES E-BANKS?
● E-banks operating inside the UK are regulated by the Financial Services Authority (FSA) and observe the Banking Code (see box, p139).
● Outside the UK, banks are regulated by the authorities in their home country, so before you open an Internet account with one, ask about protection – particularly complaints procedures and compensation arrangements if your account security is infringed or if the bank stops trading.

● In the European Economic Area (EEA – the majority of EU states plus Iceland, Liechtenstein and Norway), e-banks come under the Electronic Commerce Directive. This regulates the way in which service providers can advertise themselves online, make contracts, establish codes of conduct and make these codes known to the public. For more details, contact the Department for Trade and Industry (DTI) ▶ or you can download the Directive from the DTI's web site.

HOW SECURE IS E-BANKING?
The Banking Code (see box, p139) does not protect customers against online fraud such as attacks by hackers. So, to protect yourself, you should read the terms and conditions of an Internet account carefully to see what guarantees are offered if you are the victim of online fraud. Accounts offer four types of guarantee:
No-strings guarantee The bank guarantees that you will not be liable for any loss.
Special requirements You are not liable for

any loss provided that you comply with special requirements. For example, you must change your password every 12 months or more often, and keep your anti-virus software up to date.
Limited liability The bank initially holds you liable for a maximum sum, usually £50. Once you report the fraud, you are no longer liable.
Full liability You are liable without limit for all transactions using your security code – some banks take the view that hacking is beyond their control.

CHANGES TO THE LAW
E-banking is a form of distance-selling (the selling of goods and services when there is no face-to-face contact between the seller and the buyer – for example, when a sale is made by phone, via a catalogue or on the Internet). As a result, it will come under the Distance Marketing of Consumer Financial Services Directive when this becomes law in EEA countries in October 2004.

The Directive protects consumers who enter into financial services contracts on the Internet by stipulating that they must be given detailed, clearly understandable information about:

● the supplier
● the product offered by the supplier
● the type of distance-selling contract the buyer is being asked to agree to
● what forms of redress the consumer can draw on if a dispute occurs – for example, if the product supplied is not the one that was sold.

If the product is a bank account, the consumer must be told the current interest rates – and all deductions and charges relating to the account. The Directive also stipulates that consumers must have the right to a cooling-off period (see question, p38), when they can withdraw from the contract without charge.

GOLDEN RULE

If your property is mortgaged and you want to let it, be sure to ask for your mortgage lender's consent. If you let it without consent, the arrangement may not be binding on the lender. This means that if the property were to be repossessed, the tenant would probably not have the right to stay there.

A double debit is the bank's fault

Q I make monthly payments to a building society, but last month it debited my bank account twice. The error resulted in an unauthorised overdraft with a high interest charge and a bounced cheque. The building society says it's not liable for my bank charges. Can it do that?

A Yes. Even though your building society made the mistake, it is your bank that is responsible for operating the direct debit scheme by which you pay your mortgage, and so your bank will put the error right.

Under the direct debit guarantee (see box, p140), if an error is made by either the organisation collecting payments (in this case, your building society) or your bank, you are entitled to a full and immediate refund.

ACTION PLAN

1 Contact your bank and explain what has happened. The bank should re-credit your account and refund the charges.

2 Ask your bank to offer something as a goodwill gesture to cover the embarrassment caused by the bounced cheque. It may be willing to do so, even though the direct debit guarantee does not entitle you to compensation.

Charged for permission to let your home

Q My mortgage lenders granted approval for me to let my property, but when they wrote to me they didn't say that I would be charged administration costs. Should they have told me they would be imposing these charges?

A Yes. Under the Mortgage Code, to which most lenders subscribe (see box, p230), a lender should give you a tariff (or list) of charges before you take out a mortgage and at any time you ask. It should also send you an updated tariff each year if there have been changes to the charges.

It is normal practice for the lender to make a one-off administration charge for handling your request. There might also be other costs – for example, an increase in the interest rate you are charged.

If your lender did not tell you about the charges, you should complain. Write to the lender and ask for them to be lifted ▶ ✍. If your request is refused, you have the right to take your complaint to the Mortgage Code Compliance Board (see box, p230). It has powers to order the lender to refund the charges.

If you had known about the charges in advance, and knowing about it did not alter your decision to go ahead with the letting, it might be considered that you have not really suffered any loss.

Redemption penalties for mortgage switch

Q My mortgage lender charges a high interest rate. When I said that I wanted to switch to a lender with a lower rate I was told I'd be liable for redemption penalties. Can the lender do that?

A Yes. Most mortgages have some redemption charges. Before you took out your mortgage, you should have been given a tariff (or list) of charges.

This would have included details of any redemption penalties due if you pay off part, or all, of your mortgage before the end of its term. If there have been changes to any charges since you took out the mortgage, you should have been sent an updated tariff.

Switching your mortgage involves paying off your old loan and taking out a new loan with a new lender. You need to take into account any redemption charges on the old mortgage, along with the various other costs of switching – such as valuation and legal fees – when deciding whether making the switch is worthwhile or not.

In the early years of a mortgage, redemption charges are often high. But once the period of any special deal (such as a fixed or discounted rate) is past, redemption charges may just amount to a small administration fee.

No credit record means no loan

Q My husband died last year and I've now been denied a loan because I've no credit record in my own name. Can I be turned down like that?

A Yes. You have no automatic right to credit. The lender decides and will base the decision on information you give in the application form and which is held in files on you by credit reference agencies (see box, p153). For the lender to agree to the loan it will need to check your credit record.

If you and your late husband had any joint loans, these will appear on your personal credit files. But if all your financial arrangements were in his name rather than yours, none of them will be reflected in your record and the lender will have nothing to base its decision on.

Your lack of a credit record could cause you difficulties in other areas, too – for example, with fuel and phone bills. You may need to get the accounts changed from your husband's name to yours, and although you can usually pay fuel and phone bills quarterly in arrears, you need a good credit record to set this up. You could simply arrange to pay the bills monthly by direct debit (see box, p140).

Young people who have not yet built up a track record of borrowing can face similar problems when applying for credit for the first time.

ACTION PLAN

1 Call the lender and ask to speak to a manager. Ask if the company will reconsider if you provide relevant additional information such as proof that you now own the family home, a letter from an employer confirming that you are in regular employment, or a bank reference.

2 If the lender refuses, ask whether it is a member of a trade organisation with an appeals procedure, such as the British Bankers Association ▶ ⌂, the Building Societies Association ▶ ⌂ or the Finance and Leasing Association ▶ ⌂. If so, ask for details of the procedure and make an appeal.

3 If you cannot appeal, try other lenders. Your local Citizens Advice Bureau ▶ ⌂ can advise you on lenders to approach. ▶

4 If you cannot secure a loan, you could ask a close relative or friend who has a good credit record to act as a guarantor. This means your relative or friend would be responsible for repaying the loan if you did not keep up the payments.

Why was I turned down for a loan?

Q I applied to a loan company for a £5000 loan and was refused. I've never owed money to anyone. Can the company just turn me down?

A Yes. You have no legal right to borrow money. Deciding whether to offer a loan is a commercial decision for the lender. Typically, a lender checks your credit reference file (see box, opposite) and asks you to complete an application form. The information you give and the information in your credit reference file are used to work out a 'credit score'.

Each lender's credit-scoring system is a closely guarded commercial secret, but it is usually possible to find out why you were refused a loan, even if only in general terms – for example, there may be information such as a bad debt on your file.

ACTION PLAN

1 Check whether the lender subscribes to the Banking Code (see box, p139) or the Guide to Credit Scoring, a code of practice for members of the Finance and Leasing Association ▶ . If so, although the lender does not have to tell you why your application has been refused, you can ask to be told in broad terms why it was turned down.

2 The lender is obliged to tell you which credit reference agency it used. You can then check your credit file (see box, opposite).

Debt collectors should not harass their clients

Q Some years ago I took out a loan. I've recently had difficulty making payments on time. A debt collector has been knocking at my door at all hours. Can he do this?

A No. Even if you owe money, the law protects you from harassment (see box, p391). You should make it clear to the debt collector that you know he is breaking the law and

threaten to call the police. Creditors (the companies to which you owe money) and the companies such as debt collectors who work for them are allowed to remind you to make repayments – but not in such a way as to alarm, distress or humiliate you. They are not allowed to phone you late at night, keep phoning you at home or at work, park a vehicle marked 'debt collectors' outside your home, or contact your place of study or employment (see box, p387).

You should contact your local trading standards office (see p30) urgently with details of the collection agency, if available, and of every occasion the collector has contacted you either by visiting your home or employment, or by phoning (note the date, time and length of calls).

Finding a way to reduce your debt

Q I got myself into debt and I contacted a debt management company. Their consultant said she would negotiate with all the firms to whom I owed money and merge all my debts into one monthly payment. But the company charges very high fees, and I'm getting deeper in debt. Can I cancel the agreement with the company?

A Yes. Contact a debt counselling service (see Action Plan), or go to your local Citizens Advice Bureau ▶ ⌂, where you will receive free debt advice and help in negotiating with creditors (the people to whom you owe money). Ask the adviser to explain how you can get out of the arrangement with the debt management company.

These companies typically promise to clear all your debts through a single monthly payment. They do not themselves offer credit, but instead negotiate with all your creditors to get

a reduction in payments. They then handle the regular payments to each creditor out of a monthly payment you make to them.

Companies like this often deduct a substantial fee from the monthly payment, which reduces the amount available to pay your creditors. Moreover, some firms deal only with your unsecured loans (see box, p155), rather than taking all your loans into account when working out what you can afford to pay.

The Office of Fair Trading (OFT; see p11) lays down standards that debt management companies should follow. If you think the company is not treating you fairly, complain to your local trading standards office (see p30).

ACTION PLAN

1 Contact a debt counselling service, such as the Consumer Credit Counselling Service ▶ ⌂ or National Debtline (0808 808 4000). Explain that you are not satisfied ▶

CHECKING YOUR CREDIT FILE

There are three main credit reference agencies in the UK: Callcredit ▶ ⌂, Equifax ▶ ⌂ and Experian ▶ ⌂. Each has a file of information about virtually everyone aged 18 and over.

The file contains three broad types of information:
Publicly available information This includes your name and address from the UK electoral roll, and any potentially unfavourable information, such as county court judgments and court orders, made in the past six years.
Information about your current borrowing This shows the extent of your commitments and your repayments record.
A record of previous searches Many searches over a short period might suggest you are borrowing more than you can afford or that someone is obtaining credit in your name.

You can contact any of the credit reference agencies for a copy of your credit file. You must pay a small fee per file (currently £2). If there is an error, you have the right to correct it – the agency will tell you how to do this.

with the way your debt management company is handling your finances and you would like to switch. You will be assigned an adviser who will help you with various steps you have to take.

2 Write to the debt management company, cancelling your contract. If your agreement with the company included a refundable fee, ask for it to be returned to you.

3 If the company refuses to cancel the contract, report it to your local trading standards office (see p30) and ask for advice. Or you could

---

PERSONAL BANKRUPTCY

Bankruptcy is a legal declaration that an individual or a company cannot pay debts when they are due. In a case of personal bankruptcy, the legal process is as follows:

1 You or your creditors file a bankruptcy petition in a county court. A court fee must be paid (£120 in 2004), and a deposit (£250 by the debtor and £300 by the creditor in 2004).

2 The court issues a bankruptcy order and notifies the *London Gazette* (the official newspaper of the Crown), which will announce the bankruptcy.

3 The court appoints a trustee or an insolvency practitioner (a specialist accountant or lawyer) to protect and administer your possessions. You can no longer be pursued by creditors. The trustee or insolvency practitioner may charge fees of up to 40 per cent of the value of your assets for his services.

4 The trustee may sell your assets to raise money to pay your creditors and can apply for a court order to divert part of your income to him.

New regulations introduced in 2004 reduced the length of a bankruptcy order from three years to one year, but an order to divert income may remain in force for several years. During this period you cannot apply for credit or borrow money, practise law, or become a Justice of the Peace, a Member of Parliament or a trustee of a charity.

---

discuss with your adviser from the debt counselling service the possibility of using the small claims procedure in the county court (see p19).

Are you saying I'm bankrupt?

Q Someone who once lent me money has just sent me a 'statutory demand'. I'm told that this means I'm being made bankrupt. Is that right?

A No, but it could be a step in that direction. A statutory demand is issued under the Insolvency Act 1986 by someone to whom you owe more than £750. It is a demand for payment, not a notice of bankruptcy.

It cannot be issued for a smaller debt, or for a secured loan (see box, opposite). Anyone can issue a statutory demand through a solicitor, who will charge a fee of about £75 for completing the standard form and ensuring that the person receives it.

If you do not act in the next 21 days, the creditor – the person to whom you owe money – can apply to the court for an order to make you bankrupt (see box, left).

When you get a statutory demand, you have three options:
- repay the loan in full
- offer some possession, such as property, as security for the debt
- offer to pay the loan in instalments.

If you are not sure what you should do, contact a debt counselling service such as National Debtline (0808 808 4000) or the Consumer Credit Counselling Service ▶ 🖂 for advice.

STRATEGIES FOR DEALING WITH DEBT

All types of loan carry severe legal penalties if you fail to repay them on the due date. For this reason it is essential to sign for a loan only if you can repay it – and to take out loan insurance in case of illness or unemployment. You can be declared bankrupt for as little as £750 and the legal consequences can have far-reaching effects on your life (see box, opposite), so act decisively if you get into debt by working out a payment plan, discussing it with your creditors, and keeping up the payments.

TYPES OF LOAN

Whether it is long or short-term, interest-bearing or interest-free, a loan falls into one of two categories:

Unsecured loans You satisfy the criteria required by the lender (for example, age, income and credit record), sign an agreement and the money is yours. If you fail to repay as agreed, the lender can apply for a court judgment requiring you to repay the amount in full or by instalments.

Secured loans As well as satisfying the lender's criteria and signing an agreement, you must pledge a valuable item that belongs to you, which the lender can sell if you fail to repay. You can pledge any item that is acceptable to the lender – pawnbrokers secure loans on diverse articles of personal property – but lenders usually want large loans to be secured on property or a business.

MAKE A PAYMENT PLAN

If you find it hard to pay your debts, work out a realistic plan, and follow it:

1 Work out your monthly income and essential outgoings and draw up a budget.

2 Work out how much you can afford to pay towards your debts each month.

3 Contact your creditors and negotiate lower payments or a longer payment period, or both.

4 Concentrate on paying off the debts that have the most serious legal consequences (see panel right) and those with the highest rates of interest.

PRIORITISE YOUR PAYMENTS

Work out a priority list of the debts with serious legal consequences for non-payment. These are:

Rent Your landlord can evict you for non-payment (see box, p211).

Mortgage The lender can repossess your home or business premises if you do not keep up the mortgage payments.

Income tax The Inland Revenue can sue for bankruptcy if you do not pay on time.

Council tax A local authority can take legal action if you do not pay and you can go to prison.

Utilities bills The supplier can cut off your gas, electricity or telephone if you do not pay.

Court fines You can be imprisoned if you do not pay.

Hire purchase for items you need, such as a van for work. The lender can get a court order to reclaim it if you fall behind with the payments.

Arrange to pay unsecured personal loans and catalogue, card and non-essential hire-purchase debts at low rates over long periods.

AN ARRANGEMENT TO PAY BIG DEBTS

If your debts are so large that bankruptcy seems inevitable, consider entering into an Individual Voluntary Arrangement (IVA). To do this, you consult an insolvency practitioner (a specialist accountant or lawyer) and arrange to pay a proportion of your debts, usually in single monthly payments, over five years. The remaining debts are then written off. The arrangement must be approved by a 75 per cent vote at a meeting of your creditors. Then it is ratified by a county court and becomes legally binding. As long as you make the payments (to which the insolvency practitioner adds a fee), you cannot be declared bankrupt.

For more information call the Consumer Credit Counselling Service ▶ 🖾 or National Debtline (0808 808 4000), which can also give details of insolvency practitioners.

How a loan differs from hire purchase

Q **I paid for my hi-fi on credit but I can't keep up my payments. I'm worried that the credit company will take the hi-fi back? Can it do that?**

A No, not if you arranged a loan and used it to buy the hi-fi. The company can take court action to recover the money it lent you, but as the loan is unsecured (see box, p155), it cannot reclaim the hi-fi.

But if you bought the hi-fi through a hire-purchase agreement, the credit company can reclaim it. With a hire-purchase contract, you legally only hire the hi-fi until you have paid all the instalments and the agreement has come to an end, at which point you own it.

Until then, the finance company has various options if you stop making the payments:

• It can apply for a court order to take back the hi-fi.

• If you have not yet paid half the original purchase price, it can reclaim the hi-fi and ask you to pay an amount that brings your total payments up to the halfway mark.

• If you have paid more than half the purchase price, the company can reclaim the hi-fi and claim for the total of missed payments and for any damage to the hi-fi.

Whatever form of credit you used, seek advice by going to a debt counselling service (see question, p153). It may suggest that you contact the company to explain the problem and offer to make a smaller monthly payment over a longer period. If the company accepts, you must keep up the payments or it will take court action to recover the money or the hi-fi.

The high cost of paying off a loan early

Q **Two years ago I bought a kitchen on a five-year credit agreement, but I can now afford to pay it off in full. The credit company manager I approached quoted a settlement figure that is much higher than the amount I owe. Can he do that?**

A Yes. If you had kept the loan for the full five-year term, you would have paid the lender the original capital plus five-years' worth of interest.

The lender loses some of that interest when you pay off the loan early and the law allows the lender to recoup part of that lost interest through an early settlement charge.

Ask your local trading standards office (see p30) to check if the early settlement figure is correct.

FINANCIAL SERVICES AUTHORITY

The Financial Services Authority (FSA) ▶ 🕮 regulates financial services in the UK. It is an independent watchdog with powers to improve and maintain standards in banks, building societies, credit unions and insurance companies, and among financial advisers (see box, p159), stockbrokers and investment fund managers. It does not regulate credit, loans, debt or occupational pension schemes.

The role of the FSA is expanding. On October 31, 2004, it will take over regulation of mortgage lending (see box, p230), and from January 15, 2005, the regulation of general insurance (see box, p166).

FINANCIAL SERVICES COMPENSATION SCHEME (FSCS)

This scheme was set up by the FSA to deal with claims from customers against the banks, building societies and insurance and investment companies that it regulated but have ceased to trade or have become insolvent. The table below shows the levels of compensation you can claim for the different types of deposit and investment. To claim, contact the FSCS ▶ 🕮 and ask for an application form.

Financial product	Limit on cover provided	Maximum compensation
Deposits, such as bank and building society accounts	100 per cent of the first £2000 90 per cent of the next £33,000	£31,700
Investments, such as unit trusts and shares	100 per cent of the first £30,000 90 per cent of the next £20,000	£48,000
Long-term insurance, including investment-type life insurance and personal pensions	100 per cent of the first £2000 At least 90 per cent of the remainder (including future benefits already declared)	Unlimited
General insurance, including: • compulsory insurance such as third-party motor insurance and employers' liability insurance	Compulsory insurance: 100 per cent of claim	Unlimited
• non-compulsory insurance, for example household, travel and private medical insurance	Non-compulsory insurance: 100 per cent of first £2000 90 per cent of remainder	Unlimited
Mortgages, including advice about mortgages and arranging them	100 per cent of first £30,000 90 per cent of next £20,000	£48,000

When an adviser gives bad advice

Q I've recently lost a lot of money on investments and I think my financial adviser gave me bad advice. I complained and asked for compensation, but the adviser says he's not responsible for falling stock markets. Can he do that?

A Yes, in some cases. The Financial Services Authority (FSA; see box, above) has rules that protect investors. These do not shelter you from normal investment risks, such as falling share prices, but they might protect you if you were given bad advice.

When your adviser told you about products that are suitable for your needs, he should have: ▶

• asked you about your financial circumstances and your attitude to risk

• explained the investments he presented and checked that you were happy with the degree of risk involved

• checked that no significant changes had occurred in your circumstances if you are a longstanding customer about whom he gathered information some time ago.

If your adviser failed to do any of these things, you may have a claim against him. In particular, you will have a strong case if he recommended an investment with a higher level of risk than you could afford to take, and if you could not have been expected to understand the risks.

ACTION PLAN

1 If you think the adviser failed to follow the FSA's Code of Conduct (see box, opposite), contact the adviser and ask to use the firm's formal complaints procedure.

2 If you are unhappy with the response, take your complaint to the Financial Ombudsman Service (see box, p141).

Ways of protecting your investments

Q I'm approaching retirement. My limited assets are spread between building society deposits, investments and insurance policies. Is it possible to protect against companies going bust?

A Yes, to some extent. If you invested with a company authorised by the Financial Services Authority (FSA) ▶ ⌸ and it went bankrupt, you may be able to claim under the FSA Compensation Scheme (see box, p157). This covers you up to certain limits (see p157) when companies go bust. So you might take

these limits into account when deciding how much to invest with a company.

If you invest in a company that is not authorised by the FSA, you will not be covered by this scheme. You might not be protected at all if the firm is outside the European Economic Area (EEA – the 15 EU countries, plus Iceland, Liechtenstein and Norway). For more information, consult the FSA's Firm Check Service.

If you have put money into National Savings and Investment products, these are backed by the Treasury so the risk of losing your capital is minimal. For more information, consult an independent financial adviser (see box, opposite).

Bad service from an investment broker

Q To be sure my shares would be sold quickly if their price fell, I put in an order for my broker to sell if they dropped below a certain level. He didn't honour it, so I've lost thousands of pounds, and he won't reimburse me. Can he do that?

A No. You have a contract with your broker for his services, so contract law applies, as does the Supply of Goods and Services Act 1982 (see p53), which requires your broker to carry out the service with reasonable care and skill.

Your order to your broker is known as a 'stop-loss order', and it instructs him to sell if the share value falls below a certain figure, thereby limiting the loss you make. The order is usually valid for a specified time – the 'stop-loss' period.

You can expect the broker to carry out your instructions (for which you may have paid an extra fee) until the stop-loss period expires. If he has not done so, you have a good case for expecting him to bear the loss. ▶ p160

CONSULTING A FINANCIAL ADVISER

Financial advisers are qualified to help you to work out your various financial needs and priorities, and then recommend financial products – ranging from insurance policies to investments – that are suited to your particular situation and requirements. The best-qualified are Associates or Fellows of the Society of Financial Advisers (SOFA) ▶⌐.

Financial advisers fall into two categories:
• tied advisers, who work with banks, building societies, insurance and investment companies, and recommend the products sold by their employer
• independent financial advisers (IFAs), who are not tied, but are free to recommend products from the full range available on the market.

Authorisation and regulation
No one can operate as an independent financial adviser unless authorised by the Financial Services Authority (FSA; see box, p157). Advisers must also observe the FSA's Code of Conduct.

An IFA must:
• give you a letter at the outset, setting out the terms of business. This tells you whether an adviser is independent and, if not, which company he deals with
• be sure that products he recommends are suitable for your needs, and explain why he recommends them
• before you sign for a recommended product, give you a document listing key facts about it. This will explain charges and details of any commission the IFA expects to receive, and whether that commission will be deducted from the money you pay into the investment.

How independent financial advisers are paid
The advice you receive from your IFA is either fee-based or commission-based.

Fees You pay the adviser a fee of, usually, £75-£150 an hour for time spent on your case. Any commission received as a result of selling a product is deducted from the fee. All IFAs must offer customers the option of paying fees.

Commission The adviser recommends a product such as a bond or shares. If you buy it, the adviser receives a fee from the company that offers the product. You, the customer, may pay this fee indirectly through charges built into the product.

Complaints and compensation
If an adviser sells you a product that is different from how it was described or more expensive than you were advised, or is otherwise unsuitable for your needs, you can complain to the Financial Ombudsman (see box, p141).

If an FSA-regulated bank or building society closes down, you may be able to claim compensation under the FSA's Financial Services Compensation Scheme (see box, p157).

How to find an IFA in your area
Contact the Association of Independent Financial Advisers (AIFA) ▶⌐ or call IFA Promotion (0117 971 1177; www.unbiased.co.uk).

ACTION PLAN

1 Write to your broker and explain the position. Ask for information about the company's complaints procedure and make a formal complaint.

2 If the broker does not compensate you for the loss, or fails to reply within eight weeks, take your complaint to the Financial Ombudsman Service (see box, p141). The ombudsman can order the company to compensate you.

Dealing with an unauthorised adviser

Q I met a financial consultant at the gym and she convinced me to invest in what she claimed was a 'sure thing'. In fact, the so-called investment never existed and the woman has vanished, along with my money. Can she get away with that?

A Possibly not. By accepting the money you gave her, the woman was acting illegally and you should report her to the police.

Check whether or not she is authorised by the Financial Services Authority (FSA) ▶ 📖 to act as an independent financial adviser (see box, p159). If so, you might be entitled to compensation. On the other hand, the FSA's rules and measures to protect investors apply only to authorised advisers acting in the course of business. It could be claimed that she was only passing on a friendly tip.

Tax liability because of an accountant's error

Q Two years ago my accountant failed to declare some of my income on my tax return. Now Inland Revenue inspectors are chasing me – not my accountant – for the overdue tax and they're charging me interest on it. Can they do that?

A Yes. The Inland Revenue is acting correctly. Whether or not you use an accountant or other tax adviser, you remain ultimately responsible for reporting your tax affairs accurately and on time to the Inland Revenue.

If you do not agree with the amount the inspectors are chasing you for, contact your tax office directly. It will discuss the problem with you and explain what to do next if you cannot reach agreement. If you cannot meet the demand immediately, the tax office may allow you extra time to pay.

You may be able to recover some of the money from your accountant – for example, the interest on late payment and any penalty charges involved (see next question). But you will need to check that you gave the accountant all the necessary information correctly and did so in time to meet the Inland Revenue's tax deadlines. If you gave incomplete or inaccurate information, you will have no claim against the accountant.

Negligent accountant leads to financial strain

Q I've found that for years my accountant has been dealing wrongly with items in my accounts, so my profit position looked healthier than it was. As a result I'm having to restructure and make people redundant. The accountant says I've no grounds for claiming compensation. Is she right?

A Probably not. It all depends on the details of your case. Broadly speaking, you have a contract with your accountant for her services, and the law requires her to carry them out with reasonable care and skill.

Accountants are obliged under the rules of their professional bodies to have professional indemnity insurance in order to meet any compensation claims that may be made against them.

ACTION PLAN

1 Make an appointment to see your accountant to discuss the matter in detail. If she denies responsibility, ask to make a formal complaint through the firm's official procedure.

2 If you fail to win compensation, or if your accountant is self-employed, take your complaint to her professional body – the Institute of Chartered Accountants (ICA) ▶ 📖, Association of Chartered

---

PROTECTION AGAINST INVESTMENT SCAMS

All investments carry a risk, but you can protect yourself against bad advice, fraud, mis-selling and investment scams if you take this advice:

Check that the company you deal with is authorised
Find out through the Firm Check Service of the Financial Services Authority (FSA) ▶ 📖 that a company offering an investment product you want to buy is FSA-authorised. This gives you the protection of having recourse to a complaints procedure, an independent ombudsman service and a compensation scheme.

Do not buy without professional advice
If you are inexperienced in making investments and you invest without having the product vetted by an independent financial adviser (see box, p159), you will have no redress if the product is unsuitable.

Do your homework
You will be an easy target for bad advice, fraud and mis-selling if you do not know what type of product is suitable for you and what risks are involved.

Understand that risk and reward go hand in hand
If an investment offers a return that is higher than average, it must involve higher risk. Ask what the risks are and do not invest if you do not want to take them.

Read the small print
Find out what charges are deducted, whether you can sell or get your money back early and the potential risks of a product by reading the literature, especially the small print. Ask about anything you do not understand.

Certified Accountants (ACCA) ▶ 📖 or, if your accountant has been acting as a tax adviser, the Chartered Institute of Taxation (CIT) ▶ 📖.

3 If the professional body's complaints procedure does not settle the issue to your satisfaction, ask if it can offer low-cost outside arbitration to help you to resolve your dispute. An example is the scheme offered by ACCA in which an independent panel of assessors reviews the decision reached through ACCA's own complaints procedure.

A victim of pensions mis-selling in the past

Q **In 1993 the company where I worked advised everyone to transfer from our company pension scheme into a personal pension. We all did, but I now know it wasn't in my interest. I contacted my former employer to ask for compensation, but the company denies all responsibility. Can it do that?**

A Yes. If you were mis-sold a personal pension before June 30, 1994, it is too late now to lodge a claim.

There was a huge number of cases like this in the late 1980s and early 1990s, which caused the Financial Services Authority (FSA) ▶ ➢ to open an enquiry for the period from April 1988 to June 1994. It reviewed all cases of people who had been advised during that time to opt out of their company schemes and buy a personal pension.

If it was proved that a scheme had been mis-sold, compensation was available for the person involved. But that enquiry was completed in March 2003 and no more claims for the 1988-1994 period are being heard. For more information, you should contact the FSA and the Pensions Advisory Service ▶ ➢ (see p165).

If you have been badly advised since June 30, 1994, you should make a complaint (see question, pp158-160).

Deferring pension claims until rates rise

Q **My pension fund is about to mature, but it has suffered from recent stock market falls and I've read that the rates being paid out now are very low. My son tells me that it's better to wait until they rise before I claim the pension? Can I do that?**

A Probably. Many pensions schemes allow this – but not all. If you built up your fund in a company scheme at work, you will need to check whether the rules allow you to put back the date when you start to draw your pension. If you arranged your pension yourself, you can put off starting to receive payments until you are 75.

If you have contributed to a company or a personal pension, you will receive the money in two ways:
• a tax-free lump sum
• a sum (at least 75 per cent of your total pension fund; see p164) to buy an annuity – guaranteed income, which you

---

RECLAIMING FORGOTTEN ASSETS

Even after many years, you do not lose ownership of assets you may have forgotten you had. To trace these assets, contact the bodies listed below – most offer a free service.

Bank accounts Dormant Accounts Unit at the British Bankers' Association ▶ ➢.
Building society accounts Dormant Accounts Scheme at the Building Societies Association ▶ ➢.
Premium bonds and National Savings accounts National Savings and Investments ▶ ➢.
Occupational and personal pensions Pension Schemes Registry ▶ ➢.
Life insurance policies and personal pensions Unclaimed Assets Register ▶ ➢ – there is a charge.
Unit trusts Investment Management Association ▶ ➢.
Investment trusts Association of Investment Trust Companies ▶ ➢.
Shares Companies House ▶ ➢, which will check whether the company still exists or has merged or changed its name, and may be able to give you contact details. You can then call and ask for details of the company's registrars, who have information about shareholdings.

will receive each year until you die. It is the annuity rates – the regular payments you receive each year – that may have fallen because they depend on the ups and downs of stock markets.

An arrangement known as 'income drawdown' can help to overcome this problem. With income drawdown, you start to draw an income from the sum of money you have built up in your pension fund, but you can still postpone buying an annuity until you are 75.

By that time the pension fund will have decreased by the amount of income you have drawn from it – so consider this scheme only if you have a very large fund. Seek advice from an independent financial adviser (see box, p159).

If you decide to defer your pension, but without using 'income drawdown', your fund will have had extra time to grow. As a result, the payments, once they start, are likely to be higher than if you had not deferred.

Annuity rates depend on age as well as the stock market, since the older you are when you claim the annuity, the fewer the years in which the payments will have to be made – and so the higher the annual payments you receive.

High charges for transferring a pension

Q **My personal pension has performed very badly over the past couple of years. I was going to transfer the £21,000 remaining to a better scheme, but I've had a statement showing that the transfer value after charges have been deducted amounts to £18,000. Can the company rob me of £3000?**

A In all likelihood, yes. The charges for the personal pension should have been set out in the information you were given when you started the scheme. It would have included details of any charges payable if you transfer to another scheme.

It is common for personal pensions sold before 2001 – when the pensions industry was reformed and simplified – to have high transfer charges. This is because the costs of setting up a scheme (including commission paid to any adviser you used) are recouped by the company through charges spread over a number of years. If you transfer during the early years, a transfer charge is levied to scoop up the remainder of the setting-up costs.

You could also lose out because of a 'market value reduction'. This is a deduction the company may make with some types of scheme, reducing the transfer value of your pension when investments are performing badly.

If you are younger than about 35, it may be worth your while cutting your losses and paying the charges. They should be outweighed by better performance from a new pension scheme.

FINANCIAL & LEGAL SERVICES

Your rights with company pension schemes

If your employer runs a company (also called an occupational or superannuation) pension scheme, it is usually a good idea to join it, because:
- your employer pays some or all of the cost
- most schemes include a package of benefits including a retirement pension, dependants' pensions, a pension if you have to retire early

because of ill health, and often life insurance
- both the employer and the scheme members get tax relief on their investments and contributions.

Employers who offer a company pension scheme must also allow employees to make extra payments to boost their benefits. These are called additional voluntary contributions (AVCs).

TYPES OF COMPANY PENSION SCHEME

1 Defined benefit schemes
You are promised a pension when you leave, which is worked out according to a formula based on your pay and how long you have contributed to the scheme.

It is up to your employer to make sure that enough money is paid into the pension fund for the employees' pension promises to be met. So, for example, if the investments in the pension fund perform badly, the employer has to pay extra into the scheme.

Defined benefit schemes include:
Final salary schemes How much pension you receive is based on your pay shortly before retirement.
Career average schemes These use the average of your pay during the whole time you contribute to the scheme.

2 Money purchase schemes
These, also known as defined contribution schemes, work like savings schemes. You build up your own pension fund, and the amount of pension you get at retirement depends on what you paid into the scheme, the charges deducted, investment performance, and the market rates for an annuity (a guaranteed annual income until death) at the time you retire.

The law says that you must take 75 per cent of your pension as an annuity.

You, not your employer, bear the investment risk of this type of pension – if, for example, investments perform badly, your pension fund and the annuity you can buy with it will be smaller.

PUBLIC SECTOR SCHEMES

Most workers in the public sector, including teachers, the police and National Health Service workers, contribute to final salary pension schemes. But these are not affected by poor investment performance. Many have no pension fund. Instead employees' pensions are paid out of tax revenues.

WHEN A FINAL SALARY SCHEME CLOSES

Final salary schemes can be expensive for employers to run when the stock market falls, decreasing returns on investments. Employers may then close their schemes to new members or to new contributions from existing members.

In extreme cases, the scheme may be wound up. Employees may then be invited to join a money purchase scheme (see panel, opposite).

What if a final salary scheme closes?

In this case, employees' rights are protected by law. The pension fund must be used to pay the following benefits:

● Members who have already retired when the scheme closes are entitled to the full pension they have built up.

● Members who have not yet retired when the scheme closes are entitled to a pension, but not at the full rate. They can claim the same pension that an early leaver (someone who left the scheme before retirement) would have received under the scheme. This depends on factors such as length of service – for advice, consult the Office of the Pensions Advisory Service (OPAS) ▶⌂.

What happens if there is a shortfall?

If there is too little in the pension fund to pay all the promised benefits, the employer, if still in business, must make up the shortfall.

But if the employer has ceased trading, there is usually no way of making up the shortfall, and the pension fund is used to pay benefits in a strict order of priority:

1 The extra benefits due to members who have paid additional voluntary contributions (AVCs; see opposite) are paid first.

2 Pensions are then paid to members who have already retired.

3 Any remaining funds are shared out to meet the rights of members who have not retired.

Is there no compensation?

Members who are close to retirement and so have little time to make good any losses may be seriously affected by a shortfall. If it is because of poor investment performance, they have no redress.

But if it results from dishonest practices, you can phone or write to the Pensions Compensation Board ▶⌂, which was set up to award compensation and has the power to make good the bulk of the loss.

HOW TO COMPLAIN

If you are concerned that your occupational pension scheme is being run negligently and that this could put the scheme at risk, contact the Occupational Pensions Regulatory Authority (OPRA) ▶⌂. This is the UK regulator of pension schemes offered by employers. It can investigate and can take schemes that break pensions law to court.

If your concern relates to your own benefits under the scheme:

1 Contact your pension scheme trustees directly or through the person in your company who is responsible for the pension scheme (ask in the accounts department). Trustees must have a system for dealing with complaints.

2 If you are not happy with the trustees' response, take your complaint to the Office of the Pensions Advisory Service (OPAS) ▶⌂, a government organisation that gives advice on any aspect of occupational pensions.

3 If OPAS cannot help, contact the Pensions Ombudsman ▶⌂ (you can download a form from its web site). Decisions of the ombudsman are binding on you and the pension scheme, so you give up the right to take your complaint to court.

4 Alternatively, you can bypass the ombudsman and take your case directly to court. Contact the Law Society ▶⌂ for a list of solicitors who are experienced in complaints about pensions.

165

When a company pension scheme closes

Q I've had a letter from my company pension scheme manager saying that the scheme is closing. The rights I've built up will be preserved, but they look a lot less than I'd expected them to be. I'm told that my contributions will now go to a new scheme. Can my employer do that?

A Yes, your employer can close the company pension scheme (also called an occupational scheme) into which you have been making regular payments from your salary, and set up a new scheme into which it can direct future contributions (see feature, pp164-165).

Employers with more than five employees must by law offer employees access to a company pension scheme. The employer does not have to run the scheme – it could be managed by an insurance company, for example.

Your employment contract may specify that you can join a company pension scheme, but it is unlikely to tie your employer to providing a particular type of scheme or to maintaining any scheme indefinitely.

Contact the Office of the Pensions Advisory Service (OPAS) ▶ ⌨. It can give you advice and information on all aspects of company pension schemes.

Keeping to the terms of the insurance

Q My insurance company is refusing to meet my claim for property stolen during a recent break-in. It says that a term in the policy stipulates that locks are used on all the ground-floor doors and windows. On the night of the burglary the thieves got in by forcing a window that I'd forgotten to lock. Can the company reject my claim on these grounds?

A Yes. If you have not kept to the terms of the insurance and that failure is relevant to the claim – as in this case – the insurer will normally be justified in rejecting the claim.

The position would be different if the failure was not relevant to the particular claim – for example, you forgot to lock the window, but the thieves got in and out of the property some other way.

When a policy contains terms that are unusual or 'onerous' (see box, p21), the code of practice of the Association of British Insurers ▶ ⌨ requires the insurer to draw the terms to your attention before you take out the policy.

If the insurance company did not do this, you might have grounds to challenge its decision. Similar rules apply if you bought the policy through a broker or other adviser such as an accountant or bank.

CHANGES TO THE LAW

Most insurance companies are regulated by the General Insurance Standards Council (GISC), an independent organisation whose members must comply with a Private Customer Code. Others are regulated by the Financial Services Authority (FSA; see box, p157).

But from January 15, 2005, all insurance advisers and brokers will be regulated by the FSA. They will follow its code of practice, operate a complaints procedure, and be members of the Financial Ombudsman Service (see box, p141).

ACTION PLAN

1 If the term in the contract relating to the locks on doors and windows was not explained to you, complain in writing to the insurer ▶ ✍, and ask for your claim to be met in full.

2 If the insurer disputes your argument, ask to make a formal complaint through the company's official complaints procedure.

3 If the insurer still refuses to accept your argument or does not reply within eight weeks, contact the company to check whether it is regulated by the Financial Services Authority (FSA) ▶ 📖 or the General Insurance Standards Council (GISC) ▶ 📖, or is a member of Lloyd's ▶ 📖. If it is regulated by one of these bodies, report it to the organisation concerned.

4 If the regulatory body agrees that the term should have been brought to your attention, it can recommend that the insurer accepts your claim in full.

5 If the insurer is unregulated and has no formal complaints procedure, seek advice from a solicitor (see p20) or your local Citizens Advice Bureau ▶ 📖 or Law Centre ▶ 📖 about taking your claim against the insurer to court.

Undisclosed information in an insurance claim

Q **My car insurance company has refused to settle my claim and has cancelled my policy because I failed to mention a speeding charge for which I received penalty points on my driving licence. Can it do that?**

A Probably, because your contract with the insurer requires that you disclose all 'material facts' when you apply for insurance. These are anything that is likely to affect the insurer's decision about whether to cover you and at what price.

The questions on the proposal form help the insurer to gather this information, but you must also disclose any other details if they could be relevant. Almost all proposal forms ask whether you have had any convictions within, say, the past five years. So you should have been aware that your insurer needed to know about the speeding charge.

In such cases, the guidelines of the Financial Ombudsman Service (see p141) state that if you deliberately withheld information, your insurer can:
- refuse claims
- cancel the policy to the day it started
- try to recover money paid out under the policy for previous claims.

You can take your complaint to the ombudsman, who will look at the following factors:
- whether the insurer made it clear that such information was required
- the degree to which you should have been aware of these facts
- whether cover would have been offered if you had disclosed it
- whether the claim is related to the details you did not disclose.

GOLDEN RULE

When you renew an insurance policy, you usually do not have to fill out a new proposal form. But you must still tell your insurer about any changes that could affect your cover or the premium you pay. For instance, if you are renewing your car insurance and you have been involved in an accident, or if you are renewing house insurance and there has been subsidence locally, you must inform your insurer or you may find you are not covered.

What is excluded from a motor policy

Q **My car was stolen while I was closing my garage doors. I was only away from it for a few seconds, but my insurer has turned down my claim because my policy excludes theft when the keys are left in an unattended vehicle. Can the insurer do that?**

A Possibly. Most car insurance policies have this exclusion, which, if strictly interpreted, would rule out even a claim for a car that was hijacked as you drove it.

But the courts have considered similar cases and ruled that for a car to be 'unattended', it must be impossible for you to keep it under observation or to interfere with any attempt to steal it. If, for example, you turned your back on your car for a few seconds to open the garage it would not be 'unattended'. In these situations, insurers have been told they must meet the claim.

The Financial Ombudsman Service (see box, p141) has said that it would also take into account factors such as the neighbourhood – in some areas you might need to be more vigilant than others – and the length of time you expect to be away from the car.

ACTION PLAN

1 Write to your insurer explaining that you could not watch the car while you quickly opened the garage ▶ ✍. Point out that in similar cases the Financial Ombudsman has told insurers to meet the claim. Ask to complain through the company's complaints procedure.

2 If the insurer will not pay, take your case to the Financial Ombudsman Service (see box, p141).

Holiday insurance health risk

Q **I booked a holiday through a travel agent and bought the insurance that came with it. At the last minute I had to cancel because I had a severe asthma attack. The insurers refuse to refund the cost of the holiday because they say claims related to my asthma are excluded. I didn't know about the exclusion, so can they do that?**

A Yes, but you may be able to challenge the decision on the grounds that the exclusion was not explained to you (see box, left).

Travel insurers do not check each policy holder before offering cover and deciding the price. You buy a standard policy and the insurer relies on exclusions to weed out claims it is not prepared to cover. Such policies usually exclude claims resulting from 'pre-existing conditions' – health problems you already have, or had in, say, the past five years.

It is your responsibility to read the documents carefully to make sure that any such clauses will not affect a future claim. It is also your responsibility to disclose any facts which might be relevant to the terms of the policy, such as asthma attacks.

If you signed the insurance proposal form and it included the exclusion clause about health, you may not have any grounds for complaint, unless you feel it was not made clear to you at the time.

If you declare a pre-existing condition, the insurer may:
• charge you extra for cover
• impose a moratorium – that is, a blanket exclusion on any claim related to it until you have been free of it for two years.

ACTION PLAN

1 If you were not warned about the exclusion, write to the insurer ▸✍ saying that the exclusion was not explained to you as required by the Association of British Insurers ▸📖 and the Financial Services Authority (FSA; see box, p157). Ask for a refund of the cost of your holiday.

2 If your insurer refuses, take your complaint to its regulatory body – the Financial Services Authority (FSA) ▸📖, the General Insurance Standards Council (GISC) ▸📖 or Lloyd's ▸📖.

Increased premium for medical cover

Q I've just had my renewal form for private medical insurance and the premium is 25 per cent higher. Can the company do that without telling me in advance?

A Yes. You have no automatic right to be offered insurance cover or to be offered cover at a particular price. Many insurance contracts, including private medical insurance, run for a year.

Each time you renew, you make a new contract and the insurer can offer the insurance on different terms and at a new price. All you can do if you do not want to pay the higher premium is seek cover elsewhere.

Poor health is a reason for refusing insurance

Q I've been refused cover for life insurance because I'm HIV-positive. Can insurers do that?

A Yes. Insurers base cover and premiums on an assessment of how likely you are to make a claim.

If you are HIV-positive, this will affect the risk of you claiming against any policy that covers death or health problems. The same would be true of someone with, say, terminal cancer.

Some insurers will offer cover, but it may not be on the same terms as for non-HIV-positive people – premiums may be significantly higher. For help, contact the National AIDS Trust ▸📖.

Generally, unless there is evidence (as with HIV) to suggest that someone has a higher risk of claiming, insurers must offer people with health conditions or disabilities insurance on the same terms as others. For example, someone with a history of stress-related illness, but who has been free of symptoms for several years, should not be refused cover or made to pay a higher premium.

Do I have to pay the solicitor's fees?

Q My solicitor's bill has just arrived. It was a relatively small matter, which didn't involve going to court, and when I first saw the solicitor, she estimated that I'd have to pay around £350. But the bill she has submitted is almost double that amount. Can she do that?

A Yes. But you may be able to get the bill reduced. Under the Supply of Goods and Services Act 1982 (see p53), the solicitor should charge no more than is reasonable for the work done.

As the work did not involve going to court, you can have the bill reviewed free of charge by the Office for the Supervision of Solicitors (OSS; see box, p170). The review usually takes about three months, and if you and your solicitor have agreed a fair fee by the end of it, the OSS will issue a 'remuneration certificate' detailing how much you must pay.

If the work had involved court action, you could have had the ▸

solicitor's bill assessed by the courts. For this you would usually have to pay court costs, so it would not be worth doing if the amount involved was small. For more information, contact the Supreme Court Costs Office ▶ 🕮.

ACTION PLAN

1 Write to the solicitor, asking for the charges to be explained and justified, and for the bill to be reduced by how much it exceeded the original estimate.

2 If your solicitor disagrees with your request, ask her in writing to apply to the Office for the Supervision of Solicitors (OSS; see box, left) for a remuneration certificate. You must do this within one month of receiving the bill.

3 The solicitor will send the application form to you to add your comments. Return it promptly.

4 The OSS will send an assessment of the fee to you and the solicitor. You can ask for a reassessment if you disagree.

5 When both parties have agreed to a fee, the OSS will send a remuneration certificate. You must now pay your solicitor the amount on the certificate, deducting any part-payment you made.

Compensation for a solicitor's poor service

Q My solicitor is supposed to be helping me take legal action about my faulty central-heating system, but he hasn't reported any progress for some time now and he doesn't reply to my phone calls or letters. Can he treat me like this?

A No. You should make a formal complaint to the solicitor's office. This kind of treatment contravenes the detailed 'practice rules' (governing solicitors' conduct) and 'client's charter' (principles on customer care) issued by the Law Society ▶ 🕮. You can obtain copies of them from the society.

If you complain and the matter is not dealt with to your satisfaction, you are

---

COMPLAINING ABOUT LEGAL SERVICES

The regulatory bodies for the legal professions operate a free procedure allowing the public to complain about unnecessary delays, poor-quality work or discourtesy. They do not handle complaints about negligence or money owed to clients – in these instances, contact the Law Society for the name of an independent legal adviser. They also do not take on cases currently in the courts.

The Law Society ▶ 🕮 This is the representative and regulatory body for solicitors in England and Wales. It set up the **Office for the Supervision of Solicitors (OSS) ▶ 🕮** to deal with complaints about solicitors. To complain, first contact the helpline (0845 608 6565). Officers will investigate and help both sides to solve the problem. If they find a solicitor to be at fault, they can reduce a bill, award compensation (up to £5000 in 2003), and take disciplinary action.

The Bar Council ▶ 🕮 The governing body that regulates barristers and deals with clients' complaints. You should complain within six months of the problem arising by contacting the Bar Council for a complaints form, or downloading one from its web site. If the council upholds a complaint, it can require a barrister to apologise, repay fees or pay compensation (up to £5000 in 2003).

Legal Services Ombudsman ▶ 🕮 This deals with complaints about the Bar Council and the Office for the Supervision of Solicitors. You should complain to the ombudsman within three months of the problem arising, by letter or online at its web site. The ombudsman rarely investigates the original complaint, but he can recommend that the Office for the Supervision of Solicitors or the Bar Council should look into the matter again, or pay you compensation. He can also make a formal criticism of the professional body.

entitled to take your complaint to the Office for the Supervision of Solicitors (OSS) ▶ ⊜ . But be prepared to wait several months for an outcome.

ACTION PLAN

1 Find out who deals with complaints at your solicitor's office and ask for details of the complaints procedure. If your solicitor works alone, another firm or the local Law Society ▶ ⊜ branch may handle complaints on his behalf.

2 Make a formal complaint, asking for reimbursement of the cost of phone calls and letters, and any other compensation you wish to claim. You should receive a written reply within about 14 days. If you do not, send the firm a reminder.

3 If the firm does not accept your complaint or fails to reply within 28 days, take your case to the Office for the Supervision of Solicitors (OSS; see box, opposite).

4 If the OSS does not offer satisfactory reimbursement or compensation, ask the Legal Services Ombudsman to review the case (see box, opposite).

The hidden costs of changing solicitors

Q I was dissatisfied with my solicitor's work and decided to hire a new one. The first solicitor has refused to hand over any paperwork on my case until her bill is paid. Can she do that?

A Yes. If you owe her money, she can hold back your property, including documents relating to the case, until the bill is paid. You have several options:
• Ask the Law Society ▶ ⊜ to intervene. It may recommend that the papers should be released provided that you agree to settle the bill.
• If you are in the middle of court action and the papers are needed for your case, you may be able to get a court order for their release. Consult your new solicitor.
• Your old and new solicitors might be able to agree that the old bill is paid on completion of the case.
• If you do not agree on the bill, you could pay the amount you believe to be fair into an 'escrow' account. An escrow is money (or goods or bonds) delivered to a neutral third person and held by that person 'in escrow' – until a condition is fulfilled or a dispute settled. You can set up an escrow account with a bank and pay the money into it as a sign of good faith.

Shoddy court performance

Q The barrister who represented me in court had clearly not prepared the case and failed to marshal the evidence. Can I take any action against him?

A Yes. You should first discuss your complaint with your solicitor, who may be able to advise you about the conduct of the case. Your solicitor can tell you to which chambers (offices where ▶

171

groups of barristers work) the barrister is attached so you can make a complaint about the presentation of your case.

ACTION PLAN

1 Ask the clerk of chambers for details of its complaints procedure and make a formal complaint.

2 If you are not satisfied with the response, complain to the Bar Council ▶ 🕮 (see box, p170). If it finds in your favour, it can order the repayment of your fees or grant compensation.

3 The Bar Council cannot consider negligence claims, so if you think the barrister was negligent, ask your solicitor about taking legal action. Your claim may be referred to the barrister's professional indemnity insurer. If you and the insurer cannot agree, you should ask your solicitor about pursuing a claim in the courts.

A solicitor commits professional negligence

Q The solicitor who's handling my dispute with a builder about flood damage repairs failed to issue court proceedings within the time limit and it's now too late to sue the builder. Doesn't that count as negligence on her part?

A Yes, it is possible that in delaying proceedings your solicitor has been negligent. She must carry out her services in the time specified in her contract with you, or within a reasonable time. But negligence can be difficult to prove. You must provide evidence, such as correspondence confirming the time limit, and the dates and content of relevant phone calls.

Many complaints about solicitors are dealt with by the Law Society's Office for the Supervision of Solicitors (OSS; see box, p170). But the OSS cannot deal with claims for negligence. So in this instance, you will have to make an insurance claim.

ACTION PLAN

1 Write to your solicitor demanding compensation for the money you lost because you could not sue your builder ▶ ✍ and enclose copies of your evidence. The solicitor will refer the claim to her professional indemnity insurer. If the insurer thinks your claim is valid, it will make an offer.

2 If you refuse the offer and cannot reach agreement with the insurer, you can take your claim to court. Contact another solicitor (see p20) or your local Citizens Advice Bureau ▶ 🕮 or Law Centre ▶ 🕮 for advice.

Solicitors must avoid conflicts of interest

Q I've just discovered that the firm of solicitors acting for me in my divorce case is also acting for my husband. Can it do that?

A No. The Law Society's 'practice rules' for solicitors' professional conduct state that they may not act for two or more clients whose interests conflict or are likely to do so. Even if you had both given your consent, they would still be banned from working for you.

By breaking the practice rules, the solicitors are guilty of misconduct and you can complain to the Office for the Supervision of Solicitors (OSS; see box, p170). The OSS can investigate and take disciplinary action, but does not award compensation in cases of misconduct.

Work delegated to a trainee solicitor

Q I asked specifically for a specialist solicitor to advise me on a commercial contract. Later I discovered that my adviser was a trainee working for the solicitor I'd appointed. Can the firm do that?

A Yes. Solicitors do not consider it wrong to delegate work to a trainee, provided that the work is supervised by a qualified practitioner. As they progress, trainees are given increasingly more responsible duties, so if they are nearing the end of their training they may do most of the work relating to a case.

Solicitors have to follow a 'client's charter' – a set of principles for customer care, available from the Law Society ▶ ⌂. This says that you should receive a 'client care letter' telling you who in the firm will handle your case, and the status of that person or people. You should also be told if anyone new is brought in, or if anyone leaves.

Ask to speak to the trainee's supervisor and complain that you have discovered that a trainee is handling your case. The supervisor should explain and apologise. If you are still dissatisfied, you can make a formal complaint, asking for your fee to be returned. If you receive no redress, you can complain to the Office for the Supervision of Solicitors (OSS; see box, p170).

Assessing the work of a claims assessor

Q I broke my wrist recently when I tripped over loose paving. I've had a letter from a firm of lawyers offering to sue the council for me. The firm said it will take its fee from my compensation when it wins the case. Can it do that?

A Yes, but you should check that the writers of the letter are legally qualified before accepting. You may find that they are not lawyers but claims assessors. These are specialists in personal injury, but they are not legally qualified and so cannot bring legal action – they act as middlemen between you and a solicitor they select.

Claims assessors usually take a slice of the fee you pay to the solicitor. They also arrange insurance to cover your liability for the other party's costs should you lose the case. But the premium for this insurance is often high, and they may take, say, a 15 per cent commission out of it.

On top of that, you pay claims assessors on a 'no-win, no-fee' basis (see box, p299), which means they get nothing if you lose, but might take up to 40 per cent of any amount you win.

If you want to pursue a case against the local council, consult a solicitor (many also work on a 'no-win, no-fee' basis – see p299) or your local Citizens Advice Bureau ▶ ⌂ or Law Centre ▶ ⌂.

NOISY NEIGHBOURS

Play it softly when things get loud

Q Our neighbour plays his stereo at full volume at all hours of the day and night with the windows wide open, making our life a misery. We've asked him to turn the noise down but he takes no notice. Can he do that?

A No. Local councils have legal powers to combat noise nuisance (see box, right), but an informal approach may still work. You could speak to other neighbours who may find the noise a nuisance, and make a joint approach to the noise-maker. If your neighbour is threatening or violent when you approach him, you should inform the police. If he simply ignores you, you can contact your local council for help.

ACTION PLAN

1 Start keeping a diary of the occasions and incidents when noise has disturbed you, and any discussions you have had with your neighbour about the situation. Note down your neighbour's response.

2 Put your views in writing to your neighbour ▶ ✍, quoting instances of disturbance from your diary. Keep

KEEP THE NOISE DOWN

The Noise Act 1996:
• made it a criminal offence to cause excessive night-time noise – the Act defines night time as 11pm-7am, and the acceptable maximum noise level is 35 decibels, measured from inside the complainant's house with closed windows.
• gave local authorities the power to confiscate the music-playing or other equipment if the noise exceeds levels defined in the Environmental Protection Act 1990.

a copy of your letter and note any response to it.

3 If the noise continues, and your neighbour is a tenant, try to contact the landlord or the managing agent. Your neighbour might be in breach of the terms of the lease, in which case the landlord can warn or, as a last resort, evict him.

4 If there is still no improvement, find out whether your local council operates a mediation service (see box, opposite). Under this scheme, a skilled go-between tries to bring the two sides together to reach a solution. Council mediation services are run by volunteers and are usually free.

5 If there is no mediation service, complain to the council's public or environmental health department. Its officers can serve a noise-abatement notice on your neighbour forbidding the noise or restricting it to a certain level or time of day.

6 If your neighbour ignores the noise-abatement notice, the council can

RESOLVING DISPUTES THROUGH MEDIATION

Mediation, or 'alternative dispute resolution', can be used to settle disagreements ranging from large-scale commercial issues to divorce and quarrels between neighbours. The two parties who are in dispute speak to each other through a neutral intermediary, or mediator.

The service is offered by an increasing number of solicitors, mediation organisations such as Mediation UK, and by some courts. Most local authorities in the UK run free mediation schemes. Mediators are specially trained and should be registered with one of the bodies mentioned below. If you are dealing with a solicitor already, you should be referred to someone else who can act as

mediator – perhaps a solicitor from a firm not involved with either party in the dispute.

The process can take some time to set up, but mediation itself could be completed in a day. It does not prejudice future action through the courts or an ombudsman and is binding only when a formal agreement is reached and written into a legal contract signed by both parties.

Information is available from the UK College of Family Mediators ▶⌂, the British Association of Lawyer Mediators ▶⌂ and Mediation UK ▶⌂, any of which can put you in touch with a qualified mediator. Or you could ask your solicitor, council or library for details of local schemes.

prosecute him. The case will be heard in a magistrates' court and you should be prepared to attend to give evidence.

7 If all else fails, you could apply to the magistrates' court for a noise abatement notice to be issued (see p179). You would, in effect, be launching a private prosecution and it is advisable, though not essential, to seek advice from a solicitor (see p20) in order to do this.

A constantly blaring car alarm

Q My neighbour's car alarm has gone off every night this week and I'm losing sleep. I've asked him repeatedly to fix it but he refuses. Can he do that?

A No. The situation is much the same as with noise from a neighbour's home (see previous question), but because the source of the nuisance is movable, and there is no legal limit on how long a car alarm can continue, action is more complicated. As before, your first step should be to put your complaints in a letter. Explain that the

alarm is keeping you awake and that you would like it to stop within a week. This is usually enough to prompt a person to take the car to be repaired. If the problem persists, contact your local council for help.

Council officers will probably ask you to keep a log of when and for how long the alarm sounds – usually for a two-week period – before deciding if there is a sufficient problem to warrant action.

Dangerous behaviour that may not be illegal

Q **Our neighbour's children have air rifles and use them in the garden. We've found pellets on our side of the fence and suspect the children of shooting at birds. Can we do anything about it?**

A Yes. First, have a frank talk with your neighbour. If this does not do the trick, report the situation to the police. Your neighbours can use air rifles on their own property as long as their actions do not endanger you or cause damage to your property. If pellets are falling onto your land, you can complain.

Air rifles do not need to be licensed, but children must be 14 years old or more to carry one in the street (see Change to the Law, p180). If any damage is done to your property the parents could be liable if they have allowed their children to play with a dangerous toy that the children are too young to use responsibly, or if they have failed to control their children's behaviour. Contact the police or seek advice from a solicitor.

Also, shooting at wild birds – except for those, such as pigeons, classified as vermin – is a criminal offence. If this is happening, it would justify a complaint to the police.

Smoke from a bonfire fills the air

Q **It's impossible to enjoy our garden at the weekend as it's regularly filled with smoke from a neighbour's bonfire. We've asked him to stop, but he says he's within his rights. Can he do that?**

A Probably. Your neighbour is not committing an offence by having a bonfire, even if you live in a smokeless zone (where restrictions apply only to chimney smoke). Ask your neighbour if he will agree to have bonfires less often, or at times when you are not using the garden. As with other neighbour nuisance, start keeping a diary detailing when the problem occurs.

If it continues you could speak to your local environmental health department, but officials can do little unless the

---

COMMON WILDLIFE PROBLEMS

The Department of the Environment, Food and Rural Affairs (DEFRA) ▶🖂 issues information on the legal status of all wildlife species and advises on the measures householders are able to take to resolve problems. For instance:

• Wild birds, and their nests and eggs, are protected, but some species, such as pigeons, starlings and some members of the crow family, are recognised as pests and can be killed using certain methods, such as shooting or trapping.

• It is legal to kill foxes, but the methods for doing so – shooting, snaring or trapping – are subject to legal controls. If foxes are causing problems on

your property – for instance if they pose a health risk – call in a professional pest-control firm.

• Rats and house mice can be killed using traps or rodent poison. If significant numbers of rodents are present, the local authority must be informed.

• Moles can be killed using mole traps. The use of strychnine to poison them is not allowed in gardens.

A range of leaflets can be downloaded from the DEFRA web site (www.defra.gov.uk/wildlife-countryside). Further advice is available from the DEFRA Wildlife Management Team, contactable through the Wildlife Administration Unit ▶🖂 in England, and the National Assembly for Wales.

DOGS AND THE LAW

Dog fouling

You must clean up after your dog if it fouls public places, such as roads, pavements, parks, car parks, beaches and churchyards. If you do not, you could be liable to pay a fixed fine of £50 – or up to £1000 if you are found guilty in a magistrates' court.

Controlling your dog

• Your dog must wear a collar in public places with a tag stating your name and address.
• Local bylaws may stipulate that your dog should be on a lead in certain areas, or may ban dogs altogether from some places, such as playgrounds.
• It is an offence for a dog to be off the lead on or near a road.
• If a dog is dangerously out of control in a public place the owner or person in charge of it is guilty of an offence, whether the dog injures anyone or not. Penalties can include fines or imprisonment.
• Dogs must not worry livestock. A farmer has the right to shoot a dog if it is killing or injuring his animals, or is about to, and there is no other way of stopping it.

Dangerous breeds

It is an offence to keep a pit bull terrier, japanese tosa, dogo argentino or fila braziliero unless the dog is on the Index of Exempted Dogs ▶ ▱, a register of dogs of these breeds that the courts consider are not a risk to the public. Staff at the Index will answer general enquiries about dangerous dogs. If you want to find out whether an individual dog is on the Index, contact your local authority or the police.

Nuisance barking

Prolonged barking can be declared a 'statutory nuisance' by the local authority. The dog's owner has 21 days to stop the nuisance or face a fine.

Stray dogs

Local councils must round up strays. An owner has seven days to reclaim a dog.

Further information

• Your local council web site
• www.defra.gov.uk/environment/localenv/foul.htm
• www.defra.gov.uk/animalh/welfare/domestic/dogs

nuisance becomes serious – for instance, if it happens every weekend throughout the summer, or if what is being burnt gives off unpleasant or dangerous fumes.

You can take photographs or video footage as proof. The dog warden will probably then discuss the problem with your neighbour.

A neighbour does not control her dog

Q Our neighbour regularly allows her dog to foul the pavement outside our front gate. Can we stop this happening?

A Yes. By failing to clear up after her dog, your neighbour is probably committing an offence. Try to catch her with her dog in the act, and make the legal position clear. If this does not have any effect, speak to your local authority about the problem.

Most councils have dog wardens who can take action, but you will have to prove who is responsible for the mess.

No defence against a neighbour's cat

Q My neighbour says that my cat is constantly fouling his garden, regardless of the measures he takes to keep the cat out. Now he's threatening to take me to court over it. Can he do that?

A Yes, although any redress through the courts would be unlikely. He would have to prove that an offence has been committed under the Environmental Protection Act 1990. Pet cats are protected by law. They cannot be held guilty of trespass and it is an offence to trap, injure or kill them.

YOUR HOME, YOUR CASTLE

Neighbours from hell

Nuisance caused by a neighbour can make life a misery. The best approach, at least initially, is to talk to the person concerned to try to resolve the situation so both of you are happy. If you want to take a complaint further, you will usually be expected to have talked to the neighbour first.

Keep a diary or record of the nuisance. Depending on the situation, you should initially complain to the neighbour's landlord or the local authority, or you can take action yourself. If the nuisance you are complaining of constitutes criminal activity, contact the police.

NEIGHBOURHOOD NUISANCE

- Noise from loud music, animals, building work, factory premises or children playing or misbehaving

- Dumping rubbish

- Graffiti

- Smoke from frequent bonfires or barbecues

- Blocked drains

If the neighbour is a tenant, and the behaviour occurs in or near home

If the neighbour is a house-owner or leaseholder

Contact the landlord

Landlords can seek an eviction order against a tenant who is responsible for neighbourhood nuisance or antisocial behaviour – that is, actions likely to cause alarm, distress, nuisance or annoyance. Eviction orders can only be sought against tenants, not owner-occupiers. If the problem is not resolved by the landlord, contact your local authority.

If the problem continues

Contact your local authority

If your own attempts to reduce the nuisance fail, contact your local public or environmental health department, or environmental protection division. It is obliged to take 'all reasonable steps' to deal with your complaint under the Environmental Protection Act 1990, which covers noise and other forms of pollution.
- The environmental health officer may write to or visit the neighbour concerned.
- If this has no effect, and the officer judges the problem to be severe and persistent, he may declare the noise or other offensive behaviour a 'statutory nuisance'.
- The local authority must then issue a notice requiring the nuisance to cease. It is an offence not to comply with such a notice, and this can lead to prosecution.
- The local authority has the power to confiscate noise-making equipment.

If the council will not help

Take action yourself

- Mediation may work in some cases (see box, p175).
- You can apply direct to your local magistrates' court to complain about noise, although this will probably incur costs and is not likely to improve day-to-day relations with your neighbour.
- Before taking any action, write formally to your neighbour, setting out your complaint and giving, say, 14 days' notice of your intention to take legal action. Keep a copy of the letter.

178

CRIMINAL ACTIVITY

- Serious intimidation or threats of violence

- Damage or theft to your property

- Racist or homophobic behaviour

- Harassment or stalking

→ CONTACT THE POLICE

FURTHER INFORMATION

- Your local council web site
- The Criminal Justice System web site at www.cjsonline.org
- National Society for Clean Air (NSCA) has a number of leaflets of relevance to noise and other forms of pollution, such as *Neighbour noise problems – what you can do*. They are available on 01273 878770 or at www.nsca.org.uk/noise
For contact details for your local police force visit www.police.uk

Noise at night

Some local authorities may impose restrictions on night-time noise in addition to normal nuisance provisions, under the Noise Act 1996 (see box, p174). Powers under the Act include the ability to issue a fixed penalty notice and to confiscate the offending equipment.

Local authorities may have duty officers who are on call at night to go out and witness noise nuisance. They may also provide residents with noise-measuring equipment to help to assess the scale of the problem.

Antisocial behaviour orders

Under the Crime and Disorder Act 1998 local authorities (not individuals) can apply to a magistrates' court for an antisocial behaviour order (ASBO). An ASBO can be issued against anyone aged 16 or over, and can apply to an owner-occupier, a private tenant or a local authority tenant. It prohibits the individual from carrying out whatever form of nuisance has caused the complaint. If an ASBO is granted, any breach of it is a criminal offence, with a maximum penalty of five years' imprisonment.

- If your neighbour ignores your letter and you want to go ahead, contact the Justices' Clerks Office at your local magistrates' court and explain that you want to make a complaint under section 82 of the Environmental Protection Act 1990. The Clerk of the Court will advise you on how to proceed. A solicitor's help is advisable but not essential.
- If you are successful, the court can issue the neighbour with an abatement order forbidding or limiting the noise, and impose a fine. If you fail, you may have to pay part of the defendant's costs.

YOUR HOME, YOUR CASTLE

GRAFFITI • FENCES • HEDGES • TREES

CHANGE TO THE LAW

The Anti-Social Behaviour Act 2003, which comes into force in stages during 2004:
• makes it an offence for retailers to sell to people under 18 spray-paint of the kind used for graffiti
• bans air guns in public places and raises the age limit for owning air guns from 14 to 17
• introduces on-the-spot fines for youths aged 16 and above if they are caught committing acts of public vandalism.

Spraying graffiti may be a criminal offence

Q A group of youngsters has moved in next door. They keep spraying our wall with graffiti. Can we do anything to make them stop?

A Possibly. It will usually depend on whether the graffiti is seriously offensive, and on whether the young people or their parents own their home.

Your neighbours may be breaking the law if they paint graffiti that is racist, sexist or offensive to disabled people. If the young people or their parents rent the house or flat next to yours, you may be able to persuade their landlord to warn them about their antisocial activity. If the wall in question is yours, and if the youngsters are aged 14 (the age at which a child can be convicted of a criminal offence as if an adult) or over, they may be liable for criminal damage to your property.

ACTION PLAN

1 Contact your local police community liaison officer to ask whether charges of criminal damage are appropriate. If so, the police will decide whether to take action.

2 If the graffiti is racist, sexist or offensive to disabled people, also contact your local authority. It should send a cleaning team promptly.

3 If your neighbours are tenants, try to contact their landlord. Their behaviour may breach their lease terms, in which case the landlord may warn or, as a final resort, evict them.

4 If the wall is yours, consider covering it with graffiti protection paint.

Sudden appearance of an oversized fence

Q We returned from holiday to find that, without warning, our neighbour had put up a fence more than 6 feet high. It's ugly and cuts out a lot of light from our garden. Can he do that?

A No. A fence more than 2m (about 6ft) high in a back garden (and higher than 1m (about 3ft) in a front garden) generally needs planning permission (see box, p191), although the height limit may vary according to local bylaws and covenants.

First, check that the fence is on your neighbour's side of the boundary. The whole fence, including posts, should be on his land. If it crosses the boundary, that is a separate issue (see question, p183). Check any clauses in your title deeds that might put restrictions on the height of fencing.

Contact your council's planning office to check the local legal position and ask them to take action. They can write to

TREES IN CONSERVATION AREAS

Any tree, even if it is not subject to a tree preservation order (TPO), may be protected because it is in a conservation area. In that case the local planning authority must be given six weeks' notice in writing of any intended work. If you need professional advice about trees on your property both the Arboricultural Association and the International Society of Arboriculture ▶ ⌐ can supply lists of members in your area. Your local authority can give further information on TPOs.

your neighbour asking him to reduce the height of the fence. If he refuses, the planning office may take court action.

The hedge that's as tall as a house

Q My neighbour's leylandii hedge is now up to his rooftop. As well as blocking out the light from my garden, the hedge is making the ground very dry. I've asked him to keep it trimmed, but he's refused. Can he do that?

A Possibly not. The Anti-Social Behaviour Act 2003 gives local councils powers to intervene in disputes over high hedges (the measures do not come into force until the end of 2004). Under the Act, if you are unable to settle the matter with your neighbour, you can take your complaint to the council, who will decide whether to order the hedge to be trimmed back. More information is available from Hedgeline ▶ ⌂, a lobby group that operates on the Internet, or from the Office of the Deputy Prime Minister ▶ ⌂.

Old or landmark trees may be protected

Q I have a 150-year-old oak tree in my garden, which I want to cut down because it makes the garden too shady. I've now discovered that my neighbour asked the local council to issue a tree preservation order to prevent the tree being felled. Can the council do that?

A Yes, but your local planning authority will contact you, and you then have 28 days in which to send in your written objections to the order. The authority will take these into account

when deciding whether to issue a tree preservation order (TPO).

A TPO makes it an offence to cut down, prune, damage or destroy a tree to which it applies without the written consent of the local authority that made the order. Chopping down the tree (or deliberately poisoning it) could bring a fine of up to £20,000; even removing a branch carries a maximum fine of £2500.

If you receive a TPO, you will need the council's agreement for anything you want to do to the tree, unless it is causing immediate danger – but even then you will have to prove that the work is necessary for safety reasons.

For non-emergency work you must make a written application to the council, which can refuse to allow the work. Its tree officer will be able to offer basic advice. Similar, less stringent controls may apply to other trees in conservation areas (see box, opposite).

181

Tree pruned without permission

Q I returned from a business trip to discover that my neighbour had cut back one of my trees that overhangs his property and left the branches in a big pile beside my garage. Can he do that?

A Yes. If a plant or tree on your land overhangs a neighbour's garden, the neighbour has the right to cut it back to the boundary without asking your permission. Strictly speaking, he should also return the cut material to you (as he did), because it is your property.

Access needed to next-door garden

Q My builder is carrying out repairs to my house and needs access to the garden next door to reach the side wall. My neighbour has refused to allow him onto her land. Can she do this?

A No. You have taken the correct action by asking her permission, but since she has refused you will have to go to court to enforce your rights of access. First check the title deed of your property to see whether you have the right to enter to undertake repairs. You could also have a search carried out at the Land Registry to find out what is said about right of access to your neighbour's property. You will need to ask your local county court for a notice to be served to allow your builder onto her land under the Access to Neighbouring Land Act 1992. Seek legal advice before going ahead with this. The court will need to know when you want access and for how long.

Who pays the bill for party wall repairs?

Q There's an old brick wall between our house and the next property. It's in a state of disrepair and needs extensive work. My neighbour denies all responsibility and refuses to share the bill. Can he do that?

A No, not if the wall is a party wall as defined by the Party Wall Act 1996. A party wall is one that lies on the boundary line between two properties and forms part of the structure of both of them (see box, opposite).

ACTION PLAN

1 Get confirmation that the wall is a party wall. The title deeds of the house will usually say if this is the case. If they do not, seek advice from a surveyor.

2 Approach your neighbour again to try to reach a verbal agreement before starting formal proceedings.

3 Under the Party Wall Act 1996 you need to serve notice on your neighbour of the work to be done at least two months before the work starts. Simply give or send him a letter setting out what you propose to do, and when.

4 If your neighbour disagrees with the notice, you can agree jointly to appoint a surveyor to prepare an 'award'. This details the work to be done, when and how, and the apportionment of costs. If your neighbour fails to respond within 14 days, or will not cooperate, you have the right to appoint a second surveyor to represent his interests.

5 The Act then gives you the right to do the work, gaining access to your neighbour's property if necessary, and to take legal action against him for his share of costs under the award. Seek advice from a solicitor (see p20).

Asserting your territorial rights

Q Our neighbour's fence is a couple of metres over our boundary, but she refuses to acknowledge that this is the case or to give us back the strip of land she has 'poached'. Can she do that?

A No, as long as you are right about the boundary. Check the boundary on your house deeds, or on the Land Registry entry if the land is registered. You can get a copy of your entry and your neighbour's entries from the Land Registry ▶ 🖾 for a small charge. If the deeds are not conclusive, you may need a surveyor to do a boundary survey.

ACTION PLAN

1 If you believe your neighbour is in the wrong, send her a letter ▶ ✍ pointing out where the boundary goes according to your research or survey. Ask her to move the fence. Give her a deadline (say, two weeks) by which to respond. Keep a copy of the letter.

2 If she does not respond, write to her saying you assume she is in agreement and you will move the fence back onto her property if she has not done so herself within 14 days.

3 If she refuses you access to move the fence yourself, consult a solicitor (see p20) about what to do next.

Putting your neighbours at risk

Q I put barbed wire around my garden walls to deter burglars. My neighbour's son tried to climb in to retrieve a ball from my garden and cut his hand. His mother says the wire is illegal and she's threatening to sue me for her son's injury. Can she do that?

A Yes. It is not illegal to protect your property with barbed wire, but if someone is injured by the wire, you as the occupier could be liable to compensate the person, even if that person was not invited onto the property, and especially if the barbed wire was concealed or disguised.

One way to reduce your liability if you take any measures to keep out trespassers, such as glass or barbed wire along the tops of walls, is by putting up adequate warning signs (see box, p307). You are expected to take extra care if children might venture onto your land – even if trespassing. What might be regarded as adequate warning for an adult may not be for a child.

Force of use can become permanent

Q When I bought my flat, the lease gave me entitlement to a shed that stands on the boundary between the rear half of the garden, which is mine, and the front half, which my neighbour owns. My neighbour padlocked the shed door and has been using it to store her belongings. Now she says the shed is rightfully hers because I haven't used it for years. Is that true?

A Probably not. It depends on how long she has been storing her things in the shed without your using it; on the kind of rights you were given in your lease; and on whether she has made an official legal claim on the shed.

Under the Land Registration Act 2002, your neighbour may be able to gain possession of the shed by 'squatting' it. This is called 'adverse possession', and to gain it she must show that she has been using the shed and excluding you (for example, by padlocking the door) for ten years or more. She must also have applied to the Land Registry to have the legal title of the shed transferred from you to her. And the Land Registry should have contacted you and given you the opportunity to assert ownership. But she can only do this if you own the shed. If your lease merely gives you the right to use the shed rather than ownership of it, she cannot adversely possess your right.

Seek advice from a solicitor (see p20), who will check all the above conditions. If your neighbour has no adverse right, you can write to her to ask her to remove the padlock and her belongings. If you are happy for her to continue using the shed but want to safeguard your legal right to it, consult a solicitor about drawing up a licence agreement for her to use it.

Dividing a shared driveway

Q Our neighbours want to block a shared driveway by putting a fence down the middle. This would mean having to change our front entrance and enlarge our side of the drive in order to retain access. Can we stop them?

A Possibly. There are two issues here: ownership and rights of access. If each of you owns half the drive, and

---

OWNERS VERSUS SQUATTERS

The Land Registration Act 2002 sets out the procedure for squatters to claim possession of the property in which they have been squatting.
• Squatters need to apply to the Land Registry to be registered as owners of squatted property after using it exclusively for ten years.
• The Land Registry then contacts the existing owner, who has a chance to assert ownership.
• If the existing owner takes the necessary legal steps to assert ownership, that is usually the end of the matter.
• If the existing owner does not respond and the squatters remain in possession of the property, they can apply again to the Land Registry after a further two years to be registered as legal owners.

neither has a right of access over the other's half, your neighbours can put up a fence right to the limit of their half (the fence must be wholly on their side, which will reduce the width of their drive). They can do this even if it inconveniences you.

If each of you owns half the drive, but has rights of access over the other half – perhaps the drive is narrow and you need to use your neighbour's half to step out of your car door – your neighbour cannot put up a fence that obstructs your right of access.

You can find out about rights of access over neighbouring land from your title deeds or Land Registry entry ▶ 📖.

Commercial vehicles parked on a drive

Q **Our neighbour owns a building firm. He regularly has several large vehicles parked nose to tail in his drive, and sometimes on the road as well. Can we do anything to stop him?**

A Possibly. The amount of business use seems to be so great that your neighbour's home might be regarded as commercial premises. The person to approach is the enforcement officer at your local planning department. He will first talk to both parties to try to resolve the complaint by negotiation.

If the level of business use is considered to represent a substantial change of use, the enforcement officer can take action, ultimately by asking the local authority to issue an enforcement notice ordering your neighbour to cease business use. He will be liable to court action if he refuses to comply. He has a right of appeal against the notice, so it could take some time to resolve the dispute.

If your neighbour is a tenant or lease-holder, he will probably be in breach of his lease. You should inform the landlord or freeholder, or the managing agents.

Causing an obstruction on the footpath

Q **A neighbour who works for a building firm regularly parks his van up on the pavement. As a result I have to push my toddlers' double buggy into the road to get past – and there's lots of fast traffic. I've spoken to him, but he keeps on doing it. Can I force him to stop?**

A Yes. Obstructing a footpath is an offence which can result in a fixed penalty ticket or a summons.

ACTION PLAN

1 Talk to your neighbour. Explain the problem and ask him not to block the footpath.

2 If this has no effect, report the matter to the police.

AND WHERE DO YOU THINK YOU'RE GOING TO PARK THAT?

ANYWHERE I LIKE!

BUILDER

Neighbours' building work causes subsidence

Q My neighbours have done some building work in their basement. I'm convinced it's causing subsidence in my house, as cracks have started to appear. Repairs could cost thousands. Will I be able to get compensation?

A Yes. If your house is subject to subsidence and your insurance is in good order, your policy should cover the damage. If it is decided that your neighbours' building works are to blame, your insurer will reclaim the money from their insurance policy.

Damage caused to a neighbour's property

Q My neighbours say their roof is leaking because a creeper growing against my wall has spread over their roof and forced up the tiles. I warned them months ago that this might happen, and suggested that they cut the creeper back. They're claiming that I'm liable for the damage because the creeper is mine. Can they do that?

A Possibly. You made them aware of the situation and warned them that problems might arise, so they cannot make a claim against you for negligence, but they may be able to make a claim against you for nuisance. You should talk to them and point out that you did all that was reasonably possible to prevent damage to their property. If they persist with their claim you will need to consult a solicitor. The creeper should be cut back to their boundary to prevent ongoing damage.

If you had not warned your neighbours, they would have a stronger case for bringing a claim against you.

Damage caused by a fallen branch

Q During a recent gale a branch from a mature tree in my front garden came down on top of a car parked in the street outside. The car owner says he's holding me liable and demands that I pay for the damage. Can he do that?

A Probably not, but it depends on the state of the tree. If the tree is healthy and the gale was a freak weather event, causing several other branches to come down in your district, then you are unlikely to be liable. If the tree is rotten, you are aware of the fact and have not done anything about it, then you could be judged to be negligent.

In either case, if the car owner has a comprehensive or third-party policy he should contact his insurer, who will take the matter up with you. If you are liable, the public liability cover included in your house contents insurance should pay. If you are not liable, your insurer should fight the claim on your behalf.

A new development floods homes

Q **A new housing development next to the bottom of my garden appears to have altered the drainage in the area, as water now runs through my fence and floods my garden. Do I have any right to redress?**

A Yes, but you may have a problem proving that the new development is the cause of the flooding. And you may find it difficult to establish who is responsible – the developer or the local planning authority.

The cause of the problem may be straightforward, such as a broken or blocked culvert, and this should be relatively easy to rectify. Should the problem continue, you will need to get expert advice from a surveyor on the cause of the flooding. If other properties around you are affected, this may help in establishing the cause. If the problem is widespread, it might be a case for community action (see box, pp188-189).

If the surveyor's report suggests that the flooding was predictable and that the development should not have been given planning permission, you will have to pursue your case with your local council. The developer may have cut corners or not implemented the stipulated drainage measures properly. If so, the council will require him to remedy the situation.

ACTION PLAN
1 Take photographs and keep a diary to illustrate the problem.

EXACTLY HOW BAD DOES THE FLOODING GET SIR?

2 Speak to the developer's site manager if building is still going on. Ask him to check whether there are any obvious causes of the flooding and if so to put them right.

3 If the problem continues, get an independent assessment of the cause from a surveyor.

4 Contact your local planning authority to inform them of the problem. Send them copies of your diary and photographs as evidence, together with the surveyor's report. Ask them to investigate the matter and let you know what action they will take.

5 If the council is not proposing to take action and you want to take the matter further, seek advice from a solicitor (see p20) about pursuing your claim.

YOUR HOME, YOUR CASTLE

The fine line between self-defence and attack

Q **An attempt was made to break into my son's house recently during the night. He grabbed a hammer, rushed downstairs, caught the burglar by the back door and hit him, breaking his arm. Now the police have charged my son with grievous bodily harm. Can they do that?**

A Yes. You have the right to use 'reasonable force' to defend yourself, but you must not use excessive force. There is no hard-and-fast rule as to what constitutes 'reasonable force', but generally when you stop being the defender and become the attacker you have gone beyond reasonable force. If the burglar rushed at your son with a knife and your son responded by hitting him with a hammer, that might be thought a reasonable response. If the burglar fled and your son followed him out of the house and cracked him over the head with the hammer from behind, this would be thought excessive.

The outcome of the case will depend on the circumstances, such as whether the burglar was armed, and whether he attacked your son or was already running away.

ASSERTING YOUR RIGHTS THROUGH COMMUNITY ACTION

Whether it is to save threatened woodland, oppose plans for a new road or prevent the closure of a village school, imaginative community action by energetic volunteers can bring results.

Clarify your objectives
Have a simple message and frame it as positively as possible. If you are opposing a new scheme or a closure, suggest some alternatives.

Get a team together
• You will need a range of talents: someone with people skills to lead the team; a good talker to develop contacts; a well-organised person to keep paperwork in order; someone with media experience to write articles and adverts; people ready to distribute leaflets; someone with financial skills to act as treasurer.
• Use all local means available to attract volunteers: local papers; newsletters; radio and TV stations; other associations.

Set up a formal campaign
Depending on the nature of your campaign, it may help to have a formal constitution, well-defined responsibilities and aims, and a clear process for running the campaign. Make it clear how often the committee will meet, who can decide what, and so on. A formal structure will show that you are a bona fide organisation and may help you to get funding or grants.

Do your research
• Make sure that you have all the facts about the subject of your campaign. Research the relevant laws and regulations.

If you are protesting about the action of a council or other organisation, were they acting within their rights? Did they follow the correct procedures?
• Have plenty of facts at your fingertips about your campaign and background issues. Is your situation unique? Is it the worst example that has been seen to date? Does it threaten a type of habitat unique in your county?
• Know what your own rights are and how you can validly make your challenge. It is no use putting a case to a public inquiry that does not address the inquiry's own terms of reference, or attacking a planning application on terms that are outside the brief of the planning committee.

Speed bumps cause excessive noise

Q Speed bumps have recently been installed in our street as a traffic-calming measure. They're very high and cause a sharp jolt as you drive over them, and revving cars make a lot of noise. Can we do anything to get the bumps modified?

A Possibly. Your local authority may not respond to an individual complaint, but if a number of people in your street feel the same way you may be able to exert sufficient pressure on your local council to get the bumps altered. This is a good case for community action (see box, below).

ACTION PLAN

1 Gather together any evidence you can: noise caused by traffic going over the bumps; damage to cars; injury or discomfort to sick or disabled passengers; tradespeople refusing to cross the bumps to reach your house.

2 Ask your council what highway authority is responsible for the road, and write to the authority explaining your objection to the speed bumps. Enclose any evidence you have collected to support your claim.

3 Encourage other people to write, and try to get local press coverage.

4 If all else fails, write to your MP.

• Find out about similar campaigns and link up with them for mutual support.

Let the community know
Be as proactive as you can with local publicity. This may draw in more volunteers as well as adding to the status and effectiveness of your campaign.

Get celebrity help
• Make contact with senior members of the community or local celebrities who will add weight, credibility and even glamour to your campaign. You could ask a well-known name to chair the campaign.
• Speak to local councillors, council officials and your local MP. Even if they cannot back you, they may supply useful information. A lot can be said in an informal conversation that could not be put in a letter.

Do not give up easily
Be persistent, bold but reasonable. Aggressiveness or exaggerated claims can easily damage your case.

Write letters
A letter-writing campaign can have a big effect. A less active member of your group may be happy to sit at home and write letters. Encourage as many people as possible to write supporting letters.

Use the press
Contact the papers in person, or issue a press release. Make sure you have a good story, not just a string of opinions. For instance, '82-year-old Mary has had to give up her Wednesday lunch club because she can't cross the road' carries more weight than 'The traffic's getting really bad in our area'.

Approach possible sponsors
Think about bodies that might help you, and try to get their support – cash or otherwise. For example, insurance companies have an interest in preventing flood problems and are lobbying government to set up flood-prevention schemes.

Use the Internet
• Use it to research council and government issues, to contact experts such as academics or the technical officers of trade associations or charities, and to find other groups like your own.
• Newspapers and the BBC have Internet archives of useful press cuttings.
• Set up a web site to give supporters information and make new contacts. A good local campaign site is that of the Cambridge Cycling Campaign www.camcycle.org.uk

YOUR HOME, YOUR CASTLE

PLANNING PERMISSION • PLANNING APPEALS

Restrictions on satellite dishes

Q I want to put up a satellite TV dish, but my neighbour says I'll need planning permission. Can the authorities insist on that?

A Yes, in some circumstances, although a single dish of moderate size on an ordinary house in most locations should not need permission (see box, below).

Before you buy a dish or sign a satellite TV contract, check whether you need a landlord's permission to erect it, and whether you need planning permission. If in doubt, consult your local planning authority.

Choose a design that will blend in with your surroundings (for example, a mesh dish may be less obtrusive than a white-painted one). Position the dish so that it is as unobtrusive as possible (and below the roofline), or the planning authority may require you to resite it at your own cost or insist that you apply for planning permission.

DISH RULES

• Planning permission is needed for a satellite dish on a house in a conservation area, a national park, an Area of Outstanding Natural Beauty or the Norfolk Broads. Permission is not needed outside these areas so long as the dish meets certain rules: there must be only one dish on the property and it must conform to certain position and size restrictions. Ask your local planning department for details.
• Different restrictions on dish numbers and sizes apply to blocks of flats, depending partly on the block's height, and to houses in conservation areas, national parks and so on. But again you may not need planning permission if you comply. Again, ask your local planning department for details.
• Listed building consent is needed to install a dish on a listed property (see box, p195).

Appealing against a planning refusal

Q We sent in a planning application for a conservatory at the back of our building. The council turned us down. Can we do anything about it?

A Possibly. You need to try to resolve the situation by negotiation with the council. Study the reasons for the refusal, which will be printed on the council's decision notice. It may be that minor changes to the design or size of the conservatory would make it acceptable, in which case you can re-apply for planning permission. The reasons may also show that you do not need permission at all.

As a last resort, you have the right to appeal to the government's Planning Inspectorate ▶ ☛, which is responsible for planning appeals. First take expert advice from a surveyor about whether you have grounds for an appeal. The Inspectorate will provide details of its appeals procedures, a Planning Appeal Form and advice on what documents to submit with the form. Appeal decisions are based on government or local authority planning policies.

ACTION PLAN

1 Speak to your local planning office about whether a compromise solution would be possible. Establish which aspects of the conservatory are acceptable and which are not, and what changes you need to make before re-applying.

2 Make the necessary changes to your proposal and re-apply for planning permission. If you do this within a year, you will not have to pay a second fee.

Fighting a music licence application

Q A nearby pub is applying to extend the hours of its music licence at weekends later into the evening. We have young children and we're very worried about the noise. Can the pub do this?

A Yes, the pub's owners can apply to the local authority for a revised public entertainment licence allowing them to provide music at different times. But as a local resident you have the right to object to the pub putting on late-night music at weekends.

In considering the licence application, the council has to take into account:
• the suitability of the applicant and of the pub buildings for music events
• the safety and health of musicians and members of the public
• the need to limit noise disturbance for local residents
• the council's duty to prevent crime and disorder.

ACTION PLAN

1 Find out from your local council who to write to so you can register opposition to the licence being granted.

2 Encourage neighbours also to write in opposition; or collect signatures on a petition registering joint opposition.

3 Ask the council if you can speak at the committee or panel meeting considering licence applications; you may be allowed a few minutes to explain your objections.

CHANGE TO THE LAW

The Licensing Act 2003 (in force from 2004) changed pub licensing for entertainment. Instead of having to apply for a liquor licence, a public entertainment licence and planning consent for late opening, pub owners and landlords need only apply to the local authority for a single premises licence.

WHEN DO I NEED – OR NOT NEED – PLANNING PERMISSION?

Planning permission is needed for any development of a property. 'Development' has a wide definition in planning law, including additions and extensions, alterations, conversions and changes of use.

When planning permission may not be required
Several minor household 'developments', such as porches or small extensions, are exempted from planning permission. These are called Permitted Development Rights. They apply only to detached houses, and are subject to certain conditions, such as height, overall dimensions, percentage of the total area of the house, and proximity to a road.

As a general rule (there may be local variations) Permitted Development Rights include the following features:
• an extension that does not project beyond the front of the house, exceed the highest point of the roof or cover more than 50 per cent of the total area of land attached to the house; or a conservatory
• a porch
• gates, fences and walls that do not exceed 1m (approximately 3ft) in height beside a road and 2m (6ft) in height elsewhere
• a hard standing or patio

• a garden shed or greenhouse up to 3m (9ft) high or 4m (12ft) high with a ridge roof
• replacement doors and windows that do not extend the front of the house.

Some local authorities use an Article 4 Direction, which withdraws some or all Permitted Development Rights for a property or group of properties. They are used mainly in conservation areas, but check with the local planning department before beginning any work.

Planning permission is or may be required for:
• an extension that is more than 70m³ (2470cu ft) in area or enlarges the house by more than 15 per cent; or more than 50m³ (1770cu ft) if the house is terraced
• a garage, unless it is attached to the house or less than 5m (15ft) away (check with your local council)
• most external alterations to a flat
• most external repairs and alterations to a building in a conservation area.

Listed buildings
Consent will be needed for all external and internal alterations and repairs (see box, p195).

YOUR HOME, YOUR CASTLE

PLANNING OBJECTIONS • PLANNING BLIGHT • CHANGE OF USE

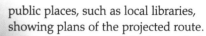

When to contest the building of a noisy road

Q **A new bypass is being built near our home and will cause a dramatic increase in noise levels. Do we have a right to object?**

A Yes. New main roads go through a lengthy process of planning and consultation, which may well take two or three years. The public have a right to comment at certain stages:

• Before a new road project goes forward several studies are commissioned by the local authority into the feasibility of different routes. These are passed to the Highways Agency, the body responsible for building and maintaining the road network, which produces plans for a 'preferred route', under government guidelines. This is taken to the public, using the local press and exhibitions in

public places, such as local libraries, showing plans of the projected route.
• There is then a consultation period of six weeks to allow objections and comments to be voiced. If significant objections are raised, the local authority may publish a modified route and hold further public consultations before deciding on the final proposed route.

If the scheme goes ahead, you may be entitled to noise-reduction measures, but you need to make your views known during the consultation period.

ACTION PLAN

1 Check the plans for the new road during the consultation stage and find out the deadline for comments.

2 Write to your council, giving details of your complaint. The council will not make a decision about compensation for traffic noise until the road has been opened but you need to register your objection at this stage.

3 Follow the advice on community action in the box on pp188-189. Be prepared to attend (and possibly address) public meetings.

Proposed road scheme devalues house

Q **One of several options for a major new road scheme would affect our house and might result in a compulsory purchase order. But we want to sell now. The threat to the house will affect the sale price. Can we do anything?**

A No, not until the proposed route of the new road is finalised and a compulsory purchase order (CPO) has been issued by the local council.

OBTAINING NOISE REDUCTION MEASURES

One of the studies made before a new road goes ahead will estimate traffic noise levels for up to 30 or 40 years ahead.

To combat noise from new roads, engineers may build in features such as embankments, or sink the road into a dip, or use road surfaces that combat tyre noise. If you want these measures included, make your views known during the consultation process.

Once a road has been open for a year, householders affected by traffic noise can apply to their council for payment for measures such as double-glazing, as long as they lodged their objections during the consultation process.

COMPLAINING TO THE LOCAL GOVERNMENT OMBUDSMAN

The Local Government Ombudsman (LGO) ▶⌂ is a free, impartial service designed to resolve complaints about the actions of district, borough, city or county councils. It covers a wide range of matters, including, planning, consumer protection, drainage, council tax, and fire and police authorities.

Types of complaint
• The LGO can only consider complaints about how the council has (or has not) done something, not, for example, about policy matters.
• To find out if your complaint is appropriate to take to the LGO, and which local LGO office to approach, call the LGO Adviceline ▶⌂.

Making a complaint
• Before approaching the ombudsman, you must first give the council the chance to sort out your complaint using its own complaints procedure.
• You must complain to the ombudsman within 12 months of the problem arising.
• Write to the LGO explaining your complaint clearly. You should not need a professional's help.
• The LGO cannot challenge a council's decision just because you disagree with it. The ombudsman looks for mistakes or delays on the part of the council, or a failure to follow the council's own rules or the law. This must have caused you 'injustice', such as a failure in getting services you are entitled to, financial loss, uncertainty or stress.

Remedies
• If the LGO decides in your favour, it might order any of a number of remedies. These can range from an apology by the council to compensation, repairs to your council house, or enforcement action on a planning issue that affects you.
• The LGO may decide to take no action if it judges the injustice concerned is minor, or the council is willing to put things right.

Further information
• The LGO ▶⌂ publishes two leaflets, which can be downloaded from the web site: *Complaint about the council? How to complain to the Local Government Ombudsman* and *How does the Ombudsman deal with your complaint?*
• If the LGO cannot deal with your complaint the British and Irish Ombudsman Association ▶⌂ can supply details of other ombudsman services.

Once planning consent for the proposed route has been given, CPOs will be issued for the areas where the council needs to acquire land. If people affected raise objections, a public inquiry will be held, and it may conclude that the road should not be built. If the route is confirmed, the council will proceed to purchase the land required,

A public inquiry is a lengthy process. While it is taking place, houses affected by CPOs may qualify as suffering from 'planning blight'. The blight rules are complicated and a surveyor's advice is needed. If your house becomes subject to 'planning blight', seek advice from a solicitor about whether you could serve (send or deliver) the council with a 'blight notice' to try to force it to buy the property. Councils can refuse to buy properties until the route is confirmed.

A change of use may need permission

Q My neighbour got planning permission to build a large detached garage on his property. He fitted it out with electricity and decorated it, and now his teenage son is living in it. Can they do that?

A No. A change of use (such as turning a garage into living space) is not allowed, but whether your local planning enforcement officer will get involved may depend on the precise details in each case.

If the garage is unchanged externally – its doors are still there, for example – your neighbour may get away with it. Seek advice from your local planning department.

193

YOUR HOME, YOUR CASTLE
PLANNING VIOLATIONS • LISTED BUILDINGS • CONSERVATION AREAS

Sudden appearance of a lurid exterior

Q A couple in our street have decorated the front wall of their house with a dramatic, brightly coloured mural. It's entirely out of keeping with the rest of the neighbourhood. Can they do that?

A Possibly. In theory, planning permission is not usually needed for external decorations unless the house is a listed building or is in a conservation area (see opposite). Restrictions may also apply in areas bordering conservation areas. Check this with your local planning department. You can check the house's title deeds at the Land Registry ▶ 🖿 for provisos about external decorations.

Changing the interior of a listed building

Q Our house, an early 19th-century former vicarage, is a listed building. Some years ago we made some improvements, converting a corner of our bedroom into a separate en-suite shower room. We assumed we wouldn't need permission, as there's no change to the outside appearance of the house, but a friend has cast doubt on this, saying we could be forced by the local authority to seek retrospective planning permission. Can they do that?

A Yes. When a building is listed the rules apply to all parts of it, internal and external, and relatively minor changes can fall foul of the rules: for example, if you removed some original ceiling cornice in the process of putting in the en-suite shower room (see box, opposite). Even changes that you might think of as repairs, such as re-roofing or replacing old windows, may need permission. So does demolishing an outbuilding or building an extension, or putting up a satellite dish or a central-heating flue.

You can apply for retrospective listed building consent, and provided that the work has been done sensitively the planning authorities will normally treat the application sympathetically. As a rule, they are less strict with Grade II buildings than Grade II* or, especially, Grade I buildings.

WORD OF WARNING
It is a criminal offence to do work without permission on a listed building, incurring stiff penalties: an unlimited fine or up to two years in prison, or both.

194

RESTRICTIONS ON LISTED BUILDINGS

A listed building may be glamorous to own, but there will be restrictions on the alterations you can make.

Types of listing
- There are three grades of listing: I, II* ('2-star') and II. Of the 500,000 or so listed buildings in the UK, 90 per cent are grade II, the 'lowest'.
- Listing applies to the whole property, outside and in, and may include features such as plasterwork, doors, staircases, panelling, and garden walls, terraces and other structures.

Regulations
- It is an offence to demolish, alter or extend a listed building without listed building consent from the local council. Offenders could be liable for unlimited fines, or imprisonment for up to two years, or both.
- Current owners are responsible for changes made by previous owners.
- Repairs do not need consent but may be considered alterations if they change the building's character – for example, replacing iron gutters with plastic, or slates with tiles.
- Once consent for any changes to a listed building is sought, further restrictions may be imposed by the council.

Buying a listed building
- Potential buyers of a listed property should consult the entry for your property in the council's central list (see below). This shows the key elements that are to be preserved. Buyers should also check with the council that any recent work to the building was done with the proper consent.

Applications for a listing
- Anyone can apply to have any building listed, even if they do not own it. Contact the Department of Culture, Media and Sport Listing Branch ▶ ⌂ and supply the building's full address, photographs and a location plan. This kind of 'spot listing' can halt insensitive renovations to important buildings.
- Owners who want to prevent spot-listing during works can apply to the local council for a five-year Certificate of Immunity from Listing. If the certificate is not granted, listing is likely to follow.

Access to lists
- You can see lists for your local area, and get copies of individual entries, at your local planning department, county council offices and most public reference libraries, or from the Department of National Heritage (see above).

Further information is available from the Department for Culture, Media and Sport ▶ ⌂ .

Changes to a property in a conservation area

Q **We've bought a house in a conservation area. Our plan was to take down the front boundary wall next to the street and remove a small tree so we could park our car off the road, but our neighbour says the council won't let us do this. Are they within their rights to stop us?**

A Yes. In conservation areas, planning applications are considered in the light of whether the proposed changes preserve or enhance the character of the area as a whole, and householders have restricted rights when it comes to altering, demolishing and extending their property. Consent is needed to put in dormer windows, external cladding and satellite dishes (see boxes, pp190 and 191). Councils can also restrict the types of material used, and can prevent you from removing a boundary wall. For more information, contact your local council's planning department or its web site.

INDEPENDENT PLANNING ADVICE

The Royal Institution of Chartered Surveyors (RICS) has a team of experts on specific types of problem who will talk through general planning queries with members of the public. Telephone 0870 333 1600 and ask for the Professional Information Team.

Insurer refuses to pay out for subsidence

Q **Some serious cracks have appeared in our house and have been diagnosed as subsidence, but our insurance company is refusing to pay our claim. It says that the survey we had done when we bought the house mentioned cracks, and because we didn't disclose this we have invalidated our policy. Can it do that?**

A Yes. When you take out a policy you have a duty to disclose all facts to the insurer that might be material to a future claim. The onus is on you to tell the insurer about anything that might be relevant, not on the insurer to ask you. Mention of cracks in your house buyer's survey, even minor ones, is relevant given that subsidence is a cause of many large insurance claims.

The insurance company will almost certainly take the view that had it known about the cracks it might have refused you cover, or restricted the amount it would pay out for a subsidence claim. So, if in doubt as to whether something is relevant, check with your insurer when you apply for cover.

If you disagree with your insurer's decision on a claim – for instance, if you think it is wrong in saying that you failed to disclose relevant information or if you believed the original cracks to be so small they were negligible – and you have pursued the matter as far as you can with the insurance company, you could try approaching the Financial Ombudsman Service ▶ ⌂. For details of how the service works, see box, p141.

Insurance value is not up to date

Q **Recently our house was damaged by flooding. Our insurer is refusing to pay out the full amount of the claim as the company says we were underinsured. We've been paying premiums to the same company for years and have never made a claim before. Can it do that?**

A Yes. Underinsurance is quite a common cause of insurance claim problems. Looked at from the insurance company's point of view, you are asking it to pay out up to a particular sum insured when you have not been paying a high enough premium to justify that amount of insurance cover.

If, for example, your house would cost £100,000 to rebuild if it were completely destroyed, but you have insured it for £80,000, this is only 80 per cent of its true rebuilding cost. If your claim for the flood damage amounts to around £30,000, the insurer will probably scale back the payout in the same proportion, to £24,000 (80 per cent of £30,000).

Talk to your insurance company. Most major companies will take some account of the circumstances leading to your being underinsured, and there may be some leeway in how they treat the case. But if you do not make sure that the

---

THE PITFALLS OF BEING UNDERINSURED

Insurers may deal with underinsurance in a number of ways:
- If you are underinsured by only a small amount, they may overlook it and pay your claim in full.
- If the underinsurance is more substantial, they may deduct the additional premiums you would have paid for full cover from the amount they pay on your claim.
- They may scale back the amount of the claim by the same percentage as the underinsurance.

insurance value of your home keeps in step with rebuilding costs – which may be higher than the market value – you are not entitled to full compensation. Some insurers automatically increase your cover (and premium) in line with average building costs (as tracked by the Royal Institution of Chartered Surveyors (RICS) ▶☜). Check every few years in case costs in your area have increased faster than average.

WORD OF WARNING

Strictly speaking, by underinsuring you have made the insurance policy – which is a contract between you and the insurance company – void. Yet most insurers will agree on a compromise.

Plumber's accident caused huge damage

Q **A plumber working on our house started a fire by accident with his blowtorch and caused thousands of pounds worth of damage. He says he's uninsured. Can we claim against him?**

A Yes, but the proper (and cheaper) way to deal with this is through your insurer. Your house (buildings) insurance will cover you for the damage even though it was caused by the plumber. If the plumber was negligent, the insurance company will seek to recover the money from him and may sue him personally as he has no public liability insurance.

WORD OF WARNING

There may be some situations where your house insurance does not cover you. For example, not all policies cover accidental damage to bathroom fittings – so if your plumber drops his hammer and breaks a basin or toilet you might be left with the bill. Check that anyone doing work in your house is fully covered.

Blacklisted by police for false call-outs

Q **Our house has a burglar alarm and we've set it off accidentally a couple of times. Now the police are refusing to come out when it goes off. Can they do that?**

A Yes. All burglar alarms should be registered with the police, who can strike you off the response list – meaning that they will not respond to your alarm going off – if there are too many false alarms. The number of false call-outs tolerated depends on the policy of the individual police force.

You may be allowed back on the list after a while, if you have cured the accidental call-out problem, but the timing and conditions imposed will depend on local policy. Discuss it with the alarms officer of your local force.

Bright light causes sleepless nights

Q **The house behind us has a security light that shines all night into our bedroom. We've had to move into another room to get some sleep. We've asked the house owner to turn the light off, but he refused. Can he do that?**

A Yes. There is nothing in law to stop someone from putting up a light, and light pollution is not covered by the laws designed to tackle other nuisances, such as noise (see box, p174). As a result, all you can do is ask your neighbour to move his security light somewhere else.

LANDLORD & TENANT

Rent Act tenant can stay put

Q **My elderly aunt has been renting from the same landlord since 1985. In 1998 he renovated the building she was living in and offered her an alternative flat in a modern block. He's claiming that she no longer has security of tenure because of the move. Can he do that?**

A No. Your aunt was probably a Rent Act tenant in the original property, with strong security of tenure (see box, opposite). Provisions of the Housing Act 1988 protect such tenants from losing their rights, even if they move to another property owned by the same landlord.

The only exception would be where there was a gap between the end of one tenancy and the beginning of another, in which case the new tenancy would probably be a shorthold one (see box, opposite). If your aunt went straight from her old property into the new one, she still has the rights of a Rent Act tenant, whatever your landlord says, and whatever the date on which she moved.

ACTION PLAN

1 Consult a solicitor (see p20) or your local Citizens Advice Bureau ▶ ⌂ or Law Centre ▶ ⌂ to confirm the status of your aunt's tenancy.

2 Write to your aunt's landlord and inform him of her rights under the Rent Act ▶ ✎.

3 If your landlord still will not accept her rights, seek advice from a solicitor. A solicitor's letter should do the trick, otherwise you may have to go to court to enforce her rights.

Dispute over type of tenancy

Q **I moved into my rented flat in January 1997. I thought I was an assured tenant with security of tenure, but my landlord now says that because of a technicality to do with the date on which I moved in, I'm a shorthold tenant with no security. Is that true?**

A No, probably not. Your landlord is almost certainly referring to the Housing Act 1996, which came into force on February 28, 1997, and made it more difficult to agree what are known as 'ordinary assured tenancies' (see box, opposite). But you moved in before that deadline, so the likelihood is that you do have an assured tenancy.

The only circumstance in which your tenancy could be shorthold, in spite of it starting before February 28, 1997, would be if:
• it had an initial fixed period of not less than six months; and
• your landlord gave you a Notice of an Assured Shorthold Tenancy before the tenancy started.

If no notice was served, or if it was served only after you moved in, you have an assured tenancy.

To be sure of your status, consult a solicitor (see p20) or your local Citizens Advice Bureau ▶ ⌂ or Law Centre ▶ ⌂.

RENT ACT AND ASSURED TENANCIES

Most private-sector tenancies, where a self-contained property – a house or flat – is let to an individual (not a company), fall into one of two groups:

- those governed by the Rent Act 1977
- those governed by the Housing Act 1988.

The Housing Act came into force on January 15, 1989. Most tenancies begun before that date were Rent Act tenancies, which confer considerable protection on the tenant. The Housing Act shifted the balance towards the landlord. This trend was reinforced by a further Housing Act in 1996.

RENT ACT TENANCIES

The main features of Rent Act tenancies – also known as protected, statutory or regulated tenancies – include strong security of tenure, a 'fair rent' that is often below the market level and the right of a spouse or partner to take over the tenancy if you die.

Security of tenure

The tenant can be evicted only if the landlord gives the tenant notice, goes to court and proves at least one of the following:

- the tenant has neglected the property
- the tenancy agreement has been breached
- the landlord needs possession of the property in order to use it himself or for an employee
- the tenant sublets the property without the landlord's consent
- the tenant is causing a nuisance to neighbours.

Charging a fair rent

The tenancy is subject to the 'fair rent' system. At any time during the tenancy the tenant can apply for a fair rent to be assessed by the local authority rent officer.

Once a fair rent is registered, it becomes the maximum chargeable for two years. This is binding, even if a higher figure was agreed in the tenancy agreement. The fixed rent does not have to reflect current market levels, and may well be below them.

Passing on the tenancy

When the tenant dies, a spouse or partner will become the tenant, with security of tenure and rent-control rights.

If there is no spouse or partner, another member of the original tenant's family can succeed to the tenancy provided that person was living in the property for two years before the death of the tenant. But in this event the family member will be an 'assured tenant' (see right).

ASSURED TENANCIES

There are two types of tenancy governed by the Housing Act 1988: assured and shorthold.

With both types, the tenancy starts with an agreed fixed period. The tenancy does not automatically finish at the end of the fixed period, but it becomes a 'periodic tenancy', which runs from week to week, or month to month, depending on the interval at which rent is paid.

The Housing Act 1996 limited the scope for creating assured tenancies, so that most tenancies agreed after it came into force on February 28, 1997, have been shorthold ones.

Assured tenants

If the landlord has served (given) notice and can prove grounds for possession under the Housing Act 1988 (see box, p211), assured tenants can be evicted.

- The rent paid is as agreed between tenant and landlord. There is no 'fair rent' arrangement as with Rent Act tenancies.
- When the tenant dies the tenancy can pass to the tenant's spouse or partner of the opposite sex, but no other family member.

Shorthold tenants

Also known as 'assured shorthold tenancies', shorthold tenancies offer no security of tenure. Shorthold tenants can be evicted after the end of the fixed period (provided it is at least six months), without any reason being given by the landlord, although the landlord still has to follow the usual possession procedures through the courts (see box, pp212-213).

- Shorthold tenants can refer excessive rents to a rent assessment committee ▶ 🕮 (see question, p202) during the first six months of the tenancy.
- Succession rights on the death of the tenant are similar to those for assured tenants.

Will the landlord allow my dog to move in too?

Q I had agreed to rent a flat from a friend of a friend. I have a well-behaved Yorkshire terrier, but the tenancy agreement states that only pets which are kept in cages are allowed. Will I have to give up the idea of moving in?

A Yes. If you keep a dog at the property, you will probably be in breach of the contract. A landlord who has known you for some time and is aware that your dog is well behaved may

HOW LONG ARE YOU IN FOR?

be prepared to give you permission to have your pet. It would be wise to get consent in writing.

A tenancy clause that excluded pet ownership altogether would probably be regarded as an unfair contract term (see box, p202), which is why the agreement you are being offered allows limited pet ownership.

Ask for a statement of tenancy terms

Q I live in private rented accommodation but have no written tenancy agreement. My landlord says I don't need one. Can he refuse to give me one?

A Yes. There is no legal requirement for a written tenancy agreement. On the other hand, it is in both tenant's

TENANCY RIGHTS AND ADVICE

In some cases it can be hard to work out what kind of tenancy – and therefore tenants' rights – you have. This is a simplified guide:
- If you moved in before January 15, 1989, you will probably be a Rent Act tenant.
- If you moved in between January 15, 1989 and February 28, 1997, and were not given any notice to the contrary, you will probably have an assured tenancy.
- The majority of modern tenancies, started on or after February 28, 1997, are shorthold tenancies.

Where to go for advice
The law on landlord and tenant matters is complex. If you have a problem it may be necessary to seek expert advice from:
- your local Citizens Advice Bureau ▶ 🏠
- your local Shelter ▶ 🏠 advice centre
- your local council housing service.

In an emergency – for example, if you get home at midnight and find that your landlord has changed the locks – phone the Shelter 24-hour helpline: 0808 800 4444.

Your local council may also have an out-of-hours phone line.

Who is a public sector tenant?

Public sector tenants are those whose landlord is a local authority.

If you live in housing association or housing cooperative accommodation, and your tenancy began before January 15, 1989, you are also a public sector tenant. If your tenancy began on or after January 15, 1989, you are an assured tenant (see box, p199).

What is a public sector tenancy?

There are two kinds of public sector tenancy:
• 'introductory' tenants are in the first year of the tenancy. During this time they have little security of tenure – the landlord does not have to prove a 'ground for possession' (see box, p211) to evict them, but does need a court possession order.

• 'secure' tenants have proved themselves to be responsible during the introductory year. They have strong tenure.

Secure local authority tenants also have the right to buy the property. They can carry out certain repairs and improvements themselves, take in lodgers without the landlord's permission, and exchange their home with another secure tenant.

Where to get help
• The Citizens Advice Bureau (CAB) web site ▶ 🖴 or your CAB local office.
• The booklet *Renting and Letting*, published by the Consumers' Association/Community Legal Service ▶ 🖴.
• For housing association members: the Housing Corporation ▶ 🖴 web site.

---

and landlord's interests to have one. It will protect both parties and make things much easier in case of any dispute. A tenancy agreement is legally binding whether or not it is written down.

If you are a shorthold tenant who moved in after February 28, 1997, you can require your landlord to give you the basic terms of your tenancy in writing.

You should ask for a 'statement of terms', which must include:
• the date the tenancy started
• the amount of the rent and when it is to be paid
• how and when the rent can be increased
• the length of any fixed term of tenancy. Your landlord is legally obliged to provide this information within 28 days.

When you can or cannot increase the rent

Q I've recently granted a shorthold tenancy on a flat I own. I understand that I can't increase the rent during the six months' initial fixed term. I feel

I have set the rent too low, and would like to raise it once the fixed term has elapsed. Can I do that?

A No, not unless there is provision for you to do so in the tenancy agreement. Under contract law, one party cannot change the contract terms unilaterally once they have been agreed.

There are, however, provisions under the Housing Act 1988 which allow a landlord to increase the rent if the tenancy has become 'periodic' (see box, p199). But they are complicated and you should seek advice from a solicitor (see p20). You would have to serve a notice on the tenant suggesting a new rent. The tenant could then refer the notice to the rent assessment committee ▶ 🖴 (see question, p202), which will determine whether it is a reasonable open market rent.

You may find it easier to terminate the current tenancy on or after the fixed term and grant a new one at a higher rent, which contains a rent review clause. The tenant would then have to choose between leaving the property or accepting the higher rent and staying on.

LANDLORD & TENANT

The tenant has stopped paying rent

Q I've granted a shorthold tenancy with a 12-month fixed term to someone who has recently moved into the area to take up a new job. She paid rent for two months, but has now missed one month's payment and is acting evasively when I try to talk to her. Can she get away with not paying?

A No. If she misses the next month's rent and has still failed to communicate, you should serve her with notice to end the tenancy.

Go to your local county court and ask for a notice known as Form 3, under Section 8 of the Housing Act. The notice must specify the grounds on which you are seeking possession – in this case Ground 8, which covers rent arrears (see box, p211). Once the notice has been served you will have to follow the 'ordinary possession procedure' (see box, pp212-213), because the alternative 'accelerated possession procedure' cannot be used during the initial fixed period of the tenancy.

WORD OF WARNING

Under Ground 8 of the Housing Act, there would have to be at least two months' arrears of rent, not only when you start legal proceedings against your tenant, but also at the date of the hearing. So your case would be jeopardised if she paid up before the hearing. Seek advice from a solicitor (see p20) or your local Citizens Advice Bureau ▶ ⌂ or Law Centre ▶ ⌂ .

Am I being overcharged?

Q I've found out that my landlord is charging a much higher rent than that paid by other tenants locally in similar accommodation. Can he do that?

A No. If you are a shorthold tenant and have not been in the accommodation for more than six months you can refer the original rent to your local rent assessment committee. For details, contact your local Rent Service office ▶ ⌂ .

There is no charge for taking your case to a rent assessment committee. The committee comprises two or three people, including a lawyer and a valuer, drawn from one of the government's six Rent Assessment Panels in England and Wales.

It will compare your rent with those of similar properties in the area and make a decision. The committee may inspect the property. Either you or the landlord can

---

UNFAIR TENANCY TERMS

A tenancy agreement is a consumer contract just like any other and is protected by the Unfair Terms in Consumer Contracts Regulations 1999. Landlords must be aware of this legislation when drawing up a tenancy agreement.

When is a term unfair?
If one of the terms in your contract is ruled by the courts to be unfair, that clause is invalid and unenforceable. Unfair terms may include:
• making you pay a large amount of interest on overdue rent
• giving the landlord sole say on how much of the deposit he can keep at the end of the tenancy.

In some cases, a total prohibition on something, such as pet ownership, may be considered unfair, whereas allowing people to do something but with conditions attached – such as allowing them to keep caged animals – would not (see question on dogs, p201). The wording of the agreement must also be in language which is easy to understand.

For further information, see the Office of Fair Trading (OFT) ▶ ⌂ leaflet *Unfair Tenancy Terms*, also available from the OFT's web site.

UNWRITTEN RIGHTS AND RESPONSIBILITIES OF LANDLORDS AND TENANTS

All landlords and tenants have rights and responsibilities known as 'expressed terms', which form part of a tenancy agreement. There are also other rights and responsibilities, known as 'implied terms', which may not be mentioned in writing in your tenancy agreement, but are still binding on both parties. Implied terms include the following:

The landlord
- is obliged to give his or her name and contact address – the address may be an agent's office rather than the landlord's own residence
- is responsible for repairs to the structure and exterior of the premises
- must make annual safety checks on gas appliances (see box, p207)
- must ensure upholstery is fire-resistant if the accommodation is let furnished (antique furnishings are exempt from this requirement)
- must make sure water, gas, electricity, sanitation, fixed heating and water-heating appliances are in good working order (and may be responsible for gas and electric cookers – see box, p207)
- may be liable for other repairs as specified in the tenancy agreement
- is usually responsible for repairs to common parts of the building, such as the stairs in a block of flats
- has a right of access to the property where there is good reason for a visit – such as for repairs or to inspect its condition – but must give reasonable notice (the notice required may be specified in the tenancy agreement)
- can usually increase the rent, depending on the type of tenancy (see box, p199), if the proper procedures are followed
- must give the correct period of notice in order to end a tenancy
- must in most cases obtain a court order before evicting the tenant (see box, pp212-213).

The tenant
- has the right to know the landlord's name and contact address
- has a right to get the basic terms of the tenancy agreement in writing from the landlord within 28 days if he or she asks for it and is a shorthold tenant who moved in after February 28, 1997 (see question, pp200-201)
- does not have a legal right to a full written tenancy agreement (a tenancy agreement is legally binding whether or not it is written down)
- must be truthful in statements made when applying for the tenancy
- must pay rent at the rate and frequency laid down by the tenancy agreement
- has a right to a rent book where rent is paid weekly
- is responsible for small day-to-day repairs
- must keep furniture, equipment and decoration in good order, allowing for general wear and tear, and must not damage the property
- must give the correct notice period to end the tenancy
- must behave in a reasonable manner, such as not causing a nuisance to neighbours
- has the right to live peacefully at the premises without harassment by the landlord or others (see question, p215)
- has the right to prevent other people entering the premises, except in an emergency or by arrangement with the landlord (see p215)
- in certain circumstances can pass on the tenancy to someone else (see box, p199), but will usually need the agreement of the landlord.

also ask for an informal hearing, which both can attend. Or you can ask for someone else, such as a lawyer, to attend it on your behalf. The advantage of a hearing is that it allows you to make your case to the committee.

If the rent assessment committee agrees that your rent is out of line with market rents in your area, it will determine the amount you should pay. The new rent applies for the rest of the fixed term, whatever the tenancy agreement says.

After the end of the fixed term, the landlord can use the procedures laid down by law for increasing the rent (see box, p199). But these procedures

▶

cannot be started until 12 months have passed from the date of the committee's assessment. Once the fixed term has finished, the landlord is entitled to end the tenancy using the correct procedure and to gain possession without giving a reason (see box, p211).

WORD OF WARNING

A rent assessment committee can propose a higher as well as a lower rent, so seek advice from a solicitor (see p20) your local Citizens Advice Bureau ▶ 🕮 or Law Centre ▶ 🕮 before you apply.

My landlord won't return my deposit

Q **I've recently moved out of my flat, but the landlord has not yet returned my deposit. As far as I'm concerned there's no reason for him to make any deductions from the deposit. Can he withhold it?**

A Yes. There are grounds on which your landlord can withhold your deposit (see box, opposite), but you are entitled to know his reasons.

ACTION PLAN

1 Check what your tenancy agreement says about the deposit. It may state when it should be returned.

2 Ask your landlord for details of the costs he has incurred which (according to him) justifies the withholding of your deposit. You are entitled to see a breakdown of the costs he is claiming, including any rent owing. If the costs sound unlikely, ask to see receipts.

3 Write to the landlord ▶ 🖎, stating whether or not you accept any of the costs he is claiming, and ask him for your deposit.

4 Failing this, you could take your landlord to court to get the money. For this you should seek advice from a solicitor (see p20) or your local Citizens Advice Bureau ▶ 🕮 or Law Centre ▶ 🕮.

Setting a sufficient deposit for a tenant

Q **My tenant has failed to pay the last instalment of rent. He says he expects the deposit to cover it, but he hasn't allowed for the cost of dilapidations and a number of outstanding bills. Can he do that?**

A No. The tenant is legally obliged to pay rent, and you can sue him to recover any that is left unpaid, although you may have trouble tracing him and

YOU SPENT IT ON WHAT?!

getting your money back once he has left the property. You can certainly keep the deposit, which gives you some protection from finding yourself seriously out of pocket. Seek the advice of a solicitor (see p20) or your local Citizens Advice Bureau ▶ 🕮 or Law Centre ▶ 🕮 .

When setting a deposit, choose a figure that is in excess of one month's rent. This allows for the cost of any repairs. On the other hand, the deposit should not be much higher than six weeks' rent, or your tenant might challenge it as an unfair contract term (see box, p202).

When the landlord will not carry out repairs

Q After waiting several months for my landlord to carry out important repairs, I feel that the only solution is to arrange and pay for the repairs myself and then deduct the cost from the rent. Can I do this?

A No, not unless you are very sure of your grounds. Withholding the rent without a cast-iron case could put you in danger of eviction by the landlord because of rent arrears. ▶

HOW TO AVOID DEPOSIT WOES

Before signing a tenancy agreement, make sure the terms relating to the deposit – such as when it will be returned and what it can be withheld for – are clearly stated. Both tenant and landlord can take basic precautions to ensure that disputes about deposits are less likely at the end of a tenancy.

What the tenant can do
- Make sure a proper inventory exists and go through it with the landlord at the start of the tenancy.
- If the landlord does not provide an inventory, produce one yourself and check it with a friend as a witness. Take photographs to record the state of the property and the condition of items such as furniture and carpets. Send copies of the inventory and photographs to your landlord.
- If you are responsible for any damage or breakages, report them to the landlord.
- Keep receipts for any work you have done or items replaced and a record of anything else to do with the property.
- Keep a record of all rent payments.

The landlord cannot withhold deposit money for:
- the effects of general wear and tear
- anything which has not caused the landlord a financial loss
- cleaning, repairing or replacing items on anything other than a 'like for like' basis – for example, you should not be expected to get rid of all the marks in a carpet which was already stained when you moved in.

What the landlord can do
- Make sure matters relating to the deposit are fully covered in the tenancy agreement.
- State the circumstances which may lead to the deposit being withheld.
- Give a time by when the deposit will be returned at the end of the tenancy.
- Make arrangements for any interest you intend to pay on the deposit amount.
- Include a clause in the tenancy agreement preventing the tenant from withholding rent against the deposit.
- Keep an inventory. Go through it with the tenant at the start of the tenancy and at the end.
- Check the property from time to time, by arrangement with the tenant, so that you are both aware of any damage which might give rise to you withholding some of the deposit.
- Do not return the deposit until the final instalment of rent and all bills have been paid.

You can withhold deposit money to cover:
- damage to the property or furnishings
- missing items
- cleaning
- unpaid rent.

You should do this only if:
• your landlord is clearly in breach of his duties to repair
• you have notified him of the problem in writing – always keep copies of your letters – and he has had a reasonable amount of time to do the repair.

ACTION PLAN

1 If your landlord is aware of the problem and has failed to act within a reasonable time, obtain at least three estimates for the work yourself.

2 Send these to the landlord and tell him that unless the work is completed by a certain date – say, in a month's time – you will have the work done yourself and deduct the costs from your rent.

3 Collect evidence of the disrepair. Take photographs. Consider commissioning a surveyor's report (see box, p222). Contact the environmental health department of your local authority, which will investigate your complaint and produce a report.

4 You could take the landlord to court, either to force him to make the repairs or to recover the cost of the repairs through a claim for damages. Seek advice from a solicitor (see p20) or your local Citizens Advice Bureau ▶ 🖂 or Law Centre ▶ 🖂.

WORD OF WARNING

As a tenant, trying to get a repair done could put your tenancy at risk if you have no security of tenure (see p199). The landlord may prefer to end the tenancy rather than make a costly repair.

Landlord is responsible for gas boiler repair

Q I agreed with my landlord that I would be responsible for repairs inside the house. Three weeks after I moved in, my gas boiler packed up. Will I have to pay for it to be repaired?

A No. Your landlord has a legal responsibility for gas appliances (except gas cookers if they belong to the tenant – see box, opposite). They should be kept in order and inspected at least annually by a plumber registered with the Council for Registered Gas Installers (CORGI; see box, p55). The plumber must provide a gas safety certificate.

The landlord should keep the certificate and details of any work done, and give you a copy of the certificate at the start of the tenancy and after every

WHEN THE LOCAL AUTHORITY STEPS IN

Local authorities have powers to take action against landlords when:
• conditions in premises are damaging to health or represent a nuisance (see box, p21)
• a building is in need of major repairs or is 'unfit for human habitation'.

Accommodation may be judged unfit by the local authority if:
• there is serious disrepair or the building is structurally unsound
• there is damp which could affect the health of the occupants
• there are inadequate facilities for preparing food, or inadequate washing or toilet facilities
• the drainage system is not working properly.

WHAT THE LANDLORD SHOULD REPAIR

Your tenancy agreement may have clauses about who is responsible for repairs. But these can be overruled by 'implied terms' (see box, p203), including the obligation to keep the property in good repair.

Whatever the contract says, it is always the landlord's responsibility to repair:
• the structure and exterior of the premises, including drains, gutters and any external pipes
• the common parts of the building, such as stairs in a block of flats
• electrical wiring, and water and gas pipes
• basins, sinks, baths and toilets
• fixed heaters and water heaters.

The landlord is responsible for gas and electric cookers, unless these belong to the tenant.

annual inspection. New landlords should have gas appliances inspected before tenants move in. If an appliance fails, the landlord is responsible for any work that needs to be done.

A property is unfit to live in

Q **My elderly mother suffers from arthritis and bronchitis. The basement flat she rents has become so damp that her health is at risk. Her landlord has refused to put things right? Can he do that?**

A No. Your mother's landlord is responsible for the repairs. If he fails to make repairs, you should approach your local authority, which has a duty to take action against him (see box, opposite).

ACTION PLAN
1 Make detailed notes of the problems which you believe are harming your mother's health and take photographs of the areas affected by damp.

2 Get a medical report on your mother's health.

3 Write to her landlord informing him of the problems ▶ ✍ .

4 If the landlord refuses to carry out the repairs, contact the environmental health department of your local council. It must investigate your complaint and, if appropriate, instruct the landlord to carry out the repairs. A landlord who does not comply could be prosecuted, and the local authority could make the repairs itself or re-house your mother.

WHEN ARE YOU GOING TO GET MY CENTRAL HEATING BOILER REPAIRED?

LANDLORD & TENANT

GETTING AN EVICTION • STUDENT ACCOMMODATION • REPOSSESSING A PROPERTY

Court appearance to evict tenant

Q **I'm letting a property under a shorthold tenancy with no written agreement. I've served notice on my tenant to leave, as I want the property vacated without delay, but he says I'll have to attend a court hearing before I can get him out. Is he right?**

A Yes. You will have to get an order to repossess your property (see box, pp212-213). This will involve a court hearing, which you and your tenant will both have to attend. The only situation in which the 'accelerated possession procedure', which does not require a court appearance, can be used is when there is a written tenancy agreement.

Responsibility for student lodgings

Q **Our daughter has just moved into a flat in the town where she's at university. The landlord lives in a separate flat in the same converted building. We're appalled at the state of her lodgings. Her room badly needs repainting and a tap in her bathroom leaks. The landlord says that none of these things is his responsibility. Can he do that?**

A Yes. Your daughter is an occupier with only 'basic protection' under the law because the landlord lives in the same building as her.

This means that she has few tenancy rights. Not only is it easy for the landlord to evict her – although he would have to get a court order to do so – it is also hard to make him carry out any repairs to the building.

With tenancies of this kind, the landlord is legally obliged to:
• maintain the outside of the property (roof, guttering, walls, windows and doors)
• provide a gas safety certificate (see question, p206)
• make sure that any furniture provided is fire-resistant
• give the tenant a rent book if the tenant pays on a weekly basis.

The tenant is responsible for most repairs inside – such as decoration and relatively minor plumbing repairs.

FINDING A GOOD TENANT

As a landlord, there are various steps you can take to increase your chances of getting a reliable tenant.

• **Ask prospective tenants to fill in an application form**
This makes a simple formality of taking down basic information such as name, current address, employment history, current employer, references, whether or not they are smokers, or have pets.

• **Take up references and check them properly**
References should include previous landlords if possible, or character references if the tenant has not rented before.

• **Check that a prospective tenant's employment is genuine**
Write to the employer yourself rather than accepting a 'to whom it may concern' letter from the applicant ▶ ✍. Check that the phone number is for a genuine company. Ask to see the tenant's last two payslips as evidence of income.

• **Do a credit check**
This will give you a guide to the tenant's financial status (see p153).

• **Have a proper written tenancy agreement**
This will prevent misunderstandings and protect your own rights as well as those of the tenant. Note that you cannot use the 'accelerated possession procedure' (see p213) against a tenant unless you have a written agreement.

For information on how to avoid problems as a landlord, see www.landlordzone.co.uk

SHORT LET

WHAT CAN A LETTING AGENT DO FOR YOU?

If you are a landlord letting property, using an agent can have advantages. A good agent will:
- have contacts, possibly including corporate clients
- deal with inventories, advertising and showing the property
- collect the rent
- make regular inspection visits
- arrange for repairs to be carried out.

The drawback is cost. Agents' fees vary hugely and Consumers' Association research has shown that their contracts can be unreasonable, for example, a requirement to give 12 months' notice to end a management agreement.

Use a reputable agent
Only use an agent who belongs to one of the professional bodies involved in the property market, such as the:
- Association of Residential Letting Agents (ARLA) ▶ ⌂ , which is the only body set up specifically to provide for this market
- National Association of Estate Agents ▶ ⌂
- Royal Institution of Chartered Surveyors ▶ ⌂.

All three bodies have their own codes of practice. They also support the National Approved Letting Scheme ▶ ⌂, which monitors and enforces its own code of conduct.

You should also check the tenancy agreement, which may specify other areas for which the tenant is responsible.

How can I get my house back?

Q Last month I granted a six-month shorthold tenancy to a visiting academic attached to the local university. I want to get possession of the house again at the end of the six months, but he says that he intends to stay and that he's not obliged to leave simply because the six-month term is up. Can he do that?

A No. Provided you give your tenant a minimum of two months' notice to end the tenancy at the end of the fixed term, he must vacate the property. If he does not leave at the end of the notice period you will have to take possession procedures through the court (see box, pp212-213).

You cannot get him out before the end of the fixed term, unless you have grounds for possession, such as rent arrears or if he is in breach of the tenancy agreement.

In some cases, tenants may agree voluntarily to end the tenancy when given notice. They may leave at the end of the fixed term anyway but do not have to give you notice that they intend to do so. If tenants leave after the end of the fixed term, they should give you written notice of at least 28 days.

Landlord proposes illegal eviction

Q My landlord has given me one month's notice to leave my flat. He says that he wants me out by the date he's given, and will change the locks on the doors if I haven't gone by then. Can he do that?

A No. There are only a few situations (see p212) where the landlord can evict a tenant without going through the courts. The situation you describe would be an illegal eviction and criminal offence.

If you are a shorthold tenant (see box, p199) and the fixed term part of your tenancy has expired, your landlord can gain possession of the flat without giving a reason, but he will have to serve notice requiring possession and then go through the proper possession proceedings and obtain a court order (see box, pp212-213).

Write to your landlord informing him that he is acting illegally ▶ ✍. If he continues to threaten you with eviction, seek an injunction against him from the county court. Consult a solicitor (see p20) or your local Citizens Advice Bureau ▶ 📖 or Law Centre ▶ 📖.

LEAVING A TENANCY EARLY

If you have to abandon a tenancy during the initial fixed period, you should:
• try to find another suitable tenant to take over the accommodation – this would have to be with the agreement of your landlord
• let your landlord know the circumstances and see if you can negotiate to pay only part of the outstanding rent.

Once the fixed period of the shorthold tenancy has ended, you will be a 'periodic tenant' (see p199). From then on, if you need to leave unexpectedly, your obligation to pay the rent will be for the normal notice period – usually one month if you pay your rent monthly.

Can I leave during the fixed period?

Q I moved into a flat in June but in July was seconded elsewhere in my job. I told the landlord I would have to leave in mid August, but he's pursuing me for payment of rent for a full six months, though I think he's since re-let the property. Can he do this?

A Yes. Assuming you have the standard type of shorthold tenancy (see box, p199) with an initial fixed period of six months, you cannot terminate the agreement before the six months is up. Your landlord may take action against you to get the money owing to him up to the end of the fixed period.

On the other hand, if it is true that after you left, but before the six months was up, he managed to rent the property to another tenant, he cannot claim money from you for that period.

Eviction of an occupier with few rights

Q My 20-year-old son has been living in a rented flat with his father. They fell out and my ex-husband asked him to leave. But, although the tenancy is in his father's name, it's my son who's been paying most of the rent for the past few years. Can his father still demand that he leaves?

A Yes. Since your son's name is not on the tenancy agreement as a joint tenant, he has few rights.

He is probably an 'excluded occupier'. This means that he is allowed to stay until asked to leave, and he can be evicted without a court order. Other

REASONS FOR TAKING BACK A PROPERTY

The Housing Act 1988 sets out lists of acceptable reasons, known as 'grounds for possession', for evicting a tenant after the end of a tenancy lasting for a fixed period. In theory, these rules apply to all tenancies governed by the 1988 Act – assured and shorthold (see box, p199). In practice, it is mostly assured tenancies that are affected. If a tenancy is shorthold, landlords can usually get possession after the initial fixed period without giving any reason, although they still need a court possession order. The 'grounds for possession' are divided into two groups: mandatory and discretionary.

Mandatory grounds

If a landlord can prove a mandatory ground, the court has no option but to grant possession. The following situations count as mandatory grounds for repossession:

- The landlord has at some time in the past used the property as his main home or can prove that the house is needed as his own or his spouse's main home. If this is established, the landlord has to give no further reason for possession.
- The mortgage lender wants to get possession of the property in order to sell it.
- The tenancy has been granted in out-of-season holiday accommodation, which is now needed again for holiday letting.
- The tenancy has been granted for the letting of student accommodation in the vacation.
- The house is owned by a religious organisation for use by ministers of religion and has, for example, been let on an interim basis between incumbencies.
- Possession is needed so that demolition or substantial redevelopment of the property can take place.
- The tenant has died. In this case the landlord can apply for possession within 12 months of finding out about the tenant's death, although this reason cannot be used against a spouse of the tenant who has succeeded to the tenancy.
- There are significant rent arrears: eight weeks or more if paid weekly, or two months or more if paid monthly.

Discretionary grounds

If the grounds are discretionary, the court may, but is not obliged to, grant possession. It will take into account the reasonableness of the case and possible hardship for either party.

The following situations count as discretionary grounds for repossession:

- Suitable alternative accommodation is available to the tenant on the same tenancy basis.
- There are some arrears of rent.
- The tenant is persistently late in paying rent.
- The tenant has breached express or implied terms under the tenancy – for example, the tenancy agreement says the tenant will keep the premises in good decorative order, and this has not been done (see box, p203).
- The tenant, or anyone sharing the accommodation with the tenant, has allowed the condition of the property to deteriorate due to abuse or neglect.
- The tenant, or someone living with or visiting the tenant, has behaved in a way which causes a nuisance to others in the neighbourhood or has been convicted in connection with illegal activities in or near the house. This ground is also available to housing associations registered with the Housing Corporation (see box, p201) in cases of domestic violence.
- Mistreatment of the landlord's furniture.
- The tenant was, but is no longer, an employee of the landlord.
- The tenant made a false statement in applying for the tenancy (for example, the tenant said he was employed when he was not).

excluded occupiers are those who share accommodation with their landlord or live in the property for a holiday.

Excluded occupiers must pay the rent they have agreed, or be evicted. Unlike other tenants (see box, p199), if the landlord imposes an increase, they do not have the right to appeal to a rent officer or rent assessment committee. Excluded occupiers have no rights to sublet or pass on a tenancy and may find the landlord reluctant to carry out repairs.

LANDLORD & TENANT
Procedures for evicting a tenant

A landlord cannot force a tenant to leave a property without following the proper possession procedures.

Even if you have a shorthold tenancy (see p199), which gives your landlord the right to repossess his property at any time after the end of the fixed term without giving a reason, he still has to follow the appropriate procedures for eviction, outlined below, and obtain a 'possession order'.

GROUNDS FOR POSSESSION

To gain possession of a property, the landlord must first give the tenant notice. If the tenant fails to leave on the due date the landlord will have to go to court to get a 'possession order' to evict the tenant.

Possession procedures vary depending on the type of tenancy, but in general the landlord must show that:
• possession can be obtained within the fixed term
• the tenant has been given the correct notice
• he has grounds for possession (such as shorthold tenancy or a breach of the tenancy agreement).

If the grounds claimed for possession are discretionary (see box, p211), the landlord has to show that the claim is reasonable. Seek advice from a solicitor (see p20) or your local Citizens Advice Bureau ▶⌂ or Law Centre ▶⌂.

GETTING A POSSESSION ORDER

The landlord can apply for a possession order by one of two different routes:

Ordinary possession (or 'fixed date' action) – this takes time and will usually involve a court hearing which the landlord or agent must attend. It is used mostly for assured or shorthold tenancies where the landlord wants the tenancy to end before the end of the fixed term. A landlord seeking rent arrears will have to use the ordinary rather than the accelerated possession procedure.

Accelerated possession – the matter is dealt with in writing without the need for a court hearing. A landlord can use the accelerated possession procedure only if he:
• has a written tenancy agreement with the tenant
• is claiming possession on a shorthold tenancy where the fixed term has ended.

Where to get the forms
The appropriate forms, and an explanatory leaflet, are available from the local county court or from the Court Service ▶⌂ web site.

WORD OF WARNING

If the landlord's claim for possession is dismissed – perhaps because the notice served was not correct – the tenant can apply for costs. If the tenant is successful in a counterclaim – for example, for repairs to the property – the court could award damages against the landlord.

ORDINARY POSSESSION
To gain possession by using the 'ordinary' route:

1 The landlord must serve the tenant with a valid notice seeking possession under Section 8 of the Housing Act 1988 (as amended by the Housing Act 1996). The notice must set out the grounds for possession that the landlord intends to use and must give notice of the landlord's intention to start proceedings. In the case of some of the grounds used, the notice period is two weeks; in others, it is two months.

2 If the tenant does not move out by the date set in the Section 8 notice, the landlord must submit the appropriate claim forms to the court and pay a fee. The court will be the one for the area in which the property is situated (your local county court will tell you which court to apply to).

3 A judge will hear evidence from both sides. The tenant may present a defence or make a counterclaim – for example, that the landlord has failed to make repairs to the property.

4 If the landlord is successful, the judge will grant either:
a possession order, requiring the tenant to move out within a specified time (usually 14 or 28 days); *or*
a suspended possession order, giving the tenant time to put right any breach of the tenancy agreement. For example, the tenant may be able to agree terms with the landlord for paying off rent arrears.

EVICTION WITH NO POSSESSION ORDER
Eviction without a possession order granted by the court is illegal for most types of tenancy, and can lead to substantial penalties against the landlord, including fines and imprisonment.

The only situations in which a landlord **does not need a court order** to repossess a property are when:
● the accommodation is shared with the landlord
● the property is a holiday let.

ACCELERATED POSSESSION
To gain possession by using the 'accelerated' route:

1 The landlord must serve the tenant with a valid notice requiring possession under Section 21 of the Housing Act 1988.

2 If the tenant does not move out by the date specified in the Section 21 notice, the landlord must submit the appropriate claim forms and pay a fee to the court. The forms ask for a witness statement.

3 The landlord must enclose:
● a copy of the tenancy agreement
● the Section 21 notice served on the tenant
● the notice of a shorthold tenancy if started before February 28, 1997.

4 If these conditions are met, the court will inform the tenant by post that legal action is being taken. The tenant can lodge an objection within 14 days of receiving the court's communication.

5 The case is referred to a judge. In some cases, such as when the tenant lodges an objection, the judge may refer the matter to a court hearing. If satisfied by the landlord's case, the judge will grant a possession order.

CALLING IN THE BAILIFFS
If a possession order is granted but the tenant still does not comply, the landlord must apply to the court for a 'warrant for possession'. The bailiffs then make arrangements to enforce the warrant and evict the tenant.

Who pays for ex-housemate's mess?

Q I share a rented house with three friends. We used to have a fifth housemate, but he left to go abroad. While he was with us, he damaged the paintwork in his room by sticking up posters. Now our landlord is saying that we must pay to have the room repainted. Can he do that?

A Yes, although it will depend on your tenancy arrangements.
• If all five of you were joint tenants, and the one who left did not end the tenancy properly, it is still valid and the one who left is still liable for rent and repairs. In his absence you will all probably be liable for any costs, and the landlord could keep your deposit.
• If you each had a separate tenancy agreement, each one of you is responsible for rent on your own part of the property and a dispute over costs should be between the landlord and the missing tenant.
• If only one of you has a tenancy agreement with the landlord and the others are subtenants, the responsibility lies with the tenant, who has to sort out the costs with the subtenants.

Mortgage lender can evict a tenant

Q My landlord rented out his house to me without the knowledge of his mortgage lender. He failed to keep up with his mortgage payments and his lender has started repossession proceedings. Can the mortgage lender evict me?

A Yes. If a landlord has a mortgage on a property and lets it without the knowledge of the lender, the lender will not be bound by the terms of the tenancy. The lender can gain possession of the property and evict you, although not without getting a court order first (see box, pp212-213).

Noise can be a cause for eviction

Q I own a flat which is rented out to students. I've received several complaints from neighbours about noisy music and doors banging late at night. Can I evict the students?

A Yes. Causing a nuisance is one of the grounds for possession (see box, p211) under the Housing Act 1988.
You can serve a notice on the tenants, then start possession proceedings (see box, pp212-213).

LETTING A MORTGAGED PROPERTY

• If you are a landlord letting a property which you are buying with a mortgage, you should make your lender and also your insurer aware of the situation. Otherwise you are violating the terms of both your loan and your insurance cover.

• If you are a prospective tenant, you should ask the landlord if there is a mortgage, and whether the lender's consent has been given for the tenancy.

• For a fee of a few pounds you can find out whether there is a mortgage on a property, assuming the property is registered, by contacting the Land Registry ▶ ⌁ (see box, p238).

When a landlord constantly intrudes

Q My partner and I recently moved into a self-contained, rented flat. The landlord keeps coming into the flat while we're out. He says he wants to check we're looking after the place. We find this very intrusive. Can he do that?

A No. You have a right to privacy in your rented accommodation, just as you would if you owned the property. Your landlord could be guilty of harassment, which is a criminal offence (see question, p389).

Your landlord does have a right of access in order to carry out repairs he is responsible for (see box, p207), but he should ask your permission and give reasonable notice – in other words, at least 24 hours. Except with your permission, he should not come in for any other reasons. The only exceptions are in an emergency or if you have an arrangement with the landlord according to which he supplies services such as cleaning.

ACTION PLAN

1 Check your tenancy agreement to see if it states the notice which the landlord must give before visiting.

2 Speak to your landlord and ask him to visit only with proper notice.

Remind him that you have a legal right to live undisturbed in the rented property.

WORD OF WARNING

If you have no security of tenure (see question, p210) there may be very little you can do in practice.

Challenging the cost of service charges

Q As a leaseholder of a flat in an apartment block I'm liable for my share of the service charges. The landlord is demanding an excessive increase. Can he do that?

A No. You can challenge an unreasonable charge, although not if you have already agreed to pay it.

Your lease will show which items you can be charged for. This may include some services – such as cleaning of the common parts and employing a caretaker – repairs and insurance. You have a right to see details of the costs being passed on by your landlord and the receipts.

If your landlord is proposing works which will cost more than a certain amount (currently £1000 or £50 multiplied by the number of flats in the building, whichever is the greater), he should get at least two estimates and notify you of this so you can make comments.

ACTION PLAN

1 Write to the owner of the property stating your views ▶ ✍ .

2 If you are not satisfied with the owner's response, consider applying to a Leasehold Valuation Tribunal (see box, right). For this, you should seek advice from the Leasehold Advisory Service (LEASE) ▶ ⌂ .

LEASEHOLD VALUATION TRIBUNALS

If you are a long-leaseholder and believe that your landlord has set too high a service charge, or the building is being mismanaged, you can apply to a Leasehold Valuation Tribunal (LVT) ▶ ⌂ either individually or as a group of tenants.

An LVT can rule on the level of the service charge and can also sack a building manager. It costs up to £500 to apply depending on the complexity of the case. A booklet, *Applying to a Leasehold Valuation Tribunal*, is available from the Office of the Deputy Prime Minister ▶ ⌂ .

Sellers have the right to gazump ...

Q My offer on a house was accepted and I paid for a survey and solicitor's fees. The day before we were due to exchange contracts the seller received a better offer and pulled out. Can he just turn his back on our agreement?

A Yes. You have been gazumped and there is nothing you can do about it. Acceptance of your offer for the house does not oblige the seller to go through with the sale, and you have no comeback.

In fact, an estate agent must pass on to a seller any offers received, even after a sale is agreed, unless the seller says he does not want them. The seller can also raise the price after you have started the necessary surveys and searches, but before you exchange contracts.

You can, however, reduce your chances of being gazumped (see box, below). For further advice on buying and selling a house, see *Using an estate agent to buy or sell your home*, published by the Office of Fair Trading (OFT) ▶ ⌂ . You can also download it from the OFT web site.

... And buyers have the right to gazunder

Q I accepted a firm offer to buy my house and the day before we were due to exchange contracts the buyer said she would only go ahead if I dropped the price by £10,000. Can she do that?

A Yes, neither buyer nor seller is legally committed until contracts are exchanged. Your buyer's action is called 'gazundering', and it is the buyer's answer to gazumping. Being a victim of either can be very frustrating because you have usually incurred costs associated with the transaction, perhaps with others in a buying chain. Gazundering typically occurs in a depressed property market when buyers have the upper hand. It may also be used if a buyer finds an alternative property, or if a survey has revealed problems with a property that the buyer will have to pay to put right.

The new home information pack (see box, p219) is intended to make house purchase more simple and reduce gazumping and gazundering. But how effective this will be is doubtful because neither practice will be illegal.

DODGING GAZUMPERS

• Apply in advance for a mortgage certificate – a document from the lenders, stating that they are prepared to give you a mortgage, so long as the valuation of the house turns out to be satisfactory – and find a solicitor. This will help you to push the sale through fast, which may enable you to dodge gazumping.
• Only use estate agents who are members of the National Association of Estate Agents (NAEA; see box, opposite) ▶ ⌂ . Its code of practice obliges agents to tell the buyer if the seller keeps the property on the market after the offer is accepted and if other offers are made.
• Try to use the schemes run by the NAEA and the Royal Institution of Chartered Surveyors (RICS) ▶ ⌂ , which stipulate that if one party to a sale pulls out, that party must compensate the other.

Suspicions about an estate agent's advice

Q It took a long time to sell my house and on the agent's advice I dropped the price three times. Eventually I received a low offer, which the agent advised me to accept. A few months after the sale had gone through I discovered that the buyer is the nephew of someone who works for the estate agency. I don't feel the agent advised me correctly. Can I complain?

A Yes. This situation is a conflict of interest for the estate agent, who should have told you that the buyer was a relative of an agency employee if he was aware of it. The code of practice of the National Association of Estate Agents (NAEA; see box, right) states that if an estate agent, an employee or an associate (a relative, spouse, cohabitee or business associate) intends to buy a property that the agency is instructed to sell, the agent must notify the client (you, the seller) in writing. The person concerned must play no part in marketing the property.

Similarly, if an agency is selling a property on behalf of one of its staff or an associate, the company must notify prospective purchasers.

ACTION PLAN

1 Write to the agent ▶ ✍, asking her to show that the price she advised you to accept reflected the average for the area. Also check the Residential Property Price Report issued free by the Land Registry ▶ 📖 and the Property Information Centre ▶ 📖. Say that the purchase by an employee's relative represents a conflict of interest and you should have been told. NAEA members have a complaints procedure and a senior person should investigate.

2 If the response is unsatisfactory, write ▶ ✍ to the Compliance Officer

NATIONAL ASSOCIATION OF ESTATE AGENTS

More than 60 per cent of UK estate agents are members of the NAEA and follow its code of practice and professional rules of conduct (mainly concerning financial matters and ethical standards). The NAEA can penalise breaches by members with a fine, reprimand, suspension or expulsion.

Members must:
- act within the law
- act in the best interests of their clients
- ensure that their staff have a good working knowledge of the law relating to buying and selling property
- ensure that statements made about a property are accurate
- ensure that advertisements are fair, decent and honest
- confirm instructions to sell a property in writing (this is required by law)
- if they hold keys, keep them secure and accompany prospective purchasers on visits to the property
- tell clients as soon as possible about all offers received, up to exchange of contracts (unless the client has stated that offers are not to be passed on; this is required by law)
- keep prospective purchasers who have made an offer (that has not been rejected) informed of the existence, but not the amount, of other offers.

Members must not:
- deliberately misrepresent the potential price of a property in order to gain the instruction to sell it
- erect a 'for sale' board without the owner's permission
- misrepresent offers or rival offers
- discriminate against a prospective purchaser
- stipulate that prospective purchasers use certain services.

More information from the NAEA ▶ 📖.
For complaints: compliance@naea.co.uk

at the NAEA. The agent could be penalised or expelled. If the agent refuses to pay you compensation, you must take your complaint to court.

3 Contact the Ombudsman for Estate Agents (OEA; see box, p235), which runs an adjudication service for disputes between NAEA members and other estate agents who are bound by the OEA scheme, and their clients.

4 Seek legal advice (see p20) if you think you are entitled to compensation.

BUYING & SELLING A HOME

JOINT TENANTS • SITTING TENANTS • NEW HOUSES

Two ways for two people to own a house

Q A friend and I want to pool our resources to buy a house together. She says that if we do so, and I die, she will inherit my share of the house. Can she be right?

A No. She can inherit only if you want her to. There are two forms of joint ownership – 'joint tenancy' and 'tenancy in common'.
• Joint tenants – both own the whole property, so if one dies, full ownership reverts to the other tenant.
• Tenants in common – each owns a share of the property, so if one dies, that person's share passes to his or her heirs. The surviving owner can buy the other share and give the heirs the money, or sell.

Before buying a property with someone else, decide what to do if one of you wants to leave, and instruct your solicitor to draw up an agreement. The one who leaves might sell his or her share, the one who stays might buy the other's share, or you can sell the property and share any profit.

ACTION PLAN

1 Discuss which form of ownership is most appropriate and instruct your solicitor to draw up the documents.

2 Make a will, particularly if you own the house as tenants in common.

Buying a house with a sitting tenant

Q The house we would like to buy has a sitting tenant. The owner assures us he will move out when the house is sold and insists that we can proceed with the sale. Can he do that?

A No, you should refuse to exchange contracts until the tenant has gone. The seller has to give vacant possession by law, unless the contract says otherwise.

You should check that your solicitor is aware that the house has a tenant, that the seller granted vacant possession, and that your solicitor uses the Law Society's TransAction Protocol (see box, p223). This includes a Seller's Property Information Form, on which the seller lists who lives at the property. It may be used to show that the seller agreed vacant possession.

If you know of the sitting tenant before completion, but the property is not vacant on handover, you can make a claim against the seller through your solicitor.

Knowing when a new house is finished

Q We paid a substantial deposit for a house on a new development and have been living in rented accommodation until we can move in. The builder said the

house was finished and we fixed our move date, but our mortgage lender won't release the money because its final inspection isn't complete. Can our lender do this?

A Yes. This is for your own protection. In April 2003 the Council for Mortgage Lenders (CML; see box, p232) tightened up its rules for new homes. Before then, as many as 70 per cent of new home buyers complained that defects remained when they moved in, and it took months of negotiation with the builder to resolve some problems.

Since the CML introduced its new rules, any house covered by a new home warranty (see box, right) must have passed its final inspection and the buyer's solicitor must have received a cover note from the warranty provider before the mortgage lender will release funds.

ACTION PLAN
1 Ask the builder to correct any defects to the warranty provider's standards, then fix a date for the final inspection.

2 Check that the warranty provider has given the builder a cover note stating that the property has passed

its final inspection and that a new home warranty will be in place on or before the completion date. The builder or builder's solicitor must fax or post a copy to your solicitor.

3 Check that your solicitor sends the Certificate of Title for your property to the mortgage provider immediately the cover note is received. The mortgage provider has a minimum of five days to release your funds.

NATIONAL HOUSE-BUILDING COUNCIL (NHBC) is a a non-profit-making company that sets standards and promotes best practice in the building of new houses and gives protection to new home-buyers. It provides about 85 per cent of the buildings warranties that come with most new homes – NHBC Buildmark cover gives a warranty against major defects in new houses for 10 years after construction. NHBC registers most UK builders of new homes and vets registered builders for technical and financial standards. It inspects homes under construction at key stages, including foundations, damp-proofing and cavity wall insulation, and inspectors can insist that defective work is removed and rebuilt. Builders registered with the NHBC must comply with NHBC rules and standards, and can be taken off the register for failure to comply. For more information contact the NHBC ▶ ⌑.

Goods damaged by a removals company

Q **When the removals company delivered our house contents to our new home, some favourite items of china had been damaged. The removers said it was because I packed that box myself and refused to compensate me. Can they do that?**

A Possibly, but not if you can show that the removals firm undertook to pack the china as part of your contract. When you hire a removals company, an estimator should visit your home and make a schedule of what you want them to do. If you want the removers to pack your possessions, the schedule should summarise the items to be packed. You should sign it, keep a copy, and confirm any later changes in writing.

If you ask the removers to pack your possessions, it is their responsibility to ensure that they arrive in perfect condition, and the company is liable for damages if they do not. If you pack the possessions yourself, and items break when being lifted, loaded or unloaded, the removers are not liable.

The removals business is not regulated, so it is wise to book a reputable company through the British Association of Removers (BAR; see box, opposite) ▶ ☞. Its code of practice protects customers and it can also offer advice – for example, on packing china.

Members of the association will also offer you – free or at a low cost – BAR's insurance policy, which will cover your possessions during the move if your house contents policy does not. In addition, many members offer BAR's Careline Guarantee against unforeseen problems – for example, if you cannot complete on time.

ACTION PLAN

1 Contact your insurer. Your house contents policy should cover your belongings during the removal.

2 If you are not covered by insurance, complain in writing to the managing director of the removals firm ▶ ✍.

3 If you do not get satisfaction, and if the company is a member of BAR, contact BAR. It will advise you and help you to resolve the dispute through conciliation.

What to do with a seller's possessions

Q **On completion, we arrived to take possession of our new house, to find it still full of the previous owner's things. Can we get rid of them?**

A Yes, but not immediately or you may expose yourself to legal action. On completion, you are legally entitled to vacant possession, and the only items that should be left in the property are those listed on the Seller's Property Information Form (see box, p223).

You can claim against the seller for the costs and inconvenience incurred in removing and disposing of the property, but if you have the seller's contact details, it may be less trouble to phone and ask for the goods to be collected.

If the seller has not moved anything out, you should contact your solicitor, who will notify the seller's solicitor that the seller is in breach of contract. You can then claim against the seller for various costs, including the costs of temporary accommodation.

ACTION PLAN

1 Store the seller's property in a safe, dry place.

2 If you cannot arrange for the seller to collect the goods, contact your solicitor who can put in motion a claim for damages and give notice for the goods to be removed.

BRITISH ASSOCIATION OF REMOVERS (BAR) is a trade association for removers. Members follow its code of practice, which covers standards of service, staff training, materials and equipment, including vehicles. They provide free written quotations, and offer customers insurance cover.

Members must have their own complaints procedure and can also use BAR's free conciliation service. If that fails, BAR will refer the complaint to a low-cost independent arbitration service.

For more information contact BAR ▶ 🖾.

BUYING PROPERTY AT AUCTION

A big attraction of buying at auction is that you cannot be gazumped. But preparatory costs can be high.

HOW TO DO IT

1 Arrange with the auctioneers to visit properties that interest you. The auctioneers may supply legal documents, such as local authority searches. Some provide a survey.

2 Have your chosen house valued and, if necessary, surveyed. Brief a solicitor. If you need a mortgage, get a lender's offer on the property and banker's drafts to cover the 10 per cent deposit – you must pay on the spot if your bidding succeeds.

3 Set a strict upper limit and if prices go higher, leave.

4 Once you hand over the 10 per cent deposit, you are legally committed to buy the property and must usually complete the sale within 28 days. Insure the property from the sale date.

More information from the Royal Institution of Chartered Surveyors (RICS) ▶ 🖾.

The seller removed fixtures and fittings

Q When we moved into our flat, we found that the sellers had removed urns, paving stones and shrubs from the garden. The look of the house is changed, and the items will cost hundreds of pounds to replace. Can they do that?

A No, unless the sellers specified in the sale contract that they would remove these items. Check the Seller's Property Information Form (see box, p223), which lists the contents, fixtures and fittings included in the sale.

ACTION PLAN

1 If the sellers have not specified that they will remove the items, instruct your solicitor to write to the sellers' solicitor to demand their return.

2 If the items cannot be returned, instruct your solicitor to initiate a claim for damages against the sellers.

Compensation for finding asbestos

Q **Soon after moving into our new home we discovered asbestos in the roof and between the floors. Can the seller just leave us to deal with it?**

A Yes. The principle of caveat emptor ('buyer beware') applies in property transactions: it is down to you, the buyer, to inspect the property and make sure there is no damp, damp rot, or hidden asbestos or dry rot. This is why a detailed survey is recommended (see box, below).

If you had the house surveyed and obvious indications of asbestos were missed, you may be able to make a claim against the surveyor (see question, pp224-225). But if you found it when, say, you lifted solid flooring, the surveyor could not have been expected to find it.

Your lender's valuation report may not give you any rights against the surveyor. The Seller's Property Information Form (see box, opposite) makes no mention of asbestos. Your solicitor can raise the question, but the seller's solicitor may refuse to answer on the basis that this information is subject to survey.

If you sell a house with a serious problem such as asbestos or subsidence (see opposite), it is best to declare the problem and get a specialist report on what has to be done. You can negotiate the price with prospective buyers in relation to the cost of the necessary work.

WHICH KIND OF SURVEY?

All buyers should commission their own survey of a property they are about to buy, even if it is a new house. A surveyor may reveal costly problems or provide a reason to renegotiate the price or reject the property. A mortgage lender's valuation is not a detailed inspection and may not reveal problems that could be expensive for you but do not affect the lender. If you rely on it as a buyer, you may be unable to claim compensation if you later discover a defect.

HOMEBUYER'S SURVEY AND VALUATION REPORT Cost: about £500

Type of survey	Provides:	Covers:	Does not test:
Format laid down by Royal Institution of Chartered Surveyors (RICS) ▶☐ – see RICS web site	• general report on condition of property, including significant defects • valuation	• damp and damp-proofing • drainage and insulation • rot and woodworm	specialist areas, such as plumbing, electrics, drains and boilers

FULL STRUCTURAL OR BUILDING SURVEY Cost: about £1000

Type of survey	Provides:	Covers:	Does not test:
A more detailed survey, suitable for: • buildings put up before 1900 • buildings of unusual construction or materials • altered and extended buildings • a building you plan to renovate	• general report on condition of property, including significant defects • information on location • technical report on structure of building	• damp • damp-proofing • drainage and insulation • rot and woodworm	specialist areas (see above), but recommends specialist inspections

For more information contact the Royal Institution of Chartered Surveyors (RICS) ▶☐.

Finding the cause of subsidence

Q **The house I recently bought has subsidence problems and the sellers say they didn't know. The surveyor denies responsibility. Can they make those claims?**

A Probably. You would have a complaint against the sellers only if you asked about subsidence before buying and they deliberately withheld key information from you. To have a valid complaint against the surveyor, you would have to show that the surveyor failed to report signs of subsidence, such as cracks in plaster.

Causes of subsidence include:
• a lowered water table resulting from reduced rainfall over a long period
• old mines beneath the property
• tunnelling for major engineering works, such as a railway underground.

In the case of subsidence caused by a lowered water table, you should be insured through your house buildings policy for any work needed.

Your solicitor should have checked for old mines beneath the house during the local authority searches (see box, p225). If he or she failed to do so and you find that mines are causing subsidence, you can make a claim against the solicitor.

Also, mining and tunnelling companies are responsible for subsidence caused by their works. If damage occurs, you can apply to the company to have your property repaired or for compensation.

ACTION PLAN

1 Contact your insurer, who will assess the problem and its cause, and agree a course of action with you.

2 If you have a claim against the person who did your conveyancing, contact the Office for the Supervision of Solicitors ▶ ▱ or the Council for Licensed Conveyancers ▶ ▱.

3 If the subsidence is caused by mining or tunnelling, report the damage to the company immediately. Your solicitor will help you to find out who is responsible, even if the original company has since been taken over.

Finding out about a boundary dispute

Q **Shortly after moving into our new home we discovered that there was a long-running dispute with the neighbours over a boundary. Shouldn't the seller have told us about it?**

A Yes. The Seller's Property Information Form (see box, right) asks for disclosure of boundary disputes, and if the seller failed to answer the question or gave misleading information you can claim damages. You should ask your solicitor to make a claim.

NOW YOU MENTION IT THERE IS A TINY BOUNDARY DISPUTE

Retrospective planning permission

Q My house has an extension built by the former owner. A neighbour tells me it was put up without planning permission and the council will make me take it down. Could they do that?

A Yes, if the extension is less than four years old. You should contact the seller, and ask if any building work has taken place. If the answer is yes, but more than four years ago, ask for evidence of the date. If your seller says that planning permission exists for the extension, local authority searches (see box, opposite) should reveal whether this is true.

If the extension was put up less than four years ago, and planning permission does not exist, call your council planning department and explain the situation. They can tell you whether permission could be granted retrospectively. If they say no – perhaps because the extension contravenes government building regulations – they could issue a notice to force you to dismantle it.

If you think your solicitor was negligent in not checking the planning records properly, you may be able to claim compensation (see question, below).

A problem you were not warned about

Q We've just discovered that there's a public right of way across the drive of our new home. Our solicitor never warned us of this, yet when we complained her assistant told us there was nothing they could do about it. Can they get away with that?

A No. Public rights of way are among the things your solicitor should have checked for as part of the local authority searches (see box, opposite). If the solicitor did not, you can seek compensation through the Office for the Supervision of Solicitors ▶ 📖 (see p170).

Making a claim against a surveyor

Q When we moved six months ago we noticed that some windows of the house dripped with condensation most mornings. We have discovered that two window frames are rotten and need replacing. Our home buyer's survey didn't reveal any major problems and the surveyors deny responsibility. Can they do that?

FEAR NOT FAIR MAIDEN THE WHOLE STRUCTURE HAS TO COME DOWN!

PLANNING

A Possibly. If you commission a homebuyer's survey or a full survey, you can claim against the surveyor if the surveyor fails to spot a significant defect:
• that was present when the survey was done; *and*
• that any surveyor could reasonably have been expected to notice.

On the other hand, a surveyor is not allowed to disturb the fabric of the building while inspecting it, and evidence of condensation can be removed by cleaning and decorating. In this case, the surveyor might not be expected to have seen the defect.

You may have a claim against the sellers if you can show that they deliberately hid defects – for example, if they denied there was a condensation problem, or if the window frames had been filled and decorated to cover up the rot.

ACTION PLAN

1 Write to the surveyor, explaining the problem ▶ ✍. Enclose a quotation for replacing your windows, and ask for compensation.

2 If you are not happy with the response, make a formal complaint. Chartered surveyors have indemnity insurance and those undertaking residential surveys should have a complaints procedure.

3 If you are dissatisfied and the surveyor is a member of the Royal Institution of Chartered Surveyors (RICS) ▶ 📖, you can use its complaints procedure.

4 If the RICS cannot resolve the matter, you can go to independent arbitration. Contact the Chartered Institute of Arbitrators ▶ 📖. The arbitrator's decision is legally binding on both sides. You will be charged a fee of at least £200 for this service, but if the arbitrator finds in your favour, it is refunded.

Storm damage before completion

Q **Between exchange of contracts and completion on our house, a storm damaged the roof. The sellers say they are not liable. Can they say that?**

A Yes. You are liable because from the moment you exchange contracts, you are committed to buy and the seller is committed to sell. The seller has only to let you know if any damage occurs.

Your house buildings insurance should cover the damage. If you paid cash and did not arrange buildings insurance from the day you exchanged contracts, you may have to pay for the damage. If you have a mortgage you will be covered: a lender will not grant a mortgage without house buildings insurance. Contact your insurer and ask for a claim form.

LOCAL AUTHORITY SEARCHES

When you buy a property, your solicitor carries out local authority searches as part of the conveyancing. The search results may affect the value of the property.

CHECKS
Make sure that the person doing your conveyancing checks:
• whether the property is affected by planning proposals, such as new roads or changes to the road layout; a development nearby such as a new supermarket; or new restrictions, such as the creation of a conservation area
• nearby areas – to find out, for example, whether there are plans to site a football stadium half a mile away.

TIMESCALE
If a search takes a long time, the results may become dated and a final check will be needed for new plans.
• Normally, your solicitor asks the local authority to carry out the search and provide the necessary documentation. This usually takes about two weeks, but in some areas it takes much longer.
• For an extra fee, you can ask for a 'personal search' in which someone commissioned by you or your solicitor carries out the search in person. Consult your solicitor.

225

BUYING & SELLING A HOME
Buying abroad

Buying and selling property abroad, especially in European countries such as France, Spain and Italy, is increasingly popular. Regular market analyses appear in the press and properties are advertised there and on web sites. Several major lenders offer mortgages for overseas properties – the financial data web site and magazine *Moneyfacts* (www.moneyfacts.co.uk) has listings of lenders and popular money magazines such as *Moneywise* publish information on foreign property. If you want to buy abroad, research the region of your choice, then stay there for a few weeks to get to know the area and make local contacts.

Further information, including links to bilingual professionals who can help you with a sale or purchase, is available through the web site of the Federation of Overseas Property Developers, Agents and Consultants ▶☐. For information about buying and selling in the EU, contact the European Consumer Centre ▶☐.

FRANCE

In France buyer and seller sign an initial contract much sooner than in the UK, but there is often a longer wait before signing the final deed of sale.

CONTRACT A *notaire* (roughly equivalent to a solicitor in the UK) or estate agent draws up a conditional contract – known as a *compromis de vente* if prepared by a *notaire*. There are various forms of contract, all binding to some degree.

DEPOSIT You pay the deposit (typically 10 per cent) when the contract is signed. It is held by the *notaire* and the property is taken off the market.

SEARCHES, DEEDS The *notaire* does the searches, deals with contractual matters and prepares the title deeds. You need a copy of your birth certificate and any marriage certificate, translated into French. The sale of properties with over 1 hectare (about 2.5 acres) of land may occasionally be disallowed by local councils to preserve the land for agricultural use. The contract is then cancelled and the deposit returned.

DEED OF SALE (*acte de vente*) This is signed in the presence of the *notaire*, who collects the balance of the purchase money, legal fees and taxes. The *notaire* ensures that buyer and seller understand the documentation, but does not give legal advice. You can appoint a power of attorney to a clerk at the *notaire*'s office to sign on your behalf.

COSTS Fees and taxes add up to about 10 per cent of the purchase price; and taxes equivalent to VAT at 20.6 per cent are imposed on new properties (sold for the first time within five years of completion). You must complete an income tax return if you have any rental income or bank interest earned in France. You may have to pay French wealth tax if you have substantial assets in the country.

INHERITANCE LAWS IN EUROPE

In some European countries you cannot leave your property to anyone you choose, so take early independent legal advice about inheritance.
• In France you may also need to plan to avoid high inheritance taxes.
• In Spain you need advice on whether or not to apply for resident status and have a Spanish will drafted. Inheritance tax can be high; a spouse does not inherit automatically and may be taxed if there is no will.

WHAT TO WATCH OUT FOR

- Always seek professional advice in the country in which you want to buy.
- Check that professionals are members of the appropriate authorised body and have financial guarantees in place if they are to handle your money.
- You need a local lawyer and a translation service.

Fees, deposits, taxes

- Legal fees and taxes can be as high as 10-15 per cent of the purchase price in popular locations.
- Check who pays the estate agent's fees – in some countries it is the buyer, not the seller.
- If you pay a fee to reserve a house on a new development, the developer may not be obliged to finish the property – if, for example, demand is low – and it can be hard to get the deposit back.
- Make sure you grasp the details of different types of contract and even different types of title (proof of ownership) in overseas property markets.
- Paying a deposit is usually a commitment to buy.
- You may be advised to set up a limited company to buy the property in your name, which could cause you tax problems in the UK. Consult a financial adviser who specialises in the field.
- Check on local taxes – you can expect annual taxes akin to council tax, and maybe also taxes linked to the letting potential of the property. In some countries, notably Spain, you are likely to have to pay capital gains tax when you sell.

SPAIN

The legal aspects of house purchase in Spain are complex and it is especially important to have thorough pre-contract searches carried out. If you are buying a property that is part of a complex, you need to be aware of rules obliging you to join the *comunidad de copropietarios* (residents' association) and pay an annual fee for the maintenance of common areas.

REGISTRATION To buy a property you must arrange through an estate agent or *abogado* (equivalent to a solicitor) to register with the tax authority and get a foreigner's identification number (*número de identificación de extranjero*, NIE).

SEARCHES Your *abogado* normally carries out pre-contract enquiries and searches, and obtains from the Registro de la Propiedad (land registry) a *nota simple*, a document proving the owner's title to the property. Searches to check that the property is free of debts are essential because debts and outstanding taxes are registered against a person's property and the new owner becomes liable.

DEPOSIT, CONTRACT The deposit is usually 10 per cent. The *abogados* agree a contract (*contrato de compraventa*) between buyer and seller, which includes penalties if either side withdraws. The deposit is legally binding unless the contract stipulates otherwise, and is paid to the estate agent.

TITLE DEED The purchase is completed when you and the seller sign the *escritura pública de compraventa* (title deed) in the presence of a *notario*, a government official who makes sure that the change of title complies with Spanish law. All property must be registered with the land registry and all related property taxes must be paid first.

COSTS Fees and taxes amount to about 10 per cent of the purchase price. Once you own the property you are liable for annual property tax of up to 1 per cent of the official registered price, in addition to local authority taxes.

ITALY

Buying property is relatively simple. The whole process usually takes 8 to 12 weeks.

CONTRACT A contract (*il compromesso*) is drawn up, stating the parties involved, the price agreed and how the money is to be paid.

DEPOSIT The size of the deposit (around 20 per cent of the purchase price) is stated in the contract and is normally paid on signing. The money order is made out to the seller, and the estate agent may hold it or give it to the seller.

SEARCHES, DEEDS An official (*il geometra*) carries out local searches. A notary public (*il notaio*) checks the title and draws up a document (*la scrittura*) for the *catasto* (land registry).

FINAL CONTRACT (*il rogito*) This must be signed in the presence of the notary public, when the balance of the purchase price is paid.

COSTS Fees and taxes, including stamp duty and purchase tax, are likely to be between 12 and 15 per cent of the purchase price.

Who can act as a mortgage broker?

Q **We're having a conservatory built by a well-known double glazing company. They have a mortgage consultant, who gave us quite a high-pressure sales talk to get us to arrange a mortgage to pay for the conservatory through them. Can the company do that?**

A Yes. Arranging mortgages and loans could be a key service for a company selling high-priced home products and you may have been given sound advice.

The mortgage would be on your home (see box, p21). Alternatively, you may prefer to arrange an unsecured loan (see box, p155), instead of a mortgage, to buy your conservatory. Under the Consumer Credit Act 1974, you would have extra rights if problems arose during its construction.

If you prefer a mortgage, you need to know whether the consultant is registered with the Mortgage Code Compliance Board (MCCB; see p230) or, after October 31, 2004, with the Financial Services Authority (see box, below).

An MCCB-registered adviser follows the MCCB code of practice, so must tell you if she represents a particular lender, or is independent and can trawl the market for best buys (see box, p157). At the beginning of the interview you must be given a leaflet, *You and your mortgage*. MCCB registration is not compulsory, but all the industry's lenders are registered with it and will not deal with advisers who are not. You could call other mortgage brokers to compare products, and check loan and mortgage rates with best buy tables in *Moneyfacts* magazine and web site (www.moneyfacts.co.uk).

The MCCB has a complaints procedure you can use if you think the consultant infringed the code of practice.

Problem with an endowment policy

Q **I have an endowment mortgage and have received a letter telling me that there's a high risk that there won't be enough money to repay my loan at the end of the term. Can the mortgage company leave me with a debt?**

CHANGES TO THE LAW

In response to complaints about the mortgage industry's low level of regulation, changes are taking place. Anyone wanting to give advice on mortgages must now pass an exam or be supervised by someone who has. And on Mortgage Day, October 31, 2004, mortgages are to come under the tougher regulatory regime of the Financial Services Authority (FSA).

The FSA will take over legal responsibility from the self-regulatory work of the Mortgage Code Compliance Board (MCCB, see p230). It will regulate mortgage lenders and advisers, control the promotion and advertising of mortgages, and have control over the sale of general insurance products. Intermediaries will have to be authorised by the FSA for mortgage business. Firms in good standing with the MCCB will be duly credited in the FSA's authorisation process. For more information, contact the FSA ▶ ⌂ .

A Yes. This is a risk with an endowment mortgage, but you may be able to complain and claim compensation (see box, right). Act quickly, or you may lose some of the recompense you may be entitled to. All endowment mortgage holders now receive regular 're-projection' letters telling them how their policy is performing. These letters may be:

- amber – on track to repay the mortgage, although this does not guarantee that it will stay on track for the future
- green – there is a significant risk that your endowment mortgage will not meet its target
- red – there is a high risk your mortgage will not repay your target amount.

The letter should be accompanied by a booklet from the Financial Services Authority (FSA; see box, p157) giving guidance on what actions to take, and by information from your endowment lender about your options. You may have grounds for complaint if you were mis-sold the policy (see box, right).

ACTION PLAN

1 If you feel you were mis-sold a policy, write to the company, saying why ▸✍. If an independent financial adviser sold you the policy, complain to the company's compliance officer, who ensures that it complies with all relevant laws and regulations. If the company is untraceable call the FSA consumer helpline (0845 606 1234). If it no longer trades, contact the Financial Services Compensation Scheme ▸▱.

2 If the lender rejects the complaint, perhaps because it is too late ('out of time'), contact the Financial Ombudsman (see box, p141).

3 If you do not accept the Financial Ombudsman's decision, contact a solicitor (see p20) urgently for advice on taking legal action against the mortgage company.

MIS-SELLING OF ENDOWMENT MORTGAGES

With an endowment mortgage, you pay interest monthly on the sum you borrowed, plus a specified sum into an investment. This is intended to grow enough to pay off the borrowed sum by the end of the loan, possibly with a surplus. But in years of poor stock market growth, the investment part of the mortgage may grow by so little that at the end of the loan period it falls short of the amount needed to pay off the mortgage. In the past, this risk was not explained to people who took on a mortgage.

WHAT YOU CAN DO

If you have an endowment mortgage, were not told the risk, and now face a debt at the end of the loan period, you may complain. You may win redress if the salesperson did not:

- tell you how your savings would be invested
- check that you understood the risks of a stock market-linked investment
- explain the fees and charges associated with the endowment and their effect on your savings.

Check the documentation you received when you took out the mortgage. If these points were not clearly laid out, you may well have a case.

WHAT THE MORTGAGE COMPANY MUST DO

If your complaint succeeds, the company must restore you to the position you would have been in if you had opted for a repayment mortgage. You may be entitled to:

- the difference between what you would now get by cashing in your endowment policy and the extra you would have paid off with a repayment mortgage
- the difference between the total payments made on the endowment policy and the total repayments you would have made with a repayment mortgage
- reimbursement of any administration fee charged for switching your mortgage now.

BUT: there may be different rules for policies sold by an independent financial adviser before April 29, 1988, when the Financial Services Act 1986 came into effect.

WORD OF WARNING

You cannot complain just because your endowment policy has performed badly. That is the risk of an investment.

Penalty on a non-transferable mortgage

Q I got a mortgage a year ago, but my job has unexpectedly been relocated. I have to move, but the mortgage isn't transferable and the lender is demanding a penalty equal to six months' payments if I terminate it. Can the lender do this?

A Yes. Some mortgages – usually those with a very low rate of interest – impose large penalties on people who move or change lender within a specified time, usually the term of the discounted interest rate.

You must be sure you will not have to move before signing up for this type of loan. There are other loans with no penalty attached, but the interest rates will be higher.

Many mortgages, even discounted ones, are now portable – that is, they can be transferred to a new property. If yours is not, you will probably have to pay the penalty, but you could check first with the Mortgage Code Compliance Board (MCCB; see box, below) to be certain.

If you take out a mortgage for a new property, commission an independent broker to find you the cheapest deals on mortgages with no penalties. It may be worth paying a little more for the flexibility that gives you.

THE MORTGAGE BOARD

The Mortgage Code Compliance Board (MCCB) ▶ ⌂, also called the **Mortgage Board, regulates the mortgage industry in the UK. Almost all mortgage lenders and brokers are registered with it.**

THE CODE OF PRACTICE

The MCCB Mortgage Code is intended to ensure that borrowers are fully informed and adequately protected. Registered members have to observe the code and are regularly inspected.

They must:
• meet all the standards of the code and comply with all related laws and regulations
• explain their products and services in plain language
• act fairly and reasonably towards you
• sell you a mortgage that fits your needs
• make sure you understand the financial implications of having a mortgage
• tell you how a mortgage account works
• give you a copy of the leaflet *You and your mortgage,* which outlines minimum standards the lender or intermediary must meet in order to comply with the code.

HELPING YOU CHOOSE A MORTGAGE

An MCCB member will:
• advise you and recommend a suitable mortgage
• tell you about the different types of mortgage on offer so you can make an informed choice
• tell you about a single mortgage product only if it is the only one available.

When you have chosen a mortgage:
• intermediaries (independent brokers) must tell you who the lender is and how it was chosen, and disclose any commission the lender will earn
• members will explain procedures for dealing with complaints
• members will consider cases of financial difficulty and mortgage arrears sympathetically and positively.

COMPLAINTS AND PENALTIES

Customers can use the MCCB's free complaints scheme, and members have professional indemnity insurance. Customer complaints must be dealt with speedily and compensation may be paid if they are upheld. The MCCB can investigate any problem with a mortgage provider or broker, and fine, suspend or deregister a company or individual that does not maintain its standards.

A bad credit record affects a mortgage

Q Some years ago I had a county court judgment against me. I've since taken out a mortgage and I'm paying much higher rates than are currently offered on mortgages. The lender refuses to offer me a cheaper loan. Can they do that?

A Not if your old debt is under control. You have what is called an 'impaired credit loan' for people who have had debt problems. The lender is taking more risk by lending to you than to someone with a perfect credit record, so the interest rate is higher. But if you have an uninterrupted record of mortgage repayments over the past few years, you should be able to switch to a cheaper loan. Write to your mortgage lender ▶ ✍, giving details of your payment record. Your case should be considered on its merits.

If the lender refuses, ask a mortgage broker to find you a cheaper loan. Some lenders offer impaired credit mortgages with interest rates that reduce over time.

The cost of a buildings insurance policy

Q When we bought our house we took the buildings insurance offered by our building society. Now I find that other lenders offer much cheaper policies, but the building society is charging me for moving from its policy. Can it do that?

A Yes. Your mortgage provider has a legitimate interest in ensuring that your property is properly insured against risk. If it did not, it could lose money if anything happened to the house. Some lenders offer 'tied-in' insurance – a policy linked to your mortgage – and may insist that you take out their buildings (and sometimes contents) insurance as a condition of the mortgage.

The premiums charged by lenders may not be competitive, however, and many have a 'lock-in' period of up to two years after you sign the mortgage, or for the period of a fixed-rate mortgage, when you cannot switch to another insurer. Some lenders charge a fee for approving alternative cover arranged by you.

ACTION PLAN

1 If you feel that the terms on which your lender will allow you to switch insurance policies are unfair, call the lender and try to renegotiate. Also check with your local trading standards office ▶ ⌂. They may refer the question to the Office of Fair Trading Unfair Contract Terms Unit.

2 Look for an insurer who offers to pay the switching fee for you, but ask if you can pay it directly. Your building society might otherwise add the fee to your mortgage account, and you will be charged interest on the fee for the life of the mortgage.

Mortgage assistance after redundancy

Q **I recently moved to a new flat, and I've been made redundant. I'm thinking of applying for help with my mortgage, but I'm told I have to wait nine months before I get any payments. Can this be right?**

A It can be, but it depends on when you took out the mortgage. Limited help with mortgage repayments is available to people in your position through jobseeker's allowance (JSA). Details vary according to individual circumstances, so you should ask for advice at your local Benefits Agency office. The rules generally applied are:
• if you took out your current mortgage before October 2, 1995, you can receive some help after eight weeks, although 100 per cent of costs will not be paid for 18 weeks after that
• if you remortgaged with the same lender after October 2, 1995, the mortgage is treated as if you took it out before that date
• if you took out the loan on or after October 2, 1995, you will get no help for the first 39 weeks of a claim, the full amount of your mortgage interest will be paid at your lender's standard rate.
   A number of restrictions apply:
• you cannot claim if your partner works 24 hours or more a week, or if you have savings of more than £8000

• there is an upper limit of £100,000 on the size of mortgage that is covered
• you get help with the interest on the loan only, not with capital repayments or endowment policy premiums.
   Apply for JSA immediately to avoid prolonging the time you have to wait for benefits to be awarded.

ACTION PLAN

1 If you have a mortgage payment protection policy, contact the insurers. Your payments should be covered for up to two years if you are unemployed.

2 Contact your local Benefits Agency ▶ 🕮 or Citizens Advice Bureau ▶ 🕮 and ask for an assessment of your benefits situation.

3 Inform your lender of the problem. To claim JSA you need forms ES1 and ES2 from a Job Centre and form MI12 from the Benefits Agency, part of which has to be completed by the mortgage lender.

Mortgage arrears raise repossession threat

Q **We're three months in arrears with our mortgage payments. I've just received a letter saying that the lender will seek a possession order if we don't now pay the whole amount of the loan outstanding – not just the arrears. Can they do that?**

A Yes, if your mortgage deed states that they can, although it is unlikely that the court to which the lender applies for the possession order would allow it.
   A mortgage gives the lender certain legal rights on your house. Among them is the right to repossess the property if

COUNCIL OF MORTGAGE LENDERS (CML) is the UK trade association for residential mortgage lenders and sponsors the Mortgage Board Code of Practice (see p230). The CML publishes useful information for borrowers, including facts about mortgage arrears and repossession. More information from the CML ▶ 🕮.

you fall behind (default) on your regular payments, and to sell it to repay the loan. When a mortgage company seeks a repossession order to sell a property, the proceeds are used first to pay off the loan; the balance, if any, is yours. Theoretically, the lender can do this even if you miss just one monthly payment.

Your charge document or mortgage deed will set out what you need to do to prevent repossession. You usually have to make up the arrears, but sometimes you must repay the whole loan. If you cannot do this, the lender will apply to the court for a possession order.

A court will usually insist that you make up the arrears rather than repay the whole loan, and it will try to give you a chance to do so. It can defer the hearing, or issue a suspended possession order that will not come into effect if you make up the deficit before a specified date. It can also postpone possession for a 'reasonable' period, which it will define, to enable you to spread the arrears, perhaps even for the remainder of the mortgage term.

ACTION PLAN

1 If you have a mortgage protection plan that will cover you, contact your insurer immediately. If not, ask for advice from your local Citizens Advice Bureau ▶ 📖 or the National Debtline (0808 808 4000).

2 Tell the lender you are taking independent advice. Your adviser may suggest that you ask the lender if you can arrange to spread the arrears over the whole mortgage term, take a capital repayment 'holiday' (you pay the interest only on the loan for a while) or increase the term of the loan to reduce monthly payments.

3 If your financial difficulties are because you lost your job, you may be able to claim benefits to help to pay the mortgage (see question, opposite). Contact the Benefits Agency ▶ 📖 .

A HOUSEBOAT? I WOULDN'T TOUCH IT WITH A BARGEPOLE!

Getting a mortgage for an unusual property

Q **I want to buy a houseboat but none of the lenders I've approached will grant me a mortgage. Can they do that?**

A Yes. Most mortgage providers will only lend money for land-based properties. You need a lender who specialises in marine mortgages, including ones for residential as well as pleasure vessels. Check the advertisements pages of a boating magazine.

Even with some land-based properties, you can have difficulties in getting a mortgage. For example, some lenders steer clear of timber-framed or thatched cottages because of the fire risk. In this case, shop around, because other lenders specialise in precisely these kinds of properties. Contact an independent mortgage broker (see box, p230), who will have a wide knowledge of different lenders' attitudes.

GOLDEN RULE

If you cannot keep up your mortgage payments, resist the temptation to abandon your property and put your keys through the lender's door. This does not free you from responsibility for the debt, so the lender may eventually pursue you through the courts. Before doing anything, ask the Citizens Advice Bureau ▶ 📖 for help.

233

Your contract with an estate agent

Q I've instructed an agent to sell my house, but so far she hasn't produced a prospective buyer. When I said I would call in another agent she said I couldn't because I would be in breach of contract. Can she be right?

A Possibly, but you need to know which of four types of contract you have with the agent.

• Sole agency – this is normally in force for a specified number of weeks, when you are tied to the agreement. If the term is too long, you can try to negotiate a shorter one. If you find a buyer privately the agent cannot claim commission, but if you ask another agent to sell the house, you will have to pay commission to both.

• Joint sole agency – two agents operate together, agreeing between them how to split the commission (say, 60:40 in favour of the agent who makes the sale).

• Sole selling rights – the agent gets commission, however the house is sold, even if you find a private buyer.

• Multiple agency – several agents are involved and the one who sells the house takes the fee.

At the outset, the agent should have given you her terms and conditions in writing, along with confirmation of your instructions to her to sell. Once you agreed the terms and instructed her to sell, the agreement was in force – even if you never confirmed it in writing.

However, if she never gave you the terms and conditions in writing, you can make a complaint.

ACTION PLAN

1 Contact the agency and ask to make a formal complaint. Agencies that are members of the National Association of Estate Agents (NAEA; see box, p217) and follow the Ombudsman for Estate Agents (OEA) scheme (see box, opposite) have a complaints procedure.

2 If the response does not satisfy you, write to the OEA ▶ ✍, who will try to arbitrate. If arbitration fails and the Ombudsman finds in your favour, the agency can be directed to pay you compensation.

COMMISSIONING AN ESTATE AGENT

• Commission an agent who is a member of the National Association of Estate Agents (NAEA; see box, p217) and the Ombudsman for Estate Agents (OEA) scheme, whose members follow a code of practice (see box, opposite).

• Ask for the agent's terms and conditions in writing, with an explanation of how you can cancel the contract. Ask for anything you do not understand to be explained in writing.

• Ask the agent to confirm your instructions in writing.

• If you cancel the contract, write a letter to the agent stating the termination date, and ask the agent to confirm in writing ▶ ✍.

Whether to accept a lock-out agreement

Q I've accepted an offer for my flat from a prospective buyer and he's asked for a lock-out agreement. Can he do that?

A Yes, but it is not obligatory, and you do not have to agree. A lock-out agreement is a contract drawn up by a solicitor through which seller and buyer agree that the buyer has an exclusive right to purchase. Any other prospective buyers are ruled out for an agreed period. There will usually be a fixed time by when the buyer must complete the sale.

A lock-out agreement is one way of combating gazumping when the property market is buoyant, but as a seller you may feel it will not benefit you.

You should decide, in consultation with your solicitor, whether a lock-out agreement is in your interests.

Your tax position if you buy to let

Q I'd like to invest in property using a buy-to-let mortgage. I've been told that the Inland Revenue will tax me on the rental income? Can they do that?

A Yes, and you will be liable for capital gains tax when you sell the property. Contact your local tax office and ask for IR150, 'Taxation of rents', which has the information you need. You can also download it from the Inland Revenue web site ▶ 🕮 .

You must consider that when you buy to let you take on the legal responsibilities of a landlord with respect to the rights of your tenants, the safety of the property, and its maintenance and condition.

Contact the Association of Residential Letting Agents ▶ 🕮 and the Council of Mortgage Lenders (CML; see box, p232) for further information.

THE ESTATE AGENTS' OMBUDSMAN

The Ombudsman for Estate Agents (OEA) is an independent service for dealing with disputes between estate agencies and their clients. More than 60 per cent of agencies are members of the OEA scheme and must follow its code of practice.

WHAT THE OEA DOES
If you are buying or selling UK residential property the Ombudsman will provide a free, fair and speedy review of a dispute.

The estate agency must have caused you inconvenience or loss of money by:
• infringing your legal rights or not complying with the OEA scheme's code of practice
• treating you unfairly
• poor administration, inefficiency or delay.

THE OEA CANNOT HELP IF
• you do not complain as a private individual
• you have a complaint against a non-member – but it will try to find an alternative service to help you
• you complain about something that happened more than a year ago
• you have not tried the agency's complaints procedure first, unless it did not respond within three months of receiving your complaint in writing.

MAKING A COMPLAINT
Write to the Ombudsman explaining your complaint and the outcome of the estate agency's complaints procedure ▶ ✍ .

The Ombudsman will try to help you and the agency find an agreement. If this fails, the Ombudsman will make a decision and inform you and the agency of it in writing. The Ombudsman can order the agency to pay up to £25,000 in compensation.

• You can reject the decision. Your right to take legal action is not affected.
• You can accept the decision. If the member agency pays you financial compensation, you must accept the payment in full and final settlement.

More information from OEA ▶ 🕮 .

Capital gains tax on a home office

Q I work from home in an office specially designed and fitted out for my business. A colleague tells me the Inland Revenue will make me pay capital gains tax for this reason when I sell my house. Can they do that?

A Yes. You may well have to pay a capital gains tax (CGT) bill if the room in which you work is used exclusively for business and you claim tax relief on a portion of heating, lighting and other household expenses as a business expense on your self-assessment tax return.

For example, if you claim one-seventh of your bills against the business, when you come to sell your house you might end up with a CGT liability on one-seventh of the sale price. Contact the Inland Revenue and ask for Help Sheet IR283 on CGT liabilities in relation to your house. You can also download it from the Inland Revenue web site ▶ ⌂ .

From the time you start working at home, consider whether it is worthwhile to claim household expenses and so risk incurring a CGT liability. Consult your local tax office or a tax adviser.

CAPITAL GAINS TAX

Capital gains are income from the sale of an investment such as shares or property. But if you own and live in only one home, you do not usually pay capital gains tax (CGT) when you sell, because it is covered by a tax relief called Principal Private Residence Relief (PPR).

If you own two homes, you can only claim PPR on one – but you can choose which. For example, if you marry and both you and your spouse have a home, which you want to keep, you should write to the Inland Revenue within two years of your marriage stating which is to be treated as your principal private residence for tax purposes. Consult a tax adviser – the rules are complex:

- If you are married (and not separated) you can claim PPR only on one main residence between the two of you.

- If you go abroad to work and let your home, you will still qualify for PPR in the UK.

- If your property consists of more than one building, or is bigger in size than half a hectare (a little more than an acre), you may not qualify for PPR on the full value.

- If you let a room in your home there will be no CGT liability as long as the room is in the part of the house where you live (that is, the lessee – lodger – has no separate entrance). If the lessee's room has a separate entrance you can claim tax relief on the income.

The way to respond to buyers' enquiries

Q The couple buying our house have sent us a list of preliminary enquiries, running to ten pages, about the sale of our house. Can they do that?

A No. You should contact your solicitor, who will very probably recommend that most of the questions are answered with 'this is a matter for survey'. Questions relating to the physical condition of a property should always be answered professionally, by the surveyor's report.

Buyers sometimes attempt to cover all possible issues through preliminary enquiries in this way. Solicitors resist giving concrete answers, because if any answer turns out to be flawed after the survey is carried out, they and the sellers of the property could be exposed to claims for damages.

You do not have to pull up the carpets

Q Our buyer's surveyor wants to check the floors, but we don't want fitted carpets pulled up – the buyer might not go ahead with the purchase. Can he ask us to do that?

A No, you are not obliged to give access to floor hidden by fitted carpets, walls covered in pine panelling or other similar features. The surveyor will mention in the report to the buyer that it was not possible to check these.

As a general rule, if the rest of the house is in good condition and there is no particular reason to suspect any kind of problem, your buyer will probably not be too worried. He is more likely to be put off if other aspects of the property give cause for concern, such as damp patches, woodwork that is in poor condition and evidence of generally sub-standard maintenance.

If your buyer is very wary, however, the fact that you will not pull pull up the carpets may put him off the purchase, since he may suspect that they could be concealing woodworm and dry rot. So your decision about whether or not pull them up might depend on the state of the market: if the market is buoyant and several buyers are interested, refusing the surveyor's request should not damage your chances of selling.

When a buyer fails to complete on time

Q Our buyer has phoned to say she can't complete on time, and she asked if I could put the completion date back. Not only will it leave us in a mess, but I don't think it's up to me to change the date. Can she do that?

SO THAT'S WHERE THE HAMSTER WENT

A Yes, but she will pay a high price for the delay. From now on, you are in the hands of the lawyers. Contact your solicitor, who will serve a notice to complete, obliging the buyer to complete by a new date. The buyer will have to pay interest at a high rate for the delay, but the transaction can still go through.

If the buyer still cannot complete by the new date, she forfeits her deposit and you are free to sell the property to another buyer. If your costs are higher than the forfeited deposit you can sue the buyer for the excess.

If you are part of a chain of buyers and sellers, a failure to complete can cause chaos. Apart from anything else, if you in turn are unable to complete you will be liable to legal action from your seller.

The best solution will probably be for you to get a short-term loan from your bank. You will be able to reclaim the interest from your buyer.

What to do if you lose the title deeds

Q We're hoping to sell my elderly father's house, so he can buy a small warden-controlled flat. But he's lost the title deeds and says that prospective sellers will refuse to complete unless he produces them. Can they do that?

A Yes, but the situation need not get to that point. Your father can apply to the Land Registry for a registration of title (see box, below). But before taking that step, your father should exhaust all possibilities of finding the deeds. If they are not among his papers, check with a solicitor, who may have the original documents or copies on file, or they may be with the original mortgage lender.

ROLE OF THE LAND REGISTRY

The title (ownership) deeds may not be the only papers that can prove you own a property. Most property in England and Wales is registered with the Land Registry, which can replace lost documents relating to property registered with it fairly easily.

IF YOUR PROPERTY IS UNREGISTERED
You must first prove that you own your property. Then the Land Registry will award one of two grades of title:

Absolute title: the Land Registry is satisfied with the evidence. It is as good as if the deeds had not been lost.
Possessory title: the Registry will grant this title if there is any uncertainty about ownership. Someone else with a stronger claim to the property could therefore emerge in the future. Possessory title can often be upgraded to absolute title after a period of 12 years. You can sell a property with only possessory title, but you will have to back it up with indemnity insurance, costing a few hundred pounds, to cover the risk of a claim of ownership.

For more information about these titles, contact HM Land Registry ▶ 🕮 .

ACTION PLAN

1 If you cannot trace the deeds, assemble all the evidence you can find that your father owns the property.

2 Apply to the Land Registry ▶ 🕮 for a registration of title. Declarations from people who can confirm that the householder has lived in the property for 12 years or more can form the basis of the claim for registration.

3 If the title document was lost and referred to a property that was registered, cancel the original deed with the Land Registry.

The risks of buying flying freehold

Q I put in an offer to buy part of a house that is split up into several units. My part includes an upstairs extension built over a single storey, part of the original house, which is owned by someone else. My solicitor says it's unwise to proceed. Can she be right?

A Yes. Your extension is what is known as a 'flying freehold' – part of a property built above land that is not part of the freehold. Another example would be a bedroom built over a common access area, such as a hall or passageway. Flying freeholds can be a problem in properties that have been divided unwisely, so that one person's share of the property overhangs a part belonging to someone else.

If the properties are both freehold, you are dependent on the other owner not to do anything that could damage your property. Yet you have limited rights to compel the owners of the dwelling beneath yours to maintain their property

so that yours is not put at risk. Most mortgage companies will not lend on properties with flying freeholds, and this makes them difficult to sell. Take your solicitor's advice and look elsewhere.

The legal position of leasehold flat-owners

Q **I'm a first-time home buyer and I want to buy a leasehold flat in a converted old house. A mortgage broker has told me that lenders often refuse a mortgage on leaseholds. Can they do that?**

A Yes. Mortgage lenders can refuse a mortgage for any property they consider a poor risk. They may judge freehold flats a better risk than leasehold.

Although a few may refuse to lend to first-time buyers who opt for leasehold flats, it is usually easy in a competitive market to find another lender.

For lease terms of less than 60 years it can be difficult to get a mortgage. But changes to the law (see box, below) have given leaseholders the right to buy an extra 90-year lease term, added to the time left on the original lease. This overcomes the problem of expiring leases, the lenders' main objection to leasehold properties.

FREEHOLD AND LEASEHOLD: TWO WAYS OF OWNING PROPERTY

There are two types of property ownership: freehold and leasehold. A freeholder owns the property for ever; whereas when you buy leasehold you own only your part of the building, and not the adjacent parts or the land. Each type of ownership carries different rights and responsibilities.

FREEHOLD

Rights and duties When you buy freehold, you own and are responsible for the building and the land it stands on.

Freehold for leaseholders
Leaseholders now have the right to buy jointly the freehold of their building. They usually form a management company, so that the residents become their own collective landlord.

New 2003 legislation has introduced:
• simplified requirements for buying the freehold or extending a lease
• the 'right to manage' – an automatic right for leaseholders to take over the management of their building
• additional consultation with leaseholders about service charges and major works
• new rights to challenge charges
• increased protection against forfeiture (enforced ending of the lease prematurely)
• financial provisions, including a new duty on the landlord to produce an annual statement of each leaseholder's service charge account.

LEASEHOLD

Rights and duties These are set out in the lease document. In properties with many occupiers, they ensure that everyone behaves responsibly towards each other and the property as a whole. For example, leaseholders typically have a right of 'quiet enjoyment' that deters neighbouring residents from acts of nuisance.

Costs Leaseholders pay a small annual ground rent to the landlord, and they must contribute to management and maintenance costs, usually through a service charge.
• If you are thinking about buying into a leasehold property, such as an apartment block, you need to know the provisions for increasing the charges.
• The landlord sets the charge and leaseholders can challenge unreasonable charges through a leasehold valuation tribunal (see question, p215).
• Leaseholders who breach the lease or fail to pay the charges due could forfeit their lease, and the landlord would be entitled to repossess the flat.

What to do about a flooding risk

Q I've been offered a new job in another part of the country, so we want to sell our house. But because it was flooded during both of the past two winters we've been having problems with our insurers, who are threatening not to provide cover any longer. Our estate agent tells us that this will make it impossible for us to sell. Can the insurers do that?

A Yes. They must continue to provide cover until your policy comes up for renewal. But then they have the option of reassessing the situation and, if they feel the risk is too great, of refusing to renew the policy.

Your estate agent is also right that your ability to sell depends on continuing cover. Buyers will find that getting a mortgage is conditional on having buildings insurance.

In most cases where flooding has been a problem, insurers have agreed to continue with cover.

But yours must be one of an estimated 200,000 properties in the UK whose future insurance cover is in question. The worst-hit areas are in Kent, Essex and Cambridgeshire.

Your insurer's decision to continue with cover depends on two main things:
• the frequency and severity of flooding
• the adequacy of flood defences.
If, for example, you make three claims in successive years, and the insurers do not think the local flood defences are effective, they could well refuse cover.

Try other insurers. New policies and conditions emerge in response to changing situations, including an increased risk of flooding. For example, an insurer may agree to insure your house at a higher premium rate, or stipulate changes to reduce the likely cost of future claims – changing from wood floors to concrete, say, or moving electric sockets to a higher position. Investigate the flood defence products on the market – for example, watertight barriers that fit over a gateway or door frame.

If you find a new insurer you will probably be able to transfer the policy to a future buyer.

HOW TO CHECK THE FLOOD RISK

Flooding has become a significant problem for some householders. But when you buy a property, the risk of flooding is not always covered in the searches, so it is worth researching any problems in the area where you intend to buy.
• Start with the Environment Agency's web site and phone floodline ▶ ⌨ .
• The local council web site should have detailed information for the area.
• Ask your insurance company to check the property's postcode. It may reveal flood or subsidence risk.

For more information contact the Association of British Insurers ▶ ⌨ .

Unsightly rubbish in a neighbour's garden

Q My neighbour is using his back garden to store old cars and furniture. I want to sell my house but I'm afraid the unsightly view will lower the price. He says he can't clear it. Can he refuse?

A Probably. If the rubbish is not a public nuisance or a hazard – for example, causing a smell or an infestation of rats – there is little you can do to force him to clear it up.

PERFECT!

PROPERTY DETAILS

A Not necessarily. A restrictive covenant is an agreement between property owners stating that one owner will refrain from doing something on her property, such as planting tall trees or erecting buildings, for the benefit of the other.

Such a covenant 'passes with the land', which means that as the current owner you are bound by it even if a previous owner made the agreement. If you are prepared to spend a little time and money you may find ways around it. This depends on the nature and age of the covenant, who now benefits from it, and whether it could be said to interfere with your reasonable use of your own land. For more information, contact the Land Registry ▶ ⌨, which publishes a fact sheet on restrictions.

ACTION PLAN

1 If possible, speak to your neighbour again. If the rubbish is not dangerous, consider offering to help to dispose of it. This might work if your neighbour does not have transport or, finds it physically tiring to clear the rubbish.

2 Failing this, write to the local environment health service ▶ ✍ (details from your local town hall). It has powers to remove rubbish if it is dangerous (for example, a fire hazard).

Restrictive covenant in the title deeds

Q I have planning permission to build a second house on my land, which I then aim to sell. But I've found a restrictive covenant in the deeds to my house that bars building or development in that area. Does that mean I've got to forget about my plan?

ACTION PLAN

1 You may be able to negotiate the terms of the restrictive covenant. The deeds should tell you who agreed to it, and you can try to discover who now benefits from it. This could be difficult if it is quite old.

2 Consult your local Citizens Advice Bureau ▶ ⌨, Law Centre ▶ ⌨ or a solicitor (see p20) about how to proceed. You may be able to apply to the Lands Tribunal – a special tribunal (see p17) set up to resolve issues like this – to have a restrictive covenant modified or even lifted. You may have to pay compensation to the person who would have been entitled to the benefit from the covenant.

3 If all options fail, you may be able to take out an insurance policy that indemnifies you (and future owners of your property) against anyone trying to enforce the restrictive covenant. This option is usually open only when a covenant restricts building development and planning permission has been granted.

BUYING & OWNING A CAR

A new car is slow arriving

Q I ordered a new car six months ago, but it still hasn't arrived. The dealer says the factory won't give a date for delivery. He has my deposit, which he refuses to repay. Can he do that?

A No. The dealer cannot withhold your deposit if the delivery date written on the form he gave you when you placed the order has long since passed. This is a binding contract. But car sales people often leave a delivery date off the form, or enter 'TBA' (to be arranged), which complicates matters.

If a delivery date is given and it has passed, the dealer is in breach of contract and you can insist that he refunds your deposit in full. If he has written 'TBA', you can ask at any point for time to be 'of the essence' to the contract (see box, p25).

ACTION PLAN

1 Write to the person in charge of the dealership ▶ ✍. Enclose a photocopy of the order form and say that you now want 'time to be of the essence' for the car's delivery (use these exact words). Ask for a reply within 14 days with a firm delivery date. Give a deadline (three months, say, for a commonly available model) after which, if it is not delivered, you will consider your contract at an end. If you signed a finance agreement or paid the deposit by credit card, copy the letter to the finance or credit card company.

2 If the dealer does not reply within 14 days or give a delivery date, you can ask him for a full refund ▶ ✍.

3 If the dealer refuses to refund your money, seek advice from your local Citizens Advice Bureau ▶ 📖 or trading standards office (see p30) about reclaiming the refund using the small claims track or fast track in the county court (see p19).

Price increase between order and delivery

Q I ordered a new car from a dealer and we negotiated a price. Yesterday she phoned to say there has been a price increase and I will have to pay extra if I still want the car. Can she do that?

A Yes. Check the small print on the order form that you signed and you will probably find that it allows the dealer to pass on the manufacturer's increase. Unless the price was guaranteed when you signed, you cannot insist that it be supplied at the pre-increase figure.

Before you agree to pay the increase, ask the dealer to reward your loyalty, for instance by including a first service for the car within the price.

If the increase is large and you wish to cancel the order for that reason, the dealer should return your deposit in full.

A new car is scratched on delivery

Q My new car has arrived with a scratch down one side. Can I reject it?

A Yes, but you must act fast because you have only a 'reasonable' time in which to reject the car (see box, p22). If you notice the damage before handover, reject the car on the spot. Under the Sale of Goods Act 1979 (as amended; see p29), a new car must be free from even

ACCEPTING A NEW CAR

Check the car
- Always time collection or delivery in daylight. Examine the car for faults outdoors and in good light. Rainwater can mask paint defects, so postpone the handover if the car is wet.
- Check the body, interior, controls and documents. Politely refuse to sign the acceptance form until you have done this.
- Take a copy of the order form you signed and check that the car is the correct model, the right colour and that whatever extras you wanted have been fitted.
- Ensure that the car has road tax and that the registration number shown is correct.

Check the paperwork
- Ask to see the dealer's pre-delivery inspection report for the car.
- If the vehicle registration document (V5) is with the dealership, ensure that the details are accurate, the date of first registration is correct and that you are listed as the car's first owner.

Test drive
- If all appears to be correct, go for a test drive in the car and ask the sales person to accompany you.

Minor defects
- If you spot a minor problem – for example, a scratch on the door trim, or a defective electric window – ask the dealer to put things right quickly and lend you another car in the meantime.
- If the fault is small, the dealer may suggest that you leave it until later to fix. Do not agree to this: a new car should be perfect. Ask the dealer to fix the fault before you accept the car.

Serious problems
- If the fault is more serious – such as rust or a badly painted door panel – reject the car on the spot.
- If there is a major fault, the dealer will probably ask for a chance to make repairs, and may even tell you that the law allows for this. It does not. The Sale of Goods Act 1979 (as amended; see p29) gives you the right to reject faulty goods outright.

minor defects. If it is not, you are entitled to a free replacement or your money back.

The dealer may offer to repair the scratch. If you agree, inspect the work carefully. Ensure the paint matches and check for specks on windows and tyres.

Take it back, we don't like the colour

Q My husband hates the colour of our new car, but the dealer refuses to take it back. Can he refuse to do that?

A Yes. If you buy from a dealer and the sales person shows you an example of the colour, and the car matches the sample, you cannot reject the car. If the manufacturer has updated its range of paints between order and delivery, and the dealer did not tell you, you can reject the car – ideally at delivery. ▶

If you bought the car over the phone or via the Internet, the transaction is governed by the Distance Selling Regulations 2001 (see p47). These allow you a week to reject goods and demand a refund. The car must be in 'as delivered' condition, so you could not hand it back having driven it even for a short time.

High charges for servicing imported cars

Q **I bought a car directly from a dealer in France and imported it myself. My local main dealer has looked after it under warranty, but now that the warranty has ended the dealer charges me more for servicing and parts than for UK cars of the same model and age. Can they do that?**

A Yes – but there is no reason why you should continue to pay your dealer's higher prices if you can find a garage whose rates are cheaper.

Before 2002, some garages charged more for servicing cars imported from the EU than for cars sold through UK dealers. There was some justification for this in that the specification for UK cars was often different from that of cars produced for other EU member states, so replacement parts often had to be specially sourced and imported.

Since 2002, such specification differences have largely been eliminated from EU imports. (But cars imported from outside the EU area, especially the Far East, are still built to different specifications from UK-built models and dealers may be justified in charging higher rates for servicing.)

The Supply of Goods and Services Act 1982 (as amended; see box, p53) says that suppliers should charge reasonable rates. 'Reasonable' is defined as what other suppliers would charge for doing the same job. If for convenience you want to continue using the same dealer, get quotes from other garages, show them to the dealer and ask for the charges for servicing your car to be reduced.

PROTECTION FOR CAR BUYERS AND OWNERS

When buying a new or a used car, or having a car repaired, choose a dealer who is a member of one of the motor trade associations:
- Retail Motor Industry Federation (RMI) ▶⌂, which also runs the National Conciliation Service
- Society of Motor Manufacturers and Traders Ltd (SMMT) ▶⌂
- Vehicle Builders and Repairers Association Ltd (VBRA) ▶⌂, for repairers who specialise in bodywork repairs.

These associations have produced a code of practice jointly with the Office of Fair Trading. The code lays down standards for buying new and used cars, advertisements for used cars, guarantees and warranties, the cost of repairs and the availability of spare parts.

If you have a complaint against a dealer or repairer who is a member of a trade association, first write to the trader. If you do not get the response you want, contact the trade association to which the trader belongs. All three associations have a code of practice that their members must follow and offer a conciliation service to help to resolve disputes between members and consumers.

WAYS OF IMPORTING A CAR

There are three main ways to buy an imported car:
• directly from a dealer abroad
• in the UK through a specialist import agency or a car supermarket
• from an online dealer on the Internet.

If you have problems, your legal rights depend on which type of outlet you bought the car from. If you bought online, for example, you are covered by the Distance Selling Regulations (see p47), so you can cancel if the supplier fails to deliver on time.

Whichever outlet you buy from, ask the supplier to confirm in writing that the car will have a UK specification and a pre-delivery quality check (see below). The car must be registered and licensed as soon as possible after it arrives in the UK. To do this, you fill in application V55/4 from the Driver and Vehicle Licensing Agency (DVLA) ▶ ⌂, and submit it with the required documents and registration fee to your local DVLA office. For a list of documents required, contact the DVLA.

POINTS TO CHECK BEFORE YOU BUY

Specification
The car should be 'UK specification', that is with the same features as cars sold by the main UK dealers, although UK specification imports may have minor differences. Get a brochure from a UK dealer and compare what is shown there with your car's specification to check whether there are any significant differences.

Type Approval Certificate
This confirms that the car meets UK and EU standards of safety and emissions. Without one you cannot register the car in the UK. The certificate may not automatically be supplied with the car, so before you confirm your order write to the supplier to make the certificate a condition of purchase. For more information, contact the Vehicle Certification Agency ▶ ⌂.

Pre-delivery quality check
Check the service book, in which the supplying dealer should stamp the pre-delivery section to say that the car is fault-free. Good car supermarkets and importers also carry out checks.

Warranty
Most cars supplied from the Continent have a two-year manufacturer's warranty from new. In most cases you can pay to extend it to three years.

REJECTING AN IMPORTED CAR

If you bought the car:
• **from an EU dealer on the Continent**
Reject it to the dealer under European Directive 1999/44/EC (see p29). Consult the European Consumer Centre (see p32).

• **from a specialist import agency/broker**
Reject the car to the import agency or broker under the Sale of Goods Act 1979 (as amended; see p29).

• **from a car supermarket or import specialist**
Reject the car to the seller under the Sale of Goods Act 1979 (as amended; see p29).

Money back for a faulty new car

Q **Our car is only a few weeks old but it has so many faults that it spends more time in the local garage than it does on our drive. I want to change it but I'm told dealers can refuse if you leave it too long. Can they do that?**

A No. Under the Sale of Goods Act 1979 (as amended), a car must be 'of satisfactory quality' (see p29), and because your car is new, it should be free from even minor defects. If a defect occurs within the first six months, it is assumed that it was present when you bought the car, and unless the dealer can prove otherwise you should be given a replacement. ▶

245

ACTION PLAN

1 Compile a diary of what has gone wrong with your car, how long it has been away for repairs and whether the dealer loaned you a vehicle to use while yours was being repaired.

2 Write a letter ▶ ✍ to the person in charge of the dealership demanding a meeting and a replacement car.

3 If you paid for the car through a hire purchase or personal contract purchase plan (PCP, see box, below), contact the finance company. It owns the car until you have paid in full and so may help you to resolve the dispute.

4 If, having tried this, you still have a faulty car, write to tell the dealer of any action you intend to take. This could include getting an independent inspection by the AA ▶ ⛖ or RAC ▶ ⛖ , who will list in a report what needs to be put right. The report may cost £100-£300 depending on its scope

and the size and type of vehicle. Give a copy of the report to the dealer, who should tackle all the faults.

5 If the dealer does not repair your car, ask your local Citizens Advice Bureau ▶ ⛖ or trading standards office (see p30) for advice.

Charged for exceeding mileage agreement

Q I bought a car using a personal contract purchase plan (PCP), but now I realise that the agreement I've signed allows for only 10,000 miles a year. I'll drive twice that, so I'm liable for a hefty extra charge. Can I avoid this?

A No, not if you exceed the agreed mileage limit. If you expect to go over the limit, do not wait until the end of the agreement to sort it out or you will be liable for excess mileage charges.

Contact the loan company offering the PCP immediately, explain the situation and ask for an increase in the mileage limit. You will pay more per month, but it should work out cheaper than the extra you would have had to pay otherwise.

Your finance company repossesses your car

Q I was unable to pay a number of instalments due on my car loan. This morning someone from the finance company towed the car away. Can the company do that?

A Possibly not. Strict procedures govern the repossession of goods. For example, the finance company may have acted illegally by repossessing the

---

PERSONAL CONTRACT PURCHASE PLANS

Personal contract purchase plans (usually called PCPs) are similar to hire purchase agreements, but payments are lower because you hand back the car at the end of the period. If you decide to keep the car, you pay an additional sum at the end of the plan.

PCPs set mileage limits, which can be as low as 7000 miles a year. You will be charged extra if you exceed the limit, but you can opt to increase it. You must keep the car in good order and serviced as the manufacturer recommends or you will face a large bill when you hand it back.

car without having sent you a default notice or applied for a court order. Contact your local Citizens Advice Bureau ▶ ▭ or trading standards office (see p30) about your rights and liabilities under the Consumer Credit Act 1974. Their advice will depend on the type of finance arrangement you have, so you should show them copies of your agreement.

If the finance company repossessed your car legally, the company may agree to revive the loan if you pay the instalments owing and the repossession costs. You may have to sign a new agreement that imposes tough penalties should you fall behind with the payments.

If you cannot afford to negotiate, tell the finance company at once. It will sell the car quickly at auction. If the sum raised is too small to repay the loan, the company will claim the balance from you, plus a fee for repossessing and selling the car. Offer to pay what you can and, provided that the amount is realistic, the lender should accept.

Repairs to brakes not covered by warranty

Q **I bought a car new. Two years and 40,000 miles later, it needs an overhaul of the brakes that will cost £600. I reckon this should be covered by the manufacturer's warranty, which is still in force, but the dealer disagrees. Can he do that?**

A Yes. No warranty will stave off all bills apart from those for routine servicing. The manufacturer's warranty provides cover for a part that fails prematurely. If, for example, a gearbox collapses after just six months' use the manufacturer will pay for its repair. But you should expect the brakes to need regular attention and replacement parts. That said, it sounds as if your car needs a lot of work given its age and mileage.

Ask your dealer to approach the manufacturer on your behalf for a goodwill payment to cover, say, half the cost of the repairs.

A used car needs major repairs

Q **The dealer promised that the second-hand car he sold me was in excellent condition. Six months later, I've taken the car to a garage and discovered that it has been in a major accident and needs hundreds of pounds worth of repairs to put it right. Can the dealer get away with that?**

A Yes, if you can prove that the car was wrongly described. Under the Sale of Goods Act 1979 (as amended; see p29), a car must be of satisfactory quality and as described. If, for instance, the car was advertised in a local newspaper as 'in excellent condition' and you can trace, or have kept, the advertisement, this will help to prove your case. If you saw the car on the dealer's web site and you have a print-out of the description, that is equally good.

You will also have to prove that the work required is a direct result of the crash. To do that, you will need a letter from the garage that has inspected your car. ▶

<aside>
GOLDEN RULE

Commission a vehicle history check on any used car before you buy (see box, p249). For about £30 you can see if it has been written off by an insurer following a crash, although less serious damage is not recorded.
</aside>

BUYING & OWNING A CAR

STOLEN CAR • BUYING SECOND-HAND • MISREPRESENTATION

ACTION PLAN

1 Ask your garage for a letter or a written report stating that the car has been in an accident and detailing the repairs that are needed as a result. Gather as much other material as possible, such as the original advertisement from which you bought the car, or descriptions of it in a sale catalogue or on a flyer.

2 When you have enough evidence, arrange to meet the dealer, show him the evidence and ask him to pay for the repairs.

3 If the dealer refuses to pay, contact your local trading standards office (see p30). Trading standards officials will investigate cases of cars that are incorrectly described.

I TOLD YOU IT WAS STOLEN... LOOK, THE LEGITIMATE OWNER IS STILL IN THE BOOT

A second-hand car is stolen property

Q The second-hand car I bought through a small ad in the local paper turns out to have been stolen. The police say it must be returned to its owner. Can that be right?

A Yes. If the person from whom it was stolen has not made an insurance claim, you will have to return the car. If that person has claimed and used the money to buy another car, ownership may have passed to the insurer. Should the insurer want the car, it would be for the courts, not the police, to decide who owns it. If the car is needed as evidence in a criminal case, the police can seize it.

You will probably have to return the car because, under the Sale of Goods Act 1979 (as amended; see p29), the seller must be the rightful owner of the item or have the agreement of the owner to sell it. Otherwise the item can be reclaimed by the true owner. If you can find the seller, you can claim a full refund. Seek advice from your local Citizens Advice Bureau ▶ ⌨ or trading standards office (see p30) about reclaiming your money.

If you had a history check done (see box, opposite), contact the company that carried out the check. Provided that it took place less than a year ago, you can claim compensation from the checking company if you lose the car.

A car may not be the seller's to sell

Q Without realising it, I bought a car privately that was still under hire-purchase. Now the finance company is threatening to collect the car. Can it do that?

A Yes. The car is legally owned by the finance company until all the instalments are paid, so the seller had no right to sell the car.

While the law entitles you to recover the full price you paid, the seller may have disappeared. If he is still around you could sue him, but there is no guarantee you will see any money even if you win.

Since you bought the car privately and the owner did not tell you that its hire purchase agreement was not terminated, you may count as an 'innocent third party' and you may have ownership rights. Contact your local trading standards office (see p30) for advice.

Had you purchased the car from a dealer or at an auction, getting a refund would be straightforward. The dealer or auctioneer should have checked the car's history before offering it for sale and, if they did, but were not told that the car was on hire purchase, they can claim compensation from the agency that did the checking (see box, right).

A used car's mileage has been 'clocked'

Q My car had 52,000 miles recorded when I bought it from a dealer. Now the engine has seized up and my garage reckons it is badly worn, suggesting that the mileage has been illegally wound back, or 'clocked'. Can I get my money back?

A Probably not, unless you can prove that the mileage was falsified and that the dealer told you that it was genuine. The Sale of Goods Act 1979 (as amended; see p29) says that you are entitled to accurate information about the car, including the mileage. A dealer who is unable to confirm that the mileage on the speedometer is correct must display a disclaimer notice saying so clearly beside the mileage reading. It

CHECK OUT A USED CAR'S HISTORY

● Data-checking agencies and motoring organisations such as the AA ▶⊟ and HPI ▶⊟ run history checks on second-hand cars for a small fee. The check will establish whether the car is recorded as stolen, is an insurance write-off, is subject to an unpaid loan or hire-purchase agreement, whether the registration number matches the chassis number, and whether the car was imported by an individual.
● If the car is given the all-clear but problems arise later, you can claim up to £10,000 in compensation from the company that did the check.
● Checks cost about £30 and can often be done over the phone with confirmation in writing.

is an offence for anyone to alter the mileage on a car, and if you suspect that this has happened, report the dealer to your local trading standards office (see p30), who will advise you on taking legal action against the dealer.

ACTION PLAN

1 If the mileage was included in the advertisement for the car, get a copy of the advertisement as proof of what was published.

2 Ask the manager of the garage that inspected your car to put what the mechanics have told you in writing.

3 Write to the dealer who sold the car to you and request a meeting.

4 At the meeting, show the dealer your evidence and ask for a refund of the difference between what you paid and what a car with higher mileage would cost (you can look up the value of this in a used-car price guide, which you can buy from a newsagent).

5 If the dealer will not give you a refund, you may have to consider suing for compensation. Seek advice from your local trading standards office (see p30).

GOLDEN RULE

If the seller of a used car cannot produce the vehicle registration document (V5), for whatever reason – including saying that it has already been sent to the DVLA – do not buy the car.

BUYING & OWNING A CAR

Buying a used car

There are several checks you can make to safeguard yourself against buying a car that has been inaccurately described by the seller, or is subject to a credit arrangement, or has been stolen or written off. Check the identity of the car and seller; look for tell-tale signs on the car; and be sure that all paperwork is in order.

1 CHECK OUT THE SELLER

Buying privately
- If the car is advertised, keep the ad. If there is a dispute, it may help to provide evidence.
- Be wary of small ads that give a mobile number only and of several ads giving the same phone number. Some professional traders masquerade as private sellers by using small ads, to dodge their legal obligations. If you answer, say 'I'm calling about the car'. A seller who has to ask 'Which one?' may be a dealer with many cars for sale.
- Insist on going to the seller's home to see the car and take someone with you. If the person offers to come to you or to meet you somewhere, refuse.
- Check that the seller's name and address are on the vehicle registration document (V5). If not, ask why – a stolen car will not be sold from the address on the V5.
- Check that extras are included in the price.
- Arrange for a history check to be carried out before you buy (see box, p249).

Buying from a dealer
- Ask whether the dealer belongs to a trade association (see p243). Members are required to carry out pre-delivery inspections and you can ask to see the inspection report.
- If the dealer is not a trade association member, ask whether the car has had a pre-sale mechanical inspection, and if so, what was checked, what faults were found and were they put right?
- Is a warranty included in the price? What does it cover?
- Will the car be serviced before delivery?
- Will the car have a year's MOT certificate?
- Will the dealer repair any scratches and other minor defects before delivering the car?

2 CHECK OUT THE CAR

- Sellers do not have to offer information, but any statements they make must be accurate.
- View the car in daylight and good weather. Take a friend along to act as a witness to what the seller tells you about the car.
- Check for uneven gaps between body panels, and differences in paint colour from one part of the car to the next, as these could indicate that a car has been seriously damaged and repaired.
- Ensure that the car sits level on its suspension and that tyre wear is even throughout (be sure to check inside edge of tread as well as outside).
- Verify that the Vehicle Identification Number (VIN) given on the V5 matches that on the car. The VIN is usually stamped on the front bodywork under the bonnet. On models built since the 1990s, the VIN appears at the base of the windscreen on the driver's side.
- Ask about the car's mileage; its history; whether it has ever been in an accident or stolen; and whether it is subject to a hire-purchase agreement or loan, and if so, whether everything has been paid.

3 ASK TO SEE

- The service history (this may be a single receipt).
- The MOT test certificate (this is required if the vehicle is at least three years old). Does it belong to the vehicle?
- The V5 (the vehicle registration document).

4 ASK FOR A RECEIPT

The receipt should include:
- a description of the car
- the registration number
- your name and the seller's name and address
- the price paid and the date.

A private seller may add phrases such as 'Sold as seen' or 'No warranty implied'. Sellers cannot legally restrict liability with such statements and you can report them to trading standards (see p30).

5 CHECK THE CAR'S IDENTITY

Check the name and address of the seller on the V5.

Check that the number of previous owners matches what you have been told.

Check the car's registration number against the V5, tax disc and MOT certificate.

Check that the make, model and colour on the tax disc and V5 match the vehicle you are looking at.

The vehicle identity number (VIN) should be the same on the car, the MOT certificate and the V5.

AS ███████ **VEHICLE REGISTRATION DOCUMENT V5**

Please write in black ink and capital letters.
Please note the shaded boxes are for official use only.

KEEPER DETAILS - if any details in section A change, please write new details in section B. *(see notes 2 to 6 overleaf)*

A Registered Keeper ~ Please note the registered keeper is not necessarily the vehicle's legal owner *(see note 1 overleaf)*

Registration Mark ███████   Validation Character **1** **3**

ACQUIRED VEHICLE ON 20 12 1996

1. NEW AT FIRST REGISTRATION.

B New keeper/ address details   Mr **1**   Mrs **2**   Miss **3**   Please tick the appropriate box **W** **4**

Title or business name
Forenames in full **5**
Surname/ DVLA Fleet Nº **6**
Address

Post Town **7**
Postcode **8**
If the keeper has changed, tick box and give the date of sale or transfer **K** **10**   **11** **12**
New keeper's ~ driver number (see note 12 overleaf)

CANCELLED

VEHICLE DETAILS If details in section D change, please write new details in section E *(see notes 12, 10 and 11 overleaf)*
You are not obliged by law to provide current information, *(see note overleaf)*

C (to last complete mile) *(see note 7 overleaf)*
Please tick the appropriate box *(see notes 8 and 9 overleaf)*   **R** **14**
Scrapped **S**   Date of Scrapping/Export Day Month Year
Exported **P** **15**   **16**
Vehicle Details- write new details only **H** **17**
18
19 **20**
21 CLR **22**
23
24
25
26
27
29
3

Declarations Please read the notes overleaf before signing
Registered Keeper: (to sign when notifying any change)
I declare that the new details I have given are true to the best of my knowledge.
Registered Keeper _____ Date _____
New Keeper *(see note 6 overleaf)*
I declare that this vehicle was sold or transferred to me on the date shown in section B and my name and address are correctly shown.
New Keeper _____ Date _____
The Law: If the vehicle is sold or transferred, both the registered keeper and the new keeper must sign this document.

D Make **FIAT**
Model/Type **BRAVO 1.4 SX**
3 DOOR HATCHBACK
Variant
Version

Date of Registration **20 12 1996**
Last Change of Keeper **05 09 1997**
Nº of Former Keepers **1**
VIN/Chassis/Frame Nº ███████
Engine Nº **0577040**
Cylinder Capacity **1370 CC**
CO₂
Type of Fuel **PETROL**
Taxation Class **PRIVATE/LIGHT GOODS (PLG)**
Type Approval Nº
Category
Revenue Weight
Seating Capacity
Colour(s) **GREY**
Document Ref. Nº ███████   **02 11 01**
Despatch Codes **3621Z051** ███████   **36**

EXPIRES 30 09 04 (tax disc) £110.00

F884UU £110.00
FIAT
1370
12
CANCELLED

Vehicle Inspectorate

MOT test certificate

Motor vehicle registration mark ███████

This certificate has been issued according to the conditions and notes on the back of this certificate.

Note: If you have doubts as to whether this certificate is valid, call our MOT enquiry line on: **0845 600 5977.**

Vehicle identification or chassis number: ███████

Colour of vehicle:	GREY
Make of vehicle:	FIAT
Approximate year the vehicle was first used:	1996
Recorded mileage:	██ 100
If it is a goods vehicle, state the maximum design gross weight:	
Type of fuel:	PETROL

Serial number of the last test certificate: ███████

Crystal Mark
Clarity approved by Plain English Campaign

CANCELLED

FIAT AUTO S.P.A.
250   kg
1-   850   kg
2-   850   kg
MOTORE·ENGINE 182A3.000
VERSION 182AA1A
4909645

MOT CHANGES

In 2004 the MOT testing scheme will be computerised, and the current MOT certificate will be replaced by a receipt-style certificate issued by computer. Records of all tests for all vehicles will be stored, so someone buying a used car will be able to trace the vehicle's MOT history. And the use of stolen and forged certificates will become more difficult.

For all vehicles with more than █ passenger seats

Seat belt installation checked this test?   Yes / No   N/A

Previous installation check date: N/A

Number of seat belts fitted at

A second-hand car is not up to standard

Q Two weeks ago, I bought a used car from a dealer. Today I called out the AA because the brakes felt strange. The AA said they were in poor condition and made the car unsafe. Yet the dealer gave me a newly issued MOT test certificate when I collected the car. Should the dealer pay for repairs?

A Yes. Under the Sale of Goods Act 1979 (as amended; see p29) a car, whether new or used, should be of satisfactory quality. It should also be roadworthy. The standard for assessing this is lower for a used car than a new one, but because your car developed a safety fault so soon after purchase, its quality may be sub-standard for its age and the price paid, or may not conform to information given by the dealer. The dealer could be committing an offence by allowing an unroadworthy car to be driven from his premises.

ACTION PLAN

1 Contact the dealer and explain what has happened and how many miles you have driven since you took delivery of the car.

2 Show the AA patrol's report on the problem to the dealer.

3 Remind the dealer of his obligations under the Sale of Goods Act and negotiate the cost of repairs.

4 If the dealer denies responsibility, contact your local trading standards office (see p30), explain the problem and ask for help. In rare cases an MOT will be re-examined if there are grounds to suspect its legitimacy, and trading standards can advise on this.

WORD OF WARNING

The MOT certificate proves only that the car met the required standard when it was examined and is no guarantee against future problems. It does not guarantee the roadworthiness of a car, even if it was issued recently.

A car does not live up to its description

Q The car I bought from a private seller was advertised as 'reliable, regularly serviced and in good condition'. But it broke down after a week, and my garage says it hasn't been serviced for years. Can I claim against the seller for the cost of the repairs?

Yes. When you buy privately, your rights in law are not as strong as they are when you buy from a dealer, and the principal 'caveat emptor', or 'buyer beware' applies.

But you are entitled to be given accurate information in advertisements and descriptions from the seller, and in answers to your questions. If you can show that the statements the dealer made were false or misleading, and that the work needed on the car is a direct result of servicing having been neglected in the past, the seller should pay most if not all of the repair costs.

ACTION PLAN

1 Ask the garage owner to write a report explaining why he says your car has not been serviced properly and how this affected its performance.

2 Show the report and the car's advertisement to the seller and ask for the repair costs to be reimbursed.

3 If the seller denies responsibility, contact your local trading standards office (see p30) about suing for the repair costs. If they are below £5000, you can use the small claims or fast track in the county court (see p19).

PRECAUTIONS WHEN YOU SELL A CAR

• Wait until you have been paid in full before handing over the car keys to anyone.
• If you accept a deposit, write a receipt. It should show the agreed total price, the amount paid as a deposit and the deadline by which the buyer must pay the balance. If you have agreed to accept cash (safer than a cheque), also make a note of this. You and the buyer should both sign the receipt and keep a copy.
• When the balance is securely in your bank account or in your hand, issue another receipt.
• Then, and only then, should you hand over the vehicle registration document V5, having first completed and posted the seller's part of the form to the Driver and Vehicle Licensing Authority (DVLA) ▶ ⌖ .

ACTION PLAN

1 If friendly persuasion does not work, write to your neighbour demanding that she pay up within a week.

2 If your neighbour fails to pay, ask your local Citizens Advice Bureau ▶ ⌖ or Law Centre ▶ ⌖ for advice. If she owes you less than £5000, you can use the small claims or fast track procedure in the county court (see p19). Your neighbour may pay as soon as the court contacts her.

The buyer refuses to pay the balance

Q I sold my old car to a neighbour, who paid a deposit and promised the balance a week later. In the meantime she crashed the car and now refuses to pay. Can she do that?

A No. Even if the agreement over the purchase of the car was reached on a hand-shake basis, it forms a contract between you both. By delivering the car, you have kept your side of the bargain and the law requires her to do the same.

The seller was not aware of a car's faults

Q I recently sold my car through an advertisement in the local paper. The buyer says the clutch has gone wrong and he's threatening to sue me. I didn't know that anything was wrong with the clutch when I sold the car. Can he do that?

A Yes. He can sue you, but you should have nothing to fear because you did not misrepresent the state of the vehicle when you sold it.   ▶

Contracts are based on the principle of 'caveat emptor' or 'buyer beware'. When the buyer agreed to exchange money for the car he entered a contract with you, and he should have satisfied himself about the car's condition before he did so.

ACTION PLAN

1 Tell the buyer that you did not know there was a problem with the clutch. Produce documents from your garage showing that MOT tests or services did not suggest the clutch was defective.

2 If the buyer sues you, seek advice from your local Citizens Advice Bureau ▶ ⌨ or trading standards office (see p30), or a solicitor (see p20) about defending yourself.

Caught over the speed limit by a camera

Q I got a speeding ticket in the post, but I'm certain I didn't exceed the speed limit. The only evidence is a picture taken by a police speed camera. Can the police fine me on that evidence?

A Yes. The technology behind speed cameras is now reliable enough to be trusted by courts. The police do not need additional evidence to prosecute. If you are certain that you were driving within the speed limit for the road, or that the car pictured is not yours, act quickly.

ACTION PLAN

1 Write to the ticket issuer straight away ▶ ✍ – the fine increases if you delay payment but it will be frozen if you reply. Explain why you think you were not speeding. If there were passengers, ask them to write down what they recollect and enclose this.

2 The police authority will check the camera. If it was faulty, the police will cancel the ticket. If it was not, the police will inform you and it is best to pay the fine. If you think you have grounds for taking the case to court and you belong to a motoring organisation such as the AA ▶ ⌨ or RAC ▶ ⌨ , ask the legal department for advice; if not, contact your local trading standards (see p30).

WORD OF WARNING

If your car is caught on camera while someone else is driving it, you will receive the ticket because you are the car's registered keeper. If this happens, you must tell the police who was driving.

Fined for speeding when out of town

Q I was surprised to receive a ticket in the post fining me for speeding when at the time I had driven to a business conference in another town. I've told the ticket issuer, but the clerk insists the data is correct and that I have to pay the fine. Can she do that?

A Yes, unless you can prove that you were elsewhere at the time. It may be that the car's number plate has been copied and used on a stolen car of the same make, model and colour. If so, the driver will flout parking and speed restrictions safe in the knowledge that you will receive the tickets.

Write to the ticket issuer and explain that you had driven to another town at the time the speeding offence was committed. Enclose copies of garage, parking, shop and other receipts or credit card vouchers as proof. You should also ask the event organisers, colleagues and anyone else who saw you or spoke to you to confirm in writing that you were with them at the stated time.

If you receive a series of tickets, contact the Driver and Vehicle Licensing Authority (DVLA ▶ 🗎), which may issue another licence plate.

The road tax disc that fell off the windscreen

Q **I received a penalty notice because a traffic warden noticed that my car wasn't displaying a road fund licence. The disc had peeled off the windscreen and fallen into the footwell. Do I have to pay?**

A Probably. The law requires you to display a valid tax disc. If you write as directed on the notice, explaining what happened, there is a chance that because you had a tax disc, you will be let off. If not, you will have to pay.

WORD OF WARNING
To catch cars without road tax discs police now use high-definition digital cameras mounted on signal gantries at busy junctions and also on police vehicles. You will probably not know that you have been caught until a penalty notice lands on your doormat.

Pulled over for a faulty brake light

Q **The police stopped me recently. They said one of my car's brake lights wasn't working and the exhaust pipe was loose. They threatened a fine but let me off with a warning. But the lights were working when I checked last weekend, and the car passed its MOT test only a month ago. Can they get away with that?**

BE CERTAIN YOUR CAR IS ROADWORTHY

It is your responsibility to check that your car is roadworthy before every trip. If the police spot one fault, they can pull you over and inspect your car for other problems. The following points are legal requirements.

Tyres
• Each tyre must have at least the minimum tread of 1.6mm around the entire diameter and three-quarters of the width.
• Each tyre must be correctly inflated.

Lights, indicators and number plates
• Must be clean and clearly visible.
• Headlights must be adjusted so they do not dazzle other road users.
• All lights and indicators must be working properly.

Windscreen and windows
• Must be clean. Check that the washer bottle for the windscreen is topped up. It is an offence to drive without washer fluid.
• Must not be blocked by obstructions.

Exhaust emissions and sound levels
• Must not exceed the legal limits – check with a garage.

A Yes. Your faulty rear light gave the police a reason to pull you over. The Road Vehicles Lighting Regulations 1989 give detailed requirements for lighting and if you infringe them you are liable to pay fines of between £60 and £2500. A similar set of regulations and lesser fines govern the exhaust pipe.

The fact that your car had just passed its MOT test does not excuse the offences here. The MOT test ensures only that the vehicle meets the set standards at the time. Although the certificate is valid for a year, it gives no promise that the car will continue to be roadworthy all through that year.

By issuing you with a warning, the police were voicing the law's view that the driver must ensure a car's roadworthiness before every journey (see box, above). They will issue a notice giving you the opportunity to rectify ▶

WHAT TO DO WHEN THE POLICE STOP YOU

Keep cool and stay polite.

Be cooperative.

Ask why they have stopped you.

If you have an important appointment and the delay is making you late, explain this politely.

If you are asked to produce your driving licence, insurance or MOT certificate (the MOT applies only if your car is more than three years old), but do not have them with you, you will be asked to present them at a police station of your choice within a week. If this is not possible (because, for instance, you have sent your licence to be updated), contact the police station immediately and explain the problem. Provided that your reasons are good ones, they will allow you more time.

To make a complaint

1 If you believe that the patrol stopped you without a good reason, or if the officers were rude to you, note their ID numbers (which appear on the shoulders of their uniforms), the number of the patrol car (shown prominently on its body or roof), and its registration number.

2 To complain, go to your local police station, where you will be seen by the senior officer on duty, or phone the station, explain that you wish to use the complaints procedure and ask for a complaints form. Fill it in and send it to your local police station.

3 If you have made a minor complaint, a senior police officer will investigate as long as you agree. If you do not agree or if you make a serious complaint, an Area Complaints Unit or the Police Anti-Corruption Group will investigate.

4 The investigating body will inform you of the outcome of the investigation.

5 If the matter is not resolved satisfactorily, write to the Police Complaints Authority ▶ 📖 or complete the complaints form on the Authority's web site. The Authority will look into your complaint and, if necessary, appoint an officer to investigate.

the faults they have found within 7 or 14 days. When you have repaired them, you must get the notice stamped by an MOT station, then you take it with all your other driving documents, to the police station specified in the notice.

The police must have a valid reason to stop a driver, and they cannot search cars or drivers without a good reason (see question, below). But once they have stopped a driver, they can inspect the car more generally for roadworthiness.

Stopped by the police for erratic driving

Q **A police traffic patrol made me pull over. They kept me for 10 minutes checking my car and asking questions. When I asked why they had stopped me, they said my driving was erratic. Eventually, they let me go without charge. Can they just stop anyone like that?**

A No. The police must have a good reason to suspect that you had committed an offence before they stop a driver. And they must tell you what the offence is. If, for example, they stopped you because they believed you to be guilty of careless driving, they must tell you that early on, not wait to be asked.

Any questions the police then ask and any checks they make must relate to the offence they think you have committed. If, for example, a car has a flickering rear light, they may check the car for roadworthiness (see question, p255); and if they think you have been drinking alcohol, they may ask you to take a breath test (see question, opposite). But they are not allowed to examine the car inch-by-inch or search the interior or boot unless they have a good reason. If the police stop you without giving a reason, and start searching your car, ask questions or want to inspect the contents, challenge them politely. Ask why they want to know or look. If you are not satisfied by their answers, you can refuse to cooperate. If you believe you have been treated improperly, you can make a complaint (see box, opposite).

Breath test shows positive

Q **Driving home after a party, I was stopped by the police and breathalysed. I had drunk one small glass of wine, but the test showed positive and I was arrested. I was taken, frantic with worry, to a police station where I took another breathalyser test, which showed I was in the clear. Can the police breathalyse anyone like that?**

A Yes, you failed the roadside test so the patrol could arrest you and take you to a police station. The equipment used for roadside testing indicates the presence of alcohol in your body and enables the officers to decide whether or not to arrest you. The decision to prosecute is not made until the results are confirmed by repeat breath tests or by blood or urine tests carried out at the police station (see box, right).

Traffic patrols have considerable scope for breath-testing motorists, but they are not allowed to test randomly. If they see you speeding, jumping a red light or driving erratically, they have the right to stop you and breathalyse you.

Breath tests are given routinely to all drivers involved in accidents to which the police are called.

BREATH TESTS AT THE STATION

If a roadside breathalyser test indicates the presence of alcohol in your body, you will be arrested and taken to a police station for a more thorough test.

- The prescribed alcohol limit is 35 microgrammes in 100 ml of breath. At the police station, two samples of breath are taken and the lower result is ignored. The machine used takes only a minute or so to produce the results and you should be shown these immediately.
- In certain cases blood or urine tests are taken, such as when a breath-testing machine is not available or is considered by the police to be unreliable, or the officer or doctor present believes there are medical reasons (perhaps the presence of drugs) why a breath test should not be taken. If urine is to be tested, two samples must be provided within an hour. The prescribed limits are 80 mg in 100 ml of blood or 107 mg in 100 ml of urine.
- If you test below the limit, you will be released.
- If you test above the limit, you will be prosecuted for driving with excess alcohol in your body. The offence will be dealt with at a magistrate's court (see p17) and carries a maximum penalty of a £5000 fine, six months in prison and a licence endorsement of up to 11 penalty points. You will also be banned from driving for 12 months, longer if you tested well in excess of the legal limit, and for three years if this is your second conviction within 10 years.
- If you refuse to give a test you have to provide a 'reasonable excuse', which is tightly defined in law, such as mental or physical incapacity, otherwise you face the same maximum penalties as if you tested over the limit.

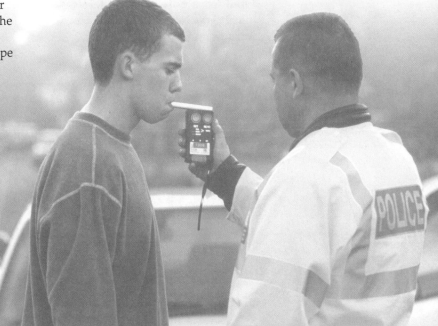

PARKING FINES: HOW TO APPEAL

The Parking and Traffic Appeals Service (London only) ▶ ⬜ and the National Parking Adjudication Service ▶ ⬜ provide an independent service for deciding disputed parking, bus lane and London congestion charge penalties. There is no charge for submitting an appeal.

When loss of licence means loss of job

Q I've been arrested and charged with drink-driving. I work in sales and need to drive to visit customers. If I lose my licence, I'll be sacked. Can I ask the magistrates not to ban me from driving?

A No. If the magistrates are satisfied that you are guilty, they have to impose at least a year's ban. There are exceptions to the rule, but very few. For example, you may not be prosecuted if you are drunk when driving on private land that is not accessible by the public, or if you could show that the police did not have a good reason to stop and breathalyse you (see question, p255).

Fined for parking at a faulty meter

Q I was given a parking ticket even though the parking meter wouldn't take my money and I had left a note on it explaining that it was broken. Can the traffic warden do that?

A Yes. You cannot park legally where there is a faulty meter, even if you discover that it is broken only when you try to insert coins into it. Most meters carry a notice warning that parking is suspended if the meter is faulty. An explanatory note placed on your car windscreen or on the meter will not be reason for a traffic warden not to give you a ticket.

If you believe you have a good case to argue, take it to the Parking and Traffic Appeals Service (London only) ▶ ⬜ or the National Parking Adjudication Service ▶ ⬜ (see box, left).

Act quickly, because most parking penalties increase if you delay payment, but will be frozen from the time you appeal until a decision is reached.

Vehicle clamped in a pub car park

Q I parked in a pub car park while I went for a walk. Two hours later, I returned to find that the car had been wheel-clamped and there was a £120 release fee. Can a clamping company do that?

A Yes, but you can challenge the clamping if the answer to any of the following questions is 'no'.
• Were there signs restricting parking to pub customers and saying that anyone else would be clamped?
• If yes, were the signs placed where anyone using the car park could be expected to see them?
• Was a telephone number for the clamping company given on the signs?
• Did the clamping company release your car promptly?
• Do other pubs in the area charge as much as £120 for being wheel-clamped? Check a few in the area.

AVOIDING PARKING FINES

• Do not park on a double yellow line. If you park on a single yellow line, check when and for how long parking is allowed. Park on a red line only if there are signs saying that parking is allowed.

• If you park at a meter, check that it works and park in the bay marked. Do not park at a meter showing an 'out of order' sign, or one that will not take your coins.

• Do not return to a meter or a pay-and-display parking bay and add more coins.

• Obey local bye-laws displayed on notices on the parking meter and at the roadside. Some prohibit moving to another parking bay or meter in the same street once your time is up, while others restrict re-parking to specified times.

• In a pay-and-display space, put the ticket where it is easily visible. Clear old tickets from the windows and dashboard so the warden sees the current one.

• Do not park and go off in search of the right coins – a traffic warden could issue a parking ticket while you are away.

ACTION PLAN

1 Quickly gather any evidence you can – photograph the site, showing the size and location of any signs.

2 Write to the clamping company and the pub landlord to demand a refund, explaining why you think the clamping was unlawful. If you belong to a motoring organisation, such as the AA ▶ 📖 or RAC ▶ 📖 , ask the legal department for advice.

3 If the company and landlord refuse a refund, write that you are prepared to take legal action against them.

4 If you do not get a refund, contact your local trading standards office (see p30) for advice on pursuing your claim against the clamping company.

Caught out for breaking down

Q My car broke down in a parking bay where parking is restricted to half an hour at a time. I left an explanatory note on the windscreen and went in search of help. When I got back, I found that my car had been wheel-clamped. Can a parking attendant do that?

A Yes. By law the car should not have been left there, even though you had no choice. Parking authorities take a tough line in such cases, but if you can prove that your problems were genuine, the ticket issuer may let you off. ▶

BUYING & OWNING A CAR

PAY & DISPLAY • RESIDENTS' PARKING • DAMAGE IN CAR PARK • CONGESTION CHARGE

ACTION PLAN

1 Pay the clamping fee in order to have your car released, but pay by credit card if possible, and write on the cheque or credit card voucher, and on the receipt 'under protest' (see p35).

2 Write to the clamping company's office (printed on the parking ticket) saying what happened ▶✍. Send proof of your breakdown – perhaps an AA or RAC patrol officer's report – and emphasise that you removed the car as quickly as you could and had intended to park for only half an hour.

3 If this fails, contact the Parking and Traffic Appeals Service or the National Parking Adjudication Service (see box, p258), who will help to resolve the dispute.

THERE! FOUND ONE!

A parking ticket paid for but not displayed

Q I bought a pay-and-display ticket and fixed it to my car windscreen. But when I returned to my car, the ticket had fallen off and I'd been given a parking fine. Do I have to pay it?

A Yes. To comply with the parking laws you must pay and display. You clearly did the first. But, even if you could prove that you stuck the ticket where it could be seen, it was your responsibility to ensure that it stayed there while you were away from the car.

You could try writing to the authority that issued the parking penalty. Explain what happened, and enclose a copy of the ticket you bought as proof that you had paid. The issuer may agree to waive the fine.

A parking permit does not guarantee a space

Q I have a resident's parking permit. The spaces outside my house are usually taken, so I have to park several streets away. I want a refund from the council, but it says that a permit does not guarantee a space. Is that true?

A Yes. Councils can and do sell more residents' parking permits than there are parking spaces. Residents merely buy the right to use a space if one is available. If more parking spaces are needed in your street, or if the council allows drivers with no permits to park in your street without ticketing them, you can make a complaint to your local councillor (details from your local town hall or library).

Hit and run in a multistorey car park

Q My car was dented while parked in a multistorey car park. The car park attendant refuses to accept liability. Can she do that?

A Yes. Paying a fee does not make the car park attendant responsible for your vehicle; you rent the parking space. In most car parks there are notices explaining this rule, and by reading them you are considered to have accepted it.

If another driver damaged your car, he should have left a note of his contact details on your windscreen, or reported the matter to the car park attendant. If he just drove off, he has broken the law.

Report the matter to the car park manager. If the car park has video cameras, these may help to identify the driver responsible. Tell the police and obtain a crime reference number. Then report the damage to your insurer.

Mistaken identity in the congestion zone

Q I live in London and have just received notice of a fine for being in the congestion charging zone on Thursday last week, but I was nowhere near the area that day. Can they make me pay?

A No. If you can prove that you were not in the zone on that day you can appeal to Transport for London ▶ 🕮 and the penalty charge will be withdrawn. Transport for London admit that a small number of people are wrongly sent fines and expect appeals from about 20 per cent of all drivers who are fined.

ACTION PLAN
1 Use the space provided on the back of the penalty charge notice to make your case against the charge. Send

---

any proof you have that you were not in the congestion zone on that day – for example, a receipt from a garage, shop or other place that you visited.

2 Transport for London will examine the facts and may waive the charge.

3 If you are unhappy with the decision, you have the right to appeal to the Parking and Traffic Appeals Service ▶ 🕮 within 28 days (see p258).

WORD OF WARNING
You are liable to pay the fine if you lent the car to a friend or relative who drove into the zone without paying.

A blue badge-holder gets a ticket

Q I can't walk far so I have a blue badge that allows disabled parking concessions. Today I left my car on a single yellow line, but when I returned an hour later, a traffic warden had given me a parking ticket. Must I pay it?

A Possibly. If you parked so as to cause an obstruction, or if the badge was not properly displayed, you are likely to be given a ticket and you would have to pay. You must check which boxes on your ticket the warden has marked. ▶

You should challenge your penalty charge only if you can prove that the traffic warden was wrong – for example, your badge was clearly on display. Write to the address given on the ticket. If your initial approach is rejected, contact the National Parking Adjudication Service or the Parking and Traffic Appeals Service (London) (see box, p258).

WORD OF WARNING

Councils issue blue (formerly orange) badge concessionary parking permits. They allow parking on single yellow lines. Misuse of a blue badge by someone other than the badge-holder is a criminal offence, subject to a fine of up to £1000 and confiscation of the badge.

A garage keeps a car in dispute over repair bill

Q **I'm disputing the amount a garage mechanic has charged for repairing my car. The garage owner refuses to let me have the car back until I've paid the bill. Can she do that?**

A Possibly. A repairer has the right to keep goods until all reasonable charges are paid, although you should be warned of this in advance. Try asking the garage manager what was done and how she charged for the work.

• If she carried out work that you did not request and that was not necessary, tell her that you do not have to pay for it and ask her to remove it from the bill.

• If the manager failed to spell out the extent of the work and the size of the bill, ask for a discount.

• If you disagree with part of the bill, offer to pay for the work you are happy with.

If the owner refuses to cooperate, you will have to pay the bill in full.

ACTION PLAN

1 Pay the bill, but if possible, pay by credit card and inform the card issuer that the amount is disputed. The card issuer may freeze the payment until the dispute is settled. Write on the bill and on the credit card slip or cheque that you are paying 'under protest'.

2 Put your complaint in writing to the garage owner, explaining the situation ▶ and ask for the disputed amount to be refunded. Copy the letter to your credit card issuer.

3 If the garage owner offers to refund some of the money, try to negotiate. If the offer is too low, or if the owner does not refund the money, contact your local trading standards office (see p30) for advice about taking legal action in the county court (see p19).

4 If you take legal action and you are successful, inform the card issuer.

A repair did not fix the problem with my car

Q I recently had an expensive repair done while I was away. The car seemed fine until I got back, but it broke down a few days ago with the same problem and I'm having it repaired by a local garage. I want to get my money back from the first garage, but they say they fixed the problem at the time and aren't liable. Can they do that?

A No. Under the Supply of Goods and Services Act 1982 (as amended; see p53), you are entitled to have the repair work done competently, using the correct parts.

But since you are dealing with two garages, you need to take action to establish that the subsequent repairs result from the first job not having been done properly – the second breakdown may not be linked to the first one even though it appears to be. You should also establish whether the first garage carried out a temporary repair, which was not intended to last a long time. If you do not do this, you may become embroiled in a dispute between the two garages.

ACTION PLAN

1 Write to the owner of the first garage ▶ 🖎 and explain what has happened. Say that under the Supply of Goods and Services Act 1982 (as amended) you can claim for any losses you incur as a result of the repairs not being done 'with reasonable care and skill'.

2 If the garage owner refuses to admit liability, find out whether he belongs to a trade organisation (see box, p244). If so, contact the organisation, whose officers will try to resolve the dispute.

3 If he does not belong to a trade association, ask your local Citizens

AVOIDING DISPUTES OVER GARAGE REPAIRS

When you ask a garage to carry out repairs, you are entering into a contract that may be legally binding. If, for instance, you simply ask the garage to repair the car, or to get it through the MOT test, you cannot complain if the garage does what you have asked and presents you with a large bill.

● Make sure the garage's service manager notes the work that is required on a work sheet. Some garages ask you to sign to say you agree to meet the bill.

● Establish whether you are being given an estimate or a quote. An estimate is the garage's best guess at the likely cost for the job and should not be relied upon; a quote is a guaranteed price.

● Agree a budget for the work and insist that the service manager phone you to ask permission to do extra jobs that will exceed the limit you have set. Insist that this condition is written on any work sheet you sign.

● Ask in advance that any worn parts that are removed be saved. When you collect the car, ask why they needed to be replaced and ask to inspect them.

Advice Bureau ▶ 🖷 or trading standards office (see p30) for advice.

A garage charges for work not done

Q I had a full service carried out on my car, which included replacing certain parts. It turns out that some parts listed on the bill haven't been replaced. Can the garage get away with this?

A No. Take the car back to the garage with a copy of the bill and ask the service manager to show you what has been done. In some garages, the service manager gives you the part that has been replaced to show that the work has been done (this also shows that the work was necessary). Ask the service manager why this was not done.

If parts have been charged for but not fitted, and the garage is reputable, the service manager should offer to replace the worn parts. ▶

ACTION PLAN

1 If the manager will not replace the worn parts, complain in writing to the garage owner ▶ ✎.

2 If you receive no response, contact your local trading standards office (see p30). It may investigate the allegations that the garage claims to have replaced parts and charged you for them when it is possible that it had not done so.

Payment for pothole damage to a wheel

Q I hit a pothole in my car, damaging a tyre and wheel. The local council refuses to pay for repairs. Can the council refuse?

A No. The council has a duty to inspect all roads regularly and make repairs promptly. You can claim compensation if it has failed to do this. Some local authorities pay out without a fight while others take a tougher stance.

ACTION PLAN

1 Phone your local council's highways department and ask for a claims form to be sent to you.

2 Photograph the pothole and the damage to your car. Do this at once – the council may patch the road soon after your call. If the pothole is not on a major road, place a pen or a ruler beside it to indicate its size and depth.

3 Get an estimate for the repair. Be realistic. If the car is old or its tyres worn, you probably cannot justify a claim for a new wheel and tyre.

4 If the council refuses your claim, you can appeal. Phone the council and ask how to appeal, or check the council's web site – many have an online appeals form.

5 As a last resort, ask your local Citizens Advice Bureau ▶ 📖 or Law Centre ▶ 📖 about suing the council for the cost of the repairs through the small claims track in the county court (see p19).

ONE MOMENT, I'LL JUST TRANSFER YOU TO OUR HOLES EXPERT

COUNCIL

Scratches caused by a car wash

Q My car was badly scratched when I used my local car wash and the operator refuses to pay for the repairs and respraying. Can it do that?

Yes, if a notice is displayed to say that you used the car wash at your own risk and it is positioned so that you could see it easily before you paid for the wash. If a notice or disclaimer is displayed close to the wash, but not at the cash desk, it could be argued that you had entered into a contract with the operator (by paying for the wash) before you were aware of any conditions – and the operator should pay for the repairs.

If you use the car wash regularly, the operator might argue that you would have seen the disclaimer on previous visits and would be aware of it when you paid for the wash that damaged your car.

But the operator cannot restrict its liability by putting up a notice. It has a duty of care for its clients, so if you can show that the operator did not maintain the car-wash equipment, it could be liable for the damage.

You cannot claim for the whole cost of the repair. The car-wash operator could claim that the repair will improve the car, so you should contribute to it.

ACTION PLAN

1 Photograph the damage to your car and of the car-wash site, including any disclaimer notices.

2 Complain in writing to the car-wash manager. Say that you hold the car-wash company responsible for the damage and you will claim for most of the cost of the repairs to the bodywork of your car ▶✍.

3 Get a written estimate from a body shop for the repairs needed. Ask the mechanics whether they consider that the damage was wholly caused by the car wash, and if so, whether they will put that in writing.

4 Ask around. Have other customers' cars been damaged? If so, contact them and suggest mounting a joint claim against the car-wash operator.

5 If the car-wash manager does not accept liability, contact your local Citizens Advice Bureau ▶ 📖 or trading standards office (see p30) about making a claim against the company.

Claiming an elusive no-claims bonus

Q After years of driving company-owned vehicles, I've changed jobs and I'm now about to buy a car. But, despite my unblemished record, insurers are asking very high premiums because I haven't built up a no-claims bonus. Can they do that?

A Yes they can, in principle. But if you have been driving for years, yet have not had an accident, most insurers will be sympathetic in their approach.

Ask the company car fleet manager at the place where you used to work to write and support your accident-free record. Many insurers will consider giving you a no-claims discount on that basis.

Your insurer cuts your no-claims bonus

Q My car was badly damaged by a hit-and-run driver. I had no choice but to claim on my own insurance even though the accident wasn't my fault. Now my insurer has cut my no-claims discount. Can an insurer do that?

A Yes. This is a no-claims not a no-blame discount. If you claim on your policy, you lose some of the discount, regardless of whose fault the accident was. To prevent this happening, most policies let you pay an extra premium when you buy or renew the insurance to protect your no-claims discount in the event of a claim.

GOLDEN RULE

If you are involved in a collision, never settle with the other driver on the spot. Even if the damage to your car looks slight and the other driver produces cash, it is always best to let your insurance company handle things. If you accept cash and then discover that the damage is worse than you thought, you will have no comeback later on.

Settling on a knock-for-knock basis

Q A driver pulled out in front of me from a side road, causing damage to both our cars. She accepts the blame, but my insurers are settling the repair bill on a knock-for-knock basis. Can they do that?

A Yes. When both drivers have comprehensive insurance and the accident is relatively minor, the big companies have agreed to settle repair bills on a knock-for-knock basis. This means that each insurer pays for its policyholder's repairs, regardless of who is to blame. Once the drivers have returned accident report forms and other paperwork, the insurers decide where the blame lies and reimburse each other if necessary. The advantage for drivers is that cars are repaired more quickly.

If your insurance policy needs to be renewed before your claim is settled, you may not get a full no-claims discount. If the other driver told her insurer that she accepts the blame, this should not arise.

Collision with an uninsured driver

Q My car has been written off in an accident with an uninsured driver and my insurance company won't pay out. Can they do that?

A Yes. Your claim is against the other driver, not the insurance company – claims are passed directly to insurers to handle for convenience. Although you have the right to pursue a claim against the driver, there may be little point in trying to sue an uninsured driver. If you want to try to, and belong to a motoring organisation such as the AA ▶ ⌂ or RAC ▶ ⌂, you could ask the legal department for advice about claiming. Otherwise, ask your local Citizens Advice Bureau ▶ ⌂ or Law Centre ▶ ⌂ or consult a solicitor (see p20) for advice.

Your best course of action is to contact the Motor Insurers Bureau (MIB) (see box, below left). The MIB has a fund for compensating drivers involved in accidents with uninsured drivers and gives legal advice on making a claim.

If the police are prosecuting the driver, you can ask them to apply for a compensation order to recover your losses. This would mean that you need not claim compensation in the courts.

UNINSURED AND UNTRACED DRIVERS

The Motor Insurers Bureau (MIB) administers a fund to which all motor insurers in the UK contribute. It is used to compensate drivers who are involved in traffic accidents with negligent, uninsured or untraced drivers. Contact MIB ▶ ⌂ for free information, advice and report forms.
• If you are involved in an accident with an uninsured driver you can claim for all losses incurred because of the accident, including damage to the vehicle and medical expenses.
• If you are involved in an accident with an untraced or unidentified driver, you can claim for losses that result from your injuries but not for damage to your vehicle or property.

Using the insurer's preferred garage

Q My car was hit by another while it was parked. Now my insurance company insists that I take my car to one of its 'preferred garages' for body repairs. I would rather use my local dealer who I know and trust. Do I have to use the insurer's repairer?

A Probably not. The answer depends on the terms of the insurance policy – but you can negotiate with your insurers and they might agree with your choice. If so you should ask them to confirm this in writing.

If you had been to blame for the damage to your car, the decision on who chooses the garage would have depended on the likely costs of the repairs and the small print in your policy.

Since you were obviously not at fault, you could insist that a franchised dealer carry out the repairs to your car. But before doing this, consider that repairs may be carried out more quickly at the insurer's preferred garage because the garage may have already had a chance to assess the damage from photographs.

Some insurance companies will pay for repairs to be done at any main dealer, but provide extras, such as a loan car or collection and delivery of your damaged car, only if their preferred repairer is used. But it is possible that your local dealer will also lend you a car and offer a collection and delivery service.

Check what services and guarantees are offered by your insurer's preferred garage and your own local dealer before making a final decision.

Challenging an insurance pay-out

Q I've been told that, following an accident, my eight-year-old car is too badly damaged to repair economically, so the insurance company has written it off. But the amount the company has offered me for it won't buy as good a car. Can they do that?

A Yes, but insurers will sometimes improve an offer if you can present a good case for doing so; for example, if you have proof, such as photographs, that the car was in good condition before

the accident, or if you can show a good servicing record, or if you have recently had major repairs done or parts replaced.

If your car has a low market value but a high value to you and a good life expectancy, another option may be to ask your insurer about the car's scrap value. If you pay this, the company will return the car and you can organise the repairs.

Whatever you claim, make it realistic. Provided that the insurance company pays you enough to buy another car of similar size, age and quality, it will have done all it should.

ACTION PLAN

1 Check the prices in used-car guides for a car of the same model, age and condition as yours. If the insurer's offer is lower, gather other evidence to support your claim. For example, look for advertisements in local newspapers for similar cars that exceed the company's offer; and if your car was in exceptionally good condition, try to find a photograph that might help to prove your point.

2 Write to the insurance company pointing out that the offer is lower than the listed market value of cars of that make, age and condition. If the car has just had new tyres fitted or undergone an expensive service, tell the company about that. Ask for an improved offer.

> ### CHECKING REPAIRS AFTER AN ACCIDENT
>
> • Check that gaps between panels are even.
> • Check that the bonnet, boot and doors open and close.
> • Ensure that body trim, mouldings and badges are complete and that paint resprays are satisfactory.
>
> If there are problems, refuse to accept the car as it is, even if the garage promises to fix them at a more convenient time. Tell the insurer that there is a problem with the repairs and ask that it inspects the car before it is returned to you.

Future employer withdraws job offer

Q I was offered a job, which I accepted. Before I started work my employer changed his mind. Can he do that?

A Probably not, but even if he persists in withdrawing the offer, you are unlikely to obtain much compensation.

As soon as a job offer is made, a contract is formed between you and the employer, even if the offer is only made and accepted verbally. Some job offers have conditions attached to them – for example, you have to pass a medical or provide good references. Others are unconditional.

If your job offer is unconditional the employer must honour it. If it is conditional the employer can withdraw the offer if you do not meet the conditions – for example, if you fail the medical or if your references are bad.

If you believe that you have been given a reference that is negligent or misleading, you may be able to sue your former employer, as an employer must give a true, accurate and fair account of you in a job reference. Consult a solicitor or your local Citizens Advice Bureau.

You have no right to see your reference, but if you start a legal case against a former employer, your lawyer or adviser will be able to see a copy of it.

ACTION PLAN
1 If the offer was unconditional, write to the employer explaining that you made an employment contract when you accepted the job offer and that he is now breaking that contract ▶ ✍. You may be offered the job, but consider whether you want to work for a company that behaves in this manner.

2 If the employer refuses to change his position, you could claim damages from him for breach of contract, although any damages awarded by the court would be minimal. Seek advice from a solicitor (see p20) or your local Citizens Advice Bureau ▶ ⌂ or Law Centre ▶ ⌂ before embarking on a claim.

WORD OF WARNING
If you receive a conditional job offer, never quit your old job before you know the results of any medical examination or search for references carried out by your new employer.

Former employer will not provide a reference

Q I have been offered a new job, but my former employer refuses to give me a reference. Can she do that?

A Yes. Your former employer is not obliged to write you a reference, unless your employment contract with the company gave you the right to one on leaving.

The only employers required to give references are those regulated by the Financial Services Authority (FSA; see box, p159). The FSA can demand references from employers because it must establish that workers providing financial services are qualified and competent.

If you are unsure whether your contract with your former employer gave you the right to a reference, check the terms carefully. If you do not have a contract, you should have a written statement of your employment terms and conditions (see box, p271).

One way out of the problem is to get a reference from another source. Contact

the human resources manager at the company that is offering you the job or the manager who interviewed you. Ask whether the company would accept a reference from one of your earlier employers or, if you are younger, from a former school teacher, a religious minister or a friend of the family.

False statements on a job application

Q I thought I had hired just the right person to fill a recent job vacancy. But now I've discovered that my new employee falsified information about a qualification on her job application. Can she get away with that?

A No. Since your employee has only been working for you for a short time, you can almost certainly fire her without legal repercussions.

Many employees are initially on probation. Did you hire her on a standard contract that included a probation clause? If she is still within her probationary period, you are free to release her.

An employee cannot bring a case for unfair dismissal to an employment tribunal before a year's continuous service has been completed. An exception is when an employee claims to have been treated less favourably than colleagues on the grounds of race, disability or sex.

If you are in doubt, before dismissing your employee seek advice from the Advisory, Conciliation and Arbitration Service (ACAS) ▶ ⌂, the Equal Opportunities Commission ▶ ⌂, the Commission for Racial Equality ▶ ⌂, or the Disability Rights Commission ▶ ⌂.

Your right to have job details in writing

Q I started a new job three months ago, but my employer won't give me written confirmation of my employment. Can she do that?

A No. Your employer does not have to give you a written contract, but she must give you a written statement of 'employment particulars' within two months of your starting work. The statement contains details of pay, holiday and sick leave entitlement, and other aspects of the job (see box, p271).

If there is any change, the employer must inform the employee of it in writing within one month of the change.

You have a contract of employment with your employer even if nothing is in writing. It was formed when you agreed to work for her in return for pay. ▶

GOLDEN RULE

When you start a new job, always ask for a written statement detailing your terms and conditions. This is your right.

ACTION PLAN

1 Write to your employer outlining your right to a written statement of employment particulars under the Employment Rights Act 1996 ▶ ✍.

2 If she still does not provide you with a written statement, make an application to an employment tribunal (see p291) to enforce your right. Seek advice from a solicitor (see p20) or your local Citizens Advice Bureau ▶ 📖 or Law Centre ▶ 📖.

3 If your employer fires you for trying to enforce your right to a written statement, you can take a case of unfair dismissal to the employment tribunal. Seek advice from a solicitor or your local Citizens Advice Bureau.

Pay deduction for shortfall in takings

Q I work on a checkout in a large store. My manager told me there was a shortfall of £22 yesterday during my shift and says she has no choice but to deduct the amount from my wage packet. Can she do that?

A Yes, if the company has warned you in advance in writing that you would be liable to make up till shortages from your wages.

But under the Employment Rights Act 1996 your manager can only take deductions from your wages:
• if she is authorised to do so by your contract; or
• if she has given you a written statement of the policy under which till shortages are reclaimed.

Before pay-day the employee must be given a written statement explaining that the shortfall will be deducted. On pay-day itself, the employee must also receive a written demand for the payment.

The maximum an employer may deduct from a single wage packet is 10 per cent of gross wages (wages before income tax and National Insurance are subtracted). For example, in the case of a £22 shortfall, if the employee earns less than £220 in the week, the employer cannot deduct the full £22 immediately. If the employee earns £110 or more per week, the employer can deduct £11 the first week and £11 the second week.

ACTION PLAN

1 If you were not given a written statement of the policy on till shortfalls, seek advice from your union or staff association representative.

2 If you do not have one, write to your manager or the human resources department to tell them that under the Employment Rights Act 1996 a deduction cannot be made from your pay because they did not inform you of the policy in advance ▶ ✍. Keep a copy of your letter together with any other paperwork.

CONTRACT TERMS

A contract between employer and employee has three main types of terms, whether written into the contract or not:
• Express terms are the ones the employee explicitly agrees to, such as the rate of pay, the number of hours to be worked and annual holiday entitlement.
• Statutory terms are ones imposed by Acts of Parliament – for example, the right of most workers to be paid the national minimum wage (see box, p272).
• Implied terms are assumed terms – for example, that the employee will not steal from the employer and that the employer will provide a safe working environment.

3 If your manager makes the deduction despite not informing you of the policy, or deducts more than 10 per cent of your gross wages in a week, or does not follow the correct procedure, contact the Advisory, Conciliation and Arbitration Service (ACAS) ▶ 🕮 or seek advice from your local Citizens Advice Bureau ▶ 🕮 or Law Centre ▶ 🕮.

Imposing a pay cut when business is slow

Q My manager says that our firm has had a very difficult year and that all members of staff will have to accept a 10 per cent drop in wages to keep the firm afloat. Can he do that?

A No. Your employer cannot force you to accept a wage cut against your will.

By asking you and your colleagues to do the same work for lower pay, your employer is varying the terms of your contract of employment. The law sees this as a breach of contract and you are within your rights to refuse to accept the change.

If you have representatives from the union or staff association, your employer should discuss the matter with them. They may be able to negotiate a better deal than the one on offer.

If you accept the drop in wages, the change to your contract terms should be recorded in writing. All employees have a legal right to a written statement of a change to their terms of employment within a month of its taking effect (see box, above). If you decide not to accept, you have a number of options:

• You can leave your job and claim constructive dismissal at an employment tribunal (see box, p291). Your case will be that you resigned because your employer broke your employment contract.

TERMS OF EMPLOYMENT

Every employee must be given a written statement of employment terms within two months of starting a job, either as part of a contract or as a statement of employment particulars, which may take the form of a letter. The statement should contain:

• employee's name and employer's name
• date the employment began
• rate of pay and when it should be paid
• hours of work
• entitlement to holiday, sick leave and sick pay
• employee's right and employer's right to be given notice if the contract is terminated
• job title or brief job description
• the length of time employment is expected to last if the job is not permanent, or, if it is fixed term, the date it will end
• the place of work or, if the work will be in many places, the employer's address
• any collective agreements (for example, agreements made between the employer and employee representatives) that affect the terms and conditions
• details of disciplinary and grievance procedures.

• You can continue to work under protest. You must make it clear, preferably in writing, that although you are continuing to work you do not accept the new terms. If you carry on working without making this clear, you will probably be regarded as having accepted the new terms. If you continue under protest you have the right to bring legal action – for example, suing your employer for breach of contract (see below).

• You can sue your employer for breach of contract in the civil courts (see p17) or at an employment tribunal (see box, p291). Or you can ask the court to declare that your employer must stick to the original rate of pay.

Seek advice before resigning or taking legal action. Contact the Advisory, Conciliation and Arbitration Service (ACAS) ▶ 🕮, an employment lawyer (see p20) or your local Citizens Advice Bureau ▶ 🕮 or Law Centre ▶ 🕮.

WORLD OF WORK

MINIMUM RATES OF PAY • HOURS

WHO IS COVERED BY THE MINIMUM WAGE?

- Workers aged 22 or over have the right to be paid the minimum wage whether they are full-time, part-time, freelance, casual, agency or temporary workers. The National Minimum Wage Regulations 1999 also apply to workers of retirement age and those drawing a state pension.
- A lower 'development rate' covers workers aged 18-21 and those aged 22 and over who are in the first six months of a job and on a training scheme.
- Workers not covered include: members of the armed forces, the self-employed, apprentices, students working as part of a sandwich course, share fishermen, au pairs, nannies.

Entitlement to the minimum wage

Q My 24-year-old son has just left university and has taken a casual job in a shop. The owner says because he's a casual she will only be paying him £2 an hour. Can she do that?

A No. Your son is entitled to be paid the national minimum wage even though he is a casual worker (meaning that he is only needed irregularly).

The law states that workers aged 22 or over must be paid a minimum amount per hour, while a lower 'development rate' covers workers aged 18-21 and those aged 22 and over who are in the first six months of a job and on a training programme. Since October 2003, the minimum wage has been £4.50 an hour and the development rate £3.80 an hour.

Your son has the right to claim the difference between his wages and the national minimum wage for every hour he has worked. If the shop-owner will not pay him this, she will be liable to a fine of twice the national minimum wage for every day he has been paid below the set level.

She faces an extra fine of £5000 if she refuses to comply with the enforcement notice, fails to keep or falsifies pay records or obstructs an Inland Revenue tax or national insurance investigation.

ACTION PLAN

1 Your son should contact his local Inland Revenue enquiry centre ▶ ⌂ or the Inland Revenue National Insurance Contributions Office ▶ ⌂, who will send an enforcement notice to the shop, setting the owner a time limit within which she must start paying workers in line with the national minimum wage.

2 If the shop owner refuses to pay, your son can take his case to the employment tribunal (see p291) or the county court and will have the money awarded to him there. Consult a solicitor (see p20) or your local Citizens Advice Bureau ▶ ⌂ or Law Centre ▶ ⌂.

3 If she sacks your son because he claims the minimum wage he will win a claim for unfair dismissal at the employment tribunal and be awarded the money he is owed as compensation.

Sunday working – a matter of choice

Q I work in a large store that opens both days at the weekend. My husband works a six-day week and only has Sunday off. I asked my boss if I could be excused Sunday working but he said 'No'. Can he do that?

A No. You have the right to choose not to work on Sunday. How you exercise this right depends on your circumstances.

It is illegal for your employer to dismiss you, select you for redundancy or treat you less favourably than your colleagues if you choose not to work on Sunday.

The Sunday Trading Act 1994 made it legal for shops to open on Sunday. If you began work for your employer later than August 26, 1994 (when the Act became law), or if your employment contract specifically requires you to work on Sunday, your employer must, within two months of your starting work, give you a written statement explaining your right to opt out of Sunday working. If he does not, you can give him one month's notice that you do not wish to work on Sunday.

WORKING HOURS, BREAKS AND HOLIDAYS

The Working Time Regulations 1998 introduced limits on the number of hours an employer can expect an employee to work.

Average hours

• Your employer cannot force you to work more than 48 hours a week on average. The average figure is normally calculated over a 17-week period.
• You can agree to work more than 48 hours a week. If so, you have to sign a written agreement stating that you are happy to do so. You can cancel this agreement but must give your employer at least seven days' notice – or longer, if specified in the agreement, to a maximum of three months.
• Your employer cannot force you to sign an opt-out agreement to work more than 48 hours a week or dismiss you for refusing to do so.

Night workers

• You are classed as a night worker if you usually work at least three hours between 11pm and 6am.
• You should not work more than eight hours at a stretch – including work during the daytime.
• If you have health problems caused by or made worse by night work, your employer should (where possible) transfer you to day work.

Rest

• You should have a minimum of 11 hours off work between working days. If you are a young worker (aged 16-18), you should have a minimum of 12 hours off between days at work.

• You should have at least one whole day off each week – or two days off every fortnight. A young worker should have two days off a week.
• Your employer must provide these days off in addition to paid annual leave.

Holidays

• The Working Time Regulations give every worker the right to four weeks' paid annual leave.

Breaks

• If you work for more than six hours a day you must be offered a break of at least 20 minutes. If you are a young worker, you should have a break of at least 30 minutes if you work for more than 4.5 hours a day.
• These breaks may not be paid – it usually depends what is in your employment contract.

If you have been notified within two months of starting employment of your right to opt out of Sunday working and you wish to exercise your right:
• you must give your employer three months' notice in a signed and dated written statement explaining that you wish to opt out of working on Sundays – you do not have to give a reason
• you must continue to work on Sundays throughout the notice period, but after this time has elapsed you can refuse to do so.

If you were working for your current employer before August 26, 1994, or if your terms of employment (see box, p271) do not require you to work on Sundays, you are considered to be an 'automatically protected worker', which means:
• you do not have to work on Sundays, even if your employer demands that you do – simply tell your manager that you do not work on Sundays
• you can choose to work on Sundays if you wish – to do so you must sign an 'opting-in' notice
• if you opt in to Sunday working, you are free to change your mind and opt out at any time – to do this, you must give your employer a signed and dated statement giving the company three months' notice.

Holiday pay for part-timers

Q I work Monday to Wednesday each week as a receptionist at a building firm. My boss says that because I'm a part-timer I can't expect to be paid when I go on holiday. Is she right?

A No. You have the right to paid holidays – just as you would if you were working full-time.

The amount of holiday you should get is in proportion to the hours you work. Because you work three days out of a possible five you are entitled to three-fifths of the paid holiday that your full-time colleagues receive. If they receive 20 days (or four working weeks) a year, you should be given 12 days' holiday or four three-day weeks.

If your full-time colleagues have paid bank holidays in addition to their annual leave, you should receive days off to balance this, calculated on a three-fifths pro rata basis. For every two bank holidays that your full-time colleagues have off work, you should receive 1.2 days' paid leave.

ACTION PLAN
1 Tell your boss or human resources manager that you have a right to paid holiday under the Part-time Workers (Prevention of Less Favourable Treatment) Regulations 2000.

2 If you are not satisfied with the outcome, you can take your case to an employment tribunal (see p291). Seek advice from a solicitor (see p20) or your local Citizens Advice Bureau ▶ ▭ or Law Centre ▶ ▭.

Holiday entitlements from year to year

Q Everyone in our department regularly works such long hours that we don't usually have a chance to take our full holiday entitlement. Now our boss says we can't carry this year's remaining holiday over to next year. Can he do that?

A Yes. You do not have a legal right to take holiday owing in one year during the next.

The Working Time Regulations 1998 (see box, p273) guarantee most workers – including part-time workers (see previous question) – a minimum of four weeks' paid annual leave. But they do not allow for this leave to be taken over from one year to the next or for employees to receive pay in place of untaken leave.

Some employers allow workers to carry a limited number of days forward, or reimburse them for untaken annual leave. If so, this should be set out in your terms of employment (see box, p271).

ACTION PLAN

1 Check your terms of employment. If carrying over holidays is not mentioned, consult your staff handbook or other written statements given to you after you started work. These may explain relevant agreements about holidays.

2 If you do have a right to carry untaken holiday over to the next year, tell your human resources manager that the company is breaking the agreed terms of employment.

Employee's right to a payslip

Q My boss pays me in cash each week, but he refuses to give me a payslip, although I've asked for one. Can he do that?

A No. If you are an employee (not self-employed; see box, p276), you have the right to a detailed statement of pay. You should be given the statement either before or when you are paid.

The payslip must include:
• what you earn before any deductions are made (your gross earnings)
• variable deductions, such as income tax and National Insurance contributions
• fixed deductions, such as your union dues or repayment on a train season-ticket loan
• what you earn after deductions (your net earnings).

If you are paid in more than one way – for example, part cash and part credited to your bank – the statement should indicate how much is paid in each way.

ACTION PLAN

1 Write or speak to your boss or the human resources manager, indicating that you have a right to an itemised payslip under the Employment Rights Act 1996 ▶ ✎.

2 If your employer still does not supply you with a payslip, contact the Advisory, Conciliation and Arbitration Service (ACAS) ▶ 📖 for advice. The ACAS representative may contact your employer.

3 As a last resort you can bring a case to an employment tribunal (see box, p291). The tribunal may award you compensation. Seek advice from a solicitor (see p20) or your local Citizens Advice Bureau ▶ 📖 or Law Centre ▶ 📖 .

WORD OF WARNING

If you suspect your employer of not paying income tax and National Insurance on your behalf, contact the Inland Revenue ▶ 📖 and the Department for Work and Pensions ▶ 📖 . Make it clear that you have not been colluding with your employer's failure to pay.

Client company will not pay up

Q I'm self-employed. I did a job for a client and sent in an invoice, but they won't pay. Can they get away with that?

A No. Once you reach an agreement with a client to do a job in return for a sum of money, you have a legally binding contract – even if it is only a verbal agreement made face-to-face or on the phone. The law requires your client to honour that contract and pay you the agreed sum. Your client may claim that you did not do the job satisfactorily, in which case you may have to negotiate a settlement or take the client to court.

ACTION PLAN

1 If your client is not disputing the quality of your work, but is simply refusing to pay, write to the accounts department ▶ ✍. Explain that your invoice for a particular job is outstanding and give details of the contract you have with the company. Add that you are willing to bring a case in the county court (see box, p19) for the money owed. Send the letter by secure post (see box, p76) and keep a copy.

2 If this does not work, you could bring the case to the county court. But if your client has no assets or is a limited company with no assets, you may not get your money even if you

---

EMPLOYEE OR SELF-EMPLOYED?

Many statutory employment rights (those introduced by Act of Parliament) are limited to employees. If you have a dispute over employment rights, a tribunal (see box, p291) will decide your status based on all the relevant information in your case. Similarly the Inland Revenue will decide your standing for tax and National Insurance purposes depending on a number of factors.

Employee
You are probably an employee if the company you work for:
• decides what work you do, when you do it, how you do it and where you do it
• has a duty to provide work for you, or to pay you if there is no work to do
• pays you by the hour or other period of time
• expects you to do the work personally – you cannot subcontract to another person
• expects you to do any work you are offered
• supplies the tools or other equipment you need to do it
• deducts your tax and National Insurance contributions through the Pay As You Earn (PAYE) scheme
• pays you holiday or sickness pay
• takes any financial risk involved in the work you do.

Self-employed
You are probably self-employed if you:
• decide whether to accept work from a company
• determine how and where you work
• are paid for providing a service or completing a task rather than by the hour
• can accept a job and then subcontract it to another person
• provide and maintain your own tools or equipment
• arrange your own tax and National Insurance contributions, dealing directly with the Inland Revenue
• can choose to do the same type of work for more than one employer at the same time
• arrange your own holiday or sickness breaks.

win. Seek advice from a solicitor (see p20) or your local Citizens Advice Bureau ▶ 📖 or Law Centre ▶ 📖 before proceeding.

Can your boss read your emails?

Q My boss sent round a memo saying that our emails and Internet use will be monitored and anyone found abusing the system will face disciplinary action. Can he do that?

A Yes. Your employer has the right to read your emails under the Regulation of Investigatory Powers Act 2000, but he must tell you that monitoring is taking place (see box, right).

The Data Protection Act 1998 requires the company to assess the impact of its monitoring. Any adverse effect on you should be balanced by benefits to the company and to others. If the company can justify the monitoring by this assessment, it does not need your consent.

Complaining about a home-working scam

Q I replied to an advertisement in the local newspaper offering high earnings for work at home. I wrote to the PO Box address given and received a letter asking me to pay a registration fee. When I sent my money I received a letter telling me to place other advertisements like the one I'd responded to, and to forward the replies. Is there any action I can take?

A Yes, but you will not recover your money. Some home-working schemes are genuine, but this one is a swindle that generates money by

collecting registration fees. Your first step should be to complain to your local trading standards office (see box, p30). Take its advice on whether to report the matter to the police.

You should also complain to the Advertising Standards Authority (ASA) ▶ 📖. This particular home-working scheme goes against the British Code of Advertising, Sales Promotion and Direct Marketing, which states that an advertisement must accurately describe the work involved, indicate any money you have to pay, give the full name and address of the person running the operation and not promise unrealistic or unattainable earnings.

You should also write to the advertising manager of the newspaper in which you saw the advertisement, pointing out that the advertisement is potentially fraudulent and breaks the ASA's code.

WHAT CAN A COMPANY DO WITH YOUR EMAILS?

Under the Data Protection Act 1998, if your emails are being monitored at work, the information gathered must be:
- fairly and lawfully processed for limited purposes
- adequate, relevant and not excessive
- accurate
- secure
- not kept for longer than is necessary or transferred to countries that do not have adequate data protection.

In 2000 the UK Information Commissioner (see box, p383) published a draft code of practice, under which:
- employees using email must be aware of the monitoring and why it is being carried out
- the company should tell workers what information on their Internet use and emails is being kept and for how long
- employers conducting monitoring must take into account that employees may access particular web sites accidentally by following misleading links
- employers should inform workers of the company policy.

If you think your employer is not following the law in monitoring your online activity, contact the Information Commissioner ▶ 📖.

HOME-WORKERS BEWARE!

If you are looking for work at home:
- never send money in advance as a registration fee or in return for a kit
- be wary of advertisements that give only a PO Box number and ask you to send a stamped addressed envelope
- try to find out more about the prospective employer – phone your local trading standards department to ask if it has had complaints about the company.

No secrets in your personal files

Q **My company's human resources department keeps files about us all. I asked to see my file but was told that I couldn't as it was privileged information. Can they withhold the file from me?**

A No. You have the right to see most of the information about you, although you will not be allowed to see any assessments or notes written by staff at your company.

The Data Protection Act 1998 gives you the right to be told what data is being held about you, whether on paper or electronically, who might see it, and why it is being kept. You also have the right to a clear and comprehensible copy of the data.

The law requires the organisation or person holding the data to respond within 40 days of your request. Your employer can charge you a fee (up to a maximum £10) for providing the information. You can change any information in your file that is incorrect.

ACTION PLAN

1 Write to your human resources manager explaining that you wish to see the information in your file under the Data Protection Act 1998 ▶ ✐ . Some information in your file may be on computer – for example, a record of your attendance based on clocking in and out. To see this material, say in your letter that you want to see 'information under section 7(1)(d) of the Data Protection Act'. Keep a copy of the letter.

2 If you have not had a reply within 40 days send a second letter as a reminder and keep a copy.

3 If you still do not receive the information, contact the government's Information Commissioner ▶ ⌒ (see box, p383). The commissioner will try to settle the matter informally, but as a last resort can serve a notice requiring your employer to supply the information.

4 If your file contains inaccurate information, ask the human resources manager to correct it. If the manager refuses, contact the Information Commissioner. The commissioner can also require your employer to correct details in your file.

How to deal with sexual harassment

Q **My supervisor tells dirty jokes and makes sexually suggestive remarks, even after I object. Is there anything I can do to stop him?**

A Yes. Your supervisor's behaviour amounts to harassment. You should be able to make a complaint under your company's complaints and grievances procedure, if there is one.

Acts of sexual harassment are illegal under the Sex Discrimination Act 1975. In addition, under the Health and Safety at Work Act 1974 your employer must make sure that your health, safety and welfare are protected.

ACTION PLAN

1 Try telling your supervisor once again that you do not appreciate his jokes and remarks. If you feel uncomfortable doing this, ask a colleague or trade union representative to speak to him on your behalf.

2 If your supervisor's behaviour continues, keep a diary: record what he says, precise times and dates, and whether there were witnesses.

3 Discuss the matter with a union representative or your company's human resources department.

4 If you want to make a formal complaint, use your employer's complaints and grievances procedure.

5 If you are unhappy with your employer's response, you could take a claim to an employment tribunal (see box, p291). Before proceeding, seek advice from your union representative, your local Citizens Advice Bureau ▶ 📖 or the Equal Opportunities Commission ▶ 📖.

6 You could resign if your employer fails to respond adequately to your complaint and you may succeed in claiming constructive dismissal (see box, p291) under the Employment Rights Act 1996. Consider this action only as a final resort. Seek legal advice before resigning.

Earning equal pay for equal work

Q My daughter discovered she is being paid thousands of pounds less than a male colleague for doing exactly the same job. Can she demand equal pay?

A Yes, but if she takes a case to an employment tribunal her employer might be able to make a number of justifications for paying her male colleague more.

Under the Equal Pay Act 1970, women have the right to receive the same pay as men if they do the same or comparable work. To win a claim under the Act your daughter must prove one of the following:
• that she and her colleague do 'like work' – the same or similar jobs
• that they both do 'equivalent-rated work' – that both their jobs have been evaluated by an external organisation (for example, a government body) as being of equal value
• that her work is of equal value to her colleague's work – for example, in effort, skill and judgment required.

Your daughter can bring a claim for equal pay in an employment tribunal (see box, p291). Before taking this step, she should seek the advice of her union representative, a solicitor or her local Citizens Advice Bureau ▶ 📖. She can bring the case at any time while she is working for the employer. If she leaves the job or has her contract terminated, she must bring the case within six months of the end of the contract.

ANY MESSAGES GORGEOUS?

YES

GET LOST!

WORLD OF WORK

AGE, SEX AND RACE DISCRIMINATION

CHANGE TO THE LAW

The government has promised to ban discrimination on the grounds of age by 2006. The UK supported the European Union Employment Directive on Equal Treatment (2000), which requires all EU member states to alter existing law or introduce new legislation to ban direct and indirect discrimination in employment on the basis of disability, sexual orientation, religion and belief, and age.

Too old to get an interview?

Q I'm 55 and looking for a job. I recently saw one for which I was extremely well qualified, but the advertisement said the company wanted 'an up-and-coming self-starter, would suit recent graduate'. This description seemed to be worded to exclude people like me, and when I applied I didn't even get an interview. Can they do that?

A Yes. The company has not acted illegally. There is currently no law banning discrimination on the grounds of age, although legislation is due to be introduced by 2006 (see box, left).

Some job advertisements are phrased in this way to indicate the wages will be low: you could tell the company that although you are 55 you are flexible and a 'self-starter' and that you would be happy to fit into the wage structure that covers such jobs. Some companies respond positively to this approach and might be willing to find another position for you or to keep your details on file.

Ask the company why you were not granted an interview – many firms will provide this information to job applicants.

Promotion deal is discriminatory

Q My employer will only offer higher-grade jobs to people under 30 who are able to work flexible hours. By doing this, he's excluding me and my female colleagues as we have family ties and aren't able to work flexible hours. Is this allowed?

A Probably not. There is no law yet against age discrimination (see box, left), but your employer may be guilty of sex discrimination. In the under-30 age group, there are more women on maternity leave or caring for children than there are men on paternity leave or caring for children. As your employer's promotion criteria excludes more women than men from higher-grade jobs, it amounts to indirect sex discrimination.

Under the Sex Discrimination Acts 1975 and 1986 it is illegal for an employer to treat a worker differently or less favourably on grounds of sex or marital status. In some circumstances an employer can claim exclusion from these laws, but unless these apply in your job, you have a good chance of winning a case at an employment tribunal.

ACTION PLAN

1 Write to your boss or the human resources department informing them that you believe the company's promotion practice amounts to indirect sex discrimination ▶ ✍.

2 If you are a member of a trade union, ask your representative for help and advice.

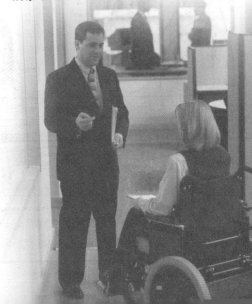

3 You can take a case to an employment tribunal (see p291). But before doing so, seek advice from your union representative or your local Citizens Advice Bureau ▶ 📖 or Law Centre ▶ 📖.

Race is a bar to promotion

Q I've been working for the same company for 15 years. I'm Asian and convinced that I've been passed over for promotion because of race discrimination. Can they do that?

A No. Under the Race Discrimination Act 1976 it is illegal to treat one worker less favourably than others on the grounds of colour, race, nationality or ethnic origins.

You may be able to bring a case to an employment tribunal (see p291), but the onus is on you to prove that racial discrimination is taking place rather than on your employer to prove that it is not.

ACTION PLAN

1 Collect evidence of occasions on which other workers were promoted rather than you. Look for cases in which your colleagues were similar to you in age, experience, status and relevant qualification, but of a different race. If they were not comparable, your employer will be able to claim that they were promoted for reasons of seniority or performance rather than race.

2 Contact the Commission for Racial Equality (CRE; see box, right) who will advise you on how strong your case is. You must bring the case to the employment tribunal within three months of the act of discrimination or the most recent of the series of discriminatory acts.

DISCRIMINATION: WHERE TO GO FOR HELP

To obtain advice about disputes over possible discrimination at work contact:

Equal Opportunities Commission (EOC)
If you think you have been discriminated against (treated less favourably than your colleagues or other people) because of your sex, contact the EOC ▶ 📖. The EOC will provide legal assistance if, after following its advice, you take a case to an employment tribunal (see box, p291) or court. You should also contact the EOC:
● in cases of sexual harassment at work
● if you are a working parent and need advice on your rights to take time off to care for your children or to request flexible working conditions (see p284).
Phone helpline: 0845 601 5901
Web site: www.eoc.org.uk

Commission for Racial Equality (CRE)
If you think you have been discriminated against, harassed or abused because of your race, skin colour, nationality or ethnic origins, the CRE ▶ 📖 can give you advice and legal help. You can also ask the CRE:
● to investigate organisations or businesses in which there is evidence of possible racial discrimination – the CRE has the power to force them to change their practices and policies
● take legal action against TV and newspaper publishers over racially discriminatory advertisements or against firms that pressurise others to practise racial discrimination – for example, a company that tells its staff to be discriminatory.
The CRE also issues codes of practice on racial equality and advises local government and other public bodies on their racial equality policy.
Phone numbers for the CRE head office and local offices are available from: www.cre.org.uk

Disability Rights Commission (DRC)
Contact the DRC ▶ 📖 if you are disabled and feel that your rights are being disregarded in employment, access to services, education, transport or housing. The DRC offers:
● advice and information
● legal support in securing your rights under the Disability Discrimination Act
● a problem-solving service that can help you to win your rights without the need to take a case to an employment tribunal or court.
The DRC also supports legal cases that clarify how courts are interpreting the Disability Discrimination Act, publishes research and runs campaigns to promote disability awareness.
Links to DRC helpline are available at: www.drc-gb.org

Facilities for disabled people at work

Q I use a wheelchair to get around, but the proprietor of the business I work for, which has five employees, refuses to modify the lavatory to make it easily accessible. I have to be helped out of my chair every time I need to use the toilet. Is his refusal to make the alterations legal?

A Yes. Although the Disability Discrimination Act 1995 requires businesses to make 'reasonable adjustments' to prevent disabled workers being at a disadvantage compared with their colleagues, the law applies only to employers with 15 or more employees.

You should point out to the proprietor that in a larger organisation the law would see his refusal to adapt the toilet as discrimination. As a matter of good practice he may wish to ensure that he does not discriminate against disabled people. Contact the Disability Rights Commission ▶ ⌨ (DRC; see box, p281) for advice.

Pregnant workers cannot be fired

Q I am employed as a waitress in an up-market restaurant. Last week I told my boss I was pregnant, and this morning she phoned me to say she is dismissing me because a pregnant waitress doesn't match the image of the restaurant. Can she do that?

A No. Being fired on the grounds of pregnancy is automatically regarded as unfair dismissal, and the law protects you even if you have only been with the company for a few days.

You can complain to an employment tribunal and expect one of three possible outcomes:
- the tribunal may order your employer to reinstate you in your old job or a similar one
- if you do not want to return to your job, or if it is not practicable for your employer to reinstate you or give you a similar job, the tribunal will order your employer to pay you compensation
- if the employer refuses, when ordered, to reinstate you, the tribunal will order a higher level of compensation to be paid to you.

ACTION PLAN

1 Before taking the case to a tribunal, try to resolve the matter by mutual agreement. Use your company's grievances and appeals procedure.

2 If there is no procedure, write to your boss to explain that the company would be breaking the law if it dismissed you for being pregnant and that you would be willing to bring a case to an employment tribunal ▶ ✎. Your boss may back down.

3 Keep any relevant letters and documents and make detailed notes of any conversations or phone calls with your boss connected to your case.

4 If you are fired, you have three months from the date of your dismissal to make your complaint of unfair dismissal to the employment tribunal (see p291). First, seek advice from a solicitor (see p20) or your local Citizens Advice Bureau ▶ ⌨.

Don't be forced to return to work early

Q I'm pregnant and due to go on maternity leave in four months. My boss says that our department can't cope without me and I must come back within a month of the birth. If I don't, he says, he may move me to a junior job at the end of my leave. Can he do that?

A No. You have the right to 26 weeks' maternity leave and to return to your original job at the end.

You can begin this leave – known as 'ordinary maternity leave' – any time after the beginning of the 11th week before you are due to give birth. You will not be paid your normal wages, but you will receive statutory maternity pay (SMP; see box, right).

If you have worked for your employer continuously for 26 weeks by the beginning of the 14th week before your expected week of childbirth, you can take a further 26 weeks of 'additional maternity leave'. This leave is usually unpaid (unless your contract states otherwise) and begins at the end of your 'ordinary maternity leave'.

When you return from maternity leave, your employer should offer you your own job with the same terms and conditions. If that is not reasonably practicable, you should be offered a suitable alternative job with terms and conditions that are no less favourable. If no suitable alternative job is available for you, you may be entitled to receive redundancy pay.

Explain to your boss that you have a right to 26 weeks' maternity leave and to return to your original job. If he does not back down, you can take your case to an employment tribunal (see box, p291). Seek advice from a solicitor (see p20) or your local Citizens Advice Bureau ▶ 🕮 or Law Centre ▶ 🕮.

MATERNITY PAY AND HOW TO CLAIM IT

There are two types of benefit for pregnant employees: statutory maternity pay and maternity allowance.

Statutory maternity pay
- To qualify for statutory maternity pay (SMP) you must have worked for your employer for 26 weeks without breaks ending with the 15th week before the week in which you are expected to give birth, and your average weekly earnings must be at least £77.
- SMP is paid for 26 weeks; the earliest you can start getting it is in the 11th week before your baby is due, the latest is from the day after the birth of your baby.
- For the first six weeks you receive 90 per cent of your weekly earnings.
- For the next 20 weeks you receive 90 per cent of your weekly earnings or £100 a week, whichever is lower.
- Your employer must pay you SMP and can claim a refund from the Inland Revenue.
- You can claim SMP even if you do not intend to return to your job after giving birth.

How to claim statutory maternity pay
- You must inform your employer of the date you want to stop work and be paid SMP at least four weeks in advance. You will have to supply a medical certificate signed by a doctor or midwife to confirm the date your baby is due.
- If you do not qualify for SMP your employer will give you an official form detailing the reasons why not. You may be able to claim maternity allowance (MA, see below).
- Further details of SMP are available from the Department for Work and Pensions ▶ 🕮.

Maternity allowance
- If you do not qualify for SMP or if you are self-employed, you may be able to claim maternity allowance (MA).
- To qualify for MA you must have been employed or self-employed for 26 weeks in the 66 weeks before the date you are due to give birth. Your average weekly earnings must be at least £30.
- MA is paid for 26 weeks.
- You receive the MA standard rate of £100 a week or 90 per cent of your average weekly earnings, whichever is lower.

How to claim maternity allowance
- You can claim MA after you have been pregnant for 26 weeks.
- Contact your local Jobcentre Plus www.jobcentreplus.gov.uk or social security office for a claim form.

WORLD OF WORK

PATERNITY LEAVE • FLEXIBLE HOURS • TIME OFF

TIME OFF TO CARE FOR A RELATIVE

Under the Employment Rights Act 1996 (amended by the Employment Relations Act 1999) workers can take a reasonable amount of time off work to look after a dependant – their child, husband, wife, partner, parent or someone such as an aunt or grandparent who lives with them. This right applies to everyone who has a contract of employment with an employer, but not to the self-employed, members of the police service and armed forces or masters/crew members on a fishing vessel paid by a share of the catch.

Father's right to paternity leave

Q My wife is having a baby in four months' time. I've worked hard for my company for five years and I recently read in the papers that fathers now qualify for 'paternity leave', but when I asked my boss for some paid time off to look after the baby he said 'No way'. Can he do that?

A No. You have the right to take up to two weeks' paid paternity leave. To qualify for paternity leave:
- you must be the baby's biological father or the partner or husband of the baby's mother, and be or expect to be responsible for the baby's upbringing
- you must have worked continuously for your present employer for 26 weeks ending with the 15th week before the birth is due.

You will be paid at the statutory rate, which is the same as that for maternity pay – £100 per week (in the tax year 2003-4) or 90 per cent of your average weekly earnings if this is less than £100. You must take the leave in one block, not a day at a time.

You have the right to return to the same job after your paternity leave, rather than to a similar job.

You also have the right to take 13 weeks' unpaid leave at any time up to your child's fifth birthday. If your child is disabled, you can take 18 weeks' unpaid leave at any time up to your child's 18th birthday.

ACTION PLAN

1 Choose how much leave you want to take, up to two weeks.

2 Choose when you want your leave to start – from the day of your partner's expected delivery date, on a fixed date that is more than a week after the birth is due or from a fixed number of days or weeks after the birth. You must complete the leave within 56 days of the birth or, if the baby is born early, within 56 days from the beginning of the week in which your wife was due to have the baby.

3 Write to your employer stating that you intend to take paid paternity leave and when you want it to start. You must do this by the end of the 15th week before the baby is due.

4 You must also sign a declaration that you are eligible to take paternity leave and to claim paternity pay.

WORD OF WARNING

If your average weekly earnings are below the lower earnings limit for National Insurance (£77 a week in the tax year 2003-4), you will not be able to claim statutory paternity pay. You still have the right to two weeks' leave from work and can probably claim income support in this period.

How to arrange flexible working

Q I'm the mother of a three-year-old boy and I asked my boss to allow me to work one day a week at home. Some of my work is self-contained and could easily be done at home. But he has refused to discuss it. Can he do that?

A No. You – and your son's father – have the right to ask for flexible working conditions because you have a child under the age of six. Your employer must give your request

serious consideration. To qualify for flexible working you have to be an employee rather than self-employed (see box, p276) and to have worked for your employer without breaks for at least 26 weeks.

You can ask to change the number of hours you work, the times you have to work, or request to work from home. This right does not apply to agency workers or members of the armed forces.

There are some circumstances in which your employer can say no – for example, if there are clear business grounds why the change cannot be made.

If your child were registered as disabled, you would have the right to ask for flexible working at any time up to his 18th birthday.

ACTION PLAN

1 Write a letter to your employer stating that you want to change your working pattern and the reasons why this will help with childcare ▶ ✍.

2 Within 28 days of receiving the letter, your employer must meet you to discuss the change. You can bring a colleague with you to this meeting to act as a witness.

3 Within 14 days of the meeting your employer must write to you, either accepting the change and giving a starting date for your new working conditions or stating the business grounds that make it impossible for the change to be made. This letter should inform you of your right to appeal against the decision.

4 If your employer denies your request, you have 14 days after receiving the letter to appeal. Alternatively, you can take your case to the Advisory, Conciliation and Arbitration Service (ACAS) ▶ ⌂. If your employer does not follow the procedure laid down by ACAS, you could take your case to an employment tribunal (see p291). Seek advice from a solicitor (see p20) or your local Citizens Advice Bureau ▶ ⌂ or Law Centre ▶ ⌂.

WORD OF WARNING

An agreed change in your working pattern will be treated as permanent unless the agreement makes it clear that the change is only temporary. You are only allowed to request to change your working pattern once a year.

Time off for a family emergency

Q **Last week I started a new job, but today I had to take a day off work to care for my elderly mother, who lives with us and had tripped and fallen. When I called my boss to explain, he threatened to fire me. Can he do that?**

A No. You have the right to take time off work to care for your mother in an emergency (see box, opposite). You can do this from the first day at work.

The law does not give you the right to take prolonged periods off work. Employees are expected to tell their employer as soon as they can how long they will be absent.

An employer cannot dismiss you because you take time off. If you and your boss are unable to settle your disagreement, use the company's grievances and appeals procedure, if there is one. If the outcome is still not satisfactory, contact the Advisory, Conciliation and Arbitration Service (ACAS) ▶ ⌂ for advice and help.

WORD OF WARNING

The law does not give you the right to be paid for the time you take off to cope with an emergency.

Help for on-screen workers

Q **I work all day at a computer as a secretary. Recently I've been suffering headaches and pains in my wrist, which I believe are caused by the work. I complained to my manager, but he said that it was up to me to perform exercises that will help to prevent the aches and pains. Can he do that?**

A No. The company has a legal duty to minimise the risks of using computer equipment for long periods.

Under the Health and Safety (Display Screen Equipment) Regulations 1992:

• Your employer must ensure that your workstation (the chair, desk, keyboard, screen and lighting) meets minimum standards – for example, the chair should be adjustable and there should be protection against glare from overhead lighting or windows.

• Your manager should plan your workload so you can take short, regular breaks from the screen. The law does not specify the number, length or timing of the breaks, but does give you some choice over when to take them.

• The company should provide health and safety information and training on how to use your workstation safely.

• You can have your eyes tested at your employer's expense. If you need glasses for screen work, your employer should pay for them. The employer must also pay for follow-up tests – say, once a year – as recommended by a doctor or optometrist.

The regulations apply to you if you regularly use computer screens at work. You are also covered if you work at home as an employee (see box, p276).

If you are self-employed, but working in a client's office, the company you are working for has to assess risks, provide a workstation that meets minimum standards and give you health and safety information.

Your rights to limit stress at work

Q **I work long hours in a responsible job. Recently I've been feeling stressed, but when I asked my boss for help or a break, she told me the company couldn't afford to give me any support staff or time off. Can she do that?**

A No. Your employer has a legal duty to make sure that your work does not make you ill. Your manager or a member of the human resources department should regularly assess employees' work demands and take steps to limit the risk of stress.

You also have the right to limit the number of hours you work. Under the Working Time Regulations 1998 your company cannot force you to work more than an average of 48 hours a week and should allow you at least 11 hours off

between working days and at least one day off a week (see box, p273).

You may have signed a document in which you agreed to work more than 48 hours on average each week, but you can cancel this as long as you give the amount of notice you agreed with your employer (ranging from seven days to three months). Check with the human resources department.

ACTION PLAN

1 Ask the human resources department whether the company can arrange counselling for you.

2 You may be able to get help through your union representative, if you have one. The Advisory, Conciliation and Arbitration Service (ACAS) ▶ ⌸ or the Health and Safety Executive (Employment Medical Advisory Service) ▶ ⌸ will also be able to advise you about your rights.

Are you entitled to sick pay?

Q I've injured my back and been off work sick for six weeks. My employer has refused me sick pay. Is this illegal?

A Yes, probably. It depends on your age, whether you are an employee or self-employed, and whether your average earnings are above a set minimum.

If you are an employee (see box, p276), you are entitled to statutory sick pay (SSP) if you are aged 16-65 and your average earnings are above the lower earnings limit for National Insurance (£77 a week in the tax year 2003-4). For the purposes of SSP you are treated as an employee if your employer has to pay employers' Class 1 National Insurance contributions on your behalf. Check your payslip to see if this is the case. To claim

SSP you must write to your employer to say that you are sick and unable to work, providing a doctor's certificate as evidence.

SSP is paid for the first 28 weeks of your sickness from the fourth day you are ill. The rate for SSP is £64.35 a week (in the tax year 2003-4). Most employers reclaim a proportion of the money from the government. Most British workers also receive sick pay guaranteed by their terms of employment, by which the employer makes up SSP to the amount of your normal weekly wages for an agreed number of weeks.

ACTION PLAN

1 Check your terms of employment (see box, p271) to see if you have the right to contractual sick pay from your employer.

2 If you qualify for contractual sick pay, write to your human resources manager or boss quoting the terms of your employment and demand sick pay backdated to the beginning of your illness ▶ ✍ .

3 If you do not qualify for contractual sick pay but you meet the conditions for SSP, write to your human resources manager or boss stating your right to the statutory amount under the Social Security and Housing Benefits Act 1982 ▶ ✍ .

4 If your employer refuses to pay SSP for all or part of your sick period, ask for a written statement of reasons, then write to the Inland Revenue ▶ ⌸ for advice.

5 If you do not qualify for SSP because of your age or your average earnings, you may be entitled to incapacity benefit – consult your local Jobcentre. Write to your employer asking for form SSP1. You will need this to apply for incapacity benefit.

Threat of dismissal over safety risk

Q When I complained to my employer that some of the equipment we use is defective and dangerous she threatened to fire me. Can she do that?

A No. It is against the law for an employer to dismiss you, select you for redundancy or treat you less favourably than your colleagues because you complain of health and safety risks.

Under the Health and Safety at Work Act 1974, employers have a duty to make sure that nothing in the workplace endangers the health, safety and welfare of their employees. They have to act 'so far as is reasonably practicable'.

In judging whether an employer should have acted to eliminate a risk, a court or tribunal would weigh up the size and nature of the risk against the difficulty and expense of eliminating it.

The Management of Health and Safety at Work Regulations 1992 add that employers must carry out a formal assessment of risks to employees' health and safety at set intervals and appoint a member of staff to be health and safety representative.

For further advice, phone the Health and Safety Executive's Infoline: 08701 545500. This can also give you the contact details for your local health and safety enforcement authority.

ACTION PLAN

1 Explain your concerns to your health and safety representative, who will discuss them with your employer and report back to you.

2 If you and your representative are not satisfied with your employer's response, contact the health and safety enforcement authority for your workplace. The Health and Safety Executive can instruct inspectors to visit your workplace and enforce the law.

3 If your employer threatens dismissal again, or actually dismisses you, you can bring a case for 'detriment' (see box, opposite) or unfair dismissal in an employment tribunal (see p291). Seek advice from your union representative, if you have one, or your local Citizens Advice Bureau ▶ 🕮 or Law Centre ▶ 🕮.

The right to set up or join a trade union

Q A group of colleagues and I want to join a trade union but the manager won't allow us to discuss it with other employees. Can he do this?

A No. Employees have the right to join a trade union. Under the Trade Union and Labour Relations (Consolidation) Act 1992 your employer cannot 'subject you to a detriment' (penalise you by treating you less favourably than your colleagues – see box, opposite) because you are, or are seeking to become, a member of a union.

Your employer does not have to give you and your colleagues time off in working hours to talk about whether or not you should join a union. However, once you and your colleagues have become union members, your employer has to give you unpaid time off in working hours to hold certain types of union meetings – for example, to meet union officials or to vote on the result of negotiations with the employer.

DEFECTIVE EQUIPMENT

You are within your rights to refuse to use defective equipment that you think might cause an injury.

You can refuse to work altogether for this reason if, for instance, you are a driver, and the vehicle your employer provides is unsafe. If you are sacked for refusing to work in this situation, an employment tribunal (see box, p291) would be likely to declare it unfair dismissal.

ACTION PLAN

1 Arrange a meeting outside working hours with your colleagues to discuss joining a trade union.

2 Once you have gauged the level of interest, contact the Advisory, Conciliation and Arbitration Service (ACAS) ▶ 📖 or the Trades Union Congress (TUC) ▶ 📖 for advice.

3 Tell your manager that you and your colleagues will be joining the union or establishing a branch of the union, as appropriate.

4 If your manager threatens to prevent you joining the union, inform him that you have the legal right to join a union and not to suffer detriment for doing so. If you prefer, ask the human resources department to advise your manager of your rights.

5 If your manager tries to prevent you joining the union, you can take the case to an employment tribunal (see box, p291) claiming detriment. The tribunal can uphold your complaint and also award you financial compensation. Seek advice from ACAS or the TUC first.

The procedures for disciplining employees

Q My manager called me into his office unexpectedly and gave me a formal written warning that I'll be dismissed if I don't improve my timekeeping. Can he do that?

A No. Your manager should have told you in advance that you were being asked to attend what was, in effect, a disciplinary hearing and that you had the right to be accompanied by a colleague or trade union representative. Under the Employment Relations Act 1999, you and your colleague or representative can address the hearing and confer together.

Your manager should follow your company's disciplinary procedure, if there is one. The Advisory, Conciliation and Arbitration Service (ACAS) ▶ 📖 code of practice on disciplinary procedures says that you should be given the chance to defend yourself before any ▶

HAVE YOU LOT BEEN READING GEORGE ORWELL?

disciplinary decisions are reached. It recommends that employers give a formal oral warning, a written warning and a final written warning before dismissing an employee. It adds that a warning should lapse after a set time – usually six months for an oral warning, 12 months for written or final ones.

Discuss the matter with your union or staff representative. If you do not have one, seek advice from your local Citizens Advice Bureau ▶ .

Stealing allegation not a cause for dismissal

Q I was wrongly accused of stealing from my employer's warehouse and my manager fired me on the spot. Can he do this?

A No, not on the spot. Your employer does have the right to dismiss you for stealing without giving you notice or payment in lieu of notice. But he is also expected to act reasonably. You should be told the detailed allegations and be allowed to put your side of the story.

Your employer should suspend you on full pay while he carries out an investigation – he must be able to show he has reasonable grounds for believing the allegations against you. If the allegations involve several people, you should all be treated in the same way.

If your company has a disciplinary procedure, your manager must follow it.

Depending on its details:
• you may have the right to a disciplinary hearing. If you do, you can be accompanied by a colleague or union representative (see question, p289)
• you may be able to have your case heard by another manager.

ACTION PLAN

1 Find out whether your company has a disciplinary procedure by looking in your contract or your terms of employment (see box, p271).

2 Write to your employer stating that the allegations against you are false and that you feel you have not been given the chance to put your side of the case. If appropriate, add that your manager has not followed agreed disciplinary procedures. Ask for help in drafting the letter from your union or staff association representative, if you have one.

3 If your employer is unwilling to change his position or does not respond, ask for a written statement of reasons for your dismissal. If you have worked for your employer continuously for at least a year you have the right to request this statement and your employer must respond within 14 days. You can use it as evidence if your case comes before an employment tribunal.

4 If you can prove that you did not steal, you might succeed in a case for unfair dismissal at an employment tribunal (see box, right). You must bring the case within three months of the date of dismissal. Before going ahead, seek advice from the Advisory, Conciliation and Arbitration Service (ACAS) ▶ ⌂ or your local Citizens Advice Bureau ▶ ⌂.

THE EMPLOYMENT TRIBUNAL

Employment tribunals settle disputes over:
- cases of unfair and constructive dismissal (when your employer breaks the employment contract by changing the terms without your consent)
- redundancy payments
- sex, race and disability discrimination
- wages
- terms and conditions of employment.

Applying to an employment tribunal
You must have worked for your employer for at least a year before you can bring a case to a tribunal, except when you are dismissed for reasons the law considers to be 'automatically unfair'.

How does the tribunal work?
An employment tribunal works like a court. You can represent yourself or you may be represented, free of charge, by a volunteer 'advocate' from, for example, a Citizens Advice Bureau.

Each tribunal generally has a legally qualified chairman and two lay members.

Time limits
You normally have to bring a case within three months of the event you are complaining about. Different time limits apply to redundancy claims.

For more information, call:
Employment Tribunals enquiry line: 0845 795 9775
Redundancy Payments Helpline: 0845 145 0004.

How to apply
- Ask for the booklet *How to Apply to an Employment Tribunal*, available from your local Jobcentre or Citizens Advice Bureau. It contains the form IT1 'Application to an Employment Tribunal'.
- Or write a letter to your nearest Employment Tribunal Office ▶ 📖, giving your name and address, the name and address of the company or person you are bringing a complaint against and the details of the complaint.
- Or download an application form from the Employment Tribunals web site ▶ 📖.

You must tell the tribunal what you want. If, for example, you have been dismissed, do you want your old job back, another job with your old employer or compensation for lost wages?

What happens next
- The tribunal sends you a case number. If you do not receive this in a week, check that the tribunal office received your application.
- Within five days of receiving your form, the tribunal sends a copy to your employer or former employer ('the respondent'), who has 21 days to reply. If there is no reply, the case goes ahead without feedback.
- The tribunal also contacts the Advisory, Conciliation and Arbitration Service (ACAS) ▶ 📖. An ACAS conciliator will liaise with you and the respondent in an attempt to resolve the matter.

If you do not agree
If you do not reach agreement through the conciliation process, the tribunal will hear the case. It will give at least 14 days' notice of the hearing date.

If you agree
The ACAS representative informs the tribunal, which issues an order stopping the case. You or the respondent can enforce the agreement in the county court.

Agreeing a date
If you cannot make the proposed date, write to the tribunal at once, giving your reasons and suggesting alternative dates. If this is acceptable the tribunal will confirm the new date.

The hearing
The tribunal will announce its decision at the hearing, and send you and the respondent a written confirmation containing reasons for its conclusions.

Appeals
- You and the respondent have the right to appeal against the decision to the Employment Appeals Tribunal ▶ 📖.
- The tribunal will provide information on how to make your appeal.

You should be paid when a firm closes

Q I've worked for a small bakery for 18 months. Today my boss announced she was closing us down, with no redundancy or payment in lieu of notice. Can she do that?

A No. Under the Employment Rights Act 1996, if you have been employed for more than one month and less than two years, you are entitled to at least one week's notice that you are losing your job.

Because you cannot work out your notice period your boss should pay you a week's wages in lieu of notice. If she refuses to do this, she is in breach of contract, and you have a case for wrongful dismissal.

You may also be entitled to more notice under your contract or terms of employment (see box, p271). Normally, you have the right to the same amount of notice that you would have to give your boss if you wanted to leave your job.

If you had worked for more than two years, you would be entitled, under the Employment Rights Act, to one week's additional notice for every complete year's service up to a maximum of 12 weeks.

You are not entitled to a redundancy payment (see p295) because you have worked for your employer for less than the two years' minimum required to qualify, but your contract or terms of employment may give you the right to a payment anyway.

ACTION PLAN

1 Check whether you are guaranteed a redundancy payment or a minimum notice period in your contract or terms of employment (see box, p271).

2 Take a claim for wrongful or unfair dismissal and redundancy payment to an employment tribunal (see p291) within three months of losing your job. The tribunal can make your employer pay you wages in lieu of notice.

3 Alternatively, make a claim in the civil courts (see p16). First, seek advice from your local Citizens Advice Bureau ▶ ⌒ or Law Centre ▶ ⌒.

Missing out on a redundancy payment

Q After 12 years working for my company I've been told that the jobs in my department are being made redundant. My colleagues are getting generous pay-offs and I would like a redundancy payment, too, but my boss says I won't receive one because he's offering me a job similar to my old one in a sister company. Can he do this?

A Probably. You do not have the right to a redundancy payment if your employer offers you a suitable alternative to your previous job. But you may be able to dispute whether the alternative job is really suitable.

Under the Employment Rights Act 1996:
• the alternative job can be with the company you already work for, with an associated company, or with another company that is taking over the business
• your employer must offer the alternative job to you before your previous employment contract expires
• the new job must either start at once or within four weeks of your old job ending
• you have the right to a four-week trial in the new job before deciding whether to accept it; you should be able to

negotiate a longer trial period if you need retraining to do the new job, but you would need a written agreement with your old employer confirming the length of the trial period. (Note that if you are still in the new job after the four-week, or otherwise agreed, period, you will be judged to have accepted it.)

• if you do not want to take the job and your employer accepts that the job is not a suitable alternative, you are entitled to a redundancy payment from the date your original job ended

• if your employer does not agree that the job is unsuitable, you can take your case to an employment tribunal (see p291). First seek advice from your trade union or staff association representative, or from your local Citizens Advice Bureau.

WORD OF WARNING

If an employment tribunal does not agree with you, it will declare that you have refused the new job without good reason and that you are not entitled to a redundancy payment.

Why have I been made redundant?

Q My employer has announced that he will be making six employees, including me, redundant. He and I have had our differences, and I suspect that this is the reason he has selected me. Can he do that?

A Yes. Your employer can choose you for redundancy because your conduct at work has been poor or you lack capability or qualifications for the job. He might be able to prove that he was justified in choosing to make you redundant on grounds of conduct if your 'differences' amounted to your being obstructive or disrespectful.

As long as your employer can show that your job is redundant, it will be very

difficult for you to prove that he is making you redundant because you do not get on. Whether you have a case or not will also depend on what your 'differences' were.

ACTION PLAN

1 Discuss your circumstances with your staff association or union representative, or seek advice from the Advisory, Conciliation and Arbitration Service (ACAS) or your local Citizens Advice Bureau.

2 If you can prove that your job is not truly redundant or that you were selected for redundancy for an automatically unfair reason (see p294), you can write to your employer in an attempt to save your job.

3 If you do not receive a satisfactory response, you can bring a case for unfair dismissal to an employment tribunal (see p291).

IF YOU DON'T MIND ME ASKING, WHY DID YOU PICK US FOUR?

REDUNDANCIES
MR EENY
MR MEENY
MR MINEY
MR MO

Redundancy: your rights

Know your redundancy rights and you may be able to save your job or appeal against your dismissal. You can ask your trade union or staff association representative for help or you can seek advice from your local Citizens Advice Bureau ▶ 📖 or Law Centre ▶ 📖.

WHAT IS REDUNDANCY?
Your job becomes redundant if your employer:
- closes the business
- closes your place of work
- needs (or expects to need) fewer employees to do a particular kind of work.

Sham redundancy
If your employer hires someone else to do the same job you were doing, you have not genuinely been made redundant. This situation is known as a 'sham redundancy'. You can claim unfair dismissal.

Unfair reasons for redundancy or dismissal
There are several reasons for dismissing employees or choosing them for redundancy that the law considers to be automatically unfair. For example, your employer cannot make you redundant because:
- you are pregnant
- you are on or are about to go on maternity leave
- you have claimed a statutory right (one guaranteed by Act of Parliament), for example, your right to an itemised payslip (see p275) or a written statement of your terms of employment (see p271)
- you acted to protect yourself or others because you were concerned about workplace health and safety (see p288)
- you are or want to become a trade union member (see p288).

For a full list of automatically unfair reasons contact the Advisory, Conciliation and Arbitration Service (ACAS) ▶ 📖 or see the booklet *Dismissal – Fair and Unfair*, which can be ordered from the Department of Trade and Industry ▶ 📖 or downloaded from www.dti.org.uk

ADVANCE CONSULTATION

An employer who is making 20 or more employees redundant within a 90-day period must consult union officials, if there are any, or other employee representatives. The employer must inform the representatives of:
- the number of redundancies
- the categories of job that are being made redundant
- how they have been selected for redundancy
- how the redundancy payments will be calculated.

The consultation should address ways of avoiding the redundancies or reducing the number. Where an employer does not consult as required, the union officials or staff representatives should bring a case to an employment tribunal (see p291).

Consultation must begin 30 days before redundancy where between 20 and 99 employees are being made redundant, and 90 days before redundancy where 100 or more employees are being made redundant.

REDUNDANCY PAYMENT

Generally, you have the right to a redundancy payment if you have worked for your employer continuously for at least two years (without breaks, such as being laid off for a time). Work when you were under 18 does not count towards the minimum amount.

When you do not have the right to redundancy

• Your employer offers you a suitable alternative job before your current contract ends (see p292).
• You resign or are dismissed for gross (serious) misconduct before the end of your period of notice.
• You are 65 or over.
• People in your company normally retire at a set age below 65 and you have reached that age.
• You are working under contract as an apprentice.
• You are working under a fixed-term contract lasting at least two years and you have given a written agreement to waive your right to redundancy at the end of the contract.
• You are in the armed services, a domestic servant in a private home, a share fisherman paid by share of the catch, an employee of an overseas government, an employee in a public office or a Crown servant.

How much should I get paid?

You have the right to a minimum amount known as statutory redundancy pay. But many employment contracts guarantee workers more than the statutory minimum.

The minimum is:
• half a week's pay for each complete year of service between the ages of 18 and 21
• one week's pay for each complete year of service between the ages of 22 and 40
• one and a half week's pay for each complete year of service between the ages of 41 and 65.

Your weekly pay is counted only up to a maximum of £260 a week (in the tax year 2003-4). If you are aged 64-65, the total you receive is cut by a twelfth for every complete month you are over 64.

NOTICE OF REDUNDANCY

You should receive notice (a written statement) that you are being dismissed from your job because of redundancy. The minimum notice is one week for each year you have worked for the company up to a maximum of 12 weeks. If you do not receive the right amount of notice, you may be able to claim pay in lieu of notice.

Looking for another job

If you have been working without breaks for your employer for two or more years you have the right to paid time off while working out your notice to look for another job.

NON-PAYMENT OF REDUNDANCY ENTITLEMENT

You can take a case to an employment tribunal (see p291) within six months of being dismissed. First get advice from ACAS ▶ 📖, the government's Redundancy Payments Service Helpline: 0845 145 0004, or your local Citizens Advice Bureau.

If your employer is in financial trouble, you may be able to get your redundancy payment from the National Insurance Fund – contact the government's Redundancy Payments Service Helpline: 0845 145 0004.

WORLD OF WORK

Who gets jobseeker's allowance?

Q **I was a self-employed decorator for ten years, paying tax and self-employed National Insurance contributions every year. My business failed and I applied for unemployment pay (jobseeker's allowance), but I was told I could only get a means-tested benefit. Is that right?**

A Yes. There are two types of jobseeker's allowance (JSA):
• Contribution-based JSA – reserved for people who have paid enough employee National Insurance contributions ('Class 1'). For details, contact your local Jobcentre or Jobcentre Plus office ▶ ⌫.
• Income-based JSA – a means-tested benefit paid to people whose income is below a set level (see box, left).

You do not qualify for contribution-based JSA if you have paid self-employed National Insurance contributions. To claim either form of JSA you have to be capable of working, available to work and actively seeking work.

Your entitlement to income-based JSA is affected by how much your partner is earning (see box, left), so you may have to make a joint claim with your partner. By contrast, you can claim contribution-based JSA even if your partner is working full-time.

It is worth claiming income-based JSA regardless of how little you may receive, because your claim may entitle you to help with mortgage interest payments.

ACTION PLAN

1 Claim JSA as soon as you can, because you may lose benefit if you delay. Ask for a claim form at your nearest Jobcentre or Jobcentre Plus office ▶ ⌫. The Jobcentre staff will make an appointment for you to have a jobseeker's interview.

2 Bring the completed form to the interview. You and the adviser will draw up a jobseeker's agreement, stating that you are available for work, the kinds of work you are looking for and what you will do to find work and improve your chances of landing a job. You cannot normally receive the benefit if you do not have a jobseeker's agreement.

3 You must attend the Jobcentre once a fortnight to state that you are still looking for work and entitled to JSA.

WORD OF WARNING

If you do not sign on as available for work you will not be entitled to National Insurance credits. You need these to safeguard your National Insurance record and for other benefits such as retirement pension. So sign on, even if you do not qualify for JSA.

Women can retire at the same age as men

Q **My manager tells me that as a woman I will have to retire next year when I reach 60 and can draw my state pension. My male colleagues generally carry on working until they are 65. Can she make me retire at 60?**

A No. Employers can set a mandatory retirement age – the age at which all employees have to retire – but they cannot set different ages for men and women. That would be illegal under the Sex Discrimination Act 1986. They are allowed to set mandatory retirement

ages for different categories of employees – for example, one for clerical workers and another for managers. But even in this case, you might be able to challenge the retirement age.

If the majority of the clerical workers are women and the majority of the managers are men, you could probably claim that your employer is guilty of indirect sex discrimination (see box, p281).

ACTION PLAN

1 Ask for a meeting with your manager or with the human resources department. Take along your union representative or a colleague to act as a witness. Tell the company that you would be willing to challenge its policy of requiring women employees to retire earlier than male employees on the grounds that it is illegal under the Sex Discrimination Act 1986. You may prefer to send a letter (keep a copy) than to have a meeting ▸✍.

2 Keep a careful record of what is said in the meeting and copies of any correspondence.

3 If your employer does not change the company retirement policy, you could bring a case of sex discrimination to an employment tribunal (see p291). Before applying to the tribunal, seek advice from the Advisory, Conciliation and Arbitration Service (ACAS) ▸ 🖾 or your local Citizens Advice Bureau ▸ 🖾.

No 'unfair dismissal' for the over-65s

Q After early retirement from my teaching job, I've worked for ten years in a large DIY store. I'm now 67 and my boss says he's letting me go because he wants to have someone younger in my place. Can he do that?

A Yes. There is no law to protect people against being treated less favourably than their work colleagues because of age – although the government is committed to introducing age discrimination legislation by 2006 (see box, p280). Once you have passed 'normal retirement age' at work (usually 65) you cannot claim unfair dismissal or redundancy.

According to the Employment Rights Act 1996, the normal retirement age is that given in your terms of employment (see box, p271), unless you can show that most employees take retirement at a different age. If there is no established retirement age at your place of work, then the Act specifies it should be 65.

If you are asked to leave at 67, but your colleagues are working on to a greater age, you may have a claim for unfair dismissal. Seek advice from a solicitor (see p20) or your local Citizens Advice Bureau ▸ 🖾 or Law Centre ▸ 🖾.

> ### CHANGE TO THE LAW
>
> Between 2010 and 2020 the government will gradually increase the age at which women can claim the state pension from the current 60 years to 65 years. From April 2020 women, like men, will only become eligible to draw the state pension when they reach the age of 65.

TYPICAL TED D.I.Y. TO THE END

INJURIES & ACCIDENTS

If somebody tries to ruin your reputation

Q **I run a physiotherapy clinic from home and a neighbour objects to the extra cars parking in the road. He's been telling people locally that I'm not fully qualified, and now he's started putting leaflets on my patients' cars saying that I'm no good. Can I sue him?**

A Probably. Your neighbour is making statements that are defamatory – that is, they may damage your reputation or standing in people's minds and could harm you professionally. This makes him liable for prosecution.

There are two types of defamation, depending on whether it is spoken or published (your neighbour has committed both):

• spoken defamation or 'slander' – to take action against slander you must show (among other things) that what your neighbour said has caused you financial loss

• published defamation or 'libel' – this may be written or broadcast. You can take action just to protect your reputation and do not have to prove financial loss.

If you sue your neighbour for defamation, the court will:

• consider your desire to protect your reputation

• examine the precise meaning of the words used by your neighbour and their context

• assess how widely the false information was spread and to whom.

In his defence, your neighbour could argue that the statements are true, but the 'burden' (see box, p21) would be on him to prove this to the court.

If you decide to take legal action, bear in mind that the costs could be very high and you will not be able to get financial

assistance to fund your case. Contact the Law Society ▶ 📖 for information about a fast-track procedure for claims involving sums of £5000-15,000, which will reduce costs (see box, p19).

ACTION PLAN

1 Talk or write to your neighbour, warning him that you will take legal action if he does not stop saying and publishing defamatory statements about you.

2 Consult a solicitor (see p20) or your local Citizens Advice Bureau ▶ 📖 or Law Centre ▶ 📖 about suing for damages and taking out an injunction (see box, p21) to stop further publication of the defamation.
For a list of solicitors specialising in defamation cases, contact the Office for the Supervision of Solicitors ▶ 📖.

Suing on a 'no-win, no-fee' basis

Q **I had an accident recently and I'm considering suing for compensation. I've seen ads from lawyers offering to take on this type of case free. My friend said I'd be falling for a scam. Can she be right?**

A No. The normal way to fund most personal injury compensation claims is now a 'conditional fee' agreement – commonly called a 'no-win, no-fee' agreement (see box, opposite).

This enables you (the claimant) to start proceedings against the person or body responsible for your injuries (the defendant) without facing mounting legal bills. Many accident victims could not afford these bills, especially if they are unable to work because of the accident.

HOW A 'NO-WIN, NO-FEE' AGREEMENT WORKS

When solicitors say they will take on a case under what is called a 'conditional fee' or 'no-win, no-fee' agreement, it means that they will agree to charge you only if you win your case. Solicitors always assess a case carefully before taking it on under 'no-win, no-fee' terms, because if you lose they do not get paid. Equally, you may be reassured that if they start proceedings on a 'no-win, no-fee' basis, they must be fairly confident that you will win.

Who pays the solicitor if you win?
Legal costs The other side – or more usually their insurers – have to pay your legal costs as well as theirs. This is on top of any compensation they have to pay you, so an award consists of compensation plus costs.
Litigation insurance Even if your solicitors are sure you have a good case, they may suggest that you take out litigation insurance. This will cover the other side's costs if you lose. There is a single premium (depending on the scale of the case, it varies from £100 to thousands of pounds), and if you win you can usually recover it from the defendant with your final settlement.

Success fee Some solicitors charge what they call a 'success fee' for winning in order to reflect the financial risk they have taken. This will be charged to the defendant as part of your total expenses (see below). The defendant can challenge the amount.

What about expenses?
These include the time your solicitor spends on your case (see question, p173), and since cases can take a long time – often years – to come to settlement, this cost can be considerable.
In addition, expenses, called 'disbursements', have to be paid for things like medical reports, court fees and expert opinions.
Solicitors discuss disbursement arrangements with their clients at the start of the case. Some ask clients to pay for disbursements, while others fund them for you. If you win, they add them to the total amount of the claim against the other side, so there is nothing for you to pay.

For more information
Contact the Law Society ▶ 🖃, which regulates the way 'no-win, no-fee' agreements work.

Claiming for an accident abroad

Q When I was on a family skiing trip I was hit by a ski lift and injured. My travel insurance covered the medical costs, but I needed time off work to recuperate when we got back to the UK. The insurance company says the policy doesn't cover this. So can I claim any compensation?

A Possibly. Some travel insurance policies exclude recuperation in the UK after an accident, but many will pay at least some of the costs if you need continuing treatment on your return. You should read the policy carefully.

If the insurer is not liable, you may still be able to claim compensation if your holiday was a package holiday booked through a tour operator. Government ▶

regulations (see box, p98) state that you can claim against the tour operator in the UK if you are injured on your holiday. You can also claim for disappointment.

If there are certain things you did not book as a part of a package – for example, if your holiday rep arranged the ski lift pass after you arrived at the resort – the situation is different. You can claim compensation only if you have grounds for legal action against the company responsible for the ski lift.

You will probably have to take action in the country where the injury occurred, which will mean hiring a lawyer who is qualified to act in that country. This can be prolonged, difficult and expensive.

ACTION PLAN

1 Read your insurance policy. If you think the insurance company is liable, write to explain why and ask for its decision to be revised ▶ ✍. Ask also to use the company's complaints procedure. If it refuses to change the decision, complain to the General Insurance Standards Council ▶ 📖 or the Financial Ombudsman Service (see box, p141).

2 If you booked the holiday through a tour operator in the UK, contact the company, explain the situation and ask how you can claim for expenses and compensation. If the company refuses, ask if it is a member of the Association of British Travel Agents (ABTA) or the Association of Independent Tour Operators (AITO; see box, pp92-93). Complain to the relevant association, which can oblige the company to act.

3 If you fail to win compensation in the UK, consult a solicitor (see p20) or your local Citizens Advice Bureau ▶ 📖 or Law Centre ▶ 📖 about how to take legal action abroad.

Dangers of ignoring a manufacturer's warning

Q My two-year-old daughter choked on a small plastic toy. The toy company says it isn't responsible because the toy came in a package with the warning 'Not for children under three years old'. Can it avoid liability in this way?

A Yes. The manufacturer made it clear that the toy your daughter choked on was unsuitable for children under three. If you choose to ignore a manufacturer's safety warning on a product, you must arrange for the child to be supervised when playing with it.

If a child is injured when playing with a toy belonging to an older sister or brother, or with a household object, the manufacturer is not liable since the parent had a responsibility to supervise the child.

To claim against the manufacturer, you would have to show that it was negligent or that it breached a duty of safety imposed by law. For example, if a new teddy bear's eye came off, this would infringe the Toys (Safety) Regulations 1995. If the eye was swallowed by a toddler, the manufacturer would be liable for any harm this caused the child, whether or not the teddy bear had a warning label saying 'not for children under five'.

An injury caused by electrical equipment

Q I was injured when my new lawnmower backfired as I started it, but the manufacturer denies any liability. Can it do that?

A No. Manufacturers are responsible for injuries caused by defective goods. As long as you followed the instructions correctly and did not alter the mower in any way, you should consider taking legal action against the mower's manufacturer for personal injury (see box, pp302-303).

The Consumer Protection Act 1987 states that you only have to prove that the lawnmower was unsafe and that it caused your injury. You do not have to prove negligence by the manufacturer. If there is any doubt about the cause of the accident, a court will consider:

- warnings and instructions about use
- the age of the machine
- what is regarded as reasonable use.

ACTION PLAN

1 Contact a solicitor (see p20) or your local Citizens Advice Bureau ▶ 🕮 or Law Centre ▶ 🕮 about pursuing a claim against the manufacturer. For a solicitor who specialises in personal injury, contact the Association of Personal Injury Lawyers ▶ 🕮.

2 If you believe that the manufacturer breached safety standards, you should also complain to your local trading standards office (see p30) or the Department of Trade and Industry (DTI) ▶ 🕮. The manufacturer may have broken one of the regulations that are designed to protect the user of electrical equipment, and if this were proved, it would help your personal injury claim.

WORD OF WARNING

If you failed to follow the operating instructions on electrical equipment or did anything to alter the equipment before using it – for example, you changed the wiring incorrectly – the manufacturer may escape liability, or your compensation could be reduced by your contributory negligence (see box, p305).

Who is liable for an uneven kerb?

Q **My mother tripped over a loose kerbstone when walking to the shops, and broke her hip. She wants to take action against the council. Can she do that?**

A Yes. According to the Highways Act 1980, the council has to keep the highways in its area, including pavements, in a safe condition. Your mother would have to prove that the kerbstone was dangerous, and a court would assess the severity of the risk. The position of the kerbstone and how irregular it was would be important. A raised kerbstone is more likely to cause harm on a busy shopping street than in a quiet cul-de-sac.

The council will have to show that it took reasonable steps to maintain the highway – perhaps with an inspection schedule. The court would assess whether the inspections were adequate. The council is more likely to be held liable if it had been informed about the hazard before your mother's accident.

If a contractor such as a cable company had left the pavement in a dangerous state after recent works, it may be liable for your mother's injury. It would strengthen her case if the council had served notice on the contractor to remedy the defect.

ACTION PLAN

1 Gather evidence. Collect statements from anyone who saw the incident and remembers any roadworks or warning signs. Measure how far the kerbstone protrudes and take photographs. Find the shoes your mother was wearing.

2 Consult a solicitor (see p20) or your local Citizens Advice Bureau ▶ 🕮 or Law Centre ▶ 🕮 about making a claim. For a solicitor specialising in personal injury, contact the Association of Personal Injury Lawyers ▶ 🕮.

INJURIES & ACCIDENTS

Making a personal injury claim

The procedures involved in taking a personal injury case to court can be long and expensive. Before starting, you need to be sure that you have a reasonable case and can raise the necessary funding.

Solicitors accept most reasonable cases on a 'conditional fee' or 'no-win, no-fee' basis (see box, p299). Household, motoring, travel and other types of insurance may include cover for legal expenses. The insurance company will fund taking a case to court if it is thought to have a reasonable chance of success. Check your insurance policies to see if you are covered before you opt for any other source of funding. Public funding – formerly called legal aid – is now only available for cases involving clinical negligence (see box, p15).

CAN YOU CLAIM?

You are not always entitled to compensation just because you have been hurt or injured. To claim for personal injury, you must usually show that someone else:
- was at fault (negligent)
- had breached a 'statutory' (legal) duty
- attacked you – you can claim compensation for injuries inflicted deliberately, in a violent attack, for example.

You can claim against:
- an individual
- a company
- an organisation
- a shop
- a manufacturer
- a local authority
- a criminal
- a driver
- your employer
- a family member
- an insurance company
- the Criminal Injuries Compensation Authority (CICA; see p319)
- the Motor Insurers' Bureau (MIB; see p266).

You may be able to claim for injuries caused by:
- a criminal attack
- medical negligence
- an occupational illness (illness brought about by your work)
- a defective product
- contaminated food
- practising a sport.

Or by an accident:
- at work
- on the roads – caused by a private vehicle
- on public transport
- in a shop or office
- at school or college
- in a public place
- in a private house or on private land
- on holiday.

TAKING LEGAL ADVICE

Take legal advice as soon as possible after an incident that could give rise to a personal injury claim. It can take years to prepare a case and any delay could reduce your chances of getting compensation. Consult a solicitor (contact the Association of Personal Injury Lawyers ▶▭) or your local Citizens Advice Bureau ▶▭ or Law Centre ▶▭.

TIME FRAME FOR CLAIMS

You can usually start a court action for personal injury compensation up to three years after the date of the incident. This 'limitation period' may be extended for:

Children The three-year period starts on their 18th birthday, so children can claim up to the age of 21, even for injuries that happened at birth.

People with a mental disability They can make a claim at any time or until they no longer need treatment – as with a temporary disability caused by, say, a head injury.

People with a condition whose symptoms do not appear immediately They must claim within three years of when they become aware:
- of the seriousness of the condition
- that it was caused by negligence
- who or which body was responsible.
Such conditions include illnesses caused by contact with asbestos.

People injured by a product they bought They must claim within three years of the date of the injury, or of the date when they located the manufacturer, and within ten years of buying the product.

Claiming after the time limit
You have to ask the court's permission to claim after the time limit expires.

WHAT ARE THE DAMAGES?

The civil courts (see p17) compensate people for losses or expenses arising from a personal injury. This compensation is known as 'damages', which may be paid as:

• a single payment – the final settlement of your claim

• interim damages – a proportion of the proposed final sum owed if the other party admits liability but disputes the final amount of damages; interim damages enable you to settle immediate bills before the court decides the final amount

• provisional damages – a sum paid if the final outcome of the injury remains uncertain. You can return to court at a later date if your condition becomes worse and the sum should be increased.

If you win a personal injury case, any award of damages will be made up of general damages and special damages (see below). Also, the defendant is usually ordered to pay your legal costs.

General damages

These are an amount of money that the court has decided is reasonable to compensate you for your suffering and 'loss of amenity' (inability to follow your normal activities). They can include compensation for mental suffering, such as the long-term psychological effects of the injury.

Each case is assessed on its merits, but general damages are worked out by comparison with past claims and by following guidelines published by the Judicial Studies Board, a body responsible for training judges and magistrates.

Factors taken into account include:
• the nature and severity of your injury
• your age
• your occupation and how much your injury interferes with your work
• your lifestyle and hobbies and how these are impaired by your injury
• your domestic responsibilities and the impact of your injury on them.

If you derived special enjoyment from your job and can no longer pursue it, you may get extra compensation for 'loss of congenial employment'.

You can also get extra damages if your injury affects your job stability, promotion prospects or ability to seek alternative employment.

Special damages

These compensate you for property damage, loss of earnings, expenses and other specific, calculable costs that you incurred because of the incident in which you were injured.

Claims for expenses may include:
• the cost of repairing your vehicle
• the reasonable costs of hiring a car while your vehicle is being repaired
• reimbursement of any insurance excess you had to pay, and loss of a no-claims bonus
• the replacement cost of clothes or damaged items of personal property
• medical expenses, including private medical fees, prescription charges and travel to attend appointments
• the costs of necessary alterations to your home – for example, to accommodate a wheelchair or to install handrails or special taps
• an hourly rate to reflect the time given by relatives, friends or neighbours to provide you with necessary nursing care – for example, helping you to wash and bathe, to get dressed or with eating
• the costs of paid help to carry out necessary tasks you can no longer perform as a result of the accident or injury – such as shopping
• sundry costs, such as postage and phone calls.

You can also claim for future losses – for example:
• expected loss of earnings or pension rights
• the costs of medical and care needs.

When a shop becomes a danger

Q At the greengrocer's shop I skidded on some squashed fruit on the floor and fell, injuring my back. The shopkeeper said the fruit must have been dropped by another customer, so she wasn't responsible. Can she do that?

A No. Shopkeepers have a duty to take reasonable care to ensure their customers' safety, and you can take legal action against the shopkeeper even if the hazard was caused by another customer's carelessness.

The Occupier's Liability Act 1957 states that if the individual or company owning the shop fails to safeguard against hazards that should not be present, such as a slippery object on the floor, they are potentially responsible for any injuries that result.

But your chance of being awarded compensation will be affected by the court's view of what reasonable circumstances are in this particular situation – for example, how long the hazard had been there, and whether or not the shopkeeper could have noticed it and removed it before you fell.

ACTION PLAN
1 Try to find witnesses to your fall or anyone who may have been aware of how long the squashed fruit had been on the floor. Find out if anyone had told the shopkeeper about it.

2 Consult a solicitor (see p20) or your local Citizens Advice Bureau ▶ 📖 or Law Centre ▶ 📖 about making a claim against the shopkeeper. For a solicitor who specialises in personal injury, contact the Association of Personal Injury Lawyers ▶ 📖.

Who is liable – landlord or tenant?

Q I live in a rented house, and last week an engineer who came to mend my washing machine was struck on the head by a loose roof tile as he was leaving. He says he's going to claim compensation for his injuries and time off work. Can he do that?

A Possibly. Two laws relate to this situation. First, the Defective Premises Act 1972 says that landlords of rented property may be held responsible if they:
• have an obligation under the lease to repair the premises or have reserved a right to enter and repair
• knew or ought to have known about a defect that resulted in a personal injury.

Under this law, your landlord may be responsible for the safety of tenants, their family, visitors, even passers-by and trespassers who are injured because the property has not been properly maintained. This makes the landlord liable for the engineer's accident.

Yet the Occupiers' Liability Act 1957 says that the occupier, who need not be the owner, is also responsible for making sure that anyone who visits the house is safe – so you, as tenant, could be liable for the engineer's injury (see box, p307).

ACTION PLAN
1 Check the terms of your lease to see whether your landlord has an obligation to repair or has reserved the right to enter and repair.

2 If the landlord is responsible for maintenance, refer the engineer to the landlord. If not and he takes legal action, ask a solicitor (see p20) or your

DEFENCES TO PERSONAL INJURY CLAIMS

If someone sues you for personal injury, you may be able to raise any of these counter-arguments:

Act of God
The injury was caused by a natural event that was not foreseeable and whose consequences were unexpected – for example, a lightning strike.

Consent
You may be able to argue that the victim consented to run the risks. For example, people may be assumed to have given their consent if they take part in a dangerous activity such as hang-gliding, provided they agree to run the risk. An employer who causes employees to undergo unnecessary risk cannot claim consent. Nor can consent be used if legal duties were not carried out, such as failing to install guards on dangerous machinery.

Contributory negligence
If you believe the victim was at least partly to blame, you can argue this in court. If you convince the court, the amount of damages it awards to the victim will be reduced accordingly.

Inevitable accident
Perhaps you can argue that the accident could not have been avoided, even if you had taken reasonable precautions – for example, if someone was hit during a pheasant shoot by a shot that ricocheted off a tree trunk.

Lawful authority
The police are allowed to use reasonable force to arrest someone – and you can use the same defence if you make a citizen's arrest to stop someone who is committing or has committed a crime.

Limitation period
Check the time limits for making a claim (see box, p302). If the limitation period is past, the claimant will have to ask the courts for special permission to pursue the action.

Necessity
The injury occurred while taking necessary measures to prevent injury or death – for example, a rescuer might break a rib while trying to resuscitate someone who had suffered a cardiac arrest.

Reasonable chastisement
This allows for moderate physical punishment of children. British law still allows this defence by parents (see question, p332) – although no longer by teachers, nor by jailers, military commanders, or husbands against their wives.

Self-defence
The injury was caused by defending yourself, your family or property, or other people (see box, p309).

---

local Citizens Advice Bureau ▶ ▭ or Law Centre ▶ ▭ about the possibility of conducting your defence in court.

Compensation in a case of negligence

Q **Builders installing a new staircase in my house left a nail sticking out of the banisters. My five-year-old daughter got a nasty gash on her ankle that turned septic and took weeks to heal. The builders claim they're not responsible. Can they say that?**

A No. To leave a nail sticking out so that someone could be injured is almost certainly negligent, so the builders failed in their 'duty of care' (see box, p21) to you and your household. It should not be difficult to show in court, with medical reports of your daughter's treatment, that the protruding nail caused her injuries.

Consult a solicitor specialising in personal injury (contact the Association of Personal Injury Lawyers ▶ ▭). The builders must compensate your daughter for the pain and any activities she missed while her ankle was healing. You can also recover any medical and travel costs you incurred as a result of the injury.

A hazard at a garden open day

Q My local horticultural society asked me to let people visit my garden for its annual open day. Unfortunately, one visitor tripped on loose paving and had a nasty fall. Can he take me to court?

A Yes, if the injury occurred because you failed to take reasonable care to ensure your visitors' safety. If the visitor decides to take action against you, consult a solicitor (see p20) about your defence.

If the paving had been loose for some time and you had done nothing about it, a court would probably hold you liable. But if the paving was loose because the path was obviously being relaid, you may not be held liable –

especially if you fenced it off or put up a warning sign. The Occupier's Liability Act 1957 (see box, opposite) says that if you allow people to enter your house or garden to take part in activities there – even if it is all for a 'good cause', such as raising money for a charity – you are responsible for their safety while they are there.

When you open your garden to visitors, consider establishing a contract between you and the public by issuing entrance tickets for a nominal fee. These tickets would give the visitors permission to enter your garden only. If they enter your house, garage or garden shed, they are trespassing (see question, opposite) and the Occupier's Liability Act 1957 states that your duty towards them is reduced.

Injured on your home ground

Q On her way to read my gas meter, an inspector fell into an unguarded hole in my drive and injured her ankle. She says she's going to sue me for compensation. Can she do that?

A Yes. As a householder you have a legal 'duty of care' (see box, p21) to lawful visitors to your property. That includes those who have a legal right to enter, such as utilities' inspectors.

The Occupier's Liability Act 1957 (see box, opposite) also says that if you do not take reasonable care, you may be liable if a visitor is injured while on your premises, or a visitor's property is damaged. For example, an unguarded hole on your drive could be considered a hazard to visitors. But if it were dug by, say, a workman while resurfacing your drive, you may not be liable if you can show that you tried to ensure the safety of visitors – for example, by hiring a reputable contractor to do the work, and putting up signs to warn people of the danger.

ACTION PLAN

1 If the gas inspector makes a claim for compensation against you, check whether your household building or contents insurance covers this type of liability to others.

2 If you have no insurance, consult a solicitor (see p20) or your local Citizens Advice Bureau ▶ 🕮 or Law Centre ▶ 🕮.

Your responsibility to safeguard an intruder

Q Someone trespassed on our property while we were on holiday. He tripped over the garden hose, which my husband hadn't put away before we left, and broke his ankle. Now he's suing us for damages. Can he do that?

A Probably. The Occupier's Liability Act 1984 (see box, right) states that you are responsible for the safety of anyone who enters your house or garden – not only people you invite but also trespassers (people who have no legal right to be on your property).

To hold you liable for his injuries, the intruder would have to convince a court that:
• you knew or had grounds to believe that the hose posed a possible danger, *and*
• you knew someone might trip over it, so you should have taken steps – such as tidying it away – to protect against injury.

The court might consider exactly where the intruder met his accident, the likelihood of his spotting the hose ▶

THE LEGAL DUTIES OF A HOUSEHOLDER

Two acts govern a householder's legal duties: the Occupier's Liability Act 1957 and the Occupier's Liability Act 1984. To restrict your liability under the acts, make sure that your household insurance covers you for occupier's liability.

Occupier's Liability Act 1957
This states that you have a duty to take care that anyone who visits your property is safe from hazards. You are not expected to achieve the highest standards of safety – such as those expected of a hospital or care home – just to take reasonable precautions. For example, you should check that electrical wiring is not dangerous and remove items that people might trip over.

Occupier's Liability Act 1984
Under this act, you are liable for injuries to people on your property, even if they have no right to be there and they are up to no good.

But your responsibility to trespassers (people who have no legal right to be on your property) is less than it is to lawful visitors. The law defines this kind of responsibility as 'humanitarian', which means that you must keep the premises in good repair. For example, you cannot leave a hazard, such as a large hole in the garden – if you were having a pond or swimming pool dug out, say, or topsoil replaced – without a warning notice and a fence around it. If there is no warning or barrier and a trespasser falls in the hole and is injured, you are liable to pay compensation.

The provisions of the act extend also to pets. If you have a guard dog – an Alsatian, say – and let it roam unmuzzled in your garden, you must put up warning signs ('Beware of the dog') on gates and fences. Then, if a trespasser ignores the signs and is bitten, you are not liable.

CHANGE TO THE LAW

According to government proposals, criminals who are injured while breaking and entering a property will be prohibited from suing the householder for damages. This proposed new legislation follows a number of cases where burglars did just that – sued householders for injuries sustained while committing their crimes. The same law would also protect the police from claims by criminals who are injured while being apprehended. The legislation is timetabled to be passed by Parliament in 2004.

INJURIES & ACCIDENTS

and realising it was a hazard, and whether you had any warning notices or other measures to discourage trespassers from entering, such as 'Private. Keep out'.

You might be held liable by the court if, for example, the hose was hidden by long grass, so the intruder was unable to see it. On the other hand, the court might consider you not liable if the hose was in plain view in your fenced-off back garden.

ACTION PLAN

1 If the area is still as it was when the incident happened, take a photograph of the hose, showing its exact position on the grass.

2 Check whether your household insurance policy covers you for occupier's liability, and if so contact the insurance company without delay.

3 Consult a solicitor (see p20) or your local Citizens Advice Bureau ▶ 📖 or Law Centre ▶ 📖 about defending the claim. For a solicitor who specialises in personal injury, contact the Association of Personal Injury Lawyers ▶ 📖 .

WORD OF WARNING
Although the law allows you to discourage intruders, even with barbed wire (see question, p183), you may be held responsible if they are injured as a result. You are not allowed to set deliberate traps to catch or hurt intruders.

Liability in an unsafe workplace

Q A fork-lift truck operator at work stacked a load so carelessly that it collapsed,

injuring my foot. I needed hospital treatment and it was weeks before I could walk properly. Can I claim compensation from my employer?

A Yes. By law, employers must provide a safe workplace and safe equipment and ensure that they have competent staff. Failure to do so gives employees the right to claim compensation for any resulting injury. In a company with more than ten employees, the employer must keep an accident book to record injuries, so check that your injury was reported and logged.

An employer is usually responsible for employees' conduct while they are at work. This is called 'vicarious liability', meaning that employer and employee are jointly responsible if the employee's negligence causes a colleague harm. It is a legal requirement for your employer to have insurance that covers vicarious liability for injuries inflicted by one employee on another. So although you have a case against the fork-lift truck operator, you would be better to claim against your employer.

ACTION PLAN

1 If you belong to a trade union, contact your representative and ask for help and advice about making a claim against your employer.

2 If you are not a trade union member, consult a solicitor (see p20) or your local Citizens Advice Bureau ▶🕮 or Law Centre ▶🕮 about making a claim. For a solicitor who specialises in personal injury, contact the Association of Personal Injury Lawyers ▶🕮.

Damaging sound-effects at work

Q I worked in a printing shop for 25 years until I retired three years ago. My hearing has deteriorated recently, and my doctor said this was probably because I was exposed to noise at work. Can I claim compensation?

A Yes. Your employer should have protected you from the harmful effects of excessive noise – for example, by offering hearing protection.

The usual three-year time limit for personal injury claims (see p302) can be extended for conditions such as industrial deafness in which damage may not become apparent for some years, or results from events such as exposure to high noise levels that take place over a long period.

If you decide to make a claim for compensation, your solicitor will want to arrange for you to see a medical specialist for tests to show that you have a noise-induced type of hearing loss.

ACTION PLAN

1 If you belong to a trade union, contact your representative and ask for help and advice about making a claim against your employer.

IF YOU INJURE SOMEONE IN SELF-DEFENCE

If you injure someone while warding off an attack, you risk being sued by the attacker or charged with a criminal offence.

Rules of self-defence
You can plead self-defence only if:
• you had to defend yourself, your family, other people or your property
• your actions were reasonable in the circumstances to deal with the threat – you used no more force than was necessary
• the abuse was verbal, you did not attack the person physically (you can use physical force only if you have no alternative – for instance, if you or the people you are protecting cannot run away)
• you attacked first, and you anticipated a violent or indecent attack and you feared for your safety
• you threatened your attacker's life, believing that your life or other people's lives were threatened.

What the courts say
Considered judgment The courts take into account the fact that acts of self-defence often occur in confusing and frightening circumstances, when you have to make rapid decisions and do not have time for 'considered judgment'.

Genuine belief The law states that if you acted in self-defence, you must have feared an imminent attack. But you need not have been right – a 'genuine belief' that you were in imminent danger is an acceptable defence.

Who has to prove self-defence?
If you face a criminal charge, but your plea of self-defence has been accepted, the prosecution must prove that your actions were not in self-defence.

Compensation for the attacker?
If a court accepts that you acted in self-defence, you are not liable for your attacker's injuries, you do not have to pay compensation, and any criminal charges will be dismissed.

---

2 If you are not a trade union member, consult a solicitor (see p20) or your local Citizens Advice Bureau ▶🕮 or Law Centre ▶🕮. For a solicitor who specialises in personal injury, you should contact the Association of Personal Injury Lawyers ▶🕮.

Lifting a heavy weight causes back injury

Q **I injured my back at work because of a heavy weight I had to lift. I've been off work intermittently since then, but my employer is unsympathetic. Can I make a claim against her?**

A Yes. Your employer must take precautions to avoid risk to her employees. If she failed to safeguard your welfare, and this was responsible for your accident, you can claim damages.

Employers have to follow many health and safety rules. In particular, the 1992 Manual Handling Operations Regulations set out their duties towards employees who have to do work that involves a risk of being injured – such as lifting or moving heavy weights or manhandling things in awkward positions.

According to the Regulations, employers should avoid, as far as possible, the need for their employees to do work with these risks. But where this is not possible, they must:

• 'take appropriate steps to reduce the risk of injury . . . to the lowest level reasonably practicable'
• where tasks involve lifting heavy weights, provide employees with details about how heavy each load is, or which side is heaviest if one side weighs more than the other.

Employers must have insurance cover for compensation in case employees injure themselves at work.

ACTION PLAN

1 Check that the incident in which you injured your back was reported to your employer. If your company has more than ten employees, it should have been recorded in its accident book (see question, p308).

2 See your doctor – you will need a medical report if you want to take action against your employer. If you have had back trouble before, you may find it hard to prove that an incident at work caused your current problems.

3 If you belong to a trade union, contact your representative and ask for advice and help with making a claim against your employer.

4 Consult a solicitor (see p20) or your local Citizens Advice Bureau ▶ 🕮 or Law Centre ▶ 🕮 about starting legal action against your employer. For a solicitor who specialises in personal injury, contact the Association of Personal Injury Lawyers ▶ 🕮 .

Who is liable for repetitive strain injury?

Q **As a newspaper subeditor I work long hours at a computer keyboard. I've recently had pains in my wrist and fingers. My GP diagnosed repetitive strain injury and advised me to stop working with computers. Have I any comeback against the newspaper?**

A Possibly. Your employer has a legal duty to provide safe working conditions, with adequate breaks.

Many UK and EU regulations cover different aspects of computer use, from how high your chair ought to be to rest periods. You should also have received training and advice about posture and position at the work station. If you can show that your employer failed in any of these duties, you may be able to claim for compensation.

To make a claim you must get expert medical opinion about the cause of your symptoms. You will also have to show that they are work-related and are not caused by some other condition. For example, you may be able to show how some change in your working conditions has caused the symptoms to appear now.

If your newspaper has an occupational health service (a doctor or nurse who specialises in work-related illnesses), make an appointment to discuss your working conditions and whether they could be altered to accommodate your injury.

It would help your case if any of your colleagues doing the same type of work have developed similar symptoms.

ACTION PLAN
1 If you belong to a trade union, contact your representative and ask for advice and help with making a claim against your employer.

2 If you are not a trade union member, consult a solicitor (see p20) or your local Citizens Advice Bureau ▶ ▭ or Law Centre ▶ ▭ about making a claim for compensation. For a personal injury solicitor, contact the Association of Personal Injury Lawyers ▶ ▭.

How stressful is your job?

Q I work long hours in a demanding administrative job and have felt so stressed recently that I can't face going to work. My doctor has given me sick leave. Can I claim compensation?

A Possibly. An employer's duty to ensure the safety and welfare of employees includes safeguarding their mental health.

To claim compensation you must prove that you are not just overworked or worried, but you have a recognised stress disorder. You would also have to show that your employer was negligent in failing to safeguard you from a type of psychological damage that could have been foreseen and prevented.

In law it is accepted that in many jobs stress is unavoidable. So an employer is generally entitled to assume that an employee can cope with the job, unless there are clear signs of excessive stress. If you claimed for compensation against your employer, a court would consider the following factors:
• the nature of your job
• whether your employer could have been expected to notice that you were stressed
• whether your co-workers were similarly affected
• whether you had a special vulnerability the employer should have known about
• the degree of risk
• the seriousness of the potential harm ▶

• what your employer could reasonably have been expected to do to prevent psychological damage.

Your employer could avoid liability by demonstrating that the company provides care for employees – for instance, by offering independent counselling at work.

Your best course of action is to consult a solicitor (see p20) about claiming compensation against your employer for personal injury (see box, pp302-303).

Injured when falling off a fairground ride

Q **My daughter fell off a fairground ride and injured her arm – so badly that we had to take her to hospital. Before leaving the fairground, I took a closer look at the ride and spotted some cracks and rust on it. My daughter insists that she was holding on tight when the accident happened, and I think the problem was the equipment, which was in poor repair. Can we sue the owner of the ride?**

A Yes, if you can show that your daughter's injuries were due to the owner's negligence or to a breach of safety regulations.

Anyone managing any public leisure facility or event has a general duty to take reasonable care that members of the public are not put at risk. In addition, there are specific regulations governing, for instance, crowd management, sporting events, fireworks, swimming pools, fairground rides and amusement parks, karting circuits, ski-slopes, water and rock activities, and adventure activities for young people – contact your local trading standards department or the Health and Safety Executive ▶ ⌯ for details.

The specific obligations of fairground operators are to:
• maintain their attractions in a safe condition
• perform regular safety checks
• ensure that users are guarded or restrained where appropriate so that children (or adults) cannot fall off and hurt themselves.

If an operator has failed to keep up with the safety provisions, the proper maintenance of equipment or routine inspections, the operator or even the safety inspector may be criminally liable and can be fined or imprisoned.

You should act quickly if you want to sue on your daughter's behalf, especially if it was a travelling fair, so that the equipment can be inspected properly. The fairground operator should carry public liability insurance to ensure that such claims, if proven, can be met.

ACTION PLAN

1 If possible, note the names and addresses of any witnesses to the accident or anyone else who might have noticed the condition of the ride.

2 Consult a solicitor (see p20) or your local Citizens Advice Bureau ▶ 🕮 or Law Centre ▶ 🕮. For a solicitor who specialises in personal injury, contact the Association of Personal Injury Lawyers ▶ 🕮.

3 Contact your local trading standards department (see box, p30) if you suspect the ride's condition breached safety standards.

A pedestrian sues a driver for compensation

Q A pedestrian stepped off the pavement, without looking, in front of my car and I couldn't avoid hitting her. Now she's asking for compensation from me for a broken leg and time off work. Can she deny all responsibility?

A No. The pedestrian can make a claim for compensation. But if you were driving safely, considering the road conditions and weather at the time, and within the speed limit, a court is likely to conclude that she was at least partly to blame – in other words, that this is a case of 'contributory negligence' (see box, p305).

Motorists have a 'duty of care' (see box, p21) towards other road users, including pedestrians. They are expected to take special care at crossings and in other areas where pedestrians are likely to want to cross the road, and where there could be children in the road – near schools and ice-cream vans, for instance.

Even so, the pedestrian you hit would have to prove that you caused the accident because you were driving negligently. If

she succeeded, she could still be held partly to blame for stepping out without looking. Any award made against you could be reduced by her contributory negligence.

Make sure you have details of any witnesses to the accident and inform your motor insurance company at once. The company should handle any legal claim against you and, if you are found not to be at fault, this should not affect your premium.

Accepting a lift with a drunk-driver

Q My son accepted a lift back from a party with someone he didn't know very well. He realised that the person giving him the lift had drunk too much, but the party was in the depths of the country and it was hard to get home any other way. They had an accident and my son suffered a minor but painful back injury. Can he claim compensation from the driver?

A Yes, if the accident was the fault of the driver. But any compensation awarded may be reduced if the court judges your son to have been partly responsible for his own misfortune by accepting the lift in the first place. As he was aware that the driver had had too much to drink, he should have foreseen a risk in travelling in the car, and so is at least partly to blame – a case of 'contributory negligence' (see box, p305).

If you want to pursue the matter, you should consult a solicitor (see p20) or your local Citizens Advice Bureau ▶ 🕮 or Law Centre ▶ 🕮. For a solicitor who specialises in personal injury, contact the Association of Personal Injury Lawyers ▶ 🕮.

Injury to a bus passenger

Q My father, a pensioner, was a passenger on a bus when it was involved in a minor accident and he was hurt. The bus company managers say they can't be held liable for his injuries because he was using a free bus pass. Can they say that?

A No. The fact that your father was using a bus pass (which is subsidised by the local authority) is irrelevant to any claim for personal injury. Public transport operators have a legal duty to do whatever is reasonable to ensure their passengers' safety, and this duty is not based on payment. So if the bus company was at fault in the accident, it could be held liable to compensate your father for his injuries.

If the accident was due to the negligence of another road user – if, for example, a car pulled out in front of the bus – your father could pursue the other driver for compensation.

Your father should contact a solicitor (see p20) or his local Citizens Advice Bureau ▶ ⌂ or Law Centre ▶ ⌂. For a solicitor who specialises in personal injury, contact the Association of Personal Injury Lawyers ▶ ⌂.

Compensation from an uninsured driver

Q As I stopped at a traffic light, my car was hit from behind, and the crash has left me with whiplash injuries. I've since been told that the driver of the other car has no insurance and I can't claim compensation? Can that be true?

A No, you can sue an uninsured driver. But if the driver does not have the money, you may not get any compensation. To protect people in this situation the Motor Insurers' Bureau (MIB; see box, p266) operates a compensation scheme funded by the insurance industry.

As an innocent third party injured by a negligent, uninsured motorist, you could claim compensation under the MIB scheme for your personal injury and for damage to your car – but an excess of £300 would be deducted, so you would have to pay the first £300 of the repair bill. You must submit your claim within three years of the accident.

The MIB scheme also applies when the driver cannot be traced – in a 'hit-and-run' accident, for example. But in these cases, the scheme compensates only for personal injury, not for vehicle damage.

ACTION PLAN

1 Report the incident to the police, since by failing to give information about insurance, the other driver may have committed a criminal offence.

2 Report the accident to your insurers, who may be able to check that the other driver had no insurance. It is important to do this, ▶ p316

MAKING AN INSURANCE CLAIM AFTER A ROAD ACCIDENT

Your chance of success with a claim will be improved if you can show the insurance company that at the time of the accident you observed the following procedures. You must:
• report the accident to the police within 24 hours if people or animals are involved or property is damaged. If you do not report an accident as soon as possible, you invalidate your insurance
• show the police your insurance certificate at the time of the accident, or at a police station within five days
• give your name, address and insurance details to anyone with reason to ask, even if no one is hurt
• where you are not the owner of the vehicle you were driving, give the registration number and the owner's name and address.

When the accident happens:

Stop the vehicle as soon as it is safe to do so. This is an essential safety procedure, and the law says that you must stop after an accident when:
• anyone has been injured
• vehicles, property or animals, such as dogs or horses, are damaged.

Call an ambulance if anyone is injured.

Call the police if:
• the accident is serious
• anyone is hurt
• vehicles are blocking the road
• it is likely that the details of what happened could be contested.

Warn oncoming traffic especially at night or on country roads:
• switch on your car's hazard lights
• set up a warning triangle
• if possible, send someone to flag down approaching vehicles.

Take the names and addresses of witnesses.

Make a note of:
• the location and approximate time of the accident
• any property damage – for example, to walls or fences, street signs or bollards
• whether anyone who was injured was wearing a seat belt.

Swap names, addresses and insurance details with the other driver or drivers, and note details of vehicle types and registrations.

After the accident:

Visit your doctor for assessment, and take photographs of visible injuries.

Report the accident to your insurers, even if you were not at fault.

Make a record of what happened. While your memory is still fresh:
• draw a sketch
• log the date, time, weather, visibility and road conditions (for example, fog, icy road)
• state whether it was daylight, dusk or dark
• estimate the width of the road
• describe any road or warning signs in the area where the accident occurred
• note whether there were street lights and if they were lit
• give the speed limit in the area and your travelling speed.

DO NOT
• admit liability or say 'sorry', even if you think the accident was your fault
• leave the scene without all the essential details
• move vehicles until the police arrive, unless there is a danger to or from other traffic. If you have to move a vehicle, try to get an independent witness to note its original position.

because before putting in your claim to the Motor Insurers' Bureau (MIB) you must be able to show that all reasonable enquiries have been made to find out if the other driver was covered by insurance.

3 If there is no evidence of the motorist having insurance, contact the MIB ▶ 🖙 and ask for a claim form. Fill it in, giving as much information as you can about the other driver together with details of your own losses.

4 The MIB will confirm receipt of your application and ask you to seek the permission of the uninsured motorist before it proceeds. So you will need to get in touch with the other driver.

5 If you cannot trace the motorist, the MIB will seek a way of proceeding without his permission. The MIB will explain what action it intends to take and will try to gain compensation within three months. If your case is likely to take longer, it will keep you informed.

Farmers have a duty to control livestock

Q When driving along a country road, I hit and killed a stray sheep, which damaged my car. The farmer is claiming compensation for her lost sheep. Can she do that?

A No. You could probably sue the farmer for the damage to your car and any injuries you suffered. But if you were infringing any motoring regulations – for example, if you were driving too fast – your compensation could be reduced because of 'contributory negligence' (see box, p305).

Livestock owners have a 'duty of care' (see box, p21) towards road users and should not compromise their safety by allowing animals to stray onto the roads. The farmer should have kept her sheep secure, and if you can show that she neglected her duty – for example, by failing to keep her fences reasonably well maintained – she may be liable to compensate you.

In most cases of this kind, the problem is sorted out by the insurance companies involved – your motor insurers and the farmer's insurers (she should have cover for this kind of eventuality). The two companies will talk to each other and both will probably want to avoid the expense of a legal case. However, if the

FIRST THE GOOD NEWS MISS BO PEEP... WE'VE FOUND ONE

farmer's insurers refuse to admit that she was at fault, you could start a legal action – if only to show you have a case. This may be enough to prompt the other side to settle out of court (see box, p18). Before embarking on this course of action, take advice from a solicitor (see p20) or your local Citizens Advice Bureau ▶ ⌂ or Law Centre ▶ ⌂.

The situation is different if you run into a sheep or pony roaming an upland or moorland area. Although they have owners, these animals are treated as wild animals. Warning signs are posted at intervals along roads the animals are likely to cross, but if incidents occur, motorists have no right to sue the animals' owners – and vice versa.

ACTION PLAN
1 Report the accident to your motor insurance company.

2 If the farmer is uninsured, consult a solicitor (see p20) or your local Citizens Advice Bureau ▶ ⌂ or Law Centre ▶ ⌂ about taking legal action against her. For a solicitor who specialises in road accidents, contact the Law Society ▶ ⌂.

WORD OF WARNING
You have a claim against a farmer whose animal causes you to crash your vehicle only if the farmer is at fault and you are not. If, for example, you are speeding around a bend in a country road and injure cattle or a horse being led along the road, you could be liable to pay compensation to the farmer.

Postman attacked by dog

Q **My dog bit the postman, who now claims that he's so scared of dogs he's had to give up his job and wants compensation for loss of earnings. Can he do that?**

A Yes. Owners and keepers of pets are responsible for the actions of their animals when it is reasonably easy to foresee that the animal might cause injury – for instance, by running into the road or biting someone. They have a duty to ensure that the animal is not a danger to anyone and to take measures such as:

• keeping the animal secure
• exerting proper control when out with the animal
• muzzling the animal when it is likely to come into contact with the public.

The postman could hold you liable for his injuries if you knew, or ought to have known, that your dog posed a danger – for example, if it belonged to a breed that was known to have attacked people before. If the attack happened on your property, you could also be held to have failed in your legal duty to take reasonable care to safeguard visitors under the Occupier's Liability Act 1957 (see box, p307).

In either case you would probably have to compensate the postman for the pain and suffering caused by the dog bite. But it does not follow that he would receive compensation for changing his job or for loss of earnings. That would be a matter for a court to decide, based on the severity of his psychological injury (see question, pp311-312).

ACTION PLAN
1 Check whether your household insurance covers you for injuries to third parties and, if so, report the matter to your insurance company.

2 If you are not insured and the postman takes action against you, contact a solicitor (see p20) or your local Citizens Advice Bureau ▶ ⌂ or Law Centre ▶ ⌂.

Overpowered in the thick of the scrum

Q During a rugby match my shoulder was badly injured following a scrum collapse, but everyone involved denies that they were responsible. Can they get away with that?

A Possibly. If individual players act in a dangerous manner, or if organisers fail to take reasonable precautions to ensure the safety of players, they may be held liable for any resulting injuries.

But in situations like this, it is often difficult to disentangle the facts of who did what, and the 'burden of proof' (see box, p21) is on you, the claimant. Unless you know who caused the injury and how, and preferably have witnesses, you will be unable to establish who was at fault and will have no one to claim against if no one owns up.

The law also takes into account how dangerous the activity is. Many sports – such as rugby, hockey, ice hockey, skiing, horse-riding, potholing, rock climbing, parachuting and hang-gliding – are recognised as dangerous by doctors and insurance companies (see box, p89), among others. The law takes the view that if you engage in a sport like this, you have consented to run the accepted risks (see box, p305).

But this does not imply that those taking party in the activity can evade all liability. Agreeing to run the risks of a game or sport does not mean that you accept the consequences of the negligence of others. You could claim compensation for an injury on the field of play caused by:
- a hazard on the field, such as frozen turf
- the reckless actions of an opponent
- the failure of a referee to apply the rules of the game correctly
- being allowed to play in a position for which you did not have enough training or experience.

Even so, the 'burden' would still be on you to show who was at fault and why, and how the other person's action or failure to act caused your injury.

ACTION PLAN

1 Gather evidence about what happened. Check whether the match was recorded on video and ask for a copy. Ask the referee, the coach, team mates and linesmen if they witnessed the scrum collapse.

2 Contact a solicitor (see p20) or your local Citizens Advice Bureau ▶ 🖙 or Law Centre ▶ 🖙 about making a claim for compensation against another player or players. For a solicitor who specialises in personal injury, contact the Association of Personal Injury Lawyers ▶ 🖙 .

IF YOU ARE INJURED IN A VIOLENT CRIMINAL ATTACK

The Criminal Injuries Compensation Authority (CICA) administers a government-backed scheme to compensate victims of violent crime, including assault, sexual attack, arson and poisoning. CICA allows you to claim compensation if you are injured in any of the ways listed below, or your parent, child, spouse or partner is killed.

Personal injuries include:
• physical or psychological injury after an attack
• psychological injury after witnessing a violent crime, or its immediate aftermath, involving someone with whom you had a close relationship.

You can claim compensation even if the person who injured you has not been arrested or convicted of the crime. But you should offer any evidence you can that you were the victim of a crime. It will help if you can show that you:
• reported the incident promptly to the police
• assisted the police in their enquiries where possible – for instance, by making a statement or attending an identity parade
• were prepared to give evidence in court.

If the person is charged, you usually have to wait for the outcome of the court case before being awarded compensation.

Are you eligible to claim?
To claim for an injury, you must have suffered:
• a serious physical or mental injury
• a combination of minor injuries from which you did not recover for at least six weeks and which caused you to visit a doctor at least twice.

If you are awarded compensation and your condition worsens afterwards, you can ask for further compensation.

The scheme does not cover minor injuries such as cuts and bruises, road traffic accidents (unless the vehicle was deliberately targeted to injure) or sexual assault within the family if this ended before 1979 – when the rules were changed to allow compensation for injuries inflicted within the family.

CICA will not offer compensation if you were injured in a fight that you started, provoked or agreed to take part in.

What can you claim for?
Compensation (to a maximum of £500,000) may include payments for:
• physical or mental pain and suffering. These payments are based on a scale (called a tariff) in which injuries are graded according to severity. Compensation payable ranges from £1000 at the bottom of the scale to £250,000 at the top
• loss of earnings if you were unable to work for more than 28 weeks after the attack
• special expenses such as medical treatment, equipment and care – only payable if you can also claim for loss of earnings
• the fatal injury of a close relative – the award is a set sum (£10,000 if one person claims, £5000 each if more than one person claims), plus funeral expenses. If you were financially dependent on the person who was killed, you can apply for a dependency award, and children can claim for loss of parental services.

How to apply for compensation
1 Ask for a compensation form from your local police station or Victim Support Scheme (see p323), or from CICA ▶⌨. You must claim within two years of the incident, except in certain circumstances, such as an application on behalf of a child.

2 Send your application to CICA's Glasgow office ▶⌨, which will allocate you a reference number. Claims relating to incidents in London and the Home Counties are then dealt with by the London office ▶⌨, and those in the rest of England, Wales and Scotland by the Glasgow office ▶⌨.

3 CICA takes eight months to one year to assess claims. A claims officer will write to tell you the decision, give reasons if compensation is not granted and if it is granted, say how it will be paid.

4 If you disagree with the decision, contact CICA for details of its appeals process.

Can executors claim compensation?

Q My brother died recently after a long illness that was almost certainly caused by exposure at work to pesticides. As an executor for his estate, I believe we should sue his former employers for compensation, but his widow thinks that we should have done it while he was still alive. Can she be right?

A No. As your brother's executor, you are entitled to pursue any action that your brother could have started had he lived – just as anyone with a claim against someone who has died can sue the dead person's estate.

To be successful, you would have to prove that it was likely that his illness was caused by pesticide exposure, and this would require expert medical opinion. You would also need to show that his employers failed in their duty to safeguard him against exposure (see questions, p308 and p310).

You can claim compensation on behalf of the estate for your brother's:
• suffering and loss of enjoyment of life from when he contracted his illness until his death
• any earnings he lost as a result
• any medical or other expenses incurred.

Also, if your brother's widow was financially dependent on him, she may have an additional dependency claim (see question, right). The estate can also claim funeral expenses.

ACTION PLAN
1 If your brother belonged to a trade union, contact the union – they may have experience of such cases and can help you to take your case to court.

2 Otherwise, consult a solicitor (see p20) who may take your case under a 'no-win, no-fee' arrangement (see p299). For a solicitor with experience of this type of claim, contact the Law Society ▶ ⌨ .

Compensation for partner's death

Q My partner died six months ago after an accident at work. We had been together for five years and had two young children. I believe the accident was a result of negligence by his employers, and I want to claim for compensation. But my friends tell me I've got no right to claim because we weren't married. Can that be right?

A No. Whether you were married is irrelevant since you were living together for more than two years.

What matters is whether you were financially dependent on your partner. If so, you can claim for yourself and on behalf of your children, since you were all 'dependants'. You will have to prove that the accident was a result of negligence by your partner's employers, or that they failed in their legal duty to ensure his safety (see questions, p308 and p310). If you can do that, you and your children can claim compensation for loss of financial support under the Fatal Accidents Act 1976.

Compensation would be awarded to cover the proportion of your partner's earnings not regarded as exclusively for his personal expenditure. There would also be an amount to cover his contributions towards domestic costs, such as child care. You can also claim a bereavement payment (see box, opposite).

ACTION PLAN

1 It can be simpler and less costly to claim compensation under the Fatal Accidents Act if you make one claim on behalf of all dependants who have a right to claim. So you should contact any other relatives towards whose maintenance your partner contributed.

2 Consult a solicitor (see p20) as soon as possible about claiming compensation. You may be able to avoid high costs by agreeing a 'no-win, no-fee' arrangement (see box, p299).

Psychological injury for witness to crime

Q **My daughter's boyfriend was horrifically injured when he resisted burglars breaking into** their flat. My daughter was there when it happened and saw it all. Since then she has suffered from severe depression and has now lost her job. I think we should claim compensation for criminal injury. Can we do that?

A Yes. You can sue a criminal for injuring you, which includes psychological injuries as well as physical ones. The only problem with seeking compensation for psychological injuries is that questions of proof may be more complicated.

If your daughter was afraid for her own safety, she could possibly claim compensation for psychological damage caused by the incident, as well as claiming for the trauma of seeing her boyfriend attacked and injured. To do this, she would need a medical report to assess the extent of her depression, and evidence to show that this contributed to her losing her job, if that is the case.

One way of claiming compensation for criminal injuries is through the Criminal Injuries Compensation Authority (CICA; see box, p319). CICA recognises that people may sustain psychological trauma as a result of witnessing a violent crime involving a relative or close friend.

Alternatively, you could pursue a legal case against the criminals – but that would involve exposing details about your daughter's psychiatric history in court. For this you should get the advice of a solicitor (see p20) or your local Citizens Advice Bureau ▶ 🕮 or Law Centre ▶ 🕮.

Consider contacting Victim Support (see box, p323). This charity helps victims of violent crime and can give you useful advice about how to proceed. It will also offer comfort and support to your daughter if she wishes. ▶

BEREAVEMENT BENEFITS

Under the Fatal Accidents Act, if your partner dies in an accident, you may be entitled to a bereavement payment (£10,000 in 2003-4). This applies to couples who had lived together for more than two years before the death or were married. For more information, consult a solicitor or your local Citizens Advice Bureau ▶ 🕮 or Law Centre ▶ 🕮. In addition, various government benefits are available to widows and widowers (but not generally to those who lived with their partners without marrying them), depending on their circumstances. They include a tax-free lump sum (£2000 in 2003-4); a bereavement allowance for a year after the spouse's death; and a widowed parent's allowance for those with dependent children. To find out whether you are eligible, contact your local Jobcentre Plus office ▶ 🕮.

ACTION PLAN

1 If the burglars responsible for the attack have been caught, ask the police if a prosecution is pending and, if so, make sure that the prosecuting lawyers are aware of your daughter's condition.

2 Contact a solicitor (see p20) or your local Citizens Advice Bureau ▶ 🕮 or Law Centre ▶ 🕮 for advice about pursuing a case directly against the criminals. Many solicitors will accept a case involving personal injury caused by a criminal act on a 'no-win, no-fee' basis (see box, p299).

3 If the burglars have not been caught or are unlikely to be able to pay compensation, ask the police or Victim Support ▶ 🕮 for a claim form for the Criminal Injuries Compensation Authority (CICA) scheme (see p319).

Compensation for a criminal attack

Q I was caught up in a fight outside a nightclub, although I had nothing to do with it. Someone hit me in the face with a bottle and I needed medical treatment, including stitches. I now have permanent scars on my face. Can my attacker get away with that?

A No, you can claim compensation. There are three main ways to do so.

First, if the person who attacked you is prosecuted and found guilty, the court may order the offender to pay you compensation. You should make full information about your injury available to the lawyers prosecuting your attacker – including loss of earnings, medical and travel expenses, and losses such as theft of your property or damage to clothing. This information can then be relayed to the judge. Victim Support (see box, opposite) can help you with this.

Second, you can sue for damages, even if the offender has been acquitted of the crime in a criminal court. You can do so up to three years after your injury if it was caused by a deliberate assault.

Third, you can apply to the Criminal Injuries Compensation Authority (CICA) for compensation (see box, p319).

Before deciding which option to take, consult a solicitor (see p20) or your local Citizens Advice Bureau ▶ 🕮 or Law Centre ▶ 🕮. For a solicitor specialising in personal injury, contact the Association of Personal Injury Lawyers ▶ 🕮.

How benefits affect compensation

Q Since I was injured in a car accident two years ago, I've been unable to walk properly and I've had to claim Disability Living Allowance. I also claimed for compensation against the driver. Eventually, the court awarded damages, but the driver's insurers deducted from it the amount I'd received in benefits payments. Can they do that?

A Yes. If you receive benefits as a result of an injury and then win compensation for that injury, you may have to pay back some of the benefits once you receive your compensation award. This is to prevent some people being paid twice for the same losses – called 'double recovery' because they would recover both benefits and compensation.

In practice, the Department of Work and Pensions requires insurers – who fund most compensation awards – to find out about your benefits payments. The insurers will then deduct the appropriate sum from your compensation before you receive it.

But the deductions can only be made from certain parts of your award. This is because an award has different components, each earmarked by the courts for different things – for example, loss of earnings, cost of care and loss of mobility (see p303). A deduction can only be made from the relevant component. So the insurers can only deduct your Disability Living Allowance from the part of your compensation that was set aside to help you with your mobility – your difficulty in walking properly.

The same thinking would apply if you had been receiving, for example, an unemployment benefit. The insurers could only make a deduction from the part of the award earmarked to cover the pay you lost because you could not work between the date of the accident and the date of the trial.

If you are worried that the amount the insurers have deducted is wrong, check with a solicitor (see p20) or your local Citizens Advice Bureau ▶ 🕮 or Law Centre ▶ 🕮. You do not have to refund any benefits paid after the date of your compensation award.

WORD OF WARNING

If you are awarded a high level of compensation, it could increase the amount of capital (money) you have in the bank so much that it reduces the level of any means-tested benefits you normally receive. Your benefits may even be stopped altogether. This problem can be avoided by setting up a trust fund before the compensation is paid – consult a solicitor (see p20).

SUPPORT FOR VICTIMS OF CRIME

Victim Support ▶ 🕮 is a national charity offering support to anyone affected by crime – victims, witnesses, families and friends. It runs a network of local schemes, providing:

- emotional support
- information
- practical help
- information about the Criminal Injuries Compensation Authority's scheme (CICA; see p319) and help with filling in CICA forms.

Witness service
Victim Support also runs a witness service, based in every criminal court, to offer support and information about court processes to victims, witnesses and their families before, during and after a trial. The service does not offer legal advice.

Helpline
The helpline (0845 303 0900) puts you in touch with local Victim Support schemes and other related organisations. You can ask Victim Support for help even if you have not reported the crime to the police. Lines are open: Monday to Friday 9am-9pm; Saturday and Sunday 9am-7pm; bank holidays 9am-5pm.

PERSONAL RELATIONSHIPS

Where a wedding can take place

Q **My fiancée and I want to get married in a marquee in the garden of her family home. But we've been told that this wouldn't be legal. Is that correct?**

A Yes, as the law stands, unless you are Jewish or a Quaker (see below). But the government proposes to change the law in 2005 (see box, right).

Under the present system, local authorities license selected buildings for religious and civil marriage ceremonies. The range of buildings that can be licensed was increased by the Marriage Act 1994 to include venues such as castles, hotels and stately homes. Since then, the list has been expanded further to include, for example, the London Eye, where a wedding first took place in 2001.

Even so, for a venue to be licensed it must have a ceiling, walls and be open to the public – which excludes a marquee in the garden of a private home.

For historical reasons dating back to the 19th century, Jews and Quakers are exempt from most laws governing wedding ceremonies and can get married anywhere – including in a garden marquee.

If you are Anglican, one option would be to have a civil marriage at your local register office, followed by a 'service of thanks' conducted by a priest or minister in the marquee.

Anglican churches – those belonging to the Church of England or the Church in Wales – are automatically licensed for weddings. Other denominations and religions, such as Baptists, Catholics and Sikhs, have to apply for their places of worship to be licensed – but once licensed, they remain licensed.

If the government adopts its proposed changes to the law in 2005, instead of licensing selected buildings for the purpose of marriage, individuals will be licensed to conduct religious and civil weddings in any venue chosen by the couple to be married.

CHANGE TO THE LAW

Under government proposals due to become law in 2005, registered 'celebrants' – religious and civil – will carry out marriages, without restrictions on the place or time of the ceremony. Civil celebrants will be appointed by the local registration authority, religious ones by their denomination.

WE WERE MARRIED IN THE LAND WHERE THE BONG TREE GROWS BY THE TURKEY WHO LIVES ON THE HILL

mmm... TRICKY

LEGALITY OF WEDDING VENUE

Counting the cost if the wedding is off

Q We planned a big wedding for our daughter. A week before the marriage her fiancé opted out. Now the marquee and car hire firms, caterer, florist, photographer, musicians and clothes hire agency are all demanding cancellation fees. Are we liable for these charges?

A Yes. If you signed contracts with these people, you are responsible. The closer to the wedding, the higher the cancellation fees will be – from 50 per cent of the quotation to the total cost.

If you took out wedding insurance, you should be covered for damage, theft or cancellation of nearly everything – from the wedding dress to car hire. The insurer might pay the cancellation charges if your daughter's fiancé opted out because he or an immediate family member was ill, but second thoughts will not be considered a valid reason.

Read the small print in each contract to see if you can renegotiate the amount owed. If there is nothing in writing, explain the situation to the suppliers and ask if, as a goodwill gesture, they can reduce the charges. You could ask the fiancé and his family to see if they would be willing to contribute towards some of the costs.

No obligation to return the engagement ring

Q I overspent on my fiancée's engagement ring. Now she has called off the wedding and refuses to return the ring. What can I do to get it back?

A Nothing. The ring was a gift. Whether the ring is returned to you or not will depend on the good graces of your former fiancée. In theory, engagement rings are given forever.

WHAT MAKES A MARRIAGE VALID?

The following requirements must be met for any marriage in England and Wales to be valid:

- you must be 18 or over, or have your parents' consent if you are 16 or 17 years old
- before the marriage, you must give the priest, minister or registrar official documentary evidence – such as a birth certificate or passport – of your name, age and nationality, the decree absolute if you are divorced, or the death certificate of your former spouse if you are a widow or widower
- the marriage must be conducted by or in the presence of a person who is authorised to register marriages in the district
- the marriage must be entered in the marriage register and signed by each spouse, two witnesses, the person who conducted the ceremony and the person who registers the marriage.

Giving notice
Before you get married, you must give notice of your marriage. If you marry in the Church of England or Church in Wales, you follow their procedures of publishing banns on three successive Sundays before the marriage. Banns (or common licences) are recognised in law.

In all other cases, you go to your local register office to 'give notice of marriage'. A notice states your name, age, whether or not you have been married before, address, occupation, nationality and where you intend to marry.

You must have lived in a registration district for at least seven days immediately before giving notice at the register office. Once you have given your notice, there has to be a 16-day waiting period before the marriage can take place.

Where and when you can marry
Anyone who is not Jewish or a Quaker (see question, opposite) is allowed to marry:
- between 8am and 6pm
- in an Anglican church (Church of England or Church in Wales)
- in any church, mosque, temple or other place of religious worship that is licensed for weddings
- in a local authority register office
- in any building licensed for weddings by a local authority under the Marriage Act 1994.

If you get married abroad
A marriage abroad is recognised in England and Wales if it does not contravene the rules of eligibility (see above). If in doubt, check with the Home Office ▶ 📖.

Concerns about fertility treatment

Q Five years ago my husband and I had a baby by IVF. We love the little boy dearly, but we're sometimes puzzled by the fact that he doesn't bear any resemblance to my husband or any member of his family. Can we check that I was impregnated with the right sperm?

A Yes. Infertility clinics licensed by the Human Fertilisation and Embryology Authority (HFEA) ▶ ⌂ operate strict codes of practice. You can ask the clinic to check its records, and if it turns out that you were impregnated with the wrong sperm, you have the option of taking action against it. This is unlikely to lead to a criminal prosecution. Instead, your complaint will be investigated by the General Medical Council (GMC) and the clinic may have its licence withdrawn by the HFEA.

ACTION PLAN

1 Write to the clinic or hospital where you received IVF treatment and explain your concerns ▶ ✍. Ask for the records to be reviewed for discrepancies.

2 If the results are unhelpful, DNA tests for your son and your husband should be more conclusive. Ask your GP.

3 If DNA tests show that you received sperm that was not from your husband, you can report the clinic to the GMC (see p110). You could also consult a solicitor (see p20) or your local Citizens Advice Bureau ▶ ⌂ or Law Centre ▶ ⌂ about claiming compensation.

The chances of tracing a sperm donor

Q My daughter was conceived by donor insemination. Now she's growing older I'm beginning to worry about what will happen when she wants to get married. Will she be able to find out who donated the sperm to check that she's not related to her future husband?

A No, she is unlikely to find out the identity of the donor, unless he waived anonymity when he gave the sperm. But she should be able to find out whether she is related to her fiancé.

Since 1991, when the Human Fertilisation and Embryology Authority (HFEA; see box, left) was set up, clinics offering fertility treatment have had to collect details about donors, patients and their treatment, and pass it on to HFEA, which keeps a confidential register.

Your daughter will be entitled to information about whether or not she is related to her fiancé, and to non-identifying details about the donor, such as eye and hair colour, occupation and interests. But the procedure for requesting such details will be fully available only from 2006, when the first children on this register reach 16.

If your daughter was born during the early days of donor insemination (DI) – before 1991 – finding out about the donor may be more difficult. All that existed then was a voluntary licensing register which kept details of clinics only, not patients and donors. She should,

HUMAN FERTILISATION AND EMBRYOLOGY AUTHORITY (HFEA) ▶ ⌂ is a government-appointed body that regulates and collects data on human embryo research and fertility treatment, including in-vitro fertilisation (IVF) and donor insemination (DI). It also supervises and licenses infertility clinics. More than half of its members must be experts in fields other than medicine or human embryo research to ensure that a wide range of opinion is taken into account in its decisions.

nevertheless, contact the HFEA, whose officers may be able to trace some information about the donor.

She could also contact the Donor Conception Network ▶ 🕮, a support network for the parents of children born by donor insemination (DI) or in vitro fertilisation (IVF) and for the children once they reach adulthood. Advisers may offer extra suggestions.

Your right to prevent an abortion

Q **My son's girlfriend is pregnant with his child. She wants an abortion, even though my son strongly objects and we're willing to bring up the child. Can she do this?**

A Yes. If your son's girlfriend is adamant about a termination, and the abortion is carried out strictly according to the terms of the law, there is no legal action you or your son can take.

There are restrictions on when an abortion can take place, and you could check that these have been observed. By law, a pregnancy can be terminated only if two doctors agree in writing that one of the following conditions applies:
- in the earlier stages of a pregnancy (up to 24 weeks), that continuing the pregnancy would risk injuring the physical or mental health of the woman or her children. At this stage, social factors such as housing and financial needs may also be taken into account
- at any stage in the pregnancy, that the termination is necessary to prevent permanent injury to the pregnant woman's physical or mental health
- that there is a risk to the life of the pregnant woman – greater than if the pregnancy were terminated
- that there is substantial risk that if the child were born it would suffer from serious physical or mental abnormalities.

A girl under 16 may have an abortion without her parents' consent if two doctors agree that she is mature enough to understand the consequences.

For more information, contact the:
- British Pregnancy Advisory Service ▶ 🕮
- FPA (Family Planning Association) ▶ 🕮
- Marie Stopes International ▶ 🕮.

Father refuses to have a DNA paternity test

Q **I'm trying to get maintenance payments for my son, but his father denies paternity and refuses to take a DNA test. Can he do that?**

A Yes. Although a court can order an alleged father to give a sample for DNA testing, it would be an assault to take the sample from him without his consent. Yet if he refuses to take the DNA test, a court may conclude that the man is the child's father.

ACTION PLAN

1 Contact the Child Support Agency (CSA; see p345). If you have applied to it to make the alleged father support the child financially, it may be able to 'presume' paternity.

2 Apply to the county court for a 'freestanding declaration of parentage' – a confirmation that the man is the child's father. You can then have the child's birth re-registered, giving the father's details. Seek advice from a solicitor (see p20) or your local Citizens Advice Bureau ▶ 🕮 or Law Centre ▶ 🕮.

Who were my birth parents?

Q **I was adopted as a baby. Now I'm about to become a father, I would like to find out who my birth parents were. Can I do that?**

A Yes. According to the Adoption Act 1976, if you were adopted through a court in England or Wales and you are 18 or over, you are entitled to information about your birth.

To access your records, contact the General Register Office ▶ ☐ or the adoption agency that placed you. The office also keeps an Adoption Contact Register, through which birth parents or other relatives can let an adopted person know that they welcome contact.

ACTION PLAN
1 Ask the Adoptions Section of the General Register Office ▶ ☐ for a form for 'access to birth records'.

2 Before information is released by the General Register Office, you will be offered counselling.
- If you were adopted after November 11, 1975, you can decline counselling.
- If you were adopted before November 11, 1975, you must attend at least one session. This is because before the 1976 Act some parents and adopters understood that the children would not be allowed to find out their birth names or who their birth parents were.

3 To find out if your birth parents or relatives have told the General Register Office they want to contact you, you pay a fee of £15 and give your name on adoption and your birth mother's name. Details of anyone who has registered will be sent to you.

Adopting a child from abroad

Q **My husband and I want to adopt a child from abroad. Can we do this?**

A Yes. According to the Adoption and Children Act 2002, anyone who is eligible to adopt a child in the UK can apply to adopt one from abroad. But you must not bring a child into the UK for adoption without prior arrangement, through official channels.

First, you must apply to a UK adoption agency to be assessed for your suitability as an adoptive parent (see box, p329). If you are approved, the Secretary of State for Health will issue a certificate to the authorities of the other country to confirm that you have been assessed and found suitable. For more information, contact the Overseas Adoption Helpline ▶ ☐.

FACTS ABOUT FOSTERING A CHILD

When you foster, you care for a child in your home on a temporary basis for a few weeks or months, and are paid a fostering allowance to do it. It differs from adoption, which is a permanent arrangement with parental responsibility (see box, p331). Foster children come from many different backgrounds: for example, their parents may be unable to care for them, or the children themselves may have behavioural problems or a disability. You do not have to be married or to own a large house to become a foster carer, but you have to be assessed by social workers for your suitability. They will look into your living arrangements, and ask about your religion, ethnic background, lifestyle and education. They will check the police records of you and members of your household over the age of 16. If they decide you are unsuitable, you will be informed. You have 28 days to appeal by contacting the local authority or agency.

For information, contact the Fostering Network ▶ ☐.

WHO CAN ADOPT A CHILD AND HOW?

Single people and heterosexual and homosexual couples can adopt a child. If a couple is married, at least one spouse must be resident in the UK. In the case of cohabiting or homosexual couples, one partner can adopt and the other can be granted a 'residence order' (see box, p341), which allows that person to share parental responsibility.

To be eligible for adoption, a child must be under the age of 18, unmarried, and must never have been married.

How to adopt

1 Apply to an adoption agency These include local authorities and voluntary organisations licensed by the Secretary of State for Health to assess and approve people to become adoptive parents. Your local authority and the British Association for Adoption and Fostering ▶ 🕮 can recommend agencies.

2 Make your application You will have to give employment references and agree to police record checks and medical examinations. Social workers will visit your home and interview you and other members of your household to assess your suitability to adopt.

3 If your application is approved, the agency will place a child with you when a child is available for adoption, or may seek a child through another agency.

4 Apply for an 'adoption order' to make the adoption official. For this, contact your local magistrates' court. The order severs all legal ties with the child's birth family and confers parental rights and responsibilities on you.

Rights after adoption

An adopted child takes your surname and assumes the same rights and privileges as if he or she had been born to you, including the right of inheritance. The birth parents cannot claim the child back.

With cohabiting couples, the child inherits if the adoptive parent dies without a will, but the partner who was granted a residence order in order to share parental responsibility will have to bequeath goods or money to the child in a will. The same applies to a homosexual couple.

Turned down by an adoption agency

Q My wife and I want to adopt a child. We applied to an adoption agency, and a representative visited our home and made us take several medical tests – then turned down our application without giving a reason. Can it do that?

A No. The agency must explain why it rejected your application, although it is not obliged to give you all the reasons. The decision will have been based on a 'home study report', compiled as part of the process of vetting you and your wife (see box, above). The agency should show you the report and then give you 28 days to comment on it. You can ask to see its files on you – used to compile the report – but in some cases it can refuse you access. For example, it is not obliged to show you the results of its police record checks (see box, above).

ACTION PLAN

1 Write to the agency, stating why you think it has reached the wrong decision ▶ ✍. You must do this within 28 days from the date you received its refusal.

2 Until the end of 2004, the decision of the agency is final. From January 2005 you can ask for an independent review under the Adoption and Children Act 2002. Call the British Association for Adoption and Fostering (BAAF) ▶ 🕮 for advice on how you can request a review.

The right to choose a child's surname

Q My partner insists that our children take his surname. Can he do that?

A No. Exactly what happens depends largely on whether or not you are married to your partner, and who has 'parental responsibility' (see box, opposite). By law, a newborn child's names have to be registered with the local registrar of births and deaths (for the address, see the phone book or ask in your local library) within 42 days of the birth.

• If you are married to your partner, both of you have parental responsibility. So either (or both) can register the child's birth. The child normally takes the father's surname, but both parents must consent.

• If you are not married, only you (the mother) have parental rights, including the responsibility to register the birth, so the choice of names is yours. This will change in 2005, when the law is due to give unmarried fathers parental responsibility (see box, opposite).

If you want to change a child's surname after having registered the birth – for example, if you are married, then separate and revert to your maiden name – contact the Deed Poll Service ▶ 🖾. You will need:

• the written consent of anyone else with parental responsibility

• the written consent of the child if the child is 16 or 17 years old.

When a mother changes a child's name, a father may appeal to the family courts to reverse the decision. The court would look at how much contact the father has with the child and the importance of maintaining the biological link to the father by having his name.

Expressing concerns about a childminder

Q Our daughter has just started taking her three-year-old son to a new childminder. Last week we went to pick up our grandson from the childminder and were shocked to find the house was dirty. There were also seven children, including the childminder's two daughters, which seemed too much for one person to handle. When we stated our concerns, the childminder implied that it wasn't our business. Can she do that?

A No. Childminders should respond to all the queries and concerns of the parents or carers of the children they look after. They must be registered with Ofsted (see box, p369) and meet its national standards, which include maintaining high levels of hygiene, decoration and cleanliness.

Childminders and their premises are inspected annually to make sure they meet the criteria.

Childminders are allowed to look after a maximum of six children – and this includes their own children aged under eight – with not more than three under-five year olds, including only one baby under 12 months.

ACTION PLAN

1 You or your daughter should look at the state of the kitchen and bathroom, and if possible check whether the childminder cleans spills, washes the children's hands regularly, and is careful about food hygiene.

2 Ask the age of the childminder's daughters. If both are under eight, she is breaking the rules.

3 If you believe that the childminder is keeping poor levels of hygiene or is caring for too many young children at once, you can contact Ofsted (see box, p369) and make an official complaint.

Punishment or physical abuse?

Q My 13-year-old son is going through a difficult phase. Yesterday he was exceptionally rude and I slapped him. He says he could report me. Can I be prosecuted?

A No. Parents are allowed to use physical punishment to discipline their children, provided it is reasonable and moderate. What counts as reasonable has been progressively narrowed, so it is no longer acceptable to beat a child with an implement, such as a belt or cane.

A slap is lawful in England and Wales (but no longer in Scotland). Provided you did not cause injury and are a caring and responsible parent, you need not worry.

WHAT IS PARENTAL RESPONSIBILITY?

Parents or those acting for them have a legal responsibility for certain aspects of a child's life, including the child's health, providing a home, protecting and maintaining the child and ensuring that the child receives a proper education.

Parental responsibility also means that your consent is needed on issues ranging from choosing the child's surname to placing the child for adoption.

Who has parental responsibility?
- A child's mother automatically has parental responsibility, as does the father if he was married to the mother at the time of the child's conception.
- If the father and mother marry at a later stage, the father will acquire parental responsibility.
- If parents separate or divorce, each remains legally responsible for the child of their marriage.
- Other individuals – for example, the unmarried father (see below), or a step-parent or grandparent who is caring for the child – can apply for parental responsibility.

How an unmarried father acquires parental responsibility
An unmarried father does not automatically have parental responsibility, but he can acquire it by:
- applying for a court order (see box, p341)
- reaching a 'parental responsibility agreement' with the mother. For this he will have to get a form from a court office or solicitor. Both parents have to sign it, witnessed by a justice of the peace, a justice's clerk or an authorised court official. He must then 'register' the agreement by sending the form, plus two photocopies, to the Principal Registry of the Family Division ▶ 🖃
- applying to the court for a 'residence order' in his favour (see box, p341), which will automatically give him parental responsibility.

When the court is deciding whether to give the father parental responsibility, it will consider:
- the degree of commitment he shows to the children
- the degree of attachment between him and them
- his reasons for applying for the order.

CHANGE TO THE LAW
According to government proposals due to become law in 2005, an unmarried father will be able to register a child's birth separately from the mother. So long as the details he gives agree with those given by the mother, he will be accepted as the registered father with parental responsibility for the child.

A legal age for babysitting?

Q **Several times recently we've used our neighbours' 15-year-old daughter as a babysitter when we've gone out. She's very reliable and our son likes her, but friends told us that it's illegal for someone under 16 to babysit. Is that true?**

A No. There is no minimum legal age at which a person is permitted to babysit. The law says only that parents must not leave their child in a situation that could be dangerous.

Nonetheless, official bodies like local councils and the NSPCC recommend that parents use babysitters aged 16 and over. This is because people aged under 16 cannot be charged with wilful neglect or ill-treatment of a child in their care, so if you ask a 15-year-old to look after a younger child, you could be charged with neglect if, as a result, that child was endangered.

Your contract with an au pair

Q **We arranged with our au pair that she would work on Saturdays. Now she has enrolled for a study course at weekends. When we protested, she said she doesn't have to fit in with our wishes on this. Can she do that?**

A Yes. The Home Office ▶ ➾ grants permits for au pairs to visit the UK and it emphasises that they are not employees, but young people taking part in a cultural exchange. Home Office guidelines say au pairs may help in the home for a maximum of five hours a day for five days a week and should be given 'appropriate opportunities' to study English. Your au pair's weekend course counts as an 'appropriate opportunity'.

Most au pair agencies try to formalise arrangements with an agreement that sets out the au pair's duties and working times in the family. The au pair is expected to ask permission before altering any of them. Yet the agreed duties are not legally binding terms of employment, so you cannot hold your au pair to them.

If you contacted your au pair through an agency, call the agency, which may be able to exert some pressure through its agreement with her.

If you suspect someone of child abuse

Q **I've a strong suspicion that my brother-in-law is sexually abusing his 12-year-old daughter. I don't want to overstep my rights but I feel I ought to do something. Can I intervene?**

A Yes. Child sexual abuse is a serious criminal offence, so you have a responsibility to take action to prevent it.

The best first step is to phone the helplines run by the NSPCC (formerly the National Society for the Prevention of Cruelty to Children) ▶ ➾ or ChildLine ▶ ➾. You can call anonymously and get advice about what to do.

If you do give names and addresses, the helpline advisers may inform your local social services department. Social services child protection teams have a legal duty to investigate child sexual abuse reported to them and, if necessary, take the child into care and notify the police.

You could also talk to your GP about your suspicions. If you find evidence of abuse, you should call your local social services department or the police.

A YOUNG PERSON'S RIGHTS TO DO WHAT?

Young people acquire rights and responsibilities at different ages. At ten, for example, a child may be tried in a youth court and found guilty of a crime. It is only at the age of 18 that you finally cease to be a 'minor', with special legal protection. In the eyes of the law, an 18-year-old has reached the 'age of majority'. But even then, there are certain things you cannot do. You cannot stand for Parliament, for example, until you are 21.

The age of majority was lowered from 21 to 18 on January 1, 1970. So, in legal documents drawn up before that date, the phrase refers to 21, not 18.

Age	Rights and responsibilities
From birth	Can have a deposit or current bank account, but not in own name, because an account holder has to be able to sign own name.
5 years	Must start full-time education.
7 years	Can have a deposit account in a National Savings Bank and draw money on own signature.
10 years	Can be: • found guilty of a crime under the Crime and Disorder Act 1998 • convicted of a criminal offence but tried in a youth court unless the offence is serious, such as murder.
11 years	Can have a deposit account in the Trustee Savings Bank and draw money on own signature.
12 years	Can buy a pet.
13 years	Can do light work as permitted under local authority by-laws: • between 7am and 7pm from Monday to Saturday • between 7am and 10am on Sunday • but not during school hours or for more than two hours on a school day or Sunday, and not lifting or carrying heavy weights.
14 years	Can be taken into a bar but must not consume alcohol there; can drink wine, beer or cider with a meal in another part of the pub or in a restaurant.
15 years	May be sentenced to time in a detention centre or in youth custody.
16 years	Can: • join the armed forces, with parents' consent • marry with the consent of parents or a magistrate • consent to have sexual intercourse – heterosexual or homosexual • buy beer, cider or perry in a restaurant or pub restaurant, but not in a bar, off-licence or supermarket • buy tobacco • ride a moped or scooter up to 50cc • leave school and take a job at the end of the spring term if 16 between September 1 and January 31 • take a job after the last Friday in May if 16 between February 1 and August 31.
17 years	Can: • drive a car or van with up to eight seats and a maximum weight of 3500kg • drive a motorbike, three-wheeler vehicle or van (up to a weight of 500kg), or a roadroller.
18 years	On reaching the 'age of majority', can: • drive a goods vehicle of up to 7.5 tonnes • apply for and obtain a passport • vote in general and local elections • join the armed forces without parents' consent • sign contracts, sue and be sued • marry without parental consent • buy alcoholic drinks in a pub, bar, off-licence or supermarket • obtain credit • be tattooed.
21 years	Can: • stand for council or Parliamentary elections • drive a lorry or bus.

Teenager in possession of cannabis

Q As I was putting my son's jeans into the washing machine, I discovered some cannabis in a pocket. He says that it's legal for him to possess a small amount of this drug. He is 17 years old. Is he within the law?

A No. Cannabis is an illegal drug under the Misuse of Drugs Act 1971. It is categorised as a Class C substance (see box, below).

In most cases the police will warn anybody found in possession of the drug and confiscate it. But if there are aggravating factors – for example, if public order is threatened or if your son is caught smoking the drug blatantly in public – he could be arrested and charged.

The maximum penalty your son could get is two years in detention and a fine. For supplying cannabis he could get up to 14 years in prison and a fine – strictly speaking, passing someone else a 'joint' counts as supplying the drug, although the police would not normally be that literal in enforcing the law. Allowing someone to take cannabis in your house is illegal (see question, below). It is also an offence to grow the cannabis plant.

For more information, contact the helpline called 'Talk to Frank' ▶ 🖅, which has been set up by the government to offer teenagers and their parents free confidential advice about drugs.

Party guests take drugs in your home

Q We gave an 18th birthday party for our daughter. Unknown to us, some of her friends were taking ecstasy, including one who'd never taken drugs before. This boy's parents are threatening to take legal action against us for allowing it to happen. Can they do that?

HOW DRUGS ARE CLASSIFIED

The Misuse of Drugs Act 1971 categorises drugs (including some drugs used in the treatment of illnesses) in a three-tiered system, in which Class A drugs are considered the most harmful if misused and Class C drugs least harmful. The Act lays down maximum penalties for possessing or supplying each class of drug or for possessing it with the intention of supplying it.

Drugs are sometimes re-classified. For example, in 2003 the government moved cannabis from a Class B drug to a Class C drug.

Class	Drugs	Maximum penalty for possession	Maximum penalty for supply
A	Cocaine, crack, ecstasy, heroin, LSD, magic mushrooms, methadone, morphine	Seven-year prison sentence and a fine	Life imprisonment and a fine
B	Amphetamines, barbiturates	Five-year prison sentence and a fine	14-year prison sentence and a fine
C	Anabolic steroids, benzodiazepines (tranquillisers such as Valium), cannabis, growth hormones	Two-year prison sentence	14-year prison sentence and a fine

A No. They could report what happened to the police, but you are not responsible if you did not know what was going on. It is unlikely that there would be sufficient evidence to press charges.

But if you allow the unlawful use of any controlled drug in your home – and this includes heroin, cocaine and ecstasy – you are liable to prosecution under the Misuse of Drugs Act 1971. It is also an offence to permit anyone on your property to produce or supply illegal drugs – and passing drugs among friends counts as supplying.

If you turn a blind eye to what is going on, you are considered to be allowing drug use. For this reason, if your daughter invites her friends to your house again, and you suspect illegal drug-taking, put a stop to the offence by finding the drug, destroying it or handing it to the police, or asking the drug-takers to leave.

Taking out a loan against the house

Q My partner is self-employed and to raise money for his business he wants to take out a secured loan on our jointly owned property. I'm anxious about forfeiting our home if he fails to keep up the repayments. Can I stop him from taking out the loan?

A Yes, if your partner is trying to borrow against your interest in the property without your consent. But he can take out a loan against his own interest.

Lenders have a legal obligation to make enquiries when a loan is being taken out with a jointly owned property as security. They must:
• establish your interest in and occupation of the property
• your relationship to the borrower
• make sure you understand that if you

consent to a secured loan on a jointly owned property and the lender later demands that it be repaid, you could lose your property
• ensure that you receive independent legal advice.

To secure the loan against the property as a whole, the lender needs the consent of both co-owners. If you object, the loan will be secured only against your partner's share in the property. You should notify the proposed lender of your interest in the property and your objection to your partner's action.

RIGHTS OF COHABITING COUPLES

Unmarried couples who live together have fewer rights than married couples. For example, if a marriage breaks up, one spouse will need a court order to evict the other from the shared home; but if one partner of an unmarried couple owns the shared home or holds the tenancy, that partner may be able to evict the other (see question, p210). For this reason, many cohabiting couples set out their rights in an agreement.

Cohabitation agreement
This is a written agreement made between heterosexual and homosexual unmarried couples to protect the interests of both partners by clarifying their rights and obligations. As long as it is dated and signed by both partners and by a witness, a cohabitation agreement has the full force of a contract in law. It should include:
• the shares each partner has in the home
• the shares each partner has in joint savings, and liability for credit card accounts and debt
• how expenses such as mortgage, repairs and insurance will be divided
• a decision about what happens if the home is sold and, if the partners separate, how each can buy out the other
• how furniture and other belongings, such as a car, should be divided if the partners separate
• if there are children, decisions such as the children's surname and, if the partners separate, how maintenance contributions will be arranged.

For advice, consult your local Citizens Advice Bureau ▶ 📖 or Law Centre ▶ 📖, or a solicitor (see p20).

Liability for a husband's debts

Q **Since losing his job, my husband has run up substantial debts. He tells me we're jointly liable for them. Is this so?**

A No, provided that the debts are in his name. Find out who your husband owes money to, and for each account establish whether it is in your joint names or your husband's sole name. This is particularly important where, for example, you have a joint bank account or joint credit card.

If your husband has run up debts on a joint account, you are jointly liable, which means that the creditor may pursue either of you for the full debt. In this case, there is a limit to what you can do. You could inform the bank and ask it to freeze the account. But this means that neither of you can make any further withdrawals from that account.

In you intend to divorce, the debts run up by a spouse are taken into account in the settlement. Often, the spouse receives less of the couple's liquid assets as a penalty for these debts. But much depends on the circumstances of the case. How did your partner run up the

debts? It may have been to pay the mortgage or to contribute towards the maintenance of the family. In that case, the court is likely to give him a more favourable settlement than if he got into debt solely for his own enjoyment.

The husband who will not leave home

Q **Our marriage is on the rocks, but my husband is refusing to leave the matrimonial home, even though I'm the legal owner of the house. Can my husband stay in the house without my consent?**

A No. If your husband refuses to leave, you can apply to the court for an 'occupation order' (see box, p341) requiring him to do so. Consult a solicitor (see p20) or your local Citizens Advice Bureau ▶ ⌐ or Law Centre ▶ ⌐.

Alternatively, you and your husband could try to agree a set of 'ground rules', allowing you to live separate lives in the house while you try to resolve the financial and other issues arising from any divorce proceedings.

Divorce without a lawyer

Q **I want a divorce but don't want to hire a lawyer. Can I obtain a divorce without one?**

A Yes. If your spouse agrees not to oppose the divorce, you can apply for an 'undefended divorce' (see box, opposite). Provided there are no children and no complicated property matters, you should be able to complete the procedure without a solicitor, but you will have to pay various

GETTING DIVORCED: THE PROCEDURES

Most divorces in England and Wales are undefended and dealt with on paper. You have no need to attend a court or use a solicitor. If one partner does not agree to the divorce, it is called a 'defended' divorce and you will need the services of a solicitor.

You must have been married for at least one year before you can file for divorce in England and Wales.

Initial steps in divorce

Either partner can apply to the court for a divorce, through an application called a 'petition'. The partner who files is called the 'petitioner' and the other partner is the 'respondent'. The court will give you the forms and you will have to pay the following fees:

- £180 when you file the divorce petition with the court
- £5-£9 for a sworn affidavit – a statement of evidence used to support your case
- £30 for the decree absolute, stating that the divorce has been granted.

Grounds for divorce

The petition has to establish that the marriage has irretrievably broken down for one of the following reasons:

- your partner has committed adultery
- your partner's behaviour is such that you cannot reasonably be expected to live with that person
- your partner has deserted you – you have not seen your partner for two years or more
- you have lived apart from your partner for two years and have both agreed to apply for a divorce
- you have lived apart from your partner for five years or more.

When children are involved

The petition must provide other information – for example, whether there are children. If you have children under the age of 16, or between 16 and 18 and in full-time education, you must fill in a form called a 'statement of arrangements for children'.

When the court comes to consider the divorce papers, it will take this information into account to ensure that the children are properly provided for.

Attending a divorce court hearing

If you and your partner fail to agree about arrangements for financial support, property and any children, or you want to ask the court for a financial order (see box, p341), you will probably have to attend a court hearing.

Decree nisi, decree absolute

Once the court is satisfied that you should have a divorce, it sets a date and time for the judge to pronounce the 'decree nisi'. This is simply a statement from the court that the divorce can go ahead and the divorce papers are approved.

Six weeks after the court grants the decree nisi, the petitioner can apply to the court for a 'decree absolute', which confirms the divorce. It will be granted so long as the court has approved the arrangements for any children.

More information from:
- your local Citizens Advice Bureau ▶ ⌨ or Law Centre ▶ ⌨
- Court Service web site: www.courtservice.gov.uk

For a solicitor specialising in divorce, contact the Office for the Supervision of Solicitors ▶ ⌨.

---

court charges to obtain the decree nisi and the decree absolute (see box, above).

ACTION PLAN

1 Check that you fulfil the criteria to start divorce proceedings (see box, above). Visit your local county court and ask for the divorce information leaflets and application forms, or download the forms from the Court Service web site ▶ ⌨.

2 Study the documents. If there is anything you do not understand, ask at your local Citizens Advice Bureau ▶ ⌨ or Law Centre ▶ ⌨. Then fill them in and hand them into your local county court.

3 The court will process the documents and send you the decree nisi and decree absolute within a few months.

A dispute over when to sell a shared home

Q My partner and I are splitting up. She wants a quick sale of our jointly owned home, but the market is at an all-time low. I want to delay the sale until we can get a better price. Can she sell the house without my consent?

A No. The property is jointly owned, so for the house to be sold, your signature is needed on the deed of sale.

If you refuse your consent, your partner could apply to a court to adjudicate, but an application may take months and legal costs can be high, so it may not be in her interest. You could buy out your partner's share (see question, p216). For this, you will need an estate agent's valuation of the property.

Deciding who gets what on divorce

Q Our marriage has broken down and we can't agree on the division of our property. My husband wants to get a court to adjudicate between us as a way out of our stalemate. Can he do that?

A Yes. If spouses are unable to agree a division of their assets, the court may adjudicate and impose a solution. You or your husband should ask your local Citizens Advice Bureau ▶ ⌷ or Law Centre ▶ ⌷, or consult a solicitor (see p20), about applying for a court order (see box, p341).

Mediation is an alternative (see box, p343). A mediator can meet both parties to agree a settlement, which they or their solicitors then put in writing and present to the divorce court for approval. This is much less confrontational and cheaper than asking for a court adjudication.

Who has custody – mother or father?

Q My partner and I are splitting up – we aren't married – and he insists that our children live with him. Can he do that?

A No. If you and your partner were not married to each other when your children were born, you as mother have parental responsibility – unless a court has granted your partner parental responsibility (see box, p331).

If you cannot agree with your partner that the children should remain with you, ask your local Citizens Advice Bureau ▶ ⌷ or Law Centre ▶ ⌷, or a solicitor (see p20), about applying for a residence order (see box, p341).

DIVORCE AND YOUR PENSION RIGHTS

Divorce can seriously affect your pension prospects, particularly if it is your spouse who has been the higher earner and who has built up more substantial pension entitlements. To ensure that you will benefit from your spouse's pension scheme after divorce, you have four options to consider:
- open-ended maintenance
- offsetting
- earmarking or attachment
- pension-sharing.

OPEN-ENDED MAINTENANCE
What it is: The ex-spouse who is a member of a pension scheme makes regular, index-linked payments to the other spouse.
Benefits: There is no need to divide the pension fund.
Disadvantages: One ex-spouse is financially dependent on the other and may lose any rights to payments on remarrying. Payments cease when the ex-spouse who makes them dies.

EARMARKING
What it is: The court hearing the divorce issues an 'attachment order', which obliges the pension scheme to pay a proportion of the fund directly to the spouse who is not a member.
Benefits: It is a way of moving forward if the spouses do not reach an out-of-court settlement.
Disadvantages: The spouse who has not contributed will have to wait for payments until the scheme member retires, and payments will cease when the scheme member dies.

OFFSETTING
What it is: The value of the pension fund at the date of divorce is worked out and added to the value of other assets, such as the family home. All these assets are taken into account when working out the compensation for the spouse without a pension scheme, as are each spouse's needs – individually and to care for children.
Benefits: It allows the couple to make a clean break – neither is financially dependent on the other.
Disadvantages: It only works fairly if the other assets are at least equivalent in value to the pension fund.

PENSION-SHARING
What it is: A proportion of the pension entitlements is transferred to the spouse who is not a member of the scheme. This spouse then has similar rights to the scheme member.
Benefits: Neither spouse is dependent on the other to receive a pension, which will continue even after the original scheme member dies. The entitlement can usually be transferred to a stakeholder or personal pension plan and the pension paid any time after the age of 50.
Disadvantages: It can be expensive to set up. The scheme providers may charge for costs, including up to £1000 for administration.

HOW A DIVORCED WOMAN CAN PROTECT HER STATE PENSION
If you married before April 6, 1977, and chose to pay a reduced rate of Class 1 National Insurance (this option was withdrawn after that date), when you get divorced you will have to start paying the full rate to protect your pension entitlement.

If you are working for an employer:
- tell your employer that you can no longer pay reduced rate contributions and ask for a 'certificate of election' (form CA4139)
- complete the certificate and send it to the Inland Revenue at the National Insurance Contributions Office ▶ ⌂.

More information from:
- your local Citizens Advice Bureau
- an independent financial adviser (see box, p157)
- Office of the Pensions Advisory Service ▶ ⌂
- Department for Work and Pensions ▶ ⌂
- Inland Revenue web site ▶ ⌂.

Father wants children to live with him

Q My ex-wife is neglecting our children and I want to step in. Can I apply to the court for an order allowing me to have the children live with me?

A Yes. You can apply for a residence order (see box, opposite) allowing you, rather than your ex-wife, to look after the children. Ask your local Citizens Advice Bureau ▶ 📖 or Law Centre ▶ 📖, or a solicitor (see p20), for help with the application.

Consider mediation before taking legal action (see box, p343). This is essential if you want to apply for public funding (see p15) to help you with your legal expenses. Public funding is not available if you have not tried mediation first.

ACTION PLAN

1 Ask at your local magistrates' or county court for Form C1, or download it from the Court Service web site ▶ 📖. Fill in the form, giving details of yourself, your children and ex-partner, and explain why you want an order.

2 Return your application to the court and pay the fee (£90 in 2003-4). The court will give you a copy of your application with a Notice of Proceedings, giving the date of the hearing.

3 You must send copies of all forms and notices to your ex-partner and tell the court when you have done so.

4 At the hearing, the judge may issue the order, or request a report from the Children and Family Court Advisory and Support Service (CAFCASS; see box, p342) and arrange a date for another hearing.

5 If the judge does not issue the order, you can appeal to a higher court. Ask for advice on doing this at your local Citizens' Advice Bureau ▶ 📖 or Law Centre ▶ 📖, or consult a solicitor (see p20).

BUT EVERY TIME I COME YOU SAY IT ISN'T A GOOD TIME TO SEE THEM!

Mother denies father access to children

Q It was stated in the contact order when I divorced that I should be able to see my son and daughter on certain days. Now my ex-wife refuses to let me be with the children. Can she do that?

A No. The contact order (see box, opposite) will stipulate that your former wife should take the children to a stated place at a certain time so that you can see them. If she refuses to do so, the order can be endorsed

Courts dealing with family proceedings (see p17) can issue a variety of orders to regulate aspects of family life, particularly orders concerning children and how divorcing couples should share property and pension rights. For example, if separated or divorced parents cannot agree on arrangements for their children, either parent may apply to the court for an order to decide on the matter.

ORDERS ABOUT CHILDREN

Before issuing an order, the court will go through a checklist of factors, the most important of which is the child's welfare. Children are legally entitled to have contact with both parents, so an order preventing a child from seeing a parent will not be granted unless there are compelling reasons for the child to be protected from that parent.

Residence orders These state where the child is to live.

Contact orders These regulate the amount of contact between a child and the parent who does not live with that child (called the 'non-resident' parent). Typically, a contact order will provide for the child to spend time during school terms and holidays with the non-resident parent. It might also provide for indirect contact by letters, email and phone.

Specific issue orders If parents cannot agree about certain aspects of a child's upbringing, either can apply for a specific issue order. It will regulate, for example, where a child should go to school, whether or not the child has certain medical treatment, or even where and with whom the child should go on holiday.

Parental responsibility orders These give the father in an unmarried couple the right to be consulted about aspects of a child's care (see box, p331), especially about education and religion.

ORDERS ON DIVORCE

When married couples divorce, court orders can resolve issues such as maintenance and pensions.

Pension-sharing orders In some cases the lower-earning spouse (usually the wife) can obtain an order obliging the higher-earning spouse to transfer a proportion of his pension fund (see box, p339). This will provide the lower earner with a pension, independent of the ex-spouse.

Financial orders (also called 'ancillary relief orders') These may provide for regular payments to be made – to an ex-wife, for instance, to keep the children. They may also specify how savings or the family home should be disposed of.

Other orders A court can order a property to be transferred from one spouse to another. It can 'freeze' property owned by one spouse, who cannot sell it until the court has decided on its future. An 'occupation order' can demand that a spouse move out of a home owned by the other spouse.

---

by the court with a 'penal notice'. Once a penal notice is issued, failure to comply with it can be punished by a fine or imprisonment.

Explain to your ex-wife that she is in breach of the contact order. If she still refuses to allow you to see the children, consult your local Citizens Advice Bureau ▶ 📖 or Law Centre ▶ 📖, or a solicitor (see p20), about applying for a penal notice to enforce your right.

Access rights for grandparents

Q Our grandchildren live with our former son-in-law and he refuses to let us see them. Can he deny us access?

A Probably not. If you cannot agree contact arrangements with your former son-in-law, you may apply ▶

to the court for a contact order (see box, p341). The court's aim will be to establish and ensure your grandchildren's best interests. Ask your local Citizens Advice Bureau ▶ 👝 or Law Centre ▶ 👝, or a solicitor (see p20), for advice.

The children do not want to see their father

Q **My partner and I never got married and now we've separated. The children say they don't want to see their father, but he insists that it's his right to see them. Is this correct?**

A No. An unmarried father has no automatic right to see his children (see box, p331), but he can apply to the court for a 'contact order' (see box, p341).

If it comes to court, this could be a finely balanced case. Courts are normally reluctant to deprive parents of all contact with their children. This is not so much because they see contact as a right of the parents, but more because contact with both parents is usually helpful for the children's emotional well-being.

The court's prime consideration is for the welfare of the child, and if your children are adamant that they do not want to see their father, the court has to take this into account. It may ask for an officer of the Children and Family Court Advisory and Support Service (CAFCASS; see box, below) to visit the children and their father and produce a report to help the court to determine what the children want and whether it is in their interests.

Father tells mother and children to move out

Q **My partner, to whom I'm not married, has started an affair with someone else. We have two young children, but my partner owns the house and says he wants me and the children to go. Can he force us to move out?**

A Yes, if he gets a court order to evict you. But you, too, can apply for a court order (see box, p341) – to prevent him from doing so.

Like you, he has a duty to house the children. Whether that should be in the present property or an alternative one depends, for example, on which of you is to be the principal carer, how much money is available and whether you own other property in which you and the children could live.

Furthermore, although the property is registered in your partner's name, if you apply for an order you may be able to show the court that you have an interest in it – for example, if you contributed to the mortgage. Seek advice from your local Citizens Advice Bureau ▶ 👝 or Law Centre ▶ 👝, or a solicitor (see p20).

HOW CAFCASS HELPS FAMILIES

The Children and Family Court Advisory and Support Service (CAFCASS) ▶ 👝 is a public body that safeguards the welfare of children in family court cases.

The courts or social services can ask CAFCASS for help when:
• separating or divorcing parents cannot reach a decision on arrangements for their children
• children have to be removed from their parents' care for safety
• children are to be adopted.

A CAFCASS officer will be asked to look into such cases and write a report advising the court on the best interests of the children concerned.

Family abandoned with no funds

Q **My partner has left me and our children. He's also left me with no money to support the children. Can he do this?**

A No. Your former partner has a duty to provide financial support for his children. There are a number of things you can do:
- If you are married, but do not want a divorce, you may apply to the court for financial provision for both you and your children.
- If you want to divorce, you may apply as part of the divorce proceedings for financial provision for both yourself and the children. This will probably consist of a combination of a lump sum and regular payments. You can also apply for a share of any pension (see box, p339).
- If you are unmarried, your former partner has no duty to maintain you. But because he is the father of your children, he can be required under the Children Act 1989 to provide for the children through regular payments, a lump sum or property. In this case, the Child Support Agency (CSA; see box, p345) ▶ 📖 can decide how much your partner should provide. The CSA will also collect the regular payments from your former partner and pass them on to you.

You should act immediately. Contact your local Citizens Advice Bureau ▶ 📖 or Law Centre ▶ 📖, or consult a solicitor (see p20):
- about applying for public funding for taking legal action (see box, p15)
- for more detailed information and advice on applying to the family courts for financial provision.

HOW MEDIATION CAN HELP

When a relationship breaks down, turning to a family mediator is a cheaper and often a more effective alternative to using solicitors or appealing to a court to resolve differences.

How mediation works
In mediation, you and your estranged spouse or partner negotiate, through a trained mediator, in order to reach decisions about your children, your property and your financial arrangements.

The role of the mediator is to act as an impartial third party, who helps both partners to:
- exchange information
- identify and discuss their options
- reach a mutual agreement in a fair way
- talk to their children about the family breakdown and their future arrangements.

What mediators cannot do
Mediators have no power to make a legally binding decision about your future. Once the mediator has helped you to reach an agreement, you and your partner must then instruct your solicitors about implementing it.

You should also keep in touch with a solicitor throughout the mediation process to explain the consequences of any agreement.

How to find a mediator
You can ask the Law Society ▶ 📖, your local Citizens Advice Bureau ▶ 📖 or Law Centre ▶ 📖, or a solicitor (see p20), to recommend a mediator.

Specialist family mediation organisations include:
- British Association of Lawyer Mediators ▶ 📖
- Mediation UK ▶ 📖
- National Family Mediation ▶ 📖
- UK College of Family Mediators ▶ 📖
- Family Mediators Association ▶ 📖
- Solicitors Family Law Association ▶ 📖
- ADR Family Mediation ▶ 📖.

PERSONAL RELATIONSHIPS

MAINTAINING STEPCHILDREN • REDUCING MAINTENANCE • PARENTAL RESPONSIBILITY

Liability to support someone else's children

Q **I'm in the process of seeking a divorce and a friend has warned me that I'll have to pay maintenance for my wife's children by a previous marriage as well as our own children. Can he be right?**

A Possibly, if the court decides that your stepchildren have been treated as part of the family. When you divorce, child maintenance will be dealt with by the divorce court or by the Child Support Agency (CSA; see box, opposite). If the children of your marriage are still in full-time education (excluding university) and are unmarried, the CSA can oblige you to pay maintenance.

In the case of stepchildren, the divorce court can order you to pay maintenance for them if it judges that you have treated them as 'children of the family' and cared for them as if they were your own. On the other hand, if their natural father is still alive, they may be entitled to maintenance from him. This will be obtained by the CSA.

If you can reach an agreement with your wife, the court may make a child maintenance order 'by consent' (agreed between you). But be warned that she can choose to opt out of the order after 12 months, provided she gives you notice, and ask the CSA to make an assessment for maintenance.

Father wants to cut maintenance

Q **My ex-partner wants to reduce the amount of child support maintenance he pays. Can he do this?**

A No, unless he applies first to the Child Support Agency (CSA; see box, opposite). If he simply fails to pay the maintenance, the CSA will take steps to enforce the payments by having the money deducted from his earnings.

If your ex-partner applies to reduce the maintenance assessment, the CSA will take various factors into account, such as:
• the number of children
• whether the children stay with him for more than 52 nights a year – if they stay with him on a regular basis for more than 52 nights a year, maintenance is likely to be reduced
• the cost of keeping in contact with the children, such as transport to visit them
• his net income
• whether he makes mortgage, insurance and loan payments on the home where you and the children live, and which he used to share with you
• the boarding element of any school fees he pays for the children
• the number of other children (referred to as 'relevant other children'), if any, that live with him.

If the maintenance is reduced, the CSA will inform you of the new amount. If you think it is too little, act quickly. You have one month to appeal by writing to the CSA office that handled your case. If the CSA cannot resolve the dispute, it will hand it over to a central appeals unit for a final decision.

The children are on the move

Q My children live with my ex-wife and I've just found out that she plans to move from the north to the south of England. Can she do this without consulting me?

A Probably. A court cannot prevent your ex-wife from living with the children anywhere in England and Wales. Yet, as the children's father, married to their mother when they were born, you have parental responsibility and should be consulted on major decisions about their upbringing and welfare, such as education and their future home.

For example, you may object to the children being removed from their present schools (because, perhaps, they are doing very well) and object to the proposed new school (because, for example, it has a poor academic record). Also, what impact will a move have on your contact with the children? Will future contact arrangements become more difficult?

ACTION PLAN

1 If you and your ex-wife cannot agree on the move, consult a solicitor or your local Citizens Advice Bureau about applying for a 'specific issue order' (see box, p341).

2 If you believe there is a real danger that your ex-wife will remove the children from their schools without regard to your wishes, ask your solicitor or Citizens Advice Bureau about applying for a 'prohibited steps order'. That would prevent her from taking the children from their schools without the consent of the court.

MAKING SURE THAT A PARENT PAYS

The Child Support Agency (CSA) ▶ 🕮, set up under the Child Support Acts of 1991, ensures that parents who live apart meet their financial responsibilities to their children. It is part of the Department for Work and Pensions.

What the CSA does
- Calculates the amount that 'non-resident' parents (the parents who do not have care of the children) should pay towards the maintenance of their children.
- Collects the maintenance payments.
- Passes the payments on to the parents who have care for the children.

If parents share care, the parent who has the children for the shorter period is counted as the non-resident parent.

Powers to investigate
The CSA has investigative powers to trace and contact a non-resident parent, as well as power to obtain detailed information about the parent's income and capital.

When parents do not pay, the CSA can have payments deducted from their wages. Where parents receive social security benefits, it works with other branches of government to ensure correct payments and to protect against fraud.

The CSA can also resolve paternity disputes if a man believes that he is not a child's father (see question on DNA testing, p327).

How payments are calculated
Payments are based on a percentage of the non-resident parent's net income:
- 15 per cent of net income for one child
- 20 per cent for two children
- 25 per cent for three children or more.

For non-resident parents with net incomes of less than £100 a week, or those receiving benefits such as income support and Jobseekers' Allowance, child maintenance is set at a flat rate of £5 a week.

Cases dealt with by the CSA before the simple percentage calculation was introduced in March 2003 will be transferred to the new system only when the government is confident that it is working well.

For further information:
- contact the CSA national enquiry line: 08457 133 133
- visit the CSA web site: www.csa.gov.uk

Parent wrongfully takes child abroad

Q My ex-partner has abducted our 14-year-old daughter from her school in Kent and taken her to Turkey. I've heard that the Foreign Office has no legal obligation to secure her return. Can that be right?

A Yes. But it can provide advice and practical assistance. For instance, it can help you to deal with authorities overseas and in obtaining passports and other travel documents.

By taking your daughter out of the jurisdiction of the courts in England and Wales, your ex-partner may be guilty of a criminal offence. Turkey has signed the two major international agreements that deal with child abduction (see box, opposite). This means that you can apply for the help of the police and courts in England and Wales and Turkey to have the child flown back to England urgently.

For help and information about abduction, contact Reunite ▶ ▭. This is a voluntary organisation for parents whose children have been abducted by the other parent.

ACTION PLAN

1 Report the incident to the police, who may notify Interpol, the international police.

2 Contact the Central Authority for England and Wales, Child Abduction Unit, at the Department of Constitutional Affairs ▶ ▭. You will need to complete a form detailing the circumstances of your child's abduction. If you can, give a recent photograph of your child and ex-partner and a copy of your child's birth certificate.

3 The Child Abduction Unit will forward your details to the equivalent body in Turkey, which will appoint a lawyer to process your application under the Hague Convention (see box, opposite).

4 Be prepared to travel to Turkey for any court proceedings and, if these are successful, to collect your child.

Does a court order have legal force abroad?

Q My ex-wife has gone back to Australia, taking our 12-year-old son with her. The court here gave me rights of access to him, but now she says I can't see him because English law doesn't apply in Australia. Can she do that?

A No. The law of the United Kingdom (England, Wales, Scotland and Northern Ireland) on international child abduction is governed by the Hague Convention (see box, opposite), which also applies in Australia.

If your ex-wife had your permission or that of the authorities to take your son to Australia, you can apply for access under Article 21 of the Hague Convention. If she did not have permission, you can apply for your son to be brought back to the UK.

Each country that has signed the Hague Convention has set up a 'Central Authority' to deal with applications for access to or the return of a child.

ACTION PLAN

1 Contact the Central Authority for England and Wales, Child Abduction Unit, at the Department of Constitutional Affairs ▶ 📖. This body will help you to fill in your Hague Convention application form. It will send it to the Central Authority in Australia, which will start the legal process there.

2 Contact Reunite ▶ 📖, a voluntary organisation for parents whose children have been abducted by a former spouse, for support and advice.

INTERNATIONAL AGREEMENTS ON ABDUCTION

Two international agreements deal with the abduction of a child from one country to another:
• **The Hague Convention on the Civil Aspects of International Child Abduction 1980.**

• **The European Convention on Recognition and Enforcement of Decisions concerning Custody of Children and on Restoration of Custody of Children.**

THE HAGUE CONVENTION

The object of the Hague Convention on the Civil Aspects of International Child Abduction 1980 is to see that children who have been abducted to another country are returned to the country they were snatched from as promptly as possible.

Countries that have signed the Convention also undertake to enforce custody and access orders issued by the courts of other signatory countries.

The following countries or territories have signed the Hague Convention:
Argentina, Australia, Austria, Bahamas, Belarus, Belgium, Belize, Bosnia & Herzegovina, Brazil, Bulgaria, Burkina Faso, Canada, Chile, Colombia, Costa Rica, Croatia, Cyprus, Czech Republic, Denmark, Ecuador, El Salvador, Estonia, Fiji, Finland, France, Georgia, Germany, Greece, Guatemala, Honduras, Hong Kong, Hungary, Iceland, Ireland, Israel, Italy, Latvia, Lithuania, Luxembourg, Macao, Macedonia, Malta, Mauritius, Mexico, Moldova, Monaco, Netherlands, New Zealand, Nicaragua, Norway, Panama, Paraguay, Peru, Poland, Portugal, Romania, Serbia & Montenegro, Slovakia, Slovenia, South Africa, Spain, Sri Lanka, St Kitts & Nevis, Sweden, Switzerland, Thailand, Trinidad & Tobago, Turkey, Turkmenistan, UK, USA, Uruguay, Uzbekistan, Venezuela, Zimbabwe.

THE EUROPEAN CONVENTION

The European Convention (on Recognition and Enforcement of Decisions concerning Custody of Children and on Restoration of Custody of Children) ensures that a court order concerning a child in one signatory country can be enforced in another.

These countries have signed the European Convention:
Austria, Belgium, Bulgaria, Cyprus, Czech Republic, Denmark, Estonia, Finland, France, Germany, Greece, Hungary, Iceland, Ireland, Italy, Latvia, Liechtenstein, Lithuania, Luxembourg, Macedonia, Malta, Moldova, Netherlands, Norway, Poland, Portugal, Slovakia, Spain, Sweden, Switzerland, Turkey, UK.

PERSONAL RELATIONSHIPS

Long-term care and your rights

Finding the right kind of care can be a pressing problem for elderly people and their families. Some are able to stay in their homes with the help of care provided by family members, local health services or voluntary organisations (see question, p350). Others reach the point where a physical illness or mental incapacity means they need the kind of long-term care provided by a home for the elderly.

Care homes may be run by the local social services department, non-profit organisations or commercial companies. Social services may contribute towards the costs – although the person receiving the care always has to pay something. To apply for financial assistance, contact your local council's social services department. Social workers will visit you to assess your care and financial needs.

TYPES OF CARE HOMES

There are several types of homes for the elderly offering varying levels of care, from sheltered housing – which has help on hand in case of an emergency – to fully staffed nursing homes.

Sheltered (or retirement) housing   You buy or rent a property in a sheltered housing complex which has a resident warden and an alarm system. All maintenance is provided and various care services are available. Usually, residence is restricted to people above a certain age, say 60.

These properties can range from small flats to luxurious homes with amenities such as swimming pools or golf courses within the complex. Some are private and others are run by local councils or housing associations. You pay a service charge which varies according to the type of facilities provided.

'Close care' or 'extra care' schemes   You buy or rent a property on the same site as a nursing or care home, often with a guarantee that your property will be bought back if you have to move into the residential home. You pay for services such as cleaning and various forms of assistance provided by the home.

Residential care homes   These provide meals and help with personal care such as dressing, as well as supervision of medication. There is someone on duty at night, but no provision for nursing care. All care homes are registered and inspected by the local social services department.

Nursing homes   These provide 24-hour nursing care, as well as residential facilities, and so are more expensive than the other types of care homes. All nursing homes are registered and inspected by the local health authority.

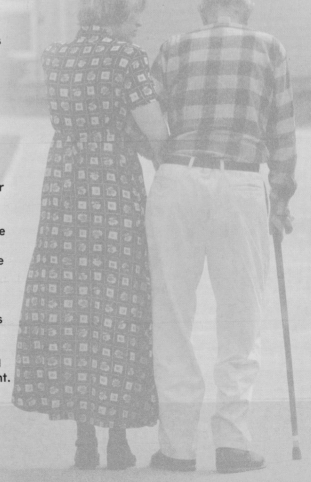

348

COMPLAINING ABOUT A CARE HOME

If you think a relative or friend is not getting adequate care, discuss the situation with the manager or proprietor of the home. Each home must have a formal complaints procedure. Homes must also be registered with the local authority, which conducts periodic inspections. In addition, there are two regulatory bodies for residential and nursing homes, which ensure that standards are maintained:
- National Care Standards Commission ▶ ⌂ in England
- Care Standards Inspectorate for Wales ▶ ⌂.

1 Ask for a copy of the home's complaints procedure, which should be available to residents and to their relatives and friends.

2 Make a formal complaint to the owner, or to the head office if the home is part of a group.

3 If you do not get a satisfactory response, raise the issue with the local authority and the appropriate regulatory body (see above). They can investigate the care being given to a particular resident and look more widely at standards in the home. They can order changes and improvements and ultimately replace managers or close homes if standards do not improve.

WORD OF WARNING
If you make a complaint about a care home to the local authority or one of the regulatory bodies, you do not have to inform the care home staff that you have done so. But, if the authority or regulatory body needs to investigate particular events or circumstances that concern one of the residents, you could find it difficult to remain anonymous. So it is better to begin by taking your complaint to the home's official complaints procedure.

BEING CARED FOR AT HOME

Getting help in the home may meet the needs of a person of any age who, because of mobility problems, a disability or long-term illness, finds it difficult to cook, bath, clean the house or get to the shops or post office.

- Local social services departments may be able to provide home care, meals and help with adaptations to the home for someone who has difficulty managing the stairs or using the bathroom.

- Many people who need home care are looked after by a family member. The local social services department may offer respite care to allow the carer a weekend or holiday break.

- Ask the local social services department for a community alarm. Alarms enable vulnerable people to call for help 24 hours a day in case of an accident or other emergency.

- The local authority housing department may be able to help with a grant if a person's home needs repairs.

- People who need extra care or have mobility problems may be entitled to disability benefit (see boxes, pp136 and 351). For information, contact the local Benefits Agency ▶ ⌂ or Citizens Advice Bureau, or call the benefits enquiry line on 0800 882 200.

- Call NHS Direct (see box, p109) for information about self-help groups.

An elderly person's right to stay put

Q I've just turned 80 and live alone. I've recently had a few accidents in my house and my son and daughter-in-law want me to move into a residential home. But I'm happy where I am and feel I can cope. Can they make me move?

A No. No one – not even the social services – can make decisions for people who are able to state and understand their own wishes.

What you or your family can do is investigate ways of making life easier for you in your home. For example, you may be entitled to help at home from your local council's social services department (see p349). The charity Age Concern ▶ 🕮 runs schemes in which local volunteers help elderly people with their shopping or collecting their pensions.

To help with any extra expenses you may incur, you might consider an 'equity release scheme'. Essentially, this is a way of releasing some of the capital that is tied up in your home:

- you take out a mortgage on your home and invest that money elsewhere to produce extra income
- interest on the loan is rolled up until you die and then paid off out of your estate – with the benefit for your heirs that it saves on inheritance tax.

ACTION PLAN

1 You or your family should contact Age Concern ▶ 🕮 to find out what volunteer schemes it runs in your area. Get in touch, too, with the Women's Royal Voluntary Service (WRVS) ▶ 🕮, which may have a meals-on-wheels service in the area.

2 Contact your local Benefits Agency ▶ 🕮 to find out what benefits you may be entitled to. If you ever need care on a daily basis, for instance, you may become eligible for attendance allowance (see box, opposite).

3 For more information about equity release schemes, contact Age Concern ▶ 🕮 and Help the Aged ▶ 🕮, both of which produce guides to them. You should also consult an independent financial adviser (see box, p159).

Preparing for the effects of Alzheimer's

Q My elderly aunt has been diagnosed with Alzheimer's. My sister and I want her to give us legal powers enabling us to look after her and her finances when the condition gets worse, but she won't. Can we oblige her to appoint someone – not necessarily one of us – to take responsibility for her when she is mentally incapable?

A No, you cannot force her to do anything while she is mentally competent to take decisions. All the same, it is sensible to try to persuade her to make advance provisions, so that decisions about important issues will be of her own choosing.

When she is ready to discuss the issue, she should take advice from a solicitor (see p20) or her local Citizens Advice Bureau ▶ 📖 or Law Centre ▶ 📖 about making an Enduring Power of Attorney (EPA). This is a document that would give one or more people power to manage her finances and property, either at once or only if and when she becomes incapable of taking decisions. An EPA can be made at any time while she is capable of understanding what it is and what it is intended to do.

If she has not already done so, your aunt should also make a will and lodge it with the Principal Registry of the Family Division (see question, p396). She might also make a living will (see box, p126) to record her wishes about health-care treatment in case she is incapacitated.

Ways of paying for residential care

Q **I'm 78 years old and need care during the day. My daughter is encouraging me to sell my house and move into a private residential home, but I'm worried about the expense. Can I claim benefits, such as attendance allowance, to help to offset the cost?**

A Yes. You can claim attendance allowance (see box, right) if you have needed care for at least six months. You or your daughter should contact your local Benefits Agency ▶ 📖 to ask for information about whether you are entitled to claim and how to do so.

You should seek expert advice on how best to invest the proceeds from the sale of your house. You could buy an:
• Impaired Life Annuity – for a capital sum, you can buy an annuity that will take care of the home's fees. An annuity gives regular payments until you die.
• Immediate Need Care Fee Payment Plan – this will guarantee to meet the costs of your residential care until you

die. The prices of these plans vary depending on your life expectancy and health.

For further information, ask the Law Society ▶ 📖 for a copy of its free guide to financial matters for the elderly.

Possible mistreatment by a carer

Q **My elderly father is in a nursing home and I think one of the carers is mistreating him. I discussed the situation with the home's manager, who refuses to do anything unless I come up with 'better' evidence. Can he do that?**

A No. The home should take your concern seriously, make enquiries to establish the circumstances, and take action as necessary. For details of how to make a complaint, see p349.

At the same time, you should make sure that what you think is mistreatment really is that. For example, physical signs of what seems to be abuse may be the result of a fall or other accident. Mental distress may be a symptom of dementia. Consider having your father examined by his GP to check for signs of abuse.

If your father has his care paid for by the Department of Work and Pensions, tell his social worker or care manager of your concerns, and ask them to investigate. If you are convinced there is imminent danger or that a serious incident has occurred, call the police.

> **ATTENDANCE ALLOWANCE is a non-taxable benefit paid to people aged 65 or over, who need help to look after themselves because of illness or disability. It is paid at different rates according to whether a person needs care during the day or night, or both. If you have needed help for at least six months, you can apply for an attendance allowance. Contact your local Jobcentre Plus office ▶ 📖 for information.**

Ageing father a danger behind the wheel?

Q **My 84-year-old father is still driving, but recently I've had some near-misses when he's been at the wheel. Despite that, he refuses to give up. Isn't there a statutory age limit on driving?**

A No. When your father reached the age of 70, he would have had to apply to the Driver and Vehicle Licensing Agency (DVLA) ▶ 🖿 to renew his licence.

The renewal form includes a number of health questions. If the DVLA is satisfied from the answers to these questions that a person is fit to drive, it will issue a new licence for up to three years, at the end of which time the process is repeated. If the DVLA renewed your father's licence the last time he applied, he is perfectly within his rights to carry on driving his car.

It is possible that his health or, for example, his eyesight has deteriorated significantly since the licence was last renewed. If that is the case, you should persuade him to discuss his driving with his GP. Remind him also to have his free annual sight tests. As a last resort, you could inform the DVLA of your concerns.

A funeral with a difference

Q **My mother has just died. She didn't belong to any church, and I don't feel that a traditional religious funeral is appropriate. Do I have the right to give her a more alternative burial?**

A Yes. First, you must apply to your local county court for a registrar's certificate or a coroner's order, without which it would be a criminal offence to bury your mother's body.

You are then free (within reason) to bury the body as you wish. For example, you can have your mother buried:
• in private land, provided it does not constitute a nuisance (see box, opposite)
• in a private cemetery
• at sea
• abroad – if she was French, say, and wanted to be buried in France.

For burials at sea, people usually have the body cremated beforehand, then they simply scatter the ashes at sea. If you want to have your mother's body buried at sea without cremating it first, you must:
• contact the Department for Environment, Food and Rural Affairs (DEFRA) ▶ 🖿 for a special licence
• let the coroner know what you are planning to do at least four days in

DID YOU KNOW YOU WERE TOUCHING 85?

YES! AND I'VE STILL GOT ALL MY OWN TEETH!

POLICE

BURIAL, CREMATION AND OTHER OPTIONS

You have no legal right to stipulate what happens to your body when you die. You can say in your will how you want it to be disposed of, but your family and executors are under no legal obligation to adhere to these wishes. In practice, what you want will usually be taken into account. The choice is usually between burial or cremation, although some people donate their body to medical research (see below) or for the organs to be used in transplants (see p125).

Burial A standard burial can take place in a local authority cemetery, churchyard or private cemetery. Burials can also take place on private land (see question, opposite and below).

Cremation Local authorities own most crematoria. Ashes can be scattered almost anywhere, including at the crematorium, but to scatter them over private land, you should ask the owner's consent.

Leaving your body for science

If you want to leave your body for medical research, you should make the arrangements while you are still alive.

Contact the anatomy department of the university or medical school of your choice. They will give you a bequest form to fill in.

Inform your family and your GP of your wish. After you die, your relatives will contact the medical school, who will advise on the next step. If your body is accepted by a medical school (not all bodies are suitable), the school can, if requested, arrange for eventual cremation.

A costly business

One way to spare your relatives undue burial expenses is to take out a pre-paid funeral plan. For more information, contact the Funeral Planning Authority ▶ ⌂.

Also, 'do-it-yourself' funerals (the funeral is arranged and the body transported by relatives and not by a professional funeral firm) are

becoming increasingly popular using low-cost, biodegradable coffins. Contact the Natural Death Centre ▶ ⌂ (see question, opposite and below).

The local authority or health authority arrange funerals for people whose bodies are not claimed by family or friends.

---

advance (ask your local authority for the coroner's contact details). This is because you cannot, by law, take a body out of England or Wales without giving the coroner four clear days' notice of removal.

Many farmers, local authorities and wildlife charities have established 'natural' or woodland burial grounds for people who want to bury relatives in private land. Often, their only condition is that you plant a commemorative tree. The Natural Death Centre ▶ ⌂ will help you to find a 'natural' burial ground and to arrange an 'ecological' burial, in which, for example, you bury your relative in a coffin made from environmentally friendly materials such as cardboard or bamboo.

Although there is no law against being buried in a private garden, if you wish to

do this, you should contact the local authority, which can issue a certificate confirming that the burial is lawful. This will avoid possible complications, including suspicions of foul play.

If you have your mother's body cremated, you can scatter the ashes in, for example, a favourite beauty spot – provided you ask the owner's consent. There is no legal restriction on taking ashes abroad, but some countries restrict the importation of ashes, so check first.

You should consult your local Citizens Advice Bureau ▶ ⌂ or Law Centre ▶ ⌂, or a solicitor (see p20), if you want to cremate your mother privately. You will need their help in negotiating the numerous legal restrictions on how and where a body can be burned.

CHOICE OF SCHOOL

Getting a child into the school you choose

Q **Our child was refused a place at the local school and offered a place at another farther away. It's a difficult bus journey and we don't like the school anyway. Can the school we want really refuse him?**

A Yes. Although the law says that parents must be given a chance to 'express a preference' – that is, to say which school they would prefer their child to attend – there is no guarantee that your preferred school will have a place.

But you can appeal against the refusal. You can ask the school or local education authority (LEA) for the decision to be reconsidered by an independent appeals panel. This is drawn from local people who are not connected with the school or its LEA. About a third of all admissions appeals are successful.

To prepare for an appeal, check the school's prospectus to make sure that the school or LEA staff have got all the facts right. For example, if distance from the school affects their decision, was the distance from your home to the school measured accurately?

Panels often respond to family difficulties. Can you show that work makes you dependent on family living near the school?

For more information, get these booklets from the Department for Education and Skills (DfES) ▶ ⌨ or its web site:
• *School Admissions Code of Practice*
• *School Admissions Appeals Code of Practice.*

ACTION PLAN

1 Contact the appeals officer of your LEA, or the head of a foundation or voluntary aided school (see box, right). Do this as soon as possible, because there may be a time limit.

2 The appeals officer or school will send you a form. Fill it in carefully, giving your reasons for appealing.

3 You will be sent a date for a hearing. Before this takes place, you will receive a statement about why your child was not given a place. Be ready with questions about this statement and whether the school really is full. You can take a friend or adviser to the hearing.

WORD OF WARNING

If the independent appeal panel finds against you, do not appeal to the DfES. No one, not even the Secretary of State, can overturn the panel's decision.

YOU'RE NOT FROM ROUND HERE ARE YOU?

SCHOOL PLAYGROUND

TYPES OF SCHOOL

Most schools in England and Wales belong to one of two categories: independent (see p357) and maintained. In state or maintained schools, the Local Education Authority (LEA, see p357) pays for all or most of the running costs – salaries, the maintenance of buildings and equipment – out of central government funding, council tax and grants.

Faith schools are schools (both maintained and independent) that have been established by religious organisations. The vast majority of maintained faith schools – all of which are voluntary schools (see below) – are Church of England or Roman Catholic. There are also some Jewish, Muslim and Sikh maintained faith schools.

MAINTAINED SCHOOLS

All LEA-maintained schools provide free education, but the ownership of the land and buildings and some aspects of funding vary from category to category.

Community schools Ordinary state schools. Land and buildings belong to an LEA. Funded and maintained entirely by the LEA.

Foundation schools Formerly known as grant-maintained schools. Land and buildings belong to the governing body. Most running costs funded by the LEA.

Voluntary schools There are two kinds of voluntary school:
• **Voluntary controlled schools** Land and buildings belong to a charitable organisation, usually a church. Running costs funded entirely by the LEA. Managed like community schools.
• **Voluntary aided schools** Land and buildings belong to a charitable organisation, usually a church. Running costs funded partly by the LEA, partly by the governing body, partly by the charitable organisation.

Special schools For pupils with special educational needs (see p372). They include:
• **Community special schools** Funded and maintained entirely by LEAs.
• **Foundation special schools** As with ordinary foundation schools, land and buildings belong to a governing body. Most running costs funded by the LEA.

HYBRID SCHOOLS

Some schools blur the distinction between maintained and independent. Although independent, they provide free schooling.

City technology colleges and city academies Independent secondary schools established by agreement between the Department for Education and Skills (DfES) and private sector sponsors. The DfES meets their running costs.

Non-maintained special schools Set up by charities for pupils with special educational needs. Funded mainly by fees paid by LEAs.

Specialist schools Secondary schools of all types can have specialist status. This allows them to select some children by aptitude – for example, aptitudes in sports, in music and drama, or in languages.

HOW PLACES ARE ALLOCATED

Who decides which children get the places available in a maintained school each year depends on the kind of school.
• In community and voluntary controlled schools, the LEA decides.
• In voluntary aided schools and foundation schools, the governing body decides.

Faith schools will usually include religious criteria in their admissions policies, such as:
• Was the child baptised?
• Do the parents attend church regularly and support the parish or religious community?
• Is there a recommendation from the parish priest or local rabbi?

Study the prospectus
When choosing a school for your child, always check the school's prospectus (published annually) for its admission arrangements.

The prospectus spells out how many places are available that year, and how they will be offered if there are more applicants than places. Factors taken into consideration usually include:
• the distance a child lives from the school
• having a brother or sister already at the school
• medical needs.

Signing a home-school agreement

Q **When the school offered my child a place they asked me to sign a home-school agreement. It asks parents to make a regular contribution to school funds. Can they insist that I sign?**

A No. The home-school agreement sets out what the school expects from parents and what parents can expect from the school. It usually covers support from parents on matters such as school rules, uniform and homework; the school takes responsibility for providing suitable education and keeping parents informed. The agreement is not legally binding.

Schools may ask parents for regular voluntary contributions, but these cannot be made compulsory. If you sign a home-school agreement, make it clear that you do not accept any financial commitment.

By contrast, the parent of a child in an independent school (see box, right) makes a formal agreement to pay the fees.

When pupils have a right to free transport

Q **We live in a rural area with very few buses. My child's school is some distance away, and the LEA says that it cannot provide transport. Can they refuse to help?**

A No. Local education authorities (LEAs) are obliged to arrange free travel to and from school for:
• children under eight years old who live more than 2 miles (3.2km) away
• children of eight and older who live more than 3 miles (4.8km) away.

The distance is measured from the front door of the child's home to the entrance of the school by a safe walking route.

Free transport may come in various forms: as bus passes, school buses or, in special cases, taxis. If the LEA provides a bus, it must also provide somebody to supervise the children during the journey.

When parents choose a school that is not the nearest one to their home – for example, a faith school – the LEA is not obliged to pay for the child's transport.

ACTION PLAN

1 Measure the distance from your home to the school by the safest walking route. Avoid short cuts across fields or parks, or roads without pavements. If the route is longer than the statutory distance, you are entitled to free transport. Contact the LEA to inform it of your findings.

2 If the LEA disputes the distance, ask for an explanation of how it is calculated. You may be able to show that a particular route is not safe.

3 If the distance is not enough to qualify, you will have to give special reasons for needing help. Find out from your LEA what the policy is on school transport and see if there are concessions you can apply for.

WORD OF WARNING

School transport eats into the budget, especially in rural areas, so LEAs apply the legislation strictly. For instance, they do not have to consider the difficulties a parent may have in escorting a child to school, although some might make a concession for parents who are disabled, cannot leave home and have no help.

The obligation to offer sporting activities

Q **My son loves sport, but the school provides scarcely any sports training. His teacher says the school prefers to concentrate on academic subjects. Can they do that?**

A No. Physical education (PE) is a national curriculum subject (see p358), and maintained schools (see p355) must follow the curriculum's rules.

At primary school, children should learn the basic skills needed for ball games, gymnastics and swimming. Secondary schools must provide games activities and at least three of the following: gymnastics, dance, swimming, athletics and outdoor adventure. Government guidelines suggest that schools should aim to provide pupils with two hours' physical activity a week.

If your child's school does not prioritise games, you can challenge it. For example, local education authorities should not sell playing fields for development without permission from the Department for Education and Skills (DfES). The DfES often gives permission, but its decision may be swayed by a campaign by parents.

ACTION PLAN

1 Ask for the PE syllabus and check the governors' annual report to parents for details of the school's sporting facilities and achievements. If they seem inadequate, ask to see the head.

2 If you are not satisfied, write to the governors to complain that they are not fulfilling their responsibilities to see that every child is able to follow a broad, balanced curriculum.

INDEPENDENT SCHOOLS 'Public' and other independent schools are funded by fees paid by parents and, in some cases, charitable trust funds. The admissions policy is set by the head and the governing body, and the governors are responsible for the school's day-to-day running.

Although independent schools have to be registered with the Department for Education and Skills (DfES), they are not subject to general education law. For example, they can teach what subjects they like, and they do not have to follow the national curriculum. For more information, contact the Independent Schools Council Information Service (ISCIS) ▶ ⌕.

3 Find out from your local authority what sports clubs are available at the school or locally. If your child's school has playing fields or a sports hall, see if a local sports organisation would set up a club there.

A school's obligation to teach languages

Q **One reason we chose our daughter's secondary school was because of its excellent German teaching. Now the head says there is not enough demand for German, and offers Spanish instead. Can he do that?**

A Yes. Schools cannot be required to teach a particular language. They have to teach the national curriculum, and this includes a modern foreign language in ▶

LOCAL EDUCATION AUTHORITIES (LEAs) are the bodies that administer the national education service in the different regions of England and Wales. Each LEA consists of elected, unpaid local politicians and paid professional officers.

LEAs provide most of the state pre-school, primary and secondary education in their area. They own, equip and maintain most local schools, and build new ones. They are financed by central government and the council tax, and allocate funds to the schools in their area. LEAs are meant to monitor, maintain and improve standards in schools through representatives who sit on the governing boards of LEA-maintained schools along with parents and other local people.

To contact your LEA, see the telephone directory or the DfES web site: www.dfes.gov.uk/leagateway

Key Stage 3 and Key Stage 4 (see box, below). But the language to be taught is not specified. As long as heads follow the national curriculum guidelines, they can decide what subjects should be taught.

ACTION PLAN

1 If your child has begun a two-year GCSE course in German, the school has to help her complete the course. Write to the head and ask how the school proposes to do this. It may be able to arrange for her to continue the course at another school or college.

2 Contact the clerk to the governors of the school expressing your concerns over the school's change in teaching policy.

Schools have different policies on homework

Q I have one daughter at primary school and another at secondary school. The one at primary school is getting stressed because of all the homework she has to do, while the other has not been given any homework since she went to her new secondary school half a term ago. Can this be right?

A Yes. There are no regulations about homework. Different schools have different policies. But the government does recommend that schools issue a written statement explaining their policy. This should be agreed by the governors and given to parents along with the home-school agreement (see p356). In this way, teachers, pupils and parents are clear about what is expected.

The Department for Education and Skills (DfES) ▶ ⌨ publishes a booklet of guidelines, *Homework: Guidelines for Primary and Secondary Schools*. You can download it from the DfES web site.

ACTION PLAN

1 Ask for a copy of each school's homework policy, which should tell you what kind of homework is suitable for children at different stages. It should also give guidance on parental help. For example, pupils may have a homework diary that parents should sign.

THE NATIONAL CURRICULUM

	Key Stage	School year	Pupils' ages
Primary and nursery schools	Foundation Stage	Nursery and reception	3-5
	Key Stage 1	Years 1 and 2	5-7
	Key Stage 2	Years 3, 4, 5 and 6	7-11
Secondary schools	Key Stage 3	Years 7, 8 and 9	11-14
	Key Stage 4	Years 10 and 11	14-16
	Sixth form	Years 12 and 13	16-18

National curriculum subjects

For each subject and key stage, programmes of study specify what pupils should be taught; levels of attainment set out the standards they should reach.

- **Key Stages 1 and 2** English, mathematics, science, technology, information and communications technology, history, geography, art, music and physical education. Welsh in Welsh schools.
- **Key Stage 3** Key Stages 1 and 2 subjects plus a modern foreign language and citizenship.
- **Key Stage 4** English, mathematics, science, physical education, technology, information and communications technology, citizenship and a modern foreign language. Welsh in Welsh schools.
- **Sixth form** Exam board syllabus.

In some cases a pupil may be exempted from modern languages and other subjects in favour of more vocational topics.

2 Keep a record of the homework set for each child over two weeks, and compare it with the policy. If homework is not marked regularly, or if the teachers set too much or too little, ask to discuss this with the child's class teacher or tutor.

3 If you remain dissatisfied, take up the matter with the parent teacher association and the governing body.

Opting out of sex education

Q I feel very strongly that sex should be within marriage. But my daughter's school takes a different line in its sex education. Can the school do this?

A Yes. But parents can opt out of all or part of sex education for their children, except when teaching about sex is part of the national curriculum – for instance, the biology of human sexual development and reproduction.
- *In primary schools*, the governors decide whether they want to offer any sex education and, if they do, what it should cover and how it should be taught. An up-to-date written statement of the policy must be available to parents. If they do not want their children to attend some or all of the sex education classes, they can withdraw them.
- *In secondary schools*, sex education (including education about sexually transmitted diseases, such as HIV/AIDS) must be provided. The governors decide the content and organisation of this provision. Parents can withdraw their children from some or all of it.

When aspects of general sex education form part of the national curriculum, parents do not have a right to withdraw their children from classes. Nor do governors have any discretion to allow children to be withdrawn from them.

> ### GUIDELINES ON SEX EDUCATION
>
> Most sex education in state schools is carefully planned and takes into account factors such as parents' anxieties and cultural and religious differences.
>
> The governors must ensure that it encourages pupils to consider the moral aspects of sex and the value of family life. Government guidelines state that heads must ensure that pupils:
> - learn about marriage and its importance for family life and the bringing up of children
> - are protected from teaching and materials that are inappropriate to the pupils' age, religion or culture.
>
> The government guidelines are set out in the booklet *Sex and Relationship Guidance* from the Department for Education and Skills (DfES) ▶ 📖.

ACTION PLAN

1 Ask the school if you can have a meeting with the teachers in order to discuss the sex education they are providing and the resources they are using to teach it. In fact, the school should have offered you this opportunity anyway. ▶

COURSE, WE DIDN'T HAVE SEX IN MY DAY

SEX EDUCATION FILE

2 If you are not happy with what is being offered, write to the clerk to the governors saying that you wish to make a formal complaint and citing reasons why the sex education does not follow government guidelines ▶ ✍.

WORD OF WARNING
Before you withdraw your child from sex education, consider the effect on her of doing this. Will she be subjected to playground misinformation and teasing?

Religious education and collective worship

Q We want to withdraw our child from religious education classes, but the head says they are compulsory. Can she be right?

A No. Although all state schools must provide religious education (RE) as well as a daily collective act of worship (which can be inter-faith), parents are entitled to withdraw their children from these activities.

According to government guidelines, the school head should establish what you object to and let you know what arrangements will be made to ensure that your wishes are followed.

Faith schools (see box, p355) often inform parents that religious belief is an essential part of the school's life and work. They may also state in their prospectus that all pupils will be expected to take part in religious education and worship. But once the child has been admitted to the school, the right to withdraw from RE and from worship cannot be withheld.

ACTION PLAN
1 If you object to all religious worship and education, write

to the head asking for your child to be withdrawn from religious classes and services. You can quote section 71 of the School Standards and Framework Act 1998, which sets out the legal right of parents to withdraw their children.

2 If you are not happy with the reply, complain in writing to the clerk to the governors. The governors have a duty to inform parents about the right to withdraw their children from RE and worship and to see that suitable arrangements are made for children who are withdrawn.

Changing the emphasis of religious education

Q Our daughter's school teaches religious education with an emphasis on comparative religion. But as Christians we would like her to have more teaching about our religion. Can we insist on this?

A No. Your best option is to find a place for your child at a school that teaches the kind of RE you prefer. Alternatively, you have the right to arrange for your child to withdraw from the RE lessons in order to attend classes with a teacher of your choice. You can ask the school for a room for private RE classes, but the head does not have to provide one if it involves extra cost. Nor does the school have to pay the teacher.

The local education authority (LEA) must be satisfied that the lessons do not interfere with the rest of your child's education – for example, by causing her to miss other classes.

With daily worship, if your child is at a state school, you can try to alter its emphasis. The school must provide a daily act of worship, but this can be changed to represent a different faith or faiths. The head can apply to the local committee on religious education (see box, below right) for permission to change the emphasis of daily worship.

ACTION PLAN

1 If you want your child to have RE classes with a private teacher, write to the head to ask for her to be withdrawn from RE classes and services (see preceding question).

2 If the head is unwilling, complain to the clerk to the governing body. The governors are responsible for the way RE is provided in the school.

Challenging a child's A-level results

Q Our daughter consistently came top of her class and we expected her to get top A-level grades. But her exam results were poor. Can we challenge them?

A Not as parents, but you can make enquiries through your child's school. You should first check that her results have surprised her teachers. If the results are not much worse than their predictions, her teachers are not likely to support an enquiry about results.

If her teachers support you, they can make an official enquiry about results to the examination board. For example,

they can ask the board to recheck the clerical procedures – perhaps to verify that all parts of her papers were marked and the marks were added up correctly. More radically, the board can be asked to have her papers re-marked by a senior examiner. It charges a fee for this service.

If you are unhappy about the outcome, the school can appeal to the examining board and, if the response is still inadequate, to the Examination Appeals Board (EAB) ▶ ▭.

For more details, check the web site of the Qualifications and Curriculum Authority: www.qca.org.uk

ACTION PLAN

1 If the school supports an enquiry, decide what kind of enquiry you want. The teachers can ask the examination board for a breakdown of your daughter's marks for each part of the exam and the boundaries between the grades, so they can tell whether or not your daughter was on the borderline.

2 Make sure that the school submits the enquiry to the board on time. It must arrive no later than September ▶

AGES AND STAGES

Maintained schools (see box, p355) in the UK cater broadly for four age groups:

Nursery schools: 3-5 years

Primary schools: 5-11 years

Secondary schools: 11-18 years

Sixth-form colleges: 16-18 years

In some areas of England, there is a system of First and Middle Schools, with children moving from First to Middle School at the age of 8 or 9.

EDUCATION AND WORSHIP

Under the law, different kinds of school (see p355) have different obligations when teaching religious education.

In community schools (and some foundation schools), RE must be taught according to an agreed non-denominational syllabus. Model syllabuses are devised by the local standing advisory committee on religious education (SACRE), which represents religious interests.

In voluntary aided schools (and some foundation schools), RE can be denominational, and is determined by the trust deed that established the school.

RE must be taught in maintained schools – classes and talks on ethics and morals cannot be substituted for RE lessons and daily worship.

20 for exams held in May or June. The board must acknowledge your enquiry within seven working days.

3 When the board's decision arrives, decide quickly with the school whether to accept it. If you want to appeal, you must do so within two weeks of receiving the decision.

4 A senior examiner with the board who has not been involved with the case will review your appeal. If you and the school are not happy with the new decision, you can appeal again.

5 A second appeal will be reviewed by an appointed panel, which will include at least one member who is not connected with the board.

6 If you remain unhappy with the response, the school can appeal to the Examination Appeals Board (EAB). They must do this within three weeks of receiving the response to the appeal to the examining board. The EAB's decision is final.

PERFORMANCE AND ACHIEVEMENT

Ofsted, the government department responsible for inspecting and reporting on schools (see p369), produces Performance and Achievement (PANDA) reports for all state schools. These give information not only about a school's exam results but also about its results in comparison with other similar schools. The reports may show, for example, that a school that seems to be failing has, in fact, helped its pupils to make more progress than one higher up the league tables, taking into account the pupils' standards when they started.

Unlike Ofsted inspection reports, PANDA reports are not available to the general public. You will have to ask the head for a copy of the school's report – you do not have an automatic right to see it.

Transferring a child from a failing school

Q **My daughter's school is low in the league tables for our area and had a bad Ofsted inspection report. I asked the LEA about finding another school, but they say they cannot do that because there are no places. Can they refuse?**

A Yes. The local education authority (LEA) has no legal duty to find another place for your daughter just because her school has weaknesses. If the other schools in the LEA area are already full, there is very little it can do to help.

You could contact other schools in the LEA area to double-check that they really are all full to the published admission number. If it turns out that one school has a spare place, you can insist that the LEA transfer your daughter to it. If not, you can only look outside the area for places in another local authority.

If a school is causing concern, the LEA has a legal obligation to give it extra resources and support. It can strengthen the governing body with its own appointments, and it can help the governors to improve the school's facilities and to make various staff changes. The school must also have an action plan to improve.

ACTION PLAN
1 If all local schools are, in fact, full, put pressure on the school to improve. Find out what the school's weaknesses are from recent Ofsted inspection reports (they are all on the Ofsted web site, see p369) and ask the school head if you can see a copy of the PANDA report (see box, left).

2 Start a campaign to support the school's improvement plan. Talk to other parents, see the teachers and the head to make suggestions, and contact the governors. You can also stand for election to the school's governing body (see p365).

A school's policy for maintaining discipline

Q **My son says that he and his classmates are doing less well in history than they ought to be, because the teacher doesn't keep control. The French teacher, on the other hand, makes fun of the slow learners. Can the school allow such inconsistency in discipline?**

A No. Governors have to issue a written statement of their principles on behaviour and discipline. This helps to establish the school's aims, and gives the pupils clear guidelines about the kind of behaviour expected of them.

It is the head's responsibility to see that this policy is enforced fairly and consistently. If a teacher fails to follow the policy, or cannot maintain order, the head may bring the teacher before a disciplinary or competency hearing.

The panel may set targets for improvements or order the teacher to undergo extra support and training. These measures will have been agreed by the teaching unions and adopted by the school's governing body. A teacher who fails to meet them may be dismissed from his job.

ACTION PLAN
1 Check the exam results, published in the school's annual report to parents. Is the school's performance worse in history and French than in other subjects in the curriculum?

2 If it is, ask to see your son's tutor – all secondary school pupils have a tutor who is responsible for their pastoral care. Explain to the tutor that you are worried about your son's progress in history.

3 If you are not satisfied with the tutor's response, ask to see the head. Discuss your worries about your son's progress – but try not to be too critical, which may arouse antagonism. Such discussions with parents often help to strengthen a head's hand in coping with an unsatisfactory teacher.

4 If there are no improvements after a term or so, seek support among other parents and write to the chair of governors, expressing your concerns.

How schools test prospective pupils

Q **My son performs below his ability level in intelligence tests, but the school we have chosen uses IQ tests in its admissions procedures. The head will not allow any other tests. Can he do that?**

A Yes. The head of a state school can refuse other tests as long as the admissions procedures are published in the school prospectus, and the tests have been applied consistently and fairly. With independent schools (see p357), the governors and head can decide their own admissions procedures.

There are, however, things you can do:
• Try another school. Not all use IQ tests in admissions.
• Prepare your son for the admissions tests. Performance in any test will improve through practice, so you can ask the school what tests are involved and make sure that your son gets some practice.
• Ask your son's teacher to write to the new school, explaining why he performs below his ability in IQ tests.
• Consider getting your son assessed by an educational psychologist. You can find one through your local education authority (LEA) or the British Psychological Society ▶ 📖.

The best education for a gifted child

Q **Our granddaughter is very gifted and is not stretched at her school. She is always in trouble because, the teacher says, she distracts other children. We think it is because she is bored, but her teacher says she's naughty and he must punish her. Can he do that?**

A Yes, as long as the teacher follows the school rules and acts reasonably. There are no regulations about support for very bright pupils. But many are thought not to realise their potential, so the government funds a nationwide programme, which includes after-school and holiday clubs and, for the top 5 per cent, a National Academy for Gifted and Talented Youth at Warwick University ▶ 📖, which since 2002 has run summer schools for gifted and talented children.

For more information about provision for gifted and talented children, contact the National Association for Gifted Children ▶ 📖.

No place at university despite good grades

Q **My son got three A grades in his A-levels, but hasn't been offered a place at any of his first three university choices. We know of children who got places with lower grades. Can a university discriminate against my son like this?**

A Yes, because admissions policies are a matter for individual universities. A-level results are a key indicator of applicants' abilities. But with a high number of students – often with similar grades – chasing a limited number of places, universities are increasingly using other criteria to help them to decide whom they will admit. These include teacher references and evidence of commitment through the personal statement on the application.

Because your son was likely to have been competing with applicants with the same grades as his own, other selection criteria would have been considered. Even if the children with lower grades were applying to the same university or

WHAT SCHOOL GOVERNORS DO

Governors are unpaid volunteers who represent parents, teachers and the community and are accountable to them for what the school does. They are responsible for its philosophy, policy and development, and they offer support to help it to improve standards. They do not get involved in the day-to-day running of the school, which is the responsibility of the head. But if serious problems emerge, it is the governors' duty to act. If they act honestly and in good faith, they cannot be held liable as individuals for mistakes, although they are liable as a corporate body if they break the law.

Budget, appointments and curriculum
Governors duties are to:
- approve the annual budget and oversee school finance. They are responsible for the care and maintenance of school premises
- appoint the head teacher and deputy head. They may also be involved in selecting and appointing other staff
- decide how many staff to employ and what they should be paid
- ensure that pupils have access to a broad and balanced curriculum and that the national curriculum is taught
- decide how sex education and other potentially controversial subjects will be taught, including religious education. They hear complaints from parents about these matters.

Discipline and prevention of discrimination
The governors must:
- lay down school disciplinary procedures. A committee of governors hears appeals against the exclusion of pupils (see p379)
- see that no one is discriminated against on grounds of sex, disability, marital status, race, colour, nationality or ethnic origin. They would be liable if the courts held that discrimination laws had been broken
- see that children with special needs or disabilities have their needs met and can take part as appropriate in school activities
- ensure that parents are kept informed about the school and their children's progress. The governors must prepare an annual report for parents and hold a meeting to discuss it.

---

universities as your son, you have no legal right to redress. The only exception would be if you felt the university was discriminating against him on grounds of sex, race or disability.

Degree withheld until student debts are paid

Q I am at the end of my degree course, which I've financed through a loan. I haven't paid my tuition fees this year – I hoped to get a job after leaving and then pay them off. But the university says it will not give me a degree unless I clear my debts. Can they do that?

A Yes. When you register for your degree course, you sign an agreement to accept the terms and conditions imposed by the university. These are set out in the universisty's student handbook, and they detail what facilities, courses (including their duration) and examinations the university agrees to provide, as well as the fees it will charge for tuition, accommodation and other services.

This agreement is legally binding. If the standard of teaching was lower than you could reasonably expect, or the department failed to teach the course as set out in the handbook, you can withhold the tuition fees and sue the university.

On the other hand, if you fail to pay, the university can withhold your degree until it receives the fees, send you down or even sue you. It has long been the practice for universities to insist on payment of fees, and even library fines, before allowing a student to attend the degree ceremony.

A school's duty to deal with bullying

Q My son has been bullied at school for the past two years. I have had several discussions with his teacher and head teacher, but the bullying is still going on and they are not taking any action. Can they just let it continue?

A No. Teachers, like doctors, have a 'duty of care' (see p21), and failing to take action when bullying has been brought to their notice can be seen as an infringement of that duty. As a last resort, you may have a case for taking the school to court.

School staff must be able to show that they have taken allegations of bullying and other harassment seriously. The governors, too, must make sure that there are effective strategies against bullying. For example, the school should start a policy of recording all incidents and the action taken to combat them. The governors should see that these policies are explained to staff, pupils and parents and enforced rigorously.

But the school's responsibility does not extend beyond its own premises. A case in West Sussex in 2000 established that parents cannot expect the school to be responsible for bullying that takes place on the bus home, even if the bullies are pupils at the school. If your son is being bullied on the way to and from school, contact the police.

The Department for Education and Skills (DfES) publishes a pack called *Don't Suffer in Silence*, which you can download from www.dfes.gov.uk/bullying. Try also the web site of the charity Bullying Online: www.bullying.co.uk

ACTION PLAN

1 Make a written complaint to the governing body. Explain what has happened and ask for an immediate investigation.

2 Send a copy of your complaint to your local councillor (details from your council offices). There are council representatives on governing bodies.

3 If the response is unsatisfactory, contact the local education authority and ask for an investigation ▶✍.

4 If you are unable to resolve the problem, consult a solicitor about taking legal action.

WORD OF WARNING

Some school bullies work by sending threatening text messages. Enforcing strict rules about the use of mobile

I WAS GETTING BULLIED SO I GOT A CHILD MINDER

phones can give pupils some protection in school. But teachers can do little to stop the practice outside school, other than to make pupils aware that it is illegal to send threatening or obscene messages, tell them the penalties and report incidents of harassment to the police.

Enforcing policy on school uniforms

Q **I am a single parent on a limited budget and find it difficult to buy my daughter's school uniform. Can the school punish her for not wearing it?**

A It depends on the severity of the punishment. Laws relating to school uniforms say only that schools can make wearing uniform a part of their rules. By accepting a place at the school, your daughter has accepted the rules and therefore any reasonable sanctions applied by the teachers to enforce them.

In practice, the governors decide whether there should be a school uniform and what it should consist of, while the head decides how wearing it should be enforced. Rules about the uniform are published in the prospectus and school rules, which are sent to the parents when a child is offered a place.

The head may impose minor punishments on pupils who break the rules by not wearing uniform. But the Department for Education and Skills (DfES) advises state schools that it would not be reasonable to impose punishments such as sending children home from school because they are not wearing the right uniform or because they disapprove of a pupil's appearance.

If a pupil is repeatedly and deliberately defiant, a head could exclude the child formally from the school (see box, p379), in which case the parents and child would have a right of appeal to the board of governors.

Bear in mind also that local education authorities (LEAs) can make grants toward the cost of clothing and sports equipment. They must publish their arrangements for this and explain how to obtain detailed information. Your LEA's Education Welfare Service will have information about publications.

ACTION PLAN
1 Contact the school office and ask for a copy of the rules about wearing the school uniform.

2 Contact your LEA, which may offer clothing grants, and the parents' association, which may run a clothing exchange scheme.

3 If you think the school requirements are unreasonable, canvass other parents for their views and write to the governors asking them to review the uniform rules.

ADAPTING THE SCHOOL UNIFORM

If you have religious or cultural reasons for not wanting your child to wear the school uniform:
● Enquire through a teacher or make an appointment to see the head and ask if the uniform can be adapted to meet your requirements.

Refusing to accept religious or cultural dress differences could put a school in breach of the Race Relations Act.

If wearing the uniform or part of it makes a disability such as asthma or eczema worse:
● Enlist the help of the school nurse or your GP to find ways in which the uniform can be modified. For example, perhaps some part of it could be made up in a different fabric. The school nurse may be able to speak to the head or school governors and arrange for it to be adapted. If not, make an appointment to see a teacher or the head and ask to be allowed to adapt the uniform.

Punishing a child for not wearing the uniform for health reasons could put the school in breach of the Disability Discrimination Act 1995 (see p375).

A teacher's right to impose detention

Q **My daughter is often late for school because of the unreliable bus service, and her teachers have threatened her with a detention. Can they do that?**

A Yes. A teacher can detain pupils after school hours and without the parents' consent, as long as the pupils are under 18 years old, and:
- detention is in the written statement of principles on behaviour and discipline published by the governors (see p363)
- it is a reasonable punishment in the circumstances
- it is imposed by the head or someone designated by the head
- the parents have at least 24 hours' written notice of the detention.

The blanket detention of a whole class for general indiscipline is permissible, but only as a last resort.

If these conditions are not met, parents may be able to claim for their child's false imprisonment.

If you can prove that your daughter could not get to school on time one day or over a period (because of a cancelled service, for example), it would not be reasonable to punish her. But bear in mind that teachers tend not to be sympathetic when parents blame poor transport. They say that children should start early enough to be sure of arriving on time.

Check that the legal conditions, particularly about notifying parents, have been followed. If not, write to the head saying that you do not agree to your child's detention and why ▶ ✍.

If you have good reasons for wanting to alter the day of the detention, you can ask for the day or time to be changed.

To forestall similar problems in future, you might encourage other parents, the school and the local education authority (LEA) to support a complaint to the transport authority.

Children need a licence to entertain

Q **My 15-year-old son has been selected for a prestigious dance programme, but the head refuses to allow him time off school for the rehearsals and performances. Can he do that?**

A Yes. Pupils under 16 must have a licence to work in entertainment from their local education authority (LEA) before they can take part in stage, film, radio or television performances and advertising. Without the licence they may not take time off school for auditions, rehearsals or performances.

Before issuing a licence, the LEA must be satisfied that your son's education will not suffer, that he is medically fit to perform and that arrangements are made for his welfare during performances.

If you apply for a licence for your son, your LEA will ask the head to advise on the desirability of issuing a licence for him. Pupils over 16 still need their head's permission to take time off.

ACTION PLAN

1 Ask your LEA for details of how to apply for an entertainment licence, and what is required to show that your son's education will not suffer.

2 Contact the head and explain that you want to apply to the LEA for a licence for your son.

3 If the head opposes the application, appeal to the LEA, which makes the final decision about issuing a licence.

GOLDEN RULE

Try to reduce the number of times your child or children are late for school. Pupils' continual lateness has been judged by the courts to amount to failure to attend school, and parents can be prosecuted if their children do not go to school. Local education authorities are increasingly exercising their right to prosecute in these circumstances.

OFSTED: MAINTAINING STANDARDS IN SCHOOLS

The Office for Standards in Education (Ofsted) ▶▭ is a government agency, headed by Her Majesty's Chief Inspector of Schools. It inspects and reports on English local education authorities (LEAs) and LEA-maintained schools, sixth form colleges and other education for 16-19 year olds, as well as teacher-training institutions and early years child care, including childminders. It also inspects independent schools when they apply for registration or there is concern about standards.

The equivalent body in Wales is Estyn, the office of Her Majesty's Inspectorate for Education and Training in Wales ▶▭.

Ofsted inspections

Ofsted is responsible for inspecting state schools every six years. Schools thought to be doing well may have only a short inspection; others need a full inspection of all national curriculum subjects and other aspects of the school's life.

The inspection teams report on:
- the quality of the work produced by the school
- the educational standards achieved by the school
- whether financial resources made available to the school are well managed
- the spiritual, moral, social and cultural development of pupils at the school.

Before an inspection:
- The school has to arrange a meeting between the inspectors and the parents of children at the school so that the inspectors can hear the parents' views.
- School governors and staff, including the head, cannot attend the meeting unless they have a child at the school.
- Parents may also be sent a questionnaire and the results of this will be included in the inspectors' report.

After an inspection:
- The inspectors meet the governors to discuss their findings.
- Within six weeks, the inspectors must send a written report and summary to the governing body, the LEA and Ofsted.
- Copies of the summary must be sent to parents.
- The full report along with the summary must be made available to anyone who asks for a copy. The full report is also available on the Ofsted web site: www.ofsted.gov.uk/reports

What the governors must do

After receiving the report, the governors have 40 working days to prepare a plan showing how they will respond to the aspects of the report's findings that need action. They must send copies of their action plan to Ofsted, the LEA, members of the school staff and all parents.

Schools with problems

In some schools, standards cause concern. The inspectors will place them in one of three groups:
- those requiring special measures, which could lead to the school being closed down
- schools with serious weaknesses, which are given a year to improve
- underachieving schools.

The governors of such schools have to make detailed proposals about how they will improve them. They must be given extra support by their LEA and be closely monitored by the LEA and by Ofsted inspectors.

What parents can do

If you, as a parent, are concerned about the inspection and its results, read a copy of the full report (see above). The crucial section is the list of recommendations.
- To help you to understand these, ask the school for a copy of the Ofsted framework document and handbook, which contain guidelines on how inspectors monitor school quality. You can also download them from the Ofsted web site: www.ofsted.gov.uk/publications
- Check the governors' action plan, which should have been sent to you. If you are still worried about what is in the report and plan, ask the governors to hold a meeting for parents so that you can express your concerns.
- Read the governors' annual report to parents, in which they must report on the progress of the action plan. If progress is too slow, ask the governors to hold a meeting for parents so that you can state your worries and ask questions.

YOUR CHILDREN'S EDUCATION

HOLIDAYS IN TERM TIME • TRUANCY • SCHOOL PHOBIA • SPECIAL MEDICAL NEEDS

When family holidays overlap with term time

Q We want to take our children for a family holiday during term time, but the school won't allow it. Can we just go?

A Probably not. By law, parents can ask the school for permission to take a child on a family holiday for ten school days during the school year – but the head can say no.

To take children away without permission, and beyond the ten-day limit, would be unauthorised absence. You could be reported to the local education authority (LEA) for this. The school cannot take action against you or your children, however, and your LEA would be unlikely to do so.

Try contacting the governors to explain your case, although they may refuse to interfere with the head's decision.

When a shopping trip is also truancy

Q I took my daughter shopping on a day when the school was closed and we were stopped by the police. Can they do that?

A Not if the school was closed – and you can complain to the police. They carry out periodic 'truancy sweeps' during term time to return children to their schools. But forces should be informed when local schools close, and it should be easy for them to check which school a child they have stopped attends. You could ask your child's teacher how the school warns the police about closing days.

Parents who often take their children out of school without permission or good reason (see box, opposite) are likely to receive a warning from the school. If the children then fail to attend regularly, parents can be prosecuted and fined or even imprisoned.

Prosecuting parents for a child's school phobia

Q My son suffers from school phobia. His teacher says the authorities will take me to court if he is absent often. Can they do that?

A Probably not, because a child who is ill cannot be forced to go to school. Parents have a legal duty to see that their children attend school regularly, arrive on time and stay for the whole session. The law is the same for all schools.

If teachers notice that a child is often absent, they have to report this to the local education authority (LEA), which can order parents to see that the child goes to school, or ask the courts to do so.

Parents who fail to obey can be fined or even sent to prison. So to avoid any risk of prosecution, you need to work with the school to help your child.

School phobia (now called 'school refusal') is a recognised medical disorder and you should begin by asking your GP for a medical report. Then arrange to see the child's teacher or the school head to explain the problem. Show the teacher or head the medical report and ask for support.

If your son is medically unfit to attend school for a long time, the LEA and his school have to provide education, perhaps through home teaching. Alternatively, you can educate him at home, but you must be able to prove to LEA inspectors that you are giving a proper education.

ACTION PLAN

1 Ask your doctor or the head to refer your child to a specialist in school refusal, who may be an educational psychologist. The specialist can plan a programme of help for your child with you and the school.

2 If teaching at home or in a special unit is recommended for a time, ask the school to refer you to the Education Welfare Family Counselling services, who can arrange it.

Providing for special medical needs

Q **My child suffers from asthma, and has a serious attack each time he faces a test or exam. We have asked if there is some other way he can be assessed, but the school says no. Can they do that?**

A No. Under the Special Educational Needs and Disability Act 2001 (see p375), schools may not treat pupils less favourably because of a disability,

---

REASONS FOR ABSENCE FROM SCHOOL

It is reasonable for a child to miss school because of an appointment with a dentist or optician, but parents who take their children shopping on a school day are helping them play truant. Prosecution is likely if this happens often, because truancy is believed to be a cause of low educational standards. Absence rates are published in the school league tables.

LEGITIMATE REASONS FOR TIME OFF SCHOOL

Medical Illness or an appointment with a doctor or a medical specialist. The school can ask for medical certificates, but these are not legally required for absences of less than two weeks.

Unavoidable cause Apart from a serious emergency, the cause must relate to the child, not the parent, so a child cannot legally be made to stay at home to look after a sick parent.

Religious observance Children may stay away on days set apart by their parents' religion – such as the Eid festival for Muslims or the Jewish Rosh Hashanah.

Transport The local education authority (LEA) must provide transport to school in certain legally defined circumstances (see p356). In these situations, lack of transport can be a valid reason for missing school.

Entertainment licences Pupils with an entertainment licence (see p368) may miss school for rehearsals and to take part in plays, films, television and radio programmes and advertising.

Interviews An interview for a job or at a school or a college.

Family holiday Parents and carers can ask the school or governing body for up to ten school days' leave of absence during term time for an annual holiday.

Exclusion When a pupil is formally excluded from the school by the head (see p379).

Special occasion Schools have discretion to allow an absence for an occasion such as a family wedding or funeral.

Since 2000 it has been possible for parents of truanting children to be fined up to £2500 or imprisoned for up to three months.

---

and they must take reasonable steps to ensure that disabled pupils are not made to suffer severe disadvantage. A child whose asthma is so severe that it handicaps his or her performance in exams could fall within the scope of the Act.

Every school must have a policy about how it helps children with special medical needs. The examining boards also make special arrangements. ▶

ACTION PLAN

1 See your GP, who may refer your son to a specialist for treatment. A consultant's report will influence his teachers to take his condition seriously.

2 Ask to see the school's policy on children with special needs. If the consultant reports that your son's disability is interfering with his progress, his teachers must do all they can to help him. For example, the teachers may rely more on course work for assessment.

3 Ask the school to report your son's disability to the examining bodies, who may then be prepared to give more weight to course work.

Help with a special educational need

Q My daughter needs extra help with reading and writing. The school says it doesn't have the staff for this, so she is falling behind with her work. Can they let this happen?

A No. By law, schools have to help all pupils, including those who find it hard to learn compared with children of the same age. All should have full access to the curriculum, and children with special educational needs (SEN) must be helped to realise their potential.

To oversee this, the school must have a SEN coordinator, to work with staff and parents to support SEN pupils. The coordinator can draw on specialist advice and training, and help the school to work out an education plan for the child in consultation with the parents.

The governing body should appoint a governor or a sub-committee to ensure that children with special needs are

identified and their requirements met. No school has a right to claim lack of funds for SEN. The local education authority (LEA) formula for allocating funds includes an element based on the number of pupils with special needs in each of its schools.

ACTION PLAN

1 Ask to see the school's written policy on SEN, then ask for a meeting with your child's teacher and the SEN co-ordinator to discuss how to support her.

2 If you are not satisfied, ask to see the governor responsible for SEN, explain your concerns and ask how the proportion of the school's budget that is given for special needs is spent. If you are not satisfied with the governor's response, make a formal complaint to the governing body.

Assessing special educational needs

Q My son has poor coordination and attention deficit disorder, but his teacher says the school doesn't have the resources for an assistant to help him. Can they refuse to support him?

A Possibly not, but you or the head must first ask your local education authority (LEA) to carry out a statutory assessment (see box, opposite). If the assessors think your son's case is severe enough, they may issue a written special educational needs (SEN) statement, obliging the LEA to provide the resources.

If the authority refuses to make an assessment, or to issue a statement, you can appeal to an independent tribunal (see p17), the Special Educational Needs

HELP FOR SPECIAL NEEDS

Help for children with special educational needs (SEN) is graded according to the child's need and the school's ability to meet it. There are three levels:

Level 1: School action
Teachers give the child appropriate extra help as part of their normal classroom role.

Level 2: School action plus
The school has to call in specialist help from outside agencies to help children make better progress in normal classes at school.

Level 3: Statutory assessment
If a child is still not making satisfactory progress, the school and parents may apply to the LEA for a 'statutory assessment'. This is an investigation by an educational psychologist and other professionals into the child's need for support (see below).

For full information, see the government's special educational needs code of practice. You can download it from: **www.dfes.gov.uk/sen**

HOW A STATUTORY ASSESSMENT IS MADE

To apply for a statutory assessment, you write to the LEA or submit a request through the school's SEN coordinator. You should be given the name of an officer at the LEA, who will advise you and keep you informed of what is happening.

The LEA will first of all ask for evidence that, despite everything the school has done, difficulties remain. Evidence includes:
- an assessment by the school of the child's needs
- a statement of the measures the school has

already taken to try to meet those needs
- reports of the child's levels of academic achievements and rate of progress at school
- an assessment of the child's behavioural, emotional and social development
- reports from professionals such as educational psychologists and specialist support teachers.

The whole process of getting a statutory assessment may take up to six months.

1 The evidence
The LEA studies the evidence, then decides that:
- a statutory assessment is appropriate for the child
OR
- the child's needs are being adequately met under existing arrangemants, so a statutory assessment is not necessary.

2 The assessment
The experts make the assessment, and then decide that:
- a 'statement of special educational needs' is necessary for the child
OR
- no extra measures are needed.

3 The statement
The LEA experts write a statement of the child's needs and of the provisions required to meet them. This statement of special educational needs is reviewed each year.

4 Transition plan
At the age of 14 a reassessment is made and a transition plan worked out to prepare the child for adult life. This plan is reviewed annually until the child leaves school.

and Disability Tribunal (SENDIST) ▶ ⌫. You can also appeal to the tribunal if you disagree with the contents of the statement, or if your LEA does not fulfil the obligations the statement imposes. For its part, the tribunal can:
- dismiss the appeal
- order the LEA to make a statement,

change a statement already made, or reconsider its position.

If you need help with your appeal, ask your LEA to put you in touch with its parent adviser or a parent partnership scheme. Or contact the Independent Panel for Special Educational Needs Advice (IPSEA) ▶ ⌫. ▶

ACTION PLAN

1 See your son's teacher and the school's SEN coordinator and ask for backing for an LEA assessment (see box, p373).

2 If the LEA refuses an assessment, or makes an assessment but decides not to issue a statement of special needs, ask the school to appeal to the Special Educational Needs and Disability Tribunal (SENDIST; see p372). If the school is unwilling, contact the parent support officer at your local LEA and ask how you can make an appeal to SENDIST.

3 If SENDIST turns down your appeal, consult a solicitor about taking legal action against the LEA.

Providing for pupils with disabilities

Q **Our son is physically disabled and in a wheelchair, but we would like him to attend a local mainstream school. I've heard that the head doesn't accept disabled children. Can he refuse?**

A Probably not. If your son has a statement of special educational needs (see box, p373), and your preferred school is named in the statement, the head is obliged to admit him. Even if he does not have a statement, it is likely that the school will have to accept him. Since April 2003, schools must have an accessibility plan showing how they plan to provide access for people with physical disabilities. Also, by law, all children with special needs should be educated in a mainstream school if the parents want it, unless catering for them involves unreasonably expensive building work or would seriously disturb the other pupils' lessons.

Check the school's prospectus for details of whether it prioritises children with particular physical disabilities and what support it offers. Check also the booklet published by your local education authority (LEA), which lists all the schools in the area and their provision for disabled children. If you are having problems with your preferred school, is there another one that might be suitable for your son?

You could also consider applying for your son to be 'statemented' (see box, p373). If successful, it would maximise his chances of getting into the school.

ACTION PLAN

1 If your son is not admitted to the school, write to the school or LEA, insisting on an explanation of why he was refused ▸ ✍. The school and LEA must be able to show that the refusal is reasonable under the Disability Discrimination Act (see box, right).

2 If you think the refusal unreasonable, you can appeal to an independent admissions appeal panel (see p354).

Discrimination and school trips

Q **Our son really wants to go on a school trip to France, but he is diabetic who needs regular insulin injections and the school does not want to take responsibility for him. Can they refuse to let him go?**

A No, because the school would be treating your son less favourably than other pupils. According to the Disability Discrimination Act (see box, right), it cannot justify this if making a reasonable adjustment would have enabled your son to go on the trip.

Staff can argue that by law they do not have to administer prescription medicines or injections. With advice from a doctor, however, they can learn to do so. In some schools, senior staff are trained to give medicines and injections.

Remember that, while responsible for a child, staff have a legal duty to act as a reasonable parent would, and that includes giving medication both in school and on school trips if it is needed.

Schools must publish a policy document setting out their plans for helping pupils with special medical needs, and you can ask your son's teacher for a copy.

For more information, consult the Code of Practice for Schools published by the Disability Rights Commission ▶☐, which explains the duties owed to disabled pupils. You can download it from the commission's web site.

ACTION PLAN

1 Tell the head of your concern that your child is getting less favourable treatment than other pupils because of his disability. If your son can inject himself, explain this to the head and get a note from your doctor to confirm it.

2 If the head is uncooperative, write to the governors ▶✎. They must ensure that discrimination does not occur in the school and are liable for the actions of staff that might be construed as discrimination.

3 If the governors support the head, appeal to the Special Educational Needs and Disability Tribunal (SENDIST; see p373).

THE DISABILITY DISCRIMINATION ACT

HOW THE ACT DEFINES DISABILITY
People are disabled if they have a physical or mental impairment that has a substantially adverse effect on their ability to carry out normal daily activities.

WHAT THE ACT SAYS
● It is unlawful to treat a disabled child less favourably than other children just because of a disability. Therefore, all reasonable steps must be taken to change policies, practices or procedures that place a disabled child at a substantial disadvantage compared with children who are not disabled.

● In certain circumstances, it may be justified to treat a disabled child less favourably than a non-disabled one. But there must be a clear connection between the reason given and the circumstances of the particular case, and the reason must be a substantial one.

Proving health and safety negligence

Q **Our son was concussed when he fell off builders' equipment that had been left in the playground. The school governors deny all liability. Can they do that?**

A No, if you can show that the accident happened because the school was negligent. The government's health and safety regulations say that schools must assess safety risks on their premises and take steps to prevent accidents.

Your son's school or the local education authority (LEA) will have public liability insurance that covers the school if it has to pay compensation for injury. But an insurance company will only pay compensation for an accident, however serious, caused by negligence.

To prove that the school was negligent, you will have to show that:
● your son was in the school's care when the accident happened – that is, during school hours or during a school activity. Ask the head for the earliest ▶

GOLDEN RULE

Only allege sexual or other misconduct by school staff if you have some evidence – never on the basis of rumour alone. Allegations made against school staff by pupils or parents can cause grave damage to the careers and reputations of school staff, even when mistaken. Also, if an allegation can be shown to have been false or malicious, the teacher could take legal action against you.

and latest times the school is responsible for supervision – usually 15 minutes before the start of the school day and 15 minutes after it ends
• the school did not provide reasonable supervision, or the premises were not safe. Most schools have lunchtime supervisors, and heads arrange for teachers to supervise children in the playground during morning and afternoon breaks
• the accident happened because the school did not take necessary steps to prevent it, and not because your son behaved exceptionally badly.

ACTION PLAN

1 Ask to see the accident report, which the school should have made, to see whether the school was responsible.

2 Ask the head whether the builders' equipment was dangerous and securely fenced off. Bear in mind that warning children not to go near the equipment may not be considered sufficient precaution.

3 Ask about the level of supervision at the time, in case the school claims that

the accident was your son's fault. Teachers must take the same care of pupils as parents normally would.

4 Gather medical reports and evidence from your son's school records that his performance has deteriorated since the accident.

5 Write a letter of complaint to the school governors ▶ ✍.

6 If the governors are unsympathetic or the insurance company will not pay, contact the Law Society ▶ 🖙 to find a solicitor specialising in negligence who will start a legal action for you.

What to do if you suspect sexual abuse

Q I have reason to believe that my son's school football coach may be abusing him. We also hear rumours about him in our area. Can we do anything?

A Yes. If you have talked the matter through with your son and are convinced that what he is telling you is true, you should make an allegation against the coach to the school. Ask to speak to the senior staff member appointed by the governors to deal with cases of suspected child abuse.

This teacher will interview you and perhaps your son, and will record your allegations as statements, which you will be asked to sign and date.

The teacher should then:
• explain to you what is likely to happen
• inform the staff member concerned about the allegation
• inform the school's chair of governors
• work with agencies such as the police.

CHECKS ON STAFF

Private individuals cannot check police records about people. But heads of schools and other educational institutions can, as can organisations such as the Scout or Guide Association.

School authorities must vet anybody who has regular contact with pupils under 19, including volunteers (such as parents who help children with reading or with sports clubs) and the staff of firms contracted by a school:
• to see that their names are not on List 99, a list held by the Department for Education and Skills (DfES) with details of teachers who are unsuitable to work with children
• by the Criminal Records Bureau, to make sure that they have no convictions that would make them unsuitable to work with young people. For more information, contact the Criminal Records Bureau ▶ 🖙.

DRUGS IN SCHOOL

Possessing and supplying 'controlled' drugs – drugs that are prohibited under the Misuse of Drugs Act 1971 – is a criminal offence, but the police have discretion to apply the law less rigorously with the possession of cannabis. Education about drugs is a compulsory part of the science national curriculum.

School policy

- Schools must have a written policy on alcohol, smoking, solvents and drugs, which should comply with legislation dealing with drug abuse. It should be published in the school handbook.
- Ultimately, it is the head's responsibility to ensure the safety and well-being of all pupils. But there should be a senior member of staff who is responsible, together with the head, for implementing the school policy on drugs.
- Many schools make a distinction between possessing and supplying prohibited drugs. Possession usually attracts a lesser punishment; pupils caught supplying drugs would normally be excluded permanently.
- Staff should be aware of the symptoms of abuse, and of the substances involved.

When a pupil is caught

- The head should tell the parents immediately if a pupil is caught with drugs.
- In drugs-related cases, schools have to take into account the school's published policy, the law and the needs of the child and other pupils.
- The school must report criminal activity to the police. The police should respond as set out in their agreements with local schools.
- Schools often work on the principle that a warning from the police can be more effective in preventing abuse than their own school sanctions.
- The governors must be informed of incidents of drug or solvent abuse.

Further information

- *Protecting young people* is a booklet on education about drugs in schools and youth organisations, published by the Department for Education and Skills (DfES) in 1998.
- **Drugscope** (www.drugscope.org.uk) is a charity providing help and information. Its booklet, *The right responses*, is about managing and making policy for drug-related incidents in schools.
- **The National Drugs Helpline** is 0800 77 66 00.
- **The Department of Health** drugs web sites are www.doh.gov.uk/drugs and www.doh.gov.uk/alcohol
- **The Health Development Agency** web site at www.hda-online.org.uk

The school will hold its own internal investigation. If your suspicions seem likely to be true, the school head will probably inform the police and give them your statements.

ACTION PLAN

1 Write down what your son told you, then try to check the facts. Ask your doctor for a medical report on your son's physical and mental condition.

2 Speak to the teacher responsible for child protection, who has a legal duty to investigate. Ask to be told the outcome of the investigation.

3 If you feel that the school has not taken the matter seriously, make a complaint to the local education authority (LEA). And if you are still dissatisfied, complain to the social services, police or NSPCC ▶▭.

How to appeal if your child is excluded

Q **Our son has been excluded permanently from his school for making what the school describes as abusive telephone calls to a teacher. We are upset because we don't think his offence merits such a harsh punishment. Can we oblige the school to take him back?**

A No, but you can appeal. Also, if you think your son has been wrongly accused, you may wish to clear his name even though you do not want him to return to the school.

Appeal to the governors' discipline committee, which in any case has to meet to consider the exclusion (see box, right).

The committee may:
- uphold the exclusion
- overthrow it and reinstate your son

OH COME ON! HE SAID HE'S SORRY!

- decide that the exclusion was unjustified, but that relationships between the school and the family have broken down to such an extent that it is in no one's interests for the child to stay at the school. The LEA would then find another school for your child.

If the committee upholds the exclusion, you can appeal to an independent appeals panel (see p354).

For more information, see the booklet, *Improving Behaviour and Attendance: Guidance on Exclusion from Schools and Pupil Referral Units*, published by the Department for Education and Skills (DfES) ▶ ▭ – you can download it from www.teachernet.gov.uk/exclusion

ACTION PLAN

1 If you feel the exclusion is unjustified write to the governors saying that you want to appeal ▶ ✎ . The governors' discipline committee will offer you a date for a hearing.

2 To prepare for the hearing, note down the ways in which you think the official guidelines have not been followed (see box, right), and the good points about your son's record at school.

3 If the committee refuses your appeal, you have 15 days to submit it to an independent appeals panel (see p354). The panel must hear the appeal within 15 days of receiving it.

4 The panel's decision is final and binding. If it confirms the exclusion, the local education authority (LEA) has to find an alternative school place for your child, or provide education outside school. In exceptional cases, the panel may adjourn without a decision – for example, if the police are involved.

WHAT HAPPENS WHEN A PUPIL IS EXCLUDED

Heads have the right to exclude pupils for a fixed period or permanently. In either case, the parents must be informed immediately of their child's exclusion. Pupils who are excluded may not enter the school premises. Their behaviour during the exclusion is not the school's responsibility but if they are excluded for a fixed period, they should be set work to do.

Fixed-period exclusion
• If a pupil is excluded for more than five days in a term, or if the exclusion would result in the pupil missing a public examination, the school must report the exclusion to the school governors and the local education authority (LEA), as well as to the pupil's parents.

• A pupil cannot be excluded from school for more than 45 days in a year unless the exclusion is permanent.

• Parents can appeal against a fixed-period exclusion.

The governors' discipline committee must meet about fixed-term exclusions only if the parents ask to make a representation such as an appeal.

Permanent exclusions
A head should exclude a pupil permanently only as a last resort or for a very serious offence. If a school excludes a pupil for misdemeanours such as poor attendance or disruptive behaviour, the head must be able to show that all other possible strategies were tried before exclusion.

A head can decide to exclude a pupil for a first or single offence if it includes:
• serious actual or threatened violence against another pupil or a member of staff
• sexual abuse or assault
• supplying an illegal drug
• carrying an offensive weapon.

The governors' discipline committee must meet within 15 school days of the exclusion being imposed, whether or not the parents appeal.

Allowing time for investigation
A pupil should not be excluded in the heat of the moment if there is no immediate risk to the safety of others or to the pupil.

The governors must ensure that:
• the incident has been properly investigated
• all the evidence has been considered, taking into account legislation on discrimination and the school's policies and rules
• the pupil has had a chance to give his or her version of events
• the incident was not provoked – for example, by bullying or racial harassment.

Ensuring an appropriate response
The school must inform the police when a pupil is excluded permanently after committing a criminal offence. But the school must weigh up a number of factors before resorting to exclusion, including:
• the age and health of the pupil
• pressure from parents or peers
• how severe the offence is and whether the pupil is likely to repeat it
• whether the pupil's behaviour affects other pupils
• whether the offending behaviour took place in school or out, and if out, whether it had a serious impact on the school
• the pupil's school record.

When exclusion is inappropriate
Exclusion should not be used as a punishment for:
• minor incidents, such as failure to do homework or to bring dinner money
• poor academic performance
• non-attendance or lateness
• pregnancy
• inappropriate dress or appearance, including hairstyles and wearing jewellery, unless this is an act of defiance and other measures have failed
• offences that took place outside school hours and away from the school, even if serious, unless they affect the school
• punishing pupils for their parents' behaviour – for example, by extending a fixed-period exclusion until the parents agree to attend a meeting.

Getting serious about a joke

Q **My employer is open about monitoring emails, as we're in a service industry where fraud or errors could cause problems. In spite of this, a few people have fun sending joke emails to colleagues. The management have now warned that even opening such emails could result in disciplinary action. Can they do that?**

A Probably not. Employees might be disciplined for sending or forwarding offensive emails – for example, ones that are obscene or make unpleasant comments about other members of staff. But it is very unlikely that disciplinary action against an employee for merely opening one would stand up in court or a tribunal (see p17). Moreover, the fact that your bosses are monitoring emails for fraud or error – which they are entitled to do (see p277) – does not allow them to do so for other purposes. So any information they gain in this way cannot be used to discipline people for circulating particular kinds of email, unless these involve fraud or error.

If your company is serious about restricting employees' access to offensive material by email or on the Internet, it must issue a written policy document. The document should state clearly what is regarded as offensive, how the policy will be monitored and what disciplinary action will be taken if anyone breaches it.

Private Internet use in the office

Q **I'm going on holiday with a friend. We've exchanged emails about our plans – marked 'Personal' to avoid confusion with work-related**

HOW TO AVOID OR BLOCK SPAM

Spam is usually defined as any unsolicited ('junk') email – whether commercial, political or pornographic. Some organisations use a narrower definition, excluding ordinary marketing emails so long as they are legal.

- Do not give your email address to anyone except personal and business contacts, and organisations you trust not to pass it on to others.
- Take particular care about giving your email address in chat rooms, news groups and forums; use a separate email address for these.
- Operate 'spam discipline'. Delete without opening any email if you do not know the name of the sender or recognise the message heading.
- Never try to 'unsubscribe' from an unwanted spam message. This just confirms that your email address is valid, and encourages the spammer.

- Consider using a spam filter – spam-blocking software – although this may have limited success. Some spam may get through, while some messages you want may be blocked.
- Consider registering with the US email preference service www.dmaconsumers.org, which is comparable with services in the UK that deal with junk mail (see box, p393). Bear in mind, though, that personal data it holds is not covered by the UK Data Protection Act.
- For more information, visit www.spam.abuse.net, www.cauce.org and www.spamhaus.org

emails – and during my lunch hour I've been using my office computer to find good package deals on the Internet. Yesterday, my boss noticed me doing this, and threatened to sack me if she caught me surfing the Web or sending personal emails again. Can she do that?

A Almost certainly not. According to the Data Protection Code on Monitoring at Work, 'intrusions [by employers] into the private lives of individual workers are not normally justified unless the business is at real risk of serious damage'. Although you have no absolute right to use your employer's computer or Internet access, banning you from making any kind of limited personal use in you own time would count as an intrusion into your private life.

If you think your boss was unaware of the circumstances, consider explaining to her that you were using the Internet only during your lunch hour. You could also use an alternative email address, rather than your office address, to receive private communications at work.

WORD OF WARNING

Your employer may be justified in monitoring your Internet use and emails (see p277), but you should be told if this is so. Also, the law is clear that employers should not open any email marked 'Private', 'Personal', 'Confidential' or 'Union business', unless they are helping the police in an investigation – for example, into suspected fraud.

A computer is swamped with unwanted emails

Q I'm finding my computer flooded with more and more email messages advertising get-rich-quick schemes or dubious-sounding products, some of which are offensive. Can I stop them?

A Probably not totally, although you can reduce the number of messages – known as 'spam' (see box, opposite). Above all, give your email address only to people and organisations you trust.

Under the European Directive on Privacy and Electronics Communications (2002/58/EC), introduced on October 31, 2003, EU companies must not send spam unless the recipient agrees in advance to receive it or is an existing customer of the sender (in which case the customer has to opt *out* of receiving spam). The same rules apply to the mobile phone equivalent of spam (see question, p393). However, spam is a worldwide problem, and EU laws have no effect on spammers in non-EU countries, many of which have no or very weak controls on spamming.

Many Internet service providers (ISPs) offer spam-filtering services, and mailservers (computers that distribute emails within a company) can use databases of known spammers to block unsolicited messages. But these are rarely entirely effective.

PROTECTING YOUR PRIVACY

COOKIES • INTERNET SAFETY • WORK REFERENCES • DATA PROTECTION

Information planted in your computer

Q **Some web sites I visit plant 'cookies' on my computer. I'm concerned about viruses, and don't want to be bombarded with these. Can they do this without my permission?**

A Yes. There is no legal bar to web sites using cookies, and many do, but you can control whether your computer accepts or keeps them.

A cookie is a short piece of text sent to your computer when you log on to a web site, which can be re-read by the site when you log on again. It may be used simply to count how many people visit a site, or to identify users – either by simply recognising you as a previous visitor, or (if you give the site personal details) by identifying you personally, so that you do not have to type in your details and password each time.

There are two basic types of cookie:
● 'persistent cookies', which last and are reactivated each time you visit a site
● 'session cookies', typically used by web sites with 'shopping carts' (which let the site keep track of your purchases). These last only for the duration of one visit.

It is almost impossible for cookies to transmit viruses because they contain only text. (A virus must be 'executable' – that is, act as a computer program, which text files cannot do.) But they can be used in ways that may infringe privacy. For example, by tracking web use, cookies let advertisers send you banner advertisements reflecting your interests.

If you object to the use of cookies as an infringement of your privacy, you can view those stored on your computer and remove any or all of them. You can then set your Internet browser software to reject any more or to notify you when you are about to receive one. But, some sites will not allow you to log on if you refuse all cookies, and others may be less convenient to use.

For more information on cookies, visit www.privacy.net, www.cookiecentral.com and www.allaboutcookies.org

Child-safe Internet access

Q **The other day I found my 11-year-old son looking at a totally unsuitable web site. I can't look over his shoulder all the time. My neighbour says there's nothing I can do about it. Is that true?**

A No. Although there is no foolproof way to make the Internet totally safe for your child, and little legal protection except against child pornography and other illegal material, you can reduce the risks by taking a number of steps:
● Keep the computer in a room where you can see what your son is doing, and limit the time he spends on the Internet.
● Explain the dangers to him. Make sure he understands the risks of using chat rooms to make friends (who may not be who they seem) and of opening emails from unknown senders (which may contain unsuitable material or viruses).
● Consider using commercial filtering software or an Internet service provider's filter. Determined children can often get round such filters, so they are not fail-safe.
● Look at the safety advice provided by the Internet Watch Foundation (IWF) ▶ 🖃 and the NCH (originally the National Children's Home) ▶ 🖃.

If you find sites you think may be illegal, because they are obscene, violent or show child pornography, report them to the IWF, which can trace the server and report the site to the police.

A full reference is not an automatic right

Q Some colleagues and I have been made redundant. When I asked for a reference the personnel manager said he would only give details of my dates of employment and job title. Surely, this could prejudice my chances of a new job. Can I insist on a full reference?

A No. Many big companies now restrict references to the basic facts. This is a result of the growing number of legal cases brought by employees who feel aggrieved because of comments made about them in references.

Employees have no right to see a reference from the organisation that *gives* it (see question, p268). But they can ask for a copy from the employer who *receives* it, so long as it is handed over in a form that does not identify who wrote it.

Need to register under the Data Protection Act

Q I'm secretary to an amateur choir, and keep basic personal data for our 100-odd members on my computer. Do I have to register under the Data Protection Act?

A No. Non-profit organisations are exempt from the legal requirement for organisations holding personal data to register with the government's Information Commissioner (see box, right). But you have to observe the Act's requirements about the lawful handling of data. For example, you must keep the information confidential and secure.

To confirm that you are exempt from registering, check the *Notification Handbook* and the leaflet *Notification Exemptions – A Self-Assessment Handbook*, both available from the Office of the Information Commissioner ▶☞.

HOW PERSONAL DATA IS PROTECTED

The Data Protection Act 1998 establishes what kind of information companies and other organisations are allowed to hold about people and how they must handle that information. It also lays down your rights to check what data organisations hold about you and to have it corrected, if necessary. A government-appointed Information Commissioner regulates and enforces the Act's provisions.

What the Act says
Data held about people must:
- be accurate
- not be excessive for the purpose for which it is held
- be kept confidential and secure, and not be kept for longer than necessary.

Bodies holding personal data – called 'data controllers' – must notify the Office of the Information Commissioner ▶☞ of their existence, pay a subscription and be listed in a public register. Exceptions to this rule are families holding data about their family members, people compiling public registers, and not-for-profit organisations.

How to check the data held about you
1 Write to the organisation that holds the data, asking for access under Section 7 of the Data Protection Act ▶✎. You have the right to be told:
- what information is being held about you
- why it is being held
- to whom it is being disclosed.

2 If the data is inaccurate, ask the organisation to correct it.

3 If the organisation fails to give you access to the data or to correct it, contact the Information Commissioner to make a formal complaint. Ask the Commissioner either to take steps to force the organisation to grant access or to correct the errors. If this is not done, consult your local Citizens Advice Bureau ▶☞ or Law Centre ▶☞, or a solicitor (see p20) about suing the organisation that holds the data.

Freedom of Information Act
The Information Commissioner also enforces the Freedom of Information Act 2000, which lays down rights of access to information held by public authorities, such as government departments, and metropolitan and local authorities.

For information on data protection
Contact the Office of the Information Commissioner ▶☞ and the Campaign for the Freedom of Information ▶☞.

PROTECTING YOUR PRIVACY

CONFIDENTIALITY • PERSONAL INFORMATION • IDENTITY FRAUD • MONEY-LAUNDERING

Idle gossip breaches confidentiality

Q I've heard that my solicitor's secretary has been talking about my pending divorce to a mutual friend. Can she do that?

A No. Solicitors have a strict duty of confidentiality towards their clients that extends to their staff. A breach of confidentiality, if reported to the solicitors' regulatory body, the Office for the Supervision of Solicitors (see p170), could result in the solicitor being disciplined. You could also sue the solicitor for damages.

There are a few exceptions to the rule of confidentiality. For example, solicitors may disclose information if they suspect their clients of money-laundering (see question, opposite) or of other criminal activities such as fraud or child abuse. The solicitors' code of conduct is available from the Law Society ▶ ⌨.

ACTION PLAN

1 Complain to your solicitor about the conduct of the secretary.

2 If you are unhappy with the solicitor's response, ask to make use of the solicitor's complaints procedure.

3 If the response seems unsatisfactory contact the Law Society's Office for the Supervision of Solicitors ▶ ⌨.

Your right to see a medical report

Q A few weeks ago I applied for life insurance. The insurer asked for a medical report from my doctor, and I agreed and signed a release form, allowing my report to be seen by a third party. Now the insurer says I have to pay a higher premium, presumably because of something in my medical record. Can I see what the record says?

A Yes. Your doctor must keep the report for six months after it is written and must let you see it if you ask to do so (see also question, p112).

The Data Protection Act 1998 (see box, p383) gives you the right to see all information about your physical or mental health recorded at any time in the past by a health professional involved with your care.

Where medical reports are produced by a doctor for reasons such as insurance or employment:
• Your insurer or employer should ask your permission before contacting your GP and tell you what your data protection rights are.
• Your doctor should wait 21 days before sending the report to the insurer or employer, so you have a chance to see it

THIS THING I'VE GOT IS IT CONTAGEOUS?

MEDICAL RECORDS

first. If you want a copy of the report, your doctor has a right to charge a fee.

For more information, see the medical section of the web site of the Information Commissioner (see box, p383) or of the human rights group Liberty ▶ 🕮.

A financial adviser is getting personal

Q When we went to a mortgage broker to discuss a loan for our new house, she asked us a number of personal questions – about our health, for example, and our plans to start a family. None of this seemed to have anything to do with house-buying, and we thought it rather intrusive. Can she do that?

A Yes. Not only is it legal, it is a requirement for financial advisers to get a full picture of your financial affairs and other relevant personal details before giving you advice. If they do not have the full picture, they might give you inappropriate advice, for which they could later be held liable.

You can refuse to give this information, but the adviser may want you to sign a letter saying you did not want to disclose your full circumstances. The purpose of this is to protect the adviser against a possible later charge of mis-selling.

Somebody pretended to be me to get credit

Q I've been refused credit to buy a TV set. When I asked why, the finance company said I was the subject of an 'identity theft' warning. Can it do that?

A No. If someone has been trying to impersonate you – 'identity theft' – to get goods or credit fraudulently – 'identity fraud' – there will probably be a

record of your name in files held by a body called the Credit Industry Fraud Avoidance System (CIFAS) ▶ 🕮. This should act only as a warning; it may slow down your application, but should not, by itself, block it.

First approach CIFAS for a copy of your file record. If there are any errors, ask the finance company that recorded the entry to correct it. If you are dissatisfied, contact CIFAS and ask to use the organisation's complaints procedure.

If you think you may be a victim of identity fraud, ask CIFAS for 'protective registration' (which shows that you yourself filed the warning). This should not be necessary if a financial institution filed a correct report that your identity was used fraudulently by someone else.

Money-laundering checks on investment

Q I recently wanted to start a personal pension plan with a lump-sum contribution. The firm asked for proof of my identity, but I don't drive, don't have a passport, and the utility bills are in my partner's name. They won't accept anything else. Can they do that?

A No, but they do have a right – in fact, a duty – to establish that you are who you say you are. Providing bank statements or paying with a personal cheque should be good enough, possibly backed up by a letter from an employer, doctor or other 'person of standing'.

By law, clients of financial institutions must give evidence of identity when they make investments of more than £10,000. The aim is to prevent the 'laundering' of money by criminals to disguise its origins. The checks can seem heavy-handed, but in your case the problem may have arisen because an employee was following rules set out in a manual. Ask to speak to a manager and explain your situation.

PROTECTING YOUR PRIVACY

OFFICIAL CALLERS • DOORSTEP CALLERS • BAILIFFS

Can you refuse to let callers into your home?

Q My grandmother lives alone. Last week a man in overalls knocked on the door, saying he was from the gas company and needed to check her supply. She asked to see his ID, but he just flashed a card at her, which she couldn't see properly. She refused to let him in, and he drove off. Can she refuse to let official callers into her house?

A Yes. People can refuse to admit anyone into their homes, with few exceptions (see box, opposite). Firefighters and engineers from gas, electricity and water companies can enter forcibly in an emergency. Callers from other bodies, such as the council, must show identification, which includes a photograph.

Utility companies will also prearrange the date and time of a visit. Many will give vulnerable people such as disabled people and elderly people and women living alone a password they can use to identify their caller.

Reputable doorstep salespeople follow the National Doorstep Cold Calling Protocol (see p39), under which they must show an identification card, which includes a photograph and the name and logo of the organisation they represent. They must say they will not enter your home without your permission.

A right to banish doorstep callers

Q I work from home and am regularly disturbed by doorstep callers selling things or wanting to do odd jobs such as re-fix crooked roof tiles. Is there any way I can stop them?

A Yes. You can put up a clear sign – for example, 'No hawkers' – showing that you do not want unsolicited callers. This removes their 'licence' to enter your land. If they do so, they are trespassing (see box, p307), and you might be able to take legal action against them or the firms they represent.

In practice, if callers persist in spite of a sign, your best course of action is to tell them firmly that you are not interested. Reputable doorstep salespeople follow the Cold Calling Protocol (see p39) and will not call again if asked.

A visit from the bailiffs

Q I've just discovered a letter to my husband from a firm of bailiffs saying that they'll be calling to take goods to pay his debts. Can they just walk into the house and help themselves?

A No. You do not have to let the bailiffs into your home and, except in specific circumstances (see box, opposite), they cannot force their way in – for example, by breaking down a door. They can enter the house by non-violent means – for example, if you let them in, or they find an open window or unlocked door.

Bailiffs can force their way into premises with no living accommodation such as a detached garage or workshop, and can climb over a wall or fence to do so.

If the bailiffs call and harass you, for example, by calling repeatedly or in the night, tell them you will complain. Bailiffs must abide by the code of conduct of the Enforcement Services Association (ESA) ▶ ⌂, which requires members to comply with regulations, maintain client confidentiality and respond to complaints. The ESA has a complaints ▶ p388

WHO CAN ENTER YOUR HOME?

A number of bodies have the right to enter your home in certain circumstances. But very few are allowed to force entry, and all of them must:
- have a legitimate reason for entry
- produce evidence of identity
- in some cases give you notice, and are then permitted to visit only at a reasonable hour
- leave your property secure after forcible entry.

The police can enter – by force if necessary – if they have a search warrant (see box, p21). If they have no warrant and ask permission to enter, that permission has to be given in writing for the search to be lawful.

The fire service can force entry into a property where there is (or is believed to be) a fire. Firefighters can also enter neighbouring premises.

Local authority housing officers can enter for various reasons, such as to enforce a compulsory purchase order or notices to repair or demolish. They need written authority and must give 24 hours' notice, but it is an offence to obstruct them.

Private landlords cannot usually enter a rented property without prior agreement with the tenant, except in an emergency (see question, p215).

Gas and electricity companies can enter in an emergency, or for other purposes with a warrant – for example, to disconnect your supply because of non-payment of bills.

Water companies can enter premises to inspect water meters, to investigate illegal use of water, or in emergencies.

Planning and rating officers can enter your house to inspect it, but only after giving notice. It is an offence to obstruct them.

Tax officers can get a warrant to enter a property if fraud is suspected.

Customs & Excise officers can enter premises without a warrant to investigate suspected VAT offences. They can enter by force, seize documents and search individuals.

TV licensing officers can enter if they have a search warrant. If you have no television it may be in your interest to let them see that this is true, but they may make repeated visits to re-check.

Bailiffs (see below).

WHAT BAILIFFS CAN AND CANNOT DO

There are two types of bailiff. County court bailiffs are official court employees who enforce court orders and judgments, often for debt. There are also private bailiffs who hold a certificate from a court to collect fines or to enforce the payment of debts, such as rent arrears on behalf of landlords.

Bailiffs must:
- follow the Enforcement Services Association ▶ 🕮 code of conduct
- carry an identity card and show it on request
- visit at a reasonable time of day
- leave premises safe after entry
- not undervalue property to be seized
- sell property they seize at the best price.

They may:
- enter a house through an open door or window
- force entry, once inside the house, into any other part of the property
- break into non-domestic premises, such as a shed

- make a charge for their services, which is added to the amount owed by the debtor
- make a forcible entry if the debtor defaults on a 'walking possession agreement', which postpones seizure of property while the debtor pays an agreed regular amount.

They must not:
- enter a house by force on a first visit – except for bailiffs for the Inland Revenue and Customs & Excise, who can get permission for forcible entry
- threaten the householder or use bad language
- seize tools, books or vehicles necessary for the debtor's employment, or items that are in use at the time they enter
- take fixtures and fittings or goods that are rented or on hire purchase – but they can take goods bought on credit
- take goods belonging to anyone except the debtor
- seize 'essential' items such as clothing, bedding or necessary household equipment.

PROTECTING YOUR PRIVACY

POLICE POWERS • CUSTOMS SEARCHES • CCTV

GOLDEN RULE

Try to rationalise debt problems at the earliest possible stage through a debt management agency (see p155). If you leave it until the bailiffs call, they will deduct their fees from the money they raise from selling your goods.

procedure through which you can ask for an apology and repair of any damage. You could also phone the head of the firm they work for or the clerk of the court or council that employed them. If they commit an illegal act, call the police.

ACTION PLAN

1 Contact your lenders to try to make an arrangement with them (see p155). If this fails, lock all doors and windows.

2 If you know when the bailiffs are coming, ask someone to be with you as a witness. Make written notes of what happens and what the bailiffs tell you.

3 Phone the bailiffs' office to try to agree a 'walking possession agreement', by which you keep the goods they want to seize and pay the debt in instalments. If you do not then pay regularly, the bailiffs can break into your home to take the goods.

Police powers to stop and search

Q Our son was coming back from a rock concert when he was stopped in the street by the police. They made him empty his pockets, saying they were searching for 'prohibited articles'. Our son has never broken the law and he felt humiliated. Can the police do that?

A Possibly, if they had 'reasonable grounds for suspicion' under the Police and Criminal Evidence Act 1984 (usually called PACE) and the code of practice issued by the Home Office ▶ 🕮 under that law.

The police do not have powers to stop and search anyone they wish. They must suspect that the person (or group) they

intend to stop has stolen or prohibited articles – including firearms, knives, other weapons or drugs. This suspicion must not be based on skin colour, age, style of dress or previous convictions known to the police. It must have some factual foundation, such as suspicious behaviour.

The human rights group Liberty ▶ 🕮 suggests that if you are stopped by police officers who clearly intend to search you, you should ask for an explanation. If the answer is unsatisfactory, you are within your rights to refuse your consent. If the police still insist on searching you, you can make a complaint.

ACTION PLAN

1 Go to any police station, ask to see the senior officer on duty, describe the search and say you want to complain. If you prefer, you can see your local Citizens Advice Bureau ▶ 🕮 or Racial Equality Council ▶ 🕮, who will forward your complaint.

2 Your complaint will be investigated by a senior police officer of the Professional Standards Department of your local police force.

3 You will be told the outcome of the investigation. If you wish, you can appeal to the Police Complaints Authority ▶ 🕮.

Stopped at port and treated like smugglers

Q We recently went on a trip to France to buy wine for my 50th birthday party. As we came back into the UK we were stopped by Customs. We tried to explain, but the car and the party drinks were seized, and we still haven't got our car back. Can they do that?

A Yes. Government guidelines allow you to bring in large quantities of alcohol and tobacco for your own use – contact HM Customs & Excise ▶ 📖 for up-to-date details. But if Customs & Excise believe you are bringing them in for commercial purposes – such as reselling them in the UK – they may seize the goods and your vehicle. Carrying goods for friends who then reimburse you – or even contribute to your travel costs – counts as a commercial purpose.

The customs officers should have asked why you had the goods, and how often you go on such shopping trips – making several trips within a few months is likely to raise their suspicions.

If you think the seizure was unjustified, you can appeal. Meanwhile – or if you do not appeal – you can ask Customs & Excise to 'restore' (return) the car and the goods. You usually have to pay the duty and VAT owing, and perhaps a fee.

ACTION PLAN

1 Write to the office that seized your car within a month of the seizure, explaining your position and asking for the return of the goods and car. Without this 'notice of claim', Customs can dispose of the car and the goods after 45 days.

2 Once you have made your claim, Customs will apply to a magistrates' court (near the port) for a magistrates' court hearing to decide if the seizure was justified. You can represent yourself or use a solicitor.

3 If the magistrates' court hearing finds in your favour, the goods and car will be returned to you. If the magistrates' court hearing finds that the Customs officers did not have good reason to make the seizure, you will be awarded costs. If the court does not find in your favour, the car and goods will not be returned to you and you will have to pay costs.

The prying eye of a closed-circuit camera

Q There's a storage depot at the bottom of our garden protected by closed-circuit TV. One of the cameras points directly towards our property. We feel it invades our privacy. Can we make the company move it?

A Possibly. Contact a manager at the company that owns the storage depot, explain the situation and ask for the camera to be re-angled.

If the company will not move it, speak to your council planning department to see if planning permission was sought to put up the camera. If permission was granted, consult your local Citizens Advice Bureau ▶ 📖 , Law Centre ▶ 📖 or a solicitor (see p20) about contesting it.

The camera may also be an 'actionable nuisance' that disturbs your peaceful ▶

LOOK! THEY'VE TRAINED THEIR CAT TO SIT ON OUR CCTV CAMERA!

PROTECTING YOUR PRIVACY

PRIVACY AND THE MEDIA • STALKERS

enjoyment of your property (see pp178-179). It may be possible to use the Protection from Harassment Act 1997 (see box, opposite) to pursue a complaint. You should take legal advice (see p20).

Unfairly treated on television

Q **I took part in a discussion on a proposed bypass for our town on a local TV programme. But I feel that I wasn't given a fair chance to present my views and was made to sound ridiculous. My complaint to the station was ignored. Can they do that?**

A No. You should complain in writing ▶ ✍ to Ofcom (the Office of Communications) ▶ 📖. Ofcom now considers all complaints about standards

COURSE, IT'S THE POOR LITTLE RABBITS I WORRY ABOUT

STOP THE BYPASS

TV

in radio and terrestrial and satellite television that used to be handled by the Broadcasting Standards Commission (BSC), the Independent Television Commission and the Radio Authority. This includes matters of fairness and privacy.

If Ofcom believes that your complaint is within its remit, its officers will study tapes of the programme, and ask each side for their comments. In some cases, a hearing may be held before a decision is made to uphold or reject the complaint. Ofcom then decides what redress you may be due, ranging from a written apology to an apology broadcast on air.

Children interviewed without permission

Q **Some of the teachers at my son's school held a one-day strike, and a number of the children staged a march in support. The local paper interviewed and photographed my son, and published a story under a rather lurid headline. Now I'm worried that he may be victimised by the headmaster or non-striking teachers. Can the editor do that?**

A Probably not. All newspaper editors agree to a voluntary code of practice administered by the Press Complaints Commission (PCC) ▶ 📖.

One of its strongest sections concerns children. It says that children under 16 must not be photographed or interviewed on 'subjects involving the welfare of the child' without permission from a parent or other responsible adult. Another clause forbids journalists and photographers from approaching or photographing pupils at school without the permission of the school authorities.

ACTION PLAN

1 Complain in writing to the editor of the newspaper, who should reply within a week ►✍. Send a copy of the letter to the PCC.

2 If you get no satisfactory response, write as soon as possible to the PCC ►✍. Enclose a copy of the publication.

3 The PCC will, if your complaint seems justified, take evidence from you and the editor of the paper, and will try to negotiate a settlement – a printed apology, perhaps. If this is not possible, and the PCC finds in your favour, it will issue an adjudication, which the newspaper will have to print in full and prominently.

Harassment by a stalker

Q A couple of times recently, on my way home from work, I've noticed a familiar face. I think it's a former boyfriend with whom I had a rather difficult break-up. I'm now afraid he may be trying to harass me. Can he do that?

A No. Harassment by stalking is illegal (see box, below). If it continues, report it to the police, who may issue a warning to the stalker or prosecute him.

If the stalker is persistent, you have the right to bring a civil case (see p17) against him. You will have to show that any reasonable person acting as the stalker ►

PROTECTION FROM HARASSMENT

The Protection from Harassment Act 1997 is known as the 'Stalker's Act' but is directed at curbing all types of harassment, not just stalking. For example, it protects against harassment by the media, neighbourhood disputes and domestic violence. The Act identifies two criminal offences:

● **causing harassment, alarm or distress** Anyone convicted faces six months in prison or a fine of up to £5000, or both.

● **causing fear of violence** Two convictions can result in a five-year prison sentence or an unlimited fine, or both.

Protection against stalking
You can sue a stalker under this Act. The court may issue an injunction (see p21) against the stalker to stop the harassment and may award cash damages and compensation.

Where to find help
The following organisations and web sites offer useful guides to the law on harassment and advice on how to deal with stalkers. They also give information on the psychology of stalking and whether a stalker is likely to become dangerous:
● www.harassment-law.co.uk
● www.lancslinks.co.uk/dv/the_law.asp
● www.met.police.uk/stalking/advice.htm
● Community Legal Service ►▱ (see p13)
● Network for Surviving Stalking ►▱
● Press Complaints Commission ►▱
● Suzy Lamplugh Trust ►▱

Protection from press harassment
If you find yourself at the centre of a news story and pestered by the media:
● Ask them formally to withdraw. Say that if they do not withdraw they are in breach of the Press Complaints Commission's code of practice, and you will complain.
● Fax or email the same statement to the editors of the publications they represent.
● If you can, give your version of the story by writing a statement and pinning it to your door with a note that you do not want to talk to journalists. Fax or email the statement to the editors.
● If the harassment continues, call the 24-hour helpline of the Press Complaints Commission (PCC) – 07659 152656. The Commission will contact the editors urgently to try to stop the harassment.
● The PCC cannot award damages. You should ask your local Citizens Advice Bureau ►▱ or Law Centre ►▱, or consult a solicitor (see p20), for advice on suing for damages.

PROTECTING YOUR PRIVACY

UNWANTED PHONE CALLS • JUNK FAXES • MAILING LISTS • TEXT MESSAGES

GOLDEN RULE

If you want to reduce the amount of junk mail you receive, take the following steps. Whenever you give personal details to a marketing organisation – when you buy something by mail order, for example, or fill in a questionnaire on the Internet – tick the box(es) saying that you do not want to receive further mailings from that or any other company. That will reduce the amount of unsolicited mail you receive.

did would have realised the likely effect of such actions. For this, you need to gather as much evidence as you can – keep letters and recorded messages, for example. Tell friends and colleagues about your suspicions, and contact a support organisation (see box, p391) for personal help and legal advice.

ACTION PLAN

1 Collect evidence that the law has been broken: keep notes and gifts from the stalker; make notes of when and where incidents occur, and what happens. Try to get a friend to witness any incidents – and, if it can be done safely and discreetly, take photographs.

2 Contact your local Citizens Advice Bureau ▶ 🖂, Law Centre ▶ 🖂 or a solicitor (see p20) about taking legal action against the stalker.

Dealing with intrusive phone calls

Q We're often disturbed just as we're sitting down to dinner by phone calls from kitchen fitters, double-glazing companies and the like. Can they do that?

A Yes, but you can take steps to stop them. The Telecommunications (Data Protection and Privacy) Regulations 1999 cover unsolicited marketing calls

(called 'cold calls'). They say that individual phone subscribers (but not companies) can opt out of receiving unsolicited direct-marketing calls. To do this, you register with the Telephone Preference Service (TPS) ▶ 🖂, which is like the Mailing Preference Service (MPS) for direct mail (see box, opposite).

Once your details are listed with the TPS, direct marketers cannot contact you by phone. If they do so, say you are registered with the TPS and tell them not to phone again. If you tell a company this and are still getting marketing calls from its representatives after 28 days, you can complain to the TPS. You can also complain to the Office of the Information Commissioner (see box, p383), but you must show evidence, such as an email or a fax, that you asked the organisation not to call.

Putting a stop to junk faxes

Q I have a fax machine at home. Lately I've started receiving unsolicited faxes advertising various products. Can companies randomly send out faxes like that?

A No. The Telecommunications (Data Protection and Privacy) Regulations 1999 (see previous question), which cover faxes, say that individuals have to give their consent ('opt in') before direct-marketing companies can send them unsolicited faxes. If you have not given consent, the sender of the fax is breaking the rules.

You can also register with a Fax Preference Service (FPS) ▶ 🖂, which works on similar lines to the Telephone Preference Service (TPS; see previous question). A company that directs its employees to contact phone subscribers whose details are listed with the FPS infringes the Telecommunications (Data Protection and Privacy) Regulations 1999.

For further information visit the web site of Ofcom (the Office of Communications) ▶ ➪.

WORD OF WARNING

Some junk faxes give a number to fax to stop receiving further unsolicited faxes. Beware: the number given may be charged at a high premium rate.

Removing details from a mailing database

Q **Last year I bought a shirt from a mail-order company. Since then I've been inundated with advertising not just from that company but also from others. When I contacted the original company to ask them to take me off their mailing list, they said they couldn't remove an individual name from their database. Is that true?**

A No. Almost all reputable direct-marketing companies belong to the Mailing Preference Service (MPS; see box, right). A condition of membership is that they agree to remove addresses registered with the MPS from their files.

Simply write to the company to say that you do not want to receive its advertising. It is legally obliged to comply with your request.

Unwanted text messages

Q **My daughter has a mobile phone, which she's always using to text her friends. She tells me she gets advertisements by text and has shown me a few of them. Some of them seem inappropriate for her. Can I stop them?**

GETTING OFF MAILING LISTS

To remove your name from direct-marketing mailing lists, register with the Mailing Preference Service (MPS). It is a registration scheme for consumers who do not want to receive unsolicited advertising by mail and is run by the Direct Marketing Association ▶ ➪ on behalf of the Office of Communications (Ofcom) ▶ ➪. The scheme is voluntary for advertisers, but it is a requirement of the Direct Marketing Association's code of practice that its members must screen their mailing lists regularly against the MPS's Mailing Preference File. The Information Commissioner (see box, p383) supports the MPS.

How the MPS works
All member companies (look for the MPS logo in advertisements) undertake to remove MPS registered addresses from their files.

When the MPS does not work
• If you are a policyholder or a customer of a direct mail advertiser – for example, if you bought something from the advertiser's catalogue or donated to a charity that uses direct mail – the MPS will not work. You must write to each company or charity to say you do not want to receive mail.
• The MPS scheme will not stop unaddressed bulk mail or items addressed to 'the occupier'. It will help only with mailings that are addressed to you.

To register
Contact the MPS ▶ ➪ and register your surname and address. Registration lasts for five years.

A Yes. Unsolicited text messages are treated in the same way as unwanted emails – 'spam' (see question, p381). The European Directive on Privacy and Electronics Communications 2002/58/EC says that you must agree ('opt in') to receive such messages unless you are a customer of the sender, when you must 'opt out'. The Information Commissioner (see box, p383) regards such messages as unsolicited phone calls under the Telecommunications (Data Protection and Privacy) Regulations 1999 (see question on faxes, opposite).

To opt out of receiving such texts, you can simply tell the sender, but it is better to register with the Telephone Preference Service (TPS) ▶ ➪.

INHERITANCE DISPUTES

Possession can be proof of a gift

Q Ten years before she died, my mother gave me some of her antique furniture as a way of reducing inheritance tax liability, and I took the furniture home. She wrote me a letter confirming the gift at the time, but I've lost it. I'm told that, as I haven't got any proof of the gift, it will be regarded as part of her estate and taxed accordingly. Can this be right?

A No. You removed the furniture to your house at the time of the gift ten years ago, so your possession of the furniture is enough to show that your mother had given you an outright gift. If you have dated photographs showing the furniture in your home, or receipts in your name and quoting your address for work such as re-upholstering or repairs, that should be ample to show that you have had use of the furniture ever since.

WORD OF WARNING
If you give a house, or furniture, to someone but keep it for your own use without paying a fee to the recipient, it will be included in your estate for inheritance tax purposes, although exceptions are made if a trust is involved.

Cheque must be cashed before giver's death

Q A few days before she died my mother gave me a cheque for £6000, in order to use her tax-exempt gift allowance for this year and last year. I failed to pay in the cheque before she died, and the bank has told me that it's now too late to cash it. Is that right?

A Yes. The sum will not qualify as a lifetime gift for inheritance tax purposes as the gift was not completely handed over (in theory the cheque could have been stopped and the gift revoked).

When a bank is notified that one of its customers has died, the mandate to operate that person's accounts are frozen immediately. Any cheques against those accounts that have not been cleared will be halted, and those for normal debts will have to be settled by the executors (see Glossary, opposite, and p401).

THE SEVEN-YEAR RULE ON GIFTS

Lifetime gifts of money, property, antiques or other valuable items are called Potentially Exempt Transfers (PETs), because if you live for seven years after making the gift, your estate will not pay inheritance tax (IHT), or 'death duties', on those gifts when you die.

If you die within three years, IHT is payable in full. If you survive between three and seven years, the percentage payable is reduced. Leaflet IHT2, *Inheritance Tax on Lifetime Gifts*, from the Inland Revenue ▶ 📖, explains how to calculate the tax on a PET.

The transfer must be an outright gift to qualify. If the giver retains an interest, it counts as a 'gift with reservation', and is included in the estate for IHT calculation. For instance, if you give away your home and continue to live in it rent-free, or hand over a holiday home and retain the right to use it free of charge, it will be included in your estate. But if you agree to pay a market rent to continue living in your home or stay in the holiday home, it will qualify as a PET.

Contesting a gift to a non-family member

Q During his final years, my father made several very large gifts to his carer. I think he was of unsound mind at the time and may have been influenced by her. Can I recover the gifts?

A Possibly. In cases where it is alleged that someone used undue influence to persuade another person to hand over large sums of money before his or her death, the burden of proof lies with the person making the allegation. You will need strong evidence for making a claim of this type.

If the case reaches court, the court will look at your father's mental capacity at the time he made the gifts, and whether it can be shown that the carer exercised undue influence over him. If the court finds in your favour, it may order the carer to return the gifts.

ACTION PLAN

1 Ask your father's doctor about his mental state, and talk to other people who had contact with him.

BUT WHAT UNDUE INFLUENCE COULD I POSSIBLY HAVE HAD OVER HIM?

2 If you think you have evidence for a claim against the carer, seek advice from your local Citizens Advice Bureau ▶ ▭ or Law Centre ▶ ▭ or consult a solicitor (see p20).

GLOSSARY

Administrator The person or firm who administers the estate of someone who died intestate; the equivalent of an executor.
Beneficiary Anyone receiving anything from a dead person's estate under a will or trust.
Bequest Gift made in a will.
Codicil A document changing the terms of a will but not forming a will itself.
Estate All the wealth and belongings of a person who has died, including cash, investments, land, property, cars and personal belongings.

Executor The person or firm (such as a bank or firm of solicitors) appointed in a person's will to administer the estate – to pay taxes, settle debts and so on, and then distribute what remains as set out in the will (see p401).
Intestate Describes a person who dies without having made a valid will (see box, p411).
Issue Children, grandchildren and other descendants.
Legacy A gift of cash or personal property made in a will.

Letters of administration Official authority to administer an intestate person's estate; the equivalent of probate.
Probate Official authority (in the form of a document issued by the Probate Registry) to administer an estate (see p399).
Residue What is left in an estate after taxes, debts and specific bequests have been paid.
Trust An arrangement by which people – trustees – own and administer all or part of an estate for the benefit of others, such as children (see box, p414).

INHERITANCE DISPUTES

A LOST WILL • INVALID WILLS

Where to look for a person's will

Q I know my mother wrote a will but I can't find it among her belongings. I've been told that if I'm unable to locate it, my mother's estate will be distributed according to rules set out by law. Is that true?

A Yes. You need to find the will. If no will can be found, it will be presumed that she destroyed it deliberately and her possessions will be distributed according to the intestacy rules (see pp412-413). It is just possible that a court may overturn this presumption if you can produce evidence that your mother did not destroy the will (see box, right).

ACTION PLAN

1 Assuming that you have looked for the will among your mother's papers and favourite hiding places around the house, contact banks where she had accounts and any firms of solicitors that she has used, to ask if she deposited her will with them.

2 Write to the Record Keeper's Department of the Principal Registry of the Family Division ▶ 📖 , asking for a search to be made of the archives. Your mother may have deposited her will there herself for safe-keeping. Enclose a copy of the death certificate. The will can only be released to one of the executors named in it.

3 If no will was lodged at the Principal Registry, write to all local banks and solicitors. Also ask at banks and security vaults whether your mother had a safe deposit box.

An out-of-date will is accidentally revived

Q Some time before my aunt died, she talked about having rewritten her will, but I can only find a much older version. It contains clauses I know she wanted to change. I've been told that if I can't find the more recent will, the earlier version will automatically be revived. Can I stop it being used?

A Possibly. If a will cannot be found, it is usually presumed that the person who wrote it must have destroyed it and intended that it should be revoked. It is possible to challenge this presumption, but only if you can produce some

RECONSTRUCTING A MISSING WILL

If a will cannot be found and there is no evidence that it has been formally revoked, the registrars at the district probate registries have powers to gather information to reconstruct its contents – for instance, by:
- referring to a copy or a completed draft of the will
- reviewing statements from people who were told about its contents by the dead person.

Evidence is needed that the will was properly signed and witnessed. The witnesses, or the solicitor who drew up the will and was present when it was signed, may confirm this. If they have died or cannot be traced, the law presumes that the will was signed and witnessed correctly.

If the will cannot be reconstructed, the intestacy rules come into play (see pp412-413).

evidence that the will existed and was not revoked. For example, your aunt may have referred to the new will shortly before she died. This information would be reinforced if there was a witness to the conversation, or if you could find a draft copy of the will.

ACTION PLAN

1 If you have evidence of the contents of the new will, you will need to swear an affidavit (make a written statement, swear that it is true and sign it in front of a commissioner for oaths). Take advice from a solicitor as soon as possible.

2 If you find the new will or any evidence of one, make a copy of it and send it with your affidavit to the probate registrar at the district probate registry handling your aunt's will. You should do this within six months of your aunt's death. Probate registrars are district judges (solicitors who are appointed judges), who can decide on the validity of the evidence.

3 The registrar will inform you of the decision, which is final.

MAKING A WILL

Making a will ensures that your belongings go where you want them to – to relatives, friends or charities – not where the intestacy rules say they should go (see pp412-413).

FOR A WILL TO BE VALID
- You must be 18 or over, and of sound mind, when you make your will.
- The will must be in writing (either typed or handwritten). It is not essential to use a solicitor.
- You must sign and date the will. Two witnesses, who must not be beneficiaries of the will or married to beneficiaries (or they will lose their right to inherit), must also sign it. They must be present when you sign the will and sign it at the same time.

CONTENTS OF THE WILL
Your will can name a single executor – a personal representative who will distribute your estate and carry out its other terms – but at least two (but not more than four) executors are preferable. You can leave your estate to whoever you want. To avoid problems over distributing your estate, make sure that your will says what should be done with:
- your house or any other property that you own either outright or jointly with another person
- stocks and shares
- money in banks and building societies
- the benefit of any insurance policies on your life
- your personal possessions and household goods.

CHANGING A WILL
Minor changes can be made by adding a codicil – a written amendment (or a separate document). This should refer to the date of the will and confirm that the original will remains in force except for the details affected by the codicil. It must be signed and witnessed in the same way as the original will. Always take legal advice on making a codicil.

If you want to make major changes to the terms, you should make a new will, which should say that all previous wills are revoked. Destroy old wills.

TO AVOID PROBLEMS
- Tell executors that you have appointed them.
- Identify beneficiaries clearly, especially when two family members have the same name.
- Destroy out-of-date wills.
- Do not tell people you have left them something in case you change your mind later.
- Do not pin, stick, clip or attach anything to the will as this can arouse suspicion, and may slow down the probate process (see box, p399).
- Do not alter the will except by adding a codicil.

A witness did not know she was a beneficiary

Q **Last year, when a friend and I visited my great-aunt, she asked us to witness her signature on her will. She has now died. I've been told that she left me a substantial legacy, but I've lost the right to it because I witnessed her will. Can they do that?**

A Yes. You lose the right to benefit under a will if you or your spouse witnessed the will. Any bequest you were left passes to the person named to receive the residue of the estate. If you were the only beneficiary, they pass to whoever benefits under the intestacy rules (see pp412-413).

You might be able to recover your inheritance if your aunt used a solicitor or a company that specialises in writing wills to help her make the will. Several court cases have established that a solicitor or a will-writer can be liable to potential beneficiaries for losses resulting from negligence. This can include failure to ensure proper witnessing of the will by people who are not beneficiaries. You should consult a solicitor (see p20).

A will with only one witness

Q **To save money, my mother wrote her will herself, but there was only one witness to the will, not two. A solicitor tells me the will isn't valid. Can that be true?**

A Yes. The will is invalid because there was only one witness, and your mother's estate will be treated as if she died intestate (see pp412-413).

A beneficiary demands immediate payment

Q **I'm the executor of my late brother's will, which names his ex-wife as a beneficiary. She is demanding that I pay her immediately, or she will take me to court. Can she do that?**

A No. An executor (or other personal representative) cannot be compelled to pay a legacy before the end of 12 months after the deceased person's death – called the 'executor's year'.

Unless you are the executor of a small estate (see box, opposite), it is prudent not to distribute the assets until six months after probate is granted (see box, right). This is because anyone not mentioned in the will who wishes to make a claim has six months from the grant of probate to do so (see box, p407).

OH, AND I'LL NEED HER PEN BACK TOO

WILL WITNESSED BY

Such a claimant who found that the estate had already been distributed could sue the executors.

Your former sister-in-law may be entitled to interest on some or all of her bequest – it depends on whether the will states when she should receive it. If no time limit is set on a cash payment, interest is also normally payable only at the end of the 'executor's year'.

Deceased's bank charges high fees

Q My sister's will names me and her bank as her executors. I'm horrified to hear how much the bank will charge for handling the estate. Can I get rid of them as executors?

A Probably not. Executors are chosen by the deceased person and have the right to act. Only the courts can remove them, and only if they are found guilty of maladministration. Executors can renounce their appointment (see next question), so you could ask the bank whether it will give up its role.

An executor's right to resign

Q My former mother-in-law, who died recently, named me as one of the executors of her will. I'm about to move to Australia and want to resign as executor; my ex-wife tells me I can't. Is she right?

A No. As long as you have not yet performed any of an executor's duties – such as collecting the estate's assets or paying debts – you can resign (or 'renounce executorship'). If you have already performed any of these duties you will be deemed to have accepted ▶

PROBATE: THE AUTHORITY TO CARRY OUT THE TERMS OF A WILL

Official confirmation that a will is valid is called a Grant of Probate. It is issued by the Probate Division of the High Court once the will, estate accounts, a probate application form and inheritance tax accounts have been sent to a district probate registry ▶⌨. The grant of probate gives the executors named in the will the legal authority to administer a large or complex estate (see p401).

If there is no will, the estate is dealt with under the intestacy rules (see pp412-413). In this case, 'letters of administration' equivalent to probate are granted by the Probate Division to an administrator – normally a close member of the family – who takes on all the tasks of an executor.

Application for probate is made through your district probate registry. You can do this yourself (see p401), but unless the deceased was intestate, a solicitor usually applies. For the address of your District Registry look in the phone directory or visit www.courtservice.gov.uk/using_courts/wills_probate

The probate registry's role ends with the granting of probate. It does not help to administer the estate.

WHEN PROBATE MAY NOT BE NEEDED
An estate worth less than £5000 is classified as a 'small estate'. There is no need to apply for probate or letters of administration – make an appointment to see a manager at the bank and take a copy of the death certificate, proof that you are an executor and personal identification, and the bank staff will assist with the administration of the estate. When a home is held in joint names by a married couple it automatically passes to the deceased person's spouse, and does not form part of the estate, so the value of the house is immaterial – if there are few other assets, an estate will still qualify as 'small'.

Further information can be found in the booklet *How to Obtain Probate* from your district probate registry or the Principal Probate Registry ▶⌨, or visit www.courtservice.gov.uk

VALUATION OF PROPERTY FOR PROBATE

Executors should employ a professional valuer such as an estate agent or an antiques dealer to give an opinion about how much a house or other valuable property (such as jewellery) is worth, and use that figure to complete the probate forms.

The value is judged as the open market value with the property being actively marketed (not, for example, an offer from a friend or relative). The valuation is taken as at the date of death, so if house prices are moving fast and some time has elapsed since the death, the valuer must ensure that the value is back-dated. If a house is sold within four years of the date of death, the sale price will usually replace the initial valuation for inheritance tax purposes. If the house is sold for less than the probate valuation on which tax was initially paid, you have the right to claim a tax refund.

the office (merely having signed a couple of cheques for small sums will not prevent you from stepping aside). You can do this even if you told your mother-in-law during her lifetime that you were willing to act as her executor.

ACTION PLAN

1 Write a letter 'renouncing' the role of executor for your mother-in-law's will. Attach the probate application to it and send it to your district probate registry ▶ 📖. Renunciation is not effective until it is filed, so you can change your mind up to that point. The district probate registry will send you a resignation form to sign.

2 Write to the other executors informing them that you have resigned as executor.

Disagreement over a house valuation

Q I'm a beneficiary of my mother's will. The probate valuation on her house seems very high compared with other properties in the area, and it has put the estate over the threshold for inheritance tax. Can I challenge the valuation?

A Yes. As you are not an executor, you can challenge the figure accepted by the executors. They will probably have employed a valuer if the property is not to be sold, or will have instructed an estate agent to find a buyer. You will need to have a valuation carried out and compare it with the figure given by the executors' valuer.

Bear in mind that if the estate is large enough for probate to be required (see box, p399), the valuation will be scrutinised by the Capital Taxes Office of the Inland Revenue. The inspectors will want to check that the correct amount of inheritance tax is paid.

The Capital Taxes Office inspectors refer a proportion of cases to the District Valuer, who has local knowledge and will be able to form an opinion about whether the valuation seems reasonable by comparing it with similar properties in the area. ▶

THE DUTIES OF EXECUTORS

The executors named in a will act as the deceased's personal representatives. They are responsible for collecting up all the deceased's money and other assets, calculating the value of the estate, paying debts and taxes, distributing the estate between the people entitled to it in the will, and carrying out any other requests mentioned in the will.

The grant of probate (see box, p399) gives the executors the legal authority to carry out their duties. Executors can apply for the grant of probate in person or through a solicitor.

Executors are not personally liable for the deceased's debts. But if they breach their legal duties, resulting in losses for beneficiaries or creditors, they will be personally liable for those losses. Examples of such breaches include paying legacies before debts are paid to creditors; failing to collect all debts due to the estate; selling assets for less than their real value; or acting carelessly so that assets are lost.

Because of the risks, many executors – particularly of complicated estates – prefer to engage a solicitor (who has professional liability insurance) to act for them.

Unlike trustees, who can retire, executors remain responsible for carrying out their duties for life – and, in extreme cases, when they die their executor duties can pass down to their own executors.

WHEN A PERSON DIES

• **Register the death** The district probate registry, and banks and building societies where accounts are held, will each need to see an original death certificate, not a photocopy. You can avoid delays by getting several certificates.
• **Find the will** If there appears to be no will, apply to the district probate registry ▶☐ for letters of administration (see box, p411).
• **Check the will** for requests about funeral arrangements and the names of other executors. Establish how the funeral expenses will be paid.
• **Collect information about assets** You may have to write for valuations of a house or other property to banks, building societies, insurance companies, National Savings, stockbrokers and investment houses. Also collect details of any liabilities such as a mortgage and other debts.
• **Draw up a rough balance sheet** to assess the value of the estate. This determines whether you need probate (see box, p399) and whether inheritance tax (IHT) is likely to be payable.
• **Complete an IHT return** and arrange for the payment of any IHT due. It can be paid directly from the deceased's bank account if the bank belongs to the Inheritance Tax direct Payments Scheme (information from the British Bankers Association ▶☐). IHT has to be paid within six months of death, or interest will be charged. But payment can be delayed for certain assets that are not to be sold, such as land, private businesses and unquoted shares. It can be paid after probate in ten annual instalments (with interest).

AFTER THE GRANT OF PROBATE

• **Collect the estate's assets** – open a bank account for the estate, and where necessary put the deceased's home and any other property that is to be sold on the market.
• **Complete tax returns** (income and capital gains) for the deceased, and pay any tax due.
• **Pay the estate's debts**, including household debts, professional fees and any outstanding mortgage. It is advisable to advertise for the creditors of the deceased in the *London Gazette* ▶☐ and a local newspaper, giving at least two months for creditors to make claims.
• **Prepare the final estate accounts** You will need a tally of assets valued at the date of death and another on the date they were paid out or realised. If the second count is lower you may be entitled to claim a refund from the Inland Revenue; if it is higher you may have to arrange for more IHT to be paid.
• **Pay legacies and distribute the residue** to beneficiaries. Ask for receipts. If ownership of a property is to be transferred you should contact the Land Registry ▶☐ and ask for form AS1.

GATHERING A SMALL ESTATE'S ASSETS

If you need to gather funds from a small estate that did not qualify for probate (see box, p399), institutions such as banks, building societies and insurance companies will require you to complete their own release forms and have them signed by all the executors in front of a solicitor or magistrate. Insurance companies will ask to see an original copy of the death certificate.

INHERITANCE DISPUTES

SOLICITOR'S FEES • EXECUTOR'S LIABILITY • CHALLENGING AN EXECUTOR • LEGACIES

ACTION PLAN

1 Contact the Royal Institution of Chartered Surveyors ▶  for details of independent local valuers who can give an independent valuation of the property at the date of your mother's death. You will have to pay a fee for the valuation.

2 If the independent valuation differs substantially from the executors' valuation, write to complain and ask the executors to reconsider their valuation.

3 If the executors do not reconsider, contact your local Citizens Advice Bureau ▶ ⌂ or Law Centre ▶ ⌂ or a solicitor (see p20) for advice.

Querying soaring solicitors' fees

Q My father named two solicitors as his executors. The probate process is dragging on and the legal fees are mounting up, cutting into our inheritance. Can we challenge their fees?

A Probably. Beneficiaries who are left a share of an estate or the residue can query the legal bill. Those who are left an item or a fixed sum do not have the right to complain, nor do those who are already involved in court proceedings against the executors.

You should discuss your concerns with the solicitors to try to negotiate a fair fee. If you fail to agree a figure, do not pay the bill. Instead, ask the solicitors to apply to the Law Society's Office for the Supervision of Solicitors (OSS – see box, p170) for a remuneration certificate. This begins the arbitration process offered by the OSS. Your right to do this should be stated on the solicitor's bill (possibly on the reverse) or in the letter sent with it. The OSS will examine the solicitors' bill or bills and either confirm that their charges are fair or say what a fair charge should be.

If a solicitor deducts money from funds held on your behalf, you should query the bill in writing within three months.

ACTION PLAN

1 Write to complain to the solicitors. Ask them to reduce the bill by the amount you think fair. The solicitors can bill you for part-payment of the reduced bill, all the VAT and any money they have paid to third parties on your behalf. If you do not pay within a month, you will be charged interest on unpaid sums. You can avoid this by paying the bill in full but writing to say that you do this on condition that the solicitors apply for a remuneration certificate.

2 If the solicitors disagree, write to ask them to apply to the Office for the Supervision of Solicitors (OSS) ▶ ⌂ for a remuneration certificate. You must do this within one month of receiving the original bill.

3 The solicitors should send the application form for the remuneration certificate to you to add your comments. Return it promptly.

4 The OSS will send an assessment of the fee to you and the solicitors within about three months. You can ask for a reassessment if you disagree.

5 When both parties have agreed a fee, the OSS will send a remuneration certificate. It is binding on both sides and you must pay the solicitor the amount stated on the certificate, less any part-payment you have already made, plus interest.

Executors may be liable for unpaid debts

Q I'm the executor of my father's estate and recently distributed the last of his bequests. Now a garage owner says my father owed £1000 on a loan agreement to buy a car, and is demanding payment from me. Can he do that?

A Yes. Executors are personally liable for making sure that all the deceased's debts are paid in full before distributing the estate to beneficiaries (see box, p401). If you did not advertise for creditors in the local press and the London Gazette (see box, p401), you are responsible for settling the loan.

Challenging the executors' actions

Q My mother's will wasn't as specific as it might have been. I'm a beneficiary and I'm sure the executors are misinterpreting some of the terms of the will. My sister says there's nothing I can do about it. Can she be right?

A No. Executors are personally responsible for carrying out the terms of a will correctly, and beneficiaries can take them to court if they believe the executors are not acting properly. If the estate is worth more than £30,000, the case is heard in the Chancery Division of the High Court, which could be costly.

Executors are entitled to take legal advice at the estate's expense, and if they are unsure how to interpret the will, they can apply to the court for rulings on ambiguous points. If this happens, the court may seek other evidence of your mother's wishes – such as letters or conversations about what she planned to do with her estate.

ACTION PLAN

1 Write to the executors stating your concerns, enclose any evidence you have of your mother's wishes, and ask them to take independent legal advice about the interpretation of the will.

2 If you remain dissatisfied, consult a solicitor (see p20) about taking court action against the executors.

Nothing left after specific legacies paid

Q I was left the residue of my aunt's estate, expecting to be the main beneficiary, but I've been told I'll receive nothing because there isn't enough money to pay all the legacies. Can that be right?

A Yes. The residue is what is left after all the other payments have been made. If there is not enough money in the estate to pay all the debts and bequests, a strict ranking is followed.

If there is a mortgage secured on your aunt's property, it must be paid off, if necessary by selling the property. The costs of administering the estate and funeral expenses take precedence over ▶

income tax and VAT payments. If money is then short, those due to receive exact sums may get only a proportion of their legacies (see next question). Anyone named to take or share the residue receives nothing.

Not enough money to pay legacies in full

Q **My uncle was very generous in his will and made cash gifts to his grandchildren, friends, neighbours and several charities, including £5000 each to his nieces and nephews. But we're only being paid £500 each because there's not enough to pay the legacies in full. Shouldn't family members receive their full share first?**

HEY! THERE'S A QUEUE YOU KNOW!

TAX | BANK | BUILD' SOC'

R.I.P UNCLE

A No. When there is not enough money to pay all the legacies in full, the executors have to follow strict rules. First come secured debts, such as a mortgage, funeral expenses and income tax or VAT owing (see question, p403).

All beneficiaries rank equally, and if there is not enough to pay them in full, the remaining money is divided in proportion to the relative size of the legacies. In your uncle's case, it appears that all the legacies he bequeathed totalled ten times what was left in the estate after the creditors were paid, so you will receive only ten per cent of the legacy specified in the will.

Varying the terms of a will after death

Q **In his will my father left the marital home to my mother, on the understanding that she would bequeath it in equal shares to my brother and I on her death. Can we alter the terms of the will to reduce our inheritance tax liability when our mother dies?**

A Yes. If all the beneficiaries agree, you can make a deed of variation or family arrangement (see box, opposite).

Under Inland Revenue rules you have up to two years from the date of death to alter the bequests, and you must then tell the Inland Revenue's Capital Taxes Office ▶ 🕮 (which handles inheritance tax) within a further six months.

The deed of variation could change the way your parent's house is inherited. For example, it could say that the house was not owned jointly by your parents, but that they owned it as 'tenants in common' (see p413), each owning a distinct half-share, and that your father's half should be placed in a trust for the whole family.

If you do this and your mother continues to live in the house without paying rent to you and your brother, she could be considered to have retained an interest in the house and you could still be liable for inheritance tax on her death.

It is essential to get advice from a solicitor specialising in this area of the law, and possibly from an accountant.

Dispute over the identity of beneficiaries

Q My father's will left £10,000 to 'be shared equally between my grandchildren living at the time of my death'. My children were his two true grandchildren. His stepson, who he never adopted as his own son, also has two children. I think the two true grandchildren should each get half of the bequest, but the executors say it should be divided four ways. Can they do that?

A No. A reference to 'children' means any child of whom your father was the biological parent, whether or not your father was married to the mother, and any child whom he adopted, but not any stepchild. 'Grandchildren' would mean the offspring of his children, but not the offspring of his stepchildren.

Unless your father's will mentions his step-grandchildren as recipients, the bequest should go to your children. This may end up in court if your grandfather treated all four children as gandchildren.

ACTION PLAN
1 Write to the executors, saying that your father's will did not refer to the children of his stepson, and that they should not be included in the bequest.

2 If the executors disagree, seek advice at your local Citizens Advice Bureau ▶ ⌂ or Law Centre ▶ ⌂ or consult a solicitor (see p20).

Facing a bill for executors' fees

Q My late mother appointed two neighbours as executors. Neither is a beneficiary of her will, but they have now produced a big bill for remuneration as well as expenses. Can they do that?

A No. Executors cannot charge fees if the will does not authorise them to do so. But they can reclaim expenses such as travel to the probate registry, phone calls and postage from the estate.

If the executors named in the will are solicitors, they can usually charge their professional fees against the estate. Non-professional executors can pass on to the estate the costs of getting legal advice from a solicitor or a barrister.

Ultimately, you could sue the neighbours for making improper deductions from the estate.

ACTION PLAN
1 Write to the executors pointing out that they are not allowed to charge a fee, only expenses. Ask them to resubmit their bill with the expenses itemised, and to enclose receipts.

2 If the executors do not comply, seek advice at your local Law Centre ▶ ⌂ or consult a solicitor (see p20).

POST-DEATH VARIATIONS

Beneficiaries have the right to make variations to a deceased person's will as long as all the adult beneficiaries (including parents and guardians of beneficiaries aged under 18) agree. They are called deeds of family arrangement or of variation. They are a good way to redistribute the assets more fairly when someone dies intestate (see pp412-413) and can be used to reduce inheritance tax liability (see question, left). A child's share of an estate cannot be reduced without a court's permission – so if one of the beneficiaries is a child, a court hearing will be necessary before the assets can be distributed.

Rights of a foster grandchild

Q **My grandfather supported me during his lifetime even though I was his son's foster child rather than a blood relation. After his death I discovered that his will provides only for his children and grandchildren. Can I contest it?**

A Possibly. You may be able to make a claim under the Inheritance (Provision for Family and Dependants) Act 1975. This includes a category for people who were being wholly or partly maintained by the deceased directly before death. But you would have to show that you had been receiving a substantial contribution to your living costs from your grandfather in the years immediately before his death.

If your grandfather had made a financial contribution to your upbringing as a child, but you are now old enough for this to have ceased and are earning a living, your claim would not succeed.

In considering your case a court would look at the basis upon which your grandfather assumed responsibility for your maintenance. It would also consider how long he had been paying towards your upkeep.

You should seek immediate advice from a solicitor (see p20). You must lodge a dependency claim within six months of the Grant of Probate being made, unless you get special permission from a court to make a late application. To lodge the claim you apply to the district probate registry that issued the Grant of Probate, or, if the estate is worth less than £50,000, to the county court.

I DESERVE IT! IT WASN'T EASY BEING RAISED BY APES YOU KNOW!

LONG LOST SON CLAIM ON ESTATE

Equal rights for an illegitimate child

Q **I discovered only after my husband's death that he had an illegitimate child. That was a bad enough shock, but now the child is claiming part of my husband's estate. Can he do that?**

A Yes, if your husband made no will, and possibly, even if he did. The Family Law Reform Act 1987 gives legitimate and illegitimate children the same rights to inherit from their parents, grandparents, sisters and brothers, or any other relation who dies intestate. So if your husband failed to make a will, this illegitimate child would have exactly the same claim as his other children under the intestacy rules (see pp412-413).

If your husband made a will, but made no provision for this child, the child could claim under the Inheritance

(Provision for Family and Dependants) Act 1975, which states that illegitimate children have a possible claim.

There are no age restrictions, so adult offspring can bring a claim as well as young children. The courts can award weekly or annual payments, normally to the end of full-time education for a child, or a lump sum. An adult who is capable of earning a living would not normally succeed in a claim, although an exception may be made if that person had remained at home to provide full-time care for an elderly or disabled relative.

Cohabitee's right to a share in the estate

Q **My partner, with whom I lived for 15 years, died without leaving a will. He always assured me that I'd want for nothing when he'd gone, but now his estranged wife insists that she has first claim on his estate. Can she do this?**

A Yes. The estranged wife has an automatic right to the bulk of the estate under the intestacy rules (see pp412-413), but you can still make a claim for financial provision.

A surviving partner can claim against the estate as long as the couple lived together for at least two years. You could claim 'reasonable provision', which is likely to be interpreted by a court as a lump sum plus an income (see box, above right). The court will take into account your age, the length of the relationship and the contribution you made to the welfare of the deceased person's family.

A court action could be costly, so seek advice before doing anything.

ACTION PLAN

1 Consult your local Citizens Advice Bureau ▶ 🏠 , Law Centre ▶ 🏠 or a solicitor (see p20) about making a claim before taking action.

MAKING A DEPENDENCY CLAIM

If you were supported by someone who has died and feel that the will fails to provide for you adequately, you can claim for weekly or monthly payments or a lump sum under the Inheritance (Provision for Family and Dependants) Act 1975.

The Act specifies four categories of claimant:
- the surviving spouse
- a cohabitee who lived with the deceased for at least two years
- children – legitimate, illegitimate or adopted, and any other child, such as a stepchild, supported by the deceased and treated as his or her own
- others supported by the deceased such as an elderly relative, or anyone receiving regular maintenance from the deceased.

If the case goes to court, it will be heard in the Chancery Division or the Family Division of the High Court unless the estate is worth less than £30,000, when it is heard in the county court. The court will consider:
- your needs and resources
- the financial status of other applicants for a claim
- the needs and resources of beneficiaries of the will
- the deceased person's obligations and responsibilities to you
- the size of the estate
- any mental or physical disabilities, such as limited mobility or dementia, you or the beneficiaries of the will may have.

The right to make an application under this law runs out six months after the Grant of Probate (see box, p399). Anyone wanting to make a claim needs to take urgent legal advice.

---

2 Write to the probate registrar at your district probate registry giving notice of your claim. You will be told if a grant of letters of administration (see p411) is made on the estate.

3 Try to negotiate an agreement with the administrators of the estate. Say that if this fails you will go to court.

4 You have six months after lodging notice of your claim to write to the executor or administrator, to say that you are putting them on notice. This means that they cannot distribute the deceased's estate without a court's permission.

GOLDEN RULE

Writing a will is the best way to ensure that your estate goes to the recipients of your choice rather than being divided up according to the intestacy rules.

INHERITANCE DISPUTES

UNUSUAL AND SUSPICIOUS BEQUESTS • SOLICITOR'S NEGLIGENCE

Contesting the validity of a will

Q **My mother left a signed and witnessed will in which she bequeathed everything to the local cats' home. I'm convinced she wasn't acting rationally when she wrote the will. Can I challenge it?**

A Yes. For a will to be valid, a person has to be of sound mind when making it. This means that a person must not have any illness or condition that would block normal reasoning.

The person making the will must understand and remember enough to know what he or she is bequeathing and to appreciate the will's terms and its impact on relatives and others. This may

disqualify someone suffering from senile dementia or Alzheimer's disease. A person under the influence of mind-altering drugs or alcohol when writing a will would also be disqualified.

The problem in challenging such a will lies in distinguishing an eccentric will made by someone of sound mind from one whose terms are the result of mental incapacity or undue pressure. The fact that your mother left her estate to the cats' home and not her family is not enough to show that she was not of sound mind.

You should get legal advice before challenging the bequest. You will need medical evidence of your mother's state of mind when she wrote the will. The Access to Health Records Act 1990 gives executors and administrators of a deceased person's estate, and any person who may have a claim, the right to apply to the health authorities for access to the deceased's health records. You should also consult your mother's doctor.

A solicitor who helped to draw up the will should be able to give evidence of your mother's mental capacity at the time.

ACTION PLAN

1 Apply in writing to any probate registry to add a caveat, or warning, to the will. This will prevent probate being issued (see p399) until you have had a chance to put your case. No special form is needed. In your letter, give the deceased's full name and address, the date of death and your own name and address ▶✍. A caveat costs £15 and lasts for six months.

2 Try to reach an agreement with the executor and the cats' home. You may be able to use mediation (see p175).

3 If you cannot agree a way forward, you or your solicitor can issue a summons, which will be heard by your

FRAUDULENT WILLS

Virtually any deception involving a will counts as fraud – a crime, as well as grounds for a claim against the perpetrator. Examples of such fraud include inserting a clause into a will before it is signed without the person making the will being aware, or reading a will to such a person with added sections that do not appear in the printed version. It is also fraudulent to lie to someone to induce them to change a will. Fraud may give rise to either civil or criminal proceedings.

district probate registrar. You will have to prove that your mother was not of sound mind when she made the will. Both sides can present medical evidence at the hearing.

Contesting a suspicious bequest in a will

Q My father's will included a legacy of £500 to the solicitor who drew it up. Can this be fraud?

A Probably not. People who draw up a will for others have a special duty to act beyond reproach. When the person who draws up a will is also a beneficiary there is always a degree of suspicion. But if the £500 bequest to your father's solicitor is a small part of his estate, it is not grounds for suspecting fraud. You would also need evidence of some dishonesty or trickery to cry foul.

If the solicitor were set to inherit a large part of the estate, the suspicion would be much greater. In that case, contact the Office for the Supervision of Solicitors (OSS; see box, p170).

Solicitor drew up a client's will carelessly

Q My father told me that I would get half the value of his country cottage on his death. But it was owned jointly by him and his second wife, so it all went to her and I got nothing. Can I take action against the solicitor who drew up the will?

A Probably. Until recently, it was thought that beneficiaries had no grounds for action in this kind of case, but several court cases have established that a solicitor advising someone about drawing up a will owes a duty of care to the beneficiaries of the will as well.

GROUNDS FOR CHALLENGING A WILL

A will can be challenged on the following grounds.
Fitness to make a will A person who does not understand the size or contents of the estate, or the terms of the will, or does not recognise people who have a moral claim on the estate, such as family members, may be considered unfit to make a will. A person with an illness that affects comprehension, such as senile dementia or Alzheimer's disease, is considered unfit to make a will (see question, opposite).

Undue influence Anyone who would benefit under the intestacy rules (see pp412-413) can contest a will if the estate is left to someone outside the family, or to an organisation, unless the deceased took independent advice before making the will.

Unfair provisions Someone who could expect to be provided for in a will, such as a spouse or child, and has not been, can make a dependency claim (see box, p407).

As a result, a beneficiary who is deprived of a legacy through an action or omission by the solicitor can claim against the solicitor. Examples of such errors include allowing a beneficiary to witness the will (see question, p398) and (as in your case) failing to appreciate that a property was jointly owned rather than held as tenants in common (see p413). Had your father and his second wife been tenants in common, your father could have left his share separately to whoever he wanted.

ACTION PLAN

1 Ask the solicitors for details of their complaints procedure and use this to make a complaint.

2 If the solicitors do not offer redress, contact the Office for the Supervision of Solicitors (OSS – see box, p170) for advice. Although the OSS does not deal with negligence cases, its helpline (0845 608 6565) can give guidance on how to make an official complaint. You must complain within six months of receiving the solicitor's final response to your complaint.

Husband's family claim part of his estate

Q **My husband died without leaving a will. He's had no contact with his parents or other members of his family for 20 years, but now they're claiming a share of his estate. Can they do that?**

A Possibly. When someone dies without leaving a will (intestate), the estate is distributed according to the rules of intestacy (see pp412-413), as set out in the Intestates' Estates Act 1952. Under this law, the value of your late husband's estate and whether or not you had children will decide whether his family has a valid claim or not. (If he had children from a former marriage, or even if he had illegitimate children, they may also have a claim.)

If your late husband left less than £125,000, you are entitled to everything, and your husband's family and children would have no claim. If the estate is worth more than £125,000 and you have children, it is divided between you and your children, and again his family would not have a valid claim.

If your husband left more than £125,000 and you have no children, your husband's family may have a claim. You are entitled to the first £200,000 and half the residue (the remainder). The other half of the residue goes to your late husband's parents. If they have both died, their part of the residue is inherited by other relatives in an order of precedence set out in the rules.

Widow's right to keep the family home

Q **My husband had not made a will when he died. As his widow, I've been told that I can't remain in the matrimonial home because it's worth more than my share of the estate. Is this right?**

A Possibly. You may have to move out if the home has to be sold in order for the estate to be divided up correctly under the intestacy rules (see pp412-413).

You, as the surviving spouse, have the right to take the matrimonial home as part of your lump-sum entitlement under the intestacy rules, as long as it does not form part of the estate's business assets. (For example, if the home is a hotel or a farm building that was owned by your husband, this right does not apply.) You have to claim this right within 12 months of letters of administration being granted (see box,

APPLYING FOR LETTERS OF ADMINISTRATION

When a person dies without leaving a valid will, the closest relative – normally a spouse, son or daughter – can apply to the local probate registry for official authority, called 'letters of administration', to handle the estate. This is equivalent to probate (see p399). If there is any dispute over who should apply, the usual order of priority is:

A surviving spouse (but not an unmarried partner)

↓

Children or their descendants

↓

Parents

↓

Brothers and sisters, or their children or grandchildren

↓

Half-brothers and sisters, or their children or grandchildren

↓

Grandparents

↓

Aunts and uncles, or their children or grandchildren

↓

Spouses of aunts and uncles, or their children or grandchildren

↓

When the list of relatives has been exhausted the role falls to the Crown

right), and it can be overridden if the estate needs cash to pay off debts.

The home may be worth more than the share of the estate you are entitled to (see question, left), so there are various solutions if you are to avoid selling up.

• You could use your own funds to bridge any difference between your entitlement and the value of the property.

• All beneficiaries could agree a different arrangement. For example, your children might concede ownership to you, or grant you a lifetime right to live in the property, possibly in return for your guarantee that they will inherit it in full on your death. This can be done through a post-death variation (see box, p405). It must be completed within two years of your husband's death and you will need to consult a solicitor (see p20) to do it.

Siblings or their children share an estate

Q My sister never married and had no children, and she died without having made a will. Our parents have died, so I'm her only close relative. My late brother's children claim that they're entitled to a share of the estate. Can they do that?

A Yes. Under the intestacy rules (see pp412-413), because your parents are both dead, half your sister's estate should go to you and the other half to your late brother's children.

WHO QUALIFIES AS INTESTATE?

A person is classified as being intestate if that person dies:
• without making a will
• leaving a will that was not properly witnessed (see box, p397)
• leaving a will that is invalid because the person married after making or altering it (see question, p414)
• leaving a will that is invalid because the person was mentally incapable when writing it (see question, p408).

A person can be declared partially intestate if, for instance, he or she leaves a valid will making various legacies but fails to say what should happen to the residue of the estate, or if the person due to receive the residue has died and has no descendants. In such cases, the residue is dealt with under the intestacy rules (see pp412-413).

INHERITANCE DISPUTES

Beneficiaries of an intestate estate

When someone dies without leaving a valid will (intestate), the estate is distributed according to the intestacy rules established by the Intestates' Estates Act 1952. The rules are complex and you should seek legal advice, particularly if you are the administrator of such an estate (see box, p399). This chart enables you to work out, in straightforward cases, who should inherit what proportions of the estate – which depends on the estate's size and who the surviving relatives are. The distribution of an intestate estate can be rearranged through a post-death variation (see box, p405).

Q Was the deceased married at the time of death?

Yes → Is the estate worth more than £125,000?

Yes → Is the deceased survived by children?

No → Is deceased survived by parents?

- Spouse receives first £200,000 + half the remainder + household goods
- Parents share the remainder

Yes (above)

No → Is deceased survived by brothers and sisters?

- Spouse receives first £200,000 + half the remainder + household goods
- Brothers and sisters share the remainder

Yes (above)

No →

No → Whole estate goes to surviving spouse

Yes →
- Spouse receives £125,000 + income on half the remainder + household goods
- Children receive other half of the remainder

No → Is the deceased survived by children?

Yes → Estate shared equally between them

No → Is deceased survived by parents?

Yes → Estate shared equally between them

No → Is deceased survived by brothers and sisters?

Yes → Estate shared equally between them

No → Is deceased survived by half-brothers and sisters?

Yes → Estate shared equally between them

No →

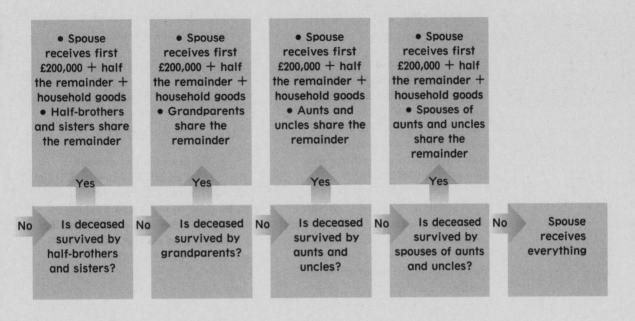

| • Spouse receives first £200,000 + half the remainder + household goods
• Half-brothers and sisters share the remainder | • Spouse receives first £200,000 + half the remainder + household goods
• Grandparents share the remainder | • Spouse receives first £200,000 + half the remainder + household goods
• Aunts and uncles share the remainder | • Spouse receives first £200,000 + half the remainder + household goods
• Spouses of aunts and uncles share the remainder | |

Yes   Yes   Yes   Yes

No → **Is deceased survived by half-brothers and sisters?** No → **Is deceased survived by grandparents?** No → **Is deceased survived by aunts and uncles?** No → **Is deceased survived by spouses of aunts and uncles?** No → **Spouse receives everything**

SPECIAL POINTS TO NOTE

- A spouse has to survive a partner by at least 28 days in order to inherit.
- If someone entitled to inherit has died, that person's share goes to his or her children.
- Illegitimate and adopted children are treated in the same way as legitimate children. Half-brothers, half-sisters, or any other relatives who share only one common ancestor, inherit only if there are no relatives descended from the same pair of ancestors.

- Many married couples hold property – especially the matrimonial home – jointly (or as 'joint tenants'). When the first spouse dies, ownership passes automatically to the survivor and does not form part of the deceased's estate.
- Some couples own property as 'tenants in common', which means that each partner owns a distinct half-share of the property. In this case the half-share goes into the estate to be dealt with under the intestacy rules.

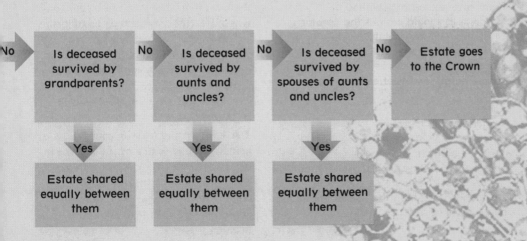

No → **Is deceased survived by grandparents?** No → **Is deceased survived by aunts and uncles?** No → **Is deceased survived by spouses of aunts and uncles?** No → **Estate goes to the Crown**

Yes   Yes   Yes

Estate shared equally between them   **Estate shared equally between them**   **Estate shared equally between them**

INHERITANCE DISPUTES

MARRIAGE • EMPTY TRUST • SECRET TRUST • TRUST TERMS

Marriage invalidates an earlier will

Q My widowed mother remarried last year, and died a few months later. She didn't make a new will after remarrying, and although her will doesn't mention her new spouse he claims he's entitled to everything she owned. Can he do this?

A Probably, but it depends how much your mother left. Marriage automatically makes any previous wills invalid. This means that your mother died intestate and her estate will be distributed according to the intestacy rules (see pp412-413). As a result your mother's new husband is entitled to a large proportion of the estate, and possibly all of it.

Even if your mother had made a will before remarrying, leaving everything to her husband-to-be, that will would be invalidated by the marriage.

An educational trust may get used up

Q My grandfather created a trust in his will to provide for my education, with the remainder to be paid to me when I reached the age of 25. On my 25th birthday I learned that all the money had gone. Can that be right?

A Possibly. It sounds as though your grandfather set up an accumulation and maintenance trust (one in which a lump sum is invested over a specified number of years) to help with your educational costs. The trust document would set out the exact terms of the trust and probably gives the trustees wide powers to advance money to pay for school fees and university costs.

It seems that the investment returns have not kept up with rising school fees and the cost of going to university. It is not unusual for all the funds in an educational trust to be used up, so that there is no lump sum left to be paid out when the trust reaches the end of its life.

The trustees are legally bound to have managed your grandfather's money prudently on your behalf and you may want to check that they have done so.

ACTION PLAN

1 Ask to see the trust accounts – as a principal beneficiary of the trust, you are entitled to do so. The trustees were probably given the right in the trust deed to charge fees, but you could check that these have not been excessive.

SETTING UP A TRUST

A trust is a legal arrangement for financial assets such as investments or property to be managed by one or more people (the trustees) on behalf of others (the beneficiaries). A trust that operates during the lifetime of the person who creates it is called a settlement; one that comes into force after the creator's death through that person's will is called a will trust.

Trusts can be created verbally and informally, but a written document is the safest and clearest method of creating one. The trust document should set out the creator's intentions clearly, and cover the following points:

- the name of the trust if it is to have one
- the names of the trustees (and who is to replace any who die or retire) and of the beneficiary or beneficiaries
- the assets held in the trust
- the duties of the trustees
- payment, if any, to be made to the trustees
- the time limit put on the existence of the trust
- the signatures of the creator and witnesses.

Take professional advice before setting up a trust. Contact the Society of Trust & Estate Practitioners ▶ 🕮 for a list of members. They are from the legal, accounting, banking and insurance professions and specialise in trusts and estates.

2 If the trustees refuse to let you see the accounts, or if you disagree with the administration of the trust, consult your local Law Centre ▶ 📖 or a solicitor (see p20) about suing the trustees for breach of trust.

The terms of a secret trust are binding

Q I had a long relationship with a married man, who promised to leave me a substantial sum of money in his will under a secret trust. The man has now died, and the person named in his will to inherit on my behalf is refusing to pass the money on to me. Can she get away with that?

A No. In a secret trust, one person (the 'nominated beneficiary') receives a bequest, but only on behalf of another person, the ultimate beneficiary. While still alive, the person who made the bequest must inform the person to whom the bequest is made that it is to be held in trust – and that person must have accepted this. The nominated beneficiary can be informed of and accept the terms of the trust verbally or in writing – merely knowing about the request and not rejecting it is enough to form a legally viable secret trust.

By allowing herself to be named as the nominated beneficiary, the person named in the will has accepted the terms of the trust and is legally bound to pass on your inheritance. If she does not, she will commit fraud and you can take legal action against her. You will be in a stronger position if you have evidence of the arrangement – perhaps if your lover talked about the terms of the will in front of a third party, who could act as a witness. Ask a solicitor for advice before taking action (see p20).

WORD OF WARNING
No one will ever know about a secret trust as long as the bequest passes from the nominated person to the eventual beneficiary as intended. But if a legal challenge is mounted, it becomes public.

Advance payment rejected by trustees

Q In her will my grandmother created a trust for me, under which I can't claim anything until my 21st birthday. I am now 18 and would like to use some of the money to pay university fees, but the trustees say I can't use the money yet. Can they do that?

A No. If the beneficiary of a trust is adult and sane, he may terminate the trust by directing the trustees to transfer the property to himself (the beneficiary) or to another person.

There are some forms of words used in trusts that attempt to prevent this, such as discretionary trusts, but it is almost impossible to create this protective form of trust in English law.

Consult a solicitor who is a trust specialist, such as a member of the Society of Trust & Estate Practitioners (STEP) ▶ 📖 .

415

INHERITANCE DISPUTES

SAME-SEX RELATIONSHIPS • UNMARRIED COUPLES • BANKRUPTCY

CHANGE TO THE LAW

In June 2003 the government issued a consultation paper proposing a civil partnership scheme under which same-sex couples could have many of the same rights as married couples.

The paper does not refer to tax, but the government says that if the proposals go ahead, registered same-sex couples might gain the same rights as married couples, including exemption from inheritance tax for gifts on death to the surviving partner.

Inheritance tax when a same-sex partner dies

Q I've been living with a same-sex partner for 20 years. My partner died recently, leaving everything to me. I thought gifts to long-term partners were exempt from tax, but I've been told that 40 per cent inheritance tax has to be paid on the estate over the tax-free allowance. Can this be true?

A Yes. Some gifts on death are exempt from tax, including anything left to a surviving spouse and gifts to charity. But this exemption does not extend to unmarried partners whether of the same sex or not.

The law may change in the future to allow same-sex couples who register their relationship broadly the same rights as married couples, and this might include the same inheritance-tax treatment (see box, left). But as the law stands, all of a deceased person's estate above the tax-free allowance (£255,000 in 2003-4) is liable for inheritance tax at 40 per cent.

Unable to get access to partner's bank account

Q The man I've been living with for 30 years has just died. Although he's been supporting me financially all these years, we had separate bank accounts. Now the bank has said that I can't have access to his bank account until the estate is settled. Can it do that?

A Yes. When someone dies, no assets can be distributed from the estate until probate is granted (see p401), and this can take months, even years. Assets that were held jointly (as 'joint tenants' rather than 'tenants in common'; see p413), are the main exception. A house or flat and a joint bank account are usually held in this way. So if you and your partner had had a joint account, the problem you face would not have arisen.

Even a surviving husband or wife has no right of access to the deceased spouse's assets, including a separate bank account, before probate is granted.

WORD OF WARNING

Relatives who suffer financial hardship as a result of bereavement can claim an allowance from the Department for Work and Pensions. But you do not have the right to claim an allowance if you were not legally married to your partner.

An unmarried partner cannot inherit a pension

Q My partner died while on a business assignment. His will stated that I should have the lump sum payable from his pension fund if he died while in employment, but the pension providers are refusing to pay me. Can they do that?

PENSION STATEMENT OF WISHES

Pension scheme members may be asked to make a statement of wishes to give the scheme's trustees guidance about what they want to happen on death. However, this statement is not legally binding. So, for instance, a man might ask for money to be paid to a new partner, but the trustees might decide to award it instead to his widow and children. Many pension schemes allow a widow's pension to be paid to a surviving partner named in the statement of wishes, and many now allow same-sex partners to be named as beneficiaries.

Check the details of your pension scheme to see what is likely to happen after your death. Ensure that your statement of wishes is up to date and reflects your current situation. But even then, the trustees of the pension fund may not carry out your wishes.

Yes. Pensions normally operate under a discretionary trust (one in which trustees have leeway to select the beneficiaries and to vary the proportion that goes to each person) and do not form part of a deceased person's estate.

This means that money in a pension scheme is not liable for inheritance tax, but the trustees have absolute discretion over who is entitled to payments. Directions in a will have no legal force. This applies to personal and company (occupational) schemes.

Write to the trustees, asking them to reconsider their decision to exclude you as a beneficiary of your deceased partner's pension. Trustees have to administer pension schemes in line with the rules, and most restrict benefits to married partners. Yet they are not inflexible, so if you can show the trustees that you and your partner shared the finances (enclose evidence of joint bank statements and household bills) – they may be able to make you an award as an unmarried partner.

Bankrupt loses his inheritance

Q **Last week I learned that I was left £10,000 in a relative's will. I'm an undischarged bankrupt, and have been told that the money will be used to pay off my creditors. Is that right?**

A Yes. Any assets, including an inheritance, which you acquired before your bankruptcy or while it is in force must be passed to whoever administers your assets during your bankruptcy – the trustee in bankruptcy or the official receiver. These assets contribute towards paying your debts. The Insolvency Act 1986 stipulates that you must tell the trustee in bankruptcy or official receiver if an inheritance or any other windfall comes your way.

The executor of your relative's will may withhold any money or valuable object left to you in the will until there is evidence that you have notified the trustee in bankruptcy or official receiver. Or the executor may pay the money into court, to be transferred through your trustee in bankruptcy or the official receiver to your creditors. An executor who paid your legacy to you directly could be held liable for part of your debt.

If the legacy is more than the amount owed to your creditors, the balance will be returned to you after the debts have been settled. But that could be any time in the future – perhaps years after your discharge – since the trustee in bankruptcy or official receiver has no obligation to deal with your assets within a specified time limit.

If your relative had died after you were discharged, you could have inherited the bequest in full.

SAMPLE LETTERS

The letters here relate to Action Plans in the preceding chapters. General advice on letters of complaint is given on pages 12 and 13.

Next to each letter is a description of its purpose and a reference to the question, or questions, to which it applies. To use a letter, follow the black type, which should apply to all situations covered by the letter, and fill in the details of your situation as indicated by the blue type, selecting the appropriate wording from the options provided. Where a list of AND/OR phrases is given, you can use just one, or any number in combination, as relevant to your problem. IF APPLICABLE indicates optional statements that may or may not apply to your situation. You can include, adapt or leave out them as necessary. Again, with EITHER/OR paragraphs, choose the one that applies to your situation.

These letters are repeated on the CD that accompanies this book. If you are taking a letter direct from the CD, fill in the parts you want to use, delete the parts you do not need, and then print the letter out.

BUYING GOODS/BUYING SERVICES/BUYING & OWNING A CAR

Rejecting goods or a car under the Sale of Goods Act 1979 (as amended) or asking for free repair or replacement under European law.

See questions, pp23, 28-30, 32, 33, 33-34, 38, 245-246

Dear [Name of person]

Re: [Product brand and model/model number if available]

I bought the above [product] from [name of store/showroom] on [date]. When I [describe when you first noticed the problem] I found that [describe problem].

IF APPLICABLE:
When I bought the [product], I [said I needed it to/was assured that it was... describe precise specifications]. This was not the case.

EITHER:
Under consumer legislation, you are required to supply goods that are [of satisfactory quality AND/OR fit for the purpose intended AND/OR as described AND/OR match the sample I was shown – choose as appropriate]. The [defect/problem] described above shows that you are in breach of contract and I would like [a full refund/compensation – explain exactly what you want], to which I am legally entitled.

▶

418

OR:
As this product was inherently faulty at the time of sale, you are required under European consumer law to replace it or to offer a free repair. I would like you to [repair/replace] it as soon as possible.

I enclose a copy of the original sales receipt.

Please respond within the next 14 days. If I do not receive a satisfactory response by then, I will take further action.

Yours sincerely…

Dear [Name of person]

Re: [Description of product/service/work/car, and contract number if available]

On [date] I [ordered/booked] [details of product/service/work/car].

IF APPLICABLE:
[Describe what was said or written into the contract at the time about the purpose or timing of the product/service/work]

Despite [describe what you have done so far]…
EITHER:…the [product] has still [not arrived/been delivered].
OR:…you/your company has still not started work.

I now consider time to be of the essence of this contract and I would like this [product/service/work] to be [supplied/carried out/started/completed] by [insert date – a reasonable time ahead]. If it is not, then I will cancel the contract and [owe you nothing/require a full refund].

Please reply within 14 days giving me a date when you will [have the item available/deliver the product/start work/complete the work].

Yours sincerely…

Stating time is of the essence for delivery of goods or car, supply of service, start or completion of work.

See questions, pp25-26, 55, 58, 74, 242

SAMPLE LETTERS

BUYING GOODS/BUYING SERVICES/BUYING & OWNING A CAR

Follow-up letter to head office if you are not offered a refund or replacement by a shop.

See question, pp33-34

Dear [Name of person]

Re: [Product brand and model/model number]

I bought this [product] from your branch in [address of shop] on [date]. When I [describe when you first noticed the problem] I found that [describe problem].

EITHER: On [date] I took the [product] back to the shop...
OR: On [date] I contacted the shop by telephone...
...and explained the problem. [Name or job title of person you spoke to] said [describe the response] and refused my request for a [refund/repair/replacement].

EITHER:
Under consumer law you are required to supply goods which are [of satisfactory quality/fit for the purpose intended/as described/match the sample I was shown]. The [defect/problem] described above shows that you are in breach of contract and I am therefore entitled to a full refund.

OR:
Under European consumer law you are required to replace this [name of product] or offer a free repair. I would like you to [repair/replace it] as soon as possible.

I enclose a copy of the original sales receipt.

Please reply within the next 14 days. If I do not receive a satisfactory response by then I will take advice on claiming a [refund/free replacement/free repair].

Yours sincerely...

Claiming compensation for damage caused as a consequence of something breaking down.

See question, pp46-48

Dear [Name of person]

Re: [Product brand and model/model number]

I bought this [product] from [name and location of store] on [date]. [When I got it home/Once it was installed/Three days later...describe when problem occurred] it [describe problem] causing [describe damage].

Under consumer legislation I am entitled to [a refund/a repair or replacement/compensation for loss of value – depending on how long you have ▶

had the item] and to compensation for the damage described above.

I enclose my [receipt/other proof of purchase] and [describe any evidence you have, such as photographs of the damage]. I have obtained three quotes for dealing with the [repeat brief nature of damage], of which the lowest is for £ [insert sum].

I would like you to [refund/replace the goods] and to compensate me for the damage done to my [brief description as above]. If I do not receive a satisfactory response within the next 14 days I will seek advice on taking further action.

Yours sincerely…

Dear [Name of person]

Re: [Description of service, contract number if available]

On [date] [you/your employees/your subcontractor – name] [describe work done] at [the above address/address of premises/garage/repair shop].[Describe the problem and how and when you discovered it]. This demonstrates that the [installation/repair/type of work – describe] was not performed [with reasonable care and skill AND/OR using materials of satisfactory quality and fit for the purpose intended].

You are [responsible for the work done by your subcontractors and are] therefore in breach of contract. Under consumer legislation, I am entitled to [compensation for the cost of putting right this defective work/withhold payment until the defective work is remedied/withhold payment for this portion of the job until the defective work is remedied].

EITHER:
I would like to give you a reasonable opportunity to rectify this problem. Please arrange for the work to be done by [insert date – allow a reasonable time].

OR:
I would like [a full refund/compensation for the cost incurred in putting this right – enclose receipt or other evidence].

Please acknowledge this letter within [14 days/less if the problem is urgent]…
EITHER:…and tell me when [you/your subcontractors] expect to start work. If I do not hear from you by then I will hire someone else to do the job and send you the bill.
OR:…If I do not hear from you by then I will take further action to recover my money.

Yours sincerely…

Asking for defective work to be remedied; or for main contractor to arrange for work by a subcontractor to be put right or pay the cost of getting it done by someone else.

See questions, pp53, 54, 68-69, 263, 263-264

SAMPLE LETTERS

BUYING GOODS/BUYING SERVICES/BUYING & OWNING A CAR

Cancelling an order if goods are not delivered by a deadline, or cancelling a contract if work is not done by the deadline.

See questions, pp58, 242

Dear [Name of person]

Re: [Description of product or service, contract number if available]

On [date] I [ordered/booked] [details of product/service/car]. By [date] this had still not [arrived/started/been carried out], and I wrote to you informing you that time was now of the essence to the contract and that I expected the [describe product or work] to be [supplied/carried out/started/completed] by [date].

As this deadline has now passed without [delivery of goods – describe/performance of service – describe], I am cancelling the contract. Therefore...
EITHER:...I am no longer bound to pay you.
OR:...I require [a full refund/the return of my deposit in full].

Please [acknowledge this letter within 14 days/ensure that this is paid as soon as possible].

Yours sincerely...

Asking for the replacement of faulty goods supplied as part of work done in the home.

See question, pp58-59

Dear [Name of person]

Re: [Description of product and/or service, contract number if available]

On [date] you [describe service]. As part of this, you supplied [describe goods]. [This/these] [is/are/is not/are not] [describe problem].

EITHER:
[When we discussed this/In our original contract] it was agreed that these fittings would be [describe exactly what you agreed].

OR:
[This/These] fittings are not [of satisfactory quality AND/OR fit for the purpose intended AND/OR as described and/or matching the sample I was shown AND/OR of a type and quality commensurate with the work – select as applicable].

You are therefore in breach of contract. Under consumer legislation you are required either to remedy this problem yourself or to pay compensation to enable me to hire someone else to do the job. I would like you to replace these fittings with [describe exactly what you want...as soon as possible/by – insert date].
I enclose a copy of [your invoice/our original agreement].

▶

Please respond within the next 14 days telling when you plan to carry out this work. If I do not receive your reply by then, I will hire another contractor and pass the costs on to you.

Yours sincerely...

- -

Dear [Name of person]

Re: [Description of service, contract number if available]

On [date] [describe nature of service].

[Describe problem that occurred, when it happened/when you noticed it, and consequences]. This demonstrates that your service was not performed with reasonable care and skill, and under consumer legislation I am entitled to [have this damage repaired/compensation for the losses involved].

IF APPLICABLE:
I entered into this contract without being aware of any conditions and I hold you responsible for the [damage to/loss of] my [goods – describe/property/car].

You are also responsible for the resulting damage [describe] to my neighbour's property.

I would like [you to rectify the damage AND/OR compensation for the damage done AND/OR a refund AND/OR compensation for my obvious disappointment (for personal items such as photographs) AND/OR compensation for the inconvenience involved (if you lost use of your car/property for a period) – select as appropriate].

I enclose a copy of [my receipt/your original invoice] and [describe your evidence and quotations for repair or replacement/costs of other losses].

I look forward to your reply. If I do not hear from you within the next 14 days I will [take/take advice on instigating] further action to [recover the money owing to me and/or my neighbour and/or have the damage repaired and send you the bill].

Yours sincerely...

Claiming compensation for damage or loss to your property while a service such as cleaning or repairs is being carried out, or damage to someone else's property caused by work done to your own.

See questions, pp59, 61, 63, 64, 77, 264-265

SAMPLE LETTERS

BUYING SERVICES • ENTERTAINMENT & TRAVEL

Claiming compensation for interruption to the water supply or other failures by utility companies to meet required standards.

See questions, pp66, 69

Dear [Name of person]

Re: [Your account number]

My [type of utility] has been [nature of problem, with dates].

IF APPLICABLE:
Your engineer was due to call on [date] at [time] but missed the appointment and did not notify me that it had been cancelled. [Describe additional consequences and losses sustained].

As a domestic consumer I am entitled to [quote relevant part of guaranteed standards]. You have not met [this/these] standards, and I [wish to make a formal complaint and/or am entitled to compensation – state amount if you know it].

IF APPLICABLE:
I would also like you to compensate me for [additional consequences as above, with estimated cost].

I look forward to your reply. Please acknowledge this letter within the next 14 days.

Yours sincerely…

Complaining to a utility company about a disputed bill and a threat to take you to court.

See question, p67

Dear [Name of person]

Re: [Your account number]

Your bill dated [give date] for my [nature of utility] supply is £ [insert sum], covering a period of [length of time].

This sum has accumulated because [explain].

[Describe what you have so far tried to negotiate with the company, and the response you got].

It is contrary to good practice for you to threaten court action in such circumstances, and I would like you to withdraw this threat immediately.

▶

In the circumstances, it would be reasonable to allow me at least [length of time – as long as the bill has been accumulating] to pay off the backlog, and I would like you to accept payment by instalments over this period.

IF APPLICABLE:
As this debt has built up due to failures on your part, and is not my fault, I would also like some form of redress [explain what you want – a reduction in the bill/writing off any debt more than a certain age].

I look forward to your response. Please acknowledge this letter within the next 14 days.

Yours sincerely…

Dear [Name of person]

Re: double-booking at [name of restaurant/hotel]

On [date] I booked a [table/room] for [date of booking, time if for a table] at your [restaurant/hotel]. When we arrived we were told that the [restaurant/hotel] was full…
EITHER:…and [describe any alternative arrangements offered]. This was [not acceptable/not as good/inconvenient/more expensive/ involved more travelling] and [describe your experience].
OR:…As a result we had to [describe what you did].

[Describe consequences: inconvenience, spoiled enjoyment, additional expenses incurred – with details].

I would like [my deposit returned/compensation for our disappointment] [IF APPLICABLE: and the extra costs we were forced to incur refunded].

I hope to receive your cheque for £ [total amount claimed] and I will wait 14 days for your reply before taking advice about claiming compensation and costs.

Yours sincerely…

Complaining to a restaurant or hotel when a table or room had been double-booked and you had to go somewhere else.

See questions, pp81, 86-87

SAMPLE LETTERS

ENTERTAINMENT & TRAVEL

Complaining to a restaurant about the bill and asking for compensation.

See question, p84

Dear [Name of person]

Re: meal at [name of restaurant], [date of meal]

On [date], [who was involved – for example, my friends and I] ate a meal in your restaurant.

[I/We] [was/were] not happy with the quality of the [food/service given] and I complained at the time that it was [describe problem].

When I came to pay the bill I deducted [the cost of the service charge/the proportion of the meal charge withheld] but your staff insisted that I must pay the whole amount charged. I did so only under protest.

Under consumer law I am entitled to compensation for this [disappointing meal/poor service]. I would like you to refund [state amount you would have withheld from the bill]. I enclose copies of your bill and my credit card receipt, which you will see are marked 'paid under protest'.

I hope this matter can be resolved and I look forward to your reply. If I do not receive a satisfactory response within the next 14 days I will take advice about reclaiming my money.

Yours sincerely…

Asking a tour operator for compensation for problems with a holiday.

See question, p94

Dear [Name of person]

Re: [name of hotel, name of resort]

My family and I have just returned from our holiday at your [name of resort], staying at [name of hotel].

We had an extremely disappointing time because [describe problem].

IF APPLICABLE:
In contrast, your brochure described the facilities as follows: [quote relevant wording from brochure].

▶

[Describe anything you did in response to the problem and any extra expenses incurred as a result.]

I am entitled to compensation for this unsatisfactory holiday and I would like [state amount claimed] to reflect [summarise nature of problem] and our disappointment and inconvenience [as well as a refund of – list any extra expenses incurred].

I enclose a copy of [our booking form/receipt/confirmation] [IF APPLICABLE: and describe any evidence, such as photographs/copies of receipts for additional expenses incurred].

I hope to receive your reply within 14 days. If I have not heard from you by then I will take this matter further with [ABTA/IATA/Trading Standards].

Yours sincerely…

- -

Dear [Name of person]

Re: refund for penalty fare

On [date] I travelled on your [time of train] service from [departure station] to [arrival station]. I had a second-class rail ticket but all the second-class seats were full. I therefore found an unoccupied seat in a first-class compartment.

Your ticket collector then charged me a penalty fare because I did not have a first-class ticket.

Under the National Rail Conditions of Carriage, because the second-class seats were all full I was entitled to sit in a first-class seat that was not needed by a first-class passenger. Your collector was entitled only to charge me a supplement for the difference between the first and second-class fares, not a penalty fare.

I would like a refund of the extra amount I was charged as a penalty fare compared with the supplement. I enclose copies of my original and penalty fare tickets.

I look forward to your reply. If I do not hear from you within the next 14 days I will contact my local Rail Passengers' Committee to pursue the matter further.

Yours sincerely…

Querying a train company's penalty fare for travelling in first class on a second-class ticket when second class was full.

See question, p104

Asking for compensation from a bus, train or other transport company for injury while travelling.

See question, p106

Dear [Name of person handling complaints]

Re: injury, [date]

On [date] I was on your [identify bus number/train departure time/ferry name and departure time] service travelling between [departure] and [destination]. The [bus/train/boat/] [describe problem] and I [describe what happened], causing injury to my [state location of injury].

In addition to pain and suffering resulting from this injury, I have incurred expenses for [list] [and had to be off work for – state how long].

This injury resulted from a failure in your duty of care towards me as a passenger, and I am entitled to compensation for my injuries and to full payment of the expenses I incurred as a direct result of the accident.

IF APPLICABLE:
I am also entitled to compensation for the amount I lost as a result of absence from work.

Fair compensation for my injury would be £ [insert amount claimed for pain and suffering] and this, together with my expenses [IF APPLICABLE: and lost earnings] comes to a total of £ [insert total amount claimed].

I attach a list of the expenses with copies of the receipts [IF APPLICABLE: and wage or salary slips/other proof of earnings lost].

I look forward to your reply. If I do not hear from you within the next 14 days I will contact a solicitor with a view to taking legal action to resolve this matter.

Yours sincerely…

Dear [Name of person]

Re: access to medical records

As allowed by law, I would like to [see/have a copy of] [my medical records/the following parts of my medical record – list the details you want].

IF APPLICABLE:
I understand that a fee may be payable for copies of the records.

Please let me know what is your procedure for this and [when I can make an appointment to look at them/when I can expect to receive my copies].

Yours sincerely…

Asking your doctor or hospital to let you see your medical records.

See question, pp112-113

Dear [Name of person]

Re: application to see medical records, [any reference number given to your application]

On [date] I asked [name of GP/practice/hospital] to let me [see/have a copy of] my medical records, as is my legal right.

IF APPLICABLE:
I [took/sent in] [the appropriate fee/signed form/proof of identity – whichever apply] on [date].

[Name of person] [refused my request/said that part of the records would be withheld from me]. When I asked why, I was told [state the reason you were given].

I am not happy with this response and would like to challenge it because [explain your reasons].

I still want access to my medical records and would like you to arrange this now.

I look forward to your reply. If I do not hear from you within 14 days I will [contact my local PALS representative or the Data Protection Commission and/or consider making a formal complaint].

Yours sincerely…

Responding when you have been refused access to your medical records.

See question, pp112-113

SAMPLE LETTERS

YOUR HEALTHCARE

Informing your local maternity unit that you want to have your baby at home.

See question, pp116-117

Dear [Name of person]

Re: home birth

I am expecting my baby on [due date] and I plan to give birth at home.

[Explain what you have already done, such as talking to your GP, and the response you got.]

I have been told that you [currently have a shortage of midwives/other reason given]. However, I do not intend to come into hospital unless unforeseen complications make this unavoidable, and I would like you to supply a midwife to attend the birth at my home. The Government supports a woman's right to choose a home birth, and if there are not enough hospital or community midwives you should arrange for an independent midwife to provide cover.

Please confirm that you will make the necessary arrangements for a midwife to attend when I go into labour. I hope to hear from you within the next 14 days [or sooner if the birth is due shortly].

Yours sincerely…

Complaining to the Health Service Ombudsman about the way in which your complaint about a service has been dealt with.

See box, p121

Dear [Name of person]

Re: complaint to [name of individual/organisation – any reference number given to your complaint]

On [date] I made a formal complaint to [name of individual/organisation] about [summarise briefly].

The response to this was [describe, with dates].

EITHER:
I do not believe this was a satisfactory response because [explain].

OR:
This complaint remains unresolved after [length of time].

▶

OR:
My request for an independent review has been refused.
I am unhappy with the way my complaint has been handled and I would like you to investigate this matter further.

I attach details of my original complaint [summarise on separate sheet] and copies of my correspondence with [name of individual/organisation].

I look forward to hearing from you.

Yours sincerely...

Stating your wishes to a surgeon regarding a forthcoming operation.

See question, p125

Dear [Name of surgeon]

Re: [nature of operation, date and any reference number]

As you know, I am due to be admitted on [date] for [nature of operation], under your care.

I confirm that we have discussed my operation, and I made it clear that I do not want [any further procedures – or describe specifically] to be carried out at the time...
EITHER:...irrespective of what is found during the operation.
OR:...unless, as we discussed, [describe specific condition] is found during the operation.

[In case I am/As I will be – depending on whether you are having a local or general anaesthetic] unable to communicate, I want my wishes to be clear, and to ensure that they are readily available during the operation.

I would be grateful if you would attach this letter to my notes, and confirm that this has been done before my admission on [date].

Yours sincerely...

Making a complaint to a complementary practitioner.

See question, pp134-135

Dear [Name of person handling complaints]

Re: treatment on [date]

I attended a [consultation/series of consultations] with you on [date(s)] at which you treated my [describe problem] by [describe what the practitioner did].

As a result [describe what has gone wrong], and since then I have [describe subsequent symptoms/problems].

[Describe any other action you have taken, such as seeing your GP, and what was said.]

This outcome represents a failure in your duty of care…
IF YOU PAID FOR THE SERVICES:…and a breach of contract.

I would like [describe what you want: money, an apology, a refund, free treatment] and I am writing to give you the opportunity to resolve this problem directly.

If I do not hear from you within 14 days I will [contact your professional body – give its name/take further advice about starting legal action against you for compensation].

Yours sincerely…

Querying with the benefits appeals service the refusal of a benefit to which you believe you are entitled.

See question, pp135-136

Dear [Name of person]

Re: [name of benefit], [your National Insurance number]

My application for [name of benefit] has been refused (reference [state reference on the letter telling you that your application had been turned down], dated [give date of letter]).

I believe I am entitled to this benefit because [explain your reasons].

I believe that it was wrong to refuse my application, and I would like to appeal against this decision.

▶

I understand that if you accept my appeal you will send me an enquiry form. I look forward to hearing from you.

Yours sincerely…

....

Dear [name of person]

Re: [your account number], [any reference number for the withdrawal]

On [date] you debited my account with £ [amount] for [nature of payment] in error [explain circumstances].

[Describe additional complications – bounced cheque, non-payment of standing orders/direct debits.]

EITHER: Under the Direct Debit Guarantee I am entitled to a full and immediate refund of this sum and associated charges and interest [give details]. In addition,…
OR: This sum has been refunded. However,…

…this episode has caused me considerable [inconvenience and/or embarrassment and/or anxiety – explain] and [took/has so far taken] [time/time and expense – detail amounts] to resolve. This merits [reimbursement of my costs and/or compensation], at least as a goodwill gesture, and I believe a sum of £ [insert amount] would be reasonable.

I look forward to your response and I would appreciate an acknowledgment of this letter within the next 14 days.

Yours sincerely…

Asking a bank for compensation for wrong direct-debit withdrawal.

See question, pp140-141

SAMPLE LETTERS

FINANCIAL & LEGAL SERVICES

Writing to a bank or credit-card company about liability for a lost or stolen card.

See question, pp144-145

Dear [Name of person]

Re: [lost/stolen card, account number]

My [cash/credit/debit] card [number] was [lost/stolen], as reported to you on [date]. Before I could report the loss, the card had been misused and £ [insert sum] [withdrawn] from my account.

I reported the loss to you as soon as I became aware of it, and...
EITHER:...I took all the usual precautions [give details if relevant] to safeguard my card and PIN number. Therefore under the Banking Code I am liable only for the first £50 of the loss.
OR:...although I accept that I did not act with reasonable care by [insert details, such as allowing your PIN number to be discovered], I am not liable for the whole loss because [explain – for example, you did not have this sum in your account at the time the card was used].

I would like you to refund the £ [amount taken/amount for which you are not liable] that has been debited to my account, together with any interest that has accrued on this sum, as quickly as possible, as recommended under the Banking Code.

Please confirm that this money has been refunded. I look forward to hearing from you.

Yours sincerely...

Querying the administration costs charged by a mortgage company.

See question, p150

Dear [name of person]

Re: [your account number]

On [date] I asked you for approval to let my house, and this was granted on [date and reference of letter].

Subsequently [give details], you charged me £ [insert sum] for [administration fee]. I was not told about this charge beforehand, and I would like you to reimburse it.

I look forward to your reply. If I do not hear from you within the next 14 days I will refer this matter to the Mortgage Code Compliance Board.

Yours sincerely...

Dear [name of person]

Re: [reference number for your claim]

On [date], [describe event and consequences], as detailed in my claim submitted to you on [date] for £ [amount of claim]. You have refused to pay this claim on the basis that [quote from insurance company's response].

EITHER:
[Explain why the company is not justified in taking this line.]

OR:
I believe this to be an [onerous term/unusual restriction on payment]. According to the Association of British Insurers' Code of Practice, I should have been warned about this before buying the policy, but this term was not explained to me.

I would therefore like to make a formal complaint about your response, and for you to settle my claim in full.

I hope to hear from you within the next 14 days. If I have not had a reply by then, I will refer this matter to the [Association of British Insurers/Financial Ombudsman Service].

Yours sincerely…

Complaining to an insurance company about its refusal to pay a claim.

See questions, pp166-167, 168, 168-169

Dear [name of solicitor]

Re: [summary details of your case]

I would like to complain about your handling of my case [give details]. Because you [explain what went wrong], [explain consequences].

This is clearly not compatible with carrying out your professional duties [as specified AND/OR within a reasonable period of time AND/OR in a reasonable manner] and represents [a breach of contract AND/OR negligence – select as appropriate].

I am therefore claiming compensation of £ [insert sum] for [specify losses]. Please refer this matter to your professional indemnity insurer.

I look forward to your response. Please acknowledge this letter within the next 14 days.

Yours sincerely…

Complaining to your solicitor about poor service or negligence.

See question, p172

SAMPLE LETTERS

YOUR HOME, YOUR CASTLE • LANDLORD & TENANT

Complaining to a neighbour about antisocial behaviour.

See question, p174

Dear [name of person]

Re: [summary description of nuisance]

I am writing formally to ask you to stop [describe the nuisance briefly].

Since we discussed this on [date if you can remember, or 'a few weeks ago'], I have kept a diary and recorded [summarise the number/type of incidents].

IF APPLICABLE:
[Add details of any further conversations you have had with the neighbour.]

IF APPLICABLE:
I have also now spoken to other neighbours nearby and [state how many, or 'several'] are also being [bothered/affected] by this.

I [or 'We', if other neighbours agree] would like you to [describe what you want: stop/reduce/limit the nuisance to reasonable times – find a compromise solution if possible].

I hope we can resolve this amicably, and I look forward to your response. If this situation continues, I will be forced to take further action.

Yours sincerely…

Telling a neighbour where the boundary between your properties is.

See question, p183

Dear [name of person]

Re: boundary, [addresses of both properties]

As we have discussed, your [hedge/fence] is currently on my property, depriving me of land which belongs to me.

According to my [house deeds/lease/boundary survey], the boundary between our properties runs [describe precise location of boundary].

IF APPLICABLE:
I enclose a copy of [the plan as shown in my deeds/the lease/the Land Registry entry] which confirms this.

▶

I would like you to move your [fence/hedge] onto your side of the boundary. I hope that we can resolve this amicably, but if this is not done within the next 14 days [or longer if it is a major job] I will take further action to repossess my land.

Yours sincerely…

Asserting security of tenure under the Rent Act 1977 or the Housing Act 1988.

See question, p198

Dear [name of person]

Re: [address of rented property]

I have been renting from you since [year], when I moved into [this address/address of first property rented].

IF APPLICABLE:
In [year] you offered me alternative accommodation at [address of subsequent property]. As there was no gap between these two tenancies, I still have a protected tenancy.

This gives me security of tenure under the [Rent Act 1977/Housing Act 1988], and you cannot evict me without grounds as specified in the Act – which do not apply in this case.

I would appreciate acknowledgement of my protected tenancy rights within the next 14 days.

Yours sincerely…

SAMPLE LETTERS

LANDLORD & TENANT

Asking a landlord to return a deposit.

See question, p204

Dear [name of person]

Re: deposit, [address of property]

I moved out of your property, [give address], on [date].
EITHER:...According to my tenancy agreement, my deposit should have been returned within [state time specified in agreement].
OR:...I have not yet had my deposit returned.

IF APPLICABLE:
Your letter of [date] details costs you have incurred. [State whether you agree with any of these or not].

EITHER:
You are not entitled to withhold my deposit and I would like it returned in full.

OR:
You are entitled to deduct only [itemise the costs you agree with] and I would like the rest of my deposit (£ [insert sum]) refunded.

I hope to hear from you within the next 14 days. If you do not refund my money by then, I will [contact the Tenancy Deposit Scheme/take further advice/instigate legal action to recover it].

Yours sincerely...

Complaining to a landlord about a property unfit to live in.

See question, p207

Dear [name of person]

Re: [address of property]

I have already approached you about [describe problem briefly] at [address of property].

IF APPLICABLE:
The problem is now sufficiently serious that it is affecting my health, and I have a medical report which confirms this.

I attach [notes on/photographs of the damp, medical report].

▶

You are legally obliged to take action to remedy these problems and I would like you to commence repair work within the next 14 days. If this does not happen, I will contact the local authority to get this matter resolved.

Yours sincerely…

Checking a prospective tenant's details with his employer.

See box, p208

Dear [name of person]

Re: reference for [name of prospective tenant]

[Name of prospective tenant] has applied to rent a [house/flat] from me and has given your details as his employer.

He states that he works as [give job title] on a [wage/salary] of £ [insert amount per week/year]. I would be grateful if you could confirm his employment status with you and that these details are correct.

I would appreciate your response within the next 14 days, and I enclose a stamped, addressed envelope for your reply.

Yours sincerely…

Opposing a landlord who is trying to evict you illegally.

See question, p210

Dear [name of person]

Re: [address of property]

Your letter of [date] gives me [notice period] to vacate my [house/flat].

This attempt to evict me without a proper possession order is against the law, and you are committing a criminal offence by doing this.

I would like you to confirm within the next 14 days that you will take no further action without going through the proper legal process. If you continue to threaten to evict me, I will seek an injunction to prevent you from doing so.

Yours sincerely…

SAMPLE LETTERS

LANDLORD & TENANT • BUYING & SELLING A HOME

Disputing a service-charge increase with your ground landlord or freeholder.

See question, p215

Dear [name of person]

Re: service charge, [address of property]

Your notice of [date] proposes an increase in the [service/maintenance] charges on the above property from £[old rate] to £[proposed new rate], to be effective from [date].

This represents an increase of [insert percentage], which seems excessively high. Please would you supply details of the actual costs of the items included in the charges, and explain why your proposed increase is so much.

I hope to receive your reply within the next 14 days.

Yours sincerely...

Complaining to an estate agent about a conflict of interest.

See question, p217

Dear [name of person]

Re: sale of [address of property]

Your company [is/was] marketing [give address of property in question] which I [am selling/sold/am interested in buying/bought]...
IF TRANSACTION HAS ALREADY TAKEN PLACE:...on [date].

I have now discovered that [describe what happened].

This represents a conflict of interest on your part. According to the National Association of Estate Agents' code of practice, you [should/should not] have [explain what the firm did/did not do that was wrong].

I would like you to investigate whether the price I [am being/was] advised to [accept/offer] represents the average for similar properties in the area.

Please confirm that you intend to investigate this matter. I will wait for 14 days for your reply before taking my complaint to the compliance officer of the National Association of Estate Agents.

Yours sincerely...

Dear [name of person]

Re: [name and location of agent]

EITHER:
I instructed [name and location of agent] to sell my [house/flat], which [is still on the market/was sold on – give date/was taken off the market on – give date].

OR:
I [bought/am interested in buying/was interested in buying] a property, [address], through [name and location of agent].

[Describe the problem].

IF APPLICABLE:
This contravenes the NAEA code of practice.

[Describe any complaints you made to the company, and the response(s) so far].

I do not think that this is acceptable practice and I would like the [NAEA/OEA] to investigate further...
IF APPLICABLE:...and consider my claim for compensation of £ [insert amount] for [give details of what you are claiming].

I look forward to your response and would appreciate an acknowledgement of this letter within the next 14 days.

Yours sincerely...

Making a formal complaint about an estate agent to the National Association of Estate Agents (NAEA) or the Ombudsman for Estate Agents (OEA).

See questions, pp217, 234, box, p235

SAMPLE LETTERS

BUYING & SELLING A HOME

Asking for compensation from a removal company for lost or damaged possessions.

See question, p220

Dear [name of person]

Re: [any reference number you were given by removal company]

Your company moved us from [old location] to [new location, address above] on [date].

When we unpacked, we discovered that [describe item(s)] [was/were] [missing/damaged – describe nature of damage].

EITHER: You are responsible for lost or missing items…
OR: As your removals personnel packed these items, the damage sustained is your responsibility…
…and I would like compensation for the cost of [replacement/repair], which is £ [insert amount].

I enclose [give evidence to support the amount you are claiming – cost of new item, quote for repair].

I hope we can settle this matter quickly. If I do not receive a satisfactory response within the next 14 days I will take advice on claiming compensation.

Yours sincerely…

Making a complaint to a surveyor about a home survey.

See question, pp224-225

Dear [name of person]

Re: [any reference number for the survey]

On [date], [you/your employee – name] conducted a survey on [my/our] house, address above, prior to purchase.

Since moving in [I/we] have discovered [describe the problem and any underlying cause]. This was not mentioned in our [survey/homebuyer's] report even though it is a significant defect which a surveyor could reasonably have been expected to notice.

I would therefore like compensation to cover the cost of [describe what needs doing to remedy the defect].

▶

I enclose a quotation for £ [insert sum] for carrying out this work.

I look forward to hearing from you and hope we can settle this matter quickly. I will wait for 14 days for your reply before taking further action.

Yours sincerely...

Dear [name of person]

Re: [account number for your mortgage]

I have just received your re-projection letter dated [insert date], telling me that you anticipate a shortfall on my policy and that it may not reach the target amount needed to repay my mortgage.

When I bought this policy in [year], I was not told [how my money would be invested/of the risks of this type of investment/about the fees and charges associated with the endowment policy and/or their effect on my savings].

I believe I was mis-sold this policy and I am entitled to compensation to restore my financial position to what it would have been had I been sold a repayment mortgage.

I look forward to your response. Please acknowledge this letter within 14 days and let me know what you intend to do to rectify this situation.

Yours sincerely...

Complaining to a company that mis-sold you an endowment mortgage.

See question, pp228-229

SAMPLE LETTERS

BUYING & SELLING A HOME • BUYING & OWNING A CAR

Asking a mortgage lender to recognise that your bad-debt record has improved and to lower your interest rate.

See question, p231

Dear [name of person]

Re: [account number of mortgage]

I took out my mortgage with you on [date]. I believe I have been paying a high interest rate since then because a past [unpaid loan/County Court judgment] left me with a bad debt record.

However, my payment history over the past [insert number of years since taking out mortgage] years has been impeccable, and I do not think I should continue to be penalised for this old problem.

I would like you to review my current record of uninterrupted mortgage payments, and to consider switching my loan to a cheaper interest rate.

I look forward to your response. Please acknowledge this letter within the next 14 days.

Yours sincerely...

Cancelling a contract with an estate agent.

See box, p234

Dear [name of person]

Re: [address of property]

I instructed you to sell my [house/flat], [address above, or give property address], on [date].

I would now like to terminate this contract [give reasons if you wish] from...
EITHER:...[give date].
OR:...the end of the period specified in our original agreement.

This letter is to give you [insert length of time] weeks' formal notice to do this, as agreed.

Please confirm in writing within the next seven days that this contract will end on [date of termination, as above].

Yours sincerely...

Dear [name of person]

Re: possible health hazard at [address of problem premises]

I live at the above address. I am concerned about a potential public health hazard at [address of problem premises] due to [describe the hazard].

[Describe any consequences which have already occurred, such as fire/rats]

[Give details of anyone else affected – for example, neighbours/local food stores.]

[Describe any action you have already taken, and any responses of the occupier to complaints.]

I would like you to investigate this matter as soon as possible, and I look forward to your response. Please acknowledge this letter within 14 days.

Yours sincerely…

Writing to a public health authority about health hazards on neighbour's property.

See question, pp240-241

Contesting a speeding fine or clamping fee.

See questions, pp254, 259-260

Dear [name of person]

Re: [speeding fine/clamping fee – give reference number]

On [date] I [received a speeding fine/had to pay a clamping fee] for [give details, including date, on notice].

However [explain why you think the fine/fee should not apply]. [Describe the circumstances if your car was clamped and explain anything you did to resolve or reduce the problem/co-operate.]

IF APPLICABLE:
I enclose [describe any evidence to back up your claim].

I would like [you to cancel/to appeal against] this charge…
IF APPLICABLE:…and to receive a full refund.

I look forward to your response. Please acknowledge this letter within 14 days.

Yours sincerely…

SAMPLE LETTERS

BUYING & OWNING A CAR • WORLD OF WORK

Disputing a garage bill and paying or partially paying it under protest.

See question, p262

Dear [name of person]

Re: [reference number on bill]

On [date] you carried out a [repair/service/alteration – give details] to my [make and model of vehicle].

[Explain what was wrong with the work and/or parts supplied.]

However, you have still charged me [for this item/the full cost of the work].

EITHER:
I am therefore deducting [the cost of this item/£ – insert amount] from your total bill to compensate for this.

OR:
I [am paying/have paid] this bill only under protest and I would like you to refund £ [insert amount] to compensate for this.

Please acknowledge this letter within the next 14 days. If I do not hear from you by then I will take advice about pursuing this matter further.

Yours sincerely…

Writing to a new employer who has withdrawn a job offer.

See question, p268

Dear [name of person]

Re: [post or job title]

On [date] I [attended a job interview for/received a letter about my application for] the post of [describe]. I was offered the job unconditionally [in writing/verbally], and I accepted [in writing/verbally].

This formed a contract of employment between us. Therefore your statement [on/in your letter of] [date] withdrawing this offer represents a breach of contract.

EITHER:
I would like this job offer to be reinstated, otherwise I will seek compensation for breach of contract.

▶

OR:
I am entitled to compensation for this breach.

IF APPLICABLE:
[Add details of any consequences you have suffered, such as giving up your previous job.]

EITHER (if you want the job):
I hope we can resolve this and I look forward to your response.

OR (if you do not):
I would like an explanation for your action in withdrawing this job offer.

I will wait 14 days for your reply before taking further action.

Yours sincerely…

Dear [name of person]

Re: [written statement of employment terms/statement of wages]

I have been working as [job title] for [length of time].

I would like…
EITHER:…a written statement of my terms of employment, including details of my [pay, holiday and sick leave entitlement/add any other details that concern you]. I have a right to such a statement under the Employment Rights Act 1996, and I [should receive/should have received] this within two months of starting work for you.
OR:…a formal statement of my wages, including my gross and net earnings and deductions [add any other details which concern you]. I have a right to such an itemised payslip under the Employment Rights Act 1996, and I should receive this before or along with my wages.

Please confirm that you will now supply this [statement/payslip]. I will wait 14 days for your reply before taking further action.

Yours sincerely…

Asking an employer for documents such as a written statement of employment terms, or a payslip.

See questions, pp269-270, 275

SAMPLE LETTERS
WORLD OF WORK

Complaining to an employer about a breach of employment terms.

See questions, pp270-271, 287

Dear [name of person]

Re: [deduction from wages/sick pay]

I have been working as [job title] for [length of time].

[On/since] [date], [describe problem, such as deduction from wages/failure to pay sick pay].

This is in breach of [FOR DEDUCTIONS: the Employment Rights Act 1996; OR FOR CONTRACTUAL SICK PAY: my contract of employment; OR FOR STATUTORY SICK PAY: the Social Security and Housing Benefits Act 1982]... IF APPLICABLE (for deductions):...because [I was not given a written statement of the company policy on till shortfalls/I was not given a written demand for the money on my pay-day/an amount more than 10 per cent of my gross wages was deducted].

EITHER (for deductions):
You are not entitled to make this deduction from my pay and I would like the sum of £ [insert] refunded to my [next – if applicable] pay packet.

OR (for sick pay):
I am entitled to [contractual/statutory] sick pay backdated to [date – 4 days after the start of your illness, or as specified in your contract].

I will wait for [14 days – or less if you need the money badly] for this money to be paid before taking further action.

Yours sincerely...

Complaining to an employer about a breach of statutory employment rights.

See questions, pp280-281, 282, 296-297

Dear [name of person]

Re: [promotion policy/dismissal for pregnancy/enforced retirement]

I have been working as [job title] for [length of time].

On [date], I was informed by [name] that [describe problem, such as being overlooked for promotion/informed that I am being dismissed because I am pregnant/told I must retire when I reach 60].

▶

448

I believe that this [is in breach of the Sex Discrimination Acts 1975 and 1986/counts as unfair dismissal] because [give reasons].

I would like [an explanation for why I have been passed over for promotion/to be reinstated in my old job or a similar one/to be paid compensation for the loss of my job/to be allowed to continue in my present job beyond the age of 60].

I look forward to hearing from you. If I do not receive a satisfactory reply within 14 days, I will seek advice on taking further action. [IF APPLICABLE: If necessary, I am willing to take my case to an employment tribunal.]

Yours sincerely…

Dear [name of person]

Re: my invoice [your reference number]

My invoice, dated [date], has still not been paid.

This invoice was for £ [insert amount] for [describe work done], as agreed with [name of contact] by [written contract – give contract reference number/ letter/telephone] [dated/on – give date].

IF APPLICABLE:
The terms were [for example, 'payment within 30 days'].

EITHER (first attempt):
This invoice is now overdue for payment. Please settle this account immediately.

OR (second or subsequent attempts if previous reminders have failed):
This invoice is now [length of time] overdue for payment despite a previous reminder [reminders] [give date(s)]. If it is not paid within the next seven days I will take legal advice on recovering the money owing to me.

Yours sincerely…

Requesting a client's accounts department to pay your invoice.

See question, p276

SAMPLE LETTERS

WORLD OF WORK/PROTECTING YOUR PRIVACY • INJURIES & ACCIDENTS • PERSONAL RELATIONSHIPS

Asking an employer or organisation for access to personal data that they hold about you.

See question, p278, box, p383

Dear [name of person]

As is my right under section 7 of the Data Protection Act 1998, I would like access to any personal data that you hold about me. I understand that I may have to pay a fee for this.

I would like to know [what information you keep AND/OR why you are holding this information AND/OR to whom you are disclosing information about me – select as appropriate].

Please acknowledge this letter within 14 days.

Yours sincerely…

Asking an employer to change your terms of employment – for example, to flexible working hours.

See question, pp284-285

Dear [name of person]

I have been working as [job title] for [length of time].

I would like to alter my terms of employment to [describe what you want]… IF APPLICABLE:…because [explain your reasons].

If you do not feel able to agree immediately, please arrange a meeting to discuss this change within the next 28 days, as required under employment law.

I look forward to your response.

Yours sincerely…

Dear [name of person]

Re: [reference number for claim]

I was injured on [date] by [describe accident] while on holiday at [location].

When I got home [describe additional consequences – time off work, costs of care, and so on]

Although [name of insurance company] covered the costs of [medical care abroad AND/OR repatriation – select as appropriate], you have stated that you will not cover [describe costs the company has refused to meet].

In fact my policy states that [quote relevant section of policy].

I would therefore like you to meet these additional costs in full. Please use your official complaints procedure to review your original decision.

I enclose [summary and evidence of amount claimed].

I will wait 14 days for your reply before referring this matter to the [General Insurance Standards Council/Financial Ombudsman Service].

Yours sincerely...

Requesting an insurance company to reimburse the costs incurred after a holiday accident.

See question, pp299-300

Dear [name of clinic director]

We received [type of infertility treatment] at [name of hospital/clinic] between [dates]. On [date] our [son/daughter] was born.

We are concerned that [he/she] [explain what worries you] and would like you to check your records to ensure that there were no errors in the source of the [egg/sperm/embryo] used.

We look forward to your response. Please acknowledge this letter within the next 14 days.

Yours sincerely...

Asking the infertility clinic where you received treatment to check your child's paternity.

See question, p326

SAMPLE LETTERS

PERSONAL RELATIONSHIPS • YOUR CHILDREN'S EDUCATION

Asking an adoption agency why you were turned down for adoption.

See question, p329

Dear [name of person]

Re: [any reference number or title for your application]

We have been through your vetting procedure following our application to adopt a child through your agency.

On [date] you informed us that you have turned down our application and we do not understand why. Your letter gave no reasons for this refusal, even though we are entitled to a broad explanation.

[Give further details about why you think the agency is wrong, if relevant.]

We would like you to review your decision and reconsider our application to adopt.

We look forward to your response. Please acknowledge this letter within 14 days.

Yours sincerely…

Making a formal complaint about sex education in a school.

See question, pp359-360

Dear [name of clerk of governors]

My [son/daughter], [name], attends [name of school], and I am unhappy about the [quality/content/emphasis] of sex education being provided for [his/her] age group.

[Give additional details if possible.]

Government guidelines on sex education state [quote relevant section] but I understand that [name of school] [description of how you think the school deviates from the guidelines].

I would like to know the reasons for this and, unless your response is satisfactory, I will be making a formal complaint. I would appreciate your reply within the next 14 days.

Yours sincerely…

Dear [name of person]

My [son/daughter], [name], attends [name of school].

[He/she] has been subjected to bullying for [length of time], and this is continuing despite my drawing it to the attention of [the school and/or the governors]…
IF APPLICABLE: …on several occasions.

[Give details of previous complaints if possible.]

The bullying has included [give examples]. I believe this represents a failure in the school's duty of care towards [child's name], and I would like you to instigate a formal investigation into the school's anti-bullying policies in general, and my [son/daughter]'s case in particular.

Please let me know how you intend to deal with this matter. I would appreciate your initial response within 5 days.

Yours sincerely…

Asking a local education authority (LEA) to investigate bullying.

See question, p366

Dear [name of head]

My [son/daughter], [name], is a pupil in class [insert] at your school.

On [date(s)] [he/she] was [describe problem] and [his/her] teacher, [name], has threatened [him/her] with detention.

EITHER:
I feel that this is an unreasonable punishment because [explain].

OR:
The law requires that parents be given formal written notice of a detention at least 24 hours in advance, and this has not happened.

I do not agree to my [son/daughter]'s detention…
IF APPLICABLE: …and I do not think that the school should penalise pupils for unavoidable [give reason].

I would be very happy to come to see you to discuss this further.

Yours sincerely…

Writing to a head teacher about your child's detention.

See question, p368

SAMPLE LETTERS

YOUR CHILDREN'S EDUCATION

Writing to the local education authority (LEA) or school head about admitting a child with disabilities.

See question, p374

Dear [name of person]

[My/our] [on/daughter], [name and age], [is/has] [briefly describe disability].

[I/we] applied for a place at [school's name] for [him/her] but were turned down. [I/we] would like an explanation of why [he/she] was refused admission.

IF APPLICABLE:
I believe [child's name] may have been treated less favourably because of [his/her] disability. [Point out the child's specific needs and abilities, suggest how these would fit in with a mainstream school and any special provisions or adaptations which would be necessary.]

[I/we] look forward to your response. Please reply within the next 5 days.

Yours sincerely…

Objecting to the governors about disability discrimination at your child's school.

See question, pp374-375

Dear [name of chair of governors]

[My/our] [son/daughter], [child's name], attends [name of school].

[He/she] has [describe condition/disability] which [describe consequences]. I am concerned that [he/she] is receiving unfavourable treatment as a result of this because [describe the problem].

[Describe your conversations with the head teacher about the issue, and what response you received.]

I would like you to investigate this matter and ensure that [child's name] is not subject to discrimination because of [his/her] [condition/disability].

EITHER:
I look forward to your response. Please acknowledge this letter within 5 days.

OR (if urgent – for example, for an imminent school trip):
Please ensure that this matter is resolved [before/in time for] [event and date]. I would appreciate your response by [date].

Yours sincerely…

Dear [name of chair of governors]

My [son/daughter], [child's name], is a pupil at [name of school].

On [date], at about [time], in [location], [he/she] [describe what happened].

As a result, [he/she] [describe consequences – immediate AND/OR ongoing].

I am concerned that this accident happened because of [a lack of reasonable supervision/poor safety considerations].

I have [discussed this with the head teacher/seen the accident report etc] and [describe any evidence you have to support your complaint].

I would like to make a formal complaint against the school for allowing this accident to happen. Please confirm that you will fully investigate the incident. If I do not hear from you within 14 days I will take further advice about pursuing a claim for compensation for [child's name]'s injuries.

Yours sincerely...

Complaining to the governors about safety in your child's school.

See question, pp375-376

Dear [name of chair of governors]

My [son/daughter], [child's name], has been excluded [permanently/for a period of – length of time] from [name of school] for [describe what prompted the exclusion].

I would like to appeal against this decision.

[Give reasons why you think the exclusion is unjustified.]

IF APPROPRIATE:
[Add any comments in support of your child – first offence/otherwise well-behaved/doing well at the school.]

I am willing to attend a hearing of the governors' discipline committee. Please acknowledge this letter within 5 days and let me know when you will be considering this issue.

Yours sincerely...

Informing the governors that you want to appeal against your child's exclusion from school.

See question, p378

SAMPLE LETTERS

PROTECTING YOUR PRIVACY • INHERITANCE DISPUTES

Complaining to Ofcom about your treatment on TV or radio.

See question, p390

Dear [name of person]

I took part in a [televised discussion/documentary/radio broadcast/interview] about [subject] on [channel/station] broadcast on [date and time].

I feel that during the programme [describe nature of your complaint]. As a result [describe the consequences – subject to ridicule, professionally compromised].

I have already raised this issue with [the producer/channel] and [I am not satisfied with their response/they have ignored my complaint]. [Add more detail if appropriate].

I would like to make a formal complaint about my treatment during this broadcast, which I believe [presented me unfairly/misrepresented what I said/invaded my privacy]. I would like you to investigate the matter.

I look forward to your reply. Please acknowledge this letter within the next 14 days.

Yours sincerely...

Writing to a newspaper or magazine editor about children interviewed without permission.

See question, pp390–391

Dear [name of person]

Your [news item/feature/article] headed [title], by [name of reporter – if applicable], published on [date], in [name of newspaper – if editor in charge of several titles], page [insert page number], included [an interview with/a picture of] my [son/daughter].

Neither I nor my child's [teacher/carer] gave permission for this [interview and/or photograph]. The [news item/feature/article] was therefore in breach of the Press Complaints Commission's Code of Practice and I would like to make a formal complaint about it.

IF APPLICABLE:
In addition I would like [an apology/a retraction, or other demand].

I look forward to your reply. If I do not hear from you within the next 7 days I will contact the Press Complaints Commission directly.

Yours sincerely...

Dear [name of person]

I am writing to complain about [an article/news item/interview] that appeared in [name of publication] on [date].

This item [describe contents]. I object strongly to [describe what concerns you about it], [IF APPLICABLE: I believe that this contravenes your code of practice for newspapers] and I would like you to investigate the matter.

IF APPLICABLE
I would also like [an apology/retraction/right of reply].

I enclose a copy of the article [and any other evidence if relevant].

I look forward to hearing from you. Please acknowledge this letter within 14 days.

Yours sincerely…

Making a complaint to the Press Complaints Commission (PCC) about a newspaper article.

See question, pp390-391

Dear [name of person]

I would like to apply for a caveat to the will of [name of deceased], of [address of deceased], who died on [date].

I am [your name and address, and relationship to the deceased], and I am concerned that [name of deceased]'s will [describe problem]. I would like further opportunity to investigate before probate is issued.

I understand the caveat will last for six months, and I enclose [a cheque/postal order] for £ [insert sum – check current fee first] in payment of the fee.

Please acknowledge this letter within 14 days.

Yours sincerely…

Asking for a caveat to be entered at a probate registry.

See question, p408

DIRECTORY OF ADDRESSES

The AA (Automobile Association)
Contact Centre, Carr Ellison House
William Armstrong Drive
Newcastle upon Tyne NE4 7YA
Information line: 0870 600 0371
Email: customer.services@theAA.com
Web: www.theAA.com

Action for Victims of Medical Accidents
44 High Street, Croydon CR0 1YB
Helpline: 020 8686 8333
Email: avma.co@virgin.net
Web: www.admin@avma.org.uk

ADR Family Mediation
Grove House, Grove Road
Redland, Bristol BS6 6UN
Tel: 0117 946 7180
Email: info@adrgroup.co.uk
Web: www.adrgroup.co.uk

Advertising Standards Authority (ASA)
2 Torrington Place, London WC1E 7HW
Tel: 020 7580 5555
Email: enquiries@asa.org.uk
Web: www.asa.org.uk

Advisory Committee on Telecommunications (ACTs)
Web: www.acts.org.uk
Consumer Communications for England
50 Ludgate Hill, London EC4M 7JJ
Tel: 020 7634 8773
Email: cce@acts.org.uk
Welsh Advisory Committee on Telecommunications
4 The Science Park, Aberystwyth
Ceredigion SY23 3AH
Tel: 01970 636 413
Email: wact@acts.org.uk

Advisory, Conciliation and Arbitration Service (ACAS)
Brandon House, 180 Borough High Street
London SE1 1LW
Helpline: 0845 747 4747
Web: www.acas.org.uk

Age Concern
England: Astral House
1268 London Road, London SW16 4ER
Tel: 020 8765 7200
Information line: 0800 009 966
Legal advice line: 020 8765 7200
Web: www.ageconcern.org.uk
Wales: 1 Cathedral Road
Cardiff CF11 9SD
Tel: 029 2037 1566
Email: enquiries@accymru.org.uk
Web: www.accymru.org.uk

Air Transport Users Council (AUC)
Room K201, CAA House
45-59 Kingsway, London WC2B 6TE
Tel: 020 7240 6061
Email: admin@auc.caa.co.uk
Web: www.caa.co.uk/auc

Air Travel Organisers Licensing (ATOL)
Room K3, CAA House
45-59 Kingsway, London WC2B 6TE
Tel: 020 7453 6430
Consumer Advice Helpline: 020 7453 6424
Email: advice@cpg.org.uk
Web: www.atol.org.uk

The Appeals Service Headquarters
5th Floor, Fox Court
14 Grays Inn Road, London WC1X 8HN
Tel: 0207 712 2600
Web: www.appeals-service.gov.uk

Arboricultural Association
Ampfield House, Romsey
Hampshire SO51 9PA
Tel: 01794 368 717
Email: admin@trees.org.uk
Web: www.trees.org.uk

Aromatherapy Organisations Council
PO Box 6522, Desborough
Kettering NN14 2YX
Tel: 0870 774 3477
Email: info@aocuk.net
Web: www.aocuk.net

Association for Improvements in Maternity Services
5 Ann's Court, Grove Road
Surbiton, Surrey KT6 4BE
Helpline: 0870 765 1433
Email: chair@aims.org.uk
Web: www.aims.org.uk

Association of British Insurers
51 Gresham Street, London EC2V 7HQ
Tel: 020 7600 3333
Email: info@abi.org.uk
Web: www.abi.org.uk

Association of British Travel Agents Ltd (ABTA)
68-71 Newman Street, London W1T 3AH
Tel: 020 7637 2444
Email: information@abta.co.uk
Web: www.abta.com

Association of Chartered Certified Accountants (ACCA)
29 Lincoln's Inn Fields
London WC2A 3EE
Tel: 020 7396 7000
Email: info@accaglobal.com
Web: www.acca.co.uk

Association of Independent Financial Advisers (AIFA)
Austin Friars House, 2-6 Austin Friars
London EC2N 2HD
Tel: 020 7628 1287
Email: info@aifa.net
Web: www.aifa.net

Association of Independent Tour Operators (AITO)
133a St Margaret's Road
Twickenham, Middlesex TW1 1RG
Tel: 020 8744 9280
Email: info@aito.co.uk
Web: www.aito.co.uk

Association of Investment Trust Companies
Durrant House, 8-13 Chiswell Street
London EC1Y 4YY
Tel: 020 7282 5555
Email: enquiries@aitc.co.uk
Web: www.aitc.co.uk

Association of Personal Injury Lawyers
11 Castle Quay,
Nottingham NG7 1FW
Tel: 0115 958 0585
Email: mail@apil.com
Web: www.apil.com

Association of Plumbing and Heating Contractors
Ensign House, Ensign Business Centre
Westwood Way, Coventry CV4 8JA
Tel: 0800 542 6060
Email: enquiries@aphc.co.uk
Web: www.aphc.co.uk

Association of Residential Letting Agents
Maple House, 53-55 Woodside Road
Amersham, Buckinghamshire HP6 6AA
Tel: 0845 345 5752
Email: info@arla.co.uk
Web: www.arla.co.uk

Banking Code Standards Board (BCSB)
33 St James's Square, London SW1Y 4JS
Tel: 020 7661 9694
Email: helpline@bcsb.org.uk
Web: www.bankingcode.org.uk

Bar Council
Complaints Department
Northumberland House
3rd Floor, 303-306 High Holborn
London WC1V 7JZ
Tel: 020 7440 4000
Email: Ethics@barcouncil.org.uk
Web: www.barcouncil.org.uk

Benefits Agency *see* **Jobcentre Plus**

Better Business Bureau,
USA-Canada-Japan Scheme *see*
Council of Better Business Bureaus

British Acupuncture Council
63 Jeddo Road, London W12 9HQ
Tel: 020 8735 0400
Email: info@acupuncture.org.uk
Web: www.acupuncture.org.uk

British and Irish Ombudsman Association
24 Paget Gardens, Chislehurst
Kent BR7 5RX
Tel: 020 8467 7455
Email: bioa@btinternet.com
Web: www.bioa.org.uk

British Association for Adoption and Fostering (BAAF)
Web: www.baaf.org.uk
England: Skyline House
200 Union Street, London SE1 0LX
Tel: 020 7593 2000
Email: mail@baaf.org.uk
Wales: 7 Cleeve House
Lambourne Crescent, Cardiff CF14 5GP
Tel: 029 2076 1155
Email: cymru@baaf.org.uk

British Association of Lawyer Mediators
The Shooting Lodge, Guildford Road
Sutton Green, Guildford
Surrey GU4 7PZ
Tel: 07000 766 422
Email: info@balm.org.uk
Web: www.lawwise.co.uk/balm.html

British Association of Nutritional Therapists
27 Old Gloucester Street
London WC1N 3XX
Tel: 0870 606 1284
Email: theadministrator@bant.org.uk
Web: www.bant.org.uk

British Association of Removers (BAR)
3 Churchill Court, 58 Station Road
North Harrow HA2 7SA
Tel: 020 8861 3331
Email: info@bar.co.uk
Web: www.bar.co.uk

British Bankers Association (BBA)
Dormant Account Unit, Pinners Hall
105-108 Old Broad Street
London EC2N 1EX
Tel: 020 7216 8909
Email: brian.white@bba.org.uk
Web: www.bba.org.uk

British Homeopathic Association
Hahnemann House, 29 Park Street West
Luton LU1 3BE
Tel: 0870 444 3950
Email: info@trusthomeopathy.org
Web: www.trusthomeopathy.org

British Massage Therapy Council
17 Rymers Lane, Cowley
Oxford OX4 3JU
Tel: 01865 774123
Email: info@bmtc.co.uk
Web: www.bmtc.co.uk

British Medical Acupuncture Society
12 Marbury House, Higher Whitley
Warrington, Cheshire WA4 4QW
Tel: 01925 730727
Email: admin@medical-acupuncture.org.uk
Web: www.medical-acupuncture.co.uk

British Medical Association (BMA)
BMA House, Tavistock Square
London WC1H 9JP
Tel: 020 7387 4499
Email: info.web@bma.org.uk
Web: www.bma.org.uk

British Pregnancy Advisory Service
Austy Manor, Stratford Road
Wootton Wawen, Solihull
West Midlands B95 6BX
Actionline: 0845 730 4030
Email: info@bpas.org
Web: www.bpas.org

British Psychological Society
St Andrews House
48 Princess Road East
Leicester LE1 7DR
Tel: 0116 254 9568
Email: enquiry@bps.org.uk
Web: www.bps.org.uk

British Reflexology Association
Monks Orchard, Whitbourne
Worcester WR6 5RB
Tel: 01886 821207
Email: bra@britreflex.co.uk
Web: www.britreflex.co.uk

Building Societies Association
Dormant Accounts Scheme
3 Savile Row, London W1S 3PB
Tel: 020 7437 0655
Email: lynne.bartlett@bsa.org.uk
Web: www.bsa.org.uk

Callcredit plc
One Park Lane, Leeds LS3 1EP
Tel: 0113 244 1555
Email: info@callcredit.plc.uk
Web: www.callcredit.plc.uk

Campaign for Freedom of Information
Suite 102, 16 Baldwins Gardens
London EC1N 7RJ
Tel: 020 7831 7477
Email: admin@cfoi.demon.co.uk
Web: www.cfoi.org.uk

Care Standards Inspectorate for Wales
4-5 Charnwood Court
Heol Billingsley, Nantgarw CF15 7QZ
Tel: 01443 848 450
Email: csiwnationaloffice@wales.gsi.gov.uk
Web: www.wales.gov.uk

Central Authority for England and Wales Child Abduction Unit
81 Chancery Lane, London WC2A 1DD
Tel: 020 7911 7047
Email: enquiries@offsol.gsi.gov.uk
Web: www.offsol.demon.co.uk/caunitfm.htm

Chartered Institute of Arbitrators
International Arbitration Centre
12 Bloomsbury Square
London WC1A 2LP
Tel: 020 7421 7444
Email: info@arbitrators.org
Web: www.arbitrators.org

Chartered Institute of Taxation
12 Upper Belgrave Street
London SW1X 8BB
Tel: 020 7235 9381
Email: post@ciot.org.uk
Web: www.tax.org.uk

ChildLine
45 Folgate Street, London E1 6GL
ChildLine: 0800 1111
Email: enquiries@childline.org.uk
Web: www.childline.org.uk

Children and Family Court Advisory and Support Service (CAFCASS)
2nd Floor, Newspaper House
8-16 Great New Street
London EC4A 3BN
Tel: 020 7210 4400
Email: webenquiries@cafcass.gov.uk
Web: www.cafcass.gov.uk

Child Support Agency
National Centre, PO Box 55
Brierley Hill, West Midlands DY5 1YL
Tel: 0845 713 3133
Email: csa-nel@childsupportagency.gsi.gov.uk
Web: www.csa.gov.uk/newcsaweb

Citizens Advice Bureau Service
Details of local offices are given in the phone directory, in local libraries and in the Adviceguide on the CAB web site: www.citizensadvice.org.uk

Commission for Racial Equality
St Dunstan's House
201-211 Borough High Street
London SE1 1GZ
Tel: 020 7939 0000
Email: info@cre.gov.uk
Web: www.cre.gov.uk

Committee of Advertising Practice
2 Torrington Place, London WC1E 7HW
Tel: 020 7828 4224
Email: enquiries@cap.org.uk
Web: www.cap.org.uk

Community Legal Service (CLS)
To find your local CLS advice centre, call 0845 608 1122 and ask for a copy of the Directory, or access the Directory on the web site: www.justask.org.uk

Companies House
Tel: 0870 333 3636
Email: enquiries@companieshouse.gov.uk
Web: www.companieshouse.gov.uk
London: PO Box 29019
21 Bloomsbury Street, London WC1B 3XD
Wales: Crown Way, Cardiff CF14 3UZ

Confederation of Passenger Transport
Imperial House, 15-19 Kingsway
London WC2B 6UN
Tel: 020 7240 3131
Email: cpt@cpt-uk.org
Web: www.cpt-uk.org

Consumer Credit Counselling Service
Wade House, Merrion Centre
Leeds LS2 8NG
Helpline: 0800 138 1111
Email: contactus@cccs.co.uk
Web: www.cccs.co.uk

Consumers' Association
2 Marylebone Road, London NW1 4DF
Tel: 020 7770 7000
Email: editor@which.net
Web: www.which.net

Consumer Support Networks
National Support Team, LACORS
10 Albert Embankment, London SE1 7SP
Tel: 020 7840 7223
Email: csn@lacors.gov.uk
Web: www.csnconnect.org.uk

Contributions Agency
see **Inland Revenue National Insurance Contributions Office**

Council for Licensed Conveyancers
16 Glebe Road, Chelmsford
Essex CM1 1QG
Tel: 01245 349599
Email: clc@theclc.gov.uk
Web: www.conveyancer.org.uk

Council for Registered Gas Installers (CORGI)
1 Elmwood, Chineham Park,
Crockford Lane, Basingstoke,
Hampshire RG24 8WG
Tel: 0870 401 2200
Email: enquiries@corgi-gas.com
Web: www.corgi-gas-safety.com

Council of Better Business Bureaus
4200 Wilson Blvd, Suite 800
Arlington, VA 22203-1838
Tel: 001 703 276 0100
Web: www.bbb.org

Council of Mortgage Lenders (CML)
3 Savile Row, London W1S 3PB
Tel: 020 7437 0075
Email: info@cml.org.uk
Web: www.cml.org.uk

Court Service
Southside, 105 Victoria Street
London SW1E 6QT
Tel: 020 7210 2266
Email: cust.ser.cs@gtnet.gov.uk
Web: www.courtservice.gov.uk

Credit Industry Fraud Avoidance System (CIFAS)
4th Floor, Tennyson House
159-165 Great Portland Street
London W1W 5PA
Email: cifas@cifas.org.uk
Web: www.cifas.org.uk

Criminal Injuries Compensation Authority (CICA)
Email: enquiries.cica@gtnet.gov.uk
Web: www.cica.gov.uk
Glasgow Office: Tay House
300 Bath Street, Glasgow G2 4LN
Tel: 0141 331 2726
London Office: Morley House
26-30 Holborn Viaduct, London EC1A 2JQ
Tel: 020 7842 6800

Criminal Records Bureau (CRB)
Customer Services, CRB
PO Box 110, Liverpool L3 6ZZ
Information Line: 0870 909 0811
Welsh Language Line: 0870 909 0223
Web: www.crb.gov.uk

Customs & Excise
see **HM Customs & Excise**

Deed Poll Service
PO Box 6788
Hatfield Peverel CM3 2WJ
Helpline: 0800 783 3048
Email: enquiries@ukdps.co.uk
Web: www.ukdps.co.uk

Department for Culture, Media and Sport (DCMS)
2-4 Cockspur Street, London SW1Y 5DH
Tel: 020 7211 6200
Email: enquiries@culture.gov.uk
Web: www.culture.gov.uk

DCMS Listing Branch
179a Tottenham Court Road
London W1T 7PA
Tel: 020 7211 2361

Department for Education and Skills
Sanctuary Buildings, Great Smith Street
London SW1P 3BT
Enquiries line: 0870 000 2288
Email: info@dfes.gsi.gov.uk
Web: www.dfes.gov.uk

Department for Environment, Food and Rural Affairs (DEFRA)
Library Enquiry Desk, Room 320
Nobel House, 17 Smith Square
London SW1P 3JR
Helpline: 0845 933 5577
Email: helpline@defra.gsi.gov.uk
Web: www.defra.gov.uk

DEFRA National Wildlife Management Team
England: Wildlife Administration Unit
Burghill Road, Westbury-on-Trym
Bristol BS10 6NJ
Tel: 0845 601 4523
Email:
enquiries.southwest@defra.gsi.gov.uk
Web: www.defra.gov.uk/wildlife-countryside
Wales: National Assembly for Wales
Agriculture Department
Food Farming Development Division
Cefn Llan Science Park
Aberystwyth, Ceredigion SY23 3AH
Tel: 01970 610 218

Department for Work and Pensions (DfWP)
Correspondence Unit, Room 540
The Adelphi, 1-11 John Adam Street
London WC2N 6HT
Tel: 020 7712 2171
Email: peo@dwp.gsi.gov.uk
Web: www.dwp.gov.uk

Department for Work and Pensions (DfWP) Disability Unit
For details of your local DfWP
Disability Centre, phone the DfWP (see above) or check the DfWP web site.

Department of Health (DoH)
Richmond House, 79 Whitehall
London SW1A 2NL
Tel: 020 7210 4850
Email: dhmail@doh.gsi.gov.uk
Web: www.doh.gov.uk

Department of Trade and Industry (DTI)
Enquiry Unit, 1 Victoria Street
London SW1H 0ET
Enquiry Unit: 020 7215 5000
Email: dti.enquiries@dti.gsi.gov.uk
Web: www.dti.gov.uk

Direct Marketing Authority (DMA)
see **Mailing Preference Service**

Disability Rights Commission
DRC Helpline, FREEPOST MID02164
Stratford-upon-Avon CV37 9BR
Tel: 0845 762 2633
Email: enquiry@drc-gb.org
Web: www.drc-gb.org

District Probate Registry
see **Probate Registry**

Donor Conception Network
PO Box 7471, Nottingham NG3 6ZR
Tel: 020 8245 4369
Email: enquiries@dcnetwork.org
Web: www.dcnetwork.org

Dormant Accounts Scheme
see **Building Societies Association**

Dormant Accounts Unit
see **British Bankers Association**

Driver and Vehicle Licensing Agency (DVLA)
Longview Road, Swansea SA6 7JL
Tel: 01792 782341
Email: drivers.dvla@gtnet.gov.uk and
vehicles.dvla@gtnet.gov.uk
Web: www.dvla.gov.uk

DTI Quality Mark Scheme
see **Quality Mark Scheme**

Employment Appeal Tribunal
Audit House, 58 Victoria Embankment
London EC4Y 0DS
Tel: 020 7273 1040
Web: www.employmentappeals.gov.uk

Employment Tribunals Offices
Local offices are listed in the phone
directory and on the Employment
Tribunals web site:
www.employmenttribunals.gov.uk
Email: Londoneat@ets.gsi.gov.uk

Energywatch
4th Floor, Artillery House
Artillery Row, London SW1P 1RT
Helpline: 0845 906 0708
Email: enquiries@energywatch.org.uk
Web: www.energywatch.org.uk

**Enforcement Services Association
(ESA)**
Ridgefield House, 14 John Dalton Street
Manchester M2 6JR
Tel: 0161 839 7225
Email: director@bailiffs.org.uk
Web: www.bailiffs.org.uk

Environment Agency
Rio House, Waterside Drive, Aztec West
Almondsbury, Bristol BS12 4UD
Tel: 0845 933 3111
Floodline: 0845 988 1188
Email: enquiries@environment-
agency.gov.uk
Web: www.environment-agency.gov.uk

Equal Opportunities Commission
Web: www.eoc.org.uk
England: Arndale House, Arndale Centre
Manchester M4 3EQ
Tel: 0845 601 5901
Email: info@eoc.org.uk
Wales: Windsor House, Windsor Lane
Cardiff CF10 3GE
Tel: 029 2034 3552
Email: wales@eoc.org.uk

Equifax
Tel: 0845 600 1772
Email:
consumer.telesalesuk@equifax.com
Web: www.equifax.co.uk

**European Advertising Standards
Alliance**
10a rue de la Pépinière
B-1000 Brussels, Belgium
Tel: 00322 513 7806
Email: library@easa-alliance.org
Web: www.easa-alliance.org

European Consumer Centre
Citizens Advice
PO Box 3308, Wolverhampton WV10 9ZS
Email:
consumer.euro@citizensadvice.org.uk
Web: www.citizensadvice.org.uk and
eei-net.org.uk

Examination Appeals Board
83 Piccadilly
London W1J 8QA
Tel: 020 7509 5995
Email: wattersk@qca.org.uk
Web: www.theeab.org.uk

Experian
Talbot House, Talbot Street
Nottingham NG1 5HF
Helpline: 0870 241 6212
Email: corps.comms@uk.experian.com
Web: www.uk.experian.com

Faculty of Party Wall Surveyors
19 Church Street
Godalming, Surrey GU7 1EL
Tel: 01424 883300
Email: enq@fpws.info
Web: www.fpws.info

Family Mediators Association
PO Box 5, Bristol BS99 3WZ
Tel: 0117 946 7062
Email: info@fmassoc.co.uk
Web: www.fmassoc.co.uk

Fax Preference Service
DMA House, 70 Margaret Street
London W1W 8SS
Tel: 0845 070 0702
Email: fps@dma.org.uk
Web: www.fpsonline.org.uk

Federation of Master Builders
Gordon Fisher House
14-15 Great James Street
London WC1N 3DP
Tel: 020 7242 7583
Email: central@fmb.org.uk
Web: www.fmb.org.uk

**Federation of Overseas Property
Developers, Agents and Consultants**
Lacey House, St Clare Business Park
Holly Road, Hampton Hill
Middlesex TW12 1QQ
Tel: 020 8941 5588
Email: info@fopdac.com
Web: www.fopdac.com

Finance and Leasing Association
2nd Floor, Imperial House
15-19 Kingsway, London WC2B 6UN
Tel: 020 7836 6511
Email: info@fla.org.uk
Web: www.fla.org.uk

Financial Ombudsman Service (FOS)
South Quay Plaza, 183 Marsh Wall
London E14 9SR
Tel: 020 7964 1000
Email: complaint.info@financial-
ombudsman.org.uk
Web: www.financial-ombudsman.org.uk

Financial Services Authority (FSA)
25 The North Colonnade
Canary Wharf, London E14 5HS
Consumer Helpline: 0845 606 1234
Email: consumerhelp@fsa.gov.uk
Web: www.fsa.gov.uk

**Financial Services Compensation
Scheme (FSCS)**
7th Floor, Lloyds Chambers
Portsoken Street, London E1 8BN
Helpline: 020 7892 7300
Email: enquiries@fscs.org.uk
Web: www.fscs.org.uk

Firm Check Service
see **Financial Services Authority**

Floodline see **Environment Agency**

Fostering Network
Email: info@fostering.net
Web: www.thefostering.net
England: 87 Blackfriars Road
London SE1 5BB
Tel: 020 7620 6400
Wales: Suite 11, 2nd Floor,
Bay Chambers, West Bute Street
Cardiff Bay CF10 5B3
Tel: 029 2044 0940

FPA (Family Planning Association)
2-12 Pentonville Road, London N1 9FP
Helpline: 0845 310 1334
Tel: 020 7837 5432
Web: www.fpa.org.uk

Frank see **Talk to Frank**

Funeral Planning Authority Ltd
Harelands, 22 Bentsbrook Park
North Holmwood, Dorking
Surrey RH5 4JN
Tel: 01306 740878
Email:
enquiries@funeralplanningauthority.com
Web:
www.funeralplanningauthority.com

General Chiropractic Council (GCC)
44 Wicklow Street, London WC1X 9HL
Tel: 020 7713 5155
Email: enquiries@gcc-uk.org
Web: www.gcc-uk.org

**General Council and Register of
Naturopaths**
Goswell House, 2 Goswell Road
Street, Somerset BA16 0JH
Tel: 0870 745 6984
Email: admin@naturopathy.org.uk
Web: www.naturopathy.org.uk

General Dental Council
37 Wimpole Street, London W1G 8DQ
Tel: 020 7887 3800
Email: complaints@gdc-uk.org
Web: www.gdc-uk.org

**General Insurance Standards Council
(GISC)**
110 Cannon Street, London EC4N 6EU
Tel: 020 7648 7800
Email: enquiries@gisc.co.uk
Web: www.gisc.co.uk

General Medical Council (GMC)
178 Great Portland Street
London W1W 5JE
Tel: 020 7580 7642
Email: gmc@gmc-uk.org
Web: www.gmc-uk.org

General Optical Council
41 Harley Street, London W1G 8DJ
Tel: 020 7580 3898
Email: rclarkson@optical.org
Web: www.optical.org

General Osteopathic Council
Osteopathy House
176 Tower Bridge Road, London SE1 3LU
Tel: 020 7357 6655
Email: info@osteopathy.org.uk
Web: www.osteopathy.org.uk

General Register Office for England and Wales
Smedley Hydro, Trafalgar Road
Southport PR8 2HH
Tel: 0870 243 7788
Email: certificate.services@ons.gov.uk
Web: www.statistics.gov.uk

Health and Safety Executive (HSE)
HSE Infoline, Caerphilly Business Park
Caerphilly CF83 3GG
Tel: 0870 154 5500
Email: hseinformationservices@natbrit.com
Web: www.hse.gov.uk

Health and Safety Executive
Employment Medical Advisory Service
see **Health and Safety Executive**

Health Professions Council
Park House, 184 Kennington Park Road
London SE11 4BU
Tel: 020 7582 0866
Email: info@hpc-uk.org
Web: www.hpc-uk.org

Health Service Ombudsman
Email:
OHSC.Enquiries@ombudsman.org.uk
Web: www.ombudsman.org.uk
England: Millbank Tower, Millbank
London SW1P 4QP
Tel: 020 7217 4051
Wales: The Health Service
Ombudsman for Wales
5th Floor, Capital Tower House
Greyfriars Road, Cardiff CF10 3AG
Tel: 029 2039 4621

Hedgeline
Tel: 0870 240 0627
Email: Clare.hdg@virgin.net
Web: http://freespace.virgin.net/clare.h

Help the Aged
Web: www.helptheaged.org.uk
England: 207-221 Pentonville Road
London N1 9UZ
Tel: 020 7278 1114
Email: info@helptheaged.org.uk
Wales: 12 Cathedral Road
Cardiff CF11 9LJ
Tel: 029 2034 6550
Email: infocymru@helptheaged.org.uk

Her Majesty's Stationery Office (HMSO)
Web: www.hmso.gov.uk

HM Customs & Excise
Contact the National Advice Service for details of your regional office.
National Advice Service: 0845 010 9000
Welsh language: 0845 010 0300
Web: www.hmce.gov.uk

HM Inspectorate for Education and Training in Wales (Estyn)
Anchor Court, Keen Road
Cardiff CF24 5JW
Tel: 029 2044 6446
Email: enquiries@estyn.gsi.gov.uk
Web: www.estyn.gov.uk

HM Land Registry
32 Lincoln's Inn Fields
London WC2A 3PH
Tel: 020 7917 8888
Email:
enquiries.pic@landregistry.gov.uk
Web: www.landreg.gov.uk

HMSO see **TSO (The Stationery Office)**

Home Office
Public Enquiry Team, 7th Floor
50 Queen Anne's Gate, London SW1H 9AT
Tel: 0870 000 1585
Email:
public.enquiries@homeoffice.gsi.gov.uk
Web: www.feedback.homeoffice.gov.uk

Housing Corporation
Maple House, 149 Tottenham Court Road
London W1T 7BN
Tel: 020 7393 2000
Email:
enquiries@housingcorp.gsx.gov.uk
Web: www.housingcorp.gov.uk

HPI Ltd
Dolphin House, New Street
Salisbury, Wiltshire SP1 2PH
HPI Check Line: 01722 422 422
Email: questions@hpi.co.uk
Web: www.hpicheck.com

Human Fertilisation and Embryology Authority (HFEA)
Paxton House, 30 Artillery Lane
London E1 7LS
Tel: 020 7377 5077
Email: admin@hfea.gov.uk
Web: www.hfea.gov.uk

Independent Committee for the Supervision of Standards of Telephone Information Services (ICSTIS)
4th Floor, Clove Building
4 Maguire Street, London SE1 2NQ
Helpline: 0800 500 212
Tel: 020 7940 7474
Email: secretariat@icstis.org.uk
Web: www.icstis.org.uk

Independent Healthcare Association
Westminster Tower
3 Albert Embankment, London SE1 7SP
Tel: 020 7793 4620
Email: info@iha.org.uk
Web: www.iha.org.uk

Independent Midwives Association
1 The Great Quarry
Guildford, Surrey GU1 3XN
Tel: 01483 821 104
Web: www.independentmidwives.org.uk

Independent Panel for Special Educational Needs Advice (IPSEA)
6 Carlow Mews
Woodbridge, Suffolk IP12 1EA
Advice line: 0800 018 4016
Web: www.ipsea.org.uk

Independent Schools Council Information Service (ISCIS)
Grosvenor Garden House
35-37 Grosvenor Gardens
London SW1W 0BS
Tel: 020 7798 1500
Email: info@iscis.uk.net
Web: www.iscis.uk.net

Index of Exempted Dogs
PO Box 47, Saffron Walden
Essex CB10 1YD
Tel: 07000 783 652
Email: indexdogs@aol.com

Information Commissioner
Wycliffe House, Water Lane
Wilmslow, Cheshire SK9 5AF
Enquiry line: 01625 545 745
Email: data@dataprotection.gov.uk
Web: www.dataprotection.gov.uk

Inland Revenue (IR)
Your nearest IR enquiry centre is listed in the phone directory or on the IR web site: www.inlandrevenue.gov.uk

Inland Revenue Capital Taxes Office
Ferrers House, PO Box 38
Castle Meadow Road
Nottingham NG2 1BB
Probate and inheritance tax helpline:
0845 302 0900
Web: www.inlandrevenue.gov.uk/cto

Inland Revenue National Insurance Contributions Office
Inland Revenue, Benton Park View
Newcastle upon Tyne NE98 1ZZ
Tel: 0191 213 5000
Web: www.inlandrevenue.gov.uk/nic

Insolvency Service
2nd Floor, West Wing
45-46 Stephenson Street
Birmingham B2 4UP
Central Enquiry Line: 020 7291 6895
Email: central.enquiryline
@insolvency.gsi.gov.uk
Web: www.insolvency.gov.uk

Institute of Chartered Accountants in England and Wales
Chartered Accountants' Hall
PO Box 433, London EC2P 2BJ
Tel: 020 7920 8100
Email: exec@icaew.co.uk
Web: www.icaew.co.uk

Institute of Plumbing
64 Station Lane, Hornchurch
Essex RM12 6NB
Tel: 01708 472791
Email: info@plumbers.org.uk
Web: www.plumbers.org.uk

Institute of Public Loss Assessors
14 Red Lion Street, Chesham
Buckinghamshire HP5 1HB
Tel: 01494 782 342
Web: www.lossassessors.org.uk

International Air Transport Association (IATA)
Central House, Lampton Road
Hounslow, Middlesex TW3 1HY
Tel: 020 8607 6262
Web: www.iata.org

International Society of Arboriculture
148 Hydes Road, Wednesbury
West Midlands WS10 0DR
Tel: 0121 556 8302
Email: enquiries@isa-uki.org
Web: www.isa-uki.org

Internet Watch Foundation
5 Coles Lane, Oakington
Cambridgeshire CB4 5BA
Tel: 01223 237700
Email: admin@iwf.org.uk
Web: www.iwf.org.uk

Investment Management Association
65 Kingsway, London WC2B 6TD
Information line: 020 8207 1361
Email: ima@investmentuk.org
Web: www.investmentuk.org

Jobcentre Plus
Your nearest Jobcentre Plus office is listed in the phone directory and on the Jobcentre Plus web site:
www.jobcentreplus.gov.uk

Land Registry see **HM Land Registry**

Law Centre
To find your nearest Law Centre, ask at your local library or contact the **Law Centres Federation.**

Law Centres Federation
Duchess House, 18-19 Warren Street
London W1T 5LR
Tel: 020 7387 8570
Email: info@lawcentres.org.uk
Web: www.lawcentres.org.uk

Law Society
113 Chancery Lane, London WC2A 1PL
Tel: 020 7242 1222
Email: info.services@lawsociety.org.uk
Web: www.lawsociety.org.uk

Leasehold Advisory Service (LEASE)
70-74 City Road, London EC1Y 2BJ
Tel: 0845 345 1993
Email: info@lease-advice.org
Web: www.lease-advice.org

Leasehold Valuation Tribunals
To apply to a Leasehold Valuation Tribunal, contact the **Leasehold Advisory Service** for the address of your regional Rent Assessment Panel.

Legal Services Commission
85 Gray's Inn Road
London WC1X 8TX
Tel: 020 7759 0000
Web: www.legalservices.gov.uk

Legal Services Ombudsman
3rd Floor, Sunlight House
Quay Street, Manchester M3 3JZ
Tel: 0845 601 0794
Email: lso@olso.gsi.gov.uk
Web: www.olso.org

Liberty
21 Tabard Street, London SE1 4LA
Tel: 020 7403 3888
Email: info@liberty-human-rights.org.uk
Web: www.liberty-human-rights.org.uk

LGO Adviceline
see **Local Government Ombudsman**

Lloyd's Complaints Department
One Lime Street, London EC3M 7HA
Tel: 020 7327 5693/6950
Email: complaints@lloyds.com
Web: www.lloyds.com

Local Government Ombudsman
For details of the Local Government Ombudsman for your region, contact your local council, ring the Local Government Ombudsman (LGO) Adviceline on 0845 602 1983, or check the LGO web site: www.lgo.org.uk

London Gazette
PO Box 7923, London SW8 5WF
Tel: 020 7394 4580
Email: london.gazette@tso.co.uk
Web: www.gazettes-online.co.uk

Mailing Preference Service (MPS)
FREEPOST 29 LON20771
London W1E 0ZT
Tel: 0845 703 4599
Email: mps@dma.org.uk
Web: www.mpsonline.org.uk

Mail Order Traders' Association (MOTA)
7th Floor, 100 Old Hall Street
Liverpool L3 9TD
Tel: 0151 227 9456
Email: m.hogarth@mota.uk.com
Web: www.adassoc.org.uk

Marie Stopes International
153-157 Cleveland Street
London W1T 6QW
Tel: 020 7574 7400
Email: info@mariestopes.org.uk
Web: www.mariestopes.org.uk

Maternity Alliance
Third Floor West, 2-6 Northburgh Street
London EC1V 0AY
Information line: 020 7490 7638
Tel: 020 7490 7639
E-mail: info@maternityalliance.org.uk
Web: www.maternityalliance.org.uk

Mediation UK
Alexander House
Telephone Avenue, Bristol BS1 4BS
Tel: 0117 904 6661
Email: enquiry@mediationuk.org.uk
Web: www.mediationuk.org.uk

Mortgage Code Compliance Board
University Court, Stafford ST18 0GN
Tel: 01785 218200
Email: enquiries@mortgagecode.org.uk
Web: www.mortgagecode.org.uk

Motor Insurers Bureau
6-12 Capital Drive, Linford Wood
Milton Keynes MK14 6XT
Tel: 01908 830 001
Email: enquiries@mib.org.uk
Web: www.mib.org.uk

National Academy for Gifted and Talented Youth
University of Warwick, Coventry CV4 7AL
Tel: 024 7657 4213
Email: gifted@warwick.ac.uk
Web: www.warwick.ac.uk/gifted

National AIDS Trust
New City Cloisters, 196 Old Street
London EC1V 9FR
Tel: 020 7814 6767
Email: info@nat.org.uk
Web: www.nat.org.uk

National Approved Letting Scheme
Tavistock House, 5 Rodney Road
Cheltenham GL50 1HX
Tel: 01242 581712
Email: info@nalscheme.co.uk
Web: www.nalscheme.co.uk

National Association for Gifted Children
Suite 14, Challenge House
Sherwood Drive, Bletchley
Milton Keynes MK3 6DP
Tel: 0845 450 0221
Email: amazingchildren@nagcbritain.org.uk
Web: www.nagcbritain.org.uk

National Association of Estate Agents
Arbon House, 21 Jury Street
Warwick CV34 4EH
Tel: 01926 496800
Email: info@naea.co.uk
Web: www.naea.co.uk

National Care Standards Commission
England: St Nicholas Building
St Nicholas Street
Newcastle upon Tyne NE1 1NB
Tel: 0191 233 3600
Email: enquiries@ncsc.gsi.gov.uk
Web: www.ncsc.gov.uk

National Care Standards Commission
Wales: *see* **Care Standards Inspectorate for Wales**

National Council for Hypnotherapy Ltd
PO Box 5779, Burton-on-the-Wolds
Loughborough LE12 5ZF
Tel: 0800 952 0545
Email: admin@hypnotherapists.org.uk
Web: www.hypnotherapists.org.uk

National Family Mediation
Alexander House, Telephone Avenue
Bristol BS1 4BS
Tel: 0117 904 2825
Email: general@nfm.org.uk
Web: www.nfm.u-net.com

National Health Service (NHS)
Department of Health Customer Service
Centre,
Room 320, Richmond House
79 Whitehall, London SW1A 2NS
Tel: 020 7210 4850
Email: dhmail@doh.gsi.gov.uk
Web: www.nhs.uk

NCT (National Childbirth Trust)
Alexandra House, Oldham Terrace
Acton, London W3 6NH
Enquiries: 0870 444 8707
Email: enquiries@national-childbirth-trust.co.uk
Web: nctpregnancyandbabycare.com

NHS Organ Donor Register see **Organ Donor Register**

National House-Building Council (NHBC)
Buildmark House, Chiltern Avenue
Amersham, Buckinghamshire HP6 5AP
Enquiries: 01494 735363
Claims: 0870 241 4329
Email: cssupport@nhbc.co.uk
Web: www.nhbc.co.uk

National Institute of Medical Herbalists
56 Longbrook Street, Exeter EX4 6AH
Tel: 01392 426022
Email: nimh@ukexeter.freeserve.co.uk
Web: www.nimh.org.uk

National Insurance Contributions Office
see **Contributions Agency**

National Parking Adjudication Service
6th Floor, Barlow House
Minshull Street, Manchester M1 3DZ
Tel: 0161 242 5252
Email: npas@parking-appeals.gov.uk
Web: www.parking-appeals.gov.uk

National Savings and Investments
Savings bondss: Glasgow G58 1SB
Premium Bonds: Blackpool FY3 9YP
TESSAS and ISAS: Durham DH99 1NS
Helpline: 0845 964 5000
Email: customerenquiries@nsandi.com
Web: www.nsandi.com

Network Rail
40 Melton Street, Euston Square,
London NW1 2EE
Helpline: 0845 711 4141
Web: www.networkrail.co.uk

Natural Death Centre
6 Blackstock Mews, Blackstock Road
London N4 2BT
Tel: 020 7359 8391
Email: ndc@alberyfoundation.org
Web: www.naturaldeath.org.uk

NCH
Helpline: 0845 762 6579
Email: supphelp@nch.org.uk
Web: www.nch.org.uk
England: 85 Highbury Park
London N5 1UD
Tel: 020 7704 7000
Wales: St David's Court
68a Cowbridge Road East
Cardiff CF11 9DN
Tel: 029 2022 2127

Network for Surviving Stalking
PO Box 7836, Crowthorne
Berkshire RG45 7YA
Email: help@nss.org.uk
Web: www.nss.org.uk

NSPCC
Weston House, 42 Curtain Road
London EC2A 3NH
English helpline: 0808 800 5000
Welsh helpline: 0808 100 2524
Email helpline: help@nspcc.org.uk
Web: www.nspcc.org.uk

Nursing and Midwifery Council
23 Portland Place, London W1B 1PZ
Tel: 020 7333 9333
Email: karen.sellick@nmc-org.uk
Web: www.nmc-uk.org

Occupational Pensions Regulatory Authority (OPRA)
Invicta House, Trafalgar Place
Brighton BN1 4DW
Tel: 01273 627600
Email: helpdesk@opra.gov.uk
Web: www.opra.gov.uk

Ofcom see **Office of Communications**

Office for Standards in Education (Ofsted)
Alexandra House, 33 Kingsway
London WC2B 6SE
Tel: 020 7421 6800
Email: geninfo@ofsted.gov.uk
Web: www.ofsted.gov.uk

Office for the Supervision of Solicitors
Victoria Court, 8 Dormer Place
Leamington Spa
Warwickshire CV32 5AE
Helpline: 0845 608 6565
Email: enquiries@lawsociety.org.uk
Web: www.oss.lawsociety.org.uk

Office of Communications (Ofcom)
Riverside House
2a Southwark Bridge Road
London SE1 9HA
Tel: 020 7981 3000
Email: mediaoffice@ofcom.org.uk
Web: www.ofcom.org.uk

Office of Fair Trading (OFT)
Fleetbank House, 2-6 Salisbury Square
London EC4Y 8JX
Tel: 020 7211 8000
Email: enquiries@oft.gov.uk
Web: www.oft.gov.uk

Office of Gas and Electricity Markets (Ofgem)
9 Millbank, London SW1P 3GE
Helpline: 0845 906 0708
Email: enquiries@energywatch.org.uk
Web: www.energywatch.org.uk

Office of the Deputy Prime Minister
26 Whitehall, London SW1A 2WH
Tel: 020 7944 4400
Web: www.odpm.gov.uk

Office of the Information Commissioner
see **Information Commissioner**

Office of the Pensions Advisory Service (OPAS)
11 Belgrave Road, London SW1V 1RB
Helpline: 0845 601 2923
Email: enquiries@opas.org.uk
Web: www.opas.org.uk

Office of the Rail Regulator (ORR)
1 Waterhouse Square, 138-142 Holborn
London EC1N 2TQ
Tel: 020 7282 2000
Email: contact.cct@orr.gsi.gov.uk
Web: www.rail-reg.gov.uk

Office of Water Services (Ofwat)
Centre City Tower, 7 Hill Street
Birmingham B5 4UA
Tel: 0121 625 1300
Email: enquiries@ofwat.gsi.gov.uk
Web: www.ofwat.gov.uk

Ofgem see **Office of Gas and Electricity Markets**

Oftel (Office of Telecommunications)
see **Office of Communications (Ofcom)**

Ofwat see **Office of Water Services**

Ombudsman for Estate Agents
Beckett House, 4 Bridge Street
Salisbury, Wiltshire SP1 2LX
Tel: 01722 333306
Email: admin@oea.co.uk
Web: www.oea.co.uk

Organ Donor Register
UK Transplant Communications
Directorate, Fox Den Road
Stoke Gifford, Bristol BS34 8RR
Tel: 0117 975 7575
Email: enquiries@uktransplant.nhs.uk
Web: www.uktransplant.org.uk

Organisation for Timeshare in Europe
Consumer Council
Rue Defacqz 78-80, 4th Floor
1060 Brussels, Belgium
Tel: 00322 533 3069
Email: info@ote-info.com
Web: www.ote-info.com

Overseas Adoption Helpline
64-66 High Street
Barnet, Hertfordshire EN5 5SJ
Tel: 0870 516 8742
Email: info@oah.org.uk
Web: www.oah.org.uk

Parking and Traffic Appeals Service
General enquiries: 020 7747 4700
Web:
www.parkingandtrafficappeals.gov.uk

**Passenger Shipping Association
(PSARA)**
Walmar House, 4th Floor
288-292 Regent Street, London W1R 5HE
Tel: 020 7436 2449
Email: admin@psa-psara.org
Web: www.psa-psara.org

Pensions Advisory Service see **Office of
the Pensions Advisory Service (OPAS)**

Pensions Compensation Board
11 Belgrave Road, London SW1V 1RB
Tel: 020 7828 9794

Pensions Ombudsman
11 Belgrave Road, London SW1V 1RB
Tel: 020 7834 9144
Email:
enquiries@pensions-omudsman.org.uk
Web: www.pensions-ombudsman.org.uk

Pensions Schemes Registry see
**Occupational Pensions Regulatory
Authority (OPRA)**

Planning Inspectorate
Web: www.planning-inspectorate.gov.uk
England: Quality Assurance Unit
Room 409, Kite Wing
Temple Quay House, 2 The Square
Temple Quay, Bristol BS1 6PN
Tel: 0117 372 8252
Email: complaints@planning-
inspectorate.gsi.gov.uk
Wales: The Planning Inspectorate
Crown Buildings, Cathays Park
Cardiff CF10 3NQ
Tel: 029 2082 3866
Email: wales@planning-
inspectorate.gsi.gov.uk

Police Complaints Authority (PCA)
10 Great George Street
London SW1P 3AE
Tel: 020 7273 6450
Email: info@pca.gov.uk
Web: www.pca.gov.uk

Postwatch
28 Grosvenor Gardens
London SW1W 0TT
Helpline: 0845 601 3265
Email: info@postwatch.co.uk
Web: www.postwatch.co.uk

Press Complaints Commission
1 Salisbury Square, London EC4Y 8JB
Tel: 020 7353 1248
English helpline: 020 7353 3732
Welsh helpline: 029 2039 5570
Email: complaints@pcc.org.uk
Web: www.pcc.org.uk

Principal Probate Registry
England: First Avenue House
42-49 High Holborn, London WC1V 6NP
Tel: 020 7947 7000
Wales: Probate Registry of Wales
2 Park Street, Cardiff CF10 1TB
Tel: 029 2037 6479

Principal Registry of the Family Division
The Court Service
Southside, 105 Victoria Street
London SW1E 6QT
Tel: 020 7210 2266
Email: cust.ser.cs@gtnet.gov.uk
Web: www.courtservice.gov.uk

Probate Registry
To find details of your district probate
office contact the **Principal Probate
Registry** or access the Law on the Web
Legal Helpline: www.lawontheweb.co.uk

Public Carriage Office
15 Penton Street, London N1 9PU
Tel: 020 7941 4500
Email: pco.tfl@gtnet.gov.uk
Web: www.tfl.gov.uk/pco

Pyramus & Thisbe Club
Rathdale House, 30 Back Road
Rathfriland, Co Down BT34 5QF
Tel: 028 4063 2082
Email: p&t@rathdale.globalnet.co.uk
Web: www.partywalls.org.uk

Quality Mark Scheme
PO Box 445, Tower Court
Foleshill Enterprise Park
Foleshill Road, Coventry CV6 5NX
Tel: 0845 300 8040
Email:
qualitymarkscheme@capita.co.uk
Web: www.qualitymark.org.uk

RAC (Royal Automobile Club)
RAC Head Office, 1 Forest Road
Feltham, Middlesex TW13 7RR
Customer Service: 0870 572 2722
Web: www.rac.co.uk

Racial Equality Council
To find the details of your nearest
Racial Equality Council, contact the
Commission for Racial Equality.

Rail Passengers Committee
To find the details of your regional Rail
Passengers Committee, contact the **Rail
Passengers Council.**

Rail Passengers Council
Whittles House, 14 Pentonville Road
London N1 9HF
Tel: 020 7713 2700
Email: info@railpassengers.org.uk
Web: www.railpassengers.org.uk

Relate
Herbert Gray College
Little Church Street, Rugby
Warwickshire CV21 3AP
Helpline: 0845 130 4010
Tel: 0845 456 1310
Email: relateonline@relate.org.uk
Web: www.relate.org.uk

Rent Assessment Committee
To find the details of your nearest Rent
Assessment Committee, contact the
Residential Property Tribunal Service.

Rent Service
Customer Services, Quality Directorate
2nd Floor, Heliting House
35 Richmond Hill, Bournemouth
Dorset BH1 6HT
Tel: 0120 255 1590
Email:
customer.service@therentservice.gov.uk
Web: www.therentservice.gov.uk

Residential Property Tribunal Service
10 Alfred Place, London WC1E 7LR
National Helpline: 0845 600 3178
Web: www.rpts.gov.uk

**Retail Motor Industry Federation
(RMI)**
201 Great Portland Street
London W1W 5AB
Tel: 020 7580 9122
Email: andrewhayes@rmif.co.uk
Web: www.rmif.co.uk

reunite
International Child Abduction Centre
PO Box 7124, Leicester LE1 7XX
Advice line: 0116 2556 234
Email: reunite@dircon.co.uk
Web: www.reunite.org

**Royal Institution of Chartered
Surveyors (RICS)**
RICS Contact Centre, Surveyor Court
Westwood Way, Coventry
Warwickshire, CV4 8JE
Tel: 0870 333 1600
Email: contactrics@rics.org.uk
Web: www.rics.org

Shelter
Helpline: 0808 800 4444
Tel: 020 7505 4699
Email: info@shelter.org.uk
Web: www.shelter.org.uk

Society of Financial Advisers (SOFA)
20 Aldermanbury, London EC2V 7HY
Tel: 020 7417 4442
Email: info@sofa.org
Web: www.sofa.org

Society of London Theatre
32 Rose Street, London WC2E 9ET
Tel: 020 7557 6700
Email: enquiries@solttma.co.uk
Web: www.officiallondontheatre.co.uk

Society of Master Shoe Repairers
St Crispin's House, 21 Station Road
Desborough,
Northamptonshire NN14 2SA
Tel: 01536 760374

Society of Motor Manufacturers and Traders Ltd (SMMT)
Forbes House, Halkin Street
London SW1X 7DS
Tel: 020 7235 7000
Web: www.smmt.co.uk

Society of Teachers of the Alexander Technique
1st Floor, Linton House
39-51 Highgate Road, London NW5 1RS
Tel: 0845 230 7828
Email: office@stat.org.uk
Web: www.stat.org.uk

Society of Ticket Agents and Retailers
PO Box 43, London WC2H 7LD
Helpline: 0870 603 9011
Email: info@s-t-a-r.org.uk
Web: www.s-t-a-r.org.uk

Society of Trust & Estate Practitioners
26 Dover Street, London W1S 4LY
Tel: 020 7763 7152
Email: step@step.org
Web: www.step.org

Solicitors Family Law Association
PO Box 302, Orpington
Kent BR6 8QX
Tel: 01689 850227
Email: louisa.cross@sfla.org.uk
Web: www.sfla.org.uk

Special Educational Needs and Disability Tribunal (SENDIST)
7th Floor, Windsor House
50 Victoria Street, London SW1H 0NW
Helpline: 01325 392555
Email:
tribunalqueries@sendist.gsi.gov.uk
Web: www.sendist.gov.uk

Strategic Rail Authority
55 Victoria Street, London SW1H 0EU
Tel: 020 7654 6000
Web: www.sra.gov.uk

Supreme Court Costs Office
The Court Service
Southside, 105 Victoria Street
London SW1E 6QT
Tel: 020 7210 2266
Email: cust.ser.cs@gtnet.gov.uk
Web: www.courtservice.gov.uk

Suzy Lamplugh Trust
PO Box 17818, London SW14 8WW
Tel: 020 8876 0891
Email: info@suzylamplugh.org
Web: www.suzylamplugh.org

Talk to Frank
Tel: 0800 776 600
Email: frank@talktofrank.com
Web: www.talktofrank.com

Telephone Preference Service (TPS)
DMA House, 70 Margaret Street
London W1W 8SS
Tel: 0845 070 0707
Email: tps@dma.org.uk
Web: www.tpsonline.org.uk

Terrence Higgins Trust
52-54 Grays Inn Road
London WC1X 8JU
Helpline: 0845 122 1200
Tel: 020 7831 0330
Email: info@tht.org.uk
Web: www.tht.org.uk

Textile Services Association
7 Churchill Court, 58 Station Road
North Harrow, Middlesex HA2 7SA
Tel: 020 8863 7755
Email: tsa@tsa-uk.org
Web: www.tsa-uk.org

Trading Standards
To find your local Trading Standards office, contact your local council or find it on the web site:
www.tradingstandards.gov.uk

Trades Union Congress (TUC)
Congress House, Great Russell Street
London WC1B 3LS
Tel: 020 7636 4030
Email: info@tuc.org.uk
Web: www.tuc.org.uk

Transport for London (TfL)
Windsor House, 42-50 Victoria Street
London SW1H 0TL
Tel: 020 7941 4500
Email: enquiries@tfl.gov.uk
Web: www.tfl.gov.uk

TrustUK
Email: secretariat@trustuk.org.uk
Web: www.trustuk.org.uk

TSO (The Stationery Office)
Offices and bookshops are listed in the phone directory or contact:
Tel: 0870 600 5522
Email: customer.services@tso.co.uk
Web: www.tso.co.uk

UK College of Family Mediators
Alexander House
Telephone Avenue, Bristol BS1 4BS
Tel: 0117 904 7223
Email: ukcfm@btclick.com
Web: www.ukcfm.co.uk

Unclaimed Assets Register
Leconfield House
Curzon Street, London W1J 5JA
Tel: 0870 241 1713
Email: search@uar.co.uk
Web: www.uar.co.uk

Vehicle Builders and Repairers Association Ltd (VBRA)
Belmont House, Finkle Lane
Gildersome, Leeds
West Yorkshire LS27 7TW
Tel: 0113 253 8333
Email: vbra@vbra.co.uk
Web: www.vbra.co.uk

Vehicle Certification Agency
1 Eastgate Office Centre
Eastgate Road, Bristol BS5 6XX
Tel: 0117 952 4235
Email: enquiries@vca.gov.uk
Web: www.vca.gov.uk

Victim Support National Office
Cranmer House, 39 Brixton Road
London SW9 6DZ
Tel: 020 7735 9166
Victim Supportline: 0845 303 0900
Email: contact@victimsupport.org.uk
Web: www.victimsupport.org.uk

WaterVoice
For details of your regional WaterVoice Committee, contact the **Office of Water Services (Ofwat).**

Women's Royal Voluntary Service (WRVS)
Milton Hill House, Milton Hill
Steventon, Abingdon
Oxfordshire OX13 6AD
Tel: 01235 442900
Email: enquiries@wrvs.org.uk
Web: www.wrvs.org.uk

INDEX

PICTURE CREDITS

T=Top; M=Middle; B=Bottom;
L=Left; R=Right

Cartoons by Robert Thompson
Photography by Roy Williams

The publishers wish to thank the
following:
Alvey and Towers 262, B
Digital Vision 109-137, T; 113, BR;
133, BR; 137, MR

Driver and Vehicle Licensing
 Agency 251, TR
Laurence Bradbury 156, BL
William Dupont 370, BL
Pip Hackett 408, ML
Mick Peel 318, B
Photodisc 38, BL; 80, BL; 84, BL;
108-137, T; 115, BR; 126, ML; 130, ML;
136, BL; 159, BR; 171, BL; 174, BL;
198-215, TL; 268-297, T; 280, BR;
290, BL; 294-95; 343, BR; 348-49;

354-379, T; 356, B; 364, ML; 374, BL;
396-417, T; 402, BL
Science Photo Library/Jim Varney
256, B
TRH Pictures/E. Partridge 99, BR
UK Transplant 125, BR
Vehicle and Operator Services
 Agency 251, BL.

CONTRIBUTORS

Contributing authors
Ray Castle
Vivien Goldsmith
Jonquil Lowe
Sheena Meredith
Charles Philips
Saundra Satterlee
Christine Stopp
Felicity Taylor

Consultants
Geoffrey Allan BA (Hons)

Louise Backhouse LLB
Solicitor, Trustee of Kennet Citizens Advice Bureau

David Crook BA, PhD
Senior Lecturer in History of Education, Institute of Education, University of London

Marie-Hélène Kutek MSc
Vice Chair of Institute of Consumer Affairs, Member of Trading Standards Institute

Claire de Than BA (Hons), LLB, LLM
Lecturer in Law, City University, London

Robert Upex MA, LLM, ACIArb, FRSA
Barrister, Head of Department of Law, University of Surrey, Guildford

Richard White LLB
Solicitor, Partner of White & Sherwin of Croydon

Toucan Books would also like to thank the following lawyers for their assistance in the preparation of this book:
Sue Bland, Ann Northover at Gordon Dadds, London
Jonathan Conder at Macfarlanes, London
Louise Spitz at Manches, London
Helen Blackburn at Reynolds Porter Chamberlain, London

Managing editors
Helen Douglas-Cooper
Andrew Kerr-Jarrett
Robert Sackville West

Consultant editor
Liz Clasen

Editors
Jane Hutchings
Michael Wright

Picture researcher
Christine Vincent

Proofreader
Barry Gage

Indexer
Laura Hicks

Design
Bradbury and Williams

For Reader's Digest, London

Project Editor
John Andrews

Art Editor
Julie Bennett

CD Compilers
Tony Rilett
Planet Three Publishing

Reader's Digest, General Books, London

Editorial Director
Cortina Butler

Art Director
Nick Clark

Executive Editor
Julian Browne

Managing Editor
Alastair Holmes

Picture Resource Manager
Martin Smith

Book Production Manager
Fiona McIntosh

Pre-press Account Manager
Penelope Grose

Origination
Colour Systems Ltd, London

Printing and binding
Mateu Cromo, Madrid, Spain

CD-Rom replication
Sonopress

CONCEPT CODE US3922/IC
BOOK CODE 400-075-01
ISBN 0 276 42769 6
ORACLE CODE 250007859H.00.24